PERSONAL INJURY AND CLINICAL NEGLIGENCE LITIGATION

David Dow LLB, Solicitor

Jeff Lill BA, MA, Solicitor

Published by

College of Law Publishing,
Braboeuf Manor, Portsmouth Road, St Catherines, Guildford GU3 1HA

© The College of Law 2006

British Library Cataloguing-in-Publication Data

A catalogue record for this book is available from the British Library.

ISBN 1 905391 08 0

Typeset by Style Photosetting Ltd, Mayfield, East Sussex

Printed in Great Britain by Ashford Colour Press Ltd, Gosport, Hampshire

PERSONAL INJURY AND CLINICAL NEGLIGENCE LITIGATION

Preface

The purpose of this book is to provide an introduction to the large and complex area of personal injury and clinical negligence litigation. It does not set out to cover the subject fully, nor does it purport to include all recent developments in this area of law.

This text has been written as an integrated element of the Legal Practice Course elective 'Personal Injury and Clinical Negligence Litigation' and its aim is to provide a framework upon which the course is built. Students are expected to carry out their own research into some aspects of the course and will receive further tuition in others and, therefore, this book is not intended to be used as a stand-alone text on the subject.

We are grateful to all of our colleagues who have contributed to the book.

Under the Civil Procedure Rules, the term 'claimant' is used to identify the person bringing the claim. Prior to this, the word 'plaintiff' was used, and thus, where quotes have been referred to in this text, the term 'plaintiff' is seen, but this is just the phrase used to identify the victim of the accident.

The Civil Procedure Rules are still being amended and it is important that readers make reference to the relevant provisions which are in place at the time of publication. The practical working of conditional fee agreements and 'success fees' are still proving difficult in practice.

Reference must be made to the relevant provisions and case law, as this is a fast-changing area of law, and practitioners must update themselves continually.

In the interests of brevity, we have used the masculine pronoun throughout to include the feminine.

The law is generally stated as at 8 July 2005.

JEFF LILL and DAVID DOW

Contents

Appendices 273

Table of Cases

S

Y

Table of Statutes

Table of Statutory Instruments

European secondary legislation

Codes of practice

List of Abbreviations

See Appendix 2 for commonly used medical abbreviations.

ABWOR	assistance by way of representation
ACOPs	Approved Codes of Practice
ADR	alternative dispute resolution
ALP	Accident Line Protect
APIL	Association of Personal Injury Lawyers
ATE	After the event
AvMA	Action against Medical Accidents
BTE	Before the event
CCFA	Collective conditional fee agreements
CFA	conditional fee agreement
CFA Regs 2000	Conditional Fee Agreements Regulations 2000
CFA Regs 2003	Conditional Fee Agreements (Miscellaneous Amendments) Regulations 2003
CHAI	Commission for Healthcare Audit and Inspection
CICA	Criminal Injuries Compensation Authority
CLS	Community Legal Service
CNST	Clinical Negligence Scheme for Trusts
CPR 1998	Civil Procedure Rules 1998
CPS	Crown Prosecution Service
CRU	Compensation Recovery Unit
CTG	cardiotachograph
DPA 1998	Data Protection Act 1998
DWP	Department for Work and Pensions
DSE	display screen equipment
ECG	electrocardiogram
FAA	Fatal Accidents Act 1976
FOIL	Forum of Insurance Lawyers
GLO	group litigation order
GMC	General Medical Council
HAVS	hand/arm vibration syndrome
HSE	Health & Safety Executive
ICTA 1988	Income and Corporation Taxes Act 1988
IRP	independent review panel
LA 1980	Limitation Act 1980
LAA	legal advice and assistance
LEI	Legal expenses insurance
LR(MP)A 1934	Law Reform (Miscellaneous Provisions) Act 1934
LSC	Legal Services Commission
MIB	Motor Insurers Bureau
MID	Motor Insurance Database
MPA	multi-party action
NHS	National Health Service
NHSLA	NHS Litigation Authority
NMC	Nursing and Midwifery Council
OLA 1957	Occupiers' Liability Act 1957
PAR	police accident report
PD	Practice Direction
PPE	personal protective equipment
PTSD	post-traumatic stress disorder

RIDDOR 1995   Reporting of Injuries, Diseases and Dangerous Occurrences Regulations 1995
RTA 1988   Road Traffic Act 1988
SSP   statutory sick pay
VWF   vibration white finger
WRULD   work-related upper limb disorders

Chapter 1

An Introduction to the Work of a Personal Injury and Clinical Negligence Solicitor

1.1 Introduction

The aim of this text is to provide an introduction to personal injury and clinical negligence litigation. It is, however, assumed that the basic civil litigation procedure has been studied before and reference to the Legal Practice Guide, *Civil Litigation* and the Civil Procedure Rules 1998 (CPR 1998) may be necessary for those unfamiliar with the essential elements of High Court and county court procedure.

The terms 'personal injury litigation' and 'clinical negligence litigation' are widely used to describe claims for compensation for injuries which a client has suffered. In this text, personal injury litigation is the term used to refer to the following types of claims.

(a) Road traffic accident claims. These are usually the most straightforward type of claim and include any case where, in addition to property damage, an injury has been suffered by the client.

(b) Employers' liability claims. This term is used for accidents that have occurred where the claimant was injured in the course of his employment and his employer is the defendant. Common examples of this type of personal injury claim are slipping accidents on the factory floor, repetitive strain injury suffered by machine operatives and clients who suffer from deafness due to their employers providing inadequate ear protection.

(c) Public liability claims. These claims arise out of public use of products or premises, for example, a person who cuts his foot on a cracked tile while using the public swimming baths.

Clinical negligence claims refer not only to the negligence of doctors but to all the related medical professions, such as nurses, physiotherapists and dentists. While the basic litigation procedure for both types of claims is the same, the skills required to pursue the claim differ. Where the procedure for a clinical negligence claim differs significantly from that of a personal injury claim, specific reference is made in the text.

This text will not deal with every type of claim that is encountered in practice. It should, however, serve as a basic introduction to a fascinating area of law which is developing quickly.

The CPR 1998 require personal injury and clinical negligence solicitors to adopt an 'approach' to litigation which requires the parties and the court to have regard to the speed and cost involved in pursuing the case. This philosophy is to be adopted at the start of any case and reference needs to be made to the relevant pre-action protocol (the full text of the protocols is set out in **Appendix 3**). It must be noted that these protocols set out the steps which should be taken by the parties *prior* to the issue of proceedings.

1.2 Personal injury claims

1.2.1 The claimant's perspective

The aim of the claimant's personal injury solicitor is to prove that the defendant was responsible for the client's injuries and to obtain the appropriate amount of compensation. The solicitor should also attempt to obtain the compensation payment as quickly as possible. Therefore, there are two essential elements to a personal injury claim: liability and quantum. This may sound obvious, but it is important that these two elements are paramount in the solicitor's mind throughout the case.

Personal injury claims can take time to progress. At the initial interview, it should be explained to the client how it is anticipated the case will proceed and a realistic timescale should be given (although this can be difficult) as to when the matter might be settled or reach trial. The client should be informed of the basic requirements of the relevant pre-action protocol and the time limits imposed on each side. It is important that the client is kept informed as the matter proceeds. Regular letters should be sent updating the client on the current position. If a proactive approach is taken, this will avoid difficulties in the future.

1.2.1.1 Liability

It is for the claimant to prove his case and the onus, therefore, will be on the client to persuade the court that the defendant is in breach of a statutory or common law duty owed to the client. The majority of personal injury claims include negligence as a cause of action and a reminder of the basic elements of negligence is included in **Chapter 3**, together with an examination of other potential causes of action. Sometimes it will be possible for the claimant's solicitor to advise the client with a degree of certainty whether a case will be made out against the defendant.

For example, if a client informs his solicitor that he was stationary in his vehicle when he was hit from behind by the defendant's vehicle, or that the client was a passenger in a car that was involved in an accident, then it is likely that the client will establish liability. However, liability can never be taken for granted.

1.2.1.2 Quantum

The claimant's solicitor should have as his aim the maximisation of damages for his client and he must do all that is possible to achieve that aim. Most solicitors working in this area acknowledge that a weariness on the part of the victims themselves can set in if months pass and the claimant perceives that little has been done, or due to anxiety at having to attend trial. This can result in the client accepting inappropriately low offers rather than instructing the solicitor to progress the matter to trial. This should be acknowledged as a factor to be dealt with by the solicitor and the client's concerns should be anticipated.

Medical evidence is required by the court to prove the injuries suffered by the client. Instructing a doctor may appear to be a simple task but the choice of the appropriate doctor is significant. The court, if the matter proceeds to trial, or the defendant's insurers, if the case is settled, will assess the value of the client's injuries on the basis of the medical evidence supplied to them. The instruction of experts is dealt with in **Chapter 8**. Those unfamiliar with this type of work will be surprised at the number and different types of experts in existence. They range from orthopaedic consultants (who can, for example, provide an opinion on a fractured bone), to consulting engineers (who can, for example, provide a report on the safety of ladders).

1.2.1.3 Active case management

The claimant's solicitor should ensure that he moves the case on with speed. A diary system is essential to ensure that deadlines are complied with. Many firms use electronic case management systems to assist in this process.

One such system popular with personal injury practices is the Proclaim system from Eclipse Software. Case management systems store client details and then use those details again and again so that time is not spent re-keying the same details into each piece of correspondence.

The essential attributes of case management are:

(a)   Data storage: the ability to store all contacts for each claim – clients, experts, solicitors, counsel, witnesses, etc – and record all correspondence, be it phone calls, letters, faxes or e-mails.

(b)   Case importation: new or amended case information received electronically can be automatically imported into the system, saving time and effort.

(c)   Guidance: some systems provides onscreen prompts to ensure that the money laundering regulations are adhered to when adding new correspondents. In fixed costs cases some systems will inform the user of cases which are not profitable.

(d)   Online case tracking: selected data can be published to a secure web site, enabling solicitors to make information available to clients, intermediaries and insurers.

(e)   Document creation and management: At the start of each case the system can generate all relevant documentation automatically.

(f)   Text messaging (SMS): messages can be sent direct to clients' mobile phones. This is often used in practice to remind clients of doctors' examination appointments.

(g)   Diary: a full diary facility is linked to all cases. Reminders can be programmed to ensure important events (such as limitation dates and deadlines for Part 36 offers and payments) are not overlooked.

1.2.2 The defendant's perspective

In many cases the defendant's personal injury solicitor will usually be instructed only when proceedings have been issued against the defendant. At all times prior to this, the claimant's solicitor will correspond with the defendant's insurance company, and many cases will be settled without the need to instruct a defence solicitor. However, if the insurance company believes that its insured can escape liability, it will defend the claim. Similarly, if it believes that liability will be established, it will attempt to dispose of the claim for as little money as possible. The insurance company's aims are clearly opposed to the aims of the claimant's solicitor.

It is important that the defendant's solicitor contacts the insured, who is the named defendant in the court proceedings. Many insurance companies require the insured to sign a letter of authority allowing them to act on the insured's behalf and to dispose of the case in any way that the defendant's solicitor sees fit. This is often a formality, as the terms of the insurance policy will allow the insurance company and its solicitor to have control of the case.

1.3 Clinical negligence claims

1.3.1 The claimant's perspective

The essential aims in a clinical negligence claim are the same as in a personal injury claim – namely, to establish liability and maximise damages. However, these are frequently not the only aims and considerations. The client's trust in a respected profession has been lost and many clients will frequently not be certain what has happened to them. It must be explained to the client that he has to prove his claim if he is to establish liability. One of the first distinctions which has to be made between personal injury and clinical negligence cases is that the issue of liability is normally far more complicated in the latter, and there is a greater chance that the claimant's claim will fail at trial. However, the law relating to the quantum of damages is the same in both personal injury and clinical negligence cases.

The costs involved in a clinical negligence case are usually higher than those incurred in a personal injury case. The clinical negligence pre-action protocol will have to be complied with and the initial investigations prior to commencing the claim will involve the solicitor taking instructions, obtaining the client's medical notes and then instructing an expert to assess the notes and evidence available. This can cost a significant amount if the client is privately funding the case. It is only then that any preliminary view on liability can be obtained. Unlike a personal injury case, the victim's clinical negligence solicitor will never be able to give a view on liability at the first interview. It will only be when the notes and an expert's view are obtained that any advice on liability can be given to the client.

A common concern expressed by clients is how they will continue to be treated by the doctor/healthcare professional if there is a continuing 'doctor/patient' relationship and an explanation of the alternatives available to clients may be required. Clients will need advice not only in respect of pursuing claims for damages but also on how to complain about the conduct of the healthcare professional or hospital, or the appropriateness of mediation in respect of their claim. The options available to the client in such circumstances should be familiar to a solicitor working in this area of the law. The solicitor will need to establish whether the client wishes to pursue a damages claim or if the client's aim is solely to report the alleged misconduct to the regulatory body.

1.3.2 The defendant's perspective

The defendant's clinical negligence solicitor will have the same basic aims as those of the defendant's personal injury solicitor. If liability can be refuted then the case will be vigorously defended and, if liability is established, the case will be settled at the lowest possible cost. However, there are also special factors that the defendant's clinical negligence solicitor must consider. The principal factor is that the defendant is a professional person and, while damages will not be paid by him personally, his reputation will be brought into question by any admission or finding of negligence on his part. This is one of the reasons why more clinical negligence claims proceed to trial than personal injury claims and, as will be seen, establishing liability in a clinical negligence case is not easy. While the patient

may complain that the treatment was unsuccessful, it does not follow that the doctor was negligent, and the arguments available to the defendant's solicitor to refute negligence are wider and more complicated than in a personal injury case.

1.4 A less adversarial culture to personal injury and clinical negligence litigation

As noted above, the aims of the claimant and defendant solicitors are opposed. However, following the implementation of the CPR 1998, solicitors should adopt a more 'open' and 'realistic' view to personal injury and clinical negligence litigation. Many solicitors report that there appears to have been a greater willingness by defendants to settle at an early stage in the litigation process and it is clear from the judicial decisions following the introduction of the CPR 1998 that the concept of the 'overriding objective' is key to all areas of litigation.

1.5 Conclusion

Personal injury and clinical negligence litigation is a diverse and expanding area. At its least complex, it may involve a claim for compensation for minor injuries suffered as a result of a road traffic accident, or, at the other extreme, it may involve representing clients in complex claims against drug manufacturers.

The increased significance of personal injury and clinical negligence work has resulted in the setting up of a number of specialist groups.

(a) It is possible for solicitors who fulfil certain criteria to apply to join the personal injury and/or clinical negligence panel set up by The Law Society. Various requirements relating to expertise must be satisfied by applicants.

(b) The Association of Personal Injury Lawyers (APIL) is an organisation which campaigns on behalf of victims of personal injuries.

(c) AvMA, Action against Medical Accidents, is a charitable organisation which gives assistance to members of the public who believe they have been a victim of a medical accident.

(d) The Forum of Insurance Lawyers (FOIL) represents defendant solicitors who act on behalf of insurance companies.

This text aims to provide an introduction to personal injury and clinical negligence litigation, but reference should also be made to practitioners' works and original sources. Where appropriate, reference must be made to the CPR 1998 and pre-action protocols.

1.6 Overviews of personal injury and clinical negligence claims

1.6.1 Overview of the main steps in a clinical negligence claim

Defendants are normally insured or part of the NHS, so normally there are no problems with enforcement.

1.6.2   Overview of the main steps in a personal injury claim, for example, a road traffic or employer's liability case

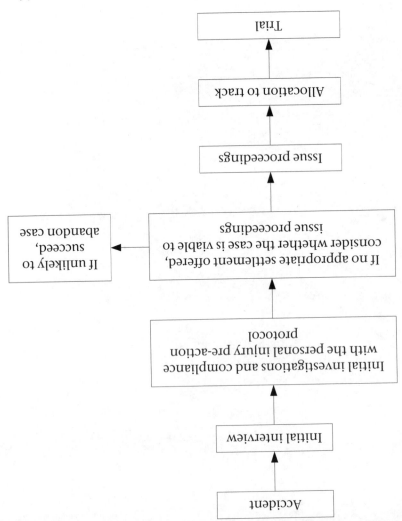

Most defendants are insured, so normally there are no problems with enforcement.

Chapter 2

Personal Injury and Clinical Negligence Jargon

2.1 Introduction

A trainee solicitor who enters the personal injury/clinical negligence department of a legal firm has to cope not only with the pressures of being able to understand fully and advise accurately on the law, but also with a barrage of unfamiliar medical terms. There can be no doubt that proficient solicitors who practise in the personal injury field have extensive medical knowledge and a detailed understanding of the terms used. This knowledge enables solicitors to understand fully clients' complaints, experts' reports and medical notes and also enables them to explain matters thoroughly to clients. For example, upon receipt of a medical report obtained following a simple road traffic accident, the solicitor must read the report carefully and then send it to the client. If the client subsequently contacts his solicitor stating that he does not understand the terms used in the medical report, it is not acceptable for the solicitor to say, 'neither do I'!

The medical profession favours abbreviations and to the trainee this can be particularly difficult. If a trainee is faced on his first day with his colleagues referring to claims dealing with work-related upper limb disorders (WRULD), vibration white finger (VWF), post-traumatic stress disorder (PTSD), etc, and if he is unfamiliar with the terminology, he will obviously be at a disadvantage. The purpose of this chapter is to assist in the understanding of the terms and abbreviations commonly found in personal injury/clinical negligence work. However, a medical dictionary is an essential requirement for the personal injury solicitor and more detailed medical texts may also be of use. See **2.3** (human skeleton) and **Appendix 2** for a list of common abbreviations.

2.2 Common injuries and medical terms used

2.2.1 Orthopaedic injuries

Orthopaedic (bone) injuries are the most common injuries encountered in a personal injury claim and are normally incurred as a result of falling or being involved in a road traffic accident.

The most common terms found in orthopaedic medical reports are as follows.

(a) *Arthrodesis* – means a joint that has been fused, either because of pre-existing joint disease or because of injury as a result of trauma to the joint.

(b) *Arthroplasty* – means that the joint has been reconstructed, often by the use of a joint implant to replace one or more parts of the components of a joint.

(c) *Contusion* – means an injury to the skin and the deeper tissues in the surrounding area which is accompanied by bleeding from damaged blood vessels. The skin, however, is not broken. The simplest form of contusion is a bruise, developing through to a contusion accompanied by a large haematoma, which is a collection of blood under the surface of the skin.

(d)   *Dislocation* – means an injury which results in the bones of a joint being out of alignment or connection with one another. There is usually associated ligament and soft tissue damage.

(e)   *Fracture* – means a break in the continuity of a bone.

(f)   *Sprain* – means an injury in the region of a joint with associated ligament and soft tissue damage.

(g)   *Subluxation* – a joint which has subluxed has undergone a partial dislocation, and subluxation is a term which is sometimes used to describe a sprain.

As a consequence of an orthopaedic injury, the client's injury may have been immobilised by a plaster of Paris cast. Certain of the terms relating to casts are self-evident (eg, below knee cast) but examples of the less obvious terms are:

(a)   *scaphoid cast* – a cast which covers the arm from just below the elbow to the start of the fingers; or

(b)   *shoulder spica cast* – a body jacket which encloses the trunk and shoulder and elbow.

A client who has an orthopaedic injury may also undergo traction – a system of weights and pulleys is used to pull muscle groups, so as to reduce/immobilise fractures and put the bones back into alignment.

In general, the most common fractures occur to:

(a)   *The clavicle (collar bone)* – these fractures are especially common in children and young adults and are almost always due to falls or direct trauma to the point of the shoulder. Treatment involves the wearing of a sling until the pain has subsided. Surgical intervention is very rarely required and is usually only indicated if there is a risk to nearby nerves or blood vessels.

(b)   *The surgical neck of the humerus (the long bone stretching from the shoulder to the elbow)* – these fractures are usually treated with a sling but, if badly displaced, are surgically treated and fixed with metal pins.

(c)   *The shaft of the humerus* – these fractures can occur at any point along the humerus and are usually treated by immobilising the fracture in a plaster of Paris cast for six to eight weeks.

(d)   *Fractures to the radius (the bone running from the elbow to the base of the thumb)* – there are many different types of radial fracture but the most common is the Colles fracture which involves fracture of the lower end of the radius with posterior displacement of the distal fragment.

(e)   *The femur (the thigh bone)* – these fractures can occur at any point along the length of the femur. The most common sites are the neck or the shaft of the femur. Treatment tends to be surgical, with surgery ranging from open fixation with metal pins to total hip replacement. Clients with fractures of the shaft of the femur will be placed in a Thomas splint, which immobilises the fracture.

(f)   *The tibia and fibula* – these two bones make up the part of the leg from beneath the knee to the ankle. Fracture of these two bones can result from direct or indirect trauma.

(g)   *The pelvis* – a number of bones which are formed together to form a ring-like structure at the base of the spine. It contains the vertebrae of the sacral spine and the hip joints and fractures can occur at any point. Because of the relative stability of the pelvis, small, undisplaced fractures can be relatively minor. Fractures to the pelvis are of two main types: first, isolated fractures of one of the bones which make up the pelvis and, secondly, double fractures of the bones which make up the pelvic rim.

Occasionally, following trauma, a client will have a limb amputated. This will have a tremendous impact on his life. It will involve a great deal of treatment and rehabilitation mainly in the form of physiotherapy in order to maintain the existing function and to maximise the potential for rehabilitation. Often, a client will have a prosthesis fitted – an artificial structure which can range from part of a limb to a complete limb.

2.2.2 Work-related upper limb disorders

Work-related upper limb disorders can occur following the constant repetition of tasks such as typing. It leads to a chronic condition which can be permanent for the sufferer. It can result in numbness, swelling and tingling.

Repetitive work can also result in tenosynovitis which is the inflammation of a tendon.

Reference should be made to the relevant regulations that govern health and safety at work in relation to work-related upper limb disorders; see **Chapter 3**.

2.2.3 Terms used to describe injuries to the skin

The following terms are used to describe injuries to the skin:

(a) *abrasion* – occurs when the surface of the skin or a mucous membrane is rubbed off due to a mechanical injury;

(b) *hypertrophic* – the overgranulation of scar tissue which can lead to disfigurement;

(c) *laceration* – a wound to the skin which has jagged, irregular edges.

2.2.4 Terms used to describe head injuries

The following terms are used in relation to head injuries:

(a) *aphasia* – the loss of power of speech;

(b) *anosmia* – the loss of the sense of smell;

(c) *cerebral oedema* – a swelling of the brain;

(d) *closed head injury* – a head injury in which there is no open skull fracture;

(e) *concussion* – instantaneous loss of consciousness due to a blow on the head;

(f) *diffuse axonal injury* – a brain injury which involves shearing of the brain tissue itself;

(g) *dysarthria* – a difficulty in the co-ordination of the speech muscles which leads to an inability to pronounce words clearly;

(h) *dysphagia* – a difficulty in swallowing;

(i) *dysphasia* – a difficulty in understanding language and in self-expression;

(j) *extradural haematoma* – a blood clot which lies immediately above the brain and its protective membranes and below the surface of the skull;

(k) *Glasgow Coma Scale* – a system of assessing neurological function;

(l) *hydrocephalus* – a condition which arises due to an increase in the amount of cerebro-spinal fluid within the cranial cavity;

(m) *hemiplegia* – paralysis of one side of the body;

(n)   *intracerebral* – within the substance of the brain itself; – *monoplegia* – a paralysis of one limb;

(o)   *open head injury* – a head injury with an associated depressed skull fracture;

(p)   *subdural haematoma* – a blood clot lying in between the brain and its protective membranes.

2.2.5 Industrial deafness

Industrial deafness claims are brought by those who have suffered hearing loss due to exposure at work to a high level of noise for a long period of time. For example, employees working in the steel industry, shipbuilding or other manufacturing industry may suffer from industrial deafness. Expert medical evidence is required to prove the loss of hearing, and evidence relating to the employees' working conditions is also required. Employers should, for example, have a system of assessing the risk from noise, provide ear protectors and have clearly marked zones where ear protection must be worn. An employer should be aware of the 'daily personal noise exposure' of its employees, which involves calculating the noise exposure to the client (the abbreviation 'Leq (8hr)' is used).

In such cases, it is important to obtain a detailed employment history and details of the client's working conditions, such as the degree of noise the client believed he encountered, for example, whether he had to shout at workmates to make himself heard, details of ear protection supplied, the types of machinery operated and any warnings given, etc. It must be remembered that the client's claim will succeed only if he can prove that his hearing loss was caused by his employment with the relevant defendant and that it was foreseeable that such a hearing loss might be sustained. It is vital to ensure that it was the client's employment which caused the deafness and not any natural degeneration or intervening illness.

2.2.6 Post-traumatic stress disorder

Post-traumatic stress disorder (PTSD) has become more prominent in recent years. This expression refers to a psychological illness where the claimant suffers from a variety of symptoms which include:

(a)   constantly reliving the initial incident which provoked the stress;

(b)   panic attacks;

(c)   palpitations;

(d)   chest pain;

(e)   nausea;

(f)   constipation;

(g)   insomnia;

(h)   lack of concentration;

(i)   loss of libido;

(j)   agoraphobia;

(k)   headaches;

(l)   indigestion;

(m)   diarrhoea;

(n)   eating disorders;

(o)   restlessness;

(p)   extreme fatigue.

It is important that medical evidence to support the injury is obtained so that the defendants cannot make the allegation that the claimant has simply been 'shaken up'. This type of injury must be considered by the claimant's solicitor, even if the client concentrates only on the physical injuries when he is asked at the first interview what injuries he has suffered as a result of the accident.

2.2.7 Asbestosis/pneumoconiosis

Asbestosis is a form of pneumoconiosis which is a general term applied to any chronic form of inflammation of the lungs affecting people who are liable to inhale irritating substances or particles at work.

Asbestosis occurs specifically following the inhalation of mainly blue or brown asbestos dust. It leads to the development of widespread scarring of the lung tissue leading to severe breathing difficulties. The main hazard, however, is the potential for the development of a type of cancer called mesothelioma, which affects the lungs, the pleura or, more rarely, the ovaries.

2.2.8 Occupational asthma

Occupational asthma may develop following exposure to a precipitating factor in the workplace, for example, flour.

Asthma is a disorder of breathing and is characterised by a narrowing of the airways within the lungs. The main symptom is breathlessness and an associated cough. It is an extremely distressing condition and, if left untreated, can be fatal.

Occupational asthma is usually treatable by the identification of the allergen which is provoking the attacks. Common allergens are flour and grain in bakeries or isocyanates found in industries involving paint-spraying.

2.2.9 Occupational dermatitis

Dermatitis is an inflammation of the skin, which is usually caused by direct contact with some irritating substance.

Occupational dermatitis is the most common of all the occupational diseases.

2.2.10 Hand injuries

In interpreting medical reports regarding hand injuries, a basic understanding of the anatomical position of the hand is required.

The functional parts of the hand are the wrist and the fingers. If the wrist is flexed, the hand is brought forward; if the hand is positioned as if to push someone away, it is said to be extended. The wrist is described as being 'pronated' if the palm of the hand is pointing towards the floor, and is described as being 'supinated' if the hand is positioned to receive something.

If the hand is made into a fist, the fingers are described as flexed; if the hand is opened out as if to receive something the fingers are described as extended.

The fingers are described as the distal half of the hand, and are made up of three joints. Working from the palm of the hand out towards the end of the fingers, the three joints are the metacarpo-phalangeal joint (the knuckles), the proximal interphalangeal joint, and the distal interphalangeal joint which is the joint nearest to the finger nails. The thumb has the same number of joints but appears shorter because it attaches to the hand lower down. 70% of the function of the hand is provided by the thumb.

If a scar to the hand is described as transverse, it runs across the hand; if it is described as longitudinal, it runs along the length of the hand.

2.2.11 Obstetrics

A normal labour and delivery takes place in three stages. The first stage refers to the period of time it takes the cervix to dilate fully to 10 cms and is the longest stage of labour. The full dilation of the cervix is also associated with the rupture of the amnion, which is the tough fibrous membrane lining the cavity of the womb during pregnancy containing amniotic fluid which supports the foetus. The rupture of the amnion is often referred to as the breaking of the waters. The second stage of labour is the actual birth of the baby. The third stage is the delivery of the placenta.

An obvious sign of foetal distress is the presence of meconium, which is a brown semi-fluid material which collects in the bowels of the baby before birth and is usually discharged either at birth or shortly afterwards. If a baby becomes distressed, it ejects the meconium into the amniotic fluid.

Cerebral palsy is a group of conditions which are characterised by varying degrees of paralysis occurring in infancy or early childhood. It is thought that the factors involved in the development of cerebral palsy are trauma to the child during birth or lack of oxygen.

If a baby is deprived of oxygen, it is said to have become hypoxic. Hypoxia refers to a state where there is an inadequate supply of oxygen to maintain normal tissue function. If a baby is deemed to be in danger, it will be intubated and ventilated. This involves the insertion of an endotracheal tube into the baby's trachea to facilitate the maintenance of the baby's airway.

Once a baby is born, it is assessed using the Apgar score. This is a method of assessing a baby's condition by giving a score of either 0, 1 or 2 to each of five signs: colour, heart rate, muscle tone, respiratory effort and response to stimulation. A total score of 10 is the best Apgar score. If a baby is described as apnoeic, it means that it is not breathing; bradycardia refers to the fact that the baby's heart is beating too slowly.

Perinatal mortality refers to the death of a foetus after the 28th week of pregnancy and to the death of the newborn child during the first week of life.

2.2.12 Occupational stress

Following the case of *Walker v Northumberland County Council* [1995] 1 All ER 737, in which a social services officer received compensation for stress induced by his employment (he suffered a nervous breakdown), there have been a number of occupational stress claims brought before the court. Careful consideration needs to be given as to whether the client will satisfy the necessary criteria to persuade the court to award damages in these circumstances.

2.3   Diagrammatic representation of the human skeleton

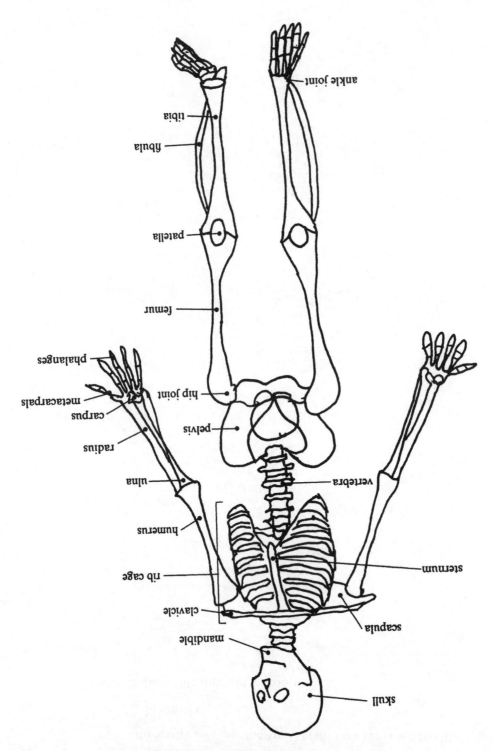

skull

mandible

clavicle

rib cage

sternum

scapula

humerus

ulna

radius

carpus

metacarpals

phalanges

vertebra

pelvis

hip joint

femur

patella

fibula

tibia

ankle joint

2.4   Conclusion

A basic understanding of the medical terms involved in personal injury and clinical negligence cases can assist the trainee in understanding medical reports and also provide an insight into the client's problems which can often be useful in the negotiation of any settlement.

2.5 Further reading

Kemp and Kemp, *The Quantum of Damages* (Sweet & Maxwell).

Medical dictionary.

Other appropriate medical textbooks.

Chapter 3

Liability: Personal Injury and Clinical Negligence

3.1 Introduction

The majority of personal injury claims arise either as the result of an accident at work or an accident on the roads. A road user may be liable to an injured person, be they a pedestrian, passenger or driver of another vehicle on the basis of common law negligence. The employer may be personally liable to an injured employee on the basis of:

(a) common law negligence; and/or

(b) breach of statutory duty, for example, under the Health and Safety at Work etc Act 1974, the Occupiers' Liability Act 1957, or European Directives covering safety by way of regulations under the Health and Safety at Work etc Act 1974. Many of the regulations also have Approved Codes of Practice (ACOPs) of which the solicitor must be aware.

The heads of liability are not mutually exclusive. For example, in certain circumstances the employer may be liable to the injured employee under both heads, while in other circumstances the employer may be liable only in common law negligence but not otherwise. The employer may be vicariously liable to the injured employee where the injury was caused by a tort (eg, negligence) of another employee who was acting in the course of his employment. However, many accidents (eg, in the construction industry) involve workers who are independent contractors working either for themselves or for an employer other than the person with control of the site itself.

3.2 Liability at common law – negligence

As with any other claim in negligence, the burden is upon the claimant to prove that:

(a) the defendant owes him a duty of care;

(b) the defendant is in breach of that duty;

(c)   the breach has caused consequential losses which are reasonably foreseeable.

It is well established that an employer owes his employee a duty of care. For losses arising out of an accident, reference should be made to **Chapter 13**. The remainder of this chapter will concentrate on the nature of the duty of care, and breach of that duty.

3.3   Establishing liability for road traffic accidents

3.3.1   The duty of one road user to another.

Road users will encompass not only those driving or riding vehicles, but also their passengers, pedestrians and owners of roadside property (such as traffic signs owned by the highway authority).

Road users have a duty of care to avoid causing injury to others whom it may reasonably be anticipated may be injured by their actions (or failure to act).

3.3.2   The standard of care

The standard of care is that of the ordinary skilful driver; therefore the standard is not lowered to take account of the fact that the driver is a learner driver (see *Nettleship v Weston* [1971] 2 QB 691). The standard of care owed by any driver is that of a driver of skill, experience and care.

3.3.3   Breach of duty

Each case must turn on its own facts. It is for the court to decide whether there has been any breach of the duty to take reasonable care in relation to other road users. When trying to answer this vital question it will be necessary to consider:

(a)   relevant legislation designed to regulate the conduct of road users (for example, the Road Traffic Acts);

(b)   the Highway Code. The code makes clear that it can be relied upon in any civil or criminal proceedings when trying to establish (or negative) any liability which is in issue in those proceedings (see Road Traffic Act 1988 s 38(7)).

3.3.4   Duty to passengers

The driver of the vehicle (whether it is a private vehicle or a public service vehicle) will owe a duty to take reasonable care to ensure the safety of his passengers for the period of the journey.

3.3.5   Seat belts and the law

The law requires seat belts to be used if they are fitted to the vehicle. It is illegal to carry an unrestrained child in the front seat of any vehicle. The law relates to the front seats of all vehicles and the rear seats of cars and small mini-buses. See the Motor Vehicles (Wearing of Seat Belts) Regulations 1993 (SI 1993/176), and the Motor Vehicles (Wearing of Seat Belts by Children in Front Seats) Regulations 1993 (SI 1993/31).

3.3.5.1   Summary of the law relating to seat belts

	Front seat	Rear seat	Whose responsibility
Driver	Seat belt must be worn if fitted	Not applicable	Driver
Child under 3 years of age	Appropriate child restraint must be used	Appropriate child restraint must be used if available	Driver
Child aged 3–11 and under 1.5m (approximately 5 ft in height)	Appropriate child restraint must be worn if available. If not, an adult seat belt must be worn if available	Appropriate child restraint must be worn if available. If not, an adult seat belt must be worn if available	Driver
Child aged 12 or 13 or younger child 1.5m or more in height	Adult seat belt must be worn if available	Adult seat belt must be worn if available	Driver
Adult passengers 14+	Seat belt must be worn if available	Seat belt must be worn if available	Passenger

Exemptions from wearing seat belts include:

(a)   persons with a current medical certificate;
(b)   disabled persons wearing a disabled persons belt;
(c)   persons carrying out a reversing manoeuvre;
(d)   taxi drivers; and
(e)   children under one year old in a carry cot, provided that the cot is restrained by straps.

See also *Jones (A Minor) v Wilkins (Wynn and Another)* (2001) *The Times,* 6 February. The claimant (aged three) was seated on her mother's lap in the front passenger seat of a car. The lap part of the seat belt was across the claimant. In assessing liability for contributory negligence at 25% by the claimant, the judge considered himself bound by *Froom v Butcher* [1976] 1 QB 286. In this case, where no seat belt was worn, the judge decided that the reduction in damages for contributory negligence should not exceed 25%.

3.3.6   Passengers using public service vehicles

The general duty outlined above applies equally to public service vehicles. For a full account of the additional responsibilities of the drivers of coaches, buses and taxis see Public Service Vehicles (Conduct of Drivers, Inspectors, Conductors and Passengers) Regulations 1990 (SI 1990/1020) and related case law.

3.3.7   Duties of the highway authority

Claims against local authorities in their capacity as highway authorities for failure to maintain the highway, range from tripping and slipping claims by pedestrians to claims by motorists for accidents caused by the poor state of roads (both the fabric of the road itself, or a failure to clear snow and ice or standing water, which might reasonably represent a hazard to those using the highway).

At common law the meaning of a highway was defined in *ex parte Lewis* (1888) 21 QBD 191, as follows:

> a highway is a way over which there exists a public right of passage ... a right ... at all seasons of the year freely and at will to pass and repass without let or hindrance.

Section 36(2) of the Highways Act 1980 defines a highway 'maintainable at public expense' as:

(a) a highway constructed by a highway authority;

(b) a highway constructed by a council within their own area or a highway constructed outside of their area for which they have agreed to be responsible;

(c) a trunk road;

(d) a footpath or bridleway created or diverted by the local authority.

Section 36(6) of the Highways Act 1980 requires that every council must compile and keep up to date a full list of all roads and traffic routes within their area for which they are responsible (for maintenance). Section 36(7) states that any person may consult the list at the council offices and that no fee may be charged for this. Therefore if there is a question over whether the location of the accident is a highway or is in private ownership and privately maintainable, recourse should be had to the relevant council record.

3.3.8 Statutory duty to maintain the highway

Section 41(1) of the Highways Act 1980 gives rise to the primary obligation of the highway authority to maintain the highway, as follows:

> The authority who are for the time being the highway authority for the highway maintainable at public expense are under a duty ... to maintain the highway.

Maintenance of the highway includes repair of it and the duty to 'maintain the highway' is construed in s 329(1) of the Highways Act 1980 accordingly.

3.3.9 Breach of duty to motorists

The highway authority will breach its duty to road users if the road is in such a condition as to be foreseeably dangerous to reasonable road users. In *Rider v Rider* [1973] 1 All ER 294 Sachs LJ concluded that:

> The highway authority must provide not merely for model drivers, but for the normal run of drivers to be found on their highways, and that includes those who make the mistakes which experience and common sense teach us are likely to occur.

3.3.10 Breach of duty to pedestrians in slipping cases

Tripping claims against highway authorities (and private companies and individuals) arising out of the presence of uneven pavements are very common. The courts have been at pains to point out that each case should turn on its own facts and that the trial judge should have discretion when interpreting what amounts to the highway being in a dangerous condition. The court in *Littler v Liverpool Corporation* [1968] 2 All ER 343 gave the following guidance:

> The test ... is reasonable foreseeability of danger. A length of pavement is only dangerous if, in the ordinary course of human affairs, danger may reasonably be anticipated from its continued use by the public who usually pass over it. It is a mistake to isolate and emphasise a particular difference in levels between flagstones unless that difference is such that a reasonable person who noticed and considered it would regard it as presenting a real source of danger. Uneven surfaces and differences

in level between flagstones of about an inch may cause a pedestrian ... to trip and stumble, but such characteristics have to be accepted.

3.3.11   Statutory defence to claims for failure to maintain a highway

There is a defence to any allegation that the authority has failed to maintain the highway in s 58 of the Highways Act 1980:

(1)   In an action against a highway authority in respect of damages resulting from their failure to maintain a highway maintainable at public expense it is a defence (without prejudice to any other defence or the application of the law relating to contributory negligence) to prove that the authority had taken such care as in all the circumstances was reasonably required to secure that the part of the highway to which the action relates was not dangerous for traffic.

(2)   For the purpose of a defence under subsection (1) above, the court shall in particular have regard to the following matters:

(a)   the character of the highway, and the traffic which was reasonably to be expected to use it;

(b)   the standard of maintenance appropriate for a highway of that character and used by such traffic;

(c)   the state of repair in which a reasonable person would have expected to find the highway;

(d)   whether the highway authority knew, or could reasonably have been expected to know, that the condition of the part of the highway to which the action relates was likely to cause danger to users of the highway;

(e)   where the highway authority could not reasonably have been expected to repair that part of the highway before the cause of action arose, what warning notices of its condition had been displayed;

but for the purposes of such a defence it is not relevant to prove that the highway authority had arranged for a competent person to carry out or supervise the maintenance of the part of the highway to which the action relates unless it is also proved that the authority had given him proper instructions with regard to the maintenance of the highway and that he had carried out the instructions.

(3)   This section binds the Crown.

3.3.12   Relevant defendant in claims relating to the state of the highway:

Generally the highway authority will be the county council or metropolitan district council. The highway authority for the City of London is the Common Council of the City of London. For other areas of London the highway authority is the council of the London Borough. For non-metropolitan areas, county councils can decide to enter into agreements to undertake maintenance of particular highways with neighbouring councils, for reasons of administrative and practical convenience.

The Secretary of State for the Environment, Transport and the Regions is the highway authority for:

(a)   any road in respect of which he is appointed highway authority by statutory instrument;

(b)   any other highway constructed by him;

(c)   any trunk road as defined by s 1 of the Highways Act 1980.

3.3.13   Duty on highway authorities to grit highways

In *Goodes v East Sussex County Council* [2000] 1 WLR 1356 the House of Lords held that there was no duty on a local authority either under the Highways Act 1980 or common law to prevent or remove snow and ice on the highway. Section 111 of the Railway and Transport Safety Act 2003 amends s 41 of the Highways Act 1980 by placing a duty on highway authorities to ensure 'so far as reasonably practicable, that safe passage along a highway is not endangered by snow or ice'. In *Sandhar v The Department of Transport, Environment and Regions* [2004] EWHC 28 (QB) the court dismissed a claim for damages from the defendant highway authority. The incident giving rise to the claim was decided after the decision in *Goodes* but before the Highways Act amendment came into force. The court concluded that the highway authority did not have a common law duty to remove ice or prevent ice forming on roads maintained by it.

3.3.14   Duty of highway authorities regarding flooding

The presence of standing water on a highway that presents a danger to traffic can give rise to liability if the flooding is due to a failure by the highway authority to maintain the drains by clearing them of leaves and debris (see *Tarrant v Rowlands* [1979] RTR 144).

3.4   Establishing liability in work-based claims

3.4.1   The nature of the duty of care

An employer is under a duty to take reasonable care of his employees' health and safety. This means providing health checks (especially if employees are engaged in hazardous work), equipment to protect employees from injury and medical equipment in order to mitigate the effects of any injury. This duty to take 'reasonable care' was explained by Lord Wright in *Wilsons and Clyde Coal Co v English* [1938] AC 57 as requiring an employer to exercise due care and skill in three particular areas, ie to provide:

(a)   competent staff;
(b)   adequate plant; and
(c)   a safe system of work.

Many of the common law duties are confirmed or strengthened by statute and regulations, but common law rules are an important indication of how courts are likely to interpret new regulations (eg, the Provision and Use of Work Equipment Regulations 1998 (SI 1998/2306) (see **3.5.2.3**)).

3.4.1.1   Competent staff

The duty is on the employer to take reasonable care to provide competent fellow workers. If an employee is injured as a result of the incompetence of a workmate, the employer may be personally liable. Whether the employer has failed to take reasonable care may depend upon the knowledge that he has (or ought to have) of the workmate's incompetence or inexperience etc (*Hudson v Ridge Manufacturing Co* [1957] 2 QB 348; *Smith v Crossley Bros* (1951) 95 Sol Jo 655).

3.4.1.2   Adequate plant

'Plant' simply means anything used in the course of work and not merely heavy machinery. It will include everything from large and complicated machinery (eg, a paper mill) to the most basic equipment (eg, an office chair). The duty rests on the employer to take reasonable steps to provide adequate equipment and materials to do the job and then to maintain that equipment. The employer will also be vicariously liable if employees fail to maintain or repair such plant or equipment. For example, if an office swivel chair gives way under an employee, the employer may be liable for failing to maintain the chair, or for having inadequate provision for maintenance or renewal.

Accidents may occur because either no plant or equipment is provided, or inadequate equipment is provided. For example, if an employee suffers injuries falling from a makeshift means of gaining access to high shelves, the employer will be liable if no ladder has been provided for this purpose. If an employee stood on an office swivel chair to gain access to the shelves and fell off the chair, it could be argued that the manufacturer would not be liable under the Employers' Liability (Defective Equipment) Act 1969 as the use was not a use that the manufacturer intended for the product.

Where plant is provided there is a duty to maintain it in good order. This duty is now supplemented by the Provision and Use of Work Equipment Regulations 1998 (SI 1998/2306) (see **3.5.2.3**). When considering whether plant has been adequately maintained the court will look to current practice, which will be different according to the type of equipment involved.

Depending on the type of equipment, all or any of the following matters may be relevant and evidence should be looked for, both when using the pre-action protocol and at the disclosure stage of litigation:

(a)   inspection and servicing records;

(b)   reports of defect, breakdown or poor running;

(c)   replacing worn-out parts or equipment;

(d)   steps taken to repair or replace equipment shown to be defective;

(e)   cleaning schedules or rotas.

The frequency and method of inspection or testing will be a question of fact depending on the equipment. Items which are subject to stress, such as ropes, should be inspected and, if necessary, replaced more regularly (see reg 6 of the Provision and Use of Work Equipment Regulations 1998) than items which are subject simply to ordinary wear and tear, such as floor coverings that might cause a person to trip.

For example, in a food processing plant, machinery and floors may become contaminated with grease if not cleaned regularly. The employer will be negligent if he fails to clean the plant; this may necessitate closing the production line down while cleaning takes place.

The requirement to provide adequate plant also extends to a duty to make reasonable provision of safety and protective equipment. This duty at common law is now supplemented by the Personal Protective Equipment at Work Regulations 1992 (SI 1992/2966) (see **3.5.2.4**).

3.4.1.3   Safe system of working

The duty to provide a safe system of working is very wide and will be a question of fact to be considered in each case. It covers such things as:

(a)   the physical layout of the plant;

(b)   the sequence in which work is to be carried out;

(c)   the method by which work is carried out;

(d)   the provision of instructions;

(e)   the provision of proper warnings, notices and instructions (*Speed v Thomas Swift & Co* [1943] KB 557).

The employer must take into account the fact that an employee may become careless after a time, especially if the work is of a repetitive nature (*General Cleaning Contractors Ltd v Christmas* [1953] AC 180).

Example

In *Morgan v Lucas Aerospace Ltd* (1997) JPIL 4/97 the claimant was employed in the defendants' factory to clean waste swarf (oil contaminated with metal waste) from trays underneath machinery. He had been given no formal training. Swarf caught in the machine cut through his heavy-duty glove, causing a cut to the hand. The claimant alleged this injury was caused by the defendants' failure to provide and maintain a safe system of work. In the first instance, it was held that the defendants were not absolved from the duty to provide a safe glove merely because it was difficult or expensive to obtain. If no better glove could be obtained at a reasonable price, the whole system was unsafe. The defendants appealed. On appeal, it was held that it was not necessary for the claimant to prove what alternative system of work could be adopted and which would have been safer. The claimant proved that the defendants allowed an unsafe practice to be adopted which they ought to have known to be unsafe and which they could have altered. If gloves provided were the best available, the obligation of the defendants was to devise a system which would remove or reduce the risk of injury.

3.4.1.4   Safe premises

It is accepted that the duty of care extends to the provision of premises. The duty applies not only to premises occupied by the employer, but also to premises occupied by a third party where the employee is working temporarily (*General Cleaning Contractors v Christmas* [1953] AC 180; *Wilson v Tyneside Window Cleaning Co* [1958] 2 QB 110). The duty is now supplemented by the Workplace (Health, Safety and Welfare) Regulations 1992 (SI 1992/3004) (see **3.5.2.6**).

Slipping and tripping cases are frequent causes of negligence claims at work, as is shown by the amount of advice and preventative information available to employers by the Health & Safety Executive (HSE). The employer must act reasonably to ensure that floors and means of access are reasonably safe.

3.4.2   The requirement of 'reasonableness'

It should be remembered that the duty on the employer is not absolute, but merely to take reasonable care. Generally, a high standard will be required but it will vary according to the circumstances. Factors to be taken into account include the following.

(a)   *Existing disabilities of the employee.* If the employer knows, or should know, of an employee's existing disability, extra precautions should be taken (*Paris v Stepney Borough Council* [1951] AC 367; cf *James v Hepworth & Grandage Ltd* [1968] 1 QB 94).

(b)   *Knowledge of the risk which the employer has or ought to have.* Due to the level and quality of safety information in the form of books, leaflets and videos from the HSE, employers may have difficulty in alleging that they were not aware of the risk, or if they were aware of it that they did not know what to do about it. The Management of Health and Safety at Work Regulations 1999 (SI 1999/3242), now require employers to carry out a risk assessment to identify potential risks and suggest precautionary measures to diminish the risk. Although employers should be aware of current improvements in matters of health and safety they are not obliged to implement them. However, once a new safety measure has proved itself practicable and reasonably available, an employer would be negligent if he failed to adopt it. For example, if there is a risk that the operator of a pneumatic drill will become deaf as a result of prolonged use of the drill, this is a matter the employer should be aware of but need not do anything to remedy. Once it is established that providing adequate ear defenders would prevent the deafness occurring, however, the employer would be negligent if he failed to adopt the precaution. The grey area is whether and to what extent the employer should take his own initiatives to try to solve the problem or look elsewhere for information to do so.

(c)   *Cost and effort of adopting precautions to overcome the risk and the seriousness of the injury risked.* If there is a high risk of serious injury, then greater (and, probably, more expensive) precautions should be taken. Conversely, if the risk of injury is small, expensive precautions may not be justified (*Latimer v AEC Ltd* [1953] AC 643). The burden is on the defendant to show that it has taken appropriate steps to reduce the risk of injury to the lowest level reasonably practicable (see *Hawkes v Southwark LBC* (CA, 20 February 1998).

(d)   *Current trade practice.* Compliance with current trade practice may indicate that the employer has acted reasonably (although this is not conclusive). It is more important that practice reflects what is accepted as correct by informed opinion. While the following were all accepted trade practices, they were still found to be negligent: failing to fence hatchways between decks of a ship at sea; failing to provide a harness for a window cleaner when standing on a windowsill; and loosely roping kegs of beer whilst lowering them, thus exposing employees to the risk that the kegs might slip out and injure them.

Section 16 of the Health and Safety at Work etc Act 1974 authorises Approved Codes of Practice (ACOPs) which will be evidence of what is good practice in a particular trade. A failure to observe an ACOP will not give rise to criminal liability but will be admissible in evidence in criminal proceedings. ACOPs will also be admissible in civil proceedings as evidence of good practice in the trade and, as such, are a reflection of current informed thinking in the health and safety industry. Similarly, Guidance Notes issued by the HSE, although not binding, will be indicative of whether good working practices were being followed.

Judicial comment has been made that defendants ought to have foreseen risks, where information was available in documents published by the HSE. It would, therefore, follow that it was questionable whether such documents had to be acted upon instantly and whether a claimant's conduct was negligent if he failed to do so (see *Foster v National Power plc* (1997) LTL, 7 May 1997).

3.4.3   Personal nature of duty

The employer will escape liability only if he shows that both he and the person to whom he delegated the duty exercised reasonable care in the discharge of that duty (*Davie v New Merton Board Mills Ltd* [1959] AC 604). Therefore, the duty is not discharged, for example, merely by delegating it to an apparently competent manager if that manager in fact fails to act competently (*Sumner v William Henderson & Sons Ltd* [1964] 1 QB 450; *McDermid v Nash Dredging & Reclamation Co Ltd* [1987] 2 All ER 878).

An employer can remain liable for the safety of an employee, even while the employee is under the control of someone else. For example, where a worker on a building site is injured whilst working on a different building site under the control and instruction of different contractors because he had been sent to work for the contractors by his own employer, his employer can be found liable for failing to ensure that he was properly trained and for failing to maintain a safe system of work even though the employer had no control over management of that site (*Morris v Breaveglen* [1993] ICR 766, CA).

3.4.3.1   Remoteness of damage

The defendant will be liable to the claimant only if it can be proved that it was foreseeable that the claimant would suffer damage of the kind that the claimant did in fact suffer. The claimant will generally recover for:

(a)   damage which was reasonably foreseeable; or

(b)   damage which can be shown to flow as a direct consequence of the breach.

Once damage is established as foreseeable (no matter how small), the claimant can recover for the full extent of the injury even if this was unforeseeable (*Smith v Leech Brain & Co Ltd* [1962] 2 QB 405).

3.4.3.2   Causation

In most straightforward personal injury claims the issue of causation will be clear. However, this may not be the case in occupational disease cases where two or more defendants have negligently exposed an employee to work practices that may prove injurious to health. This was the situation in the House of Lords ruling in *Fairchild v Glenhaven Funeral Services Ltd and Others; Fox v Spousal (Midlands) Ltd; Matthews v Associated Portland Cement Manufacturers (1978) Ltd and Others* [2002] UKHL 22, [2002] 3 All ER 305. In this case the claimant had suffered from asbestos-induced mesothelioma. During the course of his career with more than one employer the claimant had been exposed to asbestos dust which in later years manifested itself as mesothelioma, for which there is no cure. The House of Lords found that where there had been employment with more than one employer, and:

(a)   both employers had a duty to take reasonable care to prevent the claimant from inhaling asbestos dust, and

(b)   both were in breach of that duty, and

(c)   the claimant did subsequently suffer from mesothelioma,

then the claimant could recover damages from both former employers. In these circumstances it was not necessary to satisfy the 'but for' causation test. It was enough that the claimant was able to prove that a defendant had materially increased his risk of injury. In his speech to the House, Lord Bingham of Cornhill put it like this: 'such injustice as may be involved in imposing liability on a duty breaking employer is heavily outweighed by the injustice of denying redress to a victim'.

In *Barker v Saint Gobain Pipelines plc* [2004] EWCA Civ 545 the Court of Appeal applied the reasoning in *Fairchild* to a case involving a worker who had for part of his working life been self-employed and could have been exposed to asbestos during that period The court found that there were three relevant periods during which Mr Barker was exposed to asbestos: a period for which the defendant was responsible, a period during which Mr Barker was working for another company and a substantial period of self-employment. The defendant submitted that the test of causation in *Fairchild* was based on the premise that the claimant was an innocent victim of the negligent acts of the various employers.   The Court of Appeal found that *Fairchild* contained a policy element and it would be inconsistent with that policy to deprive a self-employed person of any redress in respect of the period or periods when he was employed by an employer and exposed to asbestos in breach of duty.

3.4.3.3 *Res ipsa loquitur*

It will be relatively rare that the maxim *res ipsa loquitur* (the thing speaks for itself) will be relevant. It is no more than a presumption that in the ordinary course of events the accident would not have happened. The fact of its happening is enough to raise a prima facie case in negligence if it was not possible for the claimant to show what precisely had happened, but it was more likely than not that the effective cause was some act or omission by the defendant amounting to negligence. It is therefore up to the defendant to raise evidence to explain why the accident occurred other than by his negligence (see *Widdowson v Newgate Meat Corporation and Others* [1998] PIQR P138, CA). The maxim will not apply if the employer was not in control of the operation or equipment that gave rise to the accident. For example, the claimant may seek to raise *res ipsa loquitur* if he falls from a ladder because one of the rungs gives way beneath him. However, if the ladder was his own rather than one supplied by an employer, this maxim could not be used by the claimant.

3.4.4 Defences

While *volenti non fit injuria* may be a defence in theory, in practice it is rarely successful; it is rare that an employee will consent freely to run the risk of injury with full knowledge of that risk. Contributory negligence may reduce the employee's damages under the Law Reform (Contributory Negligence) Act 1945, but in judging whether the employee has failed to take reasonable steps for his own safety, due allowance will be given for fatigue, repetition of job, etc. To a certain extent, an employee may be expected to be careless, and the employer's duty is to protect the employee from himself (*Caswell v Powell Duffryn Associated Collieries Ltd* [1940] AC 152).

3.4.5 Claimant's contributory negligence

The contributory negligence of the claimant may sometimes reduce the damages to be awarded against the defendant. It is up to the judge to decide the proportion of responsibility of the claimant and to reduce the amount of damages accordingly.

The Law Reform (Contributory Negligence) Act 1945, s 1 provides that:

> [If] any person suffers damage as a result partly of his own fault and partly of the fault of any other person ... damages recoverable in respect thereof shall be reduced by such extent as the court thinks just and equitable having regard to the claimant's share in responsibility for the damage.

'Fault' is defined by s 4 as 'negligence, breach of statutory duty, or other act or omission which gives rise to a liability in tort or, apart from this Act, gives rise to the defence of contributory negligence'.

The question for the court when considering contributory negligence is whether the claimant acted reasonably in taking the risk (*AC Billings & Son Ltd v Riden* [1968] AC 240). Whether the claim is in negligence or for breach of statutory duty, there cannot be a finding of 100 per cent contributory negligence (see *Anderson v Newham College of Further Education* [2002] EWCA Civ 505).

In assessing the claimant's conduct, allowance will be made for his working conditions. Mere inadvertence by the employee will generally not be sufficient for contributory negligence, for example, where the employee is engrossed in his work or is in a hurry to get on with his job. The relative age and experience of the claimant will also be a relevant consideration for the court when deciding questions of contributory negligence. Disobedience or reckless disregard for the employer's orders are far more likely to give rise to a finding of contributory negligence.

The following have all given rise to findings of contributory negligence:

(a)   disregarding orders to test equipment prior to use;

(b)   a machine operator placing his hand under the guard without isolating the machine;

(c)   disobeying orders by going to a part of the factory where an employee ought not to be; and

(d)   riding on a produce conveyor when this is known to be prohibited and dangerous.

Similarly, reckless disregard for one's own safety will give rise to a claim for contributory negligence. For example:

(a)   turning up for work intoxicated;

(b)   disregarding warning notices;

(c)   cleaning or adjusting machinery which is still running;

(d)   allowing loose clothing to become entangled in a machine;

(e)   failure to use safety equipment provided;

(f)   failing to use a push stick with a power saw; or

(g)   failing to use steel toe-capped boots on a building site.

When considering contributory negligence, it should be remembered that many statutory duties apply to duties of employees and not employers. For example, Management of Health and Safety at Work Regulations 1999 (SI 1999/3242), reg 14 places a duty on employees to use equipment in accordance with training and instructions.

The following are illustrations of common areas that give rise to questions of contributory negligence:

(a)   *Crash helmets.* Regulations require that every person driving or riding a motorbike on a road must wear protective headgear. See the Motor Cycles (Protective Helmets) Regulations 1980 (SI 1980/1279 (as amended)).

Exceptions include:

(i)   mowing machines;

(ii)   vehicles propelled by a person on foot; and

(iii)   members of the Sikh religion who wear a turban.

The general rule is that there will be a 25% reduction in damages if there would have been no injury had a seat belt or helmet been worn, and a 15% reduction if the injury would have been less severe.

(b)   *Intoxication.* The claimant's damages will generally be reduced if he knowingly gets into a car with a driver who is under the influence of drink or drugs. See *Stinton v Stinton and the Motor Insurers' Bureau* [1993] PIQR 135, in which damages were reduced by 33% for contributory negligence.

(c)   *Automatism.* If, for example, the claimant suffers a heart attack or hypoglycaemia, there must be total loss of voluntary control. Evidence of impairment only, no matter how severe, will not be enough to escape liability. See *Chelsea Girl Ltd v Alpha Omega Electrical* (1995) PMILL, February.

3.5   Breach of statutory duty

The relationship between an employer and employee is usually closely regulated by statute. The basic principles are set out below.

Legislation generally falls into one of the following categories:

(a)   the Health and Safety at Work etc Act 1974, ss 2 and 3 impose obligations on employers and the self-employed to ensure, so far as reasonably practicable, the health and safety of their employees and members of the public who might be affected by their activities;

(b)   regulations (made under Health and Safety at Work etc Act 1974, s 15);

(c)   Approved Codes of Practice (ACOPs) (made under Health and Safety at Work etc Act 1974, s 16);

(d)   statutes existing prior to the Health and Safety at Work etc Act 1974;

(e)   regulations existing prior to the Health and Safety at Work etc Act 1974.

Much of the legislation prior to the Health and Safety at Work etc Act 1974 has been repealed and replaced by regulations produced under that Act to comply with European Directives on health and safety. The old legislation (eg, the Factories Act 1961) applied only to employees working specifically in factories. In contrast, the Health and Safety at Work etc Act 1974, and the regulations implemented under it to comply with EU Directives, apply to employees regardless of their actual place of work.

3.5.1   Civil liability for breach of statutory duty

To be successful in a civil claim based on a breach of statutory duty, the injured employee must show that:

(a)   the breach is actionable in a civil court;

(b)   the duty is owed to the claimant by the defendant;

(c)   the claimant's loss is within the mischief of the Act;

(d)   the defendant is in breach of the duty;

(e)   the breach caused the loss.

3.5.1.1   Is the breach of duty actionable in a civil court?

A breach of statutory duty is primarily a crime, but it can also give rise to civil liability except where the statute expressly provides otherwise. There is express exclusion of civil liability for breaches of general duties under the Health and Safety at Work etc Act 1974 (s 47(1)).

The Management of Health and Safety at Work Regulations 1999 (the Management Regulations) have been amended to incorporate liability in civil proceedings if an employee suffers injury as a result of breach of the regulations.

The substituted reg 22 states:

> Breach of a duty imposed on an employer by these Regulations shall not confer a right of action in any civil proceedings in so far as that duty applies for the protection of persons not in his employment.

The Management of Health and Safety at Work and Fire Precautions (Workplace) (Amendment) Regulations 2003 (SI 2003/2457) amend the Management Regulations so that employees may bring civil claims against their employers where they are in breach of duties imposed by the Management Regulations. However, claims by non-employees are excluded. This is of particular significance as the Management Regulations include an obligation on employers to perform an adequate risk assessment (reg 3).

3.5.1.2   Has the defendant breached his statutory duty?

The standard required of the employer to fulfil his statutory duty is a question of construction of the statute. The common formulae are:

(a)   *'Absolute' (or strict) duty*: where a state of affairs is required to exist and that state does not exist, then the employer is in breach (even if he has not been negligent).

(b)   *'So far as reasonably practicable'*: when judging whether there has been a breach the court will balance the risk against sacrifice (eg, in terms of time, trouble or money) to avoid the risk. In *Davies v Health & Safety Executive* [2002] EWCA Crim 2949, [2003] IRLR 170 the court considered s 40 of the Health and Safety at Work etc Act 1974, which deals with the interpretation of 'reasonably practicable'. Section 40 imposes on the defendant the burden of proving to the court that it was not reasonably practicable to do more than was in fact done to satisfy the duty (the reverse burden of proof). This was attacked by the defendant as being incompatible with the presumption of innocence in Article 6(2) of the European Convention for the Protection of Human Rights and Fundamental Freedoms 1950. On appeal, the court found that Article 6(2) was not breached and confirmed that a defendant who wishes to raise a defence of reasonable practicability does have the legal burden of calling positive evidence to prove that it was not possible to have done more to prevent the death or injury. The court justified this stance by observing that the defence should not be difficult for a defendant to prove, as he will have this information to hand, whereas it would be unreasonable to place this burden on the prosecution.

(c)   *'As far as practicable'*: is a duty stricter than 'reasonably practicable', although more lenient than 'physically possible'. For example, current knowledge of the risk of injury will be relevant in judging whether a safety precaution was 'practicable'. The onus is on the person on whom the duty is imposed to show that compliance was not 'practicable'.

3.5.1.3   Causation

The test for causation is the same for both negligence and breach of statutory duty. The onus of proof is on the claimant to prove that there is a causal connection between the breach and the loss on the balance of probabilities.

Whether the claimant can establish causation is a question of fact to be decided by the judge in each case. The claimant is not required to show that the breach is the sole cause of the loss; it is sufficient if the breach materially contributed to the loss (*Bonnington Castings Ltd v Wardlaw* [1956] AC 613). To determine who caused the accident the courts apply common sense to the facts of the case. If a number of people can be shown to have been at fault that does not necessarily mean that they all caused the accident; it is a question of looking at the facts and deciding which factors are too remote and which are not (*Stapley v Gypsum Mines Ltd* [1953] AC 663).

3.5.2 Health and safety legislation

3.5.2.1 Management of Health and Safety at Work Regulations 1999 (implementing the 'Framework Directive')

The revised Management of Health and Safety at Work Regulations 1999 (SI 1999/ 3242) came into force on 29 December 1999 and replaced the Management of Health and Safety at Work Regulations 1992. The Regulations introduce changes to clarify the UK's implementation of the European Framework Directive (89/391/ EEC).

The Regulations implement European Health and Safety Directives relating to the employer's obligations in respect of health and safety for workers and in relation to minimum health and safety requirements for the workplace as to fire safety.

The main provisions regarding employer's duties are as follows.

Risk assessment (reg 3)

All employers are required to make a suitable and sufficient risk assessment of the risks to health and safety of their employees and persons who are not in their employment but who are affected by the conduct of their undertaking. Having made an assessment of the health and safety risks, it is incumbent upon the employer to try to diminish the risks that have been identified. In *Bailey v Commercial Security Services Ltd v TJX Inc* (2001) the first defendants were found negligent for failing to carry out a thorough risk assessment of premises.

An example of the likely approach of the courts to risk assessment can be found in *Griffiths v Vauxhall Motors* [2003] EWCA Civ 412. The court found for the claimant on the grounds that a competent employer would have performed a risk assessment, identified any risk of injury and what could be done to minimise or eradicate that risk.

Due to the large number of accidents involving young and inexperienced workers there are specific requirements in regard to assessment of risk for children and young persons. According to the Regulations, a 'child' means a person who is not over compulsory school age, and 'young person' means any person who has not attained the age of 18 (reg 1). Regulation 3 makes the further requirement that an employer shall not employ a young person unless he has, in relation to the risks to the health and safety of young persons, made or reviewed a risk assessment.

In making or reviewing the assessment, an employer who employs or is to employ a young person shall take particular account of:

(a) the inexperience, lack of awareness of risks and immaturity of young persons;

(b) the fitting-out and layout of the workplace and the workstation;

(c) the nature, degree and duration of exposure to physical, biological and chemical agents;

(d) the form, range, and use of work equipment and the way in which it is handled;

(e) the organisation of processes and activities;

(f) the extent of the health and safety training provided or to be provided to young persons (see reg 19).

The duty on employers to carry out a risk assessment is likely to be one of the areas highlighted by personal injury lawyers to substantiate whether or not the employer has acted reasonably to provide a safe system of work and to establish the question of foreseeability of harm in negligence actions. The HSE booklet *Five Steps to Risk Assessment* is available free to employers and will help to show how pro-active the employer is in regard to the Regulations. If the employer has five or more employees, there is a duty to record the risk assessment (reg 3(6)), and to note any significant findings of the assessment and whether any group of employees is identified as being especially at risk. The assessment should be carried out by consulting employees as to how they carry out their functions, together with taking advice from a relevant health and safety expert and ergonomists. The assessment should be updated and reviewed regularly.

Principles of prevention (reg 4)

According to reg 4, the principles of prevention of risk to be applied are to:

(a)   avoid risks;

(b)   evaluate the risks which cannot be avoided;

(c)   combat the risks at source;

(d)   adapt the work to the individual, especially as regards the design of workplaces, choice of work equipment and choice of working and production methods with a view to alleviating monotonous work and work at a pre-determined work rate to reduce their effects on health;

(e)   adapt to technical progress;

(f)   replace the dangerous by the non-dangerous or less dangerous;

(g)   develop a coherent overall prevention policy which covers technology, organisation of work, working conditions, social relationships and the influence of factors relating to the working environment;

(h)   give collective protective measures priority over individual protective measures; and

(i)   give appropriate instruction to employees.

Review of health and safety arrangements (reg 5)

Employers must make appropriate arrangements for planning, organisation, control, monitoring and review of preventative and protective measures.

Health surveillance (reg 6)

Employers are required to have an appropriate policy on risk surveillance, having regard to the findings of risks identified by the risk assessment. For example, if the risk assessment of employees showed that there were risks to health from airborne dust, that identified risk should be kept under review by regular health checks for rises in respiratory problems in employees.

Health and safety assistance (reg 7)

Employers must appoint competent persons to assist the employer in carrying out compliance with statutory safety provisions. The Regulations require that a safety audit be carried out by accredited auditors who are suitably qualified. The audit will identify potential hazards in the workplace.

Information for employees (reg 10)

Employers must give information which is comprehensible to employees on health and safety risks and protective measures that should be adopted.

Employers' duties to 'outside workers' (reg 12)

Employers must provide information to 'outside workers' relating to hazards and the protective and preventative measures being taken.

Employee capabilities and health and safety training (reg 13)

Employers must provide adequate health and safety training, when first recruited and subsequently on being exposed to new risks. Such training should be repeated periodically.

Risk assessment for new or expectant mothers (reg 16)

For the purpose of reg 16, 'new or expectant mother' means an employee who is pregnant who has given birth within the previous six months or who is breastfeeding. Where the workforce includes women of child-bearing age and the work is of a kind which could involve risk to the health and safety of a new or expectant mother, or of the baby, the risk assessment required by reg 3 must include an assessment of that risk. If at all possible, the employee's working conditions or hours of work should be altered so as to avoid the risk. If it is not reasonable or it is not possible to avoid the risk by these means, the employer may suspend the employee from work for so long as is necessary to avoid the risk.

Where a new or expectant mother works at night and obtains a certificate from a registered medical practitioner or registered midwife showing it is necessary for her health and safety that she should not work for any period identified in the certificate, the employer shall suspend her from work for so long as is necessary for her health and safety.

Protection of young employees (reg 19)

A 'young person' means any person who has not attained the age of 18. In relation to young persons, reg 19 states that employers are under a duty to ensure that young persons are protected from risks which are, as a consequence of the young persons' lack of experience, or absence of awareness of existing or potential risks or the fact that young persons have not yet fully matured. Subject to this, employers are not allowed to employ young persons for work which is beyond their physical or psychological capacity, or involves harmful exposure to agents which are toxic, carcinogenic, cause heritable genetic damage or harm to an unborn child or which in any other way may chronically affect human health. Employers must not allow young persons to work where they may be involved in harmful exposure to radiation; nor involve the risk of accidents which it may reasonably be assumed cannot be recognised or avoided by young persons owing to their insufficient attention to safety or lack of experience or training.

Duties of employees (reg 14)

Although the main thrust of the Regulations is to confirm the obligations on employers in relation to health and safety, there are also obligations on employees who have a duty to:

(a)   use machinery, equipment, dangerous substances or other equipment in accordance with the training and instructions which have been given to them by their employer; and

(b)   inform the employer of anything which the employee considers to represent a danger to health and safety or any shortcomings in the employer's arrangements for health and safety.

3.5.2.2 Health and Safety (Display Screen Equipment) Regulations 1992 (as amended)

The Health and Safety (Display Screen Equipment) Regulations 1992 (SI 1992/ 2792) are applicable to new display screen equipment (DSE) as from 1 January 1993, and to existing DSE from 1 January 1996. However, the requirement of ongoing risk assessment applies to both old and new DSE as from 1 January 1993.

The main provisions are:

(a)   employers must make a risk assessment of workstations used by display screen workers and to reduce risks identified (reg 2);

(b)   employers must ensure that display screen workers take adequate breaks, and must ensure that an appropriate eyesight test is carried out by a competent person (reg 5);

(c)   employers must provide users with adequate health and safety training in the use of any workstation upon which he may be required to work (reg 6);

(d)   employers must also provide adequate health and safety information to DSE operators, which should cover such things as information, and reminders on how to reduce risks such as early reporting of problems and provision of adjustable furniture (reg 7).

The main health problems associated with DSE operation are:

(a)   general fatigue caused by poor workstation design;

(b)   upper limb disorders, such as peritendonitis or carpal tunnel syndrome. Repetitive strain injury (RSI) is the most common problem experienced by keyboard users;

(c)   eyesight problems, such as temporary fatigue, sore eyes and headaches.

Employers should have, and be able to show that they have, an adequate policy designed to reduce risks associated with DSE work. The policy should identify hazards, such as visual fatigue, and action to be taken to reduce risk, such as provision of eyesight tests, screen filters and training in workstation adjustment.

3.5.2.3 Provision and Use of Work Equipment Regulations 1998 (as amended)

The Provision and Use of Work Equipment Regulations 1998 (SI 1998/2306) replace the Provision of Work Equipment Regulations 1992. The Regulations apply to all types of machine, appliance, apparatus, tool or installation for use at work (reg 2) in all types of workplaces. The Regulations are intended to ensure the provision of safe work equipment and its safe use. The main provisions are as follows.

(a)   The employer shall ensure the suitability of work equipment for the purpose for which it is provided. The equipment must be suitable by design and construction, for the place in which it will be used and for the intended purpose (reg 4).

(b)   The employer must ensure that the equipment is maintained in an efficient state (reg 5(1)) and that if machinery has a maintenance log, that the log is kept up to date (reg 5(2)).

(c)   If the work equipment must be assembled and installed correctly in order for it to be safe to use, the employer must ensure that:

(i)   it is inspected after installation and prior to being put into service; or

(ii)   it is inspected after assembly at its new location (reg 6(1)).

The wording of reg 5(1) has been considered by the Court of Appeal in *Stark v Post Office* [2000] ICR 1013. The claim concerned an accident at work where a postman was thrown from a bicycle provided by his employer when part of the front brake broke in two. It was accepted that the defect to the bicycle would not have been detected by a rigorous inspection. Nevertheless, the court found that the form of words used in the regulation gave rise to a finding of strict liability in relation to the provision of work equipment. In *Ball v Street* [2005] EWCA Civ 76 the Court of Appeal reinforced the view that reg 5(1) gives rise to liability where injury is caused by machinery that is not in an efficient state of repair. The claimant was a farmer who was injured when part of a haybailing machine fractured and ricocheted into his left eye. The Court found that notwithstanding that this was a 'freak accident' it was only necessary for the claimant to prove that the equipment failed to work efficiently and that that failure caused the accident. The court found that the machine was no longer in good repair nor was it in an efficient state and such failure caused the accident. The imposition of an absolute duty by the Regulations was designed to render the task of an injured workman easier by simply requiring him to prove that the mechanism of the machine, that is the significant part of the machine, failed to work efficiently or was not in good repair and that such failure caused the accident. In this context 'efficient' refers to its state of repair from a health and safety standpoint and not from that of productivity. However the Regulations do not extend to equipment which an employee is *working on* as distinct from the equipment which he has been *using* or been supplied with to undertake the work. In *Hammond v Commissioner of Police for the Metropolis* [2004] EWCA Civ 830, [2005] PIQR P1 the claimant was attempting to undo a wheel bolt from a vehicle owned by the defendant when the bolt sheared off causing the claimant to be injured. The issue was whether the wheel bolt was 'work equipment' within the Regulations. On appeal the Court of Appeal found that it was not, as it was neither a tool supplied by the employer, nor chosen by him for use by the employee.

(d)   The employer must ensure that employees have adequate health and safety information and, if appropriate, instruction in the use of equipment (reg 8).

(e)   The employer must ensure that anyone using the equipment has had adequate training, including any risks which use may entail and precautions to be adopted (reg 9). In particular, the ACOP attached to these Regulations states that induction training is particularly important when young people first enter the workplace.

(f)   Employers must ensure the protection of persons from dangerous parts of machinery in the following order of precedence (reg 11):

(i)   by fixed guards if practicable; but if not

(ii)   by other guards or other protection devices if practicable; but if not

(iii)   by use of jigs, holders, push-sticks or similar protective devices where practicable; but if not

(iv)   by providing information, instruction, training and supervision as is necessary.

(g)   Employers must ensure that where equipment or the substances produced are at a very high or low temperature there must be protection to prevent injury to any person (reg 13).

(h)   Employers must ensure that, where appropriate, equipment is provided with one or more easily accessible stop controls, and, where appropriate, emergency stop controls, and that they be clearly visible and identifiable (regs 15, 16 and 17 respectively).

(i)   Employers must ensure that, where appropriate, the equipment is provided with suitable means to isolate it from all sources of energy. This must be clearly identifiable and readily accessible. Appropriate measures must be taken to ensure that reconnection of the energy source to the equipment does not expose any person using the equipment to any risk (reg 19).

(j)   The equipment must be suitably stabilised and suitably lit (regs 20 and 21 respectively).

(k)   When maintenance is being carried out, equipment must be shut down if reasonably practicable (reg 22).

(l)   The equipment must be suitably marked with appropriate health and safety information and warning devices as appropriate (regs 23 and 24).

(m)   Due to the rising number of accidents arising out of the use and misuse of forklift trucks, there are comprehensive regulations relating to the use of mobile work equipment. The Regulations require employers to ensure that employees are not carried on mobile equipment unless it is both suitable, and incorporates reasonably practicable safety features (reg 25). The Regulations also seek to reduce the risk of equipment rolling over or overturning by placing on the employer an obligation to increase the stability of the equipment by making structural alterations if necessary (regs 26–28).

3.5.2.4   Personal Protective Equipment at Work Regulations 1992 (as amended)

The Personal Protective Equipment at Work Regulations 1992 (SI 1992/2966) make provision for the supply of protective and safety equipment: for example, eye-protectors, respirators, gloves, clothing for adverse weather conditions, safety footwear, safety hats, high-visibility jackets, etc.

The main provisions are as follows.

(a)   Employers must ensure that suitable personal protective equipment (PPE) is provided to employees at risk to their health and safety while at work. PPE is not suitable unless (reg 4(4)):

   (i)   it is appropriate to the risk involved, the conditions at the place where the exposure to the risk may occur, and the period for which it is worn;

   (ii)   it takes account of ergonomic requirements and the health of persons who may wear it, and of the characteristics of the workstation of each such person.

(b)   Before choosing PPE the employer should make an assessment to ensure that it is suitable and compatible with other work equipment used at the same time (reg 6).

(c)   Employers must ensure that PPE is maintained in efficient working order and good repair (reg 7). The obligation to supply protective equipment relates to identified risks. The Regulations will not be concerned with risks other than those necessitating protective equipment and no absolute duty was intended to be imposed by reg 7(1) in relation to other risks (see *Fytche v Wincanton Logistics* [2003] EWCA Civ 874). In this case the claimant suffered frostbite in the little toe of his right foot because there was a small hole in his boot where the steel cap met the sole. The steel-capped boots were personal protective equipment within the 1992 Regulations. The court found that the boots were provided for the purpose of protecting his foot from falling objects and therefore his claim must fail.

(d)   Employers must ensure that where PPE is provided, employees obtain such information, instruction and training as is adequate to ensure that they know what risks the PPE will avoid or limit, the purpose of the PPE and any action they must take to ensure efficient working of the PPE and must ensure that this information is available to employees (reg 9).

3.5.2.5 Manual Handling Operations Regulations 1992 (amended)

The Manual Handling Operations Regulations 1992 (SI 1992/2793), reg 2(1) provides a definition of manual handling operations as any transporting of a load (including the lifting, carrying and moving thereof) by hand or bodily force. Over one-quarter of accidents reported to the HSE involve manual handling. Despite moves toward mechanisation in industry there are still many jobs, such as packaging and warehouse work, requiring the day-to-day lifting of heavy objects. Many claims are brought by health service staff who may have to lift and carry heavy patients as part of their everyday duties.

The Regulations make provision as follows.

(a) So far as reasonably practicable, employers must avoid the need for employees to undertake any manual handling involving risk of injury (reg 4(1)(a)).

(b) If avoidance is not reasonably practicable, employers must make an assessment of manual handling risks, and try to reduce risk of injury. The assessment should address the task, the load, the working environment and the individual's capability (reg 4(1)(b)).

(c) If it is not reasonably practicable to avoid manual handling operations which involve risk of injury, employers must take steps to reduce manual handling to the lowest level reasonably practicable (reg 4(1)(b)(ii)). In the context of assessing manual handling risks for the purpose of complying with reg 4, the correct approach is for the employer to consider the particular task in the context of the particular place of work and the particular employee who has to perform that task; see *O'Neill v DSG Retail Ltd* [2002] EWCA Civ 1139. In this case the employer conceded that it had failed to give adequate training once it had recognised it was necessary to increase awareness of the risks in manual handling and therefore it had failed to reduce the risk of injury 'to the lowest level reasonably practicable' (as required by reg 4(1)(b)(ii)).

(d) Employees must be provided with information on the weight of each load, and the heaviest side of any load (reg 4(1)(b)(iii)).

Regulation 4 has been amended by the Health and Safety (Miscellaneous Amendments) Regulations 2002 (SI 2002/2174) by the addition of the following paragraph:

(3) In determining for the purposes of this regulation whether manual handling operations at work involve a risk of injury and in determining the appropriate steps to reduce that risk regard shall be had in particular to—

    (a) the physical suitability of the employee to carry out the operations;

    (b) the clothing, footwear or other personal effects he is wearing;

    (c) his knowledge and training;

    (d) the results of any risk assessment carried out pursuant to regulation 3 of the Management of Health and Safety at Work Regulations 1999;

    (e) whether the employee is within a group of employees identified by that assessment as being especially at risk; and

    (f) the results of any health surveillance provided pursuant to regulation 6 of the Management of Health and Safety at Work Regulations 1999.

Employees have a duty to make full use of any system of work provided by the employer to reduce manual handling risks (reg 5). As to the meaning of 'so far as reasonably practicable' in reg 4(1), see *Hawkes v Southwark LBC* (CA, 20 February 1998). In this case, it was found that the defendant had not carried out any risk assessment as required under the Regulations. The judge made it clear that the burden of proving what was 'reasonably practicable' lay on the defendant, and that failure to carry out an assessment did not by itself prove liability, rather it was the failure to take appropriate steps to reduce risk of injury to the lowest level reasonably practicable that was at issue. See also the Lifting Operations and Lifting Equipment Regulations 1998 (SI 1998/2307) which deal with health and safety requirements with respect to lifting equipment.

3.5.2.6   Workplace (Health, Safety and Welfare) Regulations 1992

The Workplace (Health, Safety and Welfare) Regulations 1992 (SI 1992/3004) are supported by an ACOP. The Regulations apply to all workplaces except ships, construction sites and mining operations (reg 3). The Regulations are concerned with the way in which the building and the facilities within it may affect employees

The main provisions are as follows:

(a)   Workplace equipment, devices and systems must be maintained in efficient working order and good repair (reg 5).

(b)   There must be adequate ventilation (reg 6).

(c)   The indoor temperature during working hours must be reasonable, and thermometers must be provided to enable employees to determine the temperature (reg 7).

(d)   Workplaces must have suitable lighting, which, if reasonably practicable, should be natural light (reg 8).

(e)   Workplaces, including furniture, fittings, floors, walls and ceilings, must be kept sufficiently clean, and waste materials must not be allowed to accumulate (reg 9).

(f)   Every workstation must be arranged so that it is suitable for any person likely to work there (reg 11).

(g)   Every floor or traffic route surface must be suitable for the purpose for which it is used. In particular, it must have no hole or slope, or be uneven or slippery so as to expose any person to a risk to his health or safety. So far as reasonably practicable, every floor or traffic route must be kept free of obstructions or articles which may cause a person to slip, trip or fall (reg 12). The claim in *Coates v Jaguar Cars Ltd* [2004] EWCA Civ 337 concerned an accident that occurred as the claimant was going up a number of steps at the defendant's factory. The claimant tripped on the third stair causing him to fall and break his arm. The claimant contended that this amounted to a breach of reg 12 as, if there had been a handrail, he would not have fallen. The Court of Appeal held that there had been no reason to find that the steps posed any real risk provided that those who had used them gave a sufficient degree of care, as had been the case for any other steps of this nature. The judge at first instance was correct to have dismissed the claim.

(h)   So far as reasonably practicable, effective measures must be taken to avoid injury to persons caused by falling or being struck by a falling object (reg 13).

(i)   Suitable and sufficient sanitary conveniences must be provided at readily accessible places. They must be adequately lit, ventilated and kept in a clean and tidy condition (reg 20).

(j)   Suitable and sufficient washing facilities must be provided, including showers if required by the nature of the work for health reasons (reg 21).

(k)   An adequate supply of wholesome drinking water must be provided at the workplace, which should be readily accessible and conspicuously marked where necessary.

3.5.2.7 Construction (Health, Safety and Welfare) Regulations 1996

The Construction (Health, Safety and Welfare) Regulations 1996 (SI 1996/1592) apply only to construction work carried out on construction sites. In the Regulations this is widely defined as 'any place where the principal work activity being carried out is construction work' and 'construction work' is similarly widely defined. The Regulations impose duties on employers, employees and the self-employed to comply with the provisions of the Regulations (reg 4). In particular there is a duty to co-operate with others to enable them to comply with the Regulations and also a duty to report any defect which may endanger the health or safety of the employee or any other person. It should be noted that the duties set out in the Regulations are not absolute but are couched in terms that the appropriate standard is that of 'reasonable practicality'.

Many of the Regulations cover matters aimed at ensuring the welfare of workers and are not covered here. The main features of the Regulations that are relevant to personal injury claims are set out below:

(a)   The Regulations require that there be safe means of access to and egress from the place of work (reg 5). Every place of work shall be made and kept safe for, and without risks to health to, any person at work there (reg 5(2)).

(b)   Preventative measures must be taken to prevent any person from falling while at work (reg 6). Falls from height (of 2 metres or more) are a common cause of injuries on construction sites. To try to combat this, the Regulations specify that there must be suitable and sufficient guard-rails and toe-boards or other similar means of protection to prevent the fall of any person. Where this is not reasonably practicable (due to the nature of the work or the short duration of the work), the employer must instead provide, and the employee must use, suitable personal suspension equipment (ie, safety harnessing). For example, it may not be reasonably practicable for a steeple jack to construct a tower with safety rails etc, in order to carry out work at height. Instead appropriate safety harnessing should be used.

(c)   Annually a significant number of injuries are caused by workers falling through roofs which have been made of materials which are too fragile to bear the weight of a person. Regulation 7 requires that where a fall would be of two metres or more, steps must be taken requiring that:

(i)   sufficient platforms, coverings or other similar means of support are provided;

(ii)   guard-rails are provided to prevent persons working nearby from falling through that material; and

(iii)   prominent warning notices be affixed at the approach to the place where the material is situated (reg 7(2))

(d)   Suitable steps must be taken to prevent, injuries caused by falling objects (reg 8).

(e)   During the demolition or dismantling of any structure, steps must be taken to ensure that it is planned and carried out so as to prevent or minimise danger to any person (reg 10).

(f)   Due to the large number of injuries caused by the collapse of trenches (excavations) being dug for the provision of foundations or pipes and services, all practicable steps must be taken to prevent any person from being buried or trapped by falling material from an excavation that has collapsed accidentally (reg 12). Generally, excavations should be supported in order to prevent the sides collapsing. Steps should also be taken to identify and prevent risk of injury caused by underground cables or other underground services (reg 12(8)).

(g)   Many injuries are caused by vehicles which inadvertently drive into or reverse into workers. Because of this danger, construction sites should be organised with designated traffic routes so that pedestrians and vehicles are separated wherever possible (reg 15). Due to the dangers of reversing vehicles reg 17(2) specifies that the person controlling the vehicle has an obligation to warn any person likely to be at risk from the vehicle reversing. Due to the dangers from workers riding on construction vehicles which are not intended or provided for that purpose reg 17(4) stipulates that this is not permissible.

(h)   Every part of a construction site must be kept in good order and in a reasonable state of cleanliness (reg 26(1). No timber or other material with projecting nails is permissible if this would result in danger to any person (reg 26(3)).

(i)   All plant and equipment used for construction work must be safe and of good construction. It should be made from sound materials of sufficient strength and suitability for the purpose for which it is used or provided (reg 27(1)). There is also a duty to maintain such equipment in such condition that it remains safe and without risks to health when it is being used (reg 27(2)).

(j)   Any person who carries out any activity involving construction work where training, technical knowledge or experience is necessary to reduce the risks of injury to any person must either have the requisite level of knowledge or experience, or if he has not, he must be under supervision by a person who does (reg 28).

3.5.2.8   Control of Substances Hazardous to Health Regulations 2002

The Control of Substances Hazardous to Health Regulations 2002 (SI 2002/2677) are concerned with substances hazardous to health, which include chemicals, airborne dusts, micro-organisms, biological agents and respiratory sensitisers.

Employers' duties are:

(a)   to carry out a formal risk assessment of risks to employees;

(b)   to prevent or control exposure to risks;

(c)   to ensure proper use of personal protective equipment;

(d)   to monitor exposure of employees;

(e)   to provide health surveillance of employees where necessary (ie, where a particular task is known to make employees susceptible to a particular injury or disease);

(f)   to provide information and training to employees regarding hazardous substances.

3.5.3 Statutory duty and common law negligence

The claimant employee's case will frequently make a claim in both common law negligence and breach of statutory duty. Although the two are distinct causes of action, they are inevitably linked. It is usually difficult, but not impossible, to show that, if the employer has complied with regulations, he has nevertheless been negligent (*Franklin v Gramophone Co Ltd* [1948] 1 KB 542; *Close v Steel Co of Wales* [1962] AC 367). However, the employer may be liable for breach of statutory duty even though he has not been negligent. The onus of proof may also be different in the two causes: in negligence the onus is upon the claimant to show a breach, but for breach of statutory duty the onus is often on the defendant to show that he acted 'as far as (reasonably) practicable' (see **3.5.1.2**).

In *Sherlock v Chester City Council* [2004] EWCA Civ 201 the claimant was a joiner who lost his thumb and index finger in an accident when using a circular saw provided by his employer. He claimed that his employer was both negligent for failing to carry out an appropriate risk assessment and also in breach of statutory duty in relation to breaches of reg 3 of the Management of Health and Safety at Work Regulations 1999, reg 20 of the Provision and Use of Work Equipment Regulations 1998, and reg 4 of the Manual Handling Operations Regulations 1992. On appeal to the Court of Appeal Arden LJ considered whether it was appropriate for there to be findings of contributory negligence in a breach of statutory duty case:

> There may be some justification for the view [that the findings of contributory negligence are not appropriate] in cases of momentary inattention by an employee. But where a risk has been consciously accepted by an employee, it seems to me that different considerations may arise. That is particularly so where the employee is skilled and the precaution in question is neither esoteric nor one which he could not take himself .... In those circumstances it seems to me that the appellant can properly be required to bear the greater responsibility. I would assess his responsibility for the accident at 60 per cent.

3.5.4 Employment tribunals and personal injury claims

When considering the appropriate forum for bringing a claim, it is important to bear in mind the concurrent jurisdiction of the employment tribunal to award damages for a claim for personal injury arising out of a discrimination claim (see *Sheriff v Klyne Tugs (Lowestoft) Ltd* [1999] ICR 707). The employee brought proceedings in the employment tribunal for unlawful racial discrimination under the Race Relations Act 1976. The employer did not admit liability but paid the employee £4,000 in full and final settlement of all claims for which an industrial tribunal had jurisdiction under a formal agreement. At a later date, the employee instructed solicitors to bring a claim in the county court for damages for personal injury caused by the racial discrimination and abusive treatment. The claim was struck out on the basis that it had been brought in breach of the earlier agreement of settlement. On appeal, the court found that both the employment tribunal and the county court had jurisdiction to award damages for the tort of racial discrimination and that included awarding damages for personal injury. In which court the claim was to be brought was a question of causation of the injury. In this case, the claim was for injury which had been sustained arising out of employment and in respect of which the employment tribunal had jurisdiction. Therefore, the settlement agreement applied and the claim could not be re-litigated in the county court. The court found that there was a principle for public policy that claims that have been *or could have been* litigated in one tribunal, should not be allowed to be litigated in another.

The Employment Appeals Tribunal has also considered the question of claims for psychiatric injury in the context of a racial discrimination claim. In *Y Essa v Laing Ltd* [2004] EWCA 02 the claimant complained to an employment tribunal about a racial remark addressed to him by his foreman. The tribunal upheld his complaint of racial discrimination under the Race Relations Act 1976. At the damages hearing the tribunal held that the employer was only liable for such reasonably foreseeable loss as was directly attributable to the discriminating act. The claimant received £5,000 for injured feelings. The employment appeal tribunal allowed the appeal in relation to compensation for psychiatric injury. The appeal tribunal held that compensation to a victim was to be assessed by reference to the loss that arose naturally and directly from the wrong. All that was needed was to establish a causal link between the racial abuse and the psychiatric illness (*Sheriff v Klyne Tugs (Lowestoft) Ltd* considered).

3.6 Occupiers' liability

3.6.1 Occupiers' liability to lawful visitors

The Occupiers' Liability Act 1957 (OLA 1957) replaces common law rules concerning the duty owed by an occupier to a lawful visitor.

Under s 1(1), 'occupier' is given the same meaning as at common law (s 1(2)), the test for which was said by Lord Denning in *Wheat v E Lacon & Co Ltd* [1966] AC 522 to be, 'who is in sufficient control?'.

A 'visitor' is a person who would be treated as an invitee or licensee at common law (s 1(2)) and who therefore is a lawful visitor (as opposed to a trespasser). The duty of care extends not only to the visitor's person but also to his property (s 1(3)).

3.6.2 The nature of the duty of care

The common duty of care is a duty to take such care as in all the circumstances of the case is reasonable to see that the visitor will be reasonably safe in using the premises for the purposes for which he is invited or permitted by the occupier to be there (s 2(2)).

The common duty of care does not impose on an occupier any obligation to a visitor in respect of risks willingly accepted as his by the visitor (s 2(5)).

3.6.3 Discharging the duty of care

The duty is to take '... such care as ... in all the circumstances ... is reasonable' taking into account the degree of care, and of want of care, which would ordinarily be looked for in such a visitor (s 2(3)). A warning may discharge the duty of care if it is enough to enable the visitor to be reasonably safe (s 2(4)).

In *Tomlinson v Congleton Borough Council and Another* [2002] EWCA Civ 309, [2003] 2 WLR 1120, the claimant was injured when diving into a lake despite signs prohibiting swimming and warning that to do so was dangerous. The defendants argued that the risk of danger was an obvious one which the claimant had willingly accepted; that they owed the claimant no duty of care; or if they did, it had been discharged by the display of warning notices.

The Court of Appeal agreed with the court of first instance and found in favour of the claimant. The House of Lords overturned the Court of Appeal decision on the basis that it would be unreasonable to impose a duty to protect people from self-inflicted injuries that they sustained when voluntarily taking risks in the face of obvious warnings. Even if the local authority had owed the claimant a duty of care, that duty would not extend to preventing the claimant from diving or warning him against dangers that were obvious. The court took the view that it was not appropriate to find in favour of the claimant and thereby impose a duty on local authorities to protect those foolish enough to ignore clear warnings. This would be at the expense of the vast majority of people who might find that they are barred from all manner of recreational activities on public land, for fear that they injure themselves and decide to sue the local authority.

3.6.4 Employing an independent contractor

Where injury is caused to a visitor by a danger due to the faulty execution of any work of construction, maintenance or repair by an independent contractor employed by the occupier, the occupier will not be treated by this reason alone as answerable for the danger if in all the circumstances (s 2(4)(b)):

(a) he had acted reasonably in entrusting the work to an independent contractor; and

(b) he had taken such steps (if any) as he reasonably ought in order to satisfy himself that:

    (i)   the contractor was competent; and

    (ii)   that the work had been properly done.

The duty of care under the Act is therefore delegable to an independent contractor. This should be contrasted with the personal nature of the common duty of care owed to an employee, which is non-delegable (see *Wilsons & Clyde Coal v English* [1938] AC 57).

3.6.5 Exclusion or modification of duty of care

By s 2(1) of the OLA 1957, an occupier may extend, restrict, modify or exclude his duty to any visitor. However, this must be read subject to s 2 of the Unfair Contract Terms Act 1977 under which, in the case of business liability:

(a) a person cannot by reference to any contract term or to a notice given to persons generally or to particular persons exclude or restrict his liability for death or personal injury resulting from negligence;

(b) in the case of other loss or damage, a person cannot so exclude or restrict his liability for negligence except in so far as the term or notice satisfies the requirement of reasonableness.

3.6.6 Occupiers' liability to non-visitors (trespassers)

The Occupiers' Liability Act 1984 replaces common law rules relating to duties owed to unauthorised visitors (ie trespassers).

Under s 1(3) of the OLA 1984 an occupier of premises owes a duty to another (not being his visitor) in respect of any danger due to the state of the premises or to things done or omitted to be done on them if:

(a) he is aware of the danger or has reasonable grounds to believe that it exists;

(b) he knows or has reasonable grounds to believe that the other is in the vicinity of the danger concerned or that he may come into the vicinity of the danger (in either case, whether he has lawful authority for being in that vicinity or not); and

(c) the risk is one against which, in all the circumstances of the case, he may reasonably be expected to offer the other some protection.

3.6.7   The nature of the duty

The duty is to take such care as is reasonable in all the circumstances of the case to see that the person does not suffer injury on the premises by reason of the danger concerned.

3.6.8   Discharging the duty

Any duty owed may be discharged by taking such steps as are reasonable in all the circumstances of the case to give warning of the danger concerned or to discourage persons from incurring the risk. Further, no duty is owed by virtue of the Act to any person in respect of risks willingly accepted by that person.

An example of a finding of liability against an occupier of premises to non-visitors is *Young v Kent County Council* [2005] EWHC 1342 (QB). The court held that the council had a duty of care to protect children from the known risk of them climbing onto the roof of a school building. There had been a breach of that duty as the council had failed to protect against that risk despite the existence of a low cost solution. The incident giving rise to the claim occurred whilst a youth club had been operating on the school's premises. The claimant climbed onto the roof of the building. The skylight was brittle and a Health and Safety Executive report indicated that there had been a problem with access to the roof prior to the incident in question. The claimant argued that the council was liable under the Occupiers' Liability Act 1984. There was a danger of which the council was aware that posed a risk of injury. There were reasonable grounds to believe that children would be in the vicinity of that danger and the council was under a duty to protect them against their own mischievous behaviour.

3.7   Vicarious liability

3.7.1   Definition

An employer will be vicariously liable for his employee's torts if committed in the course of his employment. Therefore, it falls to be established:

(a)   whether the tort was committed by an employee; and

(b)   whether that employee was acting in the course of (ie, within the scope of) his employment.

3.7.2   'Course of employment'

The employee must have committed the tort 'in the course of his employment' – which is less clear than may first appear. There are many cases on the point, but the nearest to a formulation of a rule is that the employer will be liable for acts of employees if they perform an authorised act in an unauthorised way, but will not be liable for acts not sufficiently connected with authorised acts.

3.7.3   Disobedience of orders by employees

Having established that an employer will be liable for acts of his employees if they are acting within the course of their employment, it is necessary to examine the situation where the employee disobeys the orders of his employer in relation to the way he carries out his work. In *Rose v Plenty* [1976] 1 All ER 97 a milkman had been told by his employers not to allow children to help him on his rounds. Subsequently he allowed a child to assist him and the child was injured while riding on the milk float due to the milkman's negligent driving. On appeal to the Court of Appeal, the employer was found to be vicariously liable. The court held that the employee was doing his job but was using a method that his employers had prohibited. Nonetheless, he was still found to be working within the scope of his employment as it was performed for the benefit of the defendant's business.

Contrast the above with the facts of *Lister and Others v Hesley Hall Ltd* [2001] 2 All ER 769. The facts of the case were that the warden of the school abused boys while they were resident at the school. The House of Lords held the defendant vicariously liable for the acts of their employee. The Lords said that the court should not concentrate on the nature of the actual act complained of (abuse) but that they should concentrate on the closeness of the connection between the nature of the employment and the tort complained of. The Lords found that the defendant employed the warden to care for the claimants. The abuse took place while he was carrying out the duties required by his employment. On that basis the proximity between the employment and the tort complained of was very close and therefore the defendant ought to be liable.

The Court of Appeal applied the reasoning in *Lister and Others v Hesley Hall Ltd* (2001) in the subsequent case of *Mattis v Pollock* [2003] EWCA Civ 887. In this case the claimant was stabbed by a doorman of a nightclub who was employed by the defendant nightclub owner.   The court found that the defendant expected the doorman to carry out his duties in an aggressive manner, and where an employee was expected to use violence while carrying out his duties, the likelihood of establishing that an act of violence fell within the scope of his employment was greater.

3.8 Enforcement of health and safety at work

The function of enforcement is carried out by:

(a)   the HSE, which deals broadly with industrial working environments (the Health and Safety Commission is responsible for policy development);

(b)   various specialist agencies appointed on behalf of the HSE (eg, UK Atomic Energy Authority);

(c)   local authorities, which deal broadly with non-industrial working environments.

3.8.1 Health and safety inspectors

Health and safety inspectors have wide powers to enter premises and carry out investigations. As a result of an investigation revealing a contravention, an inspector may:

(a)   issue an improvement notice requiring any contravention to be remedied;

(b)   serve a prohibition notice requring the contravention to be remedied and fixing a time after which the activity is prohibited unless remedied;

(c)   commence a criminal prosecution (which may give rise to a relevant conviction that can be used against the employer by the employee in subsequent civil proceedings).

3.8.2 The employer's duty to report, maintain and implement safety provisions

The following are the principal requirements of an employer.

(a)   An employer who employs more than five persons must have written details of his policy in regard to the organisation, control, monitoring and review of health and safety measures.

(b)   An employer is under a duty to report certain accidents, diseases and dangerous occurrences to the HSE on Form F2508. Employers are also able to report accidents to the HSE by posting information direct to their internet site at www.riddor.gov.uk. This enables the HSE to consider an investigation of the incident. All occurrences which are required to be reported must be recorded and details of the injuries must be kept in an accident book. The records must be kept for at least three years.

(c)   The employer may (and in certain circumstances must) have a safety representative to represent the health and safety interests of the employees. Such a representative has wide powers to investigate potential hazards and dangerous occurrences and to follow up complaints made by employees.

(d)   In addition to the safety representative, the employer may (and in certain circumstances must) have a safety committee, the function of which includes:

   (i)   the studying of accidents and notifiable diseases in order to recommend corrective measures to management;

   (ii)   making recommendations on safety training;

   (iii)   examining reports of the HSE and safety representatives;

   (iv)   making recommendations on developing/changing safety rules.

(e)   Where an employee is injured at work and claims benefit, in certain circumstances the employer is obliged to complete Form B176 to be sent to the Department of Work and Pensions.

(f)   Subject to certain exceptions, an employer is required by the Employers' Liability (Compulsory Insurance) Act 1969 to take out insurance against liability to his own employees.

3.8.3   Employer's liability – enforcement through criminal proceedings

The Court of Appeal established in *R v Gateway Foodmarkets Ltd* [1997] 3 All ER 78 that s 2(1) of the Health and Safety at Work etc Act 1974 imposed a duty of strict liability. This is qualified only by the defence that the employer has done everything reasonably practicable to ensure that no person's health and safety is put at risk. The defendants appealed against their conviction that they failed to do everything reasonable to ensure the safety of their employees. The court dismissed the company's appeal and held that both s 2(1) and s 3(1) of the Act were to be interpreted so as to impose liability in the event of a failure to ensure safety unless all reasonable precautions had been taken, not only by the company itself but by its servants and agents on its behalf.

Following concern at the low level of fines being imposed for offences under the Health and Safety at Work etc Act 1974, the Court of Appeal has given guidance on the factors to be taken into account by courts when considering the appropriate penalty for this type of offence. In *R v Howe & Son (Engineers) Ltd* [1999] 2 All ER 249, the Court of Appeal stated that the aim of the Act was to ensure safety for employees and the public and therefore fines needed to be large enough to convey that message. In general, they should not be so large as to put the employer out of business. In determining seriousness, the court should consider:

(a)   how far short of the appropriate standard the defendant had been;

(b)   that the standard of care was the same for small organisations as for large;

(c)   the degree of risk and extent of danger involved; and

(d)   the defendant's resources and the effect of a fine on its business.

Aggravating factors could include:

(a)   failure to heed warnings;

(b)   deliberate breach of regulations in pursuit of profit or saving money; and

(c)   loss of life.

Mitigating factors could include:

(a)   early admission of responsibility;

(b)   plea of guilty;

(c)   taking action to remedy any breach brought to the company's notice; and

(d)   a good safety record.

The court further held that it was incumbent upon a defendant seeking to make representations about its financial position to provide copies of accounts to the court and the prosecution in good time.

The above guidelines where considered by the Court of Appeal in *R v Rollco Screw & Rivet Co Ltd* [1999] 2 Cr App R (S) 436. The defendant company and two of its directors protested that the length of time given for payment of fines was inappropriate and that no distinction should be made between personal and corporate defendants (as there was a risk of double penalty if directors and shareholders where the same people). On appeal, the court agreed that a personal defendant's period of punishment had to remain within acceptable boundaries, this was not true of a corporate defendant as the same sense of anxiety was unlikely and a fine could be ordered to be payable over a longer period. The level of fines must make it clear that directors had a personal responsibility; there was a risk of double penalty in smaller companies where directors were also shareholders and would be the principal losers.

3.9   Claims for psychiatric illness or 'nervous shock'

Claims for psychiatric injury or illness have risen markedly in recent years on the basis that if the defendant would be liable for foreseeable physical injury then he ought also to be liable for foreseeable psychological injury.

3.9.1   What is nervous shock?

There must be evidence that the claimant has suffered a recognised psychiatric illness which is more than temporary grief or fright. In recent years 'nervous shock' and 'post-traumatic stress disorder' (PTSD) have become commonly used to mean psychological illness brought about by a negligent act. The Law Commission's consultation paper on liability for psychiatric illness (1995) favoured the term 'psychiatric illness'.

There are two main systems of classification of psychiatric illnesses currently used in the UK:

(a)   the Diagnostic and Statistical Manual of Mental Disorders of the American Psychiatric Association, fourth edition (DSM IV); and

(b)   The World Health Organisation International Classification of Mental and Behavioural Disorders, tenth edition (ICD-10)

One recognised psychiatric illness which forms part of the claim by claimants is PTSD. Major factors in the onset of PTSD tend to be a life-threatening experience, or exposure to grotesque death. The symptoms of PTSD are listed in **2.2.6**.

3.9.2 Primary and secondary victims

To be regarded as a primary victim the claimant must be able to show a risk of foreseeable physical harm. The key importance of this classification between primary and secondary victims is that if the claimant can show that he is a primary victim then he is likely to be treated more favourably by the courts. Primary victims will normally be involved in the events as participants, but it will be relatively rare for a primary victim directly involved in the events not to suffer any physical injury as well. Secondary victims are normally witnesses of injury caused to primary victims and have not suffered physical injury themselves.

3.9.3 Foreseeability of primary and secondary victims

3.9.3.1 Primary victims

A primary victim must show that some personal injury (ie, physical injury or psychiatric injury) was reasonably foreseeable as a result of the defendant's negligence so as to bring him within the scope of the defendant's duty of care. No distinction should be brought between a physical or a psychiatric injury.

3.9.3.2 Secondary victims

A secondary victim must show that a person of reasonable fortitude would have foreseeably suffered some psychiatric injury. Foreseeability of psychiatric injury is of critical importance to secondary victims as they will normally be outside the scope of persons who might suffer foreseeable physical injury.

If a claimant is a secondary victim, he will need to show sufficiently close ties of love and affection with a primary victim. Following the House of Lords' decision in *Alcock v Chief Constable for South Yorkshire* [1992] AC 310, there is a rebuttable presumption of sufficiently close ties between, for example, relationships as between parents, children and spouses. In *Vernon v Bosley (No 1)* [1997] 1 All ER 577, CA, although damages for normal grief and bereavement suffered as a result of another's negligence were not recoverable, the claimant in a position of a secondary victim could recover damages for PTSD or pathological grief disorder provided the two pre-conditions for recovery of damages for psychiatric illness were satisfied: namely, that the claimant was in a close and loving relationship with the primary victim and was connected with the accident in time and space, ie, the bystander and direct viewer.

If the claimant did not perceive the events in question with his own unaided senses, generally there will be no recovery for psychiatric illness. In *Frost v Chief Constable of South Yorkshire* [1997] 1 All ER 540, it was held that the claimant must witness the event with his own unaided senses, either by sight or hearing.

In *Greatorex v Greatorex* [2000] 4 All ER 769, the court considered whether or not a primary victim owed any duty of care to a third party where the third party suffers psychiatric injury. Although the case is based on a very singular set of facts, it is useful reading to anyone new to this area of law as Cazalet J considered many of the prior cases on nervous shock in the course of his judgment. The relevant facts are that the claimant was a fireman and father of the defendant who was the crash victim in a road traffic accident. It was accepted that the accident was the defendant's fault. The claimant did not witness the accident but went to the scene in the course of his employment as a fire officer. The claimant was diagnosed as suffering from post-traumatic stress disorder as a result of what he had seen. In essence the question was 'does a victim of self-inflicted injuries owe a duty of care to a third party not to cause him psychiatric injury?'. Having considered the facts the court decided that a victim does not owe a duty to a third party in circumstances where self-inflicted injuries cause psychiatric injury as to conclude otherwise would 'create a significant limitation upon an individual's freedom of action'. The judge went on to conclude that such an action would only be maintainable at all by a close relative, which would lead to undesirable litigation within the family. Such policy considerations were adjudged to outweigh arguments in favour of there being such a duty of care.

In order for a secondary victim to bring a successful claim for PTSD, the claimant must not only suffer from a recognised psychiatric illness, but it must also be as a result of some 'traumatic experience' or 'event' as opposed to a slow realisation, as can be seen from the following contrasting cases. In *Walters v North Glamorgan NHS Trust* [2002] EWHC 321 (QB), [2002] All ER (D) 65 the mother of a baby claimed psychiatric injury as a result of witnessing her child's decline and death due to misdiagnosis at the treating hospital. The period from first onset of injury to death was 36 hours. The claimant issued proceedings against the hospital for damages. The court found that although clearly not a primary victim, she could succeed as a secondary victim if her psychiatric injury was induced by shock as a result of the sudden appreciation by sight or sound of a horrifying event or its immediate aftermath. The court found that the whole period of 36 hours could be seen in law as a horrifying event and the claimant was therefore entitled to recover damages. Contrast *Sion v Hampstead Health Authority* [1994] 5 Med LR 170. The claimant's son was injured in a motorcycle accident. The father stayed at the bedside for 14 days watching his son deteriorate, fall into a coma and finally succumb to death. The claimant developed a psychiatric illness and sought to sue the hospital for negligence in the treatment of his son. The defendant applied to strike out the claim. The claim was struck out as there was no evidence of 'shock' and no sudden appreciation of a horrifying event. On the contrary, the evidence suggested a decline that continued for some time, from first arrival at the hospital to appreciation of medical negligence after the inquest. In particular, the death, when it occurred, was not surprising, but expected.

In *Atkinson v Seghal* [2003] EWCA Civ 697 the claimant appealed to the Court of Appeal following a decision dismissing her claim for nervous shock. The facts of the case were such that the claimant was present at the immediate aftermath of a road traffic accident at which her daughter had died. At that time she was told of the death of her daughter, but did not see the body until some hours later in the mortuary. It was only when she viewed the body that the claimant broke down and suffered the psychiatric condition that formed the basis of her claim. On appeal, the court found that, provided events retained sufficient proximity, the subsequent viewing of the body could be seen as part of the aftermath of the incident and on that basis the claim could succeed.

3.9.4 Employee victims

Following the House of Lords' decision in *White v Chief Constable of South Yorkshire* [1999] 2 AC 455, it is clear that unless employees can show a risk of physical injury (and therefore fall into the category of primary victims), they will be treated as secondary victims. In *Young v Charles Church (Southern) Ltd* (1998) BMLR 146, it was established that an employee who suffered psychiatric illness after seeing a workmate electrocuted close to him could recover damages against his employer as a primary victim because of the risk to himself of physical injury. The court decided that the ambit of the regulations was not limited to physical electrocution. The statute gave protection to employees from kinds of injury which could be foreseen as likely to occur when the electrical cable or equipment was allowed to become a source of danger to them. This included mental illness caused to the claimant by the shock of seeing his workmate electrocuted in circumstances where he was fortunate to escape electrocution himself.

Contrast the above case with *Hunter v British Coal* [1999] QB 89, CA. The claimant was a driver in a coalmine. His vehicle struck a hydrant causing it to leak. With the help of a workmate, he tried to stop the flow but failed. He left the scene in search of help. When the claimant was 30 metres away, the hydrant burst, and he was told that someone was injured. On his way back to the scene, he was told that the workmate who had been helping him had died. The claimant thought he was responsible and suffered nervous shock and depression. He brought proceedings for damages against his employers. It was held that a claimant who believes he has been the cause of another's death in an accident caused by the defendant's negligence could recover damages as a primary victim if he was directly involved as a participant in the incident. However, a claimant who was not at the scene could not recover damages as a primary victim merely because he felt responsible for the incident. In this case, the claimant was not involved in the incident in which the workmate died as he was 30 metres away, and only suffered psychiatric injury on being told of the death some 15 minutes later. Therefore, there was not sufficient proximity in time and space with the incident. Also, the illness triggered by the death was not a foreseeable consequence of the defendant's breach of duty of care as it was an abnormal reaction to being told of the workmate's death triggered by an irrational feeling that he was responsible.

3.9.5   Professional rescuers

In relation to psychological injury, in the case of *Frost v Chief Constable of South Yorkshire Police,* the Court of Appeal considered *Page v Smith* [1996] AC 155 and bypassed the categorisation of primary or secondary victims and held that claimants could recover on the basis of their work as rescuers. Also, it was claimed that because the claimants were employees of the defendant, the defendant owed them a duty of care to protect them from the risk of physical as well as psychiatric injury. *Frost v Chief Constable of South Yorkshire* was appealed to the House of Lords (reported as *White v Chief Constable of South Yorkshire Police and Others* [1999] 2 AC 455). The Lords rejected the police officers' claims for psychiatric injury.

The Lords disagreed with the finding in the Court of Appeal that the claimants, as rescuers, were to be treated as a special category. In his judgment, Lord Hoffmann said that the claimants asserted that they were in a special position from friends or relatives who might have developed psychiatric injuries. They claimed that, because it was admitted that the disaster had been caused by the negligence of persons for whom the defendants were vicariously liable, thus the claimants were owed a special duty as employees. The Lords debated whether it was appropriate to recognise a duty to guard employees against psychiatric injury. It was felt that it would not be fair to give police officers the right to a claim merely because the disaster had been caused by the negligence of other police officers and that, if it was given effect, the law would not be seen to be treating like cases with like.

The claimants also argued that their position was analogous to that of rescuers. The Lords rejected this argument, also stating that there was no authority for placing rescuers in a special position. The Lords decided this, based on two factors:

(a)   the problem of applying a definition to define the class of rescuers that could claim; and

(b)   if the law did allow the claims to succeed, the result would be unacceptable to the ordinary person who would think it wrong that police officers should have the right to compensation for psychiatric injury out of public funds when bereaved relatives did not. Fairness demanded that the appeal be allowed and the claims were therefore dismissed.

3.9.6 Bystanders as victims

A 'mere bystander' is someone who is not a primary victim or a secondary victim, but is merely a witness.

3.10 Occupational stress

3.10.1 The meaning of occupational stress

In trying to come to some workable definition of 'occupational stress', Hale LJ in *Hatton v Sutherland; Barber v Somerset County Council; Jones v Sandwell Metropolitan Borough Council; Bishop v Baker Refractories Ltd* [2002] EWCA Civ 76, [2002] 2 All ER 1 referred to three documents which she said the court had found particularly helpful:

(a) *Stress in the Public Sector – Nurses, Police, Social Workers and Teachers* (1988) defines stress as:

an excess of demands upon an individual in excess of their ability to cope.

(b) *Managing Occupational Stress: a Guide for Managers and Teachers in the School Sector* (Education Service Advisory Committee of the Health and Safety Commission, 1990) defines stress as:

a process that can occur when there is an unresolved mismatch between the perceived pressures of the work situation and an individual's ability to 'cope'.

(c) The Health and Safety executive booklet, *Stress at Work* (1995) defines stress as:

The reaction people have to excessive pressures or other types of demand placed upon them. It arises when they worry that they can't cope ...

Stress is not the same as ill health. But in some cases, particularly where pressures are intense and continue for some time, the effect of stress can be more sustained and far more damaging, leading to longer term psychological problems and physical ill health.

The general principles to be applied in claims for psychiatric injury, set out in the Court of Appeal decision of *Barber v Somerset County Council* (see above), have subsequently been applied in *Hartman v South Essex Mental Health and Community Care NHS Trust* [2005] EWCA Civ 06.

In *Hatton v Sutherland,* the judge concluded that harmful levels of stress are more likely to occur in situations where people feel powerless or trapped, and are therefore much more likely to affect people at junior levels, and, secondly, stress is a psychological phenomenon which can lead to either physical or mental ill health or both.

In *Barber v Somerset County Council* [2004] UKHL 13 the House of Lords overturned the Court of Appeal's earlier decision in the conjoined appeal with *Sutherland v Hatton.* In September 1995 the claimant was told that in order to maintain his salary level he would have to take on further responsibilities. He worked between 61 and 70 hours per week, and often had to work in the evenings and at weekends. In February 1996 the claimant spoke of 'work overload' to the school's deputy head teacher, and in March and April consulted his GP about stress at work, and made enquiries about taking early retirement. In May the claimant was absent from work for three weeks, his absence certified by his GP as being due to stress and depression. On his return to work he met with the head teacher and the two deputy head teachers, and discussed the fact that he was not coping with his workload. No steps were taken by the school to assist him. In November 1996 he left the school and did not return. The court ruled that the test to be applied was: had the employer fallen below the standard properly to be expected of a reasonable and prudent employer taking positive steps for the safety of its workers in the light of what was known or ought to have been known? The Lords found that the Court of Appeal had failed to give adequate weight to the fact that the claimant was an experienced and conscientious teacher who had been absent for three weeks with no physical ailment, such absence having been certified as being due to stress and depression. The Lords concluded that the local authority was in breach of its duty to the claimant to take reasonable care to avoid injuring his health as it was aware that he was having difficulties but had taken no steps to assist him.

3.10.2 Duty of care

In *Petch v Commissioners of Customs and Excise* [1993] ICR 789, it was accepted that the ordinary principles of employers' liability applied to claims for psychiatric illness arising from employment. Although the claim in *Petch* failed, Colman J, in *Walker v Northumberland County Council* [1995] 1 All ER 737, applied the same principles in upholding the claim. In this case, Mr Walker was a conscientious but overworked manager of a social work area office, with a heavy and emotionally demanding case-load of child abuse cases. Although he complained and asked for help and for extra leave, the judge held that his first mental breakdown was not foreseeable. There was, however, liability when he returned to work with a promise of extra help, which did not materialise and he experienced a second breakdown only a few months later.

Petch and *Walker* have both been cited with approval by the Court of Appeal in *Garrett v London Borough of Camden* [2001] EWCA Civ 395.

3.10.3 The foreseeability test applicable to occupational stress cases

Dillon LJ formulated the forseeablility test in *Petch:*

> ... unless senior management in the defendant's department were aware or ought to have been aware that the plaintiff was showing signs of impending breakdown, or were aware or ought to have been aware that his workload carried a real risk that he would have a breakdown, then the defendants were not negligent in failing to avert the breakdown.

In *Hatton v Sutherland* the court took the issue of foreseeability a stage further. The court found that when considering forseeability it is necessary to consider the characteristics of the employee concerned and the demands which the employer makes on him.

Factors likely to be relevant for consideration include:

(a)   the nature and extent of the work done by the employee;

(b)   how alert the employer was to picking up signs of stress from an employee;

(c)   employers should be more alert to picking up signs from an employee who is being overworked in an intellectually or emotionally demanding job;

(d)   signs that others doing the same work are under harmful levels of stress;

(e)   others who have already suffered injury to their health arising from their work;

(f)   an abnormal level of sickness or absence amongst others at the same grade or same department.

More importantly, are there signs from the employee himself?

(a)   Has the employee or his doctor made it plain that unless something is done to help, there is a clear risk of breakdown in mental or physical health?

(b)   Has there been frequent or prolonged absence from work, which is uncharacteristic of the person concerned? However, there must also be good reason to think that the underlying cause is occupational stress rather than other factors.

(c)   Unless the employer knows of some particular problem or vulnerability, the employer is usually entitled to assume the employee is up to the normal pressures of the job. Only if there is something specific about the job, or the employee, or a combination of the two, must he look further. Generally, the employer is entitled to take what he is told by or on behalf of his employee at face value.

(d)   An employee who returns to work after a period of sickness without making further disclosure or explanation to his employer is usually implying that he believes himself fit to return to the work which he was doing before. The employer is usually entitled to take that at face value unless he has other good reasons to think to the contrary.

The next question for the court was how strong should indications of stress be before an employer has a duty to act?

Courts have acknowledged that employers may have difficulties in knowing when and why a particular employee will react due to stress and whether they are susceptible to suffering injury to health brought on by stress. In *Hatton v Sutherland* the court found that the indications must be plain enough for any reasonable employer to realise that he should be doing something about it.

Young v Post Office [2002] EWCA Civ 661 was decided after *Hatton v Sutherland* and considered whether it is the responsibility of the claimant to inform the employer if he is unable to cope and whether the claimant will be contributorily negligent if he fails to do so. The claimant had worked for the Post Office for a number of years and had been promoted to workshop manager. He had no direct line manager, and when a new computer system was introduced he was expected to familiarise himself with it without formal training. The claimant began to show signs of stress and eventually suffered a nervous breakdown and subsequently took four months off work to recover. Arrangements were made to allow the claimant to return to work gradually and on a flexible basis. When the claimant returned to work he quickly shouldered the burden of the management position that had led to his breakdown. Seven weeks later the claimant was again unable to continue due to stress and left. The defendants contended that they had done all that they could in offering a less stressful work pattern for the claimant. On appeal, the court found for the claimant as it was plainly foreseeable that there might be a recurrence if appropriate steps were not taken when the claimant returned to work and the employer owed a duty to take such steps. Although the employer had told the claimant that he could adopt a flexible approach to his work, the reality was that he was a hardworking and conscientious employee and it was foreseeable that he would quickly revert to overworking and the employer had a duty to ensure help was on hand. Regarding the allegation of contributory negligence, the court found that this was not relevant in this case and would be unusual but was 'theoretically possible'.

The High Court decision of *Barlow v Broxbourne Borough Council* [2003] EWHC 50, QB, [2003] All ER (D) 208 (Jan) provides an example of the application of the principles set out by the Court of Appeal in *Hatton v Sutherland*. B had initially been employed as a gardener and had obtained several promotions to become senior operations manager in 1993. B's claim was based on two broad grounds: systematic victimisation and 'general' bullying. He alleged that from approximately 1997 he had been deliberately victimised and bullied by senior members of the council's staff which had caused him to suffer emotional distress and psychological injury. The alleged 'victimisation' and 'bullying' had included receipt of lengthy letters detailing B's non-performance, threats of disciplinary action and, at times, abusive language. Medical experts for each party were agreed that B had suffered a moderately severe depressive episode. Consequently, B had been unable to continue working for the council. B argued that he had been exposed to such stress at work that he had developed a stress-related illness which had prevented him from remaining in the council's employ. However, B's claim failed on the following grounds:

(a)   The actions of the council and its employees did not give rise to a foreseeable risk of injury. Hale LJ's guidelines in *Hatton v Sutherland* applied. In the circumstances, it was not necessary for the court to consider causation issues.

(b)   The council could not have reasonably known or foreseen that the conduct complained of by B would have caused him harm.

(c)   Nothing in B's behaviour, at the time, had given any cause for concern about the risk of psychiatric illness.

This judgment assists the defendant by confirming that the alleged incidents of bullying and/or harassment must be considered in context. In the context of the claimant's working environment, the use of bad language (which was not disputed at trial) and the actions of his line managers in highlighting areas of non-performance, did not amount to victimisation or bullying.

3.11   Liability in clinical negligence cases

The law of negligence as it relates to clinical negligence must be explained to the client in terms which are easily understood.

If the client is to be successful against a doctor, he must show that the essential elements of negligence are proved, ie:

(a)   that the doctor owed him a duty of care;

(b)   that the doctor breached that duty;

(c)   that he suffered loss as a result of that breach of duty.

The solicitor must make it clear to the client that it is for the client to prove these three elements. The client may find this difficult to accept. If he is still in pain, he may take the view that the doctor must have been negligent. However, this is not necessarily the case and the client must be made aware of this.

Each of the three elements above are examined in detail below.

3.11.1   The duty of care

3.11.1.1   The doctor

It is clear that a doctor owes a duty of care to his patients in the normal course of events.

3.11.1.2   The health authority

Does the health authority/trust owe a duty of care and can it be sued for negligence itself without proving negligence on the part of the doctor? The leading case in this area is *Wilsher v Essex Area Health Authority* [1988] AC 1074, in which it was held that a health authority has a duty to provide services of doctors of sufficient skill, and there is no reason why a health authority cannot be liable for a failure to provide such services (see also the National Health Service Act 1977, ss 1 and 3 and *Cassidy v Ministry of Health* [1951] 2 KB 343).

3.11.2   Breach of the duty of care

In the case of a clinical negligence claim, the normal 'reasonable man' test is modified. In order to show a breach of duty, the claimant must show that the doctor has followed a course of action which is not supported by any reasonable body of medical opinion – this has become known as the *Bolam* test after the case of *Bolam v Friern Hospital Management Committee* [1957] 1 WLR 582, in which it was held that:

> The test as to whether there has been negligence or not is not the test of the man on top of the Clapham omnibus because he has a special skill. The test is the standard of the ordinary skilled man exercising and professing to have that special skill. A man need not possess the highest expert skill; it is well established law that it is sufficient if he exercises the ordinary skill of an ordinary competent man exercising that particular art ... A doctor is not guilty of negligence if he has acted in accordance with a practice accepted as proper by a reasonable body of medical men skilled in that particular art ... a doctor is not negligent, if he is acting in accordance with such a practice, merely because there is a body of opinion which takes the contrary view.

Thus, if the defendants can show that the doctor acted in accordance with a reasonable body of opinion, they will have a defence to the action. Practitioners refer to the 10% rule. It is said that if 10% of the doctors in the country would have taken the same course of action then it will not be a negligent act. In *Hunter v Hanley* 1955 SLT 213, it was stated that in the realms of diagnosis and treatment there is ample scope for genuine difference of opinion and one man clearly is not negligent merely because his conclusion differs from that of other professional men: '... the true test for establishing negligence in diagnosis or treatment on the part of a doctor is whether he has been proved to be guilty of such failure as no doctor of ordinary skill would be guilty of if acting with ordinary care'.

This approach must be considered with some caution as each case will turn on its own facts.

There are a number of reported cases which suggest limits on the *Bolam* test. In *Hucks v Cole* (1968) 118 NLJ 469, Lord Denning MR said:

> A doctor is not to be held negligent simply because something has gone wrong. He is not liable for mischance or misadventure or for an error of judgment. He is not liable for taking one choice out of two or favouring one school rather than another. He is only liable when he falls below the standard of a reasonably competent practitioner in his field. On such occasions, the fact that other practitioners would have done the same thing as the defendant is a very weighty matter to be put in the scales on his behalf; but it is not conclusive. The court must be ever vigilant to see whether the reasons for putting a patient at risk are valid in the light of any well known advance to out of date ideas.

Sachs LJ added that when the evidence showed that a lacuna in professional practice existed by which risks of grave danger were knowingly taken then, however small the risks, the court must examine that lacuna, particularly if the risks could be easily and inexpensively avoided.

One of the most significant cases on the law relating to the duty owed by doctors is *Wilsher v Essex Area Health Authority* [1988] AC 1074. The facts of this case were that a junior hospital doctor was working in an intensive care neo-natal unit when he made the mistake of inserting a catheter into a vein instead of an artery. The junior doctor asked the senior registrar to check to see that what he had done was correct, but the senior registrar also failed to notice the mistake. As a result the child was given excess oxygen which the claimant alleged caused near blindness. In this case, the junior doctor had discharged the standard of care by consulting his more experienced colleague. The court suggested that there are two potential tests of liability. Mustill LJ said in his judgment that the standard for the higher test is not just that of the averagely competent and well-informed junior houseman (or whatever the position of the doctor), but of such a person who fills a post in a unit offering a highly specialised service.

Many commentators suggest that the higher test is generally used as the courts take the view that the public should be protected, that the duty of care should relate to the post and that the public should be able to rely on the doctor filling the post.

The burden of proof is on the claimant to show that on the normal balance of probabilities there was a breach of duty. The courts have given a clear message that, merely because an operation goes wrong or things turn out badly, that does not necessarily mean that there has been a breach of duty, providing the doctor has taken a course of action that a responsible body of doctors would have taken. (See *Maynard v West Midlands Regional Health Authority* [1984] 1 WLR 634.)

A good example of the position on liability in such cases was expounded by Cresswell J in *Sharpe v Southend Health Authority* [1997] 8 Med LR 299. It was contended that the defendant authority was negligent in that it had adopted a 'wait and see policy' in relation to the claimant's tumour until it was too late. It was alleged that they had failed to notice its increase in size, and had failed to operate before it became malignant. The defendants argued that they had complied with standard medical practice and that x-rays showed no significant increase in the size of the tumour. In his summing-up the judge found:

(a)   the standard of care is that of a reasonably competent radiologist/ radiotherapist *at the time;*

(b)   the defendants were not negligent if they adopted a practice accepted as reasonable by a responsible body of practitioners skilled in the relevant field;

(c)   the recommended procedure was continued observation;

(d)   the condition had been correctly identified and the advice highly competent;

(e)   the radiological changes were of negligible significance.

In those circumstances a continued policy of observation was probably a reasonable one. In the circumstances, there had been no negligence.

The *Bolam* test is concerned only with matters of clinical judgment. Clinical negligence claims can relate to errors that are clearly in breach of a doctor's duty, for example, a case where a swab is left in the patient during an operation. Such an omission will constitute a breach of duty.

The standard of care of a specialist, such as an ophthalmologist, is the standard of a reasonably competent specialist (see *Sidaway v Governors of the Bethlem Royal Hospital and Maudsley Hospital* [1985] AC 871).

3.11.3 Causation (proof of loss as a result of breach of duty)

The claimant in a clinical negligence claim will be maintaining that, as a result of the injuries he received because of the negligent treatment by the doctor or hospital, he failed to recover from his pre-existing condition, or the chances of him recovering from that condition diminished to a substantial degree. Alternatively, the claimant may argue that his original injury or condition has become worse as a result of the treatment which he received, or, where the claimant has died, the claimant's relatives may argue that the claimant's death was caused by negligent treatment.

The issue of causation was considered by the House of Lords in *Bolitho v City and Hackney Health Authority* [1997] 3 WLR 1151. In that case, the child claimant (aged two) underwent surgery to correct a heart defect. Subsequently the claimant developed croup and was admitted to hospital. The claimant suffered breathing difficulties and the nurse called for the senior registrar. The senior registrar was unable to attend and the senior house officer was paged instead. The senior house officer did not attend because the batteries of his pager were not working. The child subsequently suffered cardiac arrest, and, although he was subsequently resuscitated, he suffered brain damage. At first instance, it was accepted by the court that it was negligent not to attend the child, but the issue at stake was whether the failure was causative of any damage. It was agreed that if the child had been intubated (passing a tube into the child to create an airway) the child would not have suffered the cardiac arrest and consequently would not have become brain damaged. At this point, there was dispute as between the experts in the case as to what would have been the appropriate action to take in those circumstances. The court considered the *Bolam* test for assessing whether the doctor had been negligent (as to which see **3.11.2**). At first instance the judge decided in *Bolitho* that the defendant should succeed on the issue of causation as, on the evidence before the court, it would not have been negligent for the doctor not to have intubated the child.

The case was appealed to the Court of Appeal, where the decision at first instance was approved by a majority. The claimant then appealed to the House of Lords and the Lords dealt with the case by making a two-stage approach.

(a)   The court first considered what the doctor would have done if she had attended the child. This was a fact-finding exercise and the *Bolam* test was not relevant at this stage. From the doctor's evidence, it was accepted by the court that she would not have intubated the child.

(b)   Secondly, would that omission to intubate have been negligent? At this point the *Bolam* test is relevant. The court should consider whether a responsible body of medical opinion would support the decision not to intubate. The Lords once again found for the defendant.

It is important to remember that the appropriate test should be related to the state of knowledge in the medical profession at the time of the alleged incident. Many clinical negligence claims come to light only many years after the alleged negligence and, when an expert is instructed, it is important to remind the expert that the relevant state of medical knowledge is what prevailed at the time when the incident occurred.

In *Gregg v Scott* [2005] UKHL 2 the House of Lords decided that liability for the loss of a chance of a more favourable outcome should not be introduced into clinical negligence claims. The claimant visited Dr Scott because he had discovered a lump under his left arm. The doctor negligently misdiagnosed the lump as a lipoma or benign fatty tumour and therefore non-cancerous. After the claimant moved house he went to his new GP nine months later. However the new GP was more cautious and referred the claimant on to a specialist. It was then that the claimant discovered that he did in fact have cancer of a lymph gland. By that time the tumour had spread and the claimant had to undergo painful chemotherapy. The claimant sued Dr Scott alleging that he should have referred the claimant to hospital and that, if he had done so, the claimant's condition would have been diagnosed earlier and there would have been a high likelihood of a cure. Although the claimant could claim for the extra pain and suffering caused by Dr Scott, the claimant tried to sue on the basis that he had sufferd a loss due to diminished chances of surviving the cancer. On appeal to the House of Lords, the Lords found in favour of Dr Scott on the basis that the claimant was unable to prove that the loss was consequential on injury caused by the doctor's negligence. Causation had to be shown on the balance of probabilities. It had not been shown that, on the balance of probabilities, the delay in commencing the claimant's treatment that was attributable to the doctor's negligence had affected the course of his illness or his prospects of survival, which had never been as good as even. Further, liability for the loss of a chance of a more favorable outcome should not be introduced into personal injury claims.

Examples

(a) In *Brooks v Home Office* [1999] 2 FLR 33, the standard of obstetric care that a prisoner in prison is entitled to receive is the same as she would have received if not in prison.

(b) In *Vadera v Shaw* (1998) BMLR 162, the claimant had been prescribed a contraceptive pill in 1996 by the defendant who was her GP. Six weeks later, she suffered a stroke and sought to claim that the pill had caused the stroke, as there had been suggestions within the medical profession that this might be the case. On appeal, the claim was quickly dismissed due to lack of evidence. On the issue of causation, the judge approached the problem based on his findings of fact. He found that there was no history of hypertension or a history of headaches, therefore the issue of causation could not be proved. It was also noted that an infection or some other condition could have caused the stroke.

(c) In *Brown v Lewisham & North Southwark HA* [1999] Lloyd's Rep Med 110, the claimant alleged negligence in the use of an anti-coagulant drug (Heparin) and also in failing to diagnose deep vein thrombosis. The claimant was admitted to Guy's Hospital for quadruple bypass surgery (having been referred to Guy's from Royal Victoria Hospital, Blackpool). Heparin was administered to the claimant during the operation. The claimant was discharged from Guy's unaccompanied and travelled by train back to the Royal Victoria Hospital. The claimant experienced difficulties over the coming days and Heparin was administered to assist him. The claimant had an adverse reaction to the drug (which was not widely known about at that time), gangrene set in and the leg had to be amputated, as a consequence of the adverse reaction to Heparin.

On the question of causation, the claimant asserted that had he not been discharged he would have remained in hospital and would have received treatment earlier. Also, he would not have had to endure the effects of journey from Guy's Hospital back to the Royal Victoria Hospital. The court found that it was unlikely that the journey was an effective cause of the loss of the leg. The complex circumstances made it impossible to infer that the claimant's loss was a result of the journey. In the final analysis, the court found that there was no causal link between the negligence and the amputation, as by the time the haematologist gave his negligent advice the gangrene was evident and was an unfortunate consequence of the claimant's reasonably unrecognised reaction to Heparin. The claimant's claim therefore failed.

(d)   Cervical smear tests were taken from a number of claimants. Each of the tests was reported by the primary cytoscreeners as being negative but each of the claimants went on to develop invasive cancer. The judge found that the slides exhibited abnormalities which no reasonably competent cytoscreener would have treated as innocuous, such that a negative test would not have been given. With early detection, pre-cancerous or cancerous conditions could have been dealt with by minor surgery, but as a result of the negative smear test there was no timely follow up or therapeutic intervention (*Penney and Others v East Kent Health Authority* [2000] Lloyd's Rep Med 41).

In each of these examples, there is an issue of causation, ie, the connection between the defendant's alleged breach of duty and the claimant's eventual injury or condition.

In order to succeed in his case, a claimant must prove that the breach of duty caused his injury. If a failure to treat a patient has made no difference because he would have died in any event, his death will not have been caused by negligence.

In *Barnett v Chelsea and Kensington Hospital Management Committee* [1969] 1 QB 428, three night-watchmen attended a casualty department complaining of vomiting. As they had drunk some tea three hours previously, the doctor told them to go home and go to bed and, if necessary, tó call their own doctors. They went away but one of them died later that night and the cause of death was subsequently found to be arsenic poisoning. It was held that since the defendants provided a casualty department, they owed the deceased a duty of care to exercise such skill as ought reasonably to be expected of a nurse and casualty officer. In this instance, because the casualty officer had not exercised such skill, he was found negligent and in breach of duty. However, the court also found that the deceased would have died of the poisoning, even if he had been treated with all the necessary care. Therefore, the claimant had failed to establish on the balance of probabilities that the defendants' negligence caused the deceased's death.

The conventional doctrine, therefore, is that no claim will be successful unless the negligence causes the damage or injury.

The doctrine goes one step further in clinical negligence cases in that a claimant cannot claim for the loss of a prospect of recovery if the chance of recovery is less than probable. In *Hotson v East Berkshire Health Authority* [1987] AC 750, a 13-year-old boy was playing at school in his lunch break and, for fun, climbed a tree to which a rope was attached. He lost his grip on the rope and fell 12 feet to the ground. He was subsequently taken to hospital where the staff failed to diagnose a fracture. The boy was sent home to rest. When he returned to the hospital, the correct diagnosis was made. As a result of the initial failure to give a correct diagnosis, the boy was left with a disability of the hip and a risk of future osteoarthritis. At first instance, the trial judge, Simon Brown J, found that if the health authority had correctly diagnosed and treated the claimant when he first attended hospital, there was a high probability (which he assessed at a 75% risk) that the claimant's injury would have followed the same course as it had followed. In other words, the doctor's delay in making the correct diagnosis had denied the claimant a 25% chance that, if given immediate treatment, the avascular necrosis would not have developed and if it had not developed the claimant would have made a complete recovery. Accordingly, Simon Brown J awarded 25% of the appropriate damages. The defendants successfully appealed. The claimant received no damages in respect of his lost chances of recovery because they were less than 50% (see also *Bolitho v City and Hackney Health Authority* [1993] PIQR 334 on the issue of causation).

It can thus be said that the test applied is that 'but for' the negligence the patient would not, on the balance of probabilities, have suffered the harm in any event. Experts need to be reminded of the importance of the causation test.

In *Chester v Afshar* [2004] UKHL 41 the House of Lords considered causation issues in the context of a surgeon who failed to warn a patient of the small risk of injury inherent in the surgery which the patient was about to agree to undertake. The defendant argued that it was simply wrong to allow damages where a defendant's wrong (in this case failure to warn) had not been proved to have increased the claimant's risk and that, in any event, to succeed the claimant should prove that had she been warned she would not have consented to run the risk at all. The Lords found in the claimant's favour, and in so doing veered away from conventional causation principles. They found that the 'but for' test was satisfied, as the claimant would not have had the surgery if the warning had been given. The defendants had argued that the risk inherent in surgery was neither increased nor decreased by the failure to warn. The Lords rejected this argument, finding instead that the surgeon owed a duty to warn of the dangers inherent in surgical interventions, as this was intended to help the patient to make an informed choice about their treatment. Therefore the Lords justified their ruling on policy grounds on the basis that the loss arose, in the legal sense, out of the failure to warn the claimant.

The issue of causation is far more difficult for the claimant's clinical negligence solicitor than in normal personal injury work. In personal injury cases, the claimant is normally fit and the injury which results is due to the accident. In contrast, in clinical negligence cases, the injury complained of can be as a result of many different variables (see *McGhee v National Coal Board* [1973] 1 WLR 1).

In practice, care must be taken that if the defendants admit liability prior to trial, the claimant's solicitor should seek confirmation that the defendants also admit causation. This must be specifically considered by the claimant's solicitor.

3.12   *Res ipsa loquitur*

Can the maxim *res ipsa loquitur* be used in a clinical negligence case? The reason why this question has been raised is that, in certain circumstances, it can be very difficult to identify the specific negligent act, although it appears from the facts that negligence must have occurred. An example would be where a patient goes into hospital with a problem relating to two of his fingers on one hand but when he is discharged that hand has become completely useless (see *Cassidy v Ministry of Health* [1951] 2 KB 343). It appears from that case that although the maxim *res ipsa loquitur* may be used only in exceptional circumstances, the court, on limited occasions, will hold that the maxim is appropriate in a clinical negligence case.

The proper approach to *res ipsa loquitur* in clinical negligence litigation was reviewed by the Court of Appeal in *Ratcliffe v Plymouth and Torbay Health Authority* [1998] PIQR P170. Dismissing the appeal, the judge made the following points in relation to *res ipsa loquitur* to clinical negligence cases.

(a)   The maxim applies where the claimant relies on the happening of the thing itself to raise the inference of negligence, which is supported by ordinary human experience, and with no need for expert evidence.

(b)   The maxim can be applied in that form to simple situations in the clinical negligence field (a surgeon cutting off a right foot instead of the left; a swab left in the operation site; a patient who wakes up in the course of a surgical operation despite a general anaesthetic).

(c)   In practice, in contested clinical negligence cases the evidence of a claimant which establishes the *res* is likely to be buttressed by expert evidence to the effect that the matter complained of does not ordinarily occur in the absence of negligence.

(d)   The position may then be reached at the close of the claimant's case that the judge would be entitled to infer negligence on the defendant's part unless the defendant can then adduce some evidence which discharges the inference.

(e)   This evidence may be to the effect that there is a plausible explanation of what may have happened which does not rely on negligence on the defendant's part.

(f)   Alternatively, the defendant's evidence may satisfy the judge on the balance of probabilities that he did exercise proper care. If the untoward outcome is extremely rare, or is impossible to explain in the light of the current state of medical knowledge, the judge will be bound to exercise great care in evaluating the evidence before making such a finding.

3.13 Other common issues

3.13.1 Consent

Many of the actions of a doctor or nurse could constitute trespass to the patient if they were performed without consent. For example, a trespass may occur if, without his consent, the patient underwent an operation, was given an injection of drugs or had his body manipulated.

The patient's consent must be freely given and informed. The consent need not be in writing.

The consent will be only for the actual operation to which the patient has consented. As such, normal NHS consent forms are termed widely so as to allow a doctor to deal with any 'procedure that is necessary ... in the patient's best interests'.

If the patient asks questions about the proposed treatment then the doctor must, so far as is possible, answer any questions fully as to the risk involved in treatment and the likelihood and nature of any side-effects, however minor or unlikely.

What obligation is placed upon the doctor to tell the patient about the risks of the proposed operation? The leading case is *Sidaway v Board of Governors of the Bethlem Royal Hospital and Maudsley Hospital* [1985] AC 871, where the claimant complained of persistent pain in the right shoulder and left arm. The claimant was admitted to hospital and an operation was carried out on her back to attempt to free her from pain and discomfort. During the operation the spinal cord was damaged which left the claimant severely disabled. The claimant sued the hospital and the surgeon's estate. It was not claimed that the operation had been negligently performed. The claim was instead based on the failure to warn the claimant of the risk of damage to a nerve root and the spinal cord. The evidence produced at the trial showed a combined risk of damage of between 1% and 2%, and that the risk of damage to the spinal cord alone was less than 1%. The medical witnesses stated that they would warn a patient that there was a small risk of untoward consequences and of an increase of pain instead of relief. It was held to be accepted practice not to mention to patients the possibility of death or paralysis resulting from the operation.

The trial judge dismissed the claim and the Court of Appeal by a majority endorsed this decision. The House of Lords, by a majority of one, endorsed the medical test. Lord Diplock said that the *Bolam* test should be applied to disclosure as well as to treatment and diagnosis. Lord Scarman expressed the view that the *Bolam* principle may be taken that a doctor is not negligent if he acts in accordance with a practice accepted at that time as proper by a reasonable body of medical opinion, even though other doctors adopted a different practice.

In cases where consent to medical treatment has been obtained, it is of primary importance to ensure that the ambit of the consent is fully explained and that the subsequent surgery does not go further than was agreed to. In *Williamson v East London and City HA* [1998] Lloyd's Rep Med 6, the claimant agreed to an operation to replace a leaking silicone breast implant. The consulting surgeon noted that the situation was worse than had originally been thought, but no further consent form was signed. A mastectomy was performed without the patient's consent and the patient sued the health authority. The court found that the clinician did not properly or sufficiently inform the claimant of her intention to increase the operation, the claimant had not consented to the operation and accordingly damages were awarded for the pain and suffering caused by negligent failure to acquire consent.

In a further refinement of the law regarding consent in *Newbury v Bath DHA* (1999) 47 BMLR 138, the court found that where surgery is contemplated the nature of the operation and its risks should be explained. If the claimant was led to believe that the operation was trivial and risk free, and such was not the case, then that advice would be wrong and negligent within the terms of *Sidaway v Board of Governors of the Bethlem Royal Hospital and Maudsley Hospital* [1985] AC 871. The judge went on to give examples of circumstances where the patient was entitled to be told when surgery was not in the mainstream of treatment:

(a)   if it involved a method which was entirely new or relatively untried;

(b)   if the method had fallen out of use because it has been shown to be defective and was not accepted by a responsible body of medical opinion.

In relation to the warning of such risks, see *Lybert v Warrington HA* (1996) 7 Med LR 71 for guidance as to the form such warnings should take. In this case, the claimant claimed damages for failure to advise on the risk of the possibility of failure of a sterilisation operation. The court held that it was the duty of those running the sterilisation unit to ensure that there was a proper and effective system for warning patients at some stage. Ideally, the warning should be both oral and in writing and could have been given on admission or before she agreed to sterilisation or before discharge. There was evidence that no warning at all had in fact been given.

3.13.2   Emergency treatment

In some instances, for example in emergencies, consent may not be possible. However, where treatment is necessary to save the life or preserve the health of the patient in such circumstances, a failure to obtain consent will not render the doctor liable for an assault. In *Wilson v Pringle* [1986] 3 WLR 1, CA, the court held that a casualty surgeon who performed an emergency operation on an adult who had been brought into hospital unconscious was not liable for battery and his actions were acceptable. See also *Re C (Adult: Refusal of Medical Treatment)* [1994] 1 All ER 819, where the patient applied for an injunction preventing the hospital carrying out an operation.

In *Re F (Mental Patient: Sterilisation)* [1990] 2 AC 1, it was held that, where the patient cannot give consent, the doctor should do no more than is reasonably required in medical terms, but that it is possible for the doctor to carry out the necessary treatment. If required to examine the doctor's decision, the court is likely to hold that the doctor has acted appropriately if a 'reasonable body of the medical profession would have done likewise'. (See also *Re R (A Minor) (Wardship: Consent to Treatment)* [1992] Fam 11.)

3.13.3 Consent by children

Section 8(1) of the Family Law Reform Act 1969 provides a presumption that a child may give valid consent for medical treatment at the age of 16. This area of the law was examined closely in *Gillick v West Norfolk and Wisbech Area Health Authority and Department of Health and Social Security* [1986] AC 112, in which it was held that the important point is the degree of understanding by the child of what is going to happen (see also *Re C* (1997) Sol Jo, 4 April).

3.13.4 Refusal of consent

The basic proposition is that an adult should have a choice as to whether he wishes to undergo medical treatment. However, the case of *Re T (Adult: Refusal of Treatment)* [1992] 4 All ER 649 concerned a pregnant mother who was injured in a road traffic accident. At the hospital the mother went into labour. The mother expressed her views that she did not want a blood transfusion prior to the birth. The mother had to undergo a Caesarian section and, as a consequence, had to be admitted to the intensive care unit and was ventilated. The doctor treating her wished to give the mother a blood transfusion but was aware of the patient's views prior to the birth. The Court of Appeal held that, while an adult had the right to decide on her own treatment, even if it led to death, if the patient did not have capacity at the time of the decision and that patient was under pressure from others, a doctor was justified in exercising his clinical judgment in the patient's best interests.

The consent form is evidence of only the consent and does not imply that true consent has been given. Just because the doctor has had the form signed, it does not mean that consent has in fact been given.

3.13.5 Contractual relationship

Liability for most clinical negligence claims is under the law of tort. However, in the case of private treatment there will be a contractual relationship between the parties and both causes of action will normally be pleaded. It is important in respect of private treatment that the doctor who has been alleged to have been negligent is identified as a defendant, as no vicarious liability applies in this situation. The contract is between the patient and the doctor, not the patient and the private hospital.

3.13.6   Shared liability between healthcare professionals

It is possible for the court to hold more than one type of healthcare professional jointly responsible for personal injuries that result from negligence. This is well illustrated in the case of *Prendergast v Sam and Dee Ltd* (1989) *The Times,* 14 March, in which a pharmacist misread a prescription and gave the claimant a drug which resulted in irreversible brain damage. The pharmacist was held to be 75% responsible and the doctor who wrote the prescription was held to be 25% at fault because his handwriting was so illegible.

3.13.7   Liability of alternative healthcare practitioners

Increasing use of 'alternative' therapy for ailments has led to increased awareness of problems that can arise from use of alternative forms of healthcare. In *Shakoor v Situ (t/a Eternal Health Co)* [2000] 4 All ER 181, the court considered the appropriate standard of care by which an alternative practitioner should be judged. The court decided that, given that the alternative practitioner would often be practising alongside orthodox medicine, it would not be appropriate to simply judge him based on the standard of an ordinary practitioner 'skilled in that particular art'. Rather, it was appropriate to take account of whether the alternative practitioner had taken account of the implications of prescribing complimentary medicine, namely that any person who suffered an adverse reaction would be likely to report to a mainstream hospital and the incident was likely to be reported in orthodox medical journals. The alternative practitioner should satisfy himself that there had not been adverse reports raised in relevant journals likely to be read by an orthodox practitioner practising at the level at which the alternative practitioner held himself out to be.

3.14   Conclusion

As stated at the beginning of this chapter, the possible heads of liability of an employer are not mutually exclusive. When acting for a claimant, it is important for the solicitor to consider all heads of claim in order to maximise the client's chances of success. It is necessary to succeed under only one head for the claimant to be successful overall. In practice, it is far harder to establish liability in a clinical negligence claim than in a personal injury claim. It is important that the claimant's solicitor regularly reviews the evidence available and remembers the essential elements which need to be proved at all times.

3.15   Further reading

The above is merely an overview of the law as it relates to liability in personal injury and clinical negligence claims. For a more detailed consideration of the subject, reference should be made to the following sources of information.

Redgrave, Hendy and Ford, *Redgrave's Health and Safety* (Butterworths).

Munkman, *Employer's Liability* (Butterworths).

Tolley's Health and Safety at Work Handbook (Tolley).

Management of Health and Safety at Work Regulations 1999 (SI 1999/3242) (Stationery Office).

Health and Safety (Display Screen Equipment) Regulations 1992 (SI 1992/2792) (Stationery Office).

Provision and Use of Work Equipment Regulations 1998 (SI 1998/2306) (Stationery Office).

Personal Protective Equipment at Work Regulations 1992 (SI 1992/2966) (Stationery Office).

Manual Handling Operations Regulations 1992 (SI 1992/2793) (Stationery Office).

Workplace (Health, Safety and Welfare) Regulations 1992 (SI 1992/3004) (Stationery Office).

Lifting Operations and Lifting Equipment Regulations 1998 (SI 1998/2307) (Stationery Office).

Construction (Health, Safety and Welfare) Regulations 1996 (SI 1996/1592) (Stationery Office).

Health and Safety (Miscellaneous Amendments) Regulations 2002 (SI 2002/2174) (Stationery Office).

www.hse.gov.uk

www.safety-now.co.uk

Chapter 4

The First Interview

4.1 Introduction

The claimant's solicitor should never lose sight of the following points when making initial enquiries.

(a) He should make full enquiries as soon as possible, as this will give a tactical advantage.

(b) He should not focus on settlement being the likely outcome of the case. The assumption should be that the matter will proceed to trial and the case should be prepared accordingly.

(c) He should not give the client a firm indication of the level of damages the client is likely to receive. Clients' over-expectations as to the level of damages they can expect are often lawyer-led.

4.2 First interview

The first interview is the cornerstone of the solicitor/client relationship and it is therefore worthwhile making the effort to get it right. Reference should be made to the Legal Practice Guide, *Skills for Lawyers* which deals with how to conduct an interview. The interview will normally last at least an hour. The client should tell his own story, and the solicitor will often complete a long and detailed accident questionnaire, prior to drafting a proof of evidence. Detailed preparation at this stage will save a great deal of time later.

4.2.1 Use of questionnaires and case management tools

Client questionnaires are used frequently in personal injury work. The questionnaires are designed to elicit certain basic information about the client. A basic questionnaire is reproduced at **Appendix 4**. Increasingly, law firms 'capture' this basic data about the client by keying the details into a case management system. This has the advantage that once 'captured' the data is available for use subsequently throughout the life of the claim.

4.3 Funding

Most clients will be concerned to find out first what the claim is likely to cost and will only be happy to talk at length once they have been provided with some solid advice on this point.

4.3.1 Funding the first interview

4.3.1.1 Free initial interviews

Many firms offer a free initial half-hour interview in order to persuade clients into their offices. Many people are wary of solicitors' charges, and are put off making claims accordingly. Some solicitors therefore offer free initial advice in which they will form a view as to the viability of a personal injury or clinical negligence claim, and advise clients about the various case-funding methods available.

4.3.1.2 Accident Line – personal injury cases

The Law Society operates a scheme called 'Accident Line' under which members of the public can obtain a free first interview from members of the scheme. Only members of personal injury panels are eligible to become members of Accident Line. The benefit to the firm, if eligible to join the scheme, is that it is assured a steady stream of prospective clients for initial interview. The benefit to the public is that the service is free and carries the assurance that only those who are competent to give advice in this area are able to join the scheme.

4.3.1.3 Legal Help – under the Legal Services Commission

The Legal Services Commission (LSC) replaced the Legal Aid Board as from 1 April 2000. Under the 'Legal Help' scheme, the equivalent of up to two hours' advice may be given to the client. This can cover the first interview and initial correspondence.

4.3.2 Legal Services Commission and Community Legal Service

On 1 April 2000, the Government implemented ss 1–11 and 19–26 of the Access to Justice Act 1999. These are the key provisions which reform the public funding of civil cases. The LSC was established and replaced the Legal Aid Board. It is responsible for the Community Legal Service (CLS), which handles funding in civil matters from that date. (The criminal cases counterpart – the Criminal Defence Service – began operation in October 2000.)

4.3.2.1 The 'Funding Code'

Schedule 2 to the Access to Justice Act 1999 generally excludes personal injury (other than clinical negligence claims) from CLS funding. The CLS decides funding issues in accordance with the Funding Code published in October 1999. The Code has two parts: Part 1 defines the 'Levels of Service' which the CLS provides; Part 2 deals with the procedures for obtaining funding.

The most important Levels of Service are 'Legal Help' and 'Legal Representation'. These replace the legal advice and assistance (LAA) scheme and assistance by way of representation (ABWOR) and Civil Legal Aid respectively. Legal Representation has two sub-levels: 'Investigative Help' and 'Full Representation'.

Unlike clinical negligence cases, personal injury cases are normally outside the scope of CLS funding because they are suitable for conditional fee agreements.

However, the Code does permit public funding – 'Support Funding' – to be given in personal injury cases; chiefly, where there are the following requirements.

(a)   High investigative costs involved (Investigative Support) in order to get the case to a point where it is possible to assess whether or not it could be funded under a conditional fee agreement (ie, disbursements over £1,000 or profit costs over £3,000).

(b)   High overall costs involved (Litigation Support) (ie, disbursements over £5,000 or profit costs over £15,000).

(c)   Wider public interest issues.

The LSC *may* pay the costs or disbursements incurred in excess of the above thresholds.

The Lord Chancellor's Department has produced draft guidelines on availability of 'Exceptional Funding' in individual cases, which is designed for use in specific cases, for example, representation at inquests.

4.3.3   LSC funding in clinical negligence cases

Applications for Legal Representation for proceedings in clinical negligence cases are subject to the General Funding Code (see the criteria in s 9 of the Funding Code).

The scope of clinical negligence as defined in the Funding Code is:

(a)   a claim for damages in respect of an alleged breach of duty of care or trespass to the person committed in the course of the provision of clinical or medical services (including dental or nursing services); or

(b)   a claim for damages in respect of alleged professional negligence in the conduct of such a claim.

Only firms with a clinical negligence contract are eligible for CLS funding. Firms with a clinical negligence franchise are required to have a supervisor who is a member of either the Law Society's Clinical Negligence Panel or a member of AvMA – action against medical accidents.

4.3.3.1   Claims not exceeding £10,000

If the likely value of the claim is not more than £10,000, Investigative Help may be refused if use of the NHS complaints procedure would be in the best interests of the client rather than pursuing litigation in the first instance. Although the LSC accepts that the NHS complaints procedure was never designed to replace recourse to the court system, nevertheless it wishes it to be recognised that in small value claims (between £5,000 and £10,000) it is much more cost-effective of public funds for the claimant to seek redress in the form of explanation and apology rather than compensation through the civil court system. In claims where the likely level of damages will not exceed £5,000, the Funding Code recommends that Investigative Help should be refused on the ground that the potential cost greatly outweighs the benefit to be achieved. However, there is a caveat that the damages cut off will not apply to claims which have a significant wider public interest or are of overwhelming importance to the client (for example, claims involving the death of an infant).

If the claim is valued at less than £10,000, the solicitor will need to provide specific reasons as to why the complaints procedure is not the appropriate avenue of redress for the client. The Funding Code contains a number of examples of circumstances in which, it says, it would not be appropriate to refuse funding, which are as follows:

(a)   the NHS complaints scheme is not available to the client or clients being told a complaint may not be pursued;

(b)   the claim has overwhelming importance to the client, for example, because it relates to infant death;

(c)   there are problems with the NHS complaints scheme in the client's region, for example, there are unusually long delays in responding to complaints;

(d)   proceedings must be issued as a matter of urgency, for example, because of limitation; or

(e)   it is clear the relationship between the client and NHS has broken down to such an extent that any prospect of the complaints procedure resolving the complaint is very remote.

4.3.3.2   Investigative Help for clinical negligence claims

Investigative Help will only be granted where the prospects of success on a claim are not clear and substantial work needs to be undertaken before the prospects of success can be determined accurately. Certificates limited to Investigative Help will be subject to a limitation that the certificate covers only the obtaining of medical notes and records, obtaining one medical report per specialism, complying with all steps under the clinical disputes pre-action protocol, considering relevant evidence with counsel or an external solicitor with higher court advocacy rights and experts if necessary and thereafter obtaining counsel's opinion, up to and including settling proceedings if counsel so advises.

The cost of the above is nevertheless limited to £3,500 (including costs and disbursmeents but not VAT).

According to para 5.6.1 of the General Funding Code, the potential to obtain a conditional fee agreement will not be a ground for refusal of Investigative Help in clinical negligence claims.

4.3.3.3   Criteria for granting of Full Representation

The Funding Code makes it clear that an application for Full Representation will be refused either if:

(a)   prospects of success are unclear, or

(b)   prospects of success are borderline (ie, not better than 50%), or

(c)   prospects of success are poor (clearly less than 50%).

The cost-benefit criterion gives the minimum cost-benefit ratios for damages to costs in clinical negligence claims:

(a)   1:1 – for cases with 80% or more prospects of success – ie, the likely damages must at least break even with and should exceed the likely cost in cases with very good prospects of success.

(b)   1.5:1 – for 60–80% prospects of success – ie, the prospects of success are good, likely damages must exceed likely cost by at least 1.5.

(c)   2:1 – for cases with 50–60% prospects of success – ie, the prospects of success are moderate, likely damages must be at least twice the likely costs.

These are the minimum cost-benefit ratios in the General Funding Code.

If the prospect of success and the cost-benefit criteria set out above are satisfied, then the solicitor should make an application for Full Representation after the investigative stage. The certificate will then be issued limited to all steps up to and including exchange of statements and reports and CPR, Part 35 questioning of experts and thereafter obtaining counsel's opinion or the opinion of an external solicitor with higher court advocacy rights.

In the event that the claimant wishes to proceed to full trial, the cost-benefit criteria above are reapplied to the case and if the criteria are satisfied, then application can be made once again to amend the scope of the Full Representation certificate to cover the cost of trial.

4.3.3.4 'Exceptional funding'

Under s 6(8)(b) of the Access to Justice Act 1999, the Lord Chancellor has power to provide funding in cases which would normally be outside the scope of the scheme.

The exceptional funding provisions can be used to obtain funding for representation at an inquest. The Lord Chancellor's Guidance on Exceptional Funding states that in general cases, there will be a need to show either 'significant wider public interest' or 'overwhelming importance to the client'. Significant wider public interest is confined to cases where representation is likely to benefit the public by facilitating a real prospect of a change in the law or recommendations that will improve public safety. The 'overwhelming importance to the client' test will usually be a very difficult test to satisfy and is reserved for cases such as deaths in custody and infant death cases. The test has been revised in relation to applications for representation at inquests, so that consideration is now given to whether funded representation will assist the coroner to investigate the case effectively and establish the facts. Before requesting such funding, the LSC must be satisfied that the client is financially eligible for Legal Representation according to eligibility limits and that no alternative source of funding is available. The most likely level of funding to be granted is in the form of a one-off grant to cover only the advocacy and representation at the hearing itself as the preparation work in advance of the inquest is already covered by Legal Help. The Guidance suggests that applications for exceptional funding should address the issues set out in the Lord Chancellor's Guidance. Applications should include a breakdown of the funding required, setting out hours claimed and rates charged. As funding is by way of a one-off grant, the Lord Chancellor may approve funding retrospectively if necessary.

4.3.4 Conditional Fee Agreements

Under s 58 of the Courts and Legal Services Act 1990, a solicitor and client can agree that the client will only have to pay his own solicitor's costs under certain agreed circumstances or conditions, the condition usually being that the client wins his case (hence *Conditional* Fee Agreement (CFA)). In order to understand the following paragraphs, it is necessary first to appreciate the background to this area of law.

4.3.4.1 The success fee

If the claim is successful, the solicitor will normally expect to receive an enhanced fee to reflect his 'success' and also to help cover the cost of claims undertaken by the solicitor on a conditional fee basis which are unsuccessful. The enhancement on the fee is a percentage increase of the solicitor's normal fee and not a percentage of damages. The percentage increase on the solicitor's fee is agreed in writing between the client and the solicitor prior to the litigation and should reflect the difficulty in winning the case. In *Burton v Kingsley* [2005] EWHC 1034, QB the claimants had sustained serious injuries and liability was uncertain. The claimants entered into a CFA with their solicitors with a success fee of 100%. The claimants argued that they were entitled to recover the 100% uplift. The defendants submitted that 10 to 20% was the appropriate figure. The court found that it had been reasonable for the claimants' solicitors to enter the CFA. The court concluded that a CFA risk assessment was a fair reflection of the position in relation to the risk being undertaken by the claimant's solicitors *based on what they knew at that time*. It had been reasonable to recognise that there were uncertainties and difficulties with the case that gave rise to a significant element of risk. The instant case did not fall within the category of modest and straightforward claims specified in *Callery v Gray* (as to which see **4.3.5.4**) for compensation for personal injuries resulting from road traffic accidents and was not a case where the maximum uplift that could have been agreed was 20%. However, the 100% success fee specified by the claimants' solicitors was too high. The chances of success were higher than evens. The degree of risk was such that a reasonable figure would have been between 33% and 50%. Accordingly, a success fee of 50% under the CFA was allowed.

Under s 27 of the Access to Justice Act 1999, the success fee is recoverable from the loser to the litigation. The mechanism for recovery of the success fee is dealt with in the Civil Procedure Rules 1998. There are specific fixed costs rules operating in relation to road traffic accident claims valued at less than £10,000 and employers' liability claims, as to which see **4.36**.

If the claim is unsuccessful, the solicitor is not entitled to charge any costs at all. However, the client will still have to fund his own disbursements.

4.3.4.2   After the event (ATE) insurance

The loser's liability to pay the other side's costs and disbursements and his own disbursements can be insured against by what is often referred to as 'after the event (ATE) insurance'. As the name suggests, ATE insurance is taken out only once the need for the legal action has become apparent but before the proceedings have commenced. Here, the insurance is not against the risk of litigation but merely against the risk of having to pay the other side's costs and disbursements should the litigation fail, and can cover the cost of the party's own disbursements as well. This type of insurance can be obtained alongside a CFA or on its own as insurance against liability for the other side's costs. Under s 29 of the Access to Justice Act 1999, the premium for insuring against liability to pay the other side's costs and disbursements is recoverable from the loser.

4.3.4.3   The indemnity principle

Under s 60(3) of the Solicitors Act 1974 'a client shall not be entitled to recover from any other person under an order for payment of costs ... more than the amount payable by him to his solicitor in respect of those costs'.

It therefore followed that under the indemnity principle a solicitor may only seek to recover costs from the other party on his client's behalf, if he could first establish that his own client had an obligation to pay those costs. This meant that the CFA had to make clear to the client that he was primarily liable for his own costs. If the case was won, the solicitor would endeavour to recover those costs on his client's behalf but, if there was a shortfall, the client could, in theory, still be liable for his costs. It was not permissible for a claimant's solicitor to agree with his client not to charge anything if the claim was unsuccessful, or to limit himself to whatever costs were recovered from the losing side. Hence the term 'no win no fee' was not quite as clear as it first appeared.

4.3.5   Conditional Fee Agreements signed before 1 November 2005

In order to protect both the solicitor and the client, the Conditional Fee Agreements Regulations 2000 (CFA Regs 2000) (SI 2000/692) were introduced. These Regulations govern CFAs from 1 April 2000 to 31 October 2005.

The aim of the CFA Regs 2000 was to ensure that the circumstances under which the client did have a liability for his own costs were fully and adequately explained (ie, ensuring that the indemnity principle was complied with). Due to the relative complexity of these regulations, so-called 'satellite litigation' proliferated. Many losing parties sought to challenge the validity of CFAs based on technical grounds. They asserted that the CFA Regs 2000 had not been complied with, and thereby rendered the CFA unenforceable (and therefore no costs were liable to be paid under it).

This situation came to a head with *Hollins v Russell; Tichband v Hurdman; Pratt v Bull; Sharratt v London Central Bus Company Ltd and Accident Group Test Cases* [2003] EWCA Civ 718, [2003] 1 WLR 2487. The court held that the conditions of s 58 of the Courts and Legal Services Act 1990 were satisfied when they had been 'sufficiently met'. The court expressed it in this way. In cases where the paying party challenges whether there has been compliance, the costs judge should ask himself:

> ... has the particular departure from the regulations ... had a materially adverse effect either upon the protection afforded to the client or upon the proper administration of justice? If the answer is 'yes', the conditions have not been satisfied [and the CFA will not be enforceable].'

It became clear that the number of technical challenges to the CFA Regs 2000 were having a paralysing effect on the availability of CFAs. In an attempt to remedy matters, a new simplified CFA (termed 'CFA Simple') has been brought about by the Conditional Fee Agreements (Miscellaneous Amendments) Regulations 2003 (CFA Regs 2003) (SI 2003/1240). A solicitor can agree with his client at the outset that, if the case is won, the solicitor can agree to limit his client's liability for his own costs to that which is recovered from the losing party. The solicitor will not seek to make his own client pay any shortfall. This has effectively ended the application of the indemnity principle to this form of CFA. However, this form of CFA has not been widely adopted as the Law Society has not produced a Model Agreement applicable to this form of CFA. Because of the perceived uncertainties with this form of CFA, insurers are unwilling to provide ATE insurance cover. To date, therefore, this type of agreement has largely been ignored.

The regulations governing the two types of CFA are dealt with in detail below.

4.3.5.1   The requirements of the Conditional Fee Agreements Regulations 2000 (CFA Standard)

For CFAs entered into from 1 April 2000 to 31 October 2005, these Regulations state that the agreement must be in writing, it must contain certain prescribed information and comply with a number of technical requirements. Failure to comply with the Regulations may render the agreement unenforceable.

4.3.5.2   The requirements of the Conditional Fee Agreements Order 2000 (CFA Standard)

From 1 April 2000, CFAs are regulated by the Conditional Fee Agreements Order 2000 (SI 2000/823) and the CFA Regs 2000. The Order specifies that CFAs can be applied to all non-family and non-criminal cases and whether or not proceedings are actually commenced. Only agreements that comply with conditions set out in the Regulations are enforceable (Courts and Legal Services Act 1990, s 58(1)). In particular, all agreements are required to be in writing.

4.3.5.3   Requirements of the Conditional Fee Agreements Regulations 2000

For CFAs using the Law Society's Standard Form of CFA, based on the CFA Regs 2000, the CFA must be in writing and it must contain certain prescribed information and comply with a number of technical requirements. Failure to comply with the Regulations may render the agreement unenforceable.

Regulation 2

All agreements must specify:

(a)   the particular proceedings or part of proceedings to which it relates;

(b)   the circumstances in which the legal representative's fees and expenses or part thereof will be payable;

(c)   what payment, if any, is due:

(i)   if those circumstances only partly occur (ie, partial success);

(ii)   irrespective of whether the circumstances occur (ie, irrespective of success); and

(iii) on termination of the agreement for any reason.

The agreement must also specify the amounts which are payable in all the circumstances, the method used to calculate them and, in particular, whether amounts are limited by reference to damages which may be recovered on behalf of a client. This means that the agreement must state whether there is a 'cap' on the success fee. In other words, does the solicitor agree that, should the case be successful, the maximum that the solicitor can add by way of success fee can never be more than an agreed percentage of the claimant's damages. In this way, the claimant can be assured that, in the event of success, he will always receive *at least* the amount safeguarded by the cap.

4.3.5.4   Requirements for conditional fee agreements which provide for success fees

Regulation 3

Under reg 3, certain matters must be specified if the CFA provides for a success fee. The agreement must:

(a)   briefly specify the reason for setting the percentage increase at the level stated in the agreement; and

(b)   specify how much of that percentage increase, if any, relates to the cost to the legal representative of the postponement of his fees and expenses.

If the agreement related to court proceedings, the agreement must make provision where the success fee becomes payable as a result of the proceedings as follows:

(a) that the legal adviser or the client may, if required by the court to do so, disclose to the court, or any other person, the reasons for setting the success fee at the level stated;

(b) that if any amount of the success fee is disallowed on the ground that the level at which the increase was set was unreasonable in the light of the facts which were or should have been known to the legal adviser at the time, then that amount will cease to be payable under the agreement, unless the court is satisfied it should continue to be so payable.

This means that the level of success fee (regardless of what is in the agreement) which is payable by the client, will be limited to that which is allowed by the court on assessment.

4.3.5.5   Information for clients before the conditional fee agreement is made

Regulation 4

Under reg 4, before any CFA is entered into, the legal representative must bring certain matters to the client's attention, and, if the client requires, provide such further explanation, advice or information 'as the client may reasonably require'.

Matters that must be brought to the client's attention are:

(a) the circumstances in which the client may be liable to pay the costs of the legal representative in a accordance with the agreement;

(b) the circumstances in which the client may seek assessment of the fees and expenses of his legal representative and the procedure for doing so;

(c) whether the legal representative comes to the conclusion that the client's risk of incurring liability for costs in respect of the proceedings to which the agreement relates is insured against under an existing contract of insurance;

(d) whether other methods of financing costs are available and, if so, how they apply to that client and the proceedings in question;

(e) whether the legal representative considers any particular method, or methods of financing any or all part of those costs is appropriate, and if he considers that a contract of insurance is appropriate, or recommends a particular contract, his reasons for doing so and whether he has any interest in doing so.

The above information under reg 4 must be given to the client orally (whether or not it is also given in writing) but the information in relation to other methods of financing the costs, and the availability of insurance must be given both orally and in writing.

4.3.6   Conditional Fee Agreements signed on or after 1 November 2005

Following a review of the regulation of CFAs, the Department of Constitutional Affairs published its report on 10 August 2005. Respondents to the review from all areas of the legal community all agreed that the current CFA regulations are unnecessarily complex and should be simplified. It was also found that the detailed nature of the regulatory requirements had led to enormous problems in the operation of CFAs in practice, making them virtually impossible to explain to clients. It was thought that the client care and contractual requirements effectively duplicate the Law Society's rules, and that the proper place for regulating solicitors' use of CFAs and protecting consumers should be through the regulation of legal providers and not CFA legislation.

The conclusion of the review was that the existing CFA and collective conditional fee agreement (CCFA) regulations are to be revoked from 1 November 2005. The primary legislation will continue to be s 27 of the Access to Justice Act 1999 and the provisions in this section will continue to provide the essential regulatory requirements, namely that:

(a)   CFAs must be in writing;

(b)   they must state the percentage success fee applied; and

(c)   CFAs cannot be used in family and criminal proceedings.

On 1 November 2005 the Conditional Fee Agreements Regulations 2000 (as amended) and the Collective Conditional Fee Agreements Regulations 2000 (as amended) were repealed by the Conditional Fee Agreements (Revocation) Regulations 2005. The old 2000 Regulations continue to apply to CFAs entered into before 1 November 2005.

4.3.6.1   The reasons for the change

Much of the 2000 Regulations deal with information to be given to the client being represented under a CFA. This is already substantially covered in the Solicitors' Costs Information and Client Care Code 1999.

4.3.6.2   The new requirements:

From 1 November 2005 solicitors will be required to inform their clients, when acting under a CFA, of certain matters under the Solicitors' Costs Information and Client Care Code 1999, as amended by the Solicitors' Practice (Client Care) Amendment Rule 2005. The amended text appears below:

The Solicitors' Practice (Client Care) Amendment Rule 2005

(1)   At the end of paragraph 5 of the Solicitors' Costs Information and Client Care Code 1999 add:

'**Clients represented under a conditional fee agreement (including a collective conditional fee agreement)**

(d)   Where a client is represented under a conditional fee agreement, the solicitor should explain:

(i)   the circumstances in which the client may be liable for their own costs and for the other party's costs;

(ii)   the client's right to assessment of costs, wherever the solicitor intends to seek payment of any or all of their costs from the client; and

(iii)   any interest the solicitor may have in recommending a particular policy or other funding.'

(2)   This rule will come into force on 1 November 2005 or the date of repeal of the Conditional Fee Agreements Regulations (2000), whichever is the later.

Points (d)(i) and (ii) do not need any further explanation, as they are not new requirements, but point (d)(iii) refers to both where a solicitor may receive a commission from recommending a particular insurance policy and to where a solicitor is required, by virtue of being on a panel, to obtain funding or insurance from a particular source.

The new regulatory framework will seek to achieve the following objectives, namely that:

(a)   CFAs should be simple to understand;

(b)   the simplified regulations should deter technical challenges and bring more certainty and stability to the CFA regime.

Note that although the 2000 Regulations effectively prevent solicitors from charging clients any unrecovered success fee without the approval of the courts, the draft simplified regulations would end this requirement.

The new Law Society professional conduct requirements for use with the new model agreements will make clear the solicitors' primary obligation is to explain certain matters to the client. In particular, they must explain to the client the terms of the agreement and in what circumstances, if any, the client will be required to pay anything.

4.3.6.3   The form of the conditional fee agreement

The CFA must be in writing and signed by the client and by the legal representative.

The Law Society's Conditional Fees Committee has prepared a model agreement for use in personal injury cases post 31 October 2005. This is reproduced at **Appendix 1**.

Information for the parties about conditional fees

Information for clients on CFAs is governed by the Solicitors' Costs Information and Client Care Code, as from 1 November 2005. This information is reproduced at **Appendix 1**.

4.3.7   Costs and conditional fees

The provisions of the CPR 1998 relating to recovery of costs in conditional fees cases have been re-drafted to take account of the mechanics for recovery of the success fee and insurance premiums.

The Civil Procedure (Amendment No 3) Rules 2000 (SI 2000/1317) cover the mechanism for obtaining payment of the success fee and insurance premium from the losing party by way of costs.

According to the costs rules at CPR, Part 44 (as amended):

(a)   recovery of the success fee will not include recovery of any proportion of the success fee which relates to the cost to the solicitor of funding the case (ie, the costs to the firm of having payment of costs delayed);

(b)   recovery of the success fee will not include recovery of any part of the success fee for any period during which that party was in breach of a rule, Practice Direction or court order concerning provision of information on funding arrangements;

(c)   if the solicitor is required by the court or PD 48 to CPR 1998 – Costs, to disclose the reasons for setting a particular level of success fee and fails to do so, he may not recover the success fee;

(d)   recovery of the success fee will not be possible if a party fails to provide information regarding success fees and ATE insurance required by the Rules or a Practice Direction in any assessment proceedings;

(e)   where agreement is reached prior to issue of proceedings the procedure for resolving disputes as to costs will be by application to the court by way of a Part 8 claim form. The claim form must also be accompanied by a copy of the relevant CFA.

The Civil Procedure (Amendment No 2) Rules 2003 (SI 2003/1242) are intended to cover the mechanism for disapplying the indemnity principle to CFAs governed by the CFA Regs 2003 (CFA Simple). The rule makes provision for conditional fee agreements where the client is liable to pay his solicitor's fees and expenses only to the extent that such sums are recovered (ie, the solicitor will simply accept the costs recovered from the losing party as his full entitlement to costs).

CPR 1998, r 43.2(3) states:

> Where advocacy or litigation services are provided to a client under a conditional fee agreement, costs are recoverable under Parts 44 to 48 notwithstanding that the client is liable to pay his legal representative's fees and expenses only to the extent that sums are recovered in respect of the proceedings, whether by way of costs or otherwise.

The use of the form of words 'to pay his legal representative ... to the extent that sums are recovered ... by way of costs or *otherwise*' at the end of this sentence is thought to open up the possibility of the client having a liability to pay costs out of damages unless the CFA specifically states otherwise and uses the word 'costs' rather than 'sums'.

4.3.7.1 Legal representative's right to challenge an order that part of the percentage increase be disallowed

Where the level of success fee is subsequently disallowed on summary assessment or detailed assessment, that amount ceases to be payable (CPR 1998, PD 43–48, para 20.1).

However, under reg 3(2)(b) of the CFA Regs 2000, the legal representative may apply for an order that the disallowed amount should continue to be payable by the client.

4.3.7.2 Client's right to challenge the level of his own solicitor's costs and success fee

A client who has agreed to enter into a CFA with his solicitor and has agreed to a certain level of success fee, nevertheless has the right to have the basic costs assessed and to have the level of success fee assessed in the usual manner. If the client applies for the success fee to be reduced, the client must specify why the amount claimed is too high and what he thinks it ought to be. When assessing the application, the court will have regard to the circumstances as they appeared to the solicitor at the time when the CFA was signed. It is therefore particularly important to have a full file note available setting out the relative merits and risks on liability on the facts of the case as they appeared at that date. The court will take into account:

(a)   the risk that the case would be lost;

(b)   the inability to call for payments on account;

(c)   whether there is a CFA between solicitor and counsel;

(d)   the solicitor's liability for disbursements.

4.3.7.3 Challenging the level of success fee or ATE insurance by the losing party

At the conclusion of the case, the court will either:

(a)   make a summary assessment of all costs including any additional liability to pay a success fee/insurance premium; or

(b)   make an order for detailed assessment of the additional liability but make a summary assessment of the other costs; or

(c)   make an order for detailed assessment of all costs.

4.3.7.4   The impact on CFAs of *Callery v Gray*

The facts in *Callery v Gray*; *Russell v Pal Pak Corrugated Ltd* [2001] EWCA Civ 1117, [2001] 1 WLR 2113 were that, following a road traffic accident, the claimant instructed solicitors and entered into a CFA with a success fee of 60%. The claimant took out ATE insurance with a premium of £367.50. However, liability was quickly admitted and the claim was settled at a very early stage for £1,500 plus the claimant's reasonable costs. In the subsequent costs-only proceedings, the district judge allowed a 40% success fee and allowed the insurance premium in its entirety as a disbursement. The defendant appealed to the Court of Appeal. The court considered the issue of recoverability of the ATE insurance premium and success fee in a case which was the subject of a negotiated settlement and only came to court for the consideration of the assessment of costs. The defendant argued that he was not liable to pay the amount of the insurance premium paid by the claimant for ATE insurance. The insurance was taken out shortly after the accident and before any negotiations had taken place and before the protocol had been complied with. The defendant also argued that the success fee, which was set at 40%, was too high.

Recoverability for cost of insurance

With regard to the recoverability of the ATE insurance premium, the judge considered the wording of s 29 of the Access to Justice Act 1999. Under s 29:

> ... where in any proceedings a costs order is made in favour of any party who has taken out an insurance policy against the risk of incurring a liability in those proceedings, the costs payable to him may, subject in the case of court proceedings to rules of court, include costs in respect of the premium of the policy.

In this case, proceedings were never issued and the question arose whether the insurance premium was recoverable in circumstances where the only 'proceedings' were Part 8 proceedings which related to costs only. Where a claim had been settled on terms that the parties agreed which party was to pay the costs, and this was made or confirmed in writing, but they then failed to agree the amount of the costs, the court ruled that the ATE insurance premium could be recovered.

Time for taking out insurance

On a subsidiary point, the defendant argued that it was not right to allow any or part of the insurance premium to be recovered because it was taken out at a very early stage. On appeal, the court ruled that it would normally be reasonable for a CFA to be entered into with ATE insurance, on the first occasion that the client instructed his solicitor. If the cost of the uplift and premium were reasonable, each would be recoverable from the defendant if the claim succeeded or was settled on terms that the defendant paid the claimant's costs.

Level of success fee

In relation to the level of recoverable success fee, the court ruled that if the CFA were entered into in a modest and straightforward claim for injuries with a low risk of failure, for example, a claim by a passenger in a road traffic accident, then 20% would be the maximum uplift that could be agreed. If there were specific features or doubts about the soundness of the case, the uplift could be higher. However, if this conclusion were based on limited information, it would be better to review the situation once sufficient information was available for a 'fully informed' assessment to be made.

The decision was appealed to the House of Lords in June 2002 (*Callery v Gray (Nos 1 and 2)* [2002] UKHL 28, [2002] 1 WLR 2000), but the Law Lords declined to issue a further ruling on the issues considered by the Court of Appeal, deciding instead to state that they saw it as the role of the Court of Appeal to monitor and control this developing area. The Court of Appeal was right not to lay down rules applicable to all cases but should give provisional guidance that can be reviewed in light of increased knowledge and developing experience.

Following on from the ruling in *Callery v Gray*, senior costs Judge Hurst gave some further guidance on recoverability of ATE insurance premiums in *Re Claims Direct Test Cases* [2002] All ER (D) 76 (September). Claims Direct was a claims management company using franchised claims managers and panel solicitors, doctors and accountants. The court considered whether and to what extent the amount paid by the claimant in each case was a 'premium' within the meaning of s 29 to the Access to Justice Act 1999, and therefore recoverable as part of the costs of litigation as a disbursement. The court found that only some of the insurance premium paid by Claims Direct clients was recoverable. Of the £1,250 premium paid, less than half was recoverable as a 'premium' within the meaning of s 29 of the Access to Justice Act 1999, being the fee payable to underwriters (including commission to Claims Direct) and relevant insurance tax. The remainder of the amount claimed, which the court termed 'claims handling services', was not insurance-related and therefore not recoverable. The court also considered the extent to which the recoverable premium was reasonable. The judge expressed his concern with the way in which this area of law was developing in the following way:

> ... the test cases themselves demonstrate a far greater underlying problem. The test cases (particularly the RTA cases) are factually simple resulting in modest awards of damages for the claimants. In nearly every case the cost of obtaining those damages, even when agreed before proceedings with the defendant insurer, is greater than the amount of damages involved. This is so even before taking the recoverable insurance premium into account. The Civil Justice Council has set up a Working Party to examine the possibility of establishing a predictable costs regime for low value road traffic claims but unless and until a scheme of fixed, predictable or capped costs is introduced, satellite litigation of this type seems inevitable.

The judge concluded by finding that, particularly in road traffic claims where there is slight injury and liability is accepted at the outset, it will generally be disproportionate and unreasonable to take out an ATE insurance policy.

4.3.8 Fixed costs for straightforward road traffic accident claims valued at less than £10,000

Following on from the court's findings in *Re Claims Direct Test Cases,* the Civil Justice Council obtained agreement in principle to the introduction of a fixed costs regime to the majority of road traffic claims. CPR 1998, r 45 now provides for fixed costs to be recovered in respect of disputes, which are settled prior to proceedings being issued in respect of road traffic accidents. The scheme operates in respect of disputes arising from 6 October 2003 and is not retrospective. The scheme applies to disputes where the total agreed value of damages exceeds £1,000 but does not exceed £10,000.

4.3.8.1 Paragraph 25A road traffic accidents: fixed recoverable costs in costs-only proceedings.

According to para 25A.2 of the Practice Direction to CPR 1998, Part 45, the paragraph does not apply to disputes where the total agreed value of the damages is within the small claims limit or exceeds £10,000. The paragraph goes on to say that r 26.8(2) sets out how the financial value of a claim is assessed for the purposes of allocation to track.

CPR 1998, r 26.8(2) says:

> It is for the court to assess the financial value of a claim and in doing so it will disregard—
>
> (a)   any amount not in dispute;
>
> (b)   any claim for interest;
>
> (c)   costs; and
>
> (d)   any contributory negligence.

Therefore, it appears at first sight that, for the purpose of s 25, the formula for valuation of the claim is as used for allocation to track and contributory negligence falls to be disregarded.

However, according to para 25A.3:

> Fixed recoverable costs are to be calculated by reference to the amount of agreed damages which are payable to the receiving party. In calculating the amount of these damages—
>
> (a)   account must be taken of both general and special damages and interest;
>
> (b)   any interim payments made must be included;
>
> (c)   where the parties have agreed an element of contributory negligence, the amount of damages attributed to that negligence must be deducted;
>
> (d)   any amount required to be paid by the compensating party directly to a third party (such as sums paid by way of compensation recovery payments and National Health Service expenses) must not be included.

Therefore fixed costs are to be calculated by reference to the amount of agreed damages which are payable to the receiving party. This means that the effect of a significant degree of contributory negligence by the claimant must always be borne in mind when considering the financial viability of low value road traffic claims.

In addition to the fixed costs a success fee is applied at a rate of 12.5% of fixed recoverable costs for cases settled without trial and at a rate of 100% for cases settled at trial. The court will also allow reasonable disbursements.

Damages	Costs	Description
Up to £1,000	£1,000	£800 + 20% (of damages)
£2,000	£1,200	£800 + 20%
£3,000	£1,400	£800 + 20%
£4,000	£1,600	£800 + 20%
£5,000	£1,800	£800 + 20%
£6,000	£1,950	£800 + 15%
£7,000	£2,100	£800 + 15%
£8,000	£2,250	£800 + 15%

Damages	Costs	Description
£9,000	£2,400	£800 + 15%
£10,000	£2,550	£800 + 15%

4.3.8.2 Fixed costs in non-disease employer's liability cases

Fixed success fees apply to non-disease employer's liability claims where the injury is sustained on or after 1 October 2004 and these fees can be found at Part 45 of the CPR. The fixed success fee is 25%, unless a membership organisation has undertaken to be responsible for the claimant's costs, in which case the success fee is 27.5%. However if the case is conducted all the way to trial, the success fee is 100%.

Under CPR 1998, r 45.18(2) a party may apply for a different success fee to be applied where:

(a)   agreed damages or an award of damages are greater than £500,000; or

(b)   a court awards an amount of £500,000 or less but would have awarded damages greater than £500,000 but for a finding of contributory negligence; or

(c)   the parties agree damages of £500,000 or less but it is reasonable to expect that, but for a finding of contributory negligence, a court would have awarded damages greater than £500,000.

Note that for cases where the injury occurred after 1 October 2004 it is still necessary to complete a risk assessment in the usual way.

4.3.8.3 Access to Justice (Membership Organisation) Regulations 2000

Under the Access to Justice (Membership Organisation) Regulations 2000 (SI 2000/693), trades unions who indemnify their members in relation to costs liabilities are able to recover the amount that they have paid as 'quasi-insurance' in relation to their member. However, this sum must not exceed the cost of an equivalent insurance policy (reg 4(2)).

4.3.9 Client care

The Law Society's guide to CFAs recommends that the solicitor should read through the agreement with the client, emphasise the binding nature of the agreement and check that the client understands the agreement fully. To this end, it is good practice for the solicitor to send The Law Society's leaflet, *Conditional Fees Explained,* to the client prior to the meeting. The leaflet includes a checklist of 'questions to ask your solicitor' and it is therefore essential for the solicitor to be prepared to answer these questions, and to be able to explain those answers to the client.

4.3.10 Risk assessment and CFAs

In order to decide:

(a)   whether to take a potential claim on *at all* on a CFA basis; and

(b)   once the decision has been made to accept the client's case on a CFA basis, what is the appropriate level of success fee to apply to the agreement,

it will be necessary for the claimant's solicitor to undertake risk assessment of the potential claim in every case.

The method adopted by way of risk assessment will differ from one firm to another, with some adopting paper-based systems while others will utilise computer software to capture basic information and assist in speeding up the risk assessment process. Whichever method is used the underlying principles are the same.

4.3.10.1 Principles of risk assessment

The Oxford dictionary defines risk as: 'the chance or possibility of loss or bad consequence'. If a solicitors' firm accepts a case on a 'no win no fee' basis it exposes itself to the risk of loss in not getting paid for the work it has done on behalf of the client. However this is only half of the equation. There is equally the chance of a successful outcome. So risk assessment can be seen as the process of balancing the risk of losing against the chance of winning. That is easy enough to say, but rather more difficult to quantify objectively in a way that gives predictable and workable results. However this is exactly what a personal injury practitioner has to do when deciding whether or not to take a case on a CFA basis.

4.3.10.2 Practice of risk assessment:

In practice the skill of the personal injury practitioner will be in his ability to spot the factors relevant to risk and then go on to assess the severity of that risk. The majority of firms make use of a checklist for this purpose, which may be paper or electronically based.

The factors relevant to risk (or hazards) will include anything that could harm the claim. The risk will be the percentage chance that the factor will actually occur.

Common risk factors will include:

(a) *The facts*: is the client a credible witness and are there any other witnesses who will confirm his version?

(b) *Liability*: will the client be able to show that there was a relevant duty of care and this duty has been breached?

(c) *Causation*: will the client be able to show that the injuries sustained are causally linked to the accident?

(d) *Limitation*: are there any issues due to limitation of claims or delay (ie 'stale' evidence)?

(e) *The potential defendant*: is the opponent a 'viable' source of damages – does he carry insurance, or have funds to meet a damages claim and have insurance details been confirmed?

(f) *Loss and damage*: can the losses sustained by way of medical and other forms of evidence be proved?

The second stage in the risk assessment is to assess the chance of each of the above risk factors actually occurring and harming the viability of the case. To do this each factor needs to be categorised or 'scored' in some way. This can be done either by giving each factor a percentage, or a score between one and ten, or more simply still assessed as a high, medium or low risk.

Based on the result (or score) from the above assessment a risk assessment co-ordinator (usually a partner in the firm) will judge whether to accept the case on a conditional fee basis and if so on what level of success fee. In the event that he is unable to do so, because of insufficient information being available, he will pass the file back to the case worker for further investigation, for example, obtaining witness statements or contacting the police for clarification of key issues.

In the event that the claim is accepted on a CFA basis it is essential to record the reasoning behind the decision and the reason for the success fee claimed, as this will be needed in the event that the claim is successful and costs are assessed at the close of the case.

4.3.11 Conditional fees and counsel

Counsel's fees incurred on behalf of a client do not form part of the disbursements covered by Accident Line Protect (ALP). The Law Society model agreement at condition 6 specifies two ways of dealing with counsel's fees.

(a)   The solicitor enters into a separate CFA with the barrister:
  (i)   if the client wins the case, the barrister's basic fee will be recovered as a disbursement from the opponent. The solicitor will pay the barrister's 'uplift' agreed in the barrister's CFA, but will have regard to this expense when agreeing his own fee 'uplift' with the client;
  (ii)   if the client loses the case, he will owe the barrister nothing.
(b)   There is no CFA between the barrister and the solicitor, in which case:
  (i)   if the client wins the case and has been paying the barrister's fees on account (ie, up front), there will be no extra success fee to pay, and the barrister's fees can be recovered from the opponent as before;
  (ii)   if the client wins the case and has not been paying the barrister's fees on account, the solicitor will recover that disbursement from the opponent. Because of this greater outlay by the solicitor (and greater financial loss to the firm in the event that the client loses), the solicitor will charge an extra success fee in the event that the client wins;
  (iii) if the client loses the case and has not been paying the barrister's fees on account, the solicitor is liable to pay them, and will not be able to pass this loss on to the client.

4.3.12 Trade unions

If the client has had an accident at work and belongs to a trade union, he may be entitled to receive free access to legal advice as part of his membership. This is something that the client may not be aware of initially and the solicitor should therefore cover this point at the initial interview. If the client is entitled to advice through his union, the union may have its own legal department or nominated solicitors whom it always uses. If this is the case, the solicitor first consulted by the client is unlikely to be instructed, but should nevertheless advise the client to seek advice from his union on this point. The advantage to the client, if he is able to procure the support of union funding, is that, provided he has paid his membership fees to the union, he will have the full financial support of the union behind him. His solicitor will still have to convince the union as to the merits of the case, and will also be obliged to report on the case prior to proceeding with it. However, the claimant will not have to worry that part of his damages may be taken away to pay his legal expenses, as would be the case if he was funded either through public funding or a CFA.

4.3.13 Legal expenses insurance

The client may have legal expenses insurance (known as 'before the event' insurance) as a part of either his home or motor insurance policy, or as an extra for which he has paid an additional premium. This is something that the client may either be unaware of or have forgotten, and it is therefore important that this is considered at the first interview.

In *Sarwar v Alam* [2001] EWCA Civ 1401, [2001] 4 All ER 541, the claimant had taken out an ATE insurance policy when there was the opportunity to benefit from an existing legal expense insurance policy. In the costs-only proceedings, the issue was whether the ATE premium was recoverable. The Court of Appeal gave guidance that although a solicitor is not obliged to embark on a 'treasure hunt' in relation to pre-existing insurance, a solicitor should develop a practice of sending a standard letter requesting sight of:

(a)   any relevant motor insurance policy;

(b)   any household insurance policy;

(c)   any stand-alone before the event insurance policy belonging to the client and/or any spouse or partner living in the same household; and, if possible, their driver (if they are an injured passenger) in advance of the first interview.

A decision then needs to be made about whether any legal expenses insurance policy is satisfactory. The court emphasised that the decision related to small road traffic accident claims with a quantum of £5,000 or less and that enquiries should be proportionate. As with union-funded work, the insurer may have nominated firms of solicitors who must be instructed to undertake the insured's claim. If the insured is free to instruct the solicitor of his choice, it is usual for the insurer to require the solicitor to report to it regularly on the progress of the case. In terms of confidentiality, it is essential for the solicitor to explain to the client at the outset that a term of the insurance is that the insurer has the right to receive reports on the viability of the case and whether or not it is worthwhile to continue with it. The progress of the case can be slowed down considerably by the obligation on the solicitor to report back to the insurer to seek approval (and therefore funding) to continue with the claim to the next stage.

In *Samonini v London General Transport Services Ltd* (2005), SCCO the principal costs officer considered whether costs were recoverable under a conditional fee agreement when the solicitor did not carry out any independent enquiry as to legal expenses insurance but relied entirely on the inquiries made by a claims management company. The claimant was never asked about any policy but his motor policy. The costs officer found that the solicitor was under a duty to carry out a careful investigation as to alternative sources of insurance. If solicitors were permitted to skimp on the proper investigation of legal expenses insurance, the administration of justice would be badly served. In the circumstances, there had been a material breach of reg 4(2)(c) of the Conditional Fee Regulations 2000; the conditional fee agreement was unenforceable and therefore the solicitor could not recover any costs.

4.3.13.1   Choice of solicitor under legal expense insurance (LEI) policies

The Insurance Companies (Legal Expenses Insurance) Regulations 1990 (SI 1990/1159) give effect to European Directive 87/344. The Regulations cover, amongst other things, before the event insurance cover in respect of road traffic accidents. Regulation 6 of the 1990 Regulations specifies:

> 6.   Freedom to choose a lawyer
>
>   (1)   Where under a legal expenses insurance contract recourse is had to a lawyer . . . to defend, represent or serve the interests of the insured in any *enquiry or proceedings,* the insured shall be free to choose that lawyer (or other person). (emphasis supplied)

The interpretation given to the term 'enquiry or proceedings' will determine whether or not the insured person does have freedom to choose their lawyer. Some insurance companies providing LEI cover put a narrow interpretation on it, saying that only when there are actual court proceedings is there any freedom for the policy holder to choose. The insurer will often prefer to refer the insured's claim to its panel of solicitors only, effectively concentrating the bulk of claims to so-called 'panel firms'. Not all LEI providers operate panels of preferred solicitors but many do, citing quality assurance and consistency of claims handling as the rationale for insisting on operating panels to which to channel claims. Non-panel firms see this as damaging to their position, as they may be forced to advise clients that they should avail themselves of pre-existing LEI cover rather than take up the non-panel solicitors' offer to work on the basis of a CFA. The non-panel solicitors will often take the view that the wording of para 6(1) of the 1990 Regulations should be given a wide interpretation and 'enquiry or proceedings' will encompass the work undertaken at pre-issue stage under the pre-action protocol. Their justification for this is due to the 'front loading' of litigation where much of the work and advice is, of necessity, conducted before the issue of proceedings.

A case which illustrates many of the points outlined above is *Chappell v De Bora's of Exeter* (2004), SCCO. This is a Supreme Court Costs Office case in which the costs claim of a non-panel local firm of solicitors was allowed despite the existence of pre-existing LEI. The facts briefly are as follows. The claimant's claim was in respect of the personal injuries she suffered when she fell down some steps at the defendant's shop in Exeter. The claimant, who lived near Exeter, instructed solicitors in Exeter. They entered into a CFA with a success fee of 71%. They also arranged a policy of ATE insurance and corresponded with DAS, the legal expenses insurers with whom the claimant had an existing BTE insurance policy. DAS said that, under the terms of her policy with them, the claimant was obliged to instruct solicitors who were on their panel for any work which had to be done before the issue of proceedings, although she was entitled to instruct the solicitors of her choice for the purpose of the proceedings themselves should proceedings be necessary. The claimant's solicitors (who were not on the DAS panel) undertook the usual pre-proceedings work including sending the letter of claim, taking witness evidence and obtaining two medical reports. The defendant's solicitors eventually offered to settle the matter for £31,156 plus costs. This offer was accepted but the issue of costs could not be agreed and, following detailed assessment, the defendant was given permission to appeal on the issue of whether it was reasonable for the claimant to enter into a CFA with a success fee and ATE insurance with the solicitors of her choice, when BTE insurance was available but the claimant's chosen solicitors were not on the BTE insurers panel.

The defendant's counsel submitted that the onus was on the claimant to show why it was reasonable, on the standard basis, that the more expensive route of proceedings under a CFA with ATE insurance should have been adopted. He submitted that solicitors on the DAS panel up and down the country conducted very many cases no less serious and complex than the present case on a regular basis. He accepted what the Master of the Rolls had said in *Sarwar v Alam* (see **4.3.11**):

> In this case we are concerned only with a relatively small personal injury claim in a road traffic accident. We are not concerned with claims which look as if they will exceed about £5,000, and we are not concerned with any other type of BTE claim. We have no doubt that, if a claimant possesses pre-existing BTE cover which appears to be satisfactory for a claim of that size, then in the ordinary course of things that claimant should be referred to the relevant BTE insurers.

The claimant's counsel submitted that this was not a straightforward case and the amount of the damages in this case, in excess of £31,000, reflected those complexities. It had been reasonable for the claimant to go to solicitors in Exeter to handle her case rather than to solicitors in Bristol or Salisbury. He submitted that the costs which the district judge had allowed were proportionate in relation to a multi-track case of this nature. The judge concluded that it was reasonable in a case of this kind for the claimant to instruct the solicitors of her choice in Exeter rather than DAS panel solicitors, the nearest of whom would have been many miles away from where she lived. Accordingly he dismissed the appeal in so far as it related to the claimant's choice of solicitor.

4.3.14 Private fee-paying clients

Some clients will have no alternative but to fund their cases privately, or may choose to do so in any case. In this event the solicitor is obliged, under the Written Professional Standards, to explain to the client fully his liability for costs and disbursements. The solicitor should give the best information on costs that he can, including likely disbursements and the hourly rate that the solicitor proposes to charge (as to which see the Legal Practice Guide, *Pervasive and Core Topics*, Part II, Professional Conduct).

4.4 Urgent matters

If an urgent matter comes to light during the first interview, the solicitor should bear in mind the question of funding prior to making lengthy or expensive investigations on the client's behalf, and should consider making an application for emergency public funding if appropriate.

4.4.1 Limitation

At the first interview in a personal injury or clinical negligence claim, it may become apparent that:

(a) The three-year primary limitation period is about to expire (this is explained fully in **Chapter 6**). If so, the solicitor should consider issuing protective proceedings immediately.

(b) The three-year primary limitation period has recently expired. If so, consideration should be given to issuing proceedings as soon as possible, including in the claim form or particulars of claim, a request for a direction that the limitation period should be disapplied. Thereafter, the solicitor should inform the defendant without delay that proceedings have been issued to minimise any claim by the defendant of prejudice due to the passage of time.

(c) There is a question as to the client's 'date of knowledge' of the injury complained of. The client should be questioned closely regarding the earliest date on which he realised he might have a cause of action, and how he came to that conclusion. Proceedings can then be issued as in point (b) above and thereafter it can be argued that the limitation period has not yet expired because the client's date of knowledge of the injury is within the last three years. If this is not successful, an application should be made for the court to exercise its discretion and disapply the limitation period (see **Chapter 6**).

4.4.2 Key dates

Having established when the primary limitation period is due to expire, it is important that the time limit is recorded separately from the file in a diary system.

The file itself may be similarly marked with the date on which limitation expires. This double recording of the primary limitation period is good practice as negligence claims against solicitors in personal injury cases account for roughly 11% of claims on Solicitors' Liability. Failure to identify the correct limitation period is one of the most common pitfalls and this can be avoided.

4.4.3   Photographs

In most personal injury cases, persons seeking advice following an accident will do so relatively soon after the accident occurs. If this is the case, a task, which is often overlooked, will be to secure photographic evidence.

4.4.3.1   The client

The client may attend the interview with an array of bruises and abrasions (soft tissue injuries). These will heal or fade relatively quickly and an important piece of the claimant's evidence will be lost. The claimant's solicitor should therefore ensure that good colour photographs are taken of the client's injuries for subsequent disclosure. Such photographs will form very tangible evidence of the severity of the injuries sustained, when the case comes to be considered some months or years in the future. In cases where the client may suffer embarrassment at being photographed, or indeed in any case where a degree of sensitivity is needed, specialist medical photographers are available, for example, at larger teaching hospitals.

4.4.3.2   The location of the accident

In road traffic cases, it is usually necessary to produce photographs and plans of the location of the accident for two reasons. First, the layout of the road may change between the date of accident and the date of trial and/or the road may appear different depending on whether it is photographed in summer or in winter, especially if there are lots of trees or vegetation which could obscure a driver's view. Secondly, it may be necessary to try to show the location from the perspective of the car drivers at the time. An aerial view or plan of a road junction will do nothing, for example, to prove to a court how badly the approach of a vehicle was obscured by trees and bushes or roadside property. The solicitor should not lose sight of the fact that he must be able to prove to the court what could or could not be seen from a particular vantage point. It is open to the court to visit the site of the accident, but this may not be practicable and, in any event, would take an inordinate amount of time. The solicitor should always visit the site if possible, in order to get a feel for the case. Police accident reports (see **Chapter 5**) often contain good quality photographs which can be purchased on payment of an extra fee per print, and may prove helpful in showing not only the severity and location of the damage to each vehicle, but also the final position on the road that the vehicles were in immediately following the accident. This evidence may assume significance at a later date or may contradict the oral evidence of the witnesses. It is, however, important to read the police accident report closely, as it will confirm whether or not the vehicles were moved from their original resting position prior to the taking of the photographs.

In road traffic cases, the photographer should mark on a plan the precise location from which each photograph was taken and the direction in which the camera was pointing.

Site visits in non-road traffic cases are no less important. For example, in a case where the client has tripped on a broken pavement, it is not uncommon that, as soon as the local authority receives intimation of a possible claim, it will send a team of operatives to remedy the offending pavement to rebut any subsequent suggestion on the part of the claimant that it failed to take all reasonable care in the circumstances. It is therefore vitally important to secure good quality photographs of the pavement, etc as soon as possible, usually on the same day that the client is interviewed. Photographs must contain some indication of scale, and it is therefore necessary to place an item, such as a ruler, within the photograph.

It is not good practice to entrust the taking of photographs to the client, who may underestimate the importance of the task and forget about it until it is too late. Photographs taken by the client may be out of focus or underexposed which will not help the client's case.

4.5 Advising the client

4.5.1 Personal injury claims

It is important for the solicitor not to lose sight of the fact that the client has come into his office seeking some meaningful advice, which he hopes will lead him to a decision as to whether he has an actionable case against some other party. The client therefore needs to have the best information available, in a form that he can understand, so that he can make an informed decision as to what to do next. It is best to set out the strengths and weaknesses of the case, based on what has been said by the client. The importance of the limitation period should be explained to the client if this is likely to be an issue. The solicitor should explain to the client that it is down to him to prove his case by evidence and that anything short of this is not enough. He should be informed of the basis of his case, and the level of proof needed by the court to prove that case. The client should be left in no doubt that it is his case, to be proved by his evidence, and that he bears the risk that his case may fail. As such, he should think seriously prior to instructing his solicitor to issue proceedings. The solicitor should give an indication as to whether he believes that the case is likely to succeed, but he should make it clear that the assessment is based on the limited information available at this early stage. In any event, if the solicitor is considering taking the client's case but will be paid under a CFA, it will be necessary for the solicitor to conduct an assessment of risk at an early stage in order to decide whether or not to accept the client's instructions on that basis.

It may be that the solicitor advising the client will be required to produce to his superiors a report, from which his superiors will make a risk assessment in relation to whether or not the client should be accepted on a conditional fee basis. The risk assessment report may also consider such things as whether it is proposed that the client covers his own disbursements or whether the firm is prepared to fund them on the client's behalf. The client is likely to press for an indication of the likely level of damages that may be recovered. Giving a firm indication based on inadequate information should be resisted. Instead, the solicitor should explain to the client why an assessment would be premature at this stage.

One reason for not giving a provisional indication of the likely level of damages is that the client may be found to have been contributorily negligent. This principle should be explained to the client, first to try to elicit whether the client has any reason to believe that it will be relevant to his claim, and, secondly, to act as a warning to the client that it is likely that the opposition will try to allege that he was contributorily negligent.

The client should also be advised that he must prove every head (or type) of loss against his opponent. Although it is the case that the client is able to claim all he has lost as a direct result of the accident, he must also be in a position to prove every head of that loss to the court if he wishes to recover damages in respect of it. It should therefore be explained to the client that damages are made up of general damages (for pain, suffering and loss of amenity) and special damages (everything the client has had physically to pay for and other quantifiable losses as a direct result of the accident). For a detailed analysis of the subject of damages, see **Chapter 13**.

It will assist greatly when it comes to proving his losses if the client has kept a detailed record or account of his out-of-pocket expenses. To this end, the client should be advised at the first interview to keep all receipts for expenses incurred as a direct result of the accident, and that it is his responsibility to do so. Common examples are prescriptions, the cost of items lost or damaged beyond repair in the accident, and taxi fares to the out-patient department or physiotherapy. Similarly, with respect to general damages for pain and suffering, although the client's distress may be keen at the first interview, by the time of trial his recollection may have dimmed to the extent that he has forgotten many of the minor losses of function he suffered in the early stages of recovery from his injuries. The client should therefore be advised to keep a diary if he does not already do so, to record, for example, the fact that he is unable to sleep due to pain, or is unable to dress himself unaided or to do housework, and to record how long these disabilities last. Any number of tasks, either recreational or work-related, should be recorded so that they are not forgotten later when it comes to preparing the client's witness statement.

4.5.2 Clinical negligence claims

It is particularly important in clinical negligence cases that the client is made aware of the difficulties in pursuing the claim, and especially that he must establish not only a breach of duty, but also that the breach was causative of the damage that resulted (rather than the underlying illness or injury being the root cause of the loss). If the client is paying for the litigation privately, the high costs involved must be clearly explained to him. The solicitor should also explain the difficulty in giving a preliminary view on liability without first obtaining all the client's medical notes and at least one expert's views.

4.6 The client's proof of evidence

The client's proof of evidence should not be confused with the client's witness statement. Although they are both statements taken from the client they serve different functions. The proof is the 'rough copy', which may include irrelevant material and suspicions or 'versions' rather than facts provable by the client in court. The witness statement contains only those matters which the witness can prove, and is disclosed to the opposition at the relevant stage in the proceedings. The function of the proof is to obtain the fullest possible detail from the client, and only later to sift out what is strictly admissible as evidence. The proof can be taken at the end of the first interview when the client is still present, or from notes made at the time in conjunction with the questionnaire.

4.6.1 Contents of the proof

The proof should commence with the client's full name, address, date of birth and National Insurance number. It should state his occupation and whether he is married. If he was admitted to hospital, it should state his hospital number. The proof is intended for use by the client's solicitor and barrister, and, subsequently, in the preparation of the client's witness statement, and, as such, it should be the fullest possible statement from the client relating to the incident, the events immediately following the incident and its long-term effects. The client should begin his narrative at the earliest point in time that he feels to be relevant. Following the client's personal details, the proof should next detail the date, time and location of the incident. It should then follow through chronologically and meticulously:

(a)   the events leading up to the incident;

(b)   the circumstances of the accident itself;

(c)   what happened immediately after the incident;

(d)   why the client feels that the incident was caused by the negligence of some other person;

(e)   what medical treatment was given and injuries incurred; and

(f)   how the client feels that the incident has affected his day-to-day life.

The solicitor should bear in mind that the proof will form the basis of the witness statement, and that, usually, the witness statement will be ordered to stand as the witness's evidence-in-chief at the trial. It is important, therefore, that the proof is detailed in its description of how the incident actually happened, and the effect the incident has had on the client's day-to-day life. All aspects of the client's life should therefore be considered in the proof. The following areas should always be covered, including an estimate in weeks or months of how long the incapacity affected the client's life, or confirmation that the incapacity is still continuing.

(a)   Everyday tasks which he is unable to do for himself; for example, dressing, bathing, housework, shopping, driving. This will be important if a claim is made for loss incurred in employing someone else to carry out these tasks.

(b)   Recreational activities such as sports, hobbies, gardening, DIY in maintaining the home and the family car. The client's inability to participate in sports will have an effect on his loss of amenity claim for general damages. The client should also be asked whether he is a member of any sports team or club, and any prizes or trophies he has won as further evidence of his level of commitment. The inability to carry out maintenance jobs around the home will similarly affect his claim for loss of amenity. If the client gives evidence that DIY is a hobby, details should be obtained of any projects he has undertaken. This will also affect his special damages claim for the labour element of the cost of having to employ someone else to fulfil those tasks in the future.

(c)   Whether and to what extent the injury has affected his sex life. This area of loss of amenity should always be broached with the client, as the stress of an accident can often bring about a degree of sexual dysfunction, even if the injury itself would not immediately suggest that such was the case.

(d)   Specifically whether the incident will affect the client's ability to continue with his employment, and the extent to which he is affected. It may be obvious that the client will never work again, or will be unable to work in his pre-incident position but will have to retrain, or that he intends to return to his pre-incident employment but is unsure whether he will cope. Details should also be obtained as to the client's position if he were to be made redundant, and the degree of difficulty he would have in obtaining similar employment elsewhere because of his injuries.

It is important that all of the above issues are considered, and, if it is relevant, that they are covered in the proof in some detail, as there is little point in the client and/or his solicitor knowing the extent to which the incident has ruined the client's life, if this is not articulated sufficiently to the court. If a matter is not covered in the client's witness statement, the chances are the court will never hear of it and, if the court is not made aware of all relevant matters, the claimant's solicitor has not achieved one of his main aims, that of maximising the client's damages.

Before finishing the proof in personal injury cases, the client should always be asked whether he has had any pre-existing incident injury which may affect the current case.

The proof should always end with the client's signature and the date on which it was prepared so that, if the client dies prior to the conclusion of the case, the proof will still be of use evidentially.

4.6.2   Proofs in relation to different types of incident

The following types of incident will require the proof to cover certain areas in particular detail.

4.6.2.1   Incidents at work

The nature of the work process that gave rise to the incident must be thoroughly understood from the outset if the case is to be dealt with properly. The client should be asked to explain:

(a)   his job title;

(b)   what that involves in the work process;

(c)   the level of training or instruction received;

(d)   the level of seniority he held;

(e)   the level of supervision over him;

(f)   whether he can recall any written or oral confirmation of his work duties;

(g)   a description of his usual duties;

(h)   what he was doing on the day in question that gave rise to the incident;

(i)   whether anything out of the ordinary occurred that day;

(j)   details of other similar incidents known to the claimant;

(k)   any representations made by a trade union about the machine or system of work;

(l)   any comments made at health and safety meetings.

Example

John is an instrument artificer employed to work at a chemical plant. Part of his duties is to check the temperature of certain chemicals stored in large tanks above ground on the site. On the day of the accident, John climbed to the top of a storage tank and removed the outer cover. Without warning, John was blown backwards by excess pressure in the tank causing him to fall from the tank approximately 4 metres to the ground. Because the chemical was corrosive on contact with the skin, John suffered burns to his face and hands as well as a damaged spine and broken left leg. John tells you that he has done the same task many times before without incident, but he believes that whoever last checked that particular tank failed adequately to secure the inner seal so that when he next opened the outer seal the sudden change in pressure was like releasing a cork from a bottle. John tells you that he is usually accompanied by a fellow employee when doing these checks as the company's safety policy requires this. On the day of the incident, his colleague had telephoned in sick, but the duty manager had not called in anyone else to take his place. John also tells you that the company used to have a nurse on site to deal with minor injuries, but when the last nurse ceased to be employed she was not replaced, John believes that this was because of the expense involved. John also believes that his burns would not be so severe if he had received first aid more quickly.

In the above example, if, when describing any part of his duties, John becomes unclear, he should be asked to explain it again, perhaps drawing a sketch to assist his narrative. It is important that there is no misunderstanding at this stage as the solicitor will probably use this information as the basis for his statement of case. In addition, if the solicitor is unsure from the client's explanation precisely how the incident happened, it is also likely that a judge will be similarly confused. It is therefore vitally important that any ambiguity is resolved at this point. If ambiguity remains, facilities should be sought for a site inspection. Where the place of work is privately owned property, and may be a dangerous environment for the visitor, the solicitor must always seek permission from the employer for a site inspection. The inspection can be carried out with the claimant's expert engineer if the accident involves a piece of machinery.

In the above example, it is necessary to include in the proof John's suspicions as to:

(a)   the cause of the incident;

(b)   disregard of safety policy; and

(c)   his belief that the burns were worsened by delay in treatment.

All these matters will have to be checked, however, as the chemical engineer who inspects the plant may conclude that the incident had a completely different cause, possibly involving contributory negligence by John himself. It may be apparent to the engineer that the tank is fitted with a large pressure gauge that John should have checked prior to opening the tank. Similarly, the company safety policy may specify that rubber gloves and full face mask must be worn when working with corrosive chemicals, and that the burn time for that particular chemical is less than 30 seconds, in which case having medical personnel on site would have made no difference to John's injuries.

The function of the proof is to form the basis of the witness statement. As such, the client's assertions must be checked thoroughly in order to decide whether they are provable and can be included in the statement.

4.6.2.2 Road traffic incidents

When taking the proof in the case of a road incident, it is important first to have in mind the stretch of road in question. A large-scale map of the area in question is invaluable at this stage as it will cut short any unproductive argument as to how or where, for example, the road bends. If the client has difficulty explaining how the incident happened, it can be useful to get him to draw a sketch of the relative position of the vehicles involved, or to use toy cars to illustrate what happened. Care should be taken to ensure that the client is entirely clear about the following matters:

(a)   the direction in which he was travelling;

(b)   whether there was anyone else in the car with him;

(c)   the speed of travel;

(d)   familiarity with the car;

(e)   familiarity with the road;

(f)   whether there were any witnesses;

(g)   the make and registration numbers of all vehicles involved;

(h)   who he believes to be responsible for the incident and why;

(i)   what happened immediately after the incident;

(j)   exactly what he said to anyone after the incident;

(k)   exactly what anyone said to him, and whether anyone else heard what was said;

(l)   whether the police were called and, if not, why not;

(m)   if the police were called, which police force and the name of the officer attending;

(n)   whether the client is aware of any pending prosecutions (eg, whether he was warned that he may be prosecuted or that he may be needed as a witness in the prosecution of the other driver);

(o)   whether he is comprehensively insured and the amount of excess he has to pay on his own insurance policy (his uninsured loss);

(p)   whether he is the owner of the vehicle, and details of the owner if he is not.

If the client wrote anything down at the time of the incident, such as the name and address of the other driver(s), these should be retained. If he explains what happened, for example, by referring to the offside and nearside of his vehicle, the solicitor should check that he understands what is meant by those terms. Clients may believe that they have to speak to their solicitor using words which they would not normally use in everyday speech and, consequently, they may use words that they do not fully understand. For the avoidance of doubt, the solicitor should check with the client that when referring to a vehicle's 'offside' the client means the driver's side, and that 'nearside' refers to the side of the vehicle nearest the gutter.

In road traffic cases, it is vitally important to trace and interview witnesses as soon as possible. It is unlikely that the witnesses will be known to the client and they may prove difficult to trace if not contacted immediately, and in any event their memory of the events will fade quickly and will therefore be of less use evidentially. The question of whether there are any independent third party witnesses is of central importance because the case will be much easier to prove if an independent witness can be found who is prepared to give evidence to a court that he saw the incident and believes that the cause of the incident was the fault of the other driver. If the client does not have any details of witnesses, the police accident report may have statements from witnesses whom the solicitor can contact. The police should be notified of all incidents involving personal injury, and will prepare a report on the incident including witness statements (see **Chapter 5**).

4.6.2.3   Tripping/slipping incidents

Trips and slips make up a large proportion of incidents in the workplace, and the HSE has targeted this area in order to heighten awareness of the problem (see the HSE publication *Watch Your Step* (Stationery Office, 1985) and *Slips and Trips: Guidance for employers on identifying hazards and controlling risks* (Stationery Office, May 1996)).

Tripping incidents occurring other than at the workplace are governed by s 41 of the Highways Act 1980, under which the highway authority (usually the local district council responsible for the area in which the fall or trip took place) has a duty to maintain the highway, which includes the pavements used by the public.

It is for the claimant to show that the highway was not reasonably safe. Uneven paving stones or the sites of road improvements with poor temporary surfaces usually claim the most victims. Local authorities sometimes contract out such road works to independent contractors, in which case it may be advisable to sue both the contractor responsible for the safety of the site and the local authority which delegated the improvement work to them. If the client can show that the highway was not reasonably safe, the authority must show that it has taken such care as in all the circumstances was reasonably required to ensure that the highway was not dangerous.

Applying the above rule to the client's proof it will be necessary to ask the client:

(a)   whether he was in a hurry or was running at the time of the incident;

(b)   whether he was carrying anything which obscured his view;

(c)   whether there was a warning sign to take care and, if so, what the sign said;

(d)   whether there were any witnesses;

(e)   what sort of shoes the client was wearing; and

(f)   the exact location of the incident.

It will then be necessary to procure photographs of the location without delay, as the local authority may act quickly to repair the relevant area as soon as it becomes aware of a possible claim, in order to show that it has taken such care as in all the circumstances was reasonably required.

4.6.2.4 Clinical negligence claims

In a clinical negligence claim, the client is likely to be in a more confused or uncertain position than in a personal injury matter. While a client is normally able to explain, for example, what occurred during a road traffic incident, he may not understand the treatment and care he received from a medical practitioner. The terminology will be unfamiliar and, in the case of alleged negligence during hospital treatment, the client may not be able to recall or identify the doctors or nurses who treated him.

When obtaining a proof in a clinical negligence case, it is important that every detail is obtained, such as what exactly was said when the claimant attended at the hospital or when the client was asked to sign the consent form.

Unless the alleged negligent act arises out of an illness not previously suffered by the client, full details of any previous medical problems should be obtained. Other matters contained in the proof could be as follows:

(a)   the symptoms which led the client to seek medical advice;

(b)   the information given by the client to the doctor;

(c)   any questions asked by the doctor (eg, where the client went to his GP complaining of headaches, whether the doctor asked the client if he had hit his head or whether the client had been sick – questions which would lead a competent GP to suspect a severe head injury);

(d)   whether the client was given details of a diagnosis at that time;

(e)   what form of treatment was prescribed;

(f)   whether the treatment was explained to the client and whether he was warned of any potential risks and the likely consequences of not receiving treatment;

(g)   the name of the doctor who treated the client and his status;

(h)   whether the client was receiving treatment from different doctors;

(i)   whether the client asked for a second opinion;

(j)   whether any witnesses were present at the consultation;

(k)   any previous medical problems which could have affected the client;

(l)   whether the client has complained to the hospital/doctor;

(m)   whether the client has received any reply or relevant correspondence;

(n)   whether an apology has been received.

This should be followed by details of the injury in the normal fashion.

In certain cases, it can be useful to ask what prompted the client to contact a solicitor. In some cases, the client is advised by other medical professionals to seek legal advice as they believe that a mistake may have been made.

Example

A client injures his leg playing football and attends at the local accident and emergency department. The accident and emergency department is busy and, although the client is sent for an x-ray, the house officer fails to spot the fracture and discharges the client immediately. The client is in considerable pain for a number of weeks and eventually visits his GP's surgery, who refers him back to the hospital for another x-ray. In such circumstances, the client may be told that in fact the leg is fractured and that it was missed when the client first attended. Such information is clearly of assistance in assessing liability.

4.7   Welfare benefits

It will be necessary to advise the client of the welfare benefits he may be entitled to receive because of the incident. It may be months or years before the claim is settled, and if the client is unfit for work, he may experience financial difficulties and feel pressured into accepting the first offer of compensation from the defendant. The client may not have had any previous experience of the Benefits Agency (an executive agency of the Department for Work and Pensions (DWP)) and may initially be sceptical or even unwilling to approach the Agency. The solicitor should give the client general advice on the types of benefits that may be available to him to cover payment in respect of his inability to work, assistance with mobility, assistance with household tasks and even assistance with child care. It should be stressed that if only general guidance is given, then the client should seek detailed advice from the Agency or from the firm's welfare rights adviser, if the solicitor is not fully familiar with the current benefits available. Regulations relating to particular benefits change frequently, and up-to-date information on benefits can be obtained from the Benefits Agency on free or low-cost telephone information lines. It should be stressed to the client that he must act quickly when seeking benefits as it is not normally possible to back-date benefits and benefit may be lost due to delay.

4.7.1   Eligibility for benefits

Clients who do not have an employer because they are self-employed or unemployed may claim incapacity benefit if they have paid sufficient NI contributions. If they have paid insufficient NI contributions, they may claim income support.

The client should be advised that, although he may qualify for any of the above benefits, if his claim is successful he will be subject to recoupment under the Social Security (Recovery of Benefits) Act 1997. This area is considered in detail in **Chapter 12**.

The client's eligibility for benefits will be assessed by the Benefits Agency. People who claim incapacity or disablement benefit are examined either by doctors who work for Benefits Agency Medical Services or by health service doctors who are paid a fee. The doctor tests whether the person claiming can perform a range of tasks, and reports his findings back to the Agency. The test the doctor applies when assessing people for incapacity benefit or severe disablement allowance is called the 'all work' test. (See leaflet IB 215 Incapacity Benefit: The All Work Test – Assuring Medical Quality.)

The fact that a claimant has been in receipt of the above benefits will mean that he falls within the criteria laid down by the DWP in the 'all work' test, and this may be something which the defendant's solicitors should note. Similarly, if the claimant is claiming continuing disability in his personal injury claim, but fails the 'all work' test, or is certified unfit but is later passed as fit, this will also be a factor to be borne in mind by the parties' advisers. However, the test is not designed to be based on a 'snapshot' of the person's capabilities, but is to assess the difficulties which the person has over a sustained period of time.

When considering eligibility to benefits, it is necessary to have regard to whether the receipt of compensation will take the claimant out of financial eligibility for means-tested benefits. In *Beattie v Secretary of State for Social Security* [2001] 1 WLR 1404, Charles Beattie was injured in a road traffic accident and rendered quadriplegic. He sued by his litigation friend and Court of Protection receiver, Stephen Beattie. The claimant appealed a decision of the Social Security Commissioner that he was not entitled to income support because payments 'falling to be treated as income' under a structured settlement took him beyond the limit on income for the purpose of claiming income support. This issue was appealed because guidance from the Public Trust Office suggested that, as long as the compensation was held on trust and payments were made on a discretionary basis and were not used to fund items that would normally be paid for using benefits, then those payments would not affect benefit entitlement. In *Beattie* the court ruled that the agreement, as part of the structured settlement, to make regular payments for a fixed number of years was in fact an annuity and was therefore 'capital treated as income' under reg 41(2) of the Income Support (General) Regulations 1987 (SI 1987/1967). The essential difference in this case is that the compensation was paid to the Court of Protection who would hold the money for the benefit of the patient, rather than simply held on discretionary trust.

4.8 Road Traffic (NHS Charges) Act 1999

The Road Traffic (NHS Charges) Act 1999 (the 1999 Act) replaces an existing provision in ss 157 and 158 of the Road Traffic Act 1988.

Under the 1999 Act, when a person makes a successful claim for compensation as a result of a road traffic accident, the NHS hospital where he receives treatment can also claim an amount to cover the costs of treatment from the relevant insurer (called the compensator). This includes Motor Insurers' Bureau (MIB) cases.

The purpose of the 1999 Act is to provide a national administration system, the aim of which is to ensure that costs of treatment are, in fact, recovered in as many cases as is possible. The responsibility for collecting the NHS costs will be undertaken by the Compensation Recovery Unit (CRU) (see **Chapter 12** for a detailed consideration of the CRU and benefit recovery). The CRU was given this task as it already has extensive knowledge of the insurance industry and will therefore keep collection costs to a minimum.

In many ways, the NHS costs recovery scheme will mirror the benefit recovery scheme considered at **Chapter 12**. However, unlike the benefit recovery scheme, the NHS costs recovery scheme will not affect the amount of damages recovered by the claimant. The compensator will apply to the CRU for a Certificate of NHS Charges. The certificate may have an expiry date, depending on whether or not NHS treatment is still continuing.

The Act allows for NHS charges to be calculated according to a tariff. The tariff will allow for:

(a)   a set fee for patients treated in accident and emergency departments or out-patient clinics (the fee will be the same regardless of the number of out-patient appointments);

(b)   a daily rate for patients admitted to hospital.

The amount of the above fees has been increased for accidents occurring on or after 28 January 2002, and can be found in the Road Traffic (NHS Charges) Amendment Regulations 2001 (SI 2001/4030).

The appeal and review procedures for NHS costs recovery are designed to mirror the appeal and review provisions governing benefit recovery under the Social Security (Recovery of Benefits) Act 1997, as to which, see **Chapter 12**.

The Department of Health had planned to expand the scheme for recovery of NHS costs on 1 April 2005. This would have allowed recovery of NHS hospital costs in all cases where personal injury compensation is paid. The expanded scheme would also have covered recovery of NHS ambulance service costs under the Health and Social Care (Community Health and Standards) Act 2003.

The proposed commencement date of 1 April 2005 has been delayed at the time of writing pending consultation on the issue, and at the time of writing, the proposed date for implementation is October 2006.

The current scheme for recovery of NHS costs following road traffic accidents will continue to operate in this interim period.

4.9   Rehabilitation, early intervention and medical treatment

It has long been recognised that a claimant's long-term prognosis can be dramatically improved by the intervention of rehabilitative treatment at the earliest possible opportunity. Research by insurers has found that the UK lags behind much of Europe and North America in terms of the ability to provide restorative care for injured claimants. The result of early intervention strategies in other countries is that they have a far better rate of return to work at an earlier stage than is able to be achieved in the UK. While it is recognised that the reasons for this are complex, insurers whose operations include much of Europe are starting to question why return to work rates are so poor in the UK.

The problem in the past has been that the claimant is not able to fund the treatment adequately until after his claim for damages for personal injuries is settled. Insurance companies are now recognising that early intervention in the form of extra sessions of physiotherapy, for example, can be in their own best interests as well as the claimant's if it assists the claimant to recover sufficiently to return to employment either earlier or at all. In the long term, insurers recognise that, if they fail to co-operate in paying for rehabilitative treatment in cases where liability is unlikely to be an issue, both they and the claimant will be the ultimate losers. The claimant will lose the opportunity of therapeutic medical treatment at the earliest opportunity and the insurer (if found liable) is likely to find an increased claim for future loss as the claimant is not fit to return to work.

To alleviate this problem, the pre-action protocol for use in personal injury claims includes at Annexe D, the revised code of practice on rehabilitation, early intervention and medical treatment. This has been drafted by insurers and lawyers with the aim of ensuring that both sides are aware of the rehabilitation issue and of their respective obligations under the code. The code places responsibilities on both claimants' solicitors and insurers to consider whether rehabilitation is appropriate and places a duty on both to contact the other to raise the issue if either of them thinks that the claimant could benefit. The code is reproduced in full at **Appendix 3**.

Examples of such early treatment are: surgery, physiotherapy, counselling, occupational therapy and speech therapy. Examples may also include making adaptations to the claimant's home to make his life easier in the period prior to the settlement of the claim.

4.10 Conclusion

If the first interview is handled correctly, it should save the solicitor a great deal of time in the future. As personal injury litigation is 'front loaded', much of the essential work is covered during or shortly after the first interview. If essential matters have been missed, old ground will need to be covered again, which will lead to inevitable delay and upset for the client. If this is allowed to happen, the solicitor will have failed in one of his main objectives, that of avoiding delay, and thereby will allow the opposition to gain the advantage.

4.11 Further reading

Slips and Trips: Guidance for employers on identifying hazards and controlling risks (Stationery Office).

Statutory Sick Pay Manual for Employers.

Five Steps to Risk Assessment (HSE Publications).

A Guide to Risk Assessment Requirements (HSE Publications).

Cook on Costs (Butterworths).

The Legal Services Commission Manual (Sweet & Maxwell).

Code of Best Practice on Rehabilitation, Early Intervention and Medical Treatment in Personal Injury Claims (BICMA).

www.justask.org.uk

4.12   Overview of matters to be considered at the first interview

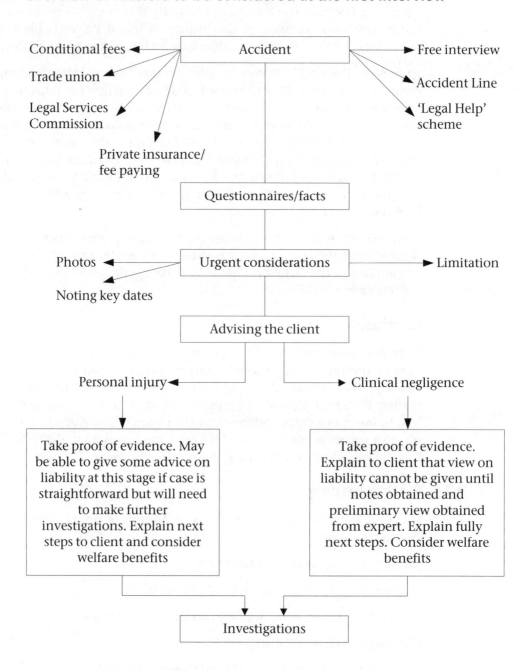

Chapter 5

Fact Gathering and Analysis

5.1 Introduction

Following the first interview, it will be necessary to gather evidence prior to advising the client whether he should commence the pre-action protocol. It is particularly important to ensure that evidence is gathered quickly as circumstances can change and important information may be lost. For example, in an incident at work involving a machine, the Health & Safety Executive (HSE) may recommend that the safety guards are upgraded. Unless a specific request is made to the employer to preserve the machine as it is, the employer may carry out the recommendations of the HSE or may even replace the machine with a new one. This can lead to enormous difficulties for the claimant later on, and therefore steps must be taken to avoid it taking place. In clinical negligence cases, it is equally important to act quickly, while events are fresh in the minds of clients and witnesses.

5.2 Identifying the defendant

In many cases, the identity of the defendant will be obvious. Nevertheless, this question should always be addressed as things are often not as straightforward as they seem. It is crucial to issue proceedings within the primary limitation period against the correct defendant. Generally, there is little point in pursuing a claim against a defendant unless he has the means with which to pay the judgment or is insured. If the defendant is a health authority or trust, it will not carry insurance provided by an insurance company, but will settle the claims itself out of its own funds.

5.2.1 Road traffic incidents

In a road traffic incident claim, it is necessary to establish not only the name of the driver of the vehicle and his insurance position, but also the name of the owner of the vehicle and of his insurer. Under the Fourth EU Motor Insurance Directive (in force from 20 January 2003) it is a requirement that the insurer of a vehicle must be readily identifiable from the vehicle registration number. Therefore when trying to trace the owner and insurer of a vehicle involved in a road traffic accident, if the claimant has taken down the registration of the other driver's vehicle, the solicitor should be able to trace the insurance details. The UK insurance industry has met this requirement by introducing the Motor Insurance Database (MID). This provides details of all vehicles and their associated insurance policies. The database was established in July 2001 and is now fully operational. Individual firms of solicitors can apply for a licence to operate the MID system allowing them almost instant access to insurance details of third parties accessed by means of the vehicle registration mark. The system is also used by the police who will be able to access the MID either from the roadside, using handheld computers, or from police stations, enabling them to check almost immediately whether or not a driver is insured.

The following details are available from the MID system:

(a)   the registration number of every vehicle insured under the policy;

(b)   the date on which cover begins for each vehicle;

(c)   the date on which cover ceases for each vehicle.

Make and model details are also usually available but are not mandatory.

Frequently, the driver of a vehicle may be using a vehicle owned and insured by his employer. In such cases, it is usual to sue the employer (or vehicle operator in the case of commercial vehicles), and a clear indication in response to the letter of claim under the pre-action protocol will usually be given by the insurance company as to whether it is prepared to deal with the claim on behalf of the proposed defendant. If such an indication is not received, or there is any reason to doubt whether the driver was acting within the course of employment, or the pre-action protocol is otherwise exhausted, it is usual to sue both the driver and the employer. Similarly, if protective proceedings are necessary to avoid the claim being statute-barred by the Limitation Act 1980, it is best, initially, to sue all potential defendants if there is a degree of uncertainty.

Example

Alice is a passenger in a car driven by her brother Peter. The car is registered in the name of their father, Harold, who also insured it in his name with Peter as a named driver on the policy. It was cheaper to insure the vehicle this way as Harold is over 50 years' old and has a good driving record, whereas Peter is under 25 years' old and has never insured a car before. Although the car is registered in Harold's name he has given it to Peter to use on a day-to-day basis. Peter crashes the car and is unhurt, but Alice suffers serious injuries. Alice will have to sue the driver of the car, her brother, who will seek to rely on his father's insurance. However, if Harold did not make it clear to his insurer that he was not the main driver of the vehicle, the insurance company is likely to avoid the policy because of non-disclosure by Harold and Peter. In that event, Alice will be left to sue Peter and will have to seek to rely on the provisions of ss 151–2 of the Road Traffic Act 1988 (RTA 1988) (see **5.4**).

5.2.1.1   European Communities (Rights against Insurers) Regulations 2002

The objective of the European Communities (Rights against Insurers) Regulations 2002 (SI 2002/3061) is to give injured parties a direct right of action in the courts against the insurer. The Regulations confer on residents of Member States of the EU a right to issue proceedings directly against the insurer of the person responsible for an accident in the UK. The Regulations give effect, in part, to the Fourth Motor Insurance Directive (which deals with the approximation of the laws of the Member States relating to insurance against civil liability in respect of the use of motor vehicles).

Under reg 3:

(1)   ... this regulation applies where an entitled party has a cause of action against an insured person in tort ... and that cause of action arises out of an accident.

(2)   Where this paragraph applies, the entitled party may, without prejudice to his right to issue proceedings against the insured person, issue proceedings against the insurer which issued the policy of insurance relating to the insured vehicle, and that insurer shall be directly liable to the entitled party to the extent that he is liable to the insured person.

5.2.2 Employers' liability

If an incident occurs at work, notwithstanding that the incident was caused by another employee or someone acting as agent for the employer, provided they were acting in the course of employment, it is usual to sue the employer only. Although the defendant will generally be the employer, a claim may also be made against the occupier of the premises or the person with control of the premises if different from the employer.

However, this is a complicated area and it will be necessary to analyse what has been agreed contractually between the parties. In *Breaveglen Ltd (t/a ANZAC Construction Co) v Sleeman Ltd* (1997) *The Times,* 10 May, A had been defending the main claim and claimed a contribution from S who was a third party to the proceedings in respect of damages claimed by an employee (M). S was the main contractor and subcontracted the supply of labour and materials to A. It was part of the agreement that A would insure and indemnify against employers' liability. M worked at S's site under the instruction of S's foreman and was injured. A claimed a contribution towards damages from S but the court found that A was under a statutory duty to insure against injury, and remained under a personal duty to M. A carried primary liability even if there was negligence on the part of S's foreman.

It will also be necessary to consider who is the appropriate defendant in cases where a business undertaking is transferred as a going concern from one owner to another. This is a common scenario, and it will be necessary to identify who is liable for the damages when an employee suffers injury prior to the transfer of the business but then sues the new employer after the transfer of the business. This was considered in *Taylor v Serviceteam Ltd and London Borough of Waltham Forest* [1998] PIQR P201. Mr Taylor was employed as a refuse collector by the council. In 1994, an incident occurred in the course of his employment. Subsequent to this, the refuse collection service was privatised to the first defendants, Serviceteam. As an employee, Mr Taylor's contract of employment was transferred to his new employer within the meaning of the Transfer of Undertakings (Protection of Employment) Regulations 1981 (SI 1981/1794). Mr Taylor was then dismissed by Serviceteam on medical grounds. Mr Taylor sued Serviceteam, notwithstanding that they were not actually his employers at the date of the incident. Not surprisingly, Serviceteam said that the council was responsible and joined them as second defendant. As a matter of law, the court had to decide who was the appropriate defendant. It was held that the correct defendant was Serviceteam, despite the fact that they were not Mr Taylor's employers at the date of injury. The court construed the Transfer of Undertakings Regulations and decided that liability for personal injury did transfer to the new employer on a relevant transfer of an undertaking or a part thereof. Although this point may now appear to be settled, it will also be necessary to establish who is the relevant insurer. In the above scenario, the council would be on risk at the time of the accident, and unless there is a clearly defined indemnity clause included in the Transfer of

Undertakings Agreement between the old employer and the new employer, the claimant may have difficulties recovering compensation.

This ruling accords with *Wilson, Holdham & Adams v West Cumbria Healthcare NHS Trust* (see **5.2.3.1**).

5.2.3 Cases involving negligence of doctors and medical staff

5.2.3.1 Claims arising out of NHS hospital treatment

If the claim arises out of treatment by a health service employee (including hospital doctors), the defendant is the health authority at district level (pursuant to National Health Service Act 1977, Sch 5, para 15, as amended by the Health Services Act 1980). Where the hospital has been granted trust status, the trust is named as the defendant. If the allegations cover the period pre- and post-trust status, it may be necessary to name both the health authority and the trust as defendants. Enquiries will need to be made as to whether liability for 'pre-trust' cases has also been transferred. It is not necessary to sue individual doctors or nurses in the direct employment of the NHS or trust.

When ascertaining the correct title of the health authority or hospital trust, it is necessary to check the Medical Register which lists all hospitals and their controlling authority/trust, or alternatively a telephone call to the 'quality control manager' at the hospital where the treatment was carried out will reveal the name of the authority. It is also necessary to check the date when the trust came into being to ensure that the correct authority is named as the defendant to the claim. Where a recently created trust is involved, there may be some apportionment in respect of the funding of the damages between the old health authority and the newly created trust. In *Wilson, Holdham & Adams v West Cumbria Healthcare NHS Trust* (1995) PMILR, 3 August, it was held that, on the transfer of an undertaking from a health authority to an NHS trust created by the National Health Service and Community Care Act 1990, liability in tort is transferred together with the contract of employment.

It may be the case, notwithstanding the granting of trust status, that individual consultants' contracts may still be held by their former employers, the regional health authority or the district health authority. This is a transitional phase and legal responsibility for all consultants' contracts has passed to trusts from the date of trust status. Thus, the contractual relationship of an individual practitioner with a trust is irrelevant to the identification of the correct defendant.

5.2.3.2 General practitioner

The general practitioner is liable for his own acts, for the acts of his employees and (arguably) for the acts of anyone else whom he employs to look after his patients, for example, nurses and allied staff.

Where the claim arises following treatment by a general practitioner, the situation may be more complicated. The general practitioner has a contract of services with the family health service authority, ie, he is an independent contractor. It is necessary to obtain the notes from a general practitioner to ascertain who supplied the treatment and whether it was one doctor, two, or more. It may be necessary to join in all the doctors in the group who were involved. This can cause some problems in that the individual general practitioners may be members of different medical defence or protection societies who may each instruct separate solicitors. This will affect the conduct of the case.

5.2.3.3   Private hospitals

A clinic or private hospital will take out its own insurance. It will employ the staff who run and administer the hospital. However, the medical staff (eg, consultants or other allied doctors) are using the services of the clinic and are independent contractors and, therefore, proceedings must identify them as defendants. The clinic will advise on the position of the doctors who use their premises and, in almost all cases, the individual doctor is sued. The doctors will be indemnified by their own defence organisations.

If the claim arises out of private treatment and is a clinical fault, then the doctor should be named as the defendant. Alternatively, if the treatment is a nursing fault, then the hospital/clinic should be named as the defendant.

5.2.3.4   Private treatment from dentists

A dentist treating private patients is not under any statutory or professional requirement to have insurance cover in respect of professional negligence – although the majority are insured.

5.2.3.5   Alternative/complementary health practitioners

An alternative health practitioner faces exactly the same risks as a general practitioner except that he is not involved in surgical intervention or, in some branches, medical prescription. The College of Osteopathy, for example, has prescribed a questionnaire which it invites its practitioners to complete before commencing any treatment and which recommends that, if the practitioner is in any doubt over the form or consequences of treatment, no treatment should be undertaken by the osteopath who should instead refer the prospective patient to a general practitioner.

5.3   Letter of claim

5.3.1   Personal injury claims

The letter of claim is the first intimation that a claim is being made against the proposed defendant; two copies are forwarded to the proposed defendant with instructions to pass one copy to his insurer. It should be written to the proposed defendant before commencing proceedings as part of the pre-action protocol. The main function of the letter is to warn the proposed defendant of possible legal proceedings if it is ignored and to alert his insurance company to the proceedings. The letter should deal with matters in sufficient detail so that the proposed defendant (and his insurer) is left in no doubt as to the position. Tactically, it is important to bear in mind that the insurance company's normal response to the letter of claim will be to send a letter requesting further information 'to enable it to investigate the claim'. This is often seen as an attempt to get as much information as possible to use subsequently against the claimant if either his statement of case or evidence contradicts the letter of claim. The letter should be constructed in such a way that further information from the solicitor is unnecessary, and the insurance company letter can therefore be answered with a polite but firm response to contact its own insured who already has all the information that the insurer needs about the incident.

Full details of the personal injury claims pre-action protocol and contents of the letter of claim are contained in **Chapter 9**.

No attempt should be made to quantify the claim (in monetary terms) in the letter – an apparently simple injury worth a few hundred pounds at the outset may unexpectedly (and quickly) develop into a serious injury worth thousands of pounds.

If possible, the proposed defendant's insurance details should be obtained. In the case of an incident at work, the insurance certificate is required to be displayed on the premises in a suitably prominent position. In the case of a road traffic incident, the proposed defendant may have volunteered his insurance details or may have been obliged to produce the documentation to the police. In the latter case, it is possible for the solicitor to ask the police to disclose the full name, address and insurance details of the proposed defendant. Although any police accident report will not be released until after any criminal proceedings have been dealt with, these limited details will be released if requested. No fee is payable for this. If the client did not manage to get any details of the proposed defendant and the police were not called out to the accident, it is possible to obtain the name and address of the owner of the vehicle if the client has the registration number. The solicitor can write to the Vehicle Enquiry Unit at DVLA Swansea SA99 1AJ which, on payment of a fee, will disclose the name and address of the registered keeper of the vehicle. Because this enquiry is being made by someone other than the current registered keeper, the DVLA requires a letter of explanation to accompany the enquiry stating why the enquirer needs this information. It is also possible to write to the proposed defendant asking him to supply his insurance details. If he fails to do so, or makes a false statement, he will be guilty of an offence under s 154 of the RTA 1988.

5.3.2 Clinical negligence claims

In clinical negligence cases, the contents of the letter of claim are dealt with in the pre-action protocol in relation to clinical negligence claims. This is dealt with in detail in **Chapter 9**.

5.4 Notice in road traffic cases

Under ss 151 and 152 of the RTA 1988, where the claimant has obtained judgment against a defendant he can enforce that judgment against the insurer notwithstanding that the insurer may be entitled to avoid or may have avoided or cancelled the policy.

5.4.1 Section 151

Section 151 applies only to a judgment obtained after insurance has been granted in respect of risks required to be compulsorily insured and either:

(a) the liability is covered by the terms of the policy and judgment is obtained against any person insured under the policy; or

(b) the liability would be covered if the policy covered all persons and the judgment is obtained against any person other than one who is insured by the policy (s 151(2)).

Matters required to be compulsorily insured are:

(a) personal injury or death of any other person;

(b) the cost of emergency hospital treatment; and

(c) damage to property (other than the insured vehicle) up to £250,000.

This means that, as long as there is an insurance certificate in respect of the vehicle and judgment is obtained against the driver, the insurer is obliged to pay damages to the claimant, even if the insurance did not cover the defendant. However, payment is only in respect of the matters required to be compulsorily insured by law.

5.4.2 Section 152

The only way in which the insurance company can avoid paying damages under the policy is under s 152 of the RTA 1988. Nothing is payable by the insurer if:

(a)   before or within seven days after commencement of proceedings the insurer was not given notice of the proceedings; or

(b)   before the event giving rise to the liability the policy was cancelled by mutual consent and before the event occurred the certificate was surrendered to the insurer, or (in certain circumstances) was declared lost or destroyed; or

(c)   the insurer commences a claim before or within three months of the commencement of (the claimant's) proceedings in which judgment was given, and the insurer obtains a declaration that he is entitled to avoid the policy on the ground that it was obtained by non-disclosure of a material fact, or by representation of a fact that was false in some material particular. To take advantage of this declaration, the insurer must also give the claimant notice of the proceedings against its own insured before or within seven days of commencement of its claim for a declaration, specifying the non-disclosure or false representation on which it proposes to rely (s 152(2)).

5.5 The Motor Insurers' Bureau

The MIB Agreements are voluntary agreements by which all motor insurers (including Lloyd's) provide a fund for compensating the victims of road incidents caused by negligent, uninsured or untraced drivers. It is not usual to name the MIB as defendant unless a ruling on the construction of the agreement itself is sought.

5.5.1 The Uninsured Drivers Agreement 1999

This Agreement replaces the 1988 MIB Agreement in relation to accidents occurring on or after 1 October 1999. The 1988 MIB Agreement will only continue to be of significance so far as claims relating to accidents which pre-date October 1999 are concerned.

5.5.2 Procedure under the Uninsured Drivers Agreement 1999

The Agreement sets out a far more complicated set of procedural steps than was previously required. A summary of those steps is set out below; however, recourse should be had to a copy of the 1999 Agreement itself and the guidance notes to that agreement as only the basic provisions are introduced below. The claim should name the uninsured driver as defendant. The claim will proceed against the named driver and, if settlement is not achieved, judgment is entered against the named driver and the MIB will satisfy the judgment if the requirements of the agreement have been complied with.

5.5.3 Notice to MIB

Claims should be made by completing the MIB's own application form. This should be completed and returned to the MIB or their nominated solicitors together with documents in support (**5.5.3.3**). The application form is currently available only from the MIB. It is important to note that the application must be signed by the claimant or his solicitor. If this is not complied with, the MIB can refuse to accept the application.

5.5.3.1   Notice of proceedings

The following notice provisions are at the heart of the 1999 Agreement and are far more complex than previous notice provisions. The claimant must give the MIB notice in writing that he has commenced proceedings. This notice together with the completed application form and documents in support must be received by the MIB no later than 14 days after commencement of proceedings.

5.5.3.2   Service of notice

The notice and supporting documentation must be served either by facsimile transmission or by registered or recorded delivery post to the MIB's registered office. Service by ordinary post and Document Exchange is not allowed. Service by facsimile is the preferred method.

5.5.3.3   Supporting documentation

The application must be supported by the following documents:

(a)   notice in writing that proceedings have been commenced by claim form or other means;

(b)   a copy of the sealed claim form or other document evidencing commencement;

(c)   a copy of any relevant insurance policy;

(d)   copies of all relevant correspondence in the possession of the claimant or his solicitor;

(e)   a copy of any particulars of claim;

(f)   a copy of all other documents required by the rules of procedure to be served on the defendant; and

(g)   such other information relevant to the proceedings as the MIB may reasonably

5.5.3.4   Requirements after the accident and prior to issue of proceedings – RTA 1988, s 154

Clause 13 of the new Agreement places a requirement on all would-be claimants to make full and timely use of their rights under s 154 of the RTA 1988. Clause 13 puts the onus on the claimant to ensure that he has as soon as reasonably practicable:

(a)   demanded the particulars specified in s 154; and if the person fails to give the information;

(b)   complained to a police officer in respect of this failure to give details following an accident; and

(c)   used all reasonable endeavours to obtain the name, address and registered keeper of the vehicle.

5.5.3.5   Notice requirements on service of proceedings

If proceedings are commenced, the claimant must inform the MIB of the date of service:

(a)   if service is effected by the court, notice must be given within seven days after the date that the claimant receives notice from the court or the defendant that service of the claim form has occurred; or

(b)   if service is effected personally, notice must be given seven days from the date of personal service; or

(c)   if recourse to deemed service is appropriate, seven days after the date when service is deemed to have occurred in accordance with the CPR 1998.

5.5.3.6   Notice requirements after service of proceedings

There are further notice requirements after service of proceedings which require notification to the MIB in writing within seven days of the occurrence of any of the following:

(a)   filing of a defence;

(b)   amendment of particulars of claim;

(c)   setting down for trial;

(d)   notification of trial date received.

In the event that the claimant intends to enter judgment the claimant must, not less than 35 days before applying for judgment, give notice in writing to the MIB of their intention so to do.

Because of the onerous nature of the notice requirements, some commentators advocate joining the MIB as second defendants at the outset of proceedings. Once they are a party to the proceedings, the claimant's solicitor can then seek written confirmation from them that they will waive reliance on the further notice provisions.

5.5.3.7   Prosecution of proceedings and judgment

The claimant must take all reasonable steps to obtain judgment against every person who may be liable (including any person who may be vicariously liable). The obligation of the MIB to pay normally arises only if a judgment is not satisfied within seven days after the claimant became entitled to enforce it.

However, the MIB is not obliged to satisfy a judgment unless the claimant has in return assigned the benefit of the unsatisfied judgment to the MIB or its nominee.

5.5.4   The Untraced Drivers Agreement 2003

The Untraced Drivers Agreement 2003 replaces the 1996 MIB Agreement in relation to accidents occurring on or after 14 February 2003. The 1996 Agreement will continue to be of significance for claims relating to accidents which pre-date 14 February 2003.

The 2003 agreement requires the MIB to consider applications for compensation for victims of 'hit and run' cases where the owner or driver cannot be traced.

The Agreement applies where:

(a)   death of, or bodily injury to, a person or damage to property of a person has been caused by, or arisen out of, the use of a motor vehicle on a road or other public place in Great Britain; and

(b)   the event giving rise to the death, bodily injury or damage to property occurred on or after 14 February 2003; and

(c)   the death, bodily injury or damage to property occurred in circumstances giving rise to liability of a kind which is required to be covered by a policy of insurance.

The applicant must make an application in writing to the MIB. If the application is signed by a person who is neither the applicant nor a solicitor acting on behalf of the applicant, the MIB may refuse to accept the application.

5.5.4.1   Time limit for making an application

The application must generally have been made not later than:

(a)   three years after the date of the event which is the subject of the application in relation to claims for compensation of death or bodily injury (whether or not damage to property has also arisen from the same event); or

(b)   nine months after the date of that event in the case of claims for compensation for damage to property (whether or not death or bodily injury has also arisen from the same event).

However, in cases where the applicant could not reasonably have been expected to have become aware of the injury or property damage, the application must be made as soon as practicable after he did become aware and in any case, not later than:

(a)   15 years after the date of the event in relation to the claim for compensation for death or bodily injury; or

(b)   two years after the date of the event in the case of claims for compensation for damage to property.

The applicant, or person acting on behalf of the applicant, must also have reported the event to the police:

(a)   in the case of claims for death or bodily injury alone, not later than 14 days after the event occurred; and

(b)   in the case of claims for property damage, not later than five days after the event occurred.

If the MIB give notice to the applicant that it has decided to make him an award it shall pay the award within 14 days of a written confirmation from the applicant that he accepts the award.

5.5.4.2   Exclusions from the Agreement

The Agreement does not apply (inter alia) where:

(a)   the claim is not made in respect of death or bodily injury, but is for property damage only;

(b)   the death, bodily injury or damage has arisen out of the use of a motor vehicle owned by the Crown;

(c)   the person suffering death, injury or damage was voluntarily allowing himself to be carried in the vehicle and before the commencement of his journey in the vehicle (or after such commencement if he could reasonably be expected to have alighted from the vehicle) he knew or ought to have known that the vehicle:

(i)   had been stolen or unlawfully taken; or

(ii)   was being used without insurance; or

(iii)   was being used in the course or furtherance of crime; or

      (iv) was being used as a means of escape from or avoidance of lawful apprehension;

(d) the death, bodily injury or damage was caused by, or in the course of, an act of terrorism;

(e) property is insured and the applicant has recovered the full amount of his loss from the insurer;

(f) the claim is for damages to a vehicle, and at the time of the incident that vehicle was uninsured;

(g) the claim is not made by a person who suffered the injury or loss nor a personal representative or dependant of such a person.

5.5.4.3   Investigation of claims

The MIB is under an obligation to make an award only if it is satisfied, on the balance of probabilities, that the death, bodily injury or damage was caused in such circumstances that the unidentified person would (had he been identified) have been held liable to pay damages to the applicant in respect of it.

The MIB shall investigate the claim and reach a decision as to whether it must make an award to the applicant. Where it decides to make an award, it will determine the amount of that award.

5.5.4.4   Calculation of compensation

The MIB shall award a sum equivalent to the amount which it would have awarded to the applicant for general and special damages if the applicant had brought successful proceedings to enforce a claim for damages against the unidentified person. In calculating the sum payable, the MIB shall adopt the same method of calculation as the court would adopt in calculating damages.

5.5.4.5   Interest

The MIB should include in its award a sum representing interest on the compensation payable at a rate equal to that which a court would award a successful litigant.

5.5.4.6   Contribution towards legal costs

The MIB is not obliged to pay the claimant's costs. In practice, it will usually include in the award a sum towards the cost of obtaining legal advice subject to a minimum of £500 and a maximum of £3,000 (plus VAT and reasonable disbursements).

5.6   Acquiring evidence

5.6.1   Expert evidence

The majority of cases will involve some expert evidence. This area is dealt with fully in **Chapter 8**.

5.6.2   Proofing witnesses

Witnesses should be contacted and interviewed as soon after the incident as possible. If the witness is not interviewed at an early stage his memory of the events may fade or he may be untraceable. In the case of an accident at work, if the witness is a fellow employee of the client he may be concerned about his employer's reaction, and may therefore have second thoughts about making a statement. Witnesses to road incidents are often initially enthusiastic, but later decide that they have little to gain and would rather not get involved. For this reason, a proof or at least a letter in reply from the witness should be obtained from the witness confirming what he saw and/or heard and that he is prepared to make a statement to that effect.

In a straightforward case, it may not be necessary to interview the witness. If his letter of response is sufficiently clear, a proof can be prepared from it and from any questionnaire he may also have been sent. A copy of the proof should be forwarded for approval and signature by the witness. This should be accompanied by a stamped addressed envelope and covering letter requesting the witness to read the proof carefully, and make any amendments or additions that he feels to be necessary before signing and dating the document for return in the envelope provided. The witness is a volunteer to the client's cause and should be thanked accordingly for the time and trouble he has taken on the client's behalf.

Having prepared a full proof of evidence from each witness at this early stage, it will not be necessary to incur the expense of preparing witness statements for disclosure if the witness evidence is irrelevant, or simply repeats what other more reliable witnesses say.

If it becomes necessary to have a formal statement drawn up for the witness, it should be checked, signed and dated by the witness. This statement will form the basis of the witness's evidence to be relied on at trial and will stand as his evidence-in-chief. The statement must conclude with a declaration of truth incorporated as the last paragraph of the statement.

Furthermore, the statement may have to be used at the trial under the Civil Evidence Act 1995 if the witness subsequently becomes unavailable. It should therefore be the best statement that the witness can produce and should deal fully with any points of evidence that only this witness would be able to state.

5.6.3   Other statements

It may be advisable for the solicitor to obtain statements from other persons, such as shop stewards or co-workers who, although they may not have seen the accident, may know of other similar accidents in the past or be able to give background information on policy changes that may have taken place within the organisation. In road incident or tripping cases, people living or working adjacent to the area of the incident may be able to give useful information relating to similar incidents that have happened in the past and even the identities of past claimants in similar incidents.

5.6.4   Employment details

The client's loss of earnings is likely to form a significant part of his claim for special damages, but may be difficult to calculate if the client is self-employed or his earnings fluctuate for some other reason. See **Chapter 13** for a detailed consideration of this point.

5.6.4.1   Obtaining details from employers

A letter to the client's employer should ask for details of earnings for 13 weeks prior to the incident and for a copy of the client's contract of employment so that the solicitor can check whether sick pay has been paid by the employer and whether it is recoverable in the event of the client recovering damages. The loss of earnings details should be set out to show weekly earnings both gross and net so as to reveal a pattern over 13 weeks.

5.6.4.2 Self-employed clients

Documentary evidence in the form of the previous year's trading accounts (or longer if appropriate) of the client should be obtained if possible, together with other evidence of contracts or offers of work that had to be turned down as a result of the incident. The client's accountant, business associates and colleagues in the same area of work should be approached to assist in this.

5.6.4.3 Unemployed clients

Even if the client is unemployed, evidence should be obtained of his last employer and of the likelihood of his obtaining suitable work which he could have undertaken but for the accident, as evidence of earning capacity. Colleagues in the same area of business and employment agencies should be approached for evidence of availability of work within the client's specialism and the level of possible earnings.

5.6.5 Obtaining a police accident report

In the case of a road traffic incident, a police accident report (PAR) should be obtained, if it exists. The following should be borne in mind.

(a) The solicitor should contact the accident records department at the police force headquarters for the area concerned (not the police officer assigned to the case). The letter should be addressed to the Chief Superintendent of the area in which the incident occurred and should include details of the date, time and place of accident, registration numbers of vehicles and full names of those involved.

(b) The PAR will contain statements from the parties, witness statements, a sketch plan, comments on condition of the vehicles, the road surface and weather conditions.

(c) The PAR will not be released until the conclusion of any criminal investigation and proceedings.

(d) A fee (which is reviewed periodically) is payable for the PAR. The solicitor should ensure that funds are available to cover this. In the case of advice under the legal advice and assistance scheme, an extension should be obtained.

(e) In addition to the usual documents contained in the PAR, the police, particularly in the case of accidents which have led to serious injury or death, may have taken photographs, copies of which are usually obtainable on payment of a further fee.

(f) Again, on payment of a further fee, the police officer who prepared the PAR may be interviewed, and will be accompanied by a senior officer. Police officers will give evidence in civil proceedings, but must be witness summonsed.

(g) If there is no PAR, it is still possible to obtain copies of police notebooks and witness statements on payment of a fee. Because reports may be destroyed (in some cases after as little as one year) a request for a report should be made promptly, notwithstanding that the report will not actually be released until the conclusion of criminal investigations.

5.6.6 Obtaining a Health & Safety Executive report

HSE reports are the equivalent of police reports in the field of industrial incidents. Generally, the same rules apply as with police reports, although, because of lack of resources, in practice it may be that in certain areas it is unlikely that an HSE report will be available except in the case of very serious injury or death.

The HSE officer responsible for the factory or workplace concerned should be approached with a request for a copy of his report. As with the PAR, the HSE report will not be available until after any criminal prosecution has been dealt with. If the HSE is unwilling to provide a copy of its report voluntarily, it may be necessary to wait until after proceedings have been commenced and then make an application for non-party disclosure.

Employers are required to report certain classes of injury or disease sustained by people at work and specified dangerous occurrences. The regulations are contained in the Reporting of Injuries, Diseases and Dangerous Occurrences Regulations 1995 (RIDDOR 1995) (SI 1995/3163). RIDDOR 1995 require the responsible person (ie, safety officer/manager) to inform HSE as soon as possible of the incident and follow it up with written confirmation within 10 days.

The reportable occurrences are:

(a)   death of any person;

(b)   any person suffering a specified major injury;

(c)   any person not at work due to an injury resulting in evacuation of the person to a hospital for treatment;

(d)   any person not at work due to an injury sustained due to working at a hospital;

(e)   where there has been a dangerous occurrence. Dangerous occurrences are listed in Sch 2 to RIDDOR 1995 and include such things as dangerous occurrences involving overhead electric lines, biological agents and radiation generators, as well as occurrences in mines, at quarries, on the railways and at off-shore installations.

Documents to request from the HSE are as follows:

Form 2508 employer's report of a dangerous occurrence;

Form 2508A report of a case of disease;

Form 2508G report of a gas incident;

Form 155 factory inspector's report;

Form 142 health and safety inspector's report.

5.6.7 The accident book

Under RIDDOR 1995, employers are required to keep an accident book of an approved type where details of all accidents that occur on the premises must be recorded. A copy of the relevant page from the accident book should be obtained and consideration should be given to inspecting the book itself for evidence of similar incidents in the past. However, from 1 May 2003, the Health & Safety Executive (HSE) launched a new form of accident book to comply with the requirements of the Data Protection Act 1998, as most accident books allow personal details and information to be seen by anyone reading or making an entry in the book. The new design allows for accidents to be recorded, while details of individual(s) can be stored separately.

5.6.8 Criminal prosecutions

If the proposed defendant is to be prosecuted, ideally the claimant's solicitor should attend the proceedings to note the evidence. The date of the proceedings may be obtained from the police or the HSE as appropriate.

Any resulting conviction of the defendant which is relevant to the issues in civil proceedings may be referred to in the civil proceedings.

5.6.9 Coroner's inquest

In certain circumstances, the coroner for the district will hold an inquest. The purpose of the inquest is not to determine civil or criminal liability of any particular person, but instead to determine how the death occurred and to ascertain the identity of the deceased. However, the inquest provides a valuable opportunity to gauge the strength of the evidence and observe a witness giving evidence. Inquests are dealt with in detail in **Chapter 14**.

5.7 Early access to documents and other items

If documents or other items are in the possession of the client, clearly the solicitor will have no trouble obtaining access to those items. The same is true if the item is in the public domain, such as the scene of a road traffic incident on a public road.

5.7.1 Pre-action disclosure and inspection

An application for pre-action disclosure is governed in the High Court by s 33(2) of the Supreme Court Act 1981; and in the county court by s 52(2) of the County Courts Act 1984, and made under r 35.16 of the CPR 1998. This area is dealt with in detail in **Chapter 9**.

It may be necessary for the client's solicitor or other advisers to gain access to information which is held only by the defendant. If the solicitor is unable to advise his client as to whether or not he has a claim without this information, a claim for pre-action disclosure and/or inspection is appropriate. This is most likely to be necessary in cases alleging clinical negligence where the health authority or trust which will be the defendant holds the client's medical notes to which the solicitor needs access before he can instruct an expert to make any judgment on the suitability of the treatment received.

5.8 Obtaining medical records in clinical negligence claims

5.8.1 Request for explanation and invitation to admit liability

Following *Naylor v Preston Area Health Authority* [1987] 1 WLR 958, claimants have been encouraged to request an explanation from the potential defendant. The advantage of this is that an early investigation may result in a prompt settlement in cases where liability is unlikely to be in issue, and this may save the necessity of issuing proceedings. The claimant's solicitor should be wary, however, of agreeing not to issue proceedings in order to see if a settlement can be reached, with the result that the matter then falls outside the limitation period. An explanation will also give an early indication of how the defendant views the case, which can then be considered with the claimant's expert. This letter often fills the role of the letter of claim in a personal injury claim, as it is the first intimation that the health authority/trust/doctor receives that there is a potential problem, and may invite an admission of liability.

5.8.2 Importance of obtaining all records

It is necessary to obtain a copy of the client's records from the general practitioner and from the hospital where he was treated to build up a full picture of the client's health records prior to the incident and of the treatment which he has received subsequently. The general practitioner's records will show a detailed record of all treatments, referrals to hospital, reports back from hospital doctors and referrals to other professionals such as occupational therapists, physiotherapists or community nurses. The hospital records will show details of the client's admission, his consents to treatment, nursing records and comments made by the doctors who were treating him. The Law Society has produced a protocol for obtaining hospital medical records which recommends the use of standard forms (set out at **Appendix 3**) when making an application for hospital records. The solicitor who is requesting the records would normally be expected to give an undertaking to be responsible for the reasonable charges incurred in supplying copies of the records to him (see below).

Until all records have been traced and disclosed, the solicitor will not be in a position to instruct an expert to review the evidence (ie, the notes) and form a view on liability/causation. Permission of the court is likely to be necessary prior to instruction of experts under the CPR 1998. Early and full disclosure is the key to successful clinical negligence litigation as, until this has been complied with, both solicitor and client are essentially in the dark as regards what actually happened.

5.8.3 Client's authority

The solicitor must obtain from his client a signed authority permitting the solicitor to make an application to the relevant doctor(s)/hospital for copies of the client's records. There is no standard form for this authority, and a short letter addressed to the solicitor and signed by the client will suffice.

5.8.4 Right of access to health records

The Data Protection Act 1998 (DPA 1998) came into force on 1 March 2000. It gives the right to living individuals to access their health records. The DPA 1998 allows individuals to gain access to personal data of which they are the subject, and therefore talks in terms of 'subject access'. A 'health record' is defined in s 68(2) of the DPA 1998, as any record which:

(a)   consists of information relevant to the physical or mental health or condition of an individual; and

(b)   has been made by or on behalf of a health professional in connection with the care of that individual.

Both written records and also other types of records such as x-rays and scans will therefore come within the definition.

Section 7 of the DPA 1998 provides that, subject to certain provisions, an individual is entitled to have communicated to him in an intelligible form information constituting any personal data of which that individual is the data subject.

5.8.4.1 Obtaining access to health records

Access to information is governed by s 7 of the DPA 1998. A written request should be made to the 'data controller' (a person or persons who decides the purpose for which data is being processed). It is likely to be doctors' surgeries, health authorities and NHS Trusts. The request should contain enough information to allow the data controller to identify the data subject (the individual) and to locate the information requested.

By s 8(2), the information must be conveyed by supplying a copy of it in permanent form unless either:

(a)   that is not possible or would involve disproportionate effort; or

(b)   the data subject agrees otherwise.

In May 2002, the Government produced notes for guidance so that all requests for subject access under s 7 would be dealt with in the same way. The guidance stresses that it is important that, in handling requests, departments adopt a consistent approach. The interpretation set out in this guidance is consistent with legal advice received from Treasury counsel and departments are instructed not to depart from the guidance unilaterally.

'Personal data' is defined in s 1(1) as data which relates to a living individual.

In *Hubble v Peterborough Hospital NHS Trust*, 16 March 2001, it was held that an x-ray was an image and constituted a visual record of the state of a person's body at the particular time when it was recorded. It therefore did include information about an individual's physical health or condition and was therefore an accessible record for the purpose of s 68 of DPA 1998. The court found that information contained in and recorded by virtue of an x-ray was readily communicated in an 'intelligible' form as was required by s 7(1)(c)(i). X-rays were clearly information and clearly part of a health record and if Parliament had intended to exclude x-rays from the 1998 Act, this intention would have been made clear.

5.8.4.2   Fees for access

By s 7(2) a data controller is not obliged to supply any information unless he has received a request in writing and such a fee (not exceeding the prescribed maximum) as he may require. The maximum fee of £50 is prescribed in reg 6 of the Data Protection (Subject Access) (Fees and Miscellaneous Provisions) Regulations 2000 (SI 2000/191).

The above fee may be charged for granting access to manual records or a mixture of manual and/or automated records where the request for access will be granted by supplying a copy of the information in permanent form.

No fee is chargeable where the individual requests access merely to inspect their health records. This provision relates to requests for access to non-automated records where some of the records were made after the beginning of the period of 40 days immediately preceding the date of the request. This provision allows individuals access to recently created health records without charge.

5.8.4.3   Human Rights Act 1998

It is likely that the Human Rights Act 1998 may be used to encourage health authorities to interpret the DPA 1998 liberally (see *Hubble v Peterborough NHS Trust* at **5.8.4.1**).

5.8.4.4   The meaning of 'health professionals'

Section 69 of the DPA 1998 sets out an exhaustive list of health professionals. Most of those listed will be employed within the NHS, such as registered medical practitioners, registered dentists, registered opticians, registered nurses and registered osteopaths. However, the list does not include alternative practitioners.

5.8.4.5   Correction of health records

Sections 12A and 14 of the DPA 1998 allow individuals to request the correction of 'inaccurate' data defined in s 70(2) as 'incorrect or misleading as to a matter or fact'. The court can order the data controller to rectify, erase or destroy such data.

Unlike its predecessor (the Access to Health Records Act 1990), the DPA 1998 is of retrospective effect. Subject to transitional provisions, it allows access to health records created before the Act was passed.

5.8.4.6   Access to health records of deceased individuals

The Access to Health Records Act 1990 continues to govern access to health records which relate to the physical or mental health of individuals who are now deceased. Access may only be requested by a personal representative or a person who may have a claim arising out of the death. A written request should be dealt with, within 40 days from the date of the request, or within 21 days if the record has been added to within 40 days preceding receipt of the written request.

5.8.5   Medical notes

Where the solicitor requires medical notes, he should ensure that he obtains all the notes, not just those which are supplied and marked relevant to the matter in hand. It is important to obtain the full set with a background history and disclosure should not be limited merely to the accident or the incident itself. In *Wickham v Dwyer* (1995) Current Law Weekly, 1 January, the court held that it was for the expert to determine whether or not there was any information of any irrelevance contained within the notes and, therefore, it was fair to allow the solicitors and experts access to the full notes.

In order to give effect to the aims of the CPR 1998, the court had jurisdiction to order a claimant to provide the defendant with a signed form of authority for release of her GP and hospital records direct to the defendant, although care had to be taken in the exercise of this jurisdiction (see *Bennett v Compass Group Ltd and Others* [2002] EWCA Civ 642, [2002] ICR 1177).

5.8.5.1   BMA/ The Law Society – Form of consent to release of health records under the Data Protection Act 1998 (July 2003)

The BMA and the Law Society have produced a consent form which should be used where solicitors are seeking access to their clients' records under the DPA 1998.

The aim of the form is to demonstrate that the patient's informed consent has been obtained before health records are disclosed and requires solicitors to sign and confirm that they need the records for a legitimate purpose.

In order to proceed with a claim, the claimant's solicitor will need to obtain a copy of all records in order to assess which parts are relevant to the claim. The form also makes it clear to the client that, in giving their consent, they understand that the defendant may also gain access to all of their health records as well. A copy of the form is included at **Appendix 7**.

5.8.6   Receipt of medical records

The following list summarises the type of information the solicitor might expect to be supplied to him in response to a request for records or notes. The exact contents of the records or notes will vary from case to case, and the following list is not exhaustive but is intended as a general guideline to the type of information which the solicitor can expect to receive.

5.8.6.1 Hospital records

(a) *Admission details/record sheet.* These should give the date and the time of admission, the record number, the name of the ward and the name of the consultant in charge of the case.

(b) *In-patient notes.* These include casualty notes (where appropriate), personal details of the patient, a detailed history of the patient and of the initial examination, daily progress and record notes, discharge notes, a copy of the letter to the GP giving details of the patient's treatment and general report to the GP.

(c) *Nursing records.* Nursing records are detailed notes made by nursing staff including temperature charts, vital signs, test results, results of all investigations carried out, and details of drugs prescribed and taken.

(d) *Letters of referral.* These include referrals from GPs, responses to GPs following consultation or complaint of a missed appointment and comments on the patient's demeanour and attitude.

(e) *Records of x-rays.* These include other films taken. Copies of the x-rays and films themselves are not supplied automatically (only the record of the fact that the x-ray was carried out) and copies of the films will have to be obtained separately.

(f) *Anaesthetic details.* These are details of the examination of the patient prior to an operation, a record of the drugs administered during pre-medication and during the operation itself.

(g) *Patient consent forms.* These forms show what treatments the patient consented to have performed on him.

(h) *Internal enquiry reports.* Where an internal enquiry has been held and the dominant purpose of that enquiry was not in contemplation of litigation, the enquiry notes will be discoverable.

(i) *Obstetric cases.* The following documents should also be supplied:
   (i) progress of labour cards;
   (ii) cardiotachograph (CTG) traces showing foetal contractions;
   (iii) partogram (showing labour in chart form);
   (iv) ante-natal records;
   (v) neo-natal records;
   (vi) paediatric notes.

5.8.6.2 General practitioner notes

General practitioner notes are usually supplied in a cardboard FP5 envelope, with the patient's name, National Insurance number and date of his registration with the named doctor written on the outside. The records are usually contained on FP7 record cards and will include the doctor's notes. Additionally, the envelope may contain reports of investigations requested by the doctor, letters of referral to hospital or consultants, the hospital or consultants' responses, letters from the hospital including out-patient clinic attendances and treatment and in-patient discharge summaries. A request should be made to the GP to preserve his original records so that they are not inadvertently destroyed or microfiched before the trial.

5.8.7   Examining the records

The solicitor should ensure (as far as possible) that the notes or records supplied to him are complete and are in date order (beginning with the earliest in time), which will show the pattern of the disease or problem and its treatment and may also highlight missing documents or records. Missing documentation should be requested since an incomplete set of records may distort the overall picture and thus give a false impression of the client's claim. Badly copied or illegible documents should be noted and a further request for clear copies made. It may be advisable to make an appointment with the GP or hospital to inspect the original documents at this stage, which will confirm whether a document is really missing and/or whether a document contains a minor clerical error. It is also helpful for the solicitor to go through the records with the client to ensure that the treatment shown on the records accords with the client's recollection of what actually occurred. The records should be supplied to the solicitor and not direct to the expert so that the solicitor has an opportunity to check them through before instructing the expert to prepare his report.

5.9   Conclusion

The essential element when gathering evidence at the preliminary stage is to act quickly. A failure to act on the client's instructions as soon as they are received can have disastrous consequences for the subsequent conduct of the litigation. In extreme cases this can seriously prejudice the client's chances of success, and can amount to negligence on the part of the solicitor.

5.10   Further reading

Motor Insurers' Bureau Agreements at www.mib.org.uk

5.11   Overview of initial liability investigations

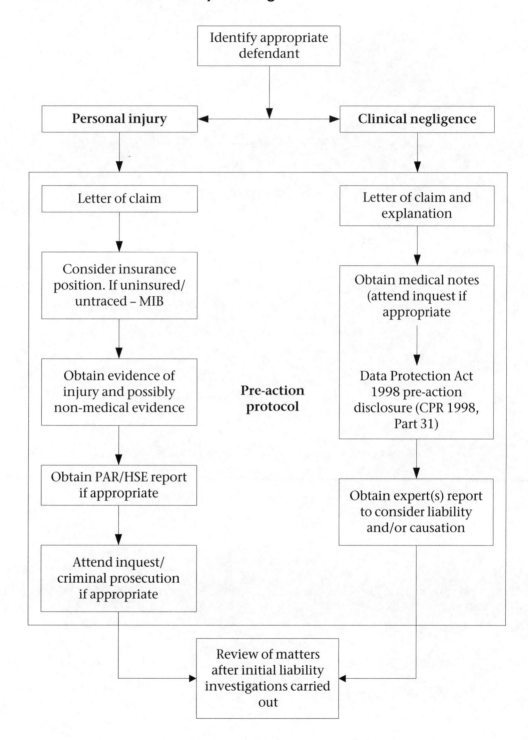

Chapter 6
Limitation of Actions

6.1 Introduction

The limitation period for claims can be a difficult area for the unwary, and the large number of negligence claims against solicitors who have allowed their clients' claims to expire by failing to issue proceedings within the limitation period is testament to this. Consequently, one of the first priorities for the claimant solicitor will be to identify when the limitation period ends and, having established this, to mark the file with that date, and enter it into the diary system.

The principal statute dealing with limitation issues is the Limitation Act 1980 (LA 1980).

For the purpose of limitation in a personal injury claim, 'personal injury' includes any disease and any impairment of a person's physical or mental condition (s 38).

6.2 The limitation period

Under ss 11 and 12 of the LA 1980, where a claimant claims damages either for negligence, nuisance or breach of duty, and that claim consists of or includes a claim for personal injuries, the claimant must normally commence his claim within three years from:

(a) the date on which the cause of action accrued; or

(b) the date of knowledge (if later) of the person injured (s 11(4)).

When calculating the three-year period (generally referred to as the 'primary' limitation period), the day on which the cause of action accrued is excluded (s 2). Therefore, in a simple road incident case, generally the claimant has three years from the incident (excluding the date of the incident) in which to commence the claim. However, in more complex claims, the claimant may seek to rely on a subsequent date of knowledge, which may enable him to commence the claim more than three years after the event complained of.

6.3   Date of knowledge

6.3.1   Section 14 of the Limitation Act 1980

Section 14 of the LA 1980 defines 'date of knowledge' for the purpose of ss 11 and 12 as the date on which the claimant first had knowledge of all of the following factors:

(a)   that the injury was significant; and

(b)   that the injury was attributable in whole or in part to the act or omission which is alleged to constitute negligence, nuisance or breach of duty; and

(c)   the identity of the defendant; and

(d)   if it is alleged that the act or omission was that of a person other than the defendant, the identity of that person and the additional facts supporting the bringing of a claim against the defendant.

In *Nash v Eli Lilly* [1993] 1 WLR 782, CA, a number of patients who had taken the drug Opren brought claims against the pharmaceutical company. The Court of Appeal considered the meaning of 'knowledge' in s 14, and decided that a claimant had knowledge when he knew enough of the various matters specified in the LA 1980 to justify taking legal advice. As regards the significance of the injury, the court held that the claimant must know of the act or omission to which the injury was attributable and, once he believed his symptoms were due to Opren, that was sufficient in terms of the 'act or omission'. Accordingly, the court refused to exercise the discretion to extend the limitation period.

According to s 14(2), an injury is significant if the person whose date of knowledge is in question would reasonably have considered it sufficiently serious to justify instituting proceedings against a defendant who did not dispute liability and was able to satisfy a judgment. In *Halford v Brookes* [1991] 3 All ER 559, it was stated that knowledge does not mean 'know for certain and beyond the possibility of contradiction' but meant 'know with sufficient confidence to justify embarking on the preliminaries to issue of proceedings, such as submitting a claim to the proposed defendant, taking legal advice and other advice and collecting evidence'. For example, a claimant may work in an environment which exposes him to excessive and injurious dust particles such as asbestos dust or coal dust. It may be many years before an injury deemed 'significant' manifests itself, and it may be some time later before the claimant realises what the cause of his illness is. Similarly, in a clinical negligence context, a patient may be fully aware of his pain and suffering, but assume that it is entirely due to an underlying illness, rather than caused by the negligence of a doctor (see *James v East Dorset Health Authority* (1999) 59 BMLR 196).

In *Dobbie v Medway Health Authority* [1994] 1 WLR 1234, CA, Mrs Dobbie had surgery to remove a lump in her breast. It was only during the operation that the surgeon took the decision to perform a mastectomy (removal of the breast), as he believed the breast was cancerous. In fact, the lump was not cancerous and the mastectomy had not been necessary. Mrs Dobbie accepted at the time that the surgeon had acted reasonably and it was her good fortune that the lump was not cancerous. Some years later when she heard about a similar case, Mrs Dobbie took advice from a solicitor. It was argued that in this case the court ought to exercise its discretion because Mrs Dobbie had not been aware that anything had gone wrong, as she did not have sufficient knowledge that she had suffered an injury, but the application failed.

In *Forbes v Wandsworth Health Authority* [1997] QB 402, the Court of Appeal held by a majority that the claimant was deemed to have constructive knowledge as soon as he had time to overcome the shock of the injury, take stock of his disability and seek advice. The facts of the case were that the claimant, who suffered from poor circulation, underwent surgery for a by-pass operation; this was not a success and a further by-pass was performed the next day. Unfortunately, the second operation was too late to be successful and the claimant was told that it was necessary to amputate his leg to prevent gangrene, to which he agreed. The sole allegation was that the authority had been negligent not to perform the second operation sooner. The claimant did not seek advice until seven years after the limitation period had expired. The court found that the amputation was a significant injury, but had to decide whether it could be attributed to some act or omission which constituted negligence. Having found that the claimant did have constructive knowledge, the court went on to decide whether to exercise its discretion under s 33 of the LA 1980. The court took into account prejudice to the defendant in that insurance arrangements and medical standards had changed and medical records were missing. The court also considered the merits of the case. It was noted that the claimant was legally aided, that there was a substantial burden on the defendants and every likelihood that the claim would fail. The court therefore declined to exercise its discretion.

However, in *Penney v British Steel*, 1 July 1997, in a refinement to the objective test for constructive knowledge used in *Forbes,* the Court of Appeal held that the claimant had taken all reasonable steps to acquire the necessary knowledge, and, although he had known for 15 years that he had significant health problems, it was not reasonable for him to disregard his GP's view and insist on a consultation with an expert, as his GP had diagnosed his condition as not linked to any negligent act or omission.

According to *Roberts v Winslow* (1999) *The Times,* 12 January (a clinical negligence case), the date from which the claimant knows that the lesser part of his injuries is attributable to the defendant is the date when time starts to run for limitation purposes, not the date when he later discovers that the greater part of his injuries are attributable to the defendant.

In relation to the method of apportionment of damage where the court finds that the relevant date of knowledge actually occurs part way through the period when the damage is being done, see *Allen v British Rail Engineering Ltd* [2001] EWCA Civ 242, [2001] ICR 942. In this case, the claimant suffered vibration white finger (VWF) injuries due to work with vibrating tools. The defendants contended that the state of knowledge as to the danger from such tools changed during the time the claimant was employed. Because of this, the defendants argued they were negligent only after they had knowledge of the problem but failed to advise the claimant of the problems and that the damage was already done by then in any event. The court decided it had to do its best to decide the correct level of apportionment and should not deny the claimant a remedy if it could not establish the proportion with accuracy. The judge was correct to try to decide how much damage was due to the defendants' negligence. Even though the figure would not be precisely accurate, that was preferable to awarding the claimant nothing because he failed to establish exactly the amount of damage that was attributable to the negligence.

6.3.2 Constructive knowledge

The claimant is expected to gain constructive knowledge by making reasonable enquiries. Under s 14(3) of the LA 1980, a person's knowledge includes knowledge which he might reasonably have been expected to acquire:

(a) from facts observable or ascertainable by him; or

(b) from facts ascertainable by him with the help of medical or other appropriate expert advice which it is reasonable for him to seek,

but he shall not be fixed with knowledge of a fact ascertainable only with the help of expert advice as long as he has taken all reasonable steps to obtain (and, where appropriate, to act on) that advice.

When trying to establish the claimant's date of knowledge for the purposes of s 14(1)(b) of the LA 1980, the court found, in *Spargo v North Essex District Health Authority* [1997] 8 Med LR 125, that to establish the date of knowledge, a subjective test was to be applied, ie, 'what did the claimant know?' and not 'what would a reasonable layman realise?'. The facts of the case were that the claimant had been diagnosed as suffering from selective brain damage and was compulsorily detained in hospital from 1975 until 1981. The damages proceedings were not issued until 1993, although the claimant had first consulted solicitors in 1986. At this time she did not know whether she had a case but felt clear in her own mind that her suffering was attributable to a mistaken diagnosis. It was held on appeal that because the claimant was clear in her own mind that a connection existed between her suffering and the misdiagnosis when she first sought legal advice in 1986, it was not necessary for the court to enquire further whether a rational lay person would have been willing to say that they knew of a connection between the suffering and the misdiagnosis without first obtaining a medical confirmation.

Further, the Court of Appeal has held that the date of a claimant's knowledge was the date on which the claimant first knew enough to begin to investigate whether he had a claim against the defendant. For example, where a specialist told the claimant that he had an inhaled disease or industrial injury, and the only source for this could be his work for the defendants (*Corbin v Penfold Metalizing* [2000] Lloyd's Rep Med 247).

When considering whether the claimant had constructive knowledge in *Sniezek v Bundy (Letchworth) Ltd* (2000) LTL, 7 July, the Court of Appeal found that a claimant could have the requisite knowledge even if medical experts advised him that this was not the case. The court ruled that the claimant had the knowledge from the date when he went to complain to his doctor of severe symptoms but was assured that there was no link between the illness and his work. The court decided that although this decision might appear harsh, the better view was that the LA 1980 was clear that time should run even when a claimant had taken reasonable steps to obtain expert advice to confirm his own belief in an injury but the advice was negative. Under such circumstances it was correct to rely on s 33. Here the claimant acted promptly and made reasonable efforts to instruct solicitors, such that the court was right to exercise its discretion under s 33 in these circumstances.

6.3.3 Knowledge of identity of defendant

The identity of the defendant may prove problematic in cases involving corporate groups. In *Simpson v Norwest Holst Southern Ltd* [1980] 2 All ER 471, the facts were that the claimant worked on a building site, and his contract of employment stated that he was employed by Norwest Holst Group. However, this did not identify his employer because at least four companies made up Norwest Holst Group, including Norwest Holst Ltd and Norwest Construction Co Ltd, and the claimant's payslips stated simply that his employer was 'Norwest Holst'. In the circumstances, the Court of Appeal found for the claimant, on the basis that neither the contract nor the payslips identified the employer and it was not reasonable to expect him to request further particulars of the identity of his employer prior to the expiry of his primary limitation period. For a case on similar facts, see *Rush v JNR (SMD) Ltd* (CA, 11 October 1999), where it was held that knowledge of a number of potential defendants was not sufficient knowledge for the purpose of s 14.

The issue of constructive knowledge of the identity of the defendant was considered in *Henderson v Temple Pier Co Ltd* (CA, 23 April 1998). In this case, it was held that, where a claimant instructed solicitors to bring a claim for damages, on the proper construction of s 14(3) of the LA 1980 the claimant was fixed with constructive knowledge of facts which the solicitor ought to have acquired.

The above is also relevant where the possibility of vicarious liability exists. For example, if the claimant sues defendant A reasonably assuming him to be responsible (where A is driving the car that hits him) and the claimant subsequently finds out that A was acting in the course of his employment with B, any claim against B can be made within three years from the date of discovery that B was the employer, or the date that the claimant reasonably ought to have discovered that fact.

6.4 Claims in fatal accidents

6.4.1 Claims under the Law Reform (Miscellaneous Provisions) Act 1934 (LR(MP)A 1934)

Section 11(4) of the LA 1980 states that the limitation period is three years from:

(a)   the date the cause of action accrued; or
(b)   the date of knowledge if later.

Section 11(5) of the LA 1980 provides that if the injured person dies before expiration of the limitation period of three years, then the limitation period shall be three years from:

(a)   the date of death; or
(b)   the date of the personal representative's knowledge,

whichever is the later. If there is more than one personal representative and they have differing dates of knowledge, time runs from the earliest date of knowledge (s 11(7)). Therefore, under s 11(4), the limitation period is three years from the date of accident or the date of knowledge. If a longer period elapses before death, the claim is statute-barred. If death occurs within three years, or having no knowledge, then s 11(5) applies a further three years from the date of death or date of knowledge of the personal representative. However, the court does have a general discretion to override the above provisions and disapply the limitation period, as to which, see s 33 of the LA 1980 (see **6.6**).

6.4.2 Claims under the Fatal Accidents Act 1976 (FAA 1976)

Section 12 of the LA 1980 provides that a claim under the FAA 1976 cannot be brought if death occurred when the person injured could no longer maintain a claim and recover damages in respect of the injury, whether because of a limitation problem or for any other reason. Therefore, the dependants of the deceased are in no better position than the deceased would have been, and, as such, if his claim would have been statute-barred under s 11 of the LA 1980, the dependants are similarly barred.

Section 12(2) provides that the limitation period for the dependants under the FAA 1976 is three years from:

(a)   the date of death; or

(b)   the date of knowledge of the person for whose benefit the claim is brought,

whichever is the later. Therefore, if the primary limitation period expires before the date of death, the dependant is statute-barred. If the primary limitation period has not expired at the date of death, s 12(2) applies and the relevant limitation period will be that of the dependants. Both LR(MP)A 1934 and FAA 1976 claims are also subject to the court's discretion under s 33 to disapply the limitation period of three years (s 28 of the LA 1980), as long as the appropriate limitation period was set by the LA 1980 and not some other statute.

It should be noted that where an FAA 1976 claim is brought on behalf of minor dependants, if that claim is dismissed for want of prosecution then even though as regards limitation, time has not run against the minor dependants, the dismissal of the claim will preclude any second claim being brought. See *Croft v Shavin & Co* (QBD, 16 November 1995).

6.5 Persons under disability

A person is under a disability while he is a child (a person who has not attained the age of 18) or is of unsound mind within the meaning of the Mental Health Act 1983 and is therefore incapable of managing his property and affairs.

Under s 28(6) of the LA 1980, while a person is under a disability, as defined above, he may bring a claim at any time up to three years from when he ceased to be under a disability.

It is important to note that according to the wording of the section:

> ... if on the date when any right of action accrued ... the person to whom it accrued was under a disability, the action may be brought at any time before the expiration of three years from the date when he ceased to be under a disability or died (whichever first occurred).

Therefore, the person must be under the disability when the cause of action first accrued. If a disability comes into existence after that date, time continues to run. However, under s 33(3) of the LA 1980 (see **6.6**) the court will have regard to any period or periods of disability when it exercises its discretion. Similarly, there is no extension of time for a person under a disability claiming through a person who was not under a disability at the time the right of action accrued (s 28(2)). This was confirmed in *Thomas v Plaistow* (1997) *The Times,* 19 May, CA. It was held that disability in s 33 of the LA 1980 has the same meaning as in s 28, that is infancy or unsound mind. There is a mandatory extension of time where the claimant has an existing disability and a discretion if there is a supervening disability.

6.6 The court's discretion to override the limitation period

Section 33 of the LA 1980 gives the court an unfettered discretion to disapply the three-year limitation period. Section 33(1) provides that:

> If it appears to the court that it would be equitable to allow an action to proceed having regard to the degree to which—
>
> (a)   the provisions of section 11 or 11A or 12 of this Act prejudice the plaintiff or any person whom he represents; and
>
> (b)   any decision of the court under this subsection would prejudice the defendant or any person whom he represents;
>
> the court may direct that those provisions shall not apply to the action, or shall not apply to any specified cause of action to which the action relates.

Under s 33(3):

> ... the court is required to have regard to all the circumstances of the case, and in particular to—
>
> (a)   the length of, and the reason for, the delay on the part of the plaintiff;
>
> (b)   the extent to which, having regard to the delay, the evidence adduced or likely to be adduced by the plaintiff or the defendant is or is likely to be less cogent than if the action had been brought within the time allowed by section 11, by section 11A or (as the case may be) by section 12;
>
> (c)   the conduct of the defendant after the cause of action arose, including the extent (if any) to which he responded to requests reasonably made by the plaintiff for information or inspection for the purpose of ascertaining facts which were or might be relevant to the plaintiff's cause of action against the defendant;
>
> (d)   the duration of any disability of the plaintiff arising after the date of the accrual of the cause of action;
>
> (e)   the extent to which the plaintiff acted promptly and reasonably once he knew whether or not the act or omission of the defendant, to which the injury was attributable, might be capable at that time of giving rise to an action for damages;
>
> (f)   the steps, if any, taken by the plaintiff to obtain medical, legal or other expert advice and the nature of any such advice he may have received.

The onus rests upon the claimant to show why the limitation period should be disapplied (*Halford v Brookes* [1991] 3 All ER 559).

In *Donovan v Gwentoys* [1990] 1 WLR 472, the House of Lords emphasised that s 33 gave the court an unfettered discretion to disapply the strict time-limits: the matters contained in s 33(3) are merely guidelines. For example, the time of notification of the claim to the defendant is of extreme importance in ascertaining prejudice, although there is no specific reference to this in s 33. Depriving the defendant of the limitation defence as such is of little importance; the matter of paramount importance is the effect of the delay on the defendant's ability to defend, as illustrated by *Hartley v Birmingham City District Council* [1992] 2 All ER 213, CA.

When considering s 33(3)(b), the extent to which evidence is less cogent, the Court of Appeal highlighted the importance of written evidence when memories of witnesses are unreliable due to the lapse of time see *Farthing v North East Essex Health Authority* [1998] Lloyd's Rep Med 37, CA. The claimant had had a hysterectomy which was negligently performed. Following her operation in 1981, she sued the defendants in 1995. When considering her application under s 33, the court found that due to the lapse of time a number of the witnesses had died or had moved abroad and could recall little of the events in question. However, the Court of Appeal further found that because there was considerable evidence available in the form of the medical records and a letter from the surgeon to the claimant's GP written shortly after the operation, there would be little need for reliance on memory alone and consequently the appeal should be allowed.

Further guidance was provided by the Court of Appeal in *Coad v Cornwall and Isles of Scilly Health Authority* [1997] 1 WLR 189, CA. The court found that s 33(3)(a) required the court to apply a subjective test to why the claimant had delayed, the length of the delay and whether the reason was good or bad. There was no requirement for the claimant to provide a 'reasonable' explanation. In relation to the conduct of the defendants, the judge is entitled to consider the conduct of the defendants, and if he establishes that the defendants have brought upon themselves the tragedies that they claim to suffer, then that should be taken into account and the prejudice should be significantly discounted. In the case of *Hammond v West Lancashire Health Authority* [1998] Lloyd's Rep Med 146, CA, the defendants claimed prejudice to their case as they had destroyed the deceased's x-rays after three years had elapsed. The court held that the destruction of the x-rays was a policy implemented by the defendants, and which had no regard for the time limits of the LA 1980. Because of this prejudice to their case, it should still be taken into account, although it would be significantly discounted.

An example of what might amount to a reasonable delay can be found in *Whittaker v Westinghouse Brake and Signal Holdings* (1996) CLR, 9 August. In this case, a widow sought to bring a claim under s 33 of LA 1980 after a delay of 31 years. The court found that there were still witnesses available and that the defendant would not be seriously prejudiced. The court found that the widow was not blameworthy in respect of the delay.

It should be borne in mind that the limitation period is important not only to the claimant personally but also to the claimant's solicitor. Where the proceedings are brought against the defendant outside the limitation period as a result of the negligence of the claimant's solicitor, and the claim is not allowed to proceed, the claimant may have a claim against his own solicitor. It has been argued that the fact that the claimant has a cast-iron claim against his own solicitor provides an overwhelming reason why the limitation period should not be disapplied; the claimant will not be prejudiced because he can pursue an alternative claim against his solicitor (rather than the defendant). However, although the ability to claim against the solicitor is a factor for the court to bear in mind, it is not an absolute bar against disapplying the limitation period (*Ramsden v Lee* [1992] 2 All ER 204; *Hartley v Birmingham City District Council* (above)):

> if the plaintiff has to change from an action against a tortfeasor, who may know little or nothing of the weak points of his case, to an action against his solicitor, who will know a great deal about them, the prejudice may well be major rather than minor ...

The court considered the above issue in *Steeds v Peverel Management Services Ltd* [2001] EWCA Civ 419, (2001) *The Times,* 16 May. In this case, solicitors failed to issue proceedings within the relevant limitation period. The court found that the proceedings were only 49 days outside of the limitation period. On appeal, the court found that the district judge at first instance was wrong to treat the claimant's good claim against his own solicitors as justification for refusing to exercise a discretion under s 33. The better view was that the existence of a claim against his own solicitors was a relevant factor in weighing the degree of prejudice suffered by the defendant in not being able to rely on the limitation period as a defence. To that end, it would always be relevant to consider when the defendant first had notification of the claim (see *Donovan v Gwentoys* (above)). On the facts of the case, the judgment was set aside and the court exercised its discretion under s 33 as it was unlikely that the defendants were caused any appreciable prejudice as it was equitable to allow the claim to continue allowing for all of the circumstances of the case.

6.7 Special periods of limitation

Although in the vast majority of personal injury cases the three-year rule will apply, it is possible that a special rule applies, for example, in regard to claims relating to aircraft under the Carriage by Air Act 1961 or the Warsaw Convention, or relating to vessels used for navigation under the Maritime Conventions Act 1911 or the Merchant Shipping Act 1995. In those cases, the limitation period is generally two years.

The most common form of special rule is in respect of contributions between tortfeasors under the Civil Liability (Contribution) Act 1978, where no claim to recover a contribution may be brought after the expiration of two years from the date on which the right accrued. This is generally the date on which judgment was given against the person who is seeking the contribution or the date when he pays or agrees to pay compensation.

6.8 Avoiding limitation problems

If limitation appears to be a problem which the solicitor becomes aware of at the first interview, the following matters should be taken into account.

(a) The date of the incident should be checked and the limitation period calculated from this date.

(b) Consideration should be given as to whether any special rule applies (date of knowledge, disability etc).

(c) If limitation will shortly expire, the solicitor should consider issuing protective proceedings to safeguard his client's position. If limitation will expire imminently, application can be made ex parte and in a real emergency the court will accept oral statements, followed by an undertaking to verify them by affidavit (see *Phillips v Taunton and Somerset NHS Trust* (1996) 33 BMLR 154).

(d) If limitation expired recently, the solicitor should consider issuing proceedings as soon as possible in order to show the court that the very minimum of delay has occurred, when making an application for the court to use its discretion under s 33 to disapply the limitation period. *Carlton v Fulchers (a Firm)* [1997] PNLR 337, CA, is a good example of how a solicitor can be found to be negligent due to a failure to be aware of limitation problems. In this case, even though the claimant did not consult the solicitor until after the three-year limitation period had expired, he was held liable due to his failure to advise of the possibility of an application under s 33.

(e) In clinical negligence cases, the solicitor should consider whether to apply for emergency assistance from the LSC.

(f) If limitation expired a long time ago, it will be too late for protective proceedings to be of any use. Therefore, the solicitor should check whether date of knowledge may be relevant and, if not, consider the likelihood of success of any application under s 33 having regard to the circumstances of the case and how they compare with the factors contained in s 33.

6.9 Conclusion

Failure to issue proceedings within the limitation period is a major source of negligence claims against solicitors. Although this chapter includes the law and procedure relevant to an application under s 33 to override the limitation period, prevention is better than cure. It is therefore essential that the solicitor establishes a routine of checking and rechecking the limitation period on the files for which he is responsible. There may also be many other files, for which he is not responsible, but which may pass through his hands on a regular basis. Such files are often the source of limitation problems, as one solicitor may assume (wrongly) that the responsibility for checking limitation resides with someone else, and the date of limitation may go unchecked. To avoid this, the solicitor should adopt a routine of checking for limitation on every file on which he is involved.

6.10 Further reading

McGee, *Limitation Periods* (Sweet & Maxwell).

Chapter 7

Complaints Procedures and Disciplinary Procedures of Health Care Providers

7.1 Introduction

When advising a client about the right to complain in relation to NHS care, and how to go about it, there are a number of matters for the solicitor to consider. While the complaint has the primary purpose of ensuring that the client's voice does not go unheard, it will also ensure that the matter is investigated quickly, while events are still fresh, and that detailed information is obtained.

Under the National Health Service Reform and Healthcare Professionals Act 2002, the Council for the Regulation of Healthcare Professionals (the Council) assumes responsibility for complaints to professional bodies from 1 April 2003.

The function of the Council is to oversee the existing complaints-handling bodies for different healthcare professions. The complaints-handling bodies regulated by the Council are the General Medical Council, the General Dental Council, the General Optical Council, the General Osteopathic Council, the Royal Pharmaceutical Society and the Nursing and Midwifery Council. The Council has power to investigate the way these regulatory bodies fulfil their complaints handling function.

7.2 The NHS complaints procedure

The complaints procedure was introduced on 1 April 1996. The procedure has two objectives: first, to simplify the method by which patients can complain about different members of the medical profession and, secondly, to separate complaints completely from disciplinary procedures. The aim is to deal with complaints simply and swiftly at local level, if possible.

The complaints procedure involves two stages:

(a) local resolution; and

(b) independent review.

From 1 April 2004 the NHS complaints procedure has been changed so that responsibility for independent reviews of complaints has passed to the

Commission for Healthcare Audit and Inspection (CHAI). Note that this body is also popularly known as the Healthcare Commission. CHAI is a public body established by the Health and Social Care (Community Health and Standards) Act 2003. Under the improved complaints procedure the responsibility to undertake independent review of complaints has been taken from the NHS and given to CHAI so that a truly independent assessment can be made of the complaint in relation to all aspects of patient care.

Under reforms to the NHS complaints procedure introduced in 2004 complainants can pursue a complaint at the same time as taking legal action.

The complaints procedure is applicable to complaints concerning NHS staff in all areas, whether they are GPs, hospital doctors, nursing staff or ambulance crew, or any other relevant NHS employee. A complaint by a patient can encompass any expression of dissatisfaction, from a complaint about the food or politeness of staff to one about the ability of a doctor properly to diagnose or treat an illness or injury (ie, a clinical complaint).

NHS staff are asked to be alert to the fact that a prompt and thorough response to a complaint as it arises, if handled correctly, may result in the complaint being nipped in the bud, before it has the chance to gain momentum. This 'local resolution' is seen by the NHS Executive as the main thrust of the procedure. Complaints are most likely to be voiced to staff on the spot, who are the people best placed to make the initial response. The aim is to resolve problems and answer concerns of patients immediately and informally if possible.

The procedure is aimed only at satisfying complaints, and will not apportion blame amongst staff. It is completely separate from disciplinary procedures. A complaint may bring a deficiency to the notice of management, which may then consider disciplinary action; however, this will involve the complainant only to the extent of possibly giving a statement to be used in the disciplinary process. Thereafter, the complainant should be informed of any outcome of any disciplinary procedure.

Assistance on how to make a complaint can be obtained from the community health council (in Scotland, the local health council). The Health Information Service gives information on the NHS complaints system. Full details of how to make a complaint can be found on the Department of Health website.

7.3 Local resolution

7.3.1 Local resolution and NHS hospitals

As part of its complaints procedure, the trust or health authority must have a clear local resolution process. If the complaint concerns a relatively minor matter, which can be resolved quickly, the person to whom the patient complains should either deal with it at the time or ensure that it is passed to an appropriate person who can respond to the complaint more fully. If the complaint is more serious and an investigation is required, it is likely that the staff member will refer the matter to the complaints manager for the hospital, who will then deal with the patient. A large number of complaints are dealt with in this way without the necessity for independent review.

However, as an alternative, under the Patients' Charter, the chief executive of the trust or health authority must respond in writing to all written complaints and all oral complaints subsequently put into writing and signed by the complainant. If the complaint is more serious, the patient may be invited to a meeting to discuss the circumstances of the incident together with those involved with it, or the hospital may hold a more formal enquiry involving examination of medical records, interviewing those involved and possibly seeking the opinion of senior doctors. The aim is to provide a full investigation within 20 working days, according to NHS targets, but there is no sanction in place if this target is not met.

If the patient remains dissatisfied, or is unwilling to voice a complaint to the person giving care, or the staff member is unable to deal with it, the complaint should be referred to the complaints manager.

If the complaint is not resolved at local level, the complainant must be informed in writing that the first stage of the complaints procedure is at an end and that the complainant has the right to independent review by CHAI.

7.3.2 Local resolution and GP or other family health service complaints

In the case of family health services (ie, GP practices and NHS dentists), local resolution is the responsibility of the practitioner. From 1 April 1996, family health service practitioners are obliged to have a practice-based complaints procedure, which they must publicise.

If the complaint concerns a GP, an NHS dentist or any person employed by their practice, it will be necessary to seek clarification from the practice as to how it operates its local complaints procedure. If the complaint cannot be dealt with immediately, the matter should be referred to the complaints manager, who in this instance is likely to be one of the other doctors or dentists in the practice or the practice manager if there is one. If the complaint is not dealt with on the spot, and requires investigation, the complaint should be acknowledged within two working days and, if possible, a written response or a meeting to try to resolve the complaint should be undertaken within 10 working days.

If the patient does not wish to complain direct to the practice, the complaints leaflet provided by the practice should include details of the complaints manager at the local health authority who can mediate between the patient and the practice.

If the complaint is not resolved at local level, the complainant must be informed in writing that the first stage of the complaints procedure is at an end and that the complainant has the right to independent review by CHAI.

7.3.3 Time limits

A complaint should be made within six months of the date of the matter complained of, or within six months of the date of discovering the problem, provided it is within 12 months of the incident.

Complaints outside the time limit may be investigated at the discretion of the health service provider.

7.4 Independent review

The Department of Health produced regulations in July 2004 (SI 2004/1768) which set out how independent review should operate. The biggest change under the reformed procedure is that every complainant has the right to have his complaint reviewed at independent review if it cannot be settled by local resolution (previously this was discretionary only).

CHAI will also deal directly with complaints which are deemed too serious to be dealt with by local resolution or where there has been a breakdown of trust between the patient and care provider. It is likely that many complaints in relation to clinical matters will fall into this category. Initially the complaint will be considered by CHAI's own complaints managers who will make an initial assessment and who are specially trained for this purpose. The complaints manager will try to resolve the situation. The complaints manager may, if he thinks it appropriate conduct his own investigation into the complaint. It is hoped that this approach will lead to faster complaint resolution and also ensure consistency of approach. If a satisfactory resolution cannot be obtained the complainant has the right to a hearing with a panel of three lay people who will review the investigation.

7.5 Independent review panel

The investigation by the independent review panel will be proportionate to both the substance of the complaint and the way in which it has been handled locally. The complainant and the complained against have the right to a panel to hear and consider the issues. A panel of three lay people will be brought together to hear the case, based on representations from the complainant, the organisation against which the complaint is made, any witnesses and on the investigation report. Panel members will be appointed from a list of lay people held by CHAI for this purpose. The panel will not be adversarial, but must uphold principles of fairness and consistency. The panel will conduct its proceedings within the following rules:

(a) proceedings should be held at a time and place that are convenient for all parties;

(b) both parties to the complaint should have access to the same information on which the panel will base it considerations, subject to the Data Protection Act 1998;

(c) both the complainant and any person complained against must be given a reasonable opportunity to express their views on the complaint;

(d) the standard of proof is the civil standard of a 'balance of probabilities' not the criminal standard of 'beyond reasonable doubt';

(e) if any of the panel members disagree about how a panel should go about its business, the majority view will prevail;

(f) accurate records approved by the panel members are kept of conclusions and recommendations and the reasons for reaching those conclusions.

Panels will normally conduct their proceedings with the complainant and the complained against together in the same room to hear the evidence given by others. This ensures that both parties know what is being said and have the opportunity to comment at the time. The panel could also be conducted as a series of interviews.

The panel will make recommendations based on its findings. Panels will be asked to make two sets of recommendations: one concerned with redress for the individual, and the other regarding improvement of the services, when called for. A full report will be available to the parties and an anonymised report will be published and available on the CHAI website.

7.6   The Health Service Commissioner (Ombudsman)

7.6.1   The role of the Ombudsman

The Ombudsman is entirely separate from the NHS. His role includes the following:

(a)   investigation of clinical complaints; and

(b)   complaints relating to family health services; and

(c)   whether the complaints procedure itself is working; or

(d)   complaints where the NHS body has refused to investigate the complaint on the basis that it is outside the time limit; or

(e)   complaints where the complaint has been dealt fully with by NHS complaints procedure and the complainant is still dissatisfied; or

(f)   complaints where the complainant is dissatisfied with the local resolution and the convener has refused to hold an independent review.

The Ombudsman has power:

(a)   to request the convener to reconsider the case; or

(b)   to investigate the matter himself.

The Ombudsman can also investigate complaints from NHS staff if they feel that they have suffered hardship or injustice as a result of the procedure, provided that established grievance procedures have been followed and the persons remain dissatisfied.

7.6.2   Time limit

The complaint should be made within one year of the event complained of.

If a client needs help to formulate a complaint, he can get help from the local community health council, which is independent and provides information and advice to the public on healthcare issues.

Investigations by the Ombudsman are published in a quarterly report, the text of which is available from the Ombudsman's Office or the Internet.

7.7   Data Protection Act 1998

If a request for access to health records has not been complied with, under the DPA 1998, it is now possible to use the complaints procedure to complain about this as an alternative to making an application to the court.

7.8   Effect of coroner's inquest

The fact that a death has been referred to a coroner does not mean that the investigation of any complaint must be suspended. The healthcare provider should initiate its own investigations, so as to be of assistance to the coroner's own enquiries, or to extend its own enquiries if the coroner so requests.

7.9   Disciplinary proceedings against doctors

7.9.1   Statutory provisions

The General Medical Council (GMC) has jurisdiction in relation to professional misconduct and criminal offences. This power was first conferred on the GMC by the Medical Act 1858, and is now regulated by ss 36–45 of and Sch 4 to the Medical Act 1983, as amended by the Medical (Professional Performance) Act 1995.

The 1983 Act provides that if a registered practitioner is:

(a) found by the Professional Conduct Committee to have committed a criminal offence in the British Isles; or

(b) is adjudged by the Professional Conduct Committee to have been guilty of serious professional misconduct,

then the Committee may direct that:

(a) the doctor's name be erased from the register; or

(b) the doctor's registration be suspended for a period of not more than 12 months; or

(c) registration be conditional on the doctor's compliance for a period of not more than three years with such requirements as the Committee thinks fit to impose in order to protect the public or in the doctor's own interests.

The GMC has power given to it by the Medical (Professional Performance) Act 1995 which amended the Medical Act 1983 to deal with less serious cases falling short of serious professional misconduct, but constituting 'seriously deficient' performance.

Where the Committee on Professional Performance finds that a doctor's professional performance has been seriously deficient, the Committee must:

(a) direct that his registration be suspended for a period not exceeding 12 months (in the first instance, but can be extended to an indefinite period); or

(b) that his registration be made conditional.

Where registration is made conditional, the condition will often specify that the doctor is to undertake re-training or refrain from a certain area of practice in future, for a period not exceeding three years. Failure to comply with conditions imposed can lead to a direction that the doctor be suspended from the register.

7.9.2 The meaning of 'conviction'

Conviction means a conviction by a criminal court in the British Isles. Any conviction in itself gives the Professional Conduct Committee jurisdiction, even if the offence does not involve professional misconduct. The Committee is, however, most concerned by convictions which affect a doctor's fitness to practice.

One of the key issues to advise a doctor about in relation to criminal offending is that, when considering convictions, the GMC is bound to accept the determination of the court as conclusive evidence of guilt of the offence for which he was convicted. Therefore, if a doctor is advised to plead guilty (eg, in order to avoid publicity), he should also be advised that admission of guilt will be conclusive evidence when the matter falls to be considered by the GMC. A doctor who has been convicted on a plea of guilty cannot subsequently argue before the Professional Conduct Committee that he was in fact innocent.

7.9.3 The meaning of 'serious professional misconduct'

The phrase 'serious professional misconduct' means serious misconduct when judged according to the rules, written or unwritten, governing the medical profession.

7.9.4 The Professional Conduct Committee and the Preliminary Proceedings Committee

The Professional Conduct Committee is elected annually and consists of 30 members. Of those, 23 are medical members and seven are lay members. It normally sits in public and its procedures are similar to those of a court of law; for example, witnesses may be witness summonsed to attend and will give their evidence on oath to the Committee. The Committee will be advised on questions of law by a legal adviser who is usually a barrister, advocate or solicitor of not less than 10 years' standing. Doctors appearing before the Committee are usually legally represented.

7.9.5 Function of the Preliminary Proceedings Committee

Cases coming before the Preliminary Proceedings Committee or Professional Conduct Committee may arise:

(a)   from a conviction before the courts; or

(b)   where it is alleged that a doctor has done something which amounts to serious professional misconduct.

Convictions of doctors are normally reported to the GMC by the police, unless the conviction is for a minor motoring offence or other trivial matter.

Complaints which may amount to serious professional misconduct are reported to the GMC and fall into two categories:

(a)   matters which have been investigated by some other procedure, for example, the NHS complaints procedure;

(b)   complaints received from other doctors or members of the public direct to the GMC.

Complaints must be supported by evidence of the facts complained of in the form of either affidavit or a statutory declaration. Having considered the allegation, if it appears that there is a question of serious professional misconduct but insufficient evidence has been put forward, the GMC's own solicitor can make further enquiries. A decision as to whether to proceed with an allegation of such serious professional misconduct will then be made by the President or other medical member of the GMC.

If a matter comes to the attention of the GMC via criminal, civil or family proceedings and an issue of disclosure of documents relied on in the case to the GMC arises, guidance on the procedure to be followed was given in *Re A (Disclosure of Medical Records to the GMC)* [1998] 2 FLR 641.

7.9.6 Procedure

Having had the matters outlined above referred to it, the Preliminary Proceedings Committee may:

(a)   refer the case to the Professional Conduct Committee; or

(b)   contact the doctor concerned by letter; or

(c)   decide to take no further action.

Most cases being considered by the Preliminary Proceedings Committee are of a less serious nature and are therefore filtered out and disposed of by way of a warning letter or a letter giving advice to the doctor concerned, for example, where a doctor has been convicted for the first time of a driving offence involving excess alcohol. However, if the doctor's fitness to practise may be impaired, the Committee may refer the matter either to the Health Committee or to the Professional Conduct Committee.

If the Preliminary Proceedings Committee decides to forward the matter to the Professional Conduct Committee or the Health Committee, it may make an interim order suspending the doctor's registration to practise or make that registration conditional. The Committee has the power to do this if it is satisfied that it is necessary to protect members of the public or that it is in the doctor's own interests so to do. However, no order can be made until the doctor concerned has had the opportunity to appear before the Preliminary Proceedings Committee and make representations in relation to whether registration should be suspended or made conditional. At such a hearing, it is normal for the doctor to be legally represented. Any order that is made can run for up to a period of six months, and thereafter can be renewed for further periods of three months.

7.9.7   Function of the Professional Conduct Committee

The function of the Professional Conduct Committee is to protect the public and uphold the reputation of the medical profession. If, having had a matter referred to it, the Committee considers that the doctor's fitness to practise may be seriously impaired because of his physical or mental condition, it may refer that question to the Health Committee for determination. If the Health Committee does find that the doctor's fitness is seriously impaired, the Conduct Committee will then take no further action.

In relation to matters referred to it, arising out of a criminal conviction, the Professional Conduct Committee is bound to accept the fact of the conviction as conclusive evidence that the doctor was guilty of the offence of which he was convicted. As such, proceedings concerning convictions are concerned only to establish the gravity of the offence and take account of any mitigating circumstances. In cases relating to conduct allegations, unless they are actually admitted by the doctor, the allegation must be proved by evidence in the usual way. The function of the Committee is to determine whether, on the facts as presented to it by evidence, the doctor has been guilty of serious professional misconduct.

7.9.8   Powers of the Professional Conduct Committee

The Professional Conduct Committee may take any of the following courses:

(a)   postpone determination of the case; or

(b)   direct that the doctor's registration be made conditional upon such matters as the Committee may think fit to impose in order to protect members of the public or in the doctor's own interests. Conditional registration may take effect for a period not exceeding three years; or

(c)   direct that the doctor's registration be suspended for a period not exceeding 12 months; or

(d)   direct that the doctor's name be erased from the register.

An example of conditional registration might be that the doctor should not engage in a specified branch of medical practice, or should only practise in that practice under supervision, or should not prescribe or possess certain drugs, or should take steps to remedy deficiencies in his knowledge or clinical skills. If a doctor's registration is suspended, he ceases to be entitled to practise as a registered medical practitioner for that period. Erasure from the register will remain effective until the doctor makes an application for restoration to the register. An application cannot be made until at least 10 months has elapsed since the order took place.

7.9.9 Appeals

In cases of erasure from the register, or suspension or subjection to conditions, the doctor has 28 days in which to give notice of appeal against that order to the Judicial Committee of the Privy Council. During the intervening period, the doctor's registration is not affected unless the Professional Conduct Committee makes a separate order that the doctor's registration should be suspended forthwith. The Committee will do this if satisfied that it is necessary to do so for the protection of members of the public or is in the interests of the doctor concerned. There is a right of appeal against this order for immediate suspension to the High Court. The doctor may make an application for restoration to the register at any time after 10 months has elapsed since the order took effect. If this is unsuccessful, a further 10 months must elapse before a further application can be made. Further information regarding disciplinary procedures can be obtained from the Fitness to Practise Directorate at the GMC.

7.10 Disciplinary proceedings against the nursing profession

7.10.1 Statutory provisions

The Nursing and Midwifery Council (NMC) has replaced the United Kingdom Central Council for Nursing, Midwifery and Health Visiting (UKCC) as the regulatory body for nurses and midwives. The NMC's jurisdiction in relation to professional misconduct is contained in the Nursing and Midwifery Order 2001 (SI 2002/253) and replaces the regulatory framework provided by the Nurses, Midwives and Health Visitors Act 1997.

7.10.2 The Conduct and Competence Committee

The Conduct and Competence Committee is set up along very similar lines to the GMC Committees. In relation to criminal offences, for example, in the same way as for doctors, the police are required to notify the NMC of any registered nurse or midwife who has been convicted of a criminal offence.

7.10.3 Functions of the Nursing and Midwifery Council

The Nursing and Midwifery Order 2001 provides for the NMC to keep a register of qualified nurses and midwives and create four committees:

(a)   the Investigating Committee;

(b)   the Conduct and Competence Committee;

(c)   the Health Committee; and

(d)   the Midwifery Committee.

The NMC is under a duty to provide for the standards of conduct, performance and ethics expected of members and trainee members. The procedure for ensuring that the requisite standard is maintained is as follows.

7.10.4 Function of the Investigating Committee

Once an allegation has been made against a member to the effect that his fitness to practise is impaired due to:

(a)   misconduct;

(b)   lack of competence;

(c)   a conviction or caution;

(d)   physical or mental health; or

(e)   a different healthcare profession has already determined that he is unfit to practise,

then the NMC has a duty to investigate the matter. A preliminary investigation may be undertaken by investigators (termed 'screeners') and the Investigating Committee. Matters referred to the screeners must be considered by a panel of at least two of them. The panel should consist of at least one lay person and one registered person drawn from the same or similar field of expertise as the person under investigation. The function of the screeners is to consider the allegation and decide whether the allegation is well founded and whether the NMC has power to deal with it.

7.10.5 Powers of the Investigating Committee

Once it has considered the available evidence before it, the Investigating Committee may deal with the matter as follows:

(a)   it may close the case having taken no action;

(b)   it may refer the case to the Conduct and Competence Committee;

(c)   it may issue a formal caution;

(d)   if the complaint refers to unfitness to practise by reason of ill-health, it may refer the matter to the Health Committee.

The Investigating Committee may issue a caution where the facts, although proven, are admitted by the practitioner and there are mitigating circumstances which mean that removal from the register would not be appropriate. The caution is retained on the practitioners' register for five years and is automatically disclosed to potential employers.

If it appears that there is a case to answer, the matter will be considered further by the Conduct and Competence Committee.

7.10.6 Function of Conduct and Competence Committee

The Conduct and Competence Committee considers allegations of professional misconduct which are referred to it by the Investigating Committee. Each Committee consists of five council members. Conduct and Competence Committee meetings are held in public, and the Committee is advised by a lawyer who advises on points of law and admissibility of evidence. The practitioner is also usually represented, by his trade union or his nominated solicitor or barrister. The practitioner may apply for the hearing to be held in private, but this will be granted only if it is necessary to protect the anonymity of a patient whom, it is alleged, is the victim, or if disclosure of confidential medical information would be involved. The future reputation of the practitioner concerned will not justify the hearing being held in private.

7.10.7 Powers of the Conduct and Competence Committee

The Conduct and Competence Committee has the following powers. It may:

(a)   declare the facts of the case not proven and take no further action;

(b)   declare the facts proven and go on to rule that the facts do not constitute professional misconduct and take no further action; or

(c)   impose an interim suspension of registration if the hearing is adjourned.

If the facts are proved and misconduct is proven, the committee may:

(a)   issue a caution;

(b)   remove the practitioner from the register indefinitely;

(c)   remove the practitioner from the register for a specified period after which the practitioner may apply for his name to be restored to the register; or

(d)   refer the case to the Health Committee in cases of ill-health of the practitioner.

7.11   Conclusion

Healthcare providers are clearly making great efforts to ensure that complaints do not go unheard, and that patients are made aware of the relevant complaints and disciplinary procedures available. Solicitors have an important role to play, not only in ensuring that patients are aware of their rights, but also that healthcare professionals are adequately advised in relation to claims which may be made against them.

7.12   Further reading

Complaints: Listening, Acting, Improving (Department of Health, March 1996).

NHS Complaints reform – Making things right (Department of Health, 2003).

Duties of a Doctor (GMC).

www.gmc-uk.org

www.healthcarecommission.org.uk

www.chai.org.uk

7.13 NHS complaints procedure

LOCAL RESOLUTION

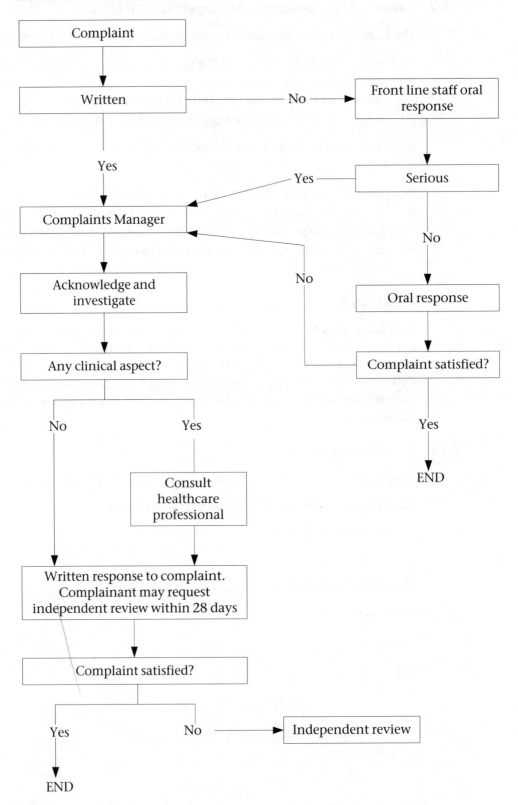

Chapter 8

Instructing Experts

8.1 Introduction

The personal injury or clinical negligence solicitor will usually instruct an expert in nearly every case. The obvious example of such an expert is a doctor who is instructed to prepare a report of the client's injuries suffered as a result of an accident at work. In a clinical negligence case, the appropriate doctors will provide a report not only on the injuries suffered as a result of the incident but also the standard of care provided/causation. The need to obtain appropriate medical evidence is vital.

While there are many different types of experts available to provide reports, the CPR 1998 are clear that expert evidence should be restricted to that which is necessary (Part 35 of the CPR 1998) and the parties should, if at all possible, co-operate in the selection of the expert.

It is clear that in each case a solicitor must consider if, and what type of, expert evidence is appropriate. In *Barings plc and Another v Coopers and Lybrand and Others*, 9 February 2001, the court held that expert evidence can be excluded if the court concludes that such evidence would not be helpful in resolving any issue in the case (see also *Regan v Chetwynd* (2001) JPIL 2/01).

It should be noted that from June 2005 there is a protocol for the instruction of experts to give evidence in the civil courts. There is also a revised code of practice for experts, which replaces the previous advice given by the Academy of Experts and the Expert Witness Institute. The protocol replaces the existing codes of guidance for expert witnesses. The code of practice is based on the EuroExpert Code published in 2001. Copies of the code of practice are available from the website of both the Academy of Experts at www.academy-experts.org and the Expert Witness Institute at www.ewi.org.uk

The protocol gives clear guidance to experts and to those instructing them in the interpretation of and compliance with Part 35 CPR and its Practice Direction. The protocol emphasises that the expert has an overriding duty to the court on matters within their expertise. It stresses that the expert's duty is to be independent and offers a 'test' for independence as being: 'would the expert express the same opinion if given the same instructions by an opposing party'. It sets out clear guidance on the matters to be covered in the instructions to experts as well as guidance to experts on the contents of their report for litigation purposes. It stresses that a summary of conclusions is a mandatory requirement with full reasons in support. This should prove useful to instructing solicitors in ensuring that the quality of reports is all that it should be.

8.2   Who is an expert?

An expert must be someone with an area of expertise which is likely to be outside the experience and knowledge of a judge and who can supply the court with objective criteria. This evidence should be presented in a clear and concise way so that the judge can use the information to reach his own conclusions. There is no requirement to accept the expert evidence (see *Armstrong and Another v First York Ltd* (2005) *The Times*, 19 January).

8.3   How to find an expert

In considering who to choose to deal with the case, the solicitor responsible must instruct the correct person. This is a vital point to note.

Many firms will have their own in-house directory of experts, which should be referred to in the first instance. Frequently, other fee earners will have inserted comments about the expert alongside the entry in the directory. Information, such as how well the expert gave evidence in court, can be vital.

8.3.1   Personal injury cases

If an in-house directory of experts is not available or is inappropriate then other sources can be used. The following sources may be of use.

(a)   The Association of Personal Injury Lawyers. This organisation provides information to members on appropriate experts.

(b)   A barrister who also practises in the personal injury/clinical negligence field may be able to assist in the choice of expert.

(c)   A search through the appropriate law reports will often reveal the name of the person who appeared as a witness in a particular case. It may be possible to approach that person directly. As an alternative, the firm of solicitors named in the report can be contacted and may offer assistance in providing the name of the relevant expert.

(d)   The Academy of Expert Witnesses.

(e)   The Society of Expert Witnesses.

(f)   Expert Witness Institute.

(g)   The *New Law Journal* and *Solicitor's Journal* regularly issue expert witness supplements which carry advertisements from experts who are prepared to provide reports for the purposes of litigation.

(h)   Many professional institutes also prepare a directory of expert witnesses.

(i)   The Medico-Legal Society publishes reports which may reveal the name of a suitable expert.

While it is possible to select an expert from one of the sources referred to above, it is important to appreciate that it is the solicitor's responsibility to choose the correct expert for his client's case.

8.3.2   Clinical negligence cases

The above sources may be useful for clinical negligence claims but, in addition, AvMA – Action against Medical Accidents – provides a very useful experts' database. The aim of this service is to provide solicitors with information for the assistance of victims of clinical negligence.

8.4   Key qualities to look for in an expert

A number of key qualities must be looked for when selecting an expert:

(a)   Is the person appropriately qualified to deal with the matter and does he have the relevant practical experience in the area?

(b)   Does the expert have experience in litigation of this type? Does he prepare reports and attend at trial regularly to give evidence? Only a small percentage of cases proceed to trial, and thus an expert may claim to have been involved in, say, 200 cases but may only have given evidence in a few of those cases (especially as, in the fast track, expert evidence is normally given in written form). It cannot be assumed that the case will settle and, however good the written report might be, convincing oral testimony (where allowed by the court) and the ability to withstand tough cross-examination is essential. The expert's general reputation should be checked with his colleagues who practise in the same area.

(c)   Does the expert have sufficient time to deal with the case properly? A good expert will refuse instructions when he has insufficient time, but this is not always the case. Whether the case is a personal injury or clinical negligence claim, the expert will have to spend considerable time examining the papers and the subject-matter of the claim.

(d)   Can the doctor provide a clear and comprehensive report?

(e)   Can the expert be regarded as impartial (see *Liverpool Roman Catholic Archdiocesan Trust v Goldberg* [2001] Lloyd's Rep PN 518).

8.5   Joint selection of experts

The CPR 1998 and the pre-action protocols require the court to exert control over the use of experts in personal injury and clinical negligence cases. The aim is to try and create a less 'confrontational' approach between experts and joint selection by both parties is encouraged by the CPR 1998. In an attempt to do this, the personal injury pre-action protocol makes reference to:

(a)   the claimant exchanging experts' names prior to instruction of the expert;

(b)   the claimant's solicitor obtaining the medical notes;

(c)   if the defendant objects to the suggested expert (which he should do within 14 days of receipt of the list of proposed experts from the claimant's solicitor), then attempts should be made to instruct an expert upon whom both parties can agree;

(d)   if an expert cannot be agreed on, then, if the defendant instructs his own expert, the court will look at this decision with care to see if it was reasonable or otherwise upon the issuing of proceedings;

(e)   if an expert is agreed upon, either party may send to the expert written questions, via the instructing solicitor. The expert should send answers to the questions to each party. The pre-action protocol confirms that the report produced is not a joint report for the purposes of Part 35 of the CPR (see also *Carlson v Townsend* [2001] EWCA Civ 511, [2001] 1 WLR 2415).

The clinical negligence pre-action protocol also emphasises the importance of the selection/instruction of experts and the need to balance each party's desire to obtain the appropriate expert evidence, with the 'overriding objective' of the CPR 1998. However, the clinical negligence protocol is less prescriptive in respect of experts than the personal injury protocol.

8.6 Particular matters relating to instructing experts in personal injury claims

In personal injury cases, the most frequently employed experts are doctors, who are employed to prepare reports on the claimant's injuries. Consulting engineers may be used in appropriate cases, to prepare reports on machinery or systems of work, and accident reconstruction experts are sometimes instructed in road traffic accidents.

8.6.1 The doctor

The importance of instructing a doctor who works in the appropriate speciality that relates to the client's case should not be underestimated, and the trainee solicitor should seek assistance from a senior colleague where appropriate, if he is uncertain as to which doctor to instruct.

8.6.1.1 Letter of instruction

Reference should be made to the pre-action protocol which sets out a specimen letter of instruction to a medical expert in a personal injury case (see **Appendix 3**).

The heading of the letter should contain: the client's full name, address, date of birth, date of the accident, his telephone number and, if considered appropriate, details of the hospital where the client was treated. It is important that the letter of instruction makes it clear on whose behalf the solicitor is acting, if the notice of appointment is to be sent directly to the client or if the appointment is to be sent via the solicitor. The doctor will need to obtain the notes from the hospital/GP where the client was treated and for this purpose a written authority for the release of his medical records will need to be obtained from the client and sent to the hospital/GP. It is not normally necessary to ask the doctor to examine all of the client's medical notes, but if there is any possibility that the injury could be due to pre-existing problems then such a request should be made (see *Bennett v Compass Group Ltd and Others* [2002] EWCA Civ 642, [2002] ICR 1177, concerning the release of GP and hospital records).

A number of specific questions relating to the injury should be asked. For example, what is the prognosis, capacity for work, and what are the likely long-term effects of the injuries?

It may be thought appropriate to ask for the doctor's opinion as to whether any other medical opinion is needed from other specialists. For example, an orthopaedic surgeon may suggest that the opinion of a radiologist is required.

If medical notes are forwarded to the doctor, every attempt should be made by the solicitor to understand what they mean as they may be vital evidence. The doctor who has been instructed may be able to assist, but the personal injury solicitor must become fully familiar with the abbreviations and symbols used by the medical profession.

It can take many months for an appointment to be made with the client and for the report to be returned to the instructing solicitor and thus the letter of instruction should include the estimate as to when the solicitor might receive the report and an invitation for the expert to contact the solicitor if the expert cannot prepare the report in the appropriate time. Once the report has been received, it should be read (and understood) by the solicitor and sent to the client for his approval.

As noted above, it is possible to send to the expert written questions and, in the case of *Mutch v Allen* [2001] EWCA Civ 76, (2001) LTL, 24 January, the Court of Appeal held that further written questions could be put to an opponent's expert to enable clarification of points not included in the expert's report, provided the questions were within the area of expert's expertise.

8.6.2 Consulting engineers' reports

Many personal injury claims involve machinery or systems of work (especially employers' liability claims) and in such cases it may be thought appropriate for a consulting engineer to be instructed to prepare a report on the machinery involved or the system of work undertaken.

Example

A client is injured while driving a fork-lift truck and alleges that the steering wheel failed to respond while he was driving it. It is part of the client's case that the employer failed adequately to maintain the fork-lift truck. If the truck has not been modified prior to the solicitor being instructed, a consulting engineer may be instructed to examine the vehicle and its maintenance records. The solicitor will therefore obtain an expert's view as to whether the appropriate system of maintenance was adopted and attempt to identify the cause of the accident.

Once a choice of consulting engineer has been made, a letter of instruction should be sent to him. Clear instructions should be given as to who is instructing the engineer and what the engineer is being instructed to do, ie, visit the premises, inspect the machinery and prepare a report for use in connection with court proceedings. If the solicitor is to attend the inspection, this should be made clear in the letter of instruction. Details of who the expert should contact to arrange a date for the inspection must also be given. Permission from the employers (who are normally the defendants in such cases) is required. If this is not granted then it will be necessary to apply to court for an order granting inspection facilities.

Frequently consulting engineers hold joint inspections, where both the claimant's and defendant's engineers attend at the scene of the accident at the same time. This has the advantage of saving costs and time, as the engineers can agree on measurements and technical details. However, while it may, in certain cases, still be appropriate to instruct two engineers, the pre-action protocol also makes reference to the joint selection of and instruction of liability experts such as consulting engineers, and thus consideration must be given to this important point.

8.6.3 Accident reconstruction experts

In more complicated road traffic cases, an accident reconstruction expert may need to be instructed. Normally, the accident reconstruction expert will attend at the scene of the accident and examine any skid marks, etc and will also consider such evidence as tachographs, if available. He will then provide an opinion as to the cause of the accident. Normally, such experts are instructed only in serious cases such as fatal road accidents and it is important that as much information as possible is obtained surrounding the events of the accident, so that the expert has full details available to him at the time the report is prepared. Frequently, the expert will want to see the police reconstruction report (if one has been prepared) and attempts must be made to obtain this as soon as possible. The appropriate police force should be contacted and a request made for the relevant documentation to be preserved.

In many cases, it is also appropriate for the expert to examine the vehicles involved in the accident and if the client has instructed the solicitor at an early stage, action must be taken to ensure that the vehicles are not disposed of or repaired prior to the expert carrying out his examination.

8.6.4   Joint instruction/joint selection

The distinction should be noted between the joint selection of an expert (as detailed by the protocol) and the joint instruction of an expert. As regards the latter, the expert can be regarded as instructed by both parties and any report would be sent to both parties once it had been prepared.

8.7   Particular matters relating to instructing experts in clinical negligence claims

The choice of expert in a clinical negligence case can be more complex than in a personal injury case. In clinical negligence cases, experts' reports can be divided into three areas.

(a)   *Reports on liability.* A doctor reviews the case and provides a report as to whether the appropriate standard of medical care has been achieved.

(b)   *Reports on causation.* A doctor reviews the case and provides an opinion as to whether the failure to act with the appropriate standard of care (if established) caused the injury.

   In certain clinical negligence cases, one doctor may be able to provide one report on both liability and causation, but whether this is appropriate will be dependent on the type of case concerned.

(c)   *Reports on quantum.* A doctor provides a report on the claimant's current and future medical condition.

In most cases, the solicitor will have no idea as to whether or not there is a case to be pursued until the first report on liability from the expert has been obtained.

It is necessary to instruct an expert in a similar speciality to that which is alleged to have given rise to the negligence. For example, if a doctor is working in accident and emergency medicine and is alleged to have been negligent, then a consultant in accident and emergency medicine should be instructed. In certain cases, there will be allegations relating to different specialities and an expert in each speciality will be required.

8.7.1   Choice of experts

Some doctors may be reluctant to provide reports for clinical negligence litigation and the views of the proposed expert must be obtained. Enquiries must also be made as to whether the doctor who is alleged to have been negligent is known to the expert preparing the report as, clearly, this may affect the contents of the report. It may also be appropriate to ensure that the expert is kept informed of who is continuing to treat the client, in case the expert knows any of the other doctors involved and does not believe that he is the appropriate person to report on the matter.

Even if the expert has been used by the solicitor before, in all clinical negligence cases it is good practice to send a preliminary letter of enquiry. Such a letter may have any of the following objectives:

(a)   to obtain confirmation that the expert deals with the appropriate speciality;

(b)   to obtain confirmation that the expert is prepared to carry out the necessary post-initial report work such as attending conference with counsel and attending experts' meetings;

(c)   to confirm that he would be willing to provide oral evidence to support his written report;

(d)   to inform the expert of the identity of the potential defendant (to establish whether the doctor is known to the expert or has worked with him in the past);

(e)   to confirm that the medical notes have been obtained (however, they must not be forwarded to the expert at this stage);

(f)   to obtain details of the likely waiting time for the report;

(g)   to obtain details of the expert's charging rate and/or to explain that the client has the benefit of public funding;

(h)   to confirm on whose behalf the solicitor is acting (but without giving any view on liability).

To avoid instructing an expert who knows the potential defendant, it is appropriate to instruct an expert out of the locality where the alleged negligent act took place.

If the expert is prepared to act in response to an initial letter of enquiry, then a full letter of instruction should be sent. It is vital that the expert has access to all medical notes prior to preparing his report (indeed, one of the points that should be raised with the expert is whether all of the necessary medical reports have been disclosed by the relevant hospital or GP). The medical notes must not be sent to the expert without first being checked by the solicitor to ensure that they are complete and in order. Identical ring binders should be prepared, with copies of paginated medical notes included, in date order, indexed and divided into relevant sections. A ring binder of notes should be prepared for each expert, counsel and the solicitor.

The full letter of instruction may include the following matters (to be amended if an expert is jointly instructed/selected):

(a)   a chronology of the events/factual resumé to which the expert can refer. A concise overview of the events should be available for the expert to consider;

(b)   a brief explanation of the relevant standard of care;

(c)   liability/causation – it will be necessary to remind the expert that there is a need to establish a causational link between the identified negligence and injury;

(d)   to provide an offer to meet the claimant, which may not be necessary but the facility should be made available;

(e)   the date by which the report is needed;

(f)   who is responsible for the fee;

(g)   a request that the expert consider whether all the relevant medical notes have been disclosed and, if not, what further notes should be obtained;

(h)   to obtain the expert's confirmation as to whether any other type of expert evidence is required in addition to his own;

(i)   the expert should be asked to make reference to medical publications to support his case. It is important to remember that the doctor who is alleged to have been negligent would not have had access to textbooks published in 2006, if the alleged incident occurred, for example, in 1990. The expert should be asked to refer to texts and authoritative works that were available at the time of the incident (see *Breeze v Ahmed* [2005] EWCA Civ 223);

(j)   specific questions that the expert is required to answer should be included in the letter of instruction. The expert should also be informed that he may be required to attend a conference with counsel at the appropriate time;

(k)   specify how the doctor should structure the report.

In the case of *Sharpe v Southend Health Authority* [1997] 8 Med LR 299, the Court of Appeal stated that an expert in a clinical negligence case should make it clear in his report that, even if the expert would have adopted a different approach, he should state whether the approach adopted by the defendant was in accordance with a responsible body of medical practitioners. If it is not known that the expert is aware of this point, then this must also be mentioned in the letter of instruction.

There have been several cases relating to the number of experts to be allowed and, in *S v A Health Authority* (2003) LTL, 25 July, the court emphasised the importance of an 'equal footing' of medical experts in clinical negligence cases and allowed the claimant's appeal for an increased number of medical experts (see also *ES (By Her Mother and Litigation Friend DS) v Chesterfield & Derbyshire Royal Hospital NHS Trust* [2003] EWCA Civ 1284).

8.7.2   Joint instruction/joint selection

In a clinical negligence case, solicitors may be more willing jointly to instruct/ select an expert in relation to quantum matters, such as future care costs, rather than in relation to liability and/or causation (see *S (A Minor) v Birmingham Health Authority* (1999) LTL, 23 November and *Daniels v Walker* [2000] 1 WLR 1382 concerning difficulties in agreeing instructions to joint experts). However, each case must be considered on its own merits. For example, in the case of *Oxley v Penwarden* (2000) MLC 0250, the Court of Appeal, in dealing with a clinical negligence claim, held:

> This was eminently a case where it was necessary for the parties to have the opportunity of investigating causation through an expert of his own choice ...

Thus, the joint instruction of an expert can be challenged where appropriate. Similarly, on occasions, despite a single joint expert being appointed under r 35.7 of the CPR 1998, the court may grant an application by a litigant to call his own expert witness (see *Cosgrove and Another v Pattison and Another* (2001) *The Times*, 13 February; *Alderson and Another v Stillorgan Sales Ltd and Another* [2001] All ER (D) 104 (June) and *Peet v Mid-Kent Healthcare Trust Practice Note* [2001] EWCA Civ 1703, [2002] 1 WLR 210).

In practice, there can be disputes as to the status of any instructions to joint experts. However, in the Court of Appeal case, *Yorke v Katra* [2003] EWCA Civ 867, (2003) LTL, 9 June, it was held that there was no obligation that a party should be bound by the instructions to a joint expert given by his opponent.

8.8   Use of experts' reports

As noted earlier, a key aim of the CPR 1998 is to attempt to encourage a less confrontational approach by the parties (especially as regards experts) and to reinforce the principle that the expert's primary duty is to the court (see also *National Justice Compania Naviera SA v Prudential Assurance Co (Ikerian Reefer)* [1993] 2 Lloyd's Rep 68, which is a pre-CPR 1998 case subsequently referred to, setting out the responsibilities of an expert).

In order to achieve these aims, Part 35 and the accompanying Practice Directions make reference to several requirements regarding expert evidence, including the following:

(a)   The duty to the court is the primary duty with which the expert should be concerned (see, for example, *Re Colt Telecom Group plc* [2002] EWHC 2815 (Ch), [2002] All ER (D) 347 (Dec)).

(b)   No expert evidence shall be used without leave of the court and details of the speciality and, if possible, the name of the expert should be provided.

(c)   In fast track cases, expert evidence will normally be given in written form and it will not be necessary for the expert to attend.

(d)   The expert's report must contain a statement that he understands and has complied with his primary duty to the court.

(e)   The expert's report must contain a statement of the substance of the instructions given to the expert. It should be noted that r 35.10(4) specifically states that the instructions are not privileged, but the court will not normally allow cross-examination of the expert on the instructions, unless it believes the statement is inaccurate (see also *Lucas v Barking, Havering and Redbridge Hospitals NHS Trust* [2003] EWCA Civ 1102, [2003] All ER (D) 379 (Jul)).

(f)   The expert may apply to the court himself for directions without reference to the parties.

(g)   The report should give details of the expert's qualifications.

(h)   The report should give details of any literature relied upon.

(i)   The report must be verified by a statement of truth.

In addition to the specific points set out above, there is also a general power (see r 32.1) which allows the court to identify the key issues and detail what evidence is required, and in what form (see also *Daniels v Walker* [2000] 1 WLR 1382 in relation to difficulties which may be encountered with jointly instructed experts). Other relevant recent cases include:

(a)   *Jackson v Davenport* [2004] EWCA 1225 in relation to the disclosure of draft reports;

(b)   *Nicos Hajigeorgian v Vassos Vasiliou* [2005] EWCA Civ 236 regarding a party's entitlement to instruct alternative experts and the status of earlier reports; and

(c)   *Phillips and Others v Symes and Others* (2004) Law Society Gazette, 18 November regarding cost penalties for experts who cause significant expenses.

8.9   Conference with experts and counsel where expert instructed by one party

8.9.1   The initial conference prior to proceedings being issued

8.9.1.1   Personal injury

An initial conference prior to proceedings being issued is not normally necessary in personal injury cases, but consideration should be given to this approach if the claimant is resistant to the solicitor's advice that the claim is likely to fail or if the matter is unusually complicated.

8.9.1.2   Clinical negligence

In clinical negligence cases, because the issues involved are likely to be complex, it may be appropriate to arrange a conference with the expert, counsel and the client after the initial medical report has been obtained. By this stage, full details of the claimant's claim should be available, together with the medical records and the expert's report. This will give the parties the opportunity to examine fully all the issues, and for the solicitor and counsel to test the expert's evidence and to ensure that he is the appropriate person to be instructed. It also provides an opportunity to assess the merits of the claim to see if proceedings should be issued. An initial conference at this stage is also appropriate when the medical report is unfavourable and it appears that the claim should not proceed.

The conference provides a valuable opportunity to satisfy the client that every possibility has been investigated and that he is not being ignored and there is no medical conspiracy against him. Consideration should be given to instructing counsel to produce a written advice following the conference, to ensure that all matters have been dealt with. During the conference, a detailed note should be taken of matters covered.

If the case is going to proceed, the next stage is the drafting of the letter of claim which is to be sent to the potential defendant.

8.9.2   Conference with counsel after proceedings issued

8.9.2.1   Personal injury

In the vast majority of personal injury cases, proceedings will be issued without the need for a conference with counsel, and many low-value cases proceed to trial without such a conference. In more complex personal injury cases, there may be a conference which will allow an assessment of the expert's knowledge of the case. The solicitor and counsel will want to be sure that the expert has studied all the papers sent to him, has understood the facts of the case, and that he has excellent communication skills. These and other matters can be assessed at the conference.

8.9.2.2   Clinical negligence

In addition to the conference prior to the issue of proceedings in a clinical negligence case, it is common to have a further conference after the exchange of lay witness statements to check whether all the experts can still support the case. A further conference is normally arranged prior to the trial to review matters.

8.10   Meeting of experts

Under the CPR 1998, the court has the power to order a meeting of the experts involved in the case and, where both parties have their own experts, this is often ordered by the court. The aim is to identify the issues that are truly in dispute and, where appropriate, to prepare a joint statement which highlights the evidence which is and which is not disputed. Certain commentators believe that these meetings (they can be done by telephone) can be of significant benefit in attempting either to resolve the case or at least identify the true issues in dispute (see *Hubbard and Others v Lambeth, Southwark and Lewisham Health Authority* [2001] EWCA Civ 1455, [2002] PIQR P14).

8.11 Types of experts

The number and variety of experts available to prepare reports is often a surprise to those unfamiliar with this area. The following are examples of experts who provide reports.

Liability – employer/public liability cases:

(a) general consulting engineers to provide reports on machinery, systems of work, slipping accidents;

(b) mining engineers;

(c) ergonomics experts;

(d) bio-engineers;

(e) pharmacologists.

Liability – road traffic accidents:

(a) accident investigators to reconstruct the events leading up to the road traffic accident;

(b) mechanical engineers to examine the vehicles involved in the accident, to identify damage or to investigate if any mechanical defects were present in the vehicle.

Liability/causation in clinical negligence cases and condition and prognosis in both clinical negligence and personal injury cases – medical specialities:

(a) orthopaedic surgeons;

(b) neurologists;

(c) psychiatrists;

(d) plastic surgeons;

(e) dental surgeons;

(f) psychologists;

(g) neuro-surgeons;

(h) oncologists;

(i) urologists;

(j) obstetricians;

(k) otorhinolaryngologists.

Quantum – condition and prognosis and costs of living with a particular injury:

(a) occupational therapists;

(b) behaviourial therapists;

(c) speech therapists;

(d) physiotherapists;

(e) employment consultants;

(f) doctors;

(g)   nurses.

Quantum – financial loss and investment of damages:

(a)   employment consultants;

(b)   accountants;

(c)   actuaries.

8.12 The role of clinical case manager

In certain high value/severe injury cases, a clinical case manager may be appointed to consider the claimant's appropriate care regime. In *Wright (by her litigation friend Karen Fay) v Kevin Sullivan* [2005] EWCA Civ 656, it was held that the clinical case manager would owe a duty to the claimant to work in his the best interests. If they gave evidence then it would be as a witness of fact.

8.13 Conclusion

The role that the expert has in a personal injury or clinical negligence case is a significant one. The importance of the selection of the correct individual cannot be underestimated.

8.14 Further reading

Kemp and Kemp, *The Quantum of Damages* (Sweet & Maxwell).

Pre-action Protocol for Personal Injury Claims.

Pre-action Protocol for the Resolution of Clinical Disputes.

8.15 Key points

Expert evidence	Will be restricted to that which is necessary and permission of the court is always required either to call an expert or use an expert's report
How to find an expert	In-house directory. Recommendation. Organisations: APIL/AvMA
Qualities of an expert	Important to pick the correct expert – experience, time, cost and availability
Who instructs?	Note: CPR 1998, Part 35 Joint instruction/selection – obligations under personal injury pre-action protocol. See example letter of instruction
Clinical negligence	More complex. Report on liability, report on causation/report on quantum. Need to be of correct speciality and status
CPR 1998 requirements	Reports need to contain certain specified points. See Part 35 and relevant PDs

Chapter 9

Pre-commencement and Commencement Steps

9.1 Introduction

9.1.1 Reasons for and against commencing proceedings early

It is usually to the claimant's advantage to begin proceedings early for the following reasons.

(a) Once the claimant has complied with the provisions of the relevant pre-action protocol (normally three months from the date of acknowledgement of the letter of claim), he is free to issue and serve the proceedings without sanctions being applied at a later date by the court on the basis that proceedings have been issued prematurely.

(b) To avoid problems with the limitation period. In personal injury litigation, proceedings must normally be commenced within three years of the accident occurring; ongoing negotiations with the proposed defendant/defendant's insurers do not have the automatic effect of extending the limitation period and, in any event, negotiations may continue after proceedings have been commenced.

(c) It will put pressure on the defendant/defendant's insurers to act in relation to the claim. In personal injury cases, it will often precipitate the defendant's file moving from the insurance company claims department to the insurer's nominated solicitors who may be more willing to negotiate.

(d) In practice, judgment usually carries entitlement to interest and costs. A settlement achieved prior to the commencement of proceedings does not carry such an entitlement (although the claimant's solicitor will always include in any such settlement an element in respect of interest and costs). After proceedings have been issued, if there is any argument by the defendant as to how much of the claimant's costs he should pay on settlement, the claimant's solicitor can have his costs assessed by the court.

(e) Commencing proceedings enables the claimant to apply to the court for an interim payment in the event that a voluntary payment cannot be negotiated.

It may not be advisable to commence proceedings in the following circumstances, which are usually beyond the control of the solicitor.

(a) The claimant is obliged to comply with the relevant pre-action protocol requiring that a detailed letter of claim be forwarded to the proposed defendant, followed by a waiting period of not less than three months.

(b)   The solicitor may not be in a position to issue proceedings because of a restriction on the client's certificate issued under the CLS Funding Code, or because of a similar restriction in relation to the client's private legal expenses insurance requiring specific authority to be granted prior to issue of proceedings.

(c)   The client may be waiting for an appointment to be medically examined in order to provide the medical report which must be filed at court on issue of proceedings.

(d)   If the amount of claim for pain, suffering and loss of amenity is not more than £1,000 and the overall value of the claim is not more than £5,000, it will be allocated to the small claims track, in which case only very limited costs can be recovered.

9.2   Pre-action protocol to be used in personal injury claims

9.2.1   Introduction

In his final report on *Access to Justice,* Lord Woolf placed emphasis on the development of what he termed pre-action protocols. He wished to 'increase the benefits of early but well informed settlement'. The aim of the protocols is to help the parties to make an informed decision on the merits of the case and lead to an increased number of pre-action settlements. This will be achieved by encouraging pre-action dialogue between the parties, exchanging better quality information and by better pre-action investigation. The net result of this will be two-fold: either a reduction in the need for recourse to litigation, or that subsequent proceedings will run more smoothly.

9.2.2   Information about funding arrangements

The Practice Direction to the protocols emphasises the requirement for potential litigants to inform their potential opponent of the existence of a funding arrangement (ie, a conditional fee agreement) within the meaning of r 43.2(1)(k). This is of particular significance as r 44.3B(1)(c) provides that a party may not recover any additional liability (ie, success fee) for any period in the proceedings during which he failed to provide information about a funding arrangement in accordance with a rule, practice direction or court order.

In order to ensure that the protocols have their desired effect, it is necessary that they be supported by sanctions for non-compliance. According to the Practice Direction to the pre-action protocols the courts will treat the standards set down in the protocols as the reasonable approach to be expected in pre-action conduct. The court has power to ensure compliance with the protocol by means of costs penalties. If the court decides that non-compliance has led to commencement of proceedings which could have been avoided with use of the protocol, or costs have been incurred needlessly, the court may penalise the party at fault in costs. The party at fault may be ordered to:

(a)   pay the costs/part costs of the other party;

(b)   pay costs on the indemnity basis;

(c)   if he is a claimant he may be penalised by not being awarded interest on all or part of the award, or interest at a lower rate;

(d)   if the party at fault is a defendant, an order for interest on damages may be awarded at a higher rate (not exceeding 10% above base rate).

There are pre-action protocols for different types of claims:

(a)   the protocol for use in personal injury claims;

(b)   the protocol for use in clinical disputes;

(c)   the protocol for disease and illness claims.

9.2.3   The protocol for use in personal injury claims

Note that this protocol was revised in March 2005, and is set out in full at **Appendix 3**.

This protocol is designed for use in:

(a)   road traffic cases;

(b)   tripping and slipping cases; and

(c)   employers' liability cases.

Because most of these cases are very likely to be allocated to the fast track, it is important that as many preliminary issues as possible are dealt with at the pre-commencement stage. This will be especially important for the defendant, who traditionally has had less time to prepare his case. However, the court will expect that in multi-track cases, the spirit if not the letter of the protocol should be adhered to as the standard of reasonable pre-action behaviour (see *Carlson v Townsend* [2001] EWCA Civ 511, [2001] 1 WLR 2415). If one or both parties consider that the protocol is not appropriate to their case, the court will expect an explanation as to why the protocol has not been followed.

9.2.4   The letter of claim

The letter of claim is most commonly sent to the proposed defendant, who will be an individual. The function of the letter of claim is to ensure that the insurer is involved at the earliest possible date and therefore stresses the importance of passing on the letter of claim to the relevant insurer. If the claimant's solicitor is not yet able to formulate a letter of claim, he may still notify the defendant or his insurer of the claim before sending a detailed letter of claim. This may be used where the defendant is unaware, or has little knowledge of the incident.

The letter of claim should contain the following:

(a)   a clear summary of the facts on which the claim is based;

(b)   an indication of the nature of all of the injuries that have been sustained; and

(c)   an indication of other financial losses.

The letter should contain enough information to enable the defendant or his solicitor to investigate the proposed claim, and put a broad valuation on the claim.

The letter should also ask the defendant to pass a copy of the letter of claim to his insurer. However, if the insurer is known, a copy of the letter of claim should also be sent to the insurer direct. Once the letter has been sent, no further investigations into liability should be conducted until a response is received.

The pre-action protocol does not currently require information about how the claim is being funded to be included in the letter of claim. It is, however, recommended that this information be given at the earliest opportunity as it is required to be given by notice with the claim form on issue of proceedings. The sooner the opposition is on notice that there is a CFA with a success fee in place, the more likely it is that there will not be a problem arguing for recovery of the success fee when an assessment of costs and success fee takes place at the conclusion of the proceedings.

Such a letter of claim is reproduced in Annexe A in **Appendix 3**.

9.2.5   The response by the defendant

The defendant should be asked to reply to the letter of claim within 21 calendar days of the date of posting, confirming the identity of his insurer, if he has one. If the defendant fails to reply within 21 days and there is no response from his insurer within the same period, then the claimant may commence proceedings.

If the defendant or his insurers do respond to the letter of claim within 21 days, they have a maximum of three months from the date of acknowledgement of claim to investigate the claim. Within that time, they must reply to the claimant, confirming whether or not they admit liability. If liability is denied, then they must give reasons for the denial. If liability is admitted, the defendant is bound by that admission for all claims up to a value of £15,000.

9.2.6   Early disclosure of documents

Disclosure of documents by the defendant is designed to clarify and resolve the issues in dispute. Either within the letter of claim, or appended to it, the claimant's solicitor can forward a list of possible documents which he considers to be relevant and which he considers the defendant ought to have in his possession. If the defendant responds to the letter of claim with a denial of liability, he should include in his reply all documents which are material to the issues between the parties and which would be likely to be ordered to be disclosed by the court. Lists of likely documents to be disclosed are reproduced at Annexe B in **Appendix 3**.

If the defendant admits liability but alleges contributory negligence on the part of the claimant, the defendant should disclose documents which are still relevant to the issue of contributory negligence.

9.2.7   Documents to be produced by the claimant

A schedule of special damages with supporting documents should be produced by the claimant for use by the defendant.

9.2.8   Selection of experts

Because, at this stage, there are no proceedings, the protocol does not require joint instruction of experts as set out in Part 35 of CPR 1998. At this stage, the instructing party only will be sent the report. The instructing party will then decide whether or not to disclose the report. If he wishes to rely on it, he discloses it to the defendant who, if he agrees with it, will not then obtain his own report. It should be noted that, in *Carlson v Townsend* [2001] EWCA Civ 511, [2001] 1 WLR 2415, the Court of Appeal confirmed that the protocol encouraged voluntary disclosure of the claimant's expert reports. However, the protocol did not require disclosure and therefore the claimant's withholding the report did not constitute non-compliance with the protocol. The defendant's non-objection to the claimant's choice of expert did not transform that expert into a single joint expert. Therefore, the report subsequently produced would not be available to the defendant as of right and the claimant could claim privilege for it.

The defendant may, after proceedings have been commenced, if he thinks that it is necessary, obtain his own report, with permission of the court. It should be borne in mind that if more than one report is prepared, the court will have to decide whether or not to allow the costs of more than one report.

Prior to instructing an expert, the claimant should give the defendant a list of names of one, or preferably more, experts within the same speciality, any of whom he considers suitable to instruct.

Within 14 days, the defendant may object to one or more of the experts proposed by the claimant. The claimant will then instruct one of the mutually acceptable experts.

If the claimant nominates his expert in the letter of claim, the defendant has 14 days to object *after* the period of 21 days within which he has to reply to the letter of claim.

If the defendant objects to all of the experts proposed by the claimant, both parties are then at liberty to instruct the expert of their own choice. If more than one expert is instructed in this way, the court must decide subsequently whether either party has acted unreasonably as to the question of recovering the costs of more than one report.

The reason for seeking the defendant's approval to the claimant's expert is that if the defendant does not object to the claimant's nominated expert he is not entitled to rely on his own evidence in the same speciality unless:

(a)   the claimant agrees;

(b)   the court so directs; or

(b)   the claimant's expert's report has been amended and the claimant is not prepared to disclose the original report.

The same reasoning will apply where it is the defendant who wishes to instruct an expert of a particular specialism and provides a list of experts to the claimant for him to agree or disagree as the case may be.

Subsequent to the expert's report having been received, either party may ask the expert to answer written questions on relevant issues via the instructing party's solicitors. The expert should then send written answers to those questions both separately and directly to each of the parties.

9.2.9   Part 36 offers

The protocol advises (para 3.21) that both parties should always bear in mind whether it is appropriate to make a Part 36 offer prior to investigating proceedings.

If a claim is not resolved at protocol stage, the parties are encouraged to 'stocktake' by considering the issues in dispute and the evidence necessary before the court will be able to decide those issues. If the defendant is insured, the insurer will normally be expected to nominate solicitors at that stage, and should do so 7–14 days prior to the intended issue date.

9.3   Pre-action protocol to be used in clinical disputes (clinical negligence)

9.3.1   Introduction

The pre-action protocol for resolution of clinical disputes is aimed at improving the pre-action communication between the parties at the earliest possible date. The protocol itself establishes a timetable for exchange of key information relevant to the dispute and provides templates for the documents to be used by both sides. The protocol has been prepared by the Clinical Disputes Forum. The Forum includes healthcare professionals, NHS management, lawyers specialising in clinical claims working for both claimant and defendant and experts. In relation to penalties for non-compliance with a protocol, the court may refuse to grant extensions of time for filing statements of case or evidence, or award or disallow costs where proceedings have been issued prematurely.

The protocol encourages a climate of openness when something has 'gone wrong' with a patient's treatment. It recommends a timed sequence of steps for claimants and healthcare providers to follow if a dispute arises. The trend in relation to healthcare disputes is that the number of complaints and subsequent litigation is on the increase, and that this trend is likely to continue as more and more patients become likely to complain about treatment and to embark subsequently on litigation. Currently, the period of delay between a suspicion by the patient that 'something has gone wrong' and receiving a response from the healthcare provider merely serves for those suspicions to take root, and for there to be reluctance of healthcare providers to reveal details to patients, especially if there has been an adverse outcome (but not necessarily as a result of negligence).

9.3.2 The protocol for use in clinical disputes

In his report on *Access to Justice,* Lord Woolf recommended that patients, their advisers and healthcare providers should work towards resolution of disputes without recourse to litigation if possible. The clinical disputes protocol works towards this by standardising not only the timetable for, but also the content of, the disclosure of information prior to litigation. Although the protocol sets strict time limits, its aim is to be flexible enough so that it may apply to all aspects of health service care, both public and private. For example, access to GP records may prove relatively easy to accomplish, whereas it may be rather more complicated and therefore slow to obtain records concerning events which may have happened many years ago from a large hospital.

9.3.3 Good practice commitments

The commitments section of the protocol summarises guiding principles that healthcare providers, patients and advisers should consider at the point where they are dealing with patient dissatisfaction.

Healthcare providers should:

(a)   ensure that key staff are appropriately trained and have some knowledge of healthcare law and the complaints procedures;

(b)   develop a system of clinical risk management;

(c)   set up 'adverse outcome reporting systems' in all specialities to record and investigate unexpected and serious adverse outcomes as soon as possible;

(d)   use the results of adverse incidents and subsequent complaints in a positive way (as a guide to how to improve service);

(e)   ensure that all patients receive a clear and comprehensible response to their complaints or concerns;

(f)   establish efficient and effective systems of recording and storing patient records, notes, diagnostic reports and x-rays and retain these in accordance with Department of Health guidance. The current minimum period for storage in the case of adults is eight years, and in the case of obstetric and paediatric notes for children, until they reach the age of 25;

(g) advise patients of a serious adverse outcome and on request provide the patient with an oral or written explanation.

According to the protocol, it is incumbent on the claimant and his advisers to:

(a) report any concerns and dissatisfactions which he may have to his healthcare provider as soon as possible;

(b) consider all of the options available to him if he is dissatisfied, including seeking clarification, and negotiation but not only to consider litigation;

(c) inform the healthcare provider when the patient is satisfied that the matter has been concluded.

9.3.4 The steps in the protocol

The following steps in the protocol should be followed once non-litigation options have been considered and litigation is proposed.

9.3.4.1 Obtaining the health records

Requests for patient records should:

(a) provide sufficient information to tell the healthcare provider where an adverse outcome has been serious or has had serious consequences;

(b) be as specific as possible about the nature of the records that are required to be disclosed.

9.3.4.2 Form of request for records

Requests for copies of patient records should be made using The Law Society and Department of Health-approved standard forms. According to the protocol, copy records should be provided within 40 days of request. The cost of copies should not exceed the charge permissible under the Data Protection Act 1998. For a detailed summary of obtaining access to health records, see **Chapter 5**.

9.3.5 The letter of claim

The protocol provides a template for the recommended contents for the letter of claim as follows.

If, following receipt and analysis of records, the patient or his adviser decide that there are grounds for claim, they should, as soon as practicable, send to the healthcare provider a letter of claim.

The letter should contain the following information:

(a) a clear summary of the facts on which the claim is based, including details of the alleged adverse outcome and main allegations of negligence;

(b) it should describe the patient's injuries, present condition and prognosis;

(c) it should describe the financial loss incurred by the claimant and indicate the heads of damage to be claimed.

If the letter of claim refers to relevant documents, and it is envisaged that normally it will, it should if possible, enclose copies of all of those documents which would not already be in the potential defendant's possession, for example, any relevant general practitioner records if the claimant is making a claim against a hospital.

In complex cases, a chronology of relevant events should be provided (eg, where a patient has been treated by a number of different healthcare professionals, and/or has been referred to a number of different hospitals and clinics).

Sufficient information must be given to enable the healthcare provider to:

(a)   commence investigations; and

(b)   put an initial value onto the claim.

Proceedings should not be issued until after three months from the letter of claim, unless there is:

(a)   a limitation problem; or

(b)   the patient's position needs protecting by early issue of proceedings.

9.3.6   Claimant's offer to settle

The claimant can make an offer to settle the claim at this stage by putting forward an amount of compensation which he would be prepared to accept in settlement of the claim. An offer to settle at this stage should be supported by:

(a)   a medical report confirming the injuries, condition and prognosis of the claimant; and

(b)   a schedule of loss, together with supporting documentation.

9.3.7   The proposed defendant's response

The proposed defendant should acknowledge the letter of claim within 14 days of receipt and should identify who is dealing with the claim. Within three months of the date of the letter of claim, the proposed defendant should provide a substantive response in the following terms:

(a)   if the claim is admitted in full, the proposed defendant should say so in clear terms;

(b)   if part is admitted, the proposed defendant should make this clear, stating which issues of breach of duty and/or causation are admitted and which issues are denied;

(c)   admissions made at this stage will be binding only if the healthcare provider has indicated that they be binding;

(d)   if the claim is denied, the response should make specific comments relating to the allegations of negligence that have been made. If a chronology of events was provided by the claimant, details in rebuttal of this should be provided;

(e)   where additional documents are referred to and relied upon, copies should be provided with the response;

(f)   if the claimant has made an offer to settle, the proposed defendant should respond to that offer in the response.

9.3.8   Proposed defendant's offer to settle

The proposed defendant may make his own offer to settle at this stage, either as a counter-offer to the claimant's offer to settle or not. Any offer of settlement should be supported by medical evidence and/or other evidence relevant to the value of the claim which the proposed defendant has in his possession.

9.3.9   Quantification of claim

If both the claimant and the proposed defendant are in agreement on liability, but, as often happens, it is necessary to wait before a clear prognosis on the injuries can be arrived at, the parties should try to agree a reasonable timescale within which to reach agreement in relation to the value of claim.

9.4   Pre-action protocol for disease and illness claims

The pre-action protocol for disease and illness claims is reproduced at **Appendix 3**. The protocol covers disease claims which are likely to be complex, and not suitable for the fast track. Detailed consideration of this protocol is beyond the scope of this book.

9.5   Pre-action disclosure

An application for disclosure prior to the start of proceedings is permitted under s 33 of the Supreme Court Act 1981 or s 52 of the County Courts Act 1984. The application must be supported by appropriate evidence, and the procedure is the same in both the High Court and county court. (This procedure is dealt with in r 31.16.) Under r 31.16 the court may make an order for disclosure only where:

(a)   the respondent is likely to be a party to subsequent proceedings;

(b)   the applicant is also likely to be a party to the proceedings;

(c)   if proceedings had started, the respondent's duty by way of standard disclosure, set out in r 31.16 would extend to the documents or classes of documents of which the applicant seeks disclosure; and

(d)   disclosure before proceedings have started is desirable in order to—

    (a)   dispose fairly of the anticipated proceedings; or

    (b)   assist the dispute to be resolved without proceedings; or

    (c)   save costs.

An order under r 31.16 must specify the documents or class of documents which the respondent must disclose and require him, when making such disclosure, to specify any of those documents which he no longer has or which he claims the right or duty to withhold from inspection. The order may also specify the time and place for disclosure and inspection to take place.

9.5.1   Orders for disclosure against a person who is not a party

Where application is made to the court, under any Act, for disclosure by a person who is not a party (but is likely to become so) to the proceedings, the application must be supported by suitable evidence.

The court may make an order under r 31.17(3) only where:

(a)   the documents of which disclosure is sought are likely to support the case of the applicant or adversely affect the case of one or other of the parties to the proceedings; and

(b)   disclosure is necessary to dispose fairly of the claim or save costs.

An order under r 31.17 must specify the documents or class of documents which the respondent must disclose, and require the respondent to make disclosure or specify any of those documents for which he no longer has or for which he claims the right or duty to withhold from inspection. Once again, the order may specify a time and place for such disclosure and inspection.

An order for an interim remedy can be made at any time prior to the proceedings being started unless there is a rule or a specific practice direction which says otherwise. The court may grant an interim remedy before a claim has been made only if:

(a)   the matter is urgent; or

(b)   it is otherwise necessary to do so in the interests of justice.

Normally the party making an application for disclosure against a non-party will bear the costs of the person making the disclosure. See *Totalise plc v The Motley Fool Ltd and Another* [2001] EWCA Civ 1897, [2002] 1 WLR 1233.

9.5.2   Procedure

The court may grant an interim remedy on application without notice if it appears to the court that there are good reasons for not giving notice to the proposed defendant. Such an application must be supported by evidence, unless the court orders otherwise. If the applicant makes an application without giving notice, the evidence in support of his application must state the reasons why no notice was given.

9.5.3   Rules in relation to inspection of property before commencement or against a non-party

The evidence in support of such an application must show, if practicable, by reference to any statement of case that has been prepared in relation to the proceedings or anticipated proceedings, that the property:

(a)   is or may become the subject-matter of the proceedings; or

(b)   is relevant to the issue that will arise in relation to those proceedings.

A copy of the application and a copy of the evidence in support must be served on the person against whom the order is sought; and every party to proceedings other than the applicant (r 25.5).

9.5.4   Offers to settle prior to commencement of proceedings under Part 36

Offers to settle and payments into court are dealt with in detail in **Chapter 10**. An offer of settlement can be made at any time by either party.

9.6   Issuing proceedings

Issuing proceedings in both the High Court and the county court uses the same procedure and the same terminology. However, cases of higher value and/or greater complexity may be issued only in the High Court.

When issuing proceedings in a case being funded by a CFA, regard must be had to the requirement to give notice that the matter is being funded in this way (see **4.3**).

The procedure for issuing proceedings is dealt with in the Legal Practice Guide, *Civil Litigation*.

9.6.1   Statements of value

In a claim for personal injuries, the claimant must state on the claim form whether the amount which he reasonably expects to recover in general damages for pain, suffering and loss of amenity is:

(a)   not more than £1,000; or

(b)   more than £1,000.

If a claim is to be issued in the High Court, it must state that the claimant reasonably expects to recover £50,000 or more; or must state that some other enactment provides that the claim may be commenced in the High Court and specify that enactment.

When calculating how much he expects to recover, the claimant must disregard any possibility:

(a)   that he may recover interest and costs;

(b)   that the court may make a finding of contributory negligence against him;

(c)   that the defendant may make a counterclaim or that the defence may include a set-off; or

(d)   that the defendant may be required to pay money which the court awards to the claimant by way of compensation recoupment under s 6 of the Social Security (Recovery of Benefits) Act 1997.

9.6.2   Particulars of claim

The particulars of claim must be contained in or served with the claim form, or be served on the defendant by the claimant within 14 days after service of the claim form. In any event, particulars of claim must be served on the defendant no later than the latest time for serving a claim form (ie, within four months after date of issue of the claim form).

The particulars of claim must include:

(a)   a concise statement of the facts on which the claimant relies;

(b)   if the claimant seeks interest, a statement detailing the interest claimed;

(c)   if the claimant is seeking aggravated damages or exemplary damages, a statement confirming the grounds on which that claim is made; and

(d)   such other matters as may be set out in the relevant practice direction.

PD 16 states that the following matters must be contained in the particulars of claim:

(a)   the claimant's date of birth;

(b)   brief details of the claimant's injuries; and

(c)   details of past and future expenses and losses.

If the claimant wishes to rely on medical evidence of a medical practitioner, such a report must be served with or attached to the particulars of claim detailing the injuries.

There are further provisions in the practice direction relevant to provisional damages claims (PD 41).

If the claim relates to a fatal accident, the claimant must state in his particulars of claim:

(a)   that it is brought under the Fatal Accidents Act 1976;

(b)   the dependants on whose behalf the claim is made;

(c)   the date of birth of each dependant; and

(d)   details of the nature of the dependency claim.

If the claimant seeks interest, he must state whether he is doing so under the terms of a contract or under an Act and, if so, which Act.

Both the claim form and the particulars of claim must contain a statement that the claimant (and if the claimant is acting as a litigation friend, the litigation friend) believes that the facts stated in the document are true.

9.6.3 Service of proceedings

After the claim form has been issued, it must be served within four months after the date of issue. If the claim form is to be served out of the jurisdiction, the period is six months.

9.6.4 Acknowledgement of service

The defendant may respond to the claim by either:

(a)   defending the claim; or

(b)   admitting the claim; or

(c)   acknowledging service of the claim form.

If the defendant makes no response to the claim, the claimant may enter default judgment.

The defendant may acknowledge service if he is unable to file a defence in time, or if he contests the court's jurisdiction.

The time for acknowledgement of service is 14 days from the service of the claim form, unless the claim form indicates that the particulars of claim are to follow separately, in which case the defendant does not have to acknowledge service until 14 days after service of those particulars of claim.

The acknowledgement of service form must be signed by the defendant or his legal representative and must include an address for service for the defendant which must be within the jurisdiction.

On receipt of such an acknowledgement of service, the court must notify the claimant in writing of this.

9.6.5 The defence

The defendant must file a defence within 14 days of service of the particulars of claim, or, if the defendant has filed an acknowledgement of service, within 28 days after service of the particulars of claim.

9.6.6 Extension of time for filing defence

The parties may agree an extension of time for filing of the defence of up to 28 days. The defendant must give the court written notice of any such agreement.

9.6.7 Contents of the defence

The defence must contain the following information:

(a)   the allegations made in the claim which are admitted;

(b)   the allegations made in the claim which are denied; and

(c)   the allegations made in the claim which are neither admitted nor denied but which the claimant is required to prove.

If the claimant has attached a schedule of past and future expenses and losses to his particulars of claim, the defendant must include with his defence a counter-schedule stating which items he agrees, disputes or neither agrees nor disputes but has no knowledge of. If items are disputed, an alternative figure must be supplied.

Where allegations are denied, the defendant must give reasons for that denial and, where relevant, give his own version of the facts. If the defendant disputes the claimant's statement of value, he must give reasons for doing so and, if possible, give his own estimate of value.

Unless the defendant has already acknowledged service, the defendant must give an address for service which is within the jurisdiction.

The defence must contain a statement that the defendant, or, if the defendant is conducting proceedings with a litigation friend, the litigation friend, believes the facts stated in it are true.

The defence must contain a statement of truth and should be signed either by the defendant or by his legal adviser.

The defence should make clear the defendant's version of the facts, in so far as it is different from that stated in the claim.

The basic function of the statements of case is to state, for the benefit of the court, the facts which are relied upon by the parties. Once the claim and defence have been filed, they will be considered by the procedural judge and, if the factual issues cannot be identified from them, directions should be given to the parties in order to rectify this. In cases where there is a case management conference (see **Chapter 10**), one of the items to be concluded either prior to or after that conference, will be to produce a comprehensive statement of the issues which are currently in dispute.

9.6.8   The counterclaim (CPR, r 20.4)

If a defendant wishes to make a counterclaim against a claimant, he should file his counterclaim with his defence. As long as the counterclaim is filed at the same time as the defence the defendant will not need permission of the court to make the counterclaim. If the claimant disputes the counterclaim he must file a defence to counterclaim within the usual 14-day period by way of a reply to the defence and a defence to the counterclaim.

Where there are co-defendants, if one of them wishes to seek a contribution or an indemnity from the other, then, once he has filed his acknowledgement of service or defence, he may proceed with his claim against the co-defendant. To proceed with a claim against the co-defendant, the Part 20 claimant must:

(a)   file a notice stating the nature and grounds of his claim; and

(b)   serve that notice on the co-defendant.

A defendant does not need leave to make a Part 20 claim if it is issued before or at the same time as he files his defence. In all other cases, he does need leave to make a Part 20 claim. The application for leave can be made without notice, unless the court otherwise directs. The defendant does not need leave to make a Part 20 claim if he serves the claim within 14 days of filing his defence.

9.6.9   The reply to defence

The claimant may file a reply to the defence, but, if he does not do so, he will not be deemed to admit the matters raised in the defence.

The claimant may file a reply and a certificate of reply when he files his allocation questionnaire (see **Chapter 10**). If he does serve a reply, he must also serve it on all other parties.

9.6.10 Contents of the reply

The reply must respond to any matters in the defence which have not been dealt with in the particulars of the claim and must also contain a statement that the maker believes the contents of the document are true.

The particulars of claim, defence and reply are said to be the statements of case. No subsequent statements of case may be filed without the court's leave.

9.6.11 Amendment to statements of case after expiry of the limitation period

In *Goode v Martin* [2001] EWCA Civ 1899, [2002] 1 WLR 1828, the claimant sought permission to amend her statement of claim after the expiry of the limitation period. The amendment consisted of a response to the defendant's version of events and no new facts were being introduced. The claimant also argued that if the amendment could not be allowed under a conventional approach to r 17.4, a less conventional approach should be adopted to comply with Article 6 of the European Convention on Human Rights.

The court found that because the claimant's new cause of action arose out of the same facts that were in issue in the original claim she should be allowed to add to her claim the alternative plea proposed. The Court of Appeal agreed with the claimant that to prevent the claimant from putting her alternative case before the court would impose an impediment on her access to the court that would have to be justified. It was possible to interpret r 17.4 in such a way as to allow the claimant's amendment and that should be done to comply with Article 6 of the Convention.

9.7 Conclusion

Because of the positive need to state a case in simple terms, solicitors acting for claimants and defendants spend more time gathering and analysing evidence in order to establish what the issues in the case are as early as possible. It should also be borne in mind that, because the statements of case are considered by the procedural judge when he makes his decision as to which track the matter should be allocated, they will be scrutinised at a much earlier date than under the old system as they will be used as the basis for a statement of issues in the case. Therefore, if the statements of case are not sufficiently clear the procedural judge will give directions to remedy this, with poorly drafted statements of case being struck out.

9.8 Further reading

Pre-action Protocol for Personal Injury Claims (see **Appendix 3**).

Pre-action Protocol for the Resolution of Clinical Disputes (see **Appendix 3**).

Chapter 10

Case Tracking and Case Management

10.1 Introduction

The 'interim stage' can be categorised as all of the stages of the litigation process, subsequent to the issue of the proceedings and prior to the trial. The interim stage is taken up mainly with obtaining and then complying with the directions issued by the court, either under the fast-track procedure or under the multi-track procedure, following the case management conference to ensure that the case is properly prepared for trial. The following paragraphs deal with this stage as it relates to personal injury and clinical negligence claims. A detailed consideration of this area is dealt with in the Legal Practice Guide, *Civil Litigation*.

10.2 Case management

Under the CPR 1998, cases are allocated within a three-tier system as follows:

(a)   small claims track – for claims of not more than £5,000 (£1,000 in personal injury claims);

(b)   fast track – for claims of more than £5,000 but less than £15,000 (more than £1,000 in personal injury cases);

(c)   multi-track – for claims of more than £15,000 and claims where the remedy is other than damages.

Where a claim is defended, on receipt of defence the court will serve each party with an allocation questionnaire. Each party must return the allocation questionnaire within 14 days. The parties must complete the allocation questionnaire indicating where they consider the case should be allocated. When allocating a case, the court may take into account the following factors:

(a)   financial value of the claim (or amount in dispute if different);

(b)   the nature of remedy sought;

(c)   the likely complexity of the facts, law or evidence;

(d)   the number of parties or likely parties;

(e)   the value of any counterclaim or other claim and the complexity of any matters relating to it;

    (f)   the amount of oral evidence that may be required;

    (g)   the importance of the claim to persons who are not parties to the proceedings;

    (h)   the views expressed by the parties;

    (i)   the circumstances of the parties.

Although the court will have regard to the above factors, it may allocate a case into an alternative track if it thinks it appropriate in the circumstances. For example, the multi-track rather than the fast track may be appropriate if either the trial is likely to last for more than one day or there will be expert evidence in more than two fields or more than one expert in any one field. This is likely to be the case in clinical negligence cases, even though the value of the claim may be quite modest.

Once the court has allocated a claim to a track, it will notify all parties and it will also serve them with:

    (a)   copies of the allocation questionnaire provided by all other parties;

    (b)   a copy of any further information provided by a party about his case.

10.2.1 Stay to allow settlement of case

A party returning his allocation questionnaire may request a stay of up to one month while the parties try to settle the case. Where all parties request a stay, or where the court, of its own initiative, considers such a stay would be appropriate, the court will direct a stay for one month. The court may also extend the period of the stay until such a date or such a period as it considers appropriate. Having stayed proceedings, if proceedings are settled, the claimant must inform the court of this.

10.3 Allocation to track

Once every party has filed an allocation questionnaire, or once the period for filing the questionnaire has expired, the court will allocate the claim to a track. Before deciding to which track to allocate the proceedings, the court may make an order for a party to provide further information (eg, if their statement of case is at all unclear). The court may also hold an allocation hearing if it thinks that this is necessary.

10.3.1 The small claims track

In relation to personal injury claims, the small claims track is the appropriate track where the financial value of the claim does not exceed £5,000 and the claim for damages for personal injuries is not more than £1,000. Rule 2.3 defines a 'claim for personal injuries' as proceedings in which there is a claim for damages in respect of personal injuries to the claimant or any other person or in respect of a person's death.

10.3.2 The fast track

The fast track is the usual track for claims for personal injuries where the financial value of the claim is not more than £15,000 but is more than £5,000 and where the claim for damages for personal injuries is more than £1,000. However, although the above is the normal rule, this assumes that:

    (a)   the trial is likely to last for no longer than one day;

    (b)   oral expert evidence at the trial will be limited to:

        (i)   one expert per party in relation to any expert field,

        (ii)   expert evidence in two expert fields.

According to the CPR 1998, 'damages for personal injuries' means damages claimed as compensation for pain, suffering and loss of amenity and does not include any other damages which are claimed.

When assessing the financial value of a claim the court will disregard:

(a)   any claim for interest;

(b)   costs;

(c)   any claim for contributory negligence.

10.3.2.1   Notice of allocation

Once the court has allocated a claim to a track, it will serve notice on every other party, together with a copy of the allocation questionnaire filed by all other parties and a copy of any further information provided by any other party about his case.

If the statements of case are later amended and it becomes clear that the case has been allocated to an inappropriate track, the court may subsequently re-allocate a claim to a different track.

When it allocates a claim to the fast track, the court will give directions for management of the case and a timetable of steps to be taken between the giving of directions and the end of the trial. When it gives directions, the court will, at that point, fix a trial date; or fix a period not exceeding three weeks in which the trial will take place. The standard period between giving directions and trial will be not more than 30 weeks.

10.3.2.2   Directions in the fast track

Matters to be dealt with by way of directions include:

(a)   disclosure of documents;

(b)   service of witness statements;

(c)   expert evidence.

10.3.2.3   Listing questionnaire

The court will send each party a listing questionnaire for completion and return to the court by the date specified in the notice of allocation. The date specified for filing a listing questionnaire is not more than eight weeks before the trial date.

If a party fails to file a completed listing questionnaire within the time limit or fails to give all of the information, or the court thinks it is necessary, the court may fix a listing hearing or give such other directions as it thinks appropriate.

10.3.2.4   Fixing trial date

As soon as practicable after filing of the completed listing questionnaires, the court will fix a date for trial, give any directions for trial and specify further steps that need to be taken by the parties prior to the trial.

The court will give each party at least three weeks' notice of the trial date. Only in exceptional circumstances will the notice period be shorter than this.

10.3.3   The multi-track

When allocating a case to the multi-track, the court will either:

(a)   give directions for case management and set a timetable; or

(b)   fix a case management conference and/or a pre-trial review, or both,

and may give such other directions relating to management of the case as it thinks fit.

10.3.4   Transfer between tracks

When considering an application to re-allocate a case from one track to another, the court has an unfettered discretion under r 26.10 of the CPR (see *Maguire v Molin* [2002] EWCA Civ 1083, [2002] 4 All ER 325). In this case proceedings were issued with damages limited to £15,000. The claim was allocated to the fast track. Part way through the trial on liability the claimant's solicitors made an application to amend the statement of case to remove the £15,000 limit. The application was refused on the grounds that it had been made very late and that allowing it would disadvantage the defendant. On appeal, the Court of Appeal found that the judge at first instance had jurisdiction to allow the amendment and continue with the hearing of the issue of liability on the fast track. However, on the facts of the case the district judge reached the right decision in refusing to re-allocate the case.

The Court of Appeal gave the following guidance. Even though the value of a claim was important in determining where it should be held in the first place, so long as a claim remained in the fast track a district judge did have the right to hear it. A claim did not cease to be in the fast track simply because its value had been increased beyond £15,000. The amount by which the financial value of a claim exceeded the normal limit for a track as a result of an amendment was highly relevant. If the amount by which the limit had been exceeded had been small then it would not usually require re-allocation to multi-track. However, if the amount were large then re-allocation would usually be necessary, even if that meant considerable delay to the litigation.

10.4   The case management conference and pre-trial review

The court may fix a case management conference and pre-trial review at any time after the defence has been filed. Where a party is legally represented, any case management conference or pre-trial review called by the court must be attended by a legal representative who is familiar with the case.

10.4.1   The case management conference

The parties may agree their own proposals for case management of the proceedings and, if the court is satisfied with these proposals, it may give directions in accordance with the proposals without the need for a court hearing.

10.4.1.1   Variation of case management timetable

If a party wishes to apply to vary any of the dates which the court has fixed for:

(a)   the case management conference;
(b)   the pre-trial review;
(c)   the return of listing questionnaires;
(d)   the trial;

he may do so only with leave of the court. However, a party cannot vary the timetable in such a way as will result in an alteration of the overall timetable mentioned above.

10.4.1.2   The listing questionnaire

The court will send each party a listing questionnaire for completion and return. The procedure and consequences of failure to return the questionnaire are the same as for the fast track listed above.

10.4.2   Pre-trial review

On receipt of the parties' listing questionnaires, the court may decide to hold a pre-trial review or cancel a pre-trial review if it has already decided to hold one, having regard to the circumstances of the case.

After filing of listing questionnaires, the court will set a timetable for the trial (unless this has already been done or is impracticable) and will notify the parties of that timetable. If it is able to do so, the court will fix or confirm the trial date and will notify the parties of it.

10.5   Group litigation

Engaging in group litigation is time-consuming, difficult and, therefore, costly. Group litigation results when there are a number of prospective claimants who have a common interest or common defendant arising out of a common incident. An example of group litigation is the litigation brought by a number of families following the *Marchioness* disaster.

The relevant rule of the CPR 1998 governing group litigation can be found at Part 19, with its accompanying PD 19B. Part 19 makes provision for the making of a group litigation order (GLO) at the request of the parties where there are, or are likely to be, a number of similar claims. The aim of the GLO is to 'steer' the group litigation by ensuring that the case is managed to suit the needs of multi-party litigation. The aim of the GLO is to ensure that all cases that are eligible to join the group do so and are then all treated in like manner to ensure consistency of result. The GLO must include specific directions for the maintenance of a group register, specify the GLO issues and appoint a particular court and particular judge to oversee the case management process. By giving one court/judge 'ownership' of the management process, the case can be more effectively managed than if all potential claimants were allowed to issue and deal with their case at any court of their choosing. The managing judge appointed to the group litigation will quickly amass specialist knowledge in relation to that particular group litigation and will therefore be able to deal with matters as they arise more quickly and effectively.

The details of group litigation are beyond the scope of this book but recourse should be had, as a starting point, to PD 19B and to the Law Society's Multi-Party Action Information Service.

10.6   Interim payments

A claimant may not seek an interim payment until after the time for acknowledging service has expired. More than one application for an interim payment may be made by a claimant.

An application for an interim payment must be supported by evidence and be served at least 14 days before the return date for the application. If a party wants to rely on a witness statement in an application for an interim payment, he must file and serve a copy of that witness statement:

(a)   at least seven days before the hearing, in the case of the respondent; or

(b)   at least three days before the hearing, in the case of an applicant who wishes to use the witness statement in reply to a respondent's submissions.

The court may order payment of an interim payment, and the court may order that such payment be by instalments.

The court may order an interim payment only if:

(a)   the defendant admits liability; or

(b)   the claimant has a judgment for damages to be assessed; or

(c)   the claimant would obtain judgment for a substantial amount of money.

In a claim for personal injuries where there are two or more defendants, the court may make an order for interim payment against any of them if it is satisfied that, if the claim went to trial, the claimant would obtain judgment for substantial damages against at least one of the defendants and the conditions specified above in relation to insurers are satisfied.

The amount of the interim payment must not exceed a reasonable proportion of the likely amount of the final judgment taking into account:

(a)   contributory negligence; and

(b)   any relevant set-off or counterclaim.

If a defendant has made an interim payment, the court may order that that sum be repaid or that another defendant reimburse that defendant.

If a defendant makes an interim payment which it transpires exceeds his liability under the final judgment, the court may award interest on the overpaid amount from the date the interim payment was made.

10.7   Disclosure and inspection of documents

A party is not required to give more than standard disclosure unless the court otherwise orders.

Standard disclosure means that a party is required to disclose only:

(a)   the documents on which he relies;

(b)   the documents which could adversely affect his own case, adversely affect another's case or support another party's case; and

(c)   all documents which he is required to disclose by any practice direction.

The court may dispense with or limit standard disclosure, and the parties can agree in writing to dispense with or limit any part of standard disclosure. As under the old rules the duty of standard disclosure continues throughout the proceedings and, if a document comes to a party's notice at any time, that party must immediately notify every other party.

10.7.1   Procedure

Each party must make and serve a list of documents in accordance with the practice form which must identify the documents 'in a convenient order and manner as concisely as possible'. A detailed consideration of the procedure on disclosure can be found in the Legal Practice Guide, *Civil Litigation*.

The list must indicate documents which are no longer in the parties' control and state what has happened to those documents.

The list must include a disclosure statement by the party:

(a)   setting out the extent of the search made to locate the documents;

(b)   certifying that he understands the duty of disclosure and that, to the best of his knowledge, he has carried out that duty.

10.7.2 Specific disclosure

An order for specific disclosure can require a party to disclose specified documents or classes of documents, or carry out a search for specified documents and disclose any documents located as a result of that search.

An application for specific disclosure must be supported by evidence. The court will order specific disclosure only if necessary to dispose fairly of the claim or save costs.

The party has a right to inspect a document mentioned in another party's:

(a)   statement of case;

(b)   witness statement or summary;

(c)   affidavit;

(d)   expert's report.

10.8 Witness evidence

As part of its management powers, the court will decide the issues on which it requires evidence, the nature of that evidence and the way in which the evidence should be placed before the court.

10.8.1 Witnesses

Facts should normally be proved at the trial by oral evidence of witnesses, and at any other hearing by the written evidence of witnesses. The court may allow a witness to give evidence by any means, which includes by means of a video link.

10.8.2 Procedure

The court may order a party to serve on any other party a witness statement containing the evidence which that party intends to rely on.

According to r 32.4(1):

> A witness statement is a written statement signed by a person which contains the evidence which that person would be allowed to give orally.

The court will normally order each party to serve the witness statements of the oral evidence on which they intend to rely at the trial. The court may give directions as to the order in which such witness statements are to be served and whether or not the statements are to be filed.

10.8.3 Use at trial of witness statements

If a witness statement has been served and a party wishes to rely on that evidence at trial, the party must call the witness to give oral evidence unless the court otherwise orders.

10.8.4 Statements to stand as evidence-in-chief

Where a witness is called to give oral evidence, his statement shall stand as evidence-in-chief, unless the court otherwise orders.

The witness giving the oral evidence may amplify the witness statement, and give evidence in relation to new matters that have arisen since the statement was served. However, he may do this only if the court considers there is a good reason not to confine his evidence to the contents of the statement that has been served.

Evidence in proceedings other than at the trial should be by witness statement, unless the court or a particular practice direction otherwise directs.

10.8.5   Witness summary

Where a party is required to serve a witness statement, if he is not able to obtain a witness statement, he may apply to the court for permission to serve only a witness summary instead. This application should be made without notice. The witness summary is a summary of the evidence which would otherwise go into a witness statement; or if the evidence is not known, matters about which the party serving the witness summary will question the witness.

Where a witness statement or a witness summary is not served, the party will not be able to call that witness to give oral evidence unless the court allows it.

10.9   Use of plans, photographs and models as evidence at trial

Where a party wishes to use evidence such as plans, photographs or models or other evidence:

(a)   which is not contained in a witness statement, affidavit or expert's report;

(b)   which is not given orally at trial;

(c)   which has already been disclosed in relation to hearsay evidence;

the party wishing to use the evidence must disclose his intention to do so not later than the latest date for serving witness statements.

If the evidence forms part of expert evidence, it must be disclosed when the expert's report is itself served on the other party. Having disclosed such evidence, the party must give every other party an opportunity to inspect it and agree its admission without further proof.

10.10   Expert evidence

The duties of experts in relation to court proceedings, and the contents of their report are dealt with in **Chapter 8**.

10.11   Offers to settle and payments into court

Under Part 36 of the CPR 1998, either party may make an 'offer to settle' to the other before the commencement of proceedings. If a party receiving the offer fails to accept it, and the offer is not beaten at trial, that party will have a costs penalty to pay for refusing to accept the offer. Once proceedings have commenced, when a defendant pays money into court in an attempt to settle a claim, he will make a Part 36 payment. When a claimant intimates an amount of money which he is prepared to accept to settle the claim, he will make a Part 36 offer. The key feature of this procedure is that it is open both to claimants and defendants. However, cases proceeding in the small claims track are not eligible for a Part 36 offer procedure.

It is important to note the difference between a Part 36 offer and a Part 36 payment. In relation to the effect of recovery of social security benefit, the rules operate differently, depending on whether there has been a payment into court or merely an offer to settle. A defendant can only claim costs protection if he makes a payment into court. Although he may make an 'offer' before proceedings are commenced, once he receives formal notice of proceedings he must make a payment into court within 14 days of an amount at least equal to the amount of the offer. If he fails to do so, the costs protection of making the offer prior to issue of proceedings will be lost. In contrast, a claimant can make an offer prior to commencement of proceedings, or at any time during proceedings but cannot make a payment into court.

10.11.1   Contents of Part 36 offers

A Part 36 offer must:

(a)   be in writing;

(b)   state whether it relates to all or part of the claim;

(c)   state whether it takes account of any counterclaim;

(d)   confirm details of interest claimed (if expressed not to be inclusive of interest, give details of interest);

(e)   be expressed to be open for not less than 21 days;

(f)   state that it can be accepted after 21 days if the parties agree liability for costs or the court so permits.

Any such offer made will be treated as being made 'without prejudice save as to costs'.

10.11.2   Contents of Part 36 payments

A Part 36 payment may relate to the whole claim or part of it.

In order to make a Part 36 payment, the defendant must file with the court and serve on all other parties a notice (a Part 36 payment notice) which states:

(a)   the amount of the payment (or increased payment);

(b)   whether the payment relates to the whole claim or part of it;

(c)   whether it takes into account any counterclaims;

(d)   details of interest (unless expressed not to be inclusive of interest).

In the terms of the above notice, the claimant can apply for an order that the defendant clarifies his notice.

Care must be taken when considering whether or not to make a Part 36 payment. It is not enough simply to make a written offer instead of a Part 36 payment into court (see *Amber v Stacey* [2001] 2 All ER 88). Here, the Court of Appeal found that, in order for an offer of payment to have the costs consequences outlined in Part 36, it was necessary for the defendant to make a Part 36 payment into court. A written offer by letter would not do.

The rules on acceptance of Part 36 payments and the costs consequences are the same as for Part 36 offers as outlined above.

10.11.3   Effect of acceptance of Part 36 offer or Part 36 payment

The effect of acceptance of an offer or payment, if it relates to the whole of the claim, is that the claim will be stayed. Where the offer relates to the whole claim, the stay will be upon the terms of the offer, and either party can apply to enforce those terms without the need for a new claim. If the offer or payment relates to only part of a claim and is accepted, the claim is stayed as to that part only; and unless the parties have agreed costs, costs shall be assessed by the court.

In the case of a minor, where court approval is required, the settlement is final, and any stay arising on acceptance of an offer or payment will take effect only when such approval has been obtained.

10.11.4   Acceptance by a defendant of a claimant's Part 36 offer

A defendant can accept a Part 36 offer made not less than 21 days before trial without need for the court's permission, if he gives the claimant written notice of acceptance not later than 21 days after the offer was made. If the claimant's offer was made less than 21 days before trial or the defendant does not accept it within 21 days of the offer being made, the court's permission will be needed only if the parties do not agree liability for costs. If the trial has not yet started, permission is sought by making an application under Part 23; if the trial has started, application is made to the trial judge.

10.11.5   Consequences where the claimant fails to match the defendant's Part 36 offer or payment

Where at the trial the claimant fails to better a Part 36 payment or fails to obtain a judgment which is more advantageous than a defendant's Part 36 offer, the court will order that claimant to pay any costs incurred by the defendant after the latest date on which the payment or offer could have been accepted without the need for the court's permission unless it considers it unjust to do so (r 36.20).

The phrase 'unless the court considers it unjust to do so' has been considered in *Ford v GKR Construction* [2000] 1 All ER 802. Here, the court considered that it was unjust to make the usual costs order against a claimant who had failed to beat the defendant's payment into court. The relevant facts of the case are that the defendants made a payment into court well in advance of the trial. Once the trial had commenced, the defendants employed video surveillance on the claimant and sought to use this evidence at the trial as it was clear that the claimant's injuries were not as severe as her evidence suggested. When giving judgment, the court made the following observations.

(a)   When exercising his discretion as to costs, the judge was required to consider the matter of late disclosure of evidence.

(b)   The guiding principle that the judge should have in mind was that the parties should conduct litigation by making full disclosure.

(c)   The parties had to be provided with the necessary information to assess whether to make or accept payments under Part 36.

(d)   Where a party failed to provide that information the court should take that into account when considering what costs order to make.

(e)   The normal costs consequences should not apply when the claimant has not been furnished with the necessary information to gauge whether to accept or reject the Part 36 payment as it would be unjust to do so.

10.11.6   Defendant's failure to obtain more than offered in a Part 36 offer

Where at trial a defendant is held liable for more than the offer, or the judgment against him is more advantageous to the claimant, the court may order interest on the whole or any part of the award not exceeding 10% above base rate from the period starting with the latest date the defendant could have accepted the offer without permission of the court.

The court may also order the claimant his entitlement to the costs on an indemnity basis from the latest date the defendant could have accepted the offer without permission of the court. The court may also grant interest on those costs at a rate not exceeding 10% above base rate.

Even if the defendant failed to beat the amount offered by a small margin, that can still be grounds for a payment of indemnity costs and interest (see *Huck v Robson* [2002] EWCA Civ 398, [2002] 3 All ER 263). The claimant made a Part 36 offer by which she offered to accept a '95:5 split on liability'. The defendant rejected the offer and proceedings were commenced. The defendant was in fact found to be 100% liable and the claimant applied for an order for costs on an indemnity basis together with interest at an enhanced rate. At first instance, the judge refused to make such an order, holding that the offer was 'illusory' because no judge would have apportioned liability in such a way. On appeal, the court found that the decision to award indemnity costs and interest at an enhanced rate was a discretionary one and it was permissible to ignore offers that were purely tactical. However, the judge had been wrong to ignore the offer. The claimant was entitled to make such an offer to achieve a quick and certain outcome to the litigation. The offer was a real opportunity to settle and it was not unjust for the defendant to be ordered to pay indemnity costs and interest at an enhanced rate.

In *Painting v University of Oxford* [2005] EWCA Civ 161 the court concluded that the claimant had deliberately exaggerated the extent of her injuries. Therefore, even though the claimant had beaten the defendant's offer to settle, the defendant should be entitled to its costs. This was because taking the conduct of the parties into account, as the court was entitled to do, the court found that the claimant had failed to take any steps to settle the matter and decided that the defendant, even though it 'lost' on liability was still entitled to its costs due to the conduct of the claimant.

10.11.7 Compensation recovery and Part 36 offers to settle

Benefit recovery (which is dealt with in detail at **Chapter 12**) must be taken into account when considering payments into court. A Part 36 payment, but not an offer, is treated as making a compensation payment for the purpose of reg 8 of the Social Security (Recovery of Benefit) Regulations 1997 (SI 1997/2205). PD 36 requires benefit recovery to be taken into account when giving notice of a Part 36 payment into court. The notice must state:

(a)   the total amount represented by the Part 36 payment (the gross compensation);

(b)   that the defendant has reduced the payment in by the amount of recoverable benefit in accordance with s 8 of the Social Security (Recovery of Benefits) Act 1997; and

(c)   that the amount paid into court is the net amount after the deduction of the amount of benefit.

PD 36 also requires the compensator (defendant) to file with the court a certificate of recoverable benefit with the notice of payment in.

The Part 36 payment should be made on court form N242A.

There are no such requirements in respect of Part 36 offers in relation to benefit recovery. However, it is advisable to set out such offers in the same way as the above in order to avoid confusion.

When seeking to establish whether or not the claimant has bettered, or obtained a judgment more advantageous than, a Part 36 payment, the court will base its decision on the gross sum specified in the Part 36 notice.

10.12 Conclusion

The above statements in relation to the CPR 1998 are correct at time of writing. However, the CPR 1998 are subject to continuing amendment. Accordingly, it will be essential to check that the version of the Rules and Practice Directions being consulted is current.

10.13 Further reading

The Civil Procedure Rules (Lord Chancellor's Department, 1998).

The Civil Court Practice (the Green Book) (Butterworths).

Civil Procedure (the White Book) (Sweet & Maxwell).

Chapter 11

Negotiations, Alternative Dispute Resolution and Trial

11.1 Introduction

Over 90% of personal injury claims and many clinical negligence claims settle without trial. It is usually the case that the solicitor's skill in arguing his client's claim with the defendant's insurer or solicitor rather than his ability to argue the case at trial will determine the level of damages. For this reason, the personal injury solicitor is more likely to become a skilled negotiator than a trial advocate.

11.2 Professional conduct

As a matter of conduct, a solicitor does not have ostensible authority to settle a client's claim until after proceedings have been issued. It is imperative for the solicitor to seek the client's specific instructions prior to settling a claim. For example, even if the client instructs his solicitor that he can settle his claim as long as the client receives at least £1,000, the solicitor should, when negotiating with the defence, stipulate that any agreement is 'subject to his client's instructions'. In this way, if the client should change his mind (which he may do at any time), the solicitor will not have committed the client to the settlement irrevocably.

Negotiations should always be entered into on an expressly 'without prejudice' basis. When talking to an insurer in person or on the telephone it is advisable for the solicitor to preface anything he says by stating expressly at the outset that the entire conversation is without prejudice to his client's claim.

11.3 Negotiating with insurance companies and defence solicitors

Claims can be settled by agreement being reached between the parties at any stage. The pre-action protocols encourage early disclosure of information to facilitate this. Claimant solicitors have in the past considered that defendant insurers will not make reasonable offers for settlement prior to issue of proceedings. For this reason, many claimant solicitors have tended to issue proceedings first and negotiate second. This strategy is not encouraged by the CPR 1998. The pre-action protocols require that attempts be made to settle disputes. For a detailed consideration of the protocols, see **Chapter 9**. If the claim is being funded by a CFA, there is also the further requirement to disclose to the insurer that the matter is being funded in this way and the identity of any after the event insurer; it is not necessary to give any further details. In particular, it is not required or desirable to disclose the level of the success fee, as this would give the insurer a good indication of how confident the claimant's solicitor was about winning the case at trial.

When negotiating with the defendant's insurer or its solicitor, a firm approach should be taken by the claimant's solicitor. He must be alert to the fact that the insurer is in business to make money for its shareholders and its employees are employed to ensure that as little money as possible is paid out in damages. Therefore, the claimant's solicitor should not delay in issuing proceedings, after the pre-action protocol has been complied with if the defendant has failed or refused to make an acceptable response. Failure to do so is likely to be a failure to act in the best interests of the client.

The technique of negotiation is contained in the Legal Practice Guide, *Skills for Lawyers*. Prior to any negotiation the claimant's solicitor should first familiarise himself with the file, noting specifically any matters likely to increase the level of damages, such as the risk of osteoarthritis or permanent scarring. There is a risk that the solicitor will fail to remember the file adequately because he may be running many very similar claims at any one time. When reviewing the file it is good practice to build up a profile of the severity of the injuries by reading the medical reports and client's statement. Matters relevant to each head of loss should be noted so that the solicitor has a list of areas of loss without having to make reference to the specifics of the claim itself.

Example

Client, A, is aged 56 and has suffered injuries to her left shoulder and abrasions to both arms and legs when she tripped over a loose paving stone in her local high street. She is a keen gardener and likes to attend aerobics once a week, and enjoys walking her dog in the countryside near her home. Her husband took early retirement due to ill-health and is not able to assist her much, but he has been driving her to the doctor and to physiotherapy and has been helping her bathe and dress herself. Day-to-day cleaning of the house and gardening has been undertaken by friends and relations.

The profile in such a case would be:

General damages claim:

(a)   female aged 56, therefore likely to take some time for injuries to mend, danger of osteoarthritis revealed in medical report;

(b)   report revealed split fracture to the clavicle (collar bone) together with a tear to the latissimus dorsi (muscle beneath the shoulder) and associated soft tissue damage;

(c)   medical intervention involved substantial and uncomfortable strapping to render the injury immobile followed by light physiotherapy. Physiotherapy continued for 20 weeks;

(d)   reasonably fit, unable to undertake pastimes such as aerobics and walking in countryside for X weeks;

Special damages:

(a)   clothes and personal items lost or damaged in the accident;

(b)   mileage claim for travel to and from hospital/physiotherapy;

(c)   prescription charges;

(d)   daily care necessary;

(e)   husband unable to care on his own due to his own ill-health;

(f)   cleaning of house and garden maintenance undertaken by others.

Having built up such a profile, the next stage is for the solicitor to become familiar with the likely level of damages to be awarded in such a claim. Such familiarity comes with experience. The method of approach to calculation of damages is considered in detail in **Chapter 13**.

The client should be aware that any form of litigation carries with it a certain amount of risk that the claim will fail because the evidence may not come up to proof at trial. Because of this 'litigation risk', it is likely that the defence solicitor will seek some reduction in damages because the claimant is being spared the upset and risk of failure at trial.

11.4 Conducting the negotiation

When conducting negotiations, it is worth bearing in mind the following.

(a) Settlement should not be entered into prematurely. If proceedings are never issued and the defendant's insurers make clear that they do not contest the case, argument will centre on quantum, and it will be fairly safe to negotiate. If, however, the matter is contested, it is unwise to negotiate prior to disclosure of each side's evidence. For this reason, many solicitors believe that settlement should not be contemplated prior to the exchange of witness evidence. Once the claimant's solicitor has considered the evidence, he can then assist the client to make an informed decision as to whether he should accept a settlement.

(b) The solicitor must never negotiate when unprepared. The file must be considered thoroughly prior to proceeding with negotiations. If the solicitor receives a surprise telephone call from a defendant insurer seeking a settlement, it is better for the solicitor to call back later after having considered the case afresh.

(c) The defence should be invited to put forward its settlement figure with supporting argument as to why that figure is correct. Comments should be kept to a minimum and further negotiations postponed while the offer is considered. This is easiest to do if negotiating over the telephone, as negotiation can be cut short and re-established later with minimum difficulty. The telephone has the added advantage that the person making an offer cannot see the reaction of the recipient of the call, and will be unable to gauge how well or how badly the offer is received. The claimant's solicitor should never disclose his valuation of the claim first in negotiations and should not put forward any figures until he believes the defendant is putting forward a realistic amount.

(d) The defence opening offer is unlikely to be the best it is prepared to come up with. All offers must, however, be put to the client. A solicitor has a duty to act in the best interests of his client, and this includes obtaining the best possible settlement figure.

(e) An offer by the defence to pay the claimant's costs to date should not sway the solicitor into advising his client to accept an offer. If the defence is offering to settle, it is effectively admitting (albeit without prejudice) that there is merit in the claim and would normally be obliged to pay the claimant's reasonable costs if the case went to trial.

(f) Often the solicitor has specific instructions to try to settle the case on the client's behalf. In such a case, he may seek confirmation that a settlement will be agreed as long as the client will receive at least £X. If this is the case, the solicitor must be careful not to jump at the first offer simply because it will secure for the client the minimum that he requires and will usually also secure payment of the solicitor's costs.

(g)   Consideration of the defendant's offer should not be rushed. Any attempt to force an agreement quickly should be regarded as spurious. The defence would not have made an offer if it was happy to take the case to trial. Therefore, regardless of whether a time limit is placed on the offer, it is likely that unless fresh evidence comes to light strengthening the defence case, an offer once made will remain open. By making an offer at all the defence is saying that it would far rather pay than fight.

(h)   When negotiating, defendant insurers will often offer to 'split the difference' if agreement cannot be reached on a particular head of loss. This is a favourite tactic that the claimant solicitor should consider carefully before accepting. On the face of it, it may appear to be a generous offer, bringing negotiations to a speedy conclusion. On closer scrutiny, it may be a ploy which results in the loss of a substantial portion of the client's legitimate expectation in a particular head of damages.

11.5 Negotiating in clinical negligence claims

When considering negotiation in the context of clinical negligence claims, the following should be borne in mind.

(a)   In many cases, the NHS complaints procedure will already have been put to use and there may therefore be greater clarity as regards what the issues of the claim are.

(b)   It is unlikely that any negotiations with a view to settlement will be made prior to full recourse to the clinical disputes pre-action protocol. Only after both sides have had access to full disclosure and expert opinion will it be possible for any meaningful negotiation to take place.

(c)   In straightforward claims of low value, negotiating tactics as outlined above may be appropriate. In relation to more complex claims, it is more likely that there would be a meeting of the parties' solicitors with or without experts to try to narrow as many issues as possible. In appropriate cases, counsel for both sides may be asked to discuss the case informally to try to narrow areas in dispute.

11.6 Alternative dispute resolution (ADR)

The use of ADR is likely to become more important in the resolution of disputes, as the overriding objective (stated in Part 1 of the CPR 1998) encourages the prompt use of ADR as a way of furthering the overriding objective, and to aid prompt settlement. Most disputes are capable of resolution either by discussion and negotiation or by trial on the issues. The rules encourage the use of alternatives to litigation as a first resort and litigation as a last resort. ADR is explained in detail in the Legal Practice Guide, *Civil Litigation*.

11.6.1 Different types of ADR

The main types of ADR available today are as follows.

Mediation

In mediation, a neutral third party is chosen by the parties as their intermediary (mediator). The mediator is likely to meet the opposing parties separately to try to establish some common ground before finally bringing the parties together to try to reach an agreement.

Conciliation

Conciliation is a similar process to mediation. However, the conciliator is likely to take a more interventionist approach by taking a more central role. He will often consider the case as put forward by both sides and then suggest terms of settlement which he feels to be most appropriate.

The mini-trial

The format and content of a mini-trial is much more like a trial. It will be chaired by a neutral mediator who will sit with a representative from each party.

All of these three methods of ADR are mechanisms which aim to bring the parties together to obtain a consensual agreement rather than a ruling which is forced upon them.

11.6.2 Case management conference

At the case management conference/pre-trial review, the parties will be told to confirm whether the question of ADR has been considered and also to confirm that, if it has not, why this is the case.

When considering the conduct of the parties, the judge is entitled to consider the parties' unreasonable refusal to use ADR, as this is central to the ethos of how to deal with disputes in accordance with Part 1 of the CPR 1998. Where ADR has been refused or where a party has later failed to co-operate with ADR, the court is entitled to take that into account when considering what costs order to make or whether to make any costs order at all.

11.6.3 ADR and personal injury claims

Use of the pre-action protocol will ensure that the parties are better able to obtain a greater depth of knowledge about the case against them than in the past. Full use of pre-action disclosure, and preliminary disclosure of key documents will enable each side to obtain a far better view on the issues of the case in relation to liability, and will therefore allow them to make a far better and earlier assessment of their client's case.

At the stage where the parties complete their allocation questionnaire, they will be asked whether they would like their proceedings to be stayed while they try to settle the case by way of ADR.

Because the court is very likely to ask whether the parties are interested in attempting ADR, and whether the possibility of ADR has been discussed with the client prior to the case management conference, it follows that the solicitor will need to ask his client at an early stage whether he would be interested in pursuing the matter by way of ADR, and must explain to the client what this will entail.

In *Halsey v Milton Keynes General NHS Trust* [2004] EWCA Civ 576 the Trust refused to refer the matter to mediation as it was of the steadfast view that there had been no negligence and therefore referral to ADR would increase costs and delay. The claim was dismissed by the court. When the court came to consider the question of costs the court stated that when deciding whether a successful party had acted unreasonably in refusing to agree to ADR the court should bear in mind the advantages of ADR over the court process and have regard to all of the circumstances of the particular case. The following factors were found to be of relevance:

(a)   the nature of the dispute;

(b)   the merits of the case;

(c)   the extent to which other settlement methods had been attempted;

(d)   whether the costs of ADR would be disproportionately high;

(e)   whether any delay in setting up and attending the ADR would have been prejudicial;

(f)   whether the ADR had a reasonable prospect of success.

11.6.4   The timing of ADR

It is likely that in complicated cases ADR will not be appropriate until such time as statements of case and disclosure of documents by both sides have been dealt with. Only then will ADR be a practical alternative to a trial. It is therefore likely that parties in cases which were initially felt to be unsuitable for ADR may find that ADR is a possibility once the case is at the case management conference stage.

11.6.5   Procedure following failed ADR

Where the parties have attempted ADR and this has failed to produce a settlement, the parties are likely to wish to fall back on their original court proceedings or intended court proceedings.

At this stage, if proceedings have already been issued, the solicitor for the claimant will need to apply promptly for further directions in the case so that the matter may proceed swiftly to trial.

However, although ADR may fail to produce a settlement, it may produce a degree of information about the other side's case which prior to ADR had not been clear. If this is the case, it may be that an offer to settle or payment should be considered by either or both parties.

11.6.6   ADR in clinical negligence cases

The *Legal Services Commission Manual* recommends the use of ADR techniques to resolve clinical negligence disputes. Guidance notes make the point that although most successful claims settle, they do so at a very late stage. Because many clinical negligence claims are very complex, lengthy and very costly, a settlement reached earlier would have the effect of saving significant amounts of CLS funding. The NHS Litigation Authority which handles large clinical negligence claims also encourages the use of ADR. The Clinical Disputes Forum has also produced a guide on the use of mediation in clinical negligence disputes.

The guidance aims to:

(a)   ensure the use of ADR is considered by clients and solicitors at key points in clinical negligence claims;

(b)   require solicitors to report to their regional office at various stages in the litigation, explaining why ADR has not been pursued if appropriate;

(c)   explain the approach regional offices should take in deciding whether to limit a certificate to work necessary to progress ADR;

(d)   help the parties set up mediation.

11.6.6.1   When should ADR be considered in clinical negligence claims?

The parties should keep the possibilities of ADR in mind at all times. However, at the outset of litigation ADR is not likely to be appropriate until the pre-action protocol for use in clinical negligence claims has been complied with because the client and his solicitor are unlikely to have information available to enter into a fair settlement of the claim.

According to the *LSC Manual*, once the clinical negligence pre-action protocol has been complied with, solicitors should consider with their clients the use of ADR at the following stages:

(a)   prior to issue of proceedings;

(b)   before and immediately after a case management conference;

(c)   before and immediately after pre-trial review;

(d)   whenever the other side offers ADR;

(e)   whenever the new parties are specifically asked to consider ADR by the court or the LSC.

If at any of the above points it is decided by the client or solicitor not to pursue ADR, the reason for that decision should be recorded on the solicitor's file. Following on from this, where application is made by the solicitor for the certificate to be extended, the reason for not pursuing ADR must be reported to the regional office when submitting Form APP 8 for amendment of certificate.

11.6.6.2   Cases where ADR may not be appropriate

The *LSC Manual* gives the following specific guidance and examples of types of claims that may not be suitable for ADR:

(a)   where essential basic information (such as relevant medical records, key expert evidence on liability and causation) is not available;

(b)   where there is no clear prognosis for the condition of the client and time is needed to see how the client progresses before settlement can be considered;

(c)   ADR is unnecessary as all parties are already negotiating effectively;

(d)   proceedings need to be issued urgently in order for the claim to be within the relevant limitation period;

(e)   the claim includes a future cost of care claim and information is needed as to quantum before any settlement can be discussed;

(f)   the case is a 'test case' and requires a ruling from a court in order to lay down a precedent for future claims;

(g)   ADR would not be a cost effective way of dealing with the claim because there is no reason to believe that the claim will be resolved more quickly or cheaply by using it.

Although the LSC in its *Manual* states that it does not wish to impose ADR as a condition of funding, it does make it clear that it will consider limiting a certificate so that it only covers participation in ADR in the following circumstances:

(a)   when it receives a report that ADR has been refused;

(b)   where the opponent or the NHS Litigation Authority suggests ADR has been unreasonably refused;

(c)   where an application is made to extend the scope of a clinical negligence certificate to full representation or to cover the costs of a trial.

In any of the above cases, the regional office will consider the reason given for not pursuing ADR. In the guidance notes, the LSC states that the following reasons are not good reasons for refusing ADR:

(a)   the client refuses ADR and still wishes to have their day in court;

(b)   that there are important, outstanding facts or legal issues between the parties;

(c)   the parties feel that their positions are so far apart that they cannot foresee settling;

(d)   further information or exchange of evidence is required but this information is not sent forward to the client's case.

Once ADR has been attempted, the LSC will lift restrictions on the certificate if the ADR, having been attempted in good faith, breaks down.

In cases where ADR is not successful the LSC expects both sides to be able to put forward their most realistic Part 36 offers as a result of having taken part in the ADR.

11.6.7   NHS complaints procedure

The complaints procedure (which is dealt with in detail in **Chapter 7**) is designed specifically to provide an explanation to patients in cases where they have felt sufficiently concerned about the healthcare received to make a complaint. The procedure is not designed or able to give compensation to patients. It is useful if the only or main issue at stake is for an explanation or an apology to be obtained, or simply to find more information to help the patient to come to terms with an event, or to help him decide whether he should take further action, and, if so, what form this should take.

11.6.8   Mediation

Mediation may be appropriate in some cases where the parties agree. This may be seen as particularly useful when there are allegations of clinical negligence, as ADR will be conducted in private, and this is something which is likely to appeal to medical practitioners who may not wish the allegations to be made public and reportable, as would be the case if the matter were to proceed in open court to a trial.

11.7   Funding any settlement

In nearly all personal injury cases, there will not be a problem with the financing of any settlement, as the defendant will have been required to be insured in respect of the potential liability. Thus a commercial insurer will normally meet any settlement.

In clinical negligence cases, also, the defendant will normally not have a problem with the financing of any settlement but the administration of the settlement can be rather more complicated in certain cases. The NHS Litigation Authority (NHSLA) administers the Existing Liability Scheme and Clinical Negligence Scheme for Trusts (CNST). The CNST came into being as a result of concern over the financing of damages claims and the object of the scheme is to protect NHS trusts and improve the quality of risk management. The CNST is not an insurance scheme but a mutual fund.

The administration of any settlement is normally of little concern to claimant solicitors, but many practitioners become frustrated by the delays which can arise with insurance companies in personal injury cases and also the NHSLA, as they operate a system whereby certain levels of claims have to be given specific approval.

11.8 Court orders

It is good practice to obtain a court order formally stating the terms of the settlement. A settlement on behalf of a minor should always be contained in a court order (see **Chapter 16**).

11.8.1 Advantages of obtaining a court order

The advantages of obtaining an order are:

(a)   payment of interest and costs can be specifically dealt with;

(b)   if the amount stated in the order is not paid the order can be enforced in the same way as any other judgment;

(c)   if costs cannot be agreed they can be assessed by the court if there is provision in the order;

(d)   if the client has CLS funding, he will need an order for CLS assessment.

The order should contain a provision that the claim be stayed rather than dismissed, and the stay should contain provision for a return to court in the event that the terms of the stay are not complied with.

11.8.2 Drawing up the consent order

The procedure for drawing up a consent order is:

(a)   it must be drawn up in the agreed terms;

(b)   it must be expressed as being 'by consent';

(c)   it must be signed by solicitors or counsel for the parties;

(d)   it must be presented to the court for entry and sealing.

An order takes effect from the date given, unless the court orders otherwise. An order for payment of money (including costs) must be complied with within 14 days unless the order or any of the CPR rules specifies otherwise. When drafting a consent order, the guiding principle is that the order shows where the money is to come from to satisfy the order and where that money will go.

Example

In a case where there has been a payment in of £2,000 which was not accepted, and later a settlement is achieved by which the defendant agrees to pay £3,000 plus costs to be assessed if not agreed, the order should state:

(a)   that the claim is stayed on payment of £3,000;

(b)   where that £3,000 is to come from, ie, partly from money already in court and the balance to be paid by the defendant within a given timescale (usually 14 days);

(c)   that an order for payment out will be needed because the money in court was not accepted;

(d)   who is to have the interest earned on the money while in court (normally the defendant);

(e)   where the money is to go (in this case to the claimant). In a case involving a minor the money will usually be ordered to be invested by the court;

(f)   who is to bear the costs. If this has been agreed the figures should be stated with a time limit for payment. Usually, the provision will be for costs to be assessed if not agreed;

(g)   whether CLS assessment is needed; and

(h)   liberty to apply – which simply allows the parties to return to the court if there is subsequently a disagreement as to what the terms of the order mean or because the terms have not been complied with.

If there had been an interim payment in the above example, this should also be reflected in the terms of the order. The order should state that the amount agreed in full and final settlement takes into account the interim payment, specifying the amount and the date it was given or the date of the court order so ordering it to be paid.

11.9   Preparation for trial

11.9.1   Outstanding orders

Once it becomes apparent that the case will proceed to trial as no Part 36 payment has been made nor any satisfactory Part 36 offer received, the claimant's solicitor should undertake a thorough stocktaking of the file to ensure that all directions or other orders of the court have been complied with. Any outstanding matters in the claimant's own file should be attended to without further delay, and any outstanding matters for the defendant to attend to should be chased by issuing an interim application for judgment in default of compliance with the direction/ other order if necessary.

11.9.2   Experts

Experts' reports will usually have been exchanged in accordance with directions. Provision of joint experts and agreed expert evidence is dealt with in **Chapter 8**.

11.9.3   Use of counsel

The solicitor may not have instructed counsel before this stage if the claim has been straightforward. If the case has been complex, as is likely in a clinical negligence case, counsel will probably have been involved at an early stage from drafting documents to advising on evidence. It is usual for the barrister who drafted the statements of case also to be briefed for the trial. As counsel will be handling the witnesses at trial, it may be thought to be appropriate to send the witness statements to counsel for approval before exchange to ensure that an important area concerning the conduct of the case at trial is not overlooked. It may be more cost-efficient to brief counsel for the trial than for the solicitor himself to attend. However, with trial on the fast track limited to one day, and with fixed costs of trial, it may be that many more solicitor-advocates will undertake the advocacy of this type of claim. If the case involves complex elements, such as clinical negligence, catastrophic injuries or difficult questions of fact or law, consideration should be given to whether it would be appropriate to instruct leading counsel; junior counsel will usually advise the solicitor if he thinks that this would be appropriate. The solicitor should advise the client accordingly of the extra cost involved and, if the client is CLS funded, seek authority from the CLS to instruct leading counsel. The client should also be advised that if leading counsel is instructed, and this is disallowed on assessment, the cost will ultimately be borne by the client in the form of the statutory charge on the client's damages.

11.9.4   Narrowing the issues

When preparing for trial the solicitor should ask himself, 'what do I have to prove?'. A review should be made of the case file to ascertain areas of agreement, which are no longer in issue. One useful device may be a list comprising two columns: the left-hand column listing the facts which have to be proved (eg, that the claimant was driving the car; that an accident occurred; the date of the accident; the place of the accident; an itemised list of the losses, etc); and the right-hand column indicating whether the fact is admitted by the opponent.

Admissions will normally be found in the statements of case or in open correspondence.

11.9.5 Schedule of special damages

The claimant's solicitor must check that the schedule of special damages is up to date and, if necessary, serve an updated schedule of special damages. Ideally, this should be the final schedule (although it may have to be revised again if there is a significant delay before the trial), the purpose of which is to identify the areas of agreement and disagreement between the parties. With this in mind, the following format could be usefully employed (the figures are merely for illustration):

Item of claim	Claimant's figure	Defendant's figure	Discrepancy
Purchase of wheelchair	£350	£350	Nil
Loss of future earnings	£50,000 (multiplicand = £5,000, multiplier = 10)	£32,000 (multiplicand = £4,000, multiplier = 8)	£18,000

The defendant's solicitor should be sent the updated schedule of special damages, with a covering letter requesting that he agrees it or specifies the items he is not prepared to agree, and giving a time limit for the reply. It should be pointed out that, if he fails to reply, the claimant's solicitors will have to issue a witness summons for any persons necessary to prove the amounts claimed, and the claimant will ask for the costs of this exercise be paid by the defendant in any event.

In clinical negligence claims, where special damages claims are likely to involve substantial amounts of money, it is more likely that the defence will seek to query items claimed as special damages. For this reason the directions will normally require that the defendant also provide a counter-schedule of special damages itemising the areas of disagreement.

11.9.6 Trial bundles

In both the High Court and the county court, bundles of documents upon which the parties intend to rely must be lodged within the appropriate time, for use by the trial judge.

The bundle must be paginated and indexed. The medical records must be complete and in good order to enable medical experts to study them easily. X-rays or scans included in the bundle should be clearly identified. Scans may be several feet long and should be professionally copied if possible.

The quality of preparation of bundles varies enormously, and this can have serious implications for the client's case if preparation is not undertaken properly. Although there are rules governing the content of the bundles, there is very little guidance on how the documents should be presented. When preparing the bundle the aim should be to enable whoever is conducting the trial to turn to any document at any time with the minimum of fuss or delay, and that all others concerned with the case can do likewise. The more documents there are in the bundle, the more difficult this task becomes. In a straightforward road traffic claim, there will be few documents and, as such, the bundle should be relatively easy to prepare. In serious cases involving multiple injuries or in clinical negligence cases, however, the documents are likely to extend to many hundreds of pages. In such cases, it is even more important that the court is not hindered by trying to find documents that should be readily to hand. Poor preparation of the case will not impress the judge, nor will it go unnoticed. Documents will need to be split into a number of smaller bundles which are easier to handle. Using colour-coded lever arch files is often a good method, with a separate file for each class of document. As a matter of courtesy, if counsel has been instructed, the solicitor may wish to send the proposed index to the core bundle of documents to counsel in advance of the trial, so that counsel has the opportunity to ask for further items to be included if necessary.

11.9.7   Use of visual aids

Plans, photographs and models can be of enormous value at the trial as an aid to clarity, thereby shortening the length of the trial (avoiding long testimony of a witness) and saving costs. A judge may more readily understand the testimony of a witness if that witness is allowed to refer to a plan or photograph. Medical experts can often supply good quality colour diagrams, anatomical illustrations or models to make their testimony more comprehensible. In clinical negligence cases, it is worth the extra time and effort to find good visual aids. A judge is unlikely to have in-depth medical knowledge, and attempts to help the judge fully comprehend the circumstances giving rise to the alleged negligence are likely to be gratefully received.

Visual aids must be disclosed to the opponent in advance. No plan, photograph or model will be receivable in evidence at trial unless the party wishing to use the evidence discloses it no later than the latest date for serving witness statements.

A video-recording is more useful than photographs in the case of 'movement'. Two common examples are:

(a)   a video-recording of an industrial process;

(b)   a video-recording showing the difficulties of the claimant in coping with his injuries (a 'day in the life'). Although the claimant should call, in addition to his own evidence, members of his family or friends to give evidence as to how he manages with his injuries (evidence of his bodily and mental condition before and after the accident), a video film (eg, showing the medical assistance required, such as physiotherapy or even surgery) may illustrate the situation more graphically.

If the photographs or other visual aids are agreed, they are admissible in the absence of the maker. If the aids are not agreed, the maker must be called to prove their authenticity.

The solicitor should ensure at the trial that there are enough copies of photographs for the use of the judge, advocates and witnesses.

11.10   The trial

11.10.1   The morning of the trial

The solicitor should arrive early to ensure that he has time:

(a) to check with the clerk to the court that the court has the trial bundles, and place a bundle in the witness-box;

(b) to ensure that counsel has arrived and consider any last minute questions he may have;

(c) to meet the client on his arrival and attempt to put him at his ease;

(d) to introduce counsel to the client (if they have not already met in conference);

(e) to ensure that an interview room is reserved for the pre-trial conference with counsel.

11.10.2 Advice to clients and witnesses

The case will usually turn on how well or how badly the witnesses give their evidence and how they are perceived by the judge. The client and other witnesses should be reminded that they will not be able to take their statements into the witness-box. The solicitor should run through the procedure to be adopted when giving oral evidence with the witnesses, as follows:

(a) explain the procedure on taking the oath, and whether the client wishes to affirm;

(b) remind the witness that all responses should be addressed to the judge regardless of who asked the question; and

(c) that the judge must be addressed in the appropriate manner; and

(d) go through the order in which the witnesses will be examined.

Each witness's statement will normally stand as evidence-in-chief, in which case the witness's evidence will move to being cross-examined almost immediately.

It is important to allay the client's fears about giving oral evidence. The solicitor should advise the client to speak slowly and directly to the judge, just as if there was no one else in the room. The judge will be writing notes and therefore the witness should watch the judge's pen and only resume speaking when the judge has finished writing.

It is unlikely that the client and lay witnesses will have given evidence before. They should be advised that if they do not understand the question they should say so, and to take their evidence slowly, answer only the question put to them and not to engage in questioning opposing counsel or offer unsolicited opinions of their own. It is up to the solicitor to keep his witnesses in check and ensure that they do not embarrass the client or harm his case.

11.10.3 Conduct of the trial

Counsel (if instructed) will have the conduct of the trial, and the solicitor's function will be to sit behind counsel and take full notes of evidence. For the purpose of costing, a note should be made of the start time, any adjournments and the time the trial finishes. The questions asked by counsel should be noted, as well as the responses given, as counsel will not be able to make any notes himself while on his feet.

11.10.4 Order of evidence

Although evidence is usually given by the claimant first, followed by the defence, in clinical negligence cases all witnesses of fact may be called first, followed by witnesses giving evidence of opinion. This is because the facts themselves are often complex and it assists the judge greatly if the facts are laid out clearly by hearing evidence from the witnesses of fact for the claimant, followed directly by those of the defence. The object is to clarify the areas of disagreement so that experts can concentrate their efforts there, and shorten the length of trial. However, the parties must apply to the trial judge on the first day of the trial to use this procedure, as the order of evidence in the judge's court will be decided by the individual judge as a matter of discretion.

11.10.5   Judgment

The solicitor should take a careful note of the judgment delivered by the judge at the end of the case, as it may be crucial if the client decides to appeal.

Counsel must be made aware of any specific orders which may be necessary.

The solicitor should also check the pre-trial orders to see if costs were reserved in any interim proceedings, and, if so, that this is brought to the attention of the judge so that a costs order can be made in relation to that application.

The judgment should be fully explained to the client, which can be undertaken by counsel.

11.10.6   The order

Following trial in the county court, the court will draw up the order, which should be checked carefully to ensure that it reflects the judge's decision, as mistakes are sometimes made by the court staff.

11.11   Conclusion

Taking a case to trial will be the exception rather than the rule in personal injury litigation. Nevertheless, every case must be approached from the standpoint that it will go to trial, and must be prepared accordingly.

11.12   Further reading

The Civil Procedure Rules (Lord Chancellor's Department, 1998).

Civil Court Practice (the Green Book) (Butterworths).

Civil Procedure (the White Book) (Sweet & Maxwell).

Chapter 12

Clawback of Benefits — Social Security (Recovery of Benefits) Act 1997

12.1 Introduction

The claimant may receive State benefits as a result of the accident. The purpose of this chapter is to examine how the receipt of such sums affects the claimant's damages.

The Department for Work and Pensions (DWP) operates the recovery of benefits system, via the Compensation Recovery Unit (CRU).

12.2 The legislation

The legislation is predominantly contained in the Social Security (Recovery of Benefits) Act 1997 (the 1997 Act). The key features of the 1997 Act are as follows:

(a) Recoupment is not allowed against general damages for pain, suffering and loss of amenity.

(b) Recoupment is allowed only against certain special damages, ie, those for loss of earnings, damages for costs of care and damages for loss of mobility.

(c) Certain benefits can only be recouped against the above and only on a 'like-for-like basis' (ie, benefits paid as a result of loss of earnings can only be recouped out of damages awarded in respect of past loss of earnings).

(d) The burden of recoupment is shifted onto the 'compensator' (usually the defendant's insurer). The compensator is responsible for repayment of all relevant benefits paid to the injured person even if they are unable to recoup the full amount out of that person's damages.

(e) There is no deduction from damages for future loss.

(f) There is no deduction from damages in respect of medical expenses (not included in cost of respite or nursing care and attendance).

The main Regulations relevant to the Scheme are found in the Social Security (Recovery of Benefits) Regulations 1997 (SI 1997/2205), as amended by paras 148–52 of Sch 7 to the Social Security Act 1998.

12.3 Definitions

12.3.1 The meaning of 'compensation payment'

A compensation payment is a payment made by a person (whether on his own behalf or not) to or in respect of any other person in consequence of any accident, injury or disease suffered by the other (s 1 of the 1997 Act). This is a very wide definition and is designed to cover payments whether made by the tortfeasor or his insurer. The 1997 Act also applies to all claims settled or judgments given on or after 6 October 1997, regardless of whether proceedings were issued prior to that date.

12.3.2 The meaning of 'compensator'

The compensator means the person, company or agent who is paying the compensation, usually an insurance company, on behalf of their insured.

12.3.3 The meaning of 'recoverable benefit'

A recoverable benefit is any listed benefit which has been or is likely to be paid in respect of an accident, injury or disease (s 1 of the 1997 Act).

'Recoverable benefits' are listed in Sch 2 to the 1997 Act and are reproduced at 12.7.

12.4 Compensation subject to recoupment

The reforms introduced by the 1997 Act are designed to spread the burden evenly between claimants and compensators.

Further safeguards in respect of recoupment out of special damages are also provided by the 1997 Act. Recoupment is allowed only against specified areas of loss (see below).

The three specified areas subject to recoupment are:

(a)   compensation for loss of earnings;

(b)   compensation for cost of care; and

(c)   compensation for loss of mobility.

Scope for recoupment is further limited by the fact that recoupment out of the above three types of compensation is allowed only on a 'like-for-like' basis.

In relation to all three of the above, recoupment can occur only in respect of losses during what the 1997 Act terms 'the relevant period'.

The relevant period is defined in s 3 as:

(a)   five years from the date of the accident or injury; or

(b)   in the case of a disease, five years beginning with the date on which a listed benefit was first claimed; or

(c)   the period ending with a compensation payment in final discharge of the claim (if less than five years).

Therefore, the overall effect of the legislation is that:

(a)   it allows recoupment against certain items of special damage; and

(b)   it should ensure that general damages are protected from recoupment.

Note that claims for future loss including cost of care and mobility *beyond* the above five-year period are *not* subject to recoupment.

12.5 'Like-for-like' recoupment

Having established that only special damages can be the subject of recoupment, Sch 2 to the 1997 Act further safeguards special damages as it allows only 'like-for-like' recoupment. This means that only benefits which closely correspond to the relevant head of loss can be recouped from damages awarded in respect of that head of loss.

For example, if you consider the schedule at **12.7**, you will see that attendance allowance can be recouped only from compensation for cost of care, and not from compensation for loss of earnings.

If compensation for cost of care is less than the amount actually paid out in listed benefits during the relevant period, the claimant will receive nothing in respect of that head of loss; *however,* any excess in benefits for cost of care which has not so far been recouped, cannot be recouped from any other head of compensation. In this instance, the burden of paying off the excess falls on the compensator (usually the insurance company), and will be refunded to the DWP, so that the State will always achieve 100% recoupment, the only question being how much will be out of compensation, and how much will be paid by the compensator.

For example, due to an accident at work six years ago, John (who is aged below 65) has received severe disablement allowance and reduced earnings allowance over the entire six-year period. He has also received disability living allowance.

Severe disablement allowance and reduced earnings allowance are both recoupable in full, but only for the first five years and only from compensation paid in respect of lost earnings. Similarly, disability living allowance will be recoupable, as regards the care component only, from compensation paid in respect of cost of care.

12.6 The role of the compensator

(a)   In most cases, the claimant's solicitor will supply to the compensator the necessary Compensatory Recovery Unit (CRU) information.

(b)   Within 14 days, the compensator informs the CRU on Form CRU 1 giving required particulars.

(c)   The CRU acknowledges receipt of the notification and issues Form CRU 4 to the compensator.

(d)   The claim then progresses to the settlement stage.

(e)   When ready to make an offer of compensation, the compensator submits Form CRU 4 to obtain a certificate of recoverable benefit.

(f)   The CRU acknowledges receipt of Form CRU 4 (within 14 days).

(g)   The CRU sends the certificate of recoverable benefit to the compensator. A copy will also be sent to the claimant's solicitor. The compensator will then settle the compensation claim and then pay the relevant amount to the DWP within 14 days of the settlement.

12.6.1   Notifying the DWP

Section 4 of the 1997 Act requires that the compensator inform the DWP not later than 14 days after receiving the claim. The notification is made on Form CRU 1 which is sent to the DWP.

The information required by the compensator to complete Form CRU 1 includes:

(a)   the full name and address of the claimant;

(b)   (if known) the date of birth and national insurance number of that person;

(c)   the date of the accident or injury (or in the case of disease the date of diagnosis);

(d)   the nature of the accident, injury or disease (as alleged by the claimant);

(e)   (if known) the name and address of the claimant's employer and his payroll number at the relevant time.

On receipt of Form CRU 1, the CRU will send Form CRU 4 to the defendant. This has a twofold function:

(a)   it acknowledges receipt of the notification of claim; and

(b)   the compensator should retain it safely on the file as it will be needed later to obtain the certificate of recoverable benefit (ie, the details of the benefit paid or to be paid to the claimant).

Despite the requirement that the DWP be informed of the claim within 14 days of notification of the claim, this is sometimes overlooked by insurance companies. If proceedings are issued and the insurer instructs solicitors, Form CRU 1 should be completed immediately, if this has not already been done. In such circumstances, it may be appropriate for the address of the compensator given on Form CRU 1 to be care of the solicitors, to ensure that the certificate of recoverable benefit is forwarded to the solicitors, who are likely to make the compensation payment to the claimant.

When the matter is lodged with the DWP, the claimant's solicitor will be notified and a Form CRU 4R will also be sent to the claimant's representative, which can be used to obtain benefit information (the claimant's solicitor can also obtain benefit details by writing to the DWP). It is important that, prior to negotiating any settlement or accepting any payment into court, the claimant himself examines the benefit details to ensure that they are correct.

12.6.2   The certificate of recoverable benefit

The provision central to the whole system is that no compensation is to be paid until the defendant has obtained a 'certificate of recoverable benefit'. If compensation is paid without obtaining a certificate, the DWP can still take steps against the defendant to recover the benefits.

The defendant obtains the certificate by completing and returning Form CRU 4 to the CRU. The defendant must ensure that all the information required by Forms CRU 1 and CRU 4 is given, after which the CRU will acknowledge the form in writing and send a certificate to the defendant and a copy to the claimant.

The certificate details:

(a)   the amount of relevant benefits paid or likely to be paid by a specified date;

(b)   the details of any continuing benefit; and

(c)   the amount to be recouped in the event of a compensation payment being made.

12.7 The meaning of 'recoverable benefits'

A schedule of recoverable benefits and the heads of damage which they are recoverable against on a like-for-like basis (see **12.5** for explanation of 'like-for-like' recoupment) is contained in Sch 2 to the 1997 Act as:

Head of compensation	*Benefit**
1. Compensation for earnings lost during relevant period	Disability working allowance Disablement pension payable under section 103 of the 1992 Act Incapacity benefit Income support Invalidity pension and allowance Jobseeker's allowance Reduced earnings allowance Severe disablement allowance Sickness benefit Statutory sick pay before 6 April 1994 Unemployability supplement Unemployment benefit
2. Compensation for cost of care incurred during the relevant period	Attendance allowance Care component of disability living allowance Disablement pension increase payable under section 104 or s 105 of the 1992 Act
3. Compensation for loss of mobility during the relevant period	Mobility allowance Mobility component of disability living allowance

(* The names of the various benefits have changed over the years. However, there are still claims involving certain of these benefits despite them no longer being available.)

DWP Leaflet Z1 provides further details of damages that do and do not fall within Sch 2 (see also case law such as *Clenshaw v Tanner* [2002] EWHC 184, QB, dealing with housing benefit, and *Lowther v Chatwin* [2003] EWCA Civ 729) and see also *Eagle v Chambers* [2004] EWCA Civ 1033 concerning benefits and the claimant's duty to mitigate.

Note: References to incapacity benefit, invalidity pension and allowance, severe disablement allowance, sickness benefit and unemployment benefit also include any income support paid with each of those benefits.

Any reference to statutory sick pay:

(a)   includes only 80% of payments made between 6 April 1991 and 5 April 1994; and

(b)   does not include payments made on or after 6 April 1994.

In the case of *Griffiths and Others v British Coal Corporation and the Department of Trade and Industry* [2001] 1 WLR 1493, it was held that an award of interest on damages for past loss of earnings fell within the expression 'compensation for earnings lost' in Sch 2 to the 1997 Act and was therefore subject to reduction on account of payments by the tortfeasor to the DWP. In the same case, it was also held that any compensation for services in the nature of care, gratuitously rendered, fell within the term 'compensation for cost of care incurred during the relevant period', and allowed the tortfeasor to set off the benefits paid against the damages.

12.8   Exempt payments

Schedule 1, Pt 1 of the 1997 Act and reg 2 of the Social Security (Recovery of Benefits) Regulations 1997, contain the payments which are exempt from recoupment under the Act. These include payments by or under the following:

(a)   Fatal Accidents Act 1976.

(b)   Criminal Injuries Compensation Authority payments.

(c)   Vaccine damage payments.

(d)   The Macfarlane Trust (established partly under funds from the Secretary of State to the Haemophilia Society) and the Eileen Trust.

(e)   British Coal, in accordance with the NCB Pneumoconiosis Compensation Scheme.

(f)   Cases of hearing loss, where the loss is less than 50db in one or both ears.

(g)   The National Health Service (Injury Benefits) Regulations.

(h)   Criminal Court Compensation Orders, s 35 of the Powers of Criminal Courts Act 1973.

(i)   Certain trust funds (in particular 'disaster funds', where more than half of the fund is raised by public subscription).

(j)   Certain private insurance contracts between the victim and his insurer entered into before the contract.

(k)   Any redundancy payment already accounted for in the assessment of damages.

(l)   Any amount which is referable to costs.

(m)   Any contractual amount paid to an employee by an employer in respect of incapacity for work (eg, occupational sick pay).

(n)   Any small payment, as defined in Pt II of Sch 1 to the Social Security (Recovery of Benefits) Act 1997. There are currently no small payment exceptions.

12.9   Contributory negligence

Since 'compensation payment' is defined as the sum falling to be paid to the claimant, it follows that the relevant sum is that which is paid to the claimant after any deduction for contributory negligence by the claimant. However, the case of *Williams v Devon County Council* [2003] EWCA Civ 365 should be considered as the Court of Appeal gave guidance on the interrelation of r 36.23 and the provisions of benefit deduction, in respect of contributory negligence.

12.10   Multiple defendants ('compensators')

In certain cases, the claimant will sue two or more defendants, and, as such, all defendants are jointly and severally liable to reimburse the CRU. However, in practice, it is usual for a sharing agreement as between defendants to be made, whereby the defendants reach an agreement as to how they are to pay the claimant and the CRU.

12.11   Clinical negligence

The rules relating to the clawback of benefit apply to clinical negligence claims and, due to their complexity, especially with regard to causation, the CRU has set up a specialist group to deal with the claims and makes a special request that compensators inform the CRU about clinical negligence claims as soon as the pre-action correspondence is received.

12.12 Part 36 payments

If the defendant wishes to place pressure on the claimant to settle the case and proceedings have been commenced, the defendant will make a Part 36 payment into court. PD 36 requires the notice of payment into court to state:

(a)   the amount of the gross compensation;

(b)   that the gross amount has been reduced by the amount of benefits in accordance with s 8 of and Sch 2 to the Social Security (Recovery of Benefits) Act 1997, specifying the name of the benefit and the amount; and

(c)   the net amount paid in after the reduction.

The compensator must obtain a Certificate of Recoverable Benefits and lodge it with the payment into court.

Form N424A should be used for the Part 36 payment and the compensator should file with the court a Certificate of Recoverable Benefits.

12.13 Interim payments

It should be noted that if an interim payment is made, then the compensator is liable to repay any relevant recoverable benefits at that stage.

12.14 Appeals system

The grounds for appeal include:

(a)   that any amount, rate or period in the Certificate of Recoverable Benefits is incorrect;

(b)   against the calculations in the Certificate of Recoverable Benefits relating to benefits not paid in consequence of accident, injury or disease.

An appeal can be made only after final settlement of the compensation claim and payment of the recoverable benefits has been made. The basic time limit for the appeal is one month from the date on which the compensator makes the full payment of recoverable benefits and is dealt with by an independent tribunal administered by the Appeals Service.

Appeal can be made by:

(a)   the person who applied for the certificate, ie, the compensator; or

(b)   the injured person whose compensation payment has been reduced.

There is a less formal procedure that can be adopted and that is known as a 'review'. This can be requested at any time and as a result the CRU will look at the matter again and clear the benefits that are listed as recoverable.

12.15 Conclusion

Solicitors should exercise care when dealing with this area to ensure that it is clear whether any offer put forward is net or gross of benefits, and that the benefit figures are correct. In *Hilton International v Martin-Smith* (2001) LTL, 12 February, it was held that, where a party made an error of judgment (in this case, in relation to the amount stated on the Certificate of Recoverable Benefits), it did not follow that the court would permit that party to escape its consequences. Similarly, defendant solicitors also need to ensure that benefits listed as recoverable benefits are as a consequence of the accident (see *Eagle Star Insurance v Department of Social Development (Northern Ireland)* (only persuasive) (2001) NICE, 12 February; *Secretary of State for Social Security v Oldham MBC and Others*, 15 May 2001 and see *Quantum* 4/2004 (Sweet & Maxwell). See also *Williams v Devon County Council* [2003] EWCA Civ 365, [2003] All ER (D) 255 (Mar), concerning details to be included on a notice of payment into court and details of the benefits to be included and *Bruce v Genesis Fast Food Ltd* [2003] EWHC 788 concerning whether defendants are entitled to take the benefit on any reduction in recoverable benefits when an appeal takes place.

12.16 Further reading

Department for Work and Pensions/CRU leaflet Z1, *A Recovery of Benefits Guide for Companies and Solicitors – Procedures for Liaison with the Compensation Recovery Unit.*

Kemp and Kemp, *The Quantum of Damages* (Sweet & Maxwell).

12.17 Overview of clawback of benefits

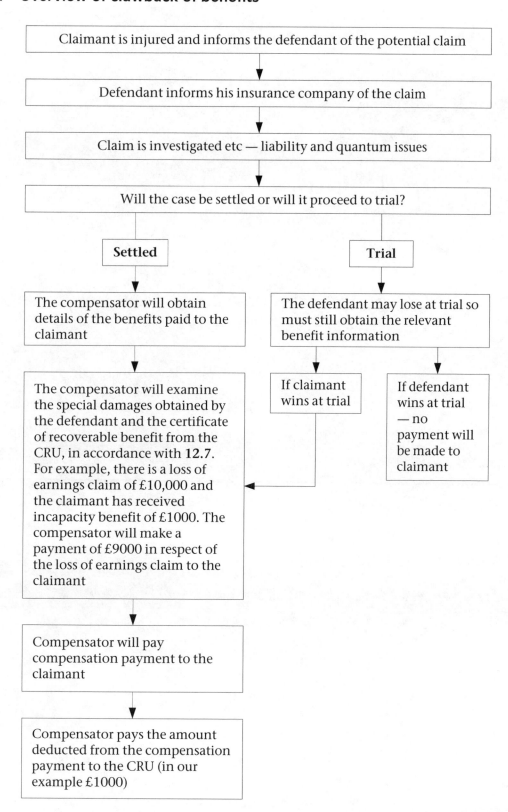

Chapter 13

Quantification of Damages

13.1 Introduction

The claimant's solicitor has as his aim the achievement of the highest possible level of damages for his client. This chapter explains how these damages are calculated.

In tort, the aim of the award of damages in a personal injury claim is to restore the claimant to the position that he was in prior to the accident. In practice, for a personal injury claim this clearly cannot be achieved. For many clients, the award of damages is recompense not only for the injuries that they have suffered but compensation for the stress and inconvenience of being involved in a litigation process which can take many years. Many victims of clinical negligence complain that the difficulties that they have encountered in pursuing their investigation of the potential negligence can result in continued illness or failure to recover within the expected period of time. However, the award of monetary compensation is the only available remedy to the court.

Many claimants' solicitors believe that the level of damages awarded in personal injury cases does not adequately compensate the injured claimant, and organisations such as the Association of Personal Injury Lawyers (APIL) campaign on this issue.

The court can make true recompense for the financial losses which the claimant has incurred prior to trial, as these can be calculated precisely. Such losses are referred to as 'special damages'. (The phrase 'past pecuniary loss' is also used but the meaning is the same.) The element of the compensation award that cannot be calculated specifically, for example, the pain and suffering which the claimant suffered, are referred to as 'general damages'. The distinction is significant not only in the method of calculation but also with regard to the level of interest awarded by the court (see **13.4**). Although the claimant regards his compensation payment as one lump sum, the personal injury solicitor must fully understand on what basis the court will award damages, to ensure that he can maximise the level of damages awarded to his client, where appropriate.

The claimant's damages are assessed as at the date of the trial, and it is therefore important that sufficient and up-to-date evidence is available in respect of special and general damages. For example, an up-to-date loss of earnings calculation must be put before the court, together with up-to-date medical evidence on the client's condition, where appropriate.

The following basic guidance applies to both personal injury and clinical negligence claims.

13.2   Special damages

Special damages are the items of loss that can be specifically calculated, and represent the claimant's financial loss from the date of the accident until the date of trial.

The main heads of special damages are:

(a)   items of specific loss;

(b)   loss of earnings to the date of trial;

(c)   medical expenses prior to trial;

(d)   cost of services provided by a third party prior to the trial;

(e)   expenses relating to the cost of living with disabilities prior to trial.

13.2.1   Items of specific loss

In the majority of personal injury cases, there will be certain one-off losses incurred by the claimant. In a road traffic accident, the claimant will normally have several items of specific loss, for example:

(a)   the cost of repair of the vehicle;

(b)   policy excess if the car was comprehensively insured;

(c)   hire car charges;

(d)   bus fares;

(e)   damage to clothing;

(f)   taxi fares;

(g)   prescription charges;

(h)   recovery or storage charges relating to the car;

(i)   damaged items in the vehicle;

(j)   pre-accident value of the car (less salvage if the car is written off);

(k)   loss of petrol if the car is written off.

It is for the claimant to prove the items of loss, and he should be reminded at the outset of the case that he should retain documentary evidence (such as receipts) in support of as many items as possible. Insurance companies often deny payment for items that cannot be supported by documentary evidence, but it is open to the claimant to attempt to prove the loss by evidence at trial (see *Hughes v Addis* (2000) LTL, 23 March).

All of the above items are frequently claimed for in a road traffic case and many are uncontroversial. However, there can be difficulties in advising as regards to hire charge claims, especially where the claimant wishes to hire a different type of vehicle from that involved in the accident or the hire charges are for a long period of time. It is clear that hire car charges can be claimed while the claimant's vehicle is being repaired but the claimant must show that he has acted reasonably. For example, if the hire car is being hired by the claimant at a daily rate (which is frequently the most expensive charging rate) rather than at a weekly rate (which is often cheaper), then the court may take the view that only the weekly rate should be recoverable, unless the claimant can show a good reason for using the daily rate (see *Usher v Crowder* [1994] CLY 1494).

It appears that the claimant is able to claim for losses from the defendant that were due to the claimant's lack of money. For example, the defendants admit liability for a road traffic accident but the claimant cannot afford to pay for the repairs out of his own funds. As a result, the claimant hires a car until the defendants pay for the repairs to the claimant's car. Following *Mattocks v Mann* [1993] RTR 13, such a claim is recoverable. However, in certain circumstances, the claimant may use a vehicle supplied by a 'credit hire' company. However, for any such agreement to be enforceable, it must comply with the Consumer Credit Act 1974 (or be exempt) and the amount recoverable should be the 'market rate'; see *Dimond v Lovell* [2000] 2 WLR 1121.

If a claim for hire charges is made then, generally, a claim for loss of use (see **13.3.7**) will not be made as the claimant has not been without a vehicle.

It may also be possible to recover as special damages the loss of any non-recoupable benefits which are no longer being paid to the client as a result of the injury (see *Neal v Bingle* [1998] 2 All ER 58, CA).

13.2.2 Loss of earnings up to the date of the trial

This is the most common example of special damages. Only in the most simple of personal injury cases will there be no claim for lost earnings. The claimant is allowed to recover his net loss of earnings; this represents the figure which he would have earned after tax, national insurance and contractual pension payments (if his pension is left unaffected see *Dews v National Coal Board* [1988] AC 1, HL).

The claimant's solicitor should contact his client's employer and ask for details of the client's wages prior to the accident (providing the employer is not the defendant, in which case such detail will be provided via the defendant's insurance company). It is common to obtain the details for the period of 13 weeks prior to the accident and a standard form is often used for such a purpose. However, if there is any evidence that the average of the 13 weeks prior to the accident is not representative of the claimant's average pre-accident wage, then further enquiries should be made and a longer period of pre-accident wage details should be obtained, for example six months. In particular, it must be ensured that any overtime, bonus payments or commission that the claimant would have earned if he had been at work are included in the net loss of earnings figure. Enquiries also need to be made as to whether the client would have received any pay increase, promotion, or obtained any other benefits such as a company car had he not been absent from work.

In appropriate cases, it is good practice to obtain details of a comparative earner when calculating the loss of earnings figure. This involves obtaining the wages details of another employee of the client's employer who is on the same wages as the client. For example, where a solicitor represents a factory operative who is paid a basic wage of £200 net per week, but the client can also earn additional overtime, details can be obtained of another employee who is on the same pay scale and who has the same opportunity for overtime work as the client, and the amount that the comparative employee has earned while the client has been absent from work can be put to the defendants as the figure that the client would have earned had he not been involved in the accident. This can be particularly useful in cases where the claimant has only recently obtained a job and a clear pattern of pre-accident earnings cannot be established. The comparative figures must be shown to the client for confirmation that they represent a true comparison.

Very few employees receive no income whatsoever while absent from work and so the calculation of the claimant's lost earnings is not simply: weekly net loss of earnings × period of absence = net loss. A detailed examination of what income the claimant received while absent from work is required as certain types of income have to be credited in calculating the net loss figure, for example:

Net pre-accident earnings × 10 weeks' absence from work	£100 / £1,000

Claimant received £50 per week from his employer while
absent, in accordance with his contract of employment.
The contract does not make any provision for the money
paid while absent to be repaid to the employer.   £500

Total net loss of earnings   £500

13.2.2.1 Most common items dealt with in net loss of earnings calculation

The following are the most common items which must be accounted for in the net loss of earnings figure (for both past and future loss of earnings calculations).

Tax refunds received due to absence from work as a result of the accident

A claimant who is an employee will generally pay income tax on the Pay As You Earn (PAYE) system. To a certain extent this system is a payment of tax in advance, as it assumes that the claimant's earnings will continue throughout the whole of the forthcoming year. In the event of the claimant's absence from work, he may then have paid too much tax. In this case, the claimant may receive a tax rebate via his employer. An amount equivalent to the whole of the rebate has to be given credit for in the calculation of wage loss (*Hartley v Sandholme Iron Co Ltd* [1975] QB 600). Occasionally, instead of a 'cash-in-hand' tax rebate, the claimant may receive a tax credit against future tax liability so that on his return to work he pays no tax for a period (a 'tax holiday'). A sum equivalent to this tax credit also has to be given credit for in the calculation of the wage loss (*Brayson v Wilmot-Breedon* [1976] CLY 682).

Sums paid to the claimant by his employer

Whether sums equivalent to such payments fall to be deducted from the damages depends on:

(a)   the basis of the payment; and

(b)   who is the tortfeasor.

The following are the most common situations:

(a)   The sum is paid under a legal obligation (eg, under the claimant's contract of employment) and is not refundable by the claimant to his employer. An amount equivalent to the whole of the payment should be deducted from the damages.

(b)   The sum is paid under a legal obligation (eg, under the contract of employment) and must be repaid by the claimant to his employer out of any damages the claimant receives from the defendant. Such a payment is effectively a loan and, as such, is not deducted when assessing the damages.

(c)   The sum is paid ex gratia by the employer who is not the tortfeasor. Such a payment is effectively a 'charitable' payment and is not to be deducted when assessing the damages (*Cunningham v Harrison* [1973] 3 All ER 463).

(d)   The sum is paid ex gratia by the employer who is the tortfeasor. An amount equivalent to the whole of the payment may (in certain circumstances) be deducted from the damages (*Hussain v New Taplow Paper Mills Ltd* [1988] AC 514).

(e)   The claimant receives statutory sick pay from his employer. This is not a recoverable benefit to the DWP (see **Chapter 12**) and therefore an amount equivalent to the whole payment should be deducted (the contract of employment may need to be examined in case the employer is entitled to clawback the SSP in some way). See also *Palfrey v Greater London Council* [1985] ICR 437 (and see **4.7.1.1** for further details of SSP).

Any saving to an injured person attributable to his maintenance wholly or partly at public expense

This would apply where the claimant was, for example, admitted into an NHS hospital, nursing home or other institution. The savings must be calculated and set off against any claim for income lost as a result of the injuries (Administration of Justice Act 1982, s 5). In practice, this deduction is overlooked because in most cases the sums saved are *de minimis* (while in hospital the claimant will generally have to meet the same household expenses such as rent, mortgage and council tax; any saving will usually only be in regard to the cost of food. This saving is then so small as to be ignored). For private medical expenses, see **13.2.3**.

Redundancy payments

An equivalent amount is to be deducted in full from the damages calculation when redundancy occurs as a result of the injury caused by the accident (*Colledge v Bass Mitchells & Butlers* [1988] 1 All ER 536).

13.2.2.2   Most common items excluded from net loss of earnings

The following items are the most common payments to be left out of account in assessing an award for loss of past (and future) earnings.

State retirement pension

The State retirement pension is ignored in assessing an award for loss of past and future earnings (*Hewson v Downs* [1970] 1 QB 73).

Pensions received

The general rule is that if the claimant receives a pension, this cannot be set against the claim for loss of earnings. However, if there is a separate claim for loss of pension rights, for example since the claimant is unable to work he will receive less pension in the future, any pension he does receive may be offset against the claim for loss of pension rights (*Parry v Cleaver* [1970] AC 1; *Smoker v London Fire and Civil Defence Authority* [1991] 2 All ER 449; *Longden v British Coal Corporation* [1997] 3 WLR 1336; see also **13.3.6**).

Insurance moneys

The claimant may have the benefit of an insurance policy under which he is entitled to receive payment in the event of his sustaining injury. The claimant may have taken out the policy specifically to cover such eventualities or the personal injury cover may be an 'incidental' benefit (eg, to a comprehensive motor insurance policy).

In such cases, the payment is usually a fixed sum according to the type of injury; for example, in the event of a loss of a limb the insurance company will pay the insured the sum of £5,000. The claimant need not give credit for moneys received under such a policy against the damages payable by the defendant. The justification is that the defendant should not benefit from the fact that the claimant had the foresight to take out the cover and pay the premium (*Bradburn v Great Western Railway Co* (1874) LR 10 Exch 1; *McCamley v Cammell Laird Shipbuilders Ltd* [1990] 1 All ER 854). The claimant, however, should check the terms of his insurance policy. It is often the case (particularly in motor insurance) that there is a provision that if the claimant recovers damages in respect of a loss for which the claimant's insurance company has paid the claimant compensation, the claimant must reimburse his insurance company. In this case, although the claimant may claim for the losses from the defendant, he will receive no personal benefit if he does so.

This issue was considered by the Court of Appeal in *Pirelli v Gaca* [2004] EWCA Civ 373, in relation to the situation where an employer sets up a non-contributory group personal accident insurance policy. In this case the claimant received substantial payments from the insurance policy and it was held that the claimant must give credit for the payments in these circumstances. Care should be taken to examine the exact basis on which payments have been made and reference made to *Pirelli v Gaca*.

Charitable payments

If money is received by the claimant as a charitable payment (even if it is on an informal basis such as the proceeds of a collection taken among his friends) then the claimant is not required to give credit for such payments against the damages received. The justification is that as a matter of policy people should not be discouraged from making such payments to the victims of accidents (*Parry v Cleaver* (above)). However, the exact circumstances and sources of the ex gratia payment must be considered. In *Williams v BOC Gases Ltd* [2000] PIQR Q253, the Court of Appeal held that, where an employer (who was the tortfeasor) made an ex gratia payment on termination of the claimant's employment and 'it is to be treated as an advance against damages that may be awarded ... in respect of any claim ...', credit had to be given for that amount in a subsequent personal injury claim.

13.2.2.3   Clients with unusual employment histories

Not all claimants are employees nor have they all had stable employment backgrounds. In such circumstances, further enquiries must be made in an attempt to provide evidence of pre-accident income. Self-employed claimants should be asked to supply copies of their accounts for the year prior to the accident, or a longer period if one year's figures are not representative. Unfortunately, this information can be difficult to obtain from the client, and the defendants will argue the validity of the claim. In certain cases, it will be necessary to obtain a report from an accountant (the term 'forensic accountant' is often used for those who specialise in this area). It may also be necessary to contact the claimant's tax office to obtain copies of his tax returns. In an attempt to establish details of how much the claimant would have earned between the accident and trial in cases where an erratic employment history is presented (eg, this can often be the situation with building labourers who had just commenced employment at the time of the accident), reference can be made to the New Earnings Survey produced by the Office for National Statistics, which is a statistical analysis of earnings throughout the country. The Survey can provide details of average earnings for particular industries or occupations on a national or regional basis and can be useful in attempting to persuade the defendant to accept that the claimant would have received a particular wage. (The Survey is also of particular use in connection with future loss claims.) The claimant must adduce as much evidence as possible to establish what he would have earned if it had not been for the accident.

It is still possible for an accident victim who was, prior to the accident, receiving earnings from a lawful source but failing to pay tax or National Insurance, to bring a claim for past and future loss of earnings (although adjustments will have to be made to the past and future loss of earnings calculation) (see *Newman v Marshall and Dunlop Tyres Ltd* (2001) LTL, 19 June and *Duller v South East Lincs Engineers* (1985) CLY 585).

13.2.3 Medical expenses prior to trial

In certain cases, where there are long waiting lists under the NHS, the claimant solicitor should suggest that the client undergo private medical treatment in an attempt to speed the recovery period. Indeed, the defendant's solicitors in serious cases will suggest further medical treatment in an attempt to reduce the level of damages payable if the claimant establishes liability.

Example

A 10-year-old girl is injured and has to undergo major abdominal surgery at the local hospital, which leaves her with a large surgical incision. As part of her general damages award she will claim for pain and suffering relating to the scarring. It is also likely that she will claim that she will suffer psychological problems in relation to the embarrassment of wearing swimming costumes throughout her teenage years and perhaps in later life. In such a case, it is likely that the defendant's solicitors will suggest that the claimant undergo specialist plastic surgery in an attempt to reduce the significance of the scarring and the potential psychological problems, which, in turn, will reduce the level of damages that the defendant will pay.

A claimant may claim for the reasonable cost of private medical care actually incurred. The availability of free NHS treatment is ignored (Law Reform (Personal Injuries) Act 1948; see also *Eagle v Chambers* [2004] EWCA Civ 1033). However, the claimant cannot be treated free under the NHS system and then claim what it would have cost to have been treated privately. Future private medical care may also be claimed (if long term, on a multiplicand and multiplier system – see **13.3.3**) provided it is reasonably likely to be incurred (*Hodgson v Trapp* [1988] 3 WLR 1281). However, only the cost of the medical care may be claimed; the claimant cannot claim for the 'hotel' element in the expenses, for example, the proportion of the fees that relate to the provision of meals, heating and lighting (*Lim Poh Choo v Camden and Islington Area Health Authority* [1979] 2 All ER 910).

Medical expenses incurred pre-trial are claimed as special damages; those incurred post-trial are claimed as general damages.

13.2.4 Losses incurred and services rendered by third parties as a result of the claimant's injuries

13.2.4.1 General principle

The general principle is that a third party cannot claim against the defendant for losses incurred by a third party as a result of injury to the claimant.

Example 1

An employer cannot claim for the loss of services of the claimant who is a 'non-menial servant', for example, an employee who is not part of the employer's household, eg, a butler (*IRC v Hambrook* [1956] 3 All ER 338). Therefore, if Fred employed Tom in his factory and Tom is injured in a road traffic accident as a result of Eric's negligence, Fred has no right of action against Eric.

Example 2

An employee cannot sue for loss of lucrative employment caused by injury to his employer (*Best v Samuel Fox & Co Ltd* [1952] 2 All ER 394). For example, Tom is employed by Fred. Fred is seriously injured in an accident as a result of Eric's negligence and subsequently Tom loses his job when Fred's firm ceases to trade. Tom has no right of action against Eric for the loss of his job.

13.2.4.2   Value of services rendered

The claimant (but not the third party) may recover the value of services provided to him by a third party, so long as such services were rendered necessary by the act of the tortfeasor (*Kirkham v Boughey* [1958] 2 QB 338; *Schneider v Eisovitch* [1960] 2 QB 430; *Lowe v Guise* [2002] EWCA Civ 197, [2002] 3 WLR 562).

In practice, a common example of such services is nursing (or quasi-nursing) services rendered to the claimant by his relatives or friends.

Example

Tom is injured in an accident caused by Eric's negligence. Tom is admitted to hospital for six weeks. Tom's wife, Ann, visits Tom each day that he is in hospital. Tom is discharged from hospital and spends three months convalescing at home. During that time, Ann cares for Tom by cooking his meals, giving him his medication and generally seeing to his personal needs. Ann cannot claim against Eric for the value of the services rendered to Tom. However, as part of his claim against Eric, Tom can claim for the value of the services rendered to him by Ann in respect of the visits to hospital (on the basis that the visits speeded his recovery) and the nursing care after his discharge from hospital.

The following should be noted:

(a)   The value of the services may be claimed by the claimant irrespective of whether the third party has been put to actual expense in rendering those services, for example, by incurring loss of earnings (*Cunningham v Harrison* [1973] 3 All ER 463; *Daly v General Steam Navigation Co* [1980] 3 All ER 696; *Roberts v Johnstone* [1988] 3 WLR 1247).

(b)   It is unnecessary (and undesirable) for there to be any agreement between the claimant and the third party as to the reimbursement of the third party for the services (*Cunningham v Harrison* (above)).

(c)   The claim for the value of the services is made by the claimant, not by the third party. Similarly, the award is to the claimant, not to the third party, as it is the claimant's loss which is being compensated. This was explained by Megaw LJ in *Donnelly v Joyce* [1973] 3 All ER 475 in the following terms: 'The plaintiff's loss is not the expenditure of money to buy the special boots or to pay for the nursing attention. This loss is the existence of the need for those special boots or for those nursing services'.

(d)   Although the claimant claims the value of the services, the damages awarded to him in respect of those services are held by the claimant in trust for the person who provided those services (the carer). Therefore, where the carer is also the defendant (eg, where a wife is injured as a result of her husband's negligent driving and the husband provides quasi-nursing services to the wife during her convalescence) the claimant cannot recover the value of those services from the defendant/carer, since otherwise the claimant would have to repay the damages to the defendant/carer (*Hunt v Severs* [1994] 2 All ER 385, HL).

(e)   If, for example, a mother (who is severely injured) and child (only minor injury) are involved in a road traffic accident, then it is not possible for the child to claim damages for the care element from the defendant. The appropriate course is for the mother to claim, as part of the case, the costs of care of the child (see *Buckley v Farrow and Buckley* [1997] PIQR Q78).

(f)   It is not normally possible to recover damages for a spouse of an accident victim who does work for the victim's business on a 'gratuitous' basis. See *Harwick v Hindson and Another* (1999) NLJ, 28 May.

(g)   A claimant whose injury prevented him from caring for his disabled brother, but did not affect his entitlement to an invalid care allowance, has still suffered a loss which he can claim for. See *Lowe v Guise* [2002] EWCA Civ 197, [2002] 3 WLR 562.

Valuing the services rendered

Megaw LJ, in *Donnelly v Joyce* (above), stated that 'the value of [the services] for the purposes of damages – for the purpose of the ascertainment of the amount of his loss – is the proper and reasonable costs of supplying those needs'.

In the case of professional services (eg, professional nursing care), the claimant is entitled to the reasonable fee for those services. In the case of the services rendered by non-professionals (eg, nursing care rendered by the claimant's spouse), where there is no fee incurred, the valuation may be more problematical. O'Connor LJ, in *Housecroft v Burnett* [1986] 1 All ER 332, stated:

> Where the needs of an injured plaintiff are and will be supplied by a relative or friend out of love and affection (and, in cases of little children where the provider is a parent, duty) freely and without regard to monetary reward, how should the court assess 'the proper and reasonable cost'? There are two extreme solutions:
>
> (i)   assess the full commercial rate for supplying the needs by employing someone to do what the relative does;
>
> (ii)   assess the cost at nil, just as it is assessed at nil where the plaintiff is cared for under the National Health Scheme;
>
> 'each' case must be considered on its own facts ... the court should look at it as a whole and consider whether, on the facts of the case, it is sufficient to enable the plaintiff, among other things, to make reasonable recompense to the relative.

In some cases, the relative or spouse may have given up work in order to look after the claimant and therefore incurred an actual loss of earnings. In *Housecroft v Burnett*, O'Connor LJ went on to say that 'in [such] cases ... I would regard it as natural that the plaintiff would not wish the relative to be the loser so that the court would award sufficient to enable the plaintiff to achieve that result'.

Where there is no actual loss by the third party the court may take as the value of the services that which it would have cost to employ professional help (*Roberts v Johnstone* (above); but contrast *Daly v General Steam Navigation Company* (above), where there was no actual loss and the value of the services was awarded as part of the claimant's loss of amenity). It should also be noted that the defendant's solicitor will argue that it is inappropriate to put forward a commercial rate as a figure representing the loss in these circumstances, because that rate includes an element of profit for the care organiser, such as a nursing agency. However, the ceiling for the value of the services would normally be the commercial rate (*Housecroft v Burnett*). If the claimant is claiming that the value of the services should exceed the commercial rate then the claimant has the onus of proving the higher value (*Rialas v Mitchell* (1984) *The Times*, 17 July where the claimant justified care at home which was approximately twice the cost of care in an institution) (see also *Fitzgerald v Ford* [1996] PIQR Q72).

Subject to the comments in *Daly* set out above, the value of services claimed pre-trial are special damages, and post-trial are general damages (and, where the services are likely to be necessary over a long period of time, a multiplicand and multiplier system will be used – see **13.3.3**).

In serious injury cases the cost of care claim can be significant and it can be a contentious issue between the parties. The court is reluctant to adopt a strict formula or impose a 'straitjacket'. Each case will be dealt with on its own facts (see *Evans v Pontypridd Roofing Ltd* [2001] EWCA Civ 1657, (2001) LTL, 9 November and *Newman v Folkes and Dunlop Tyres Ltd* [2002] EWCA Civ 591).

In *Giambrone & Others v JMC Holidays Ltd (formerly t/a Sunworld Holidays Ltd)* [2004] EWCA Civ 158 the Court of Appeal confirmed that awards for gratuitous care as a result of contracting gastroenteritis or similar illness while on holiday were not reserved for very serious cases and that the judge had been correct in principle to make an award for cost of care in such cases. It is therefore important to remember to include claims for cost of care where appropriate.

Local authorities

In certain circumstances a local authority may have provided care to the client. As a consequence the authority may want to recover the cost of care services supplied, from those to whom such services have been supplied. If a local authority has provided such care to a client (and recoupment is relevant) then an indemnity must be obtained from the defendant in respect of any such claim by the authority, or the local authority's claim should be paid by the defendant prior to the settlement of the claim (see *Avon County Council v Hooper* [1997] 1 WLR 1605 and *Thrul v Ray* [2000] PIQR Q44).

In relation to serious injury cases, reference should also be made to the following cases: *Ryan v Liverpool City Council* [2002] Lloyd's Rep Med 23; *Bell v Todd* [2002] Lloyd's Rep Med 12 and *Firth v Ackroyd* [2000] Lloyd's Rep Med 312, which all concern local authority 'claw back'. See also *Crookdake v Drury; Sowden v Lodge* [2004] EWCA Civ 1370 regarding local authority services.

13.2.5   Expenses relating to cost of living with disabilities prior to trial

In more serious cases, the claimant will incur specific items of cost relating to the disabilities resulting from the accident. These may be only one-off payments, but if these items are frequently required throughout the claimant's life the replacement cost must be included within any future loss calculation. It may be necessary to use an occupational therapist to provide a rehabilitation cost report. This will involve the occupational therapist assessing the claimant in his own home to see whether the client can carry out 'the activities of daily living'. Where someone has suffered extensive injuries, the expenses relating to the costs of living with a disability can be significant. Few clients will be able to afford the necessary equipment and the possibility of making an application for an interim payment must be considered throughout the case.

The following are examples of the types of items which may have to be purchased after an accident by a seriously injured client:

(a)   adaptation of the family car to allow the claimant to drive;

(b)   the cost of a wheelchair (defendants will argue that this can be provided free by the State but this may not be suitable for the client);

(c)   beds ruined due to incontinence;

(d)   incontinence pads;

(e)   extra costs of laundry;

(f)   odour control in the house due to incontinence;

(g)   additional fuel costs due to the claimant being at home all day;

(h)   installation of a stairlift;

(i)   installation of a shower if clients are unable to use a bath;

(j)   installation of a downstairs toilet;

(k)   adapted furniture;

(l)   therapy ball – to help with mobility.

In respect of adaptations to the claimant's home (eg, ramp access for a wheelchair or the purchase of a vehicle to help cope with his disability), the claimant will have to give credit for any enhanced value of the house or vehicle as a result of the adaptation. Calculating the loss resulting from alternative accommodation to cope with the claimant's disability may be problematical. If the claimant buys alternative (more expensive) property he has, to a certain extent, acquired an investment, ie, a valuable item that can be eventually sold. In such circumstances, the claimant can claim only a proportion of the amount of capital spent, see *Roberts v Johnstone* [1988] 3 WLR 1247; *Page v Sheerness Steel Co Ltd*; *Wells v Wells*; *Thomas v Brighton Health Authority* [1998] 3 WLR 329; see also *M v Leeds Health Authority* [2002] PIQR Q46.

13.2.6   Evidence of special damages

Details of the client's special damages and evidence in connection with them must be included in the appropriate witness statement(s) prepared for exchange.

13.3   General damages

General damages are those which are not capable of precise mathematical calculation. The main heads of general damages are:

(a)   pain, suffering and loss of amenity;

(b)   handicap in the labour market;

(c)   loss of earnings post-trial;

(d)   loss of congenial employment;

(e)   future cost of care/future cost of specialist equipment;

(f)   lost pension;

(g)   loss of use of a motor vehicle.

13.3.1   Pain, suffering and loss of amenity

Awards of damages under this head are designed to compensate the claimant for the pain and suffering attributable to the injury both immediately after the accident and in the future if the injury is serious. It will cover not only physical injury but also psychological illness.

The award is made on the basis of a subjective test, ie, 'what was the pain and suffering of this particular claimant?'. If there is no evidence that the claimant actually experienced pain then no award will be made – there must be evidence. If the claimant's expectation of life has been reduced by the injuries, he will be compensated under this head of general damages.

When the court comes to assess damages, it will examine the claimant's position as at the date of trial. The relevant compensation payment will include a sum for past and future pain (if applicable).

13.3.1.1   Damages for loss of amenity

Strictly speaking, there is a separate head of damages known as 'loss of amenity', but compensation for this loss is usually included with compensation for pain and suffering. This element is designed to compensate the claimant for the loss of enjoyment of life which has resulted from the accident. Examples under this head include interference with the claimant's sex life, or the loss or impairment of enjoyment of holidays, sports, pursuits and hobbies, as a result of injuries.

The award for loss of amenity is based on an objective test (in contrast to pain and suffering) and thus may be awarded irrespective of whether the claimant is personally aware of his loss, for example, if he is unconscious (*West v Shephard* [1964] AC 326).

Although the test is primarily objective, it does have subjective overtones in so far as the court will have regard to the claimant's former lifestyle. This may be particularly pertinent where the claimant was formerly a very active person (eg, a keen sportsman) and can no longer pursue his sport. Although his pain and suffering may be the same as another person with a similar disability, his loss of amenity may be greater and, as such, the total award for pain and suffering and loss of amenity may be greater.

Damages for loss of congenial employment (see **13.3.4**) may also be argued under this head, but, increasingly, the courts are making separate reference to these types of damages.

13.3.1.2   Quantification of damages for pain and suffering and loss of amenity

It is impossible to give a precise figure of what an injury is worth in regard to pain, suffering and loss of amenity. General damages are incapable of precise mathematical calculation. Even the most experienced personal injury lawyer would probably quantify the damages only approximately.

It should be remembered that there is no minimum award of damages which must be made (however, only exceptionally would an injury not be worth, for example, £500 or £750); nor is there any maximum.

In attempting to value the claim, reference should be made to specialist texts. Few cases are reported in general law reports such as the All England or Weekly Law Reports, and the following are the most likely sources:

(a)   Kemp and Kemp, *The Quantum of Damages* (Sweet & Maxwell);

(b)   *Butterworths Personal Injury Service*;

(c)   *Personal Injuries and Quantum Reports* (Sweet & Maxwell);

(d)   *Guidelines for the Assessment of General Damages in Personal Injury Cases* (Judicial Studies Board) (Oxford University Press);

(e)   *Current Law* (Sweet & Maxwell);

(f)   *Personal and Medical Injuries Law Letter* (IBC).

Increasingly, information technology is also being used in the valuation of general damages by means of CD-ROM packages such as the Kemp and Kemp CD-ROM (Sweet & Maxwell), *Current Legal Information* and Butterworths PI on-line service.

A useful starting point is the Judicial Studies Board *Guidelines* which is an analysis of previous judgments and provides an easy reference to broad bands of damages awards. However, reference should be made to previous cases where the court has made an award for similar injuries to those suffered by the client. In *Dureau v Evans* [1996] PIQR Q18, the Court of Appeal commented that, in relation to claimants who have suffered multiple injuries, the *Guidelines* are of limited assistance as it is necessary to take an overall view of all the injuries and, if at all possible, the court should consider a comparable case. The court should also decide which was the most serious injury (to try to find a comparable award) and build on the other heads of injury from there. Similarly, in *Reed v Sunderland Health Authority* (1998) *The Times,* 16 October, it was held that while the *Guidelines* were an important source of information, they did not have the force of law and the Court of Appeal is unlikely to overturn a decision if the *Guidelines* are not followed precisely (see *Davis v Inman* [1999] PIQR Q26).

It should be remembered when looking at previous cases that it is the general damages figure which is significant and it must then be inflated to present-day values. The inflation table in Kemp and Kemp *The Quantum of Damages,* can be used for that purpose. It is important to note, when examining the previous cases reported in Kemp and Kemp or other such practitioner works, that the phrase 'general damages' is sometimes given a restricted meaning of general damages 'for pain and suffering and loss of amenity' (and occasionally an element is identified for a *Smith v Manchester* award – see **13.3.2**); it does not normally include the figure awarded in the case for future loss of earnings (if appropriate) as this will differ in each case.

The following points should be considered when examining the medical report obtained in support of the case prior to attempting to identify analogous cases in the sources referred to above:

(a)   Identify the date of the accident and calculate how many years post-accident the report has been prepared. It is clearly a more significant injury if the doctor reports that the claimant is still in considerable pain two years after the accident, as opposed to merely six months afterwards.

(b)   Calculate for how long the client was in hospital and how many operations (if any) he had to undergo.

(c)   Calculate how long the client will suffer a major disability.

(d)   Calculate how long the client will suffer with residual problems.

(e)   Identify any future degeneration (eg, osteoporosis).

When attempting to value the award, the following points should be considered when examining the previous cases:

(a)   *Sex* – for example, scarring (especially scars on the face) on a female carries a higher award than on a male (see Judicial Studies Board *Guidelines*).

(b)   *Age of the victim* – in cases of permanent disability, younger victims tend to get more compensation than older victims as the young will suffer longer.

(c)   *Loss of amenity* – is heavily influenced by whether the victim had a previously active lifestyle.

(d)   *Limb injuries* – injuries to dominant limbs attract higher awards than injuries to non-dominant limbs.

(e)   Consideration must be given to the case of *Heil v Rankin and Another* [2000] 2 WLR 1173. In this case, the Court of Appeal considered the level of damages for pain and suffering. Also, in this case, the court held that, in cases where the level of damages for pain and suffering was in excess of £10,000, there should be a gradual increase of up to one-third in value for serious injuries. It is important to consider this landmark decision when considering any earlier decision on damages for pain and suffering in law reports or legal texts. The decision was incorporated into the 5th edition of the *Guidelines*. It is important to note that if an earlier case is to be relied on, then a conversion table (such as that found in *Quantum* 2/2000, 18 April 2000 (Sweet & Maxwell)) should be used.

When valuing pain and suffering, a solicitor should, if at all possible, rely on recent cases, not only because of *Heil v Rankin* (see above), but if older reports are relied upon, the level of damages may not be analogous. It is unlikely that an identical case will be found, and a number of cases will need to be examined. The approach that should be taken is to focus on the most significant injury and then look at the overall position. The court will not adopt a strictly mathematical approach of adding up the value of the different injuries sustained by the client.

13.3.1.3   Evidence

Although the medical evidence will be the primary matter which the court will have regard to in determining the award for pain, suffering and loss of amenity, the claimant will also give evidence of his injuries at trial. It is important that details are contained within the client's witness statement. It is surprising how many clients forget the exact details of the difficulties they had immediately post-accident, and it is good practice for the claimant's solicitor to suggest that a diary is kept by the client detailing the pain and practical difficulties that were suffered. In serious cases, it may also be necessary to obtain evidence from the claimant's spouse and family of the effect of the injuries on the claimant.

13.3.2   Handicap in the labour market

The purpose of this award is to compensate the claimant for the potential difficulties he may suffer in obtaining another job due to the injuries that he sustained in the accident, if he loses his current job. In practice, this is referred to as a *Smith v Manchester* claim (see *Smith v Manchester Corporation* [1974] 17 KIR 1).

For the court to award such damages, the claimant should have suffered a 'weakening' of his competitive position in the open labour market – or, in other words, what are his chances are of obtaining comparable employment in the open labour market if he should lose his job?

The case of *Moeliker v A Reyrolle & Co Ltd* [1977] 1 WLR 132 considered the award of damages under this head, where it was stated that:

> The consideration of this head of damages should be made in two stages:
> (1)   Is there a 'substantial' or 'real' risk that the plaintiff will lose his present job at some time before the estimated end of his working life?
> (2)   If there is (but not otherwise), the court must assess and quantify the present value of the risk of the financial damage which the plaintiff will suffer if that risk materialises, having regard to the degree of risk, the time when it may materialise, and the factors, both favourable and unfavourable, which in a particular case will, or may, affect the plaintiff's chance of getting a job at all or an equally well paid job.
>
> It is impossible to suggest any formula for solving the extremely difficult problems involved in stage 2 of the assessment. A judge must look at all the factors which are relevant in a particular case and do the best he can ...

The claimant must establish first that there is a risk that he will lose his job. However, the courts have given the words 'substantial or real' a liberal interpretation and what is required to be shown is that the risk is 'real' rather than 'speculative'. Evidence is required to support the contention that the claimant may lose his job, and a useful source of information may be the client's trade union, which will have details of any redundancies that have been made by the employer in recent years. It may also be able to provide information about the employer's future plans, of which the client may not have been aware. If the client does not belong to a trade union, evidence should be obtained from the client's workmates or managers. (If the defendant is the claimant's employer, such information should be obtained from the defendant's insurers or solicitor.) The solicitor representing the defendant must obtain clear evidence concerning the claimant's job security in an attempt to refute the *Smith v Manchester* claim.

Once the first test has been satisfied, the court attempts to quantify the risk and calculate the appropriate damages. The court has to anticipate what would be the claimant's chances of getting an equally well paid job if he was forced onto the labour market. This head of damages is notoriously hard to quantify as the court will consider each individual case on its own facts; but a common approach is to award between zero to two years' net loss of earnings as at the date of trial. However, the Court of Appeal in *Foster v Tyne and Wear County Council* [1986] 1 All ER 567 stated that there was no 'conventional' figure for damages under this head, and awarded a sum equivalent to four years' net salary. This is, therefore, a particularly difficult element to value.

The fact that the claimant is suffering a handicap on the labour market should normally be put in the particulars of claim (*Chan Wai Tong v Li Ping Sum* [1985] AC 446).

Examples of cases where a *Smith v Manchester* award may be considered appropriate include the following:

(a)   The claimant has returned to work after the accident and thus he has no continuing loss of earnings claim. However, if there is a risk that the claimant will lose his job in the future and he will have difficulty in obtaining a job as equally well paid due to his injuries, then a *Smith v Manchester* award will be claimed for.

(b)   The claimant has returned to work and is earning, say, 20% less than he did prior to the accident. As a result, the claimant will have a continuing partial loss of earnings claim that could be calculated by using the multiplier/ multiplicand approach (see **13.3.3**). In addition, if the court is satisfied that the claimant will lose his job and he will have difficulty in obtaining a job equally well paid due to his injuries, then a *Smith v Manchester* award will be claimed for.

(c)   The claimant is still absent from work at the time of the trial as a result of the injuries suffered in the accident but he expects to return to his job in a few years, when he has recovered further from his injuries. The medical evidence suggests that he may still have problems in obtaining equally well paid work due to his injuries should he lose his job. In these circumstances, a *Smith v Manchester* award will be claimed.

The above are only a few illustrations as to when a *Smith v Manchester* award may be claimed. The medical evidence in every case must be examined to see whether a *Smith v Manchester* award can be justified. Although a *Smith v Manchester* claim should normally be claimed in the particulars of claim, the Court of Appeal in *Thorn v Powergen* [1997] PIQR Q71 upheld a decision allowing a *Smith v Manchester* award in a case where it had not been claimed specifically but was found by the trial judge to be implied due to the nature of the injuries revealed by the medical evidence.

This type of award is not normally appropriate where the claimant will never be able to return to work, as he will be compensated by his claim for lost earnings. However, the number of cases where the claimant is unable to work at all in the future will be small.

13.3.2.1 Evidence

Evidence must be obtained concerning the claimant's future job prospects including any skills he possesses (eg, a labourer of 50 years of age with no qualifications will find it difficult to retrain if he loses his job), the prospects of the industry in which the claimant works and any unusual local problems that may be relevant to the claimant. It may be necessary to instruct an employment consultant to provide information about these matters, or obtain relevant information from other sources, ie, New Earnings Survey. If an employment consultant is instructed, this will normally involve the expert considering the client's injuries, personal qualifications and forming an analysis of employment statistics and local press advertisements to provide a report to assist the court in determining the severity of the handicap on the labour market. In other cases, the trial judge will be aware of the employment situation in his area and be able to formulate the appropriate award (see *Goldborough v Thompson and Crowther* [1996] PIQR Q86) – see also **Chapter 8** on experts.

Any evidence relating to handicap on the labour market claim must be included within the witness statements for exchange.

13.3.3 Future loss of earnings

Damages for loss of earnings after the trial will be general damages.

The existing system

Under the head 'future loss of earnings', a lump sum is awarded which is arrived at by means of a 'multiplicand' and 'multiplier' system, which allows for:

(a)   the contingencies of life; and

(b)   the accelerated receipt of a sum which is available for investment.

No allowance is made for inflation (*Auty v National Coal Board* [1985] 1 All ER 930).

The same principles apply as to pre-trial lost earnings: they must be proved, necessary and reasonable. The object in assessing future earnings loss is to assess the amount of money which can be invested today to represent a fund which should last for precisely the period of the lost earnings. The compensation payment which the claimant receives at trial for future loss involves the court awarding today what the claimant would have earned in the future and is, therefore, extremely difficult to asses.

13.3.3.1 The multiplicand

The multiplicand is the claimant's net annual earnings that he would have been receiving at the date of the trial. No increase is allowed for inflation, but allowance may be made for likely increased earning capacity as a result, for example, of the acquisition of greater skills or promotion. Conversely, a likely decrease in earning capacity may be taken into account. The items to be included or ignored in the calculation of the multiplicand are the same as for pre-trial earnings, as identified at **13.2.2.**

13.3.3.2   The multiplier

The multiplier is based on the period of likely future loss. This will depend on the facts of the case. For example, in the case of a male claimant who will never work again, the period of loss will normally extend until his likely retirement age (normally 60 or 65, or longer in the case of a professional person). The multiplier is therefore taken from the date of trial.

The period of loss is then converted into a multiplier. Following the House of Lords' decision in the joint appeals of *Page v Sheerness Steel Co Ltd; Wells v Wells; Thomas v Brighton Health Authority* [1998] 3 WLR 329, it can now be assumed that the starting point when attempting to identify the multiplier is to use the Government's actuarial tables (the Ogden tables; see **Appendix 5**).

For example, a male claimant is aged 45 at trial and is to retire at 65. He earns £10,000 net per annum. Using the Ogden tables (fifth edition, Table 9), a multiplier of 15.22 is identified (using the 2.5% column). Future loss = 15.22 × £10,000 = £152,200. However, actuarial multipliers are, in certain circumstances, discounted. The precise amount of the discount depends upon the exact circumstances of the case and full details are contained within the Ogden tables.

The House of Lords' decision confirmed that it may still be appropriate to discount multipliers for future loss of earnings calculations in certain circumstances, but that if the tables are used to identify a 'whole life multiplier' (which may be relevant in identifying a multiplier for the cost of care – see **13.3.5**), there is no reason to discount.

In June 2001, the Lord Chancellor set the 'discount rate' that should be referred to when using the Ogden Tables at 2.5%. The term 'discount rate' is identified in each set of the tables and it represents the real rate of return (ie, after tax and making allowance for inflation) calculated over the appropriate period of time. As the Lord Chancellor has now set the 'discount rate' to be used, he should have eliminated scope for uncertainty and argument about the applicable rate (although the Lord Chancellor does acknowledge it is open to the courts under s 1(2) of the Damages Act 1996 to adopt a different rate if there are exceptional circumstances). In *Warriner v Warriner* [2002] EWCA Civ 81, [2002] 1 WLR 1703, the Court of Appeal re-affirmed that the appropriate discount rate was 2.5% as there was nothing 'unusual on the facts'.

13.3.3.3   Reduced expectation of life

The period of loss is assessed on the basis of the claimant's expectation of life as it was before the accident, not on the expectation of life as shortened by the accident. Therefore, if the claimant (aged 40), at the date of the accident, was expected to die at the age of 55 (whereas formerly the claimant would have been expected to work until the age of 65), the period of loss would remain 25 years. However, in respect of the period actually lost from his life (the 'lost years') the claimant must give credit for the amounts which would have been spent on his own maintenance (*Pickett v British Rail Engineering Ltd* [1980] AC 136, overruling *Oliver v Ashman* [1962] 2 QBD 210).

In the case of *Phipps v Brookes Dry Cleaning Services Limited* [1996] PIQR Q100, it was held that in assessing a claim over the 'lost years' by a claimant, the correct approach in calculating expenses during the lost years was to divide the common expenses equally between the claimant and his partner. If there were any children, the division should be pro rata. The value of the claimant's DIY and gardening skills were not recoverable for the lost years, as they were amenities falling to be assessed in general damages.

The system after April 2005

As noted later (see **16.4**) a new system of awarding damages was introduced in April 2005. The court now has a duty to consider whether a periodical payment order is appropriate. If the court adopts such an order then, instead of the court 'making a guess' at the claimant's future needs for the entirety of the claimant's life, the court will look at the annual needs of the claimant. This could result in a move away from the use of the traditional multiplier/multiplicand (Ogden tables) approach as explained in **13.3.3.1** and **13.3.3.2**.

13.3.3.4 Future loss of earnings in practice

In only relatively few cases will the claimant be physically unfit to carry out any type of work in the future. In the majority of cases, the claimant will have to give credit for potential future earnings that he may receive against his future loss of earnings.

> **Example**
>
> The claimant has suffered an amputation to his non-dominant hand as a result of an accident at work. He is 45 years of age at the date of the trial and was previously employed as a manual worker in the steel industry. The court may consider taking the following approaches.
>
> (a)   That the claimant is totally unemployable and should be given his net annual earnings × a multiplier of, say (just as an example), 13.
>
> (b)   That the claimant should have a period of full loss of earnings, say two years' post-trial but from that time it is likely that the claimant will obtain some form of work, say as a car park attendant, and the claimant must give credit therefore for this income, and a reduced multiplicand should be calculated.

Although much would depend on the medical evidence, if the claimant was otherwise healthy it is likely that the court will adopt the second approach. The enormous difficulties in quantifying such a claim can be appreciated, as the court has to pick a date by which time it considers it reasonable for the claimant to have obtained work. Assistance can be provided by an employment consultant's report, but trade unions can also be of assistance in respect of employment prospects within a particular region. It will also be necessary to refer to the New Earnings Survey (see also its successor, the Annual Survey of Hours and Earnings) which will provide details of earnings for particular occupations, such as car park attendants (as an example of work that can be undertaken by an amputee) so as to provide a figure which has to be credited against the net loss of earnings from the original employer.

As can be seen the method of calculating the claimant's future loss of earnings set out above is an imprecise science.

13.3.3.5 Evidence

The importance of expert evidence in such a case is vital. Medical evidence can provide an indication as to what work the claimant will be capable of undertaking both at present and in the future. This, together with evidence of the claimant's employment prospects, will assist the court in determining what will happen to the claimant in the future, which, while often appearing unsatisfactory to many clients, is usually the approach that the court will take.

13.3.4 Loss of congenial employment

Traditionally, an element for loss of job satisfaction was included under the head of pain, suffering and loss of amenity. However, the courts in certain cases are now prepared to make a separate award under this heading. In *Morris v Johnson Matthey & Co Ltd* (1967) 112 SJ 326, Edmund-Davies LJ stated:

> the joy of the craftsman in his craft is beyond price. But the court had to give some monetary value to the loss of craft. The court should give consideration to the fact that a craftsman had to replace his craft with humdrum work.

In that case, a precious metal worker, aged 52, sustained a serious injury to his left hand, which left him incapable of continuing his craft. His employers found him alternative employment as a storeman.

The leading case in this area is *Blamey*, 16 December 1988, in which a fireman was awarded £3,250. This case increased awareness of awards for loss of congenial employment. The court felt that there was an advantage in identifying such loss as a separate head of damages, to ensure that it was properly compensated. A table of awards under this heading is referred to in Kemp and Kemp *The Quantum of Damages* (Sweet & Maxwell). It can be seen in the case reports that the courts are more likely to make such an award where the claimant's job at the time of the accident involved a vocational element, ie, nurse, actor, firefighter, etc (see also *Willbye (by her mother and next friend) v Gibbons* [2003] EWCA Civ 372).

13.3.4.1 Evidence

Any evidence relating to a loss of congenial employment claim must be included within the witness statements for exchange, together with details of the loss of job satisfaction.

13.3.5 Future cost of care/specialist equipment

In many cases, the cost of future expenses will exceed the multiplier used for loss of earnings, because the need for care will often exceed the claimant's normal retirement age. It must be remembered that the cost and type of care may change in the future.

For example, a severely injured child's costs of care will increase as he becomes older because it is unlikely that his parents will be able to look after him when they are elderly and, as such, increased professional help will be required.

The cost of care can normally be worked out on an annual basis and can be dealt with in a similar manner to the loss of earnings multiplicand. The cost of specialist equipment must be dealt with differently. For example, the claimant may include the cost of a wheelchair as part of his special damages claim. That wheelchair will not last the claimant for the rest of his life and, therefore, the replacement cost will need to be annualised. For example, where the cost of a wheelchair is £1,000 and it would have a life span of, say, five years, it is therefore necessary to include the annual cost of £200 within the multiplicand figure (£1,000/5).

In respect of the cost of care and other expenses (if lifelong), the multiplier is based on life-expectancy and, when examining the actuarial tables, care must be taken to refer to the 'Multipliers for pecuniary loss for life male/female' referred to in the Ogden tables, rather than 'Multipliers for the loss of earnings to pension age males/females' tables, to ensure that the correct multiplier is obtained. Medical evidence on life expectancy is vital if it is not a 'normal life expectancy' case. Following the House of Lords' decision in *Page v Sheerness Steel Co Ltd; Wells v Wells; Thomas v Brighton Health Authority* (see **13.3.3.2**), it is not appropriate to discount whole life multipliers.

13.3.6 Loss of pension

In more serious cases, where the claimant does not return to work or returns on a lower wage, consideration must be given for a claim for lost pension. The claimant's pension is normally based upon his period of service with the company and the salary that he would have earned at retirement age. Reference should be made to specialist texts on this subject.

13.3.7 Loss of use of a motor car

Loss of use of a motor car is included in damages claims in connection with road traffic accidents (with or without a personal injury), for example, where the client's vehicle is damaged and is off the road for four weeks while being repaired, and the client uses an alternative method of transport and claims compensation for the 'loss of use' of his vehicle. On occasions, solicitors can include this item in the schedule of special damages and claim a weekly figure, but it is for the court to decide on the exact level of compensation, which will depend upon the facts of the case and the claimant's actions while he was without the car (see *Lagden v O'Connor* [2003] UKHL 64).

13.4 Interest

A claim for interest should be included in the court proceedings. In the majority of personal injury cases, the court will award interest in addition to the basic damages. The purpose of an interest award is to compensate the claimant for having to wait to receive his compensation. Interest in a personal injury claim is generally awarded in accordance with the following guidelines.

(a)   Special damages carry interest at half the short-term investment/special account rate from the date of the accident to the date of trial. In *Roberts v Johnstone* [1989] QB 878, it was held that damages for unpaid past services of care and attendance should be awarded in a similar manner to any other items of special damages.

It should also be noted that following the case of *Wadley v Surrey County Council* (2000) *The Times,* 7 April, the House of Lords confirmed that, when calculating interest on special damages, the court should disregard deductible State benefits and interest is claimed on the gross amount (see **Chapter 12**).

(b)   Damages for pain and suffering and loss of amenities carry interest from date of service of proceedings to the date of trial at 2% per annum following the case of *Felmai Lawrence v Chief Constable of Staffordshire* (2000) *The Times,* 25 July.

(c)   Damages for future losses carry no interest (as, by definition, the losses have not yet been incurred).

(d)   General damages for a handicap on the labour market carry no interest.

It should be noted that these are general guidelines, but the court does have a discretion to depart from them in exceptional cases. In Kemp and Kemp *The Quantum of Damages,* it is argued that while the general approach for special damages stated above is appropriate for regular losses between the accident and trial (eg, weekly wage loss), it is not satisfactory where there has been a one-off significant payment by the claimant just after the accident as the claimant is being under-compensated and, therefore, interest should be awarded at the full rate (see *Prokop v Department of Health and Social Security*, 5 July 1983).

Interest is awarded to mitigate the effects of delay. However, if the delay is the fault of the claimant, this may be a 'special reason' not to award full interest (*Birkett v Hayes* [1982] 2 All ER 70). This point was raised in the case of *Beahan v Stoneham* (2001) LTL, 16 May, where an appeal from an assessment of damages in a claim for personal injuries was allowed in part where the trial judge failed to reduce interest on damages. The matter concerned a case where there was a significant delay in proceeding with the claim (see also *Spittle v Bunney* [1988] 1 WLR 847). The court held that the judiciary should be more ready to mark their disapproval of delay in this matter.

13.4.1 Calculation of interest

The calculation of interest on general damages should not present any problem. However, the calculation of interest on special damages can be more difficult. In practice, solicitors use the Nelson–Jones table which is printed annually in the Law Society Gazette and reference should be made to the latest table when calculating interest on special damages.

The inclusion of interest on the settlement of a case must not be forgotten by the claimant's solicitor.

13.5 The award of damages at trial

In conclusion, at the trial of a personal injury case the judge will award a lump sum figure to the claimant, but each head will be identified as separately appealable (*Jefford v Gee* [1970] 2 QBD 130). The Court of Appeal also held in *Coates v Curry* (1998) *The Times*, 22 August that it was necessary to identify past and future loss of earnings as specific figures for the purpose of the calculation of interest.

Personal injury damages are not chargeable gains and therefore the damages themselves are not subject to tax (however, the returns from the investment of those damages are subject to tax).

While this chapter has examined special damages, general damages and interest separately, there are certain circumstances where payments received by the claimant have to be given credit from the total amount of damages. For example, in the case of *Ballantine v Newalls Insulation Co Ltd* [2001] ICR 25, it was held that in a claim brought by a claimant who suffered malignant mesothelioma (and subsequently died), the estate had to give credit for the payment of an award under the Pneumoconiosis etc (Workers' Compensation) Act 1979.

Care must also be taken to see if any other benefits are deductible from the claimant's damages, even though they are not included within the Social Security (Recovery of Benefits) Act 1997 (see **Chapter 12**).

In a small number of personal injury cases the court finds that the claimant has been dishonest and has attempted to inflate the level of damages by lying or deliberately exaggerating his injuries. In these cases, the court is likely to take a dim view. One illustration of this is the case of *Molloy v Shell UK Ltd* [2001] EWCA

Civ 1272, (2001) LTL, 6 July, where the claimant was ordered to pay the defendant's costs in full.

13.6 Periodic payments

As noted earlier in this chapter (see **13.3.3.3**), in April 2005 a new system of periodic payments was introduced under the CPR. Reference should be made to **16.4** for further details.

13.7 Further reading

The text provides a basic introduction to this complex topic and further reference should be made to Kemp and Kemp, *The Quantum of Damages* (Sweet & Maxwell).

Chapter 14

Post-death Investigations

14.1 Introduction

The personal injury/clinical negligence solicitor must, on occasion, advise either the family of an accident victim who has died or, alternatively, the person who it is claimed is responsible for the death. This can be very demanding work for the solicitor as the client is likely to make considerable demands both professionally and emotionally. There are three main processes in which the solicitor may become involved:

(a) the coroner's inquest;

(b) criminal prosecution for manslaughter or prosecution under the Health and Safety at Work etc Act 1974;

(c) criminal prosecution for death by dangerous driving.

Although each process has its own purpose, post-death investigations offer an important opportunity to gain evidence on liability for the civil claim.

14.2 The coroner's court

If acting for the claimant, the solicitor is likely to be instructed by a relative who may be upset and in a state of complete despair. The relative may also be looking to identify the person responsible for the death. It is important that the solicitor explains the post-death process thoroughly to the client, who, although he may recognise the phrases 'coroner's court' and 'inquest', may not understand the purpose of the process.

While the claimant's solicitor may wish to use the inquest to examine the evidence surrounding the accident and to obtain full details of the circumstances leading to the death, the coroner is concerned only with how the death occurred (see **14.2.6**) and this should be made clear to the client.

Prior to advising a client on this area, reference must be made to the Coroners Act 1988 and the Coroners Rules 1984 (SI 1984/552). (See also **14.2.10** where the impact of Article 2 of the ECHR is considered.)

If acting for the defendant, the solicitor is likely to have been instructed by the defendant's insurance company, or, in the case of clinical negligence, by the hospital or defence union. In these circumstances, the solicitor's aim is:

(a) to protect the interests of the client (eg, by making sure he does not incriminate himself); and

(b)   to obtain as much evidence as possible relating to the issue of liability.

A fatal accident which leads to an inquest is one of the occasions where a defendant's solicitor is instructed close to the time of the accident. He can therefore obtain details of any potential claims so that the insurance company can establish a reserve in its accounts for any potential liability.

Normally, the coroner will formally open the inquest and then immediately adjourn for enquiries to be made. The inquest will take place at the coroner's court (if the district has a specific court) or in the magistrates' court, council offices or at another public building. The inquest will be held in public unless matters of national security are being considered.

14.2.1   Personnel involved at an inquest

14.2.1.1   The coroner

The coroner is responsible for the inquest procedure and, although appointed by the local government body responsible for the area where the coroner sits, he is an independent judicial officer. A number of coroners are qualified both as doctors and (normally) as barristers, although this is not a strict requirement of obtaining the post. Those who are legally qualified only, normally have significant knowledge of medical matters.

In certain cases, the coroner may sit with an 'assessor' who is a person with specialist knowledge of the matters being considered, for example, a consultant anaesthetist in a case where a patient died due to an airway not being maintained. However, the assessor must remain under the control of the coroner and cannot give expert evidence (see *R v Surrey Coroner, ex p Wright* [1997] 2 WLR 16).

14.2.1.2   The coroner's officer

The coroner will be assisted by the coroner's officer, who is usually a serving or ex-police officer and will often be the first person with whom the personal injury solicitor will communicate about the case. The coroner's officer will obtain evidence relating to the accident or liaise with the police if they are carrying out investigations. His role is important to the solicitor as he can provide information regarding the investigations which are being carried out, details of the incident and may provide details of any witnesses the coroner intends to call.

The coroner's officer will notify the relevant parties, and/or their solicitors of the inquest date. In certain specified circumstances, the deceased's trade union and the HSE will also be notified.

14.2.1.3   The deputy coroner

A coroner will appoint a deputy coroner, who will normally stand in when the coroner is absent. Provided specific requirements for allowing a deputy to act are fulfilled, the deputy has all the powers of the coroner.

14.2.2   Circumstances which lead to an inquest

The circumstances where a coroner will become involved in a death are set down in s 8(1) of the Coroners Act 1988.

If the coroner is informed that a dead body is within his jurisdiction (it is the fact that there is a body in his jurisdiction and not where the death occurred that is important), the coroner will hold an inquest as soon as practicable, where it is reasonable to suspect that a person has died:

(a)   a violent or unnatural death; or

(b)   a sudden death of which the cause is unknown; or

(c)   in prison; or

(d)   in such place or such circumstances as to require an inquest in pursuance of any Act.

Normally, the police, the GP or the hospital will contact the coroner's officer and inform the coroner of the death. However, there is a wider duty to report the matter (see below) and, on occasions, the relatives of the deceased will contact the coroner's officer if they believe that there has been an act of clinical negligence.

In addition to the criteria set down in s 8(1), there is an obligation on a GP to inform the Registrar of Births and Deaths stating the cause of the death if the GP was treating the 'last illness' or the hospital doctor if a patient dies undergoing surgery.

Once the coroner has been informed of the death, the coroner's officer will make preliminary enquiries and the coroner may then require a post-mortem examination to be made.

14.2.2.1   Post-mortem examinations

Although no absolute obligation is placed upon the coroner, usually he will request that a post-mortem takes place (see *R v HM Coroner for Greater Manchester Northern District, ex p Worch and Another* [1988] QB 513). Care should be taken to ensure that if the death occurred in hospital, the pathologist should not be connected with the hospital where the death occurred. There are detailed provisions contained in Coroners Rules 1984, r 6 on this point. The claimant's solicitor must make strong representations on this point if there is any possibility of a clinical negligence claim and, in certain circumstances (if the first report is unsatisfactory), consideration should be given to having a second post-mortem carried out.

Consideration should be given to making a request that blood and tissue samples taken at the post-mortem are preserved, as they may provide important information.

Section 21(3) of the Coroners Act 1988 provides:

> Where a person states upon oath before the coroner that in his belief the death of the deceased was caused partly by or entirely by the improper or negligent treatment of a medical practitioner or other person, that medical practitioner or other person shall not be allowed to perform or assist at the post-mortem examination of the deceased.

The coroner must inform the relatives of the deceased, the GP and the hospital (if the deceased died in hospital) of the arrangements of the post-mortem. These are normally referred to as the 'interested parties' and can be represented at the post-mortem by a doctor. The coroner can, in his discretion, also allow any other person to attend at the post-mortem (Coroners Rules 1984, r 7(4)).

The post-mortem report is vital evidence and an immediate request should be made to the coroner for a copy (but see **14.2.5**). The report can contain evidence which will assist in establishing civil liability. For example, if the death resulted from a road traffic accident the pathologist will give a detailed description of the injuries, and photographs will be taken of the body. The pathologist's investigations in respect of this may be vital evidence in indicating the events prior to the accident, for example, whether the deceased was wearing a seat-belt. In fatal accident at work cases, the pathologist's report may also be of use in identifying whether the cause of the death resulted from exposure to dangerous materials at work, such as coal dust or asbestos. While the Coroners Rules 1984, r 57(1) makes provision for a copy of the post-mortem report to be provided to 'interested parties', it is unclear if the right relates to any request prior to the inquest, but many coroners do provide a copy of the post-mortem prior to the inquest (see below).

If acting for the defendant, the post-mortem may reveal whether there are any intervening illnesses from which the deceased may have died. This may then be used in negotiations in an attempt to reduce the multiplier in the future loss calculation. In addition, in a road traffic case, it is important to check the blood alcohol levels to see if the deceased had been drinking at the time of the accident. Such evidence can provide important arguments regarding liability and quantum.

14.2.3   The criteria for an inquest

As noted above, the coroner will hold an inquest only if the criteria in s 8(1) of the Coroners Act 1988 are satisfied. The personal injury/clinical negligence solicitor will be concerned only with the first two criteria.

The first limb of s 8(1) requires that there must have been a violent or unnatural death. What exactly is meant by this term?

(a)   A violent death is normally regarded as one where an injury has occurred and will normally be apparent. For example, when a factory operative falls into machinery and dies.

(b)   An unnatural death is not legally defined and it will be a question for the coroner to decide. Certain coroners believe that the phrase should be given its 'ordinary meaning'.

The coroner decides whether the death is natural or unnatural at his discretion, and this decision may need to be challenged. For example, in *R v Poplar Coroner, ex p Thomas* [1993] 2 WLR 547, a woman died following an asthma attack after there had been a considerable delay in an ambulance reaching her. There was evidence that if she had reached hospital earlier she might have survived. Was this an unnatural death? The Court of Appeal overturned the decision of the Divisional Court that it was an unnatural death and stated that 'unnatural' was an ordinary word whose meaning should be left to the coroner (unless his decision was unreasonable). If a solicitor believes that the death was unnatural, the coroner's officer must be contacted immediately and informed of the solicitor's interest. See also *R v Inner London North Coroner, ex p Touche* [2001] 3 WLR 148 and *R v HM Coroner for Avon, ex p Smith* (1998) 162 JP 403.

The second limb of s 8(1) requires that there must have been a sudden death of which the cause is unknown. In the context of a personal injury claim, this is less likely to be a significant cause, but may be appropriate in certain circumstances.

If the coroner refuses to call an inquest, the following options can be considered:

(a)   to make an application to the Divisional Court of the High Court;

(b)   to make an application for judicial review.

14.2.4   Funding representation at the inquest

It may be possible for a solicitor (with an appropriate contract) to provide assistance under the 'Legal Help' scheme for the initial preparations for an inquest. A solicitor may not represent the family at the inquest under the scheme using this method of funding. However, on 1 November 2001, the Lord

Chancellor published *Revised Guidance on Applications for Exceptional Funding* and this brings representation at certain inquests within the scope of Community Legal Service funding (see *R (on the application of (1) Challender and (2) Morris) v Legal Services Commission* [2004] EWHC 925); and see the Community Legal Service (Financial) (Amendment No 2) Regulations 2003 (SI 2003/2838).

It should be noted that in exceptional cases the Secretary of State for Constitutional Affairs has power under s 6(8)(b) of the Access to Justice Act 1999 to provide funding on an individual basis to cover advocacy and representation at an inquest. Consideration should be given to this option where the matter has a 'significant wider public interest' or 'overwhelming importance to the client'. Interestingly in the case of *King (Administatrix of the Estate of Robert Gadd deceased) v Milton Keynes General NHS Trust* (2004) LTL, 4 June it was held that when assessing the costs of civil proceedings the court did have jurisdiction to award the costs of attending at an inquest if the material purpose was to obtain information or evidence for use in civil proceedings. Similarly, in *Stewart and Hubbard v Medway NHS Trust* (2004) LTL, 20 September the cost of counsel attending an inquest in a clinical negligence case was held to be recoverable. All possible alternative methods of funding representation need to be considered in appropriate circumstances.

The importance of funding at inquests was also considered in *R (on the application of Khan) v Secretary of State for Health* [2003] EWCA Civ 1129 where the Court of Appeal held on the facts that the inquest would not be an effective one unless the deceased's family could play an effective part in it. The absence of legal representation in matters involving Article 2 of the ECHR needs to be specifically considered.

All possible alternative sources of finance should be considered (eg, in a fatal road traffic accident, the deceased's legal expense insurance may cover the cost of representation for the estate). Immediate enquiries must be made in respect of any claim on any insurance policy and, if appropriate, prior authorisation should be obtained from the insurer. Enquiries should also be made as to whether a trade union will fund representation at the inquest or whether any *pro bono* service may be able to provide assistance.

If there is a possibility of a clinical negligence claim being brought, any doctor who is required to give evidence will be represented by the hospital's solicitors or his defence union. Similarly, in a personal injury case, if a civil claim is likely to follow as a result of the death, the employers (eg, in a factory accident) or the driver of the other vehicle (in a road traffic accident) will be represented by solicitors instructed by their respective insurers.

14.2.5 Preparation for the hearing

Only the coroner can decide which documents should be placed before the court. This makes preparation for the inquest difficult for the solicitor as he may have little idea of what evidence will be called. The coroner's officer may be able to assist informally and he should be contacted to see what view the coroner may be taking in respect of the evidence. The coroner may decide to release documents before the inquest and a request should be made in each case.

In the case of *R (Bentley) v HM Coroner for Avon* [2001] EWHC 170 (Admin), (2001) LTL, 23 March, it was held that, on the facts, the request for advanced disclosure was reasonable and, since straightforward disclosure was requested by a party who would, in the end, be entitled to see it, the document should be disclosed. The court has emphasised that while there was no requirement for advanced disclosure in the Coroners Rules, there was a requirement of natural justice and fairness.

In certain complicated matters, the coroner may be willing to hold a 'pre-inquest review' to allow the parties and the coroner to consider matters prior to the actual inquest. The coroner may summarise the evidence that he proposes to call and give the parties the opportunity to suggest any other witnesses that they may wish to call.

Normally, statements have been taken from the proposed witnesses by the coroner's officer or police and it can be of considerable advantage if these can be obtained beforehand. At the hearing of the inquest, further evidence or information can become available. If such information leads the solicitor to believe that he cannot represent his client adequately, he should request an adjournment.

In an attempt to overcome the above difficulties, prior to the hearing detailed enquiries must be made of such bodies as the police, trade union or HSE, which may be able to provide general background information. The more information that is obtained prior to the hearing the better.

In a clinical negligence case, the deceased's medical records should be obtained (see *Stobart v Nottingham Health Authority* [1992] 3 Med LR 284). Once received, they should be placed in an ordered, paginated file, and legible copies made. If the solicitor is instructed by an insurance company on behalf of the deceased's estate, in-depth research should be carried out into the nature of the illness, the usual treatment which is prescribed for the illness, and the usual consequences and recovery time of the illness. This research will include relevant medical literature, and copies should be taken of any appropriate material. Medical school libraries are generally very helpful with this form of research and can provide assistance and copying facilities. Research may reveal whether the treatment fell below the level which can be expected and required of the medical staff.

In addition, a solicitor may seek assistance from an expert who can advise him on how to examine any medical experts giving evidence on behalf of the doctor. Informed examination will test a witness's evidence, and may be useful if civil proceedings are later issued. It is important for the claimant's solicitor to make such detailed preparation, because solicitors acting for a doctor will be experienced in this field and have access to a wide range of sources, including many experts.

14.2.6   Procedure at the inquest

The inquest is formally opened without any significant evidence being given, and the formalities are carried out by the coroner sitting alone (who, eg, will take initial evidence, evidence of identification of the body, issue an order for disposal of the body and adjourn until a more suitable time). Evidence will be called concerning the death at the resumed full hearing, with legal representatives for both sides attending. If appropriate, a jury (see **14.2.6.1**) will also be in attendance at that time.

The coroner will not proceed with the inquest until the relevant authority has been contacted (see Coroners Rules 1984, r 26(3) – eg, in the case of industrial diseases) or after certain criminal proceedings have been brought (eg, in the case of death by dangerous driving). In the latter case, the claimant's solicitor should attend the criminal proceedings and take notes of the trial (see below), as useful evidence may be obtained which can assist in identifying any civil liability for the death.

The majority of evidence at the resumed inquest will usually be given orally by witnesses on oath, but the coroner has power to admit documentary evidence if he believes that the evidence is unlikely to be disputed. However, it is possible to object to such a decision, and a solicitor should do this where he believes that a witness should be called to answer questions (see also *R (Bentley) v HM Coroner for Avon* [2001] EWHC 170 (Admin), (2001) LTL, 23 March).

The actual order of calling the witnesses lies entirely within the discretion of the coroner. However, the pathologist may be the first substantive witness to give evidence (see *R v HM Coroner for Kent (Maidstone District), ex p Johnstone* (1994) 158 JP 1115). When the pathologist gives evidence, he will undoubtedly use medical language and it is important that the solicitor is able to understand the evidence which is given. Thus, research should be carried out prior to the inquest, so as to become familiar with the potential medical terms that may be used. The solicitor should not be afraid to ask the doctor to explain himself fully.

The coroner will normally then examine each witness so that the evidence is heard in the same order as the events leading to the death occurred. The solicitor should make careful notes as these witnesses may need to be contacted in relation to a potential civil claim. If the witness does not give evidence in accordance with his previous written statement to the coroner, and the interested party is not aware of this, then the coroner must deal with this point (see *R v HM Coroner for Inner London North District, ex p Cohen* (1994) 158 JP 644, DC). Once the coroner has dealt with the witness, each interested party (or their legal representatives) will be allowed to question them. A witness is examined by his own representative last (r 21).

14.2.6.1 Juries

A jury will be used at the coroner's court if the death:

(a)   occurred in prison;

(b)   occurred while the deceased was in police custody or resulted from injury caused by a police officer in the execution of his duty;

(c)   was caused by an accident, poisoning or disease, notice of which is required to be given under any Act to a government department or to any inspector or other officer of a government department, or to an inspector appointed under s 19 of the Health and Safety at Work etc Act 1974 (see *R (on the application of Aineto) v HM Coroner for Brighton and Hove* (2003) LTL, 21 July); and

(d)   occurred in circumstances the continuance or possible reoccurrence of which is prejudicial to the health and safety of the public or any section of the public.

A personal injury solicitor is most likely to be involved in cases coming within heads (c) and (d) above.

The jury will consist of between 7 and 11 people.

14.2.6.2 Witnesses

The coroner is the only person who has the power to call witnesses (the interested parties cannot), but if a solicitor believes that a particular witness should be called, representation can be made to the coroner (see *R (Nicholls) v Coroner for the City of*

Liverpool [2001] EWHC 922 (Admin), where an application for judicial review was successful where the coroner's reasons for not allowing a medical expert requested by the deceased's family could not be sustained). Enquiries need to be made of the coroner's officer (prior to the hearing) as to which witnesses the coroner intends to call. On occasion, the solicitor will make representations that other witnesses should be called. For example, the coroner may not have intended to call a nurse manager who may have been responsible for the system of work adopted on a hospital ward, because she was not present at the time of death, but she may have vital evidence. However, it is for the coroner to decide which witnesses to call.

Persons entitled to examine witnesses at an inquest are as follows:

(a)   the parent, child, spouse or any personal representative of the deceased;

(b)   any beneficiary under a policy of insurance issued on the life of the deceased;

(c)   the insurer who issued such a policy of insurance;

(d)   any person whose act or omission or that of his agent or servant may, in the opinion of the coroner, have caused, or contributed to, the death of the deceased;

(e)   any person appointed by a trade union to which the deceased belonged at the time of his death, if the death of the deceased may have been caused by an injury received in the course of his employment or by an industrial disease;

(f)   an inspector appointed by, or a representative of, an enforcing authority, or any person appointed by a government department to attend the inquest;

(g)   the chief officer of police;

(h)   any other person who, in the opinion of the coroner, is a properly interested person.

The Coroners Rules 1984 provide that the above persons can either examine witnesses in person or through counsel or solicitors. In *R v Portsmouth City Coroner, ex p Keane* (1993) 153 JP 658, the coroner refused leave to a brother of the deceased to examine certain witnesses through counsel on the basis that the brother was not a properly interested person within r 20(2) of Coroners Rules 1984. It was held that the coroner was entitled by use of his discretion to come to that decision.

The questioning of witnesses at the inquest can be a difficult matter as the strict purpose of the inquest is limited to finding:

(a)   who the deceased was;

(b)   how, when and where the deceased came by his death (see **14.2.10**);

(c)   the particulars required by the Registration Acts to be registered concerning the death.

The Divisional Court has repeatedly reaffirmed that these are the only matters that the coroner's court is concerned with and the coroner will wish to concentrate on these fundamental points. However, there can be no doubt that many solicitors attend the inquest with a slightly wider agenda, that of trying to identify who was liable for the death and to examine the evidence surrounding the case. Much will depend upon the individual coroner as to the types of questions which are allowed, but the coroner will always limit questions concerned with civil liability.

To prevent the inquest apportioning blame, the Coroners Rules 1984, r 22 specifically provides that a witness is not obliged to answer any questions tending to incriminate himself. The witness may be called to the witness box and asked merely to give his name and address. On occasion, no further questions will be put to him. However, practice varies widely on this point and, in *R v Lincolnshire Coroner, ex p Hay* (1999) 163 JP 666, it was held that the privilege against self-incrimination did not give the witness complete immunity against further questioning. The privilege against self-incrimination is against criminal proceedings (and not civil proceedings) and this should be borne in mind when the coroner is deciding if the witness is entitled to claim self-incrimination. The solicitor may have to remind the coroner about this point. If the coroner allows the witness to be questioned, it is for the witness's representative to make the objection if a question is put which might lead to self-incrimination. If the witness answers the question, he will waive the privilege.

In certain cases, it is desirable for a witness's identity to be protected, as in the case of *R v Newcastle-upon-Tyne Coroner, ex p A* (1998) 162 JP 387, where a police officer was allowed to give evidence from behind a screen. (See also *R (A and Another) v Inner South London Coroner* (2004) *The Times*, 12 July and 11 November and *Family of Derek Bennett v (1) HM Coroner and (2) Commissioner of Police for the Metropolis* [2004] EWCA Civ 1439.)

14.2.6.3 Summation

If a jury is present, the coroner will sum up the evidence to the jury after the witnesses have given evidence and will direct the jury on points of law. In *R v HM Coroner for Inner London South District, ex p Douglas-Williams* (1998) 162 JP 751, it was held that, in complex cases, it would be good practice for the coroner to prepare a written statement of matters which the law requires in relation to possible verdicts. If such a policy is followed, a solicitor should request to inspect the statement prior to summing up. The jury may wish to make other comments outside its terms of reference (normally with the motive of trying to prevent another death occurring), but the coroner will not allow this.

If no jury is present the coroner normally sums up by means of a revision of the evidence and states his conclusions.

14.2.6.4 Expressing an opinion

Rule 43 of the Coroners Rules 1984 allows a coroner, who believes that action should be taken to prevent the recurrence of fatalities similar to that in respect of which the inquest was held, to announce at the inquest that he is reporting the matter in writing to whoever has power to take such action.

14.2.6.5 Verdicts

Strictly, a verdict is not given by the coroner who, instead, gives a summary of the results of the inquisition (see below and **14.2.10**).

If a jury is present, it will retire to consider its verdict. No communication is permitted with the jury once it has retired. A majority verdict is allowed where the minority is not more than two. The coroner may accept a majority verdict, but is not bound to do so (see *R (Dawson and Others) v HM Coroner for East Riding and Kingston-upon-Hull Coroners District* [2001] EWHC 352 (Admin) – a coroner need not leave all possible verdicts to a jury).

A document called an 'inquisition' is completed by the coroner at the end of the inquest, and is signed by the coroner and jury members who concur with it. The form requires five matters to be dealt with:

(a)   the name of the deceased;

(b)   the injury or disease causing death;

(c)   the time, place and circumstances at or in which the injury was sustained;

(d)   the conclusion of the jury/coroner as to the death; and

(e)   the particulars under the Registration Acts.

(The above vary depending on the particular type of case – see the Coroners Rules 1984, Sch 2, Form 22.)

The standard inquisition form gives a comprehensive list of suggested verdicts, of which the most significant in personal injury/clinical negligence cases are:

(a)   industrial disease (this is given no defined meaning);

(b)   want of attention at birth;

(c)   accident/misadventure (the courts have taken the view that any distinction between the two words is undesirable);

(d)   unlawful killing;

(e)   open verdict;

(f)   suicide;

(g)   natural causes.

(The notes to Form 22 have no binding effect whatsoever and are merely advisory.) The following points should be noted in relation to possible verdicts.

In *R (Mowlem plc) v Avon Assistant Deputy Coroner* (2005) LTL, 13 May, the court reinforced the appropriateness of r 43 rather than the coroner making improper comments following the verdict in that case.

Accident/accidental death

Even if such a verdict is given it does not mean that a civil case cannot be brought.

An open verdict

This means simply that there is insufficient evidence to reach a conclusion.

Neglect

This is a controversial verdict and, following the case of *R v Surrey Coroner, ex p Wright* [1997] 2 WLR 16, it appears that a coroner cannot return a verdict of 'lack of care', but the term 'neglect' may be used to describe a situation where there has been a period of neglect which resulted in the death. In this context, neglect means continuous, or at least 'non-transient' neglect (see also *R v HM Coroner for North Humberside and Scunthorpe, ex p Jamieson* [1995] QB 1, CA). This verdict does not necessarily mean that negligence can be established as it does not necessarily mean that the three elements of negligence required to be proved in a civil court can be established (see also *R v HM Coroner for Swansea and Gower, ex p Tristram* (2000) 164 JP 191; *R v HM Coroner for Coventry, ex p Chief Constable of Staffordshire Constabulary* (2000) LTL, 28 September and *R (Amin) v Secretary of State for the Home Department; R (Middleton) v Secretary of State for the Home Department* [2002] EWCA Civ 390, [2002] 3 WLR 505 – concerning Article 2 of the European Convention on Human Rights and returning a verdict of neglect).

Some commentators state that neglect can rarely, if ever, be a verdict on its own. Rather, it is ancillary to any verdict where there is a link between the relevant conduct and the cause of death. In *R (S) v HM Coroner for Inner West London* [2001] EWHC 105 (Admin), (2001) 61 BMLR 222, a fresh inquest was allowed due to the fact that the coroner had not left a verdict incorporating an element of neglect to the jury (see also *R v Coroner for Western Somerset, ex p Middleton* [2004] UKHL 10; *R v HM Coroner for West Yorkshire, ex p Sacker* [2004] UKHL 11; *R (Mumford) v HM Coroner for Reading and Secretary of State for the Home Department* [2002] EWHC 2184 (Admin).

Following *Middleton* (above), it is arguable that the term 'neglect' should be avoided. Certain coroners now, where appropriate, provide narrative verdicts that comment on the factual issues and thus avoid the need for short phrases.

Suicide or unlawful killing

The standard of proof required for a suicide or unlawful killing verdict to be returned is that of beyond reasonable doubt. See *R (on the application of Neil Sharman) v HM Coroner for Inner London* [2005] EWHC 857 concerning the returning of a verdict of unlawful killing and *R (on the application of Anderson and Others) v HM Coroner for Inner North Greater London* [2004] EWHC 2729.

All other verdicts require a burden of proof based on the balance of probabilities.

The Divisional Court (and the Coroners Rules 1984 themselves) have made it clear that the coroner's court does not decide the responsibility for the death. Therefore, verdicts in the coroner's court are framed so as not to identify any individual as being responsible (see also *R v HM Coroner for Derby and South Derbyshire, ex p John Henry Hart Jnr* (2000) 164 JP 429 and *R v Director of Public Prosecutions, ex p Manning and Another* [2000] 3 WLR 463).

14.2.6.6   Transcripts

At the conclusion of the inquest, the coroner's officer will collect any documents or copy statements which were used during the hearing. A copy of the transcript of the case can be obtained on payment of a fee. (See also *R (on the application of the Ministry of Defence) v Wiltshire and Swindon Coroner* [2005] EWHC 889.) It is possible for this transcript to be used for limited purposes at the civil trial if the appropriate procedure is used in the civil proceedings.

14.2.7   Representing the family

The inquest can be difficult for lay persons to understand. Lay persons will be unfamiliar with the role of the coroner and may expect that the purpose of the inquest is not to establish how the deceased died but to establish fault. Because of potential problems with lack of advance disclosure of evidence, the family of the deceased may not be aware in advance what evidence will be given and may be upset by the evidence disclosed at the inquest.

The procedure that the coroner will follow during the inquest must be explained to the family of the deceased. It will be necessary to discuss the evidence with them and, in particular, to discuss the verdict. The verdict should be explained thoroughly and the deceased's family reminded that the purpose of the inquest and the verdict is not to apportion blame, but to establish by what means the deceased came by his death.

14.2.8   Representing the potential defendant

14.2.8.1   Clinical negligence cases

Requesting records and taking statements

The solicitor for the health authority or health trust should obtain all relevant records and obtain statements from any medical and nursing staff who have been called by the coroner to give evidence at the inquest.

The solicitor should help the staff by reviewing their statements prior to submission to the coroner. The solicitor should ensure that the statements contain only relevant facts and do not offer any opinion which the witness is not competent to give. For example, a house officer should not give an opinion on whether specific parts of the treatment contributed to the death, but should restrict his statement to the facts alone.

If it appears from the statements that disciplinary action might be taken against a member of the medical staff (eg, because a mistake in treatment has been made), that person should be advised to seek his own representation from his defence organisation as his interests will conflict with those of the hospital.

The solicitor should advise the medical and nursing staff that the original records will be available at the inquest and that they are permitted to refer to these.

Purpose, form and limits of inquest

The solicitor should advise the medical and nursing staff about the purpose and form of an inquest and encourage an attitude of openness and co-operation at the inquest.

Expert evidence

The solicitor may consider obtaining the specialist opinion on the issues arising at the inquest from a hospital consultant (but not from a consultant who is directly involved in the case).

14.2.8.2   Personal injury cases

In a personal injury case, as soon as the solicitor is instructed, he will make contact with the insured and attempt to investigate the matter further. This will normally involve attending at the insured's premises, if the accident was work-based, or at the scene of the accident with the insured, in the case of a road traffic accident. The defendant's solicitor will be under strict instructions from the insurer to formulate a view on liability and attempt to find out as much as possible about the deceased, so that some idea can be obtained about quantum. In a road traffic accident, the inquest will provide early access to the police investigation report (which may have involved a partial reconstruction) and useful information, such as whether a seat-belt was worn, may become apparent. In the case of an industrial accident, the solicitor investigating the case will normally be concerned with the system of work used or the employment history of the deceased. This may be particularly useful in asbestosis claims where it may become apparent that the deceased's main exposure to asbestos was during his employment with another employer.

14.2.9   Publicity at the inquest

There is often publicity attached to inquests. Reporters may request an interview with the key witnesses and, in particular, the family. The appropriate advice to witnesses is at the discretion of the solicitors acting for the parties. Usually, the solicitor representing the hospital or doctors will decline to say anything to the press to avoid saying anything amounting to an admission in subsequent proceedings, or which may be upsetting to the family. The solicitor should also advise the doctors and nursing staff not to make any comments to the media. In some cases, it may be appropriate, from a public relations point of view, for the hospital to issue a brief statement offering sympathy to the family following the death of the deceased.

If the family wishes to express its anger in a more public forum, the press is usually happy to provide this opportunity. If there are any concerns to which the inquest gave rise, these could be expressed to the press. It is important, however, that the family's solicitor does not get carried away on the tide of emotion and risk slandering any of the individuals concerned.

14.2.10 The impact of the Human Rights Act 1998

In the cases of *R v HM Coroner for Western Somerset, ex p Middleton* [2004] UKHL 10 and *R v Coroner for West Yorkshire, ex p Sacker* [2004] UKHL 11 the House of Lords examined the relationship between Article 2 of the ECHR and the role of inquests where the deceased dies while under the control of the State or as a consequence of the actions of a State agent. Although full reference to the cases must be made, the following points should be noted:

(a)   Acts or omissions may be recorded, but expressions that suggest civil liability, in particular 'neglect' or 'carelessness' should be avoided.

(b)   There are some cases where short verdicts in the traditional form did not enable the inquest jury to express their conclusion on the central issues in the case and this did not meet the requirements of the Convention. Where a short form verdict was not satisfactory, it would be for the coroner to decide how best to elicit the jury's conclusion.

(c)   The rules for conducting inquests enacted by Parliament should be respected save for the interpretation of 'how' in the phrase 'how, when and where the deceased came by his death' in r 36 of the Coroners Rules 1984. The phrase should be interpreted in the broad sense, meaning 'by what means and in what circumstances' rather than simply 'by what means'.

Other recent cases relating to Article 2 of the ECHR include *R (on the application of (1) Challender and (2) Morris) v Legal Services Commission* [2004] EWHC 925 concerning a refusal of funding by the Legal Services Commission; *R (on the application of (1) A and (2) B) v HM Coroner for Inner South District of Greater London* [2004] EWHC 1592 (Admin) concerning a coroner's refusal to grant anonymity to two police officers; and Re *McKerr* [2004] UKHL 12 where the duty to investigate an unlawful killing under Article 2 did not arise in domestic law in respect of deaths before 2 October 2000 when the Human Rights Act 1998 came into force. See also *R (Wilson) v Secretary of State for the Home Department* [2004] EWHC 2462 and *Pearson v HM Coroner for Inner London North* [2005] EWHC 833.

Coroners are clearly having regard to Article 2 in their day-to-day work. However, such cases as *Plymouth City Council v HM Coroner for Devon (defendant) and the Secretary of State for Education and Skills* (2005) illustrate that there can be difficulties in the interpretation of the Article 2 requirements. In *Plymouth City Council* the coroner decided to hold a 'broad inquest' (by including certain statutory child protection agencies) in relation to a child's death, but it was held on judicial review that the investigation duty under Article 2 had not been activated and there was no need for a broad inquest. See also *Goodson v HM Coroner for Bedfordshire and Luton* [2004] EWHC 2931 in relation to when the State's procedural obligation under Article 2 is invoked.

14.2.11   Proposals for change

It should be noted that, at the time of writing, there are proposals to change the role of the coroner and the latest position should be checked.

14.3   Prosecution for manslaughter or prosecutions under the Health and Safety at Work etc Act 1974

Personal injury solicitors will need to be familiar with the law surrounding prosecutions under criminal law, and the health and safety legislation concerning accidents that result in death. The defendant personal injury solicitor may be instructed by the insurers to represent the insured in criminal proceedings at a very early stage, to enable investigations to take place quickly and to take a view on the case. The insurers will be concerned not only with obtaining details on civil liability but also that a successful defence of the criminal case, and the absence of any criminal conviction, may assist in the defence of the civil claim.

The prosecution of employers for deaths resulting from workplace fatal accidents is normally under the Health and Safety at Work etc Act 1974.

Another possible prosecution is for manslaughter. However, prosecutions of a company for manslaughter have been difficult. The most famous prosecution for corporate manslaughter was in *R v P & O European Ferries (Dover) Ltd* (1991) 93 Cr App R 72, following the *Herald of Free Enterprise* disaster when the ship capsized with the loss of 188 passengers and crew. The prosecution against the individuals concerned and the company failed.

However, in December 1994 a prosecution was brought against OLL Ltd for manslaughter. In that case, four teenagers drowned while taking part in a canoeing exercise and evidence was given of exceedingly poor safety provisions. Convictions were successful against the company, which was fined £60,000, and the managing director, who was imprisoned for three years.

In *R v Adomako* [1995] 1 AC 171, an anaesthetist was convicted of manslaughter. The facts concerned an eye operation, which left the patient paralysed when the supply of oxygen to the patient ceased which resulted in a cardiac arrest. The doctor had not noticed the disconnection of the tube supplying the oxygen. Approximately 4½ minutes after the disconnection, an alarm sounded on one of the machines in the operating theatre, which prompted the doctor into action but at no stage did he check the tube. The prosecution alleged that the doctor failed to notice other clinical signs that the patient was displaying. The House of Lords held that in cases of manslaughter involving breach of duty, the ordinary principles of the law of negligence apply to ascertain whether the defendant had been in breach of duty of care to the victim. If so, the next question was whether it had caused the death and could be characterised as gross negligence and therefore a crime. Lord MacKay held:

> The essence of the matter which is supremely a jury question is whether, having regard to the risk of death involved, the conduct of the defendant was so bad in all the circumstances as to amount in their judgment to a criminal act or omission.

Although such prosecutions are rare, the above cases should be borne in mind when considering responsibility for fatal accidents. (See also *R v Kelly and Frear* [2005] EWCA Crim 1061.)

14.3.1 Future proposals

This is an area where the Government and commentators have called for changes to the current law and in March 2005 a draft corporate manslaughter Bill was published together with a consultation document entitled *Corporate Manslaughter: the Government's Draft Bill for Reform*. The consultation is still ongoing at the time of writing.

14.4 Criminal prosecution for causing death by dangerous driving

Causing death by dangerous driving is an indictable offence. The maximum penalty in the Crown Court is 14 years' imprisonment and/or an unlimited fine. The offence carries obligatory disqualification from driving for two years or obligatory endorsement on the driving licence of 3–11 points (if disqualification is avoided but not endorsement) and compulsory re-testing before recommencement of driving (see s 1 of the Road Traffic Act 1988 (as amended)). Forfeiture of the motor vehicle may be ordered.

The definition of dangerous driving is found in s 2A of the Road Traffic Act 1988:

(1) For the purpose of sections 1 and 2 above a person is to be regarded as driving dangerously if (and, subject to subsection 2 below, only if)—

    (a) the way he drives falls far below what would be expected of a competent and careful driver; and

    (b) it would be obvious to a competent and careful driver that driving in that way would be dangerous.

(2) A person is also to be regarded as driving dangerously for the purpose of sections 1 and 2 above if it would be obvious to a competent and careful driver that driving the vehicle in its current state would be dangerous.

The procedure adopted in the magistrates' courts and Crown Court for such a prosecution is dealt with in the Legal Practice Guide, *Criminal Litigation*. If such a prosecution occurs following a fatal road accident, the claimant's solicitor should attend at court to obtain details of the circumstances of the accident and take notes of the evidence. If a conviction is obtained, this will be very useful for the civil proceedings, and in these circumstances the relevant insurance company will often settle any claim.

Many motor insurance policies provide for the cost of defending such an offence, and the insurance company will nominate solicitors to act on the insured's behalf. The defendant's insurers will use the proceedings to establish a view on criminal, as well as civil liability. In such circumstances, the defendant's solicitor will usually instruct an accident reconstruction expert to assist in the investigations.

14.5 Conclusion

Evidence must be gathered as quickly as possible in all fatal accident claims and it is important that the above processes are used to protect the client's interests at all times.

14.6 Further reading and information

Matthews, *Jervis on Coroners* (Sweet & Maxwell) and the cumulative supplement.

Advice can be obtained from the organisation 'Inquest', which can be contacted at Alexandra National House, 330 Seven Sisters Road, Finsbury Park, London N4 2PJ.

14.7 Key points

Chapter 15

Introduction to Fatal Accident Claims — Procedure and Quantification

15.1 Introduction

This chapter sets out the basic principles involved in assessing damages in personal injury and clinical negligence cases where the victim has died before trial.

There are two main causes of action in such circumstances:

(a) the Law Reform (Miscellaneous Provisions) Act 1934, which allows a claim for the benefit of the deceased's estate; and

(b) the Fatal Accidents Act 1976, which allows a claim for the benefit of the dependants and those entitled to an award of bereavement damages.

It will be assumed that the death occurred on or after 1 January 1983 as the above Acts were amended substantially relating to deaths after that date. While the Acts provide two separate causes of action they are commonly brought together.

In certain cases, specific statutes provide for recompense for the deceased's family, such as the Carriage by Air Act 1961 in cases of death arising out of civil aviation accidents (these are not dealt with in this text).

15.2 Limitation period

The main limitation time limits are as follows.

(a) If a claim is brought under the Law Reform (Miscellaneous Provisions) Act 1934, the claim should be commenced three years from: (i) the date of death; or (ii) the date of knowledge of the deceased's personal representative, whichever is the later, or if there is more than one personal representative and their dates of knowledge are different, from the earliest date of knowledge of any of them. It should be noted, however, that if the injured person dies after the period in which he could have brought the claim, the case will be prima facie statute-barred (although the court has a power to override this time limit under s 33 of the Limitation Act 1980).

(b)   If a claim is brought under the Fatal Accidents Act 1976, the limitation period is: (i) three years from the date of death; or (ii) the date of knowledge of the persons for whose benefit the claim is brought. If a claim brought under the Fatal Accidents Act 1976 is out of time by virtue of this provision, the court can use its discretion under s 33 of the Limitation Act 1980. It must be remembered, however, that a claim under the Fatal Accidents Act 1976 cannot be brought if at the time of the injured person's death he could not have brought his own claim for damages for the injuries that he sustained because, for example, he had failed to comply with the time limit under the Carriage by Air Act 1961 (see also *Young v Western Power Distribution (South West) plc* [2003] EWCA Civ 1034. The power to extend the limitation period will apply only where there has been a failure to comply with the initial limitation period set by the Limitation Act 1980. (See *Clack v Thames Television Ltd* (2004) LTL, 16 September for an example where the court has disapplied the limitation period in relation to asbestos claims. See also *Young (deceased) v Western Power Distribution (South West) plc*.)

15.3   Cause of action

The Law Reform (Miscellaneous Provisons) Act 1934 (LR(MP)A 1934) provides (for the benefit of the deceased's estate) for the continuation of the cause of action to which the deceased was entitled the instant before he died (LR(MP)A 1934, s 1(2)). It does not create a separate cause of action.

The Fatal Accidents Act 1976 (FAA 1976) does create a separate cause of action for the dependants (and those entitled to the award of bereavement damages), but it is based on the pre-condition that the deceased, had he lived, would have been able to sue successfully (FAA 1976, s 1).

Three things follow from this, namely:

(a)   if the deceased had no cause of action then the estate and the dependants have no cause of action;

(b)   any defence that could have been used against the deceased can be used against the estate and the dependants;

(c)   if the deceased was contributorily negligent then the damages of the estate and the dependants are reduced accordingly.

Example 1

Tom is driving his car when it collides with a car driven by Sharon. Tom dies as a result of his injuries. He is survived by his widow, Elaine, and his son, Christopher. The accident is entirely the fault of Tom. As a result, neither Tom's estate, Elaine nor Christopher have any right of action against Sharon.

Example 2

Lucy is killed in an accident at work. She is survived by her husband, Michael, and daughter, Patricia. Lucy and her employers are equally to blame for the accident. Although Lucy's estate, Michael and Patricia may claim against the employers, the damages awarded to each will be reduced by 50%.

In the case of *Jameson and Another v Central Electricity Generating Board and Another* [2000] AC 455, the House of Lords held that in a case where the second co-defendant had paid a compensation payment to the injured person when he was still alive (on a less than full liability basis), this did prevent the dependants bringing a claim under FAA 1976 against the first co-defendant (who was a concurrent tortfeasor) and did amount to a settlement of claim.

15.4 The appointment of personal representatives

Fatal accident claims are normally representative actions. This means that the personal representative normally brings a claim simultaneously on behalf of the estate under LR(MP)A 1934 and on behalf of the dependants under FAA 1976. The grant of probate or letters of administration should therefore be obtained before the claim is commenced.

15.5 Damages under the Law Reform (Miscellaneous Provisions) Act 1934

Generally, the damages awarded to the estate under LR(MP)A 1934 are based on the losses for which the deceased could have claimed at the instant before he died. In essence, the estate inherits the deceased's right to sue in respect of the death. Any head of damages that is duplicated between LR(MP)A 1934 and FAA 1976 is only recoverable once.

The following heads of damages may be appropriate.

15.5.1 Pain, suffering and loss of amenity

There must be evidence that there was suffering. This will mean, in practice, that there must be a period of survival. If there is no significant period of survival (eg, in the case of instantaneous death) an award will not be made (*Hicks v Wright* [1992] 2 All ER 65). If the victim enters an immediate coma after the accident and subsequently dies without regaining consciousness then, again, no damages for pain and suffering will be awarded under this head. However, if there is a period of survival and, during that period, the victim becomes aware of impending death, the award for pain and suffering will be increased. The most common example of a case where the deceased has a long and painful death is that of mesothelioma (lung cancer by asbestosis). In such a case, the victim will suffer haemoptysis (coughing up blood), shortness of breath, loss of weight and loss of appetite. In the case of lingering death (eg, a protracted death as a result of disease), the amount of the award for pain and suffering and loss of amenity will depend upon the actual level of pain and the length of time over which the pain was experienced.

15.5.2 Loss of income

The estate is entitled to claim the lost net earnings of the deceased from the time of the accident until death, calculated in the same way as for a living claimant (see **Chapter 13**). No claim can be made for loss of income in respect of any period after that person's death (LR(MP)A 1934, s 1(2)(a)(ii), as amended by the Administration of Justice Act 1982).

15.5.3 Funeral expenses

Funeral expenses are specifically provided for in s 1(2)(c) of LR(MP)A 1934. The expenses may be claimed provided they are:

(a)   reasonable; and

(b)   incurred by the estate.

If the expenses are incurred by a dependant of the deceased rather than by the deceased's estate, the dependant may claim the expenses as part of the fatal accidents claim.

15.5.4 Value of services rendered by third parties

Services rendered by third parties may include, for example: nursing services rendered by a relative to the deceased up to the time of death; expenses incurred by a third party in assisting in bringing the deceased's body home from abroad; or the costs incurred by relatives in visiting the hospital. The quantum is the proper and reasonable cost of supplying the need (for the general principles involved, see **Chapter 13**).

15.5.5 Other losses

Other losses may include, for example, damage to chattels such as the car the deceased was driving at the time of the incident, or the clothing which he was wearing. (See *Batt v Highgate Private Hospital* [2004] EWHC 707.)

15.5.6 Distribution of damages

Damages under LR(MP)A 1934 pass to the deceased's estate, and from there to the deceased's beneficiaries according to the deceased's will or the rules of intestacy.

Damages under LR(MP)A 1934 are, in appropriate cases (eg, where there was a long interval between the accident and the death, and the deceased had been in receipt of recoverable benefits), subject to the Social Security (Recovery of Benefits) Act 1997 (see **Chapter 12**) but are not subject to any other loss or gains to the estate, such as the receipt of insurance money (LR(MP)A 1934, s 1(2)).

15.5.7 Conclusion

In the case of instantaneous death, damages under LR(MP)A 1934 will normally be limited to damages for funeral expenses and damage to chattels. Where there is a period of survival, the damages may be more extensive but will normally still be severely curtailed by the inability of the estate to claim the lost future income of the deceased.

15.6 Damages under the Fatal Accidents Act 1976

In general terms, there are three possible heads of damages, namely:

(a) a dependency claim for the financial losses suffered by the dependants of the deceased;

(b) an award of bereavement damages; and

(c) a claim for the funeral expenses if paid by the dependants.

15.6.1 Loss of dependency

The broad requirements under the loss of dependency head are that the claimant must be a 'dependant', as defined by the FAA 1976, who suffers financial loss as a result of the deceased's death which is referable to a personal family relationship with the deceased.

15.6.1.1 The statutory meaning of 'dependant'

The definition of 'dependant' at s 1(3) of the FAA 1976, is as follows:

(a) the wife or husband or former wife or husband of the deceased;

(b) any person who:

(i) was living with the deceased in the same household immediately before the date of the death; and

(ii)   had been living with the deceased in the same household for at least two years before that date; and

(iii)   was living during the whole of that period as the husband or wife of the deceased;

(c)   any parent or other ascendant of the deceased;

(d)   any person who was treated by the deceased as his parent;

(e)   any child or other descendant of the deceased;

(f)   any person (not being a child of the deceased) who, in the case of any marriage to which the deceased was at any time a party, was treated by the deceased as a child of the family in relation to that marriage;

(g)   any person who is, or is the issue of, a brother, sister, uncle or aunt of the deceased.

The requirement to come within the statutory definition of 'dependant' has resulted in adverse judicial comment (see *Shepherd v Post Office* (1995) *The Times*, 15 June), and the introduction of the cohabitee ((b) above) by the Administration of Justice Act 1982 as a possible claimant was controversial.

In *Fretwell v Willi Betz* (2001), the definition of a 'dependant' was challenged, by virtue of the Human Rights Act 1998. The case was settled without any admission as regards the claimant's status as a 'dependant' (the argument concerned a child of the girlfriend who was living with the deceased prior to the accident), but it does illustrate the possibility of using the Human Rights Act 1998 to challenge the narrow statutory definition of a 'dependant' (see also *Ogur v Turkey* (2001) 31 EHRR 912).

The requirement to have been living together for two years prior to the death should be noted, and evidence should be obtained on this point if it is anticipated that the defendant will challenge this (see *Kotke v Saffarini* [2005] EWCA Civ 221). The FAA 1976 contains a provision that the cohabitee's lack of enforceable right to support is to be taken into account (FAA 1976, s 3(4)). This may mean that a cohabitee will receive less compensation than a lawful spouse, as the court may use a lower multiplier in determining the dependency claim. For example, a multiplier of 13 was used for a cohabiting couple, instead of 15 which would have been used if they were married.

15.6.1.2   Further provisions with regard to the meaning of 'dependant'

Section 1(4) of the FAA 1976 (as amended by the Administration of Justice Act 1982) provides:

> ... former wife or husband ... includes a reference to a person whose marriage to the deceased has been annulled or declared void as well as a person whose marriage to the deceased has been dissolved.

Section 1(5) of the FAA 1976 (as amended by the Administration of Justice Act 1982) provides:

(a)   any relationship by affinity shall be treated as a relationship by consanguinity, any relationship of the half blood as a relationship of the whole blood, and the stepchild of any person as his child;

(b)   an illegitimate person shall be treated as the legitimate child of his mother and reputed father.

Thus, for example, the stepbrother of the deceased is treated as his true brother; the uncle of a wife is treated as the husband's uncle.

The Adoption Act 1976 provides that, generally, an adopted child is treated as the natural child of the adopters.

15.6.1.3   Identifying the dependants

It is important to identify all prospective dependants as s 2(3) of the FAA 1976 provides that 'not more than one action shall lie' and, as a result, only one claim will be brought. A defendant is entitled to full particulars of all those on whose behalf the claim is being brought. In practice, the particulars of the dependants are set out in the court documentation and generally include details of:

(a)   the age of the dependants;

(b)   their relationship with the deceased;

(c)   the nature of the dependency (eg, the dependant was a minor son wholly supported by the deceased father who was the family breadwinner and who had good promotion prospects).

In the case of *Cachia v Faluyi* [2001] EWCA Civ 998, [2001] 1 WLR 1966, the Court of Appeal held that it was possible to interpret s 2(3) of the FAA 1976 under the European Convention on Human Rights, so as to prevent a dependent child's claim from becoming statute-barred for limitation purposes.

On occasions, the defendants will argue that a claimant is not a true 'dependant' under the FAA 1976, and this is often resolved by the court ordering a trial of the point as a preliminary issue.

15.6.1.4   The requirement of 'financial loss'

It is not sufficient that the claimant merely satisfies the statutory meaning of 'dependant'. It must be shown in addition that there is a reasonable likelihood that the claimant has or will suffer financial loss as a result of the death of the deceased. In the case of *Thomas v Kwik Save Stores Ltd* (2000) *The Times,* 27 June, the Court of Appeal reaffirmed the principle that, when awarding damages under the FAA 1976, the court was concerned with the financial loss and not the emotional dependency of the claimant on the deceased.

In many cases, the dependants will have a clear and immediate financial loss. For example, where a husband before his death was maintaining his wife and children, the fact that they will suffer financial loss as a result of the husband's death is obvious.

The loss may still be regarded as 'financial' even if there was no expenditure by the deceased, provided the support can be quantified in monetary terms (eg, where the deceased's elderly mother was allowed to live rent-free in the deceased's house before his death, the mother would be able to claim a quantifiable financial loss).

In the case of *Cox v Hockenhill* (1999) *Law Society Gazette,* 30 June, the Court of Appeal held that the important point in assessing the dependency was to identify the loss the claimant has suffered as a result of a death. In that case, the deceased's income had been certain State benefits which she and her husband had relied upon. The court allowed the husband's claim for dependency on the basis that he was dependent on certain benefits that had been received prior to the death and which he no longer obtained after his wife was killed in a road traffic accident.

15.6.1.5 The loss must be as a result of a personal family relationship with the deceased

If the loss to the dependant is, in reality, a loss attributable to a business relationship with the deceased, then the claim for loss of dependency will fail (*Burgess v Florence Nightingale Hospital for Gentlewomen* [1955] 1 QB 349).

Example

Tom is killed in a car accident as a result of the negligent driving of Keith. Tom is survived by his widow, Sally, and his six-month-old son, Brian. Tom was the sole financial support of Sally and Brian. Tom worked in business with his brother, Joe. As a result of Tom's death, the business fails and Joe suffers heavy financial losses. Tom's married sister, Edwina, is very upset at the news of her brother's death.

Sally and Brian may claim as defined dependants who suffer financial losses as a result of a family relationship with Tom.

Joe cannot claim because, although he is a defined dependant, his financial losses are as a result of a business relationship with Tom.

Edwina cannot claim because although she is a defined dependant, she has suffered no financial losses (merely grief and sorrow).

15.6.2 Assessing loss of dependency – the traditional method

The award for loss of dependency is ascertained by a multiplicand and multiplier system. The multiplicand is the net annual loss of the dependants; the multiplier is based on the number of years' loss of dependency (ie, the length of time that the claimant would have been dependent on the deceased). The approach taken by the court is similar to that adopted by the court in determining the living claimant's loss of future earnings.

15.6.2.1 The multiplicand – the net annual loss to the dependants

The deceased wage earner

The starting point is to calculate the amount of the deceased's earnings and deduct the estimated amount of how much was required or spent by the deceased on his own personal and living expenses (*Davies v Powell Duffryn Associated Collieries* [1942] AC 601 at 617).

The deceased's net annual earnings

The deceased's net annual earnings must be calculated as at the date of the trial (*Cookson v Knowles* [1979] AC 556). In order to ascertain that sum, it may be necessary to adjust the deceased's earnings at the date of death.

Sums spent on the deceased's own maintenance

A figure must be ascertained for sums spent exclusively on the maintenance of dependants or on items which benefited both the deceased and the dependants jointly (eg, mortgage or rent payments are left out of account) (*Harris v Empress Motors* [1984] 1 WLR 212).

Calculating the dependency figure

There are two approaches that the courts have considered:

(a)   The 'old' system for calculating the dependency figure is to add up all the financial benefits received by the dependants from the deceased. It is necessary to produce a list of the items which contributed to the annual value of dependency and for the claimant to provide documentary evidence, bills, etc for the year prior to the death. A proportion is then deducted for the deceased's own expenses. For example, the following items have been considered: How much housekeeping money was paid to the wife? How much was spent on the deceased's food? How much was spent on the food for the rest of the family? Who paid how much for the children's shoes, etc?

(b)   The customary modern practice is to deduct a percentage from the net income figure to represent what the deceased would have spent exclusively on himself. Conventional percentages are adopted. Where the family unit was husband and wife, the usual figure is one-third. Where the family unit was husband, wife and children the usual figure is one-quarter. However, it is important to note that each case must be judged on its own facts. The court is willing to depart from the conventional figures where there is evidence that they are inappropriate (*Owen v Martin* [1992] PIQR Q151), for example, where the deceased was particularly frugal or a spendthrift. In such circumstances, less or more than the conventional figure should be deducted (see also *Coward v Comex Houlder Diving Ltd*, 18 July 1988 and *Dhaliwal v Personal Representatives of Hunt (Deceased)* [1995] PIQR Q56, CA).

Furthermore, it is quite possible that different multiplicands may have to be selected according to different times in the period of dependency. Had he lived, the deceased's financial affairs would not have remained constant throughout his life. Similarly, therefore, the multiplicand will not remain constant either. For example, in the case of a husband with wife and children, 75% of the husband's earnings may be the appropriate initial multiplicand while his children are likely to be dependent. However, from the point where the children can be expected to become independent the multiplicand may be merely two-thirds of the husband's earnings (see also *Coward v Comex Houlder Diving Ltd*).

Frequently, both husband and wife would have been earning at the time of death, and in such circumstances the approach adopted is to calculate the dependency as two-thirds or 75% (as the case may be) of the total joint net income less the continuing earnings (see also *Coward v Comex Houlder Diving Ltd*).

Other relevant factors

(a)   *Change in earning capacity.* No allowance is made for inflation (*Auty v National Coal Board* [1985] 1 All ER 930), but allowance is made for a likely increase in the deceased's earning capacity (eg, as result of promotion). Evidence will be needed in support of this, and the best evidence may be from a comparative employee or employees who have gone, or who are going through, the same career structure as the deceased would have done. This evidence could be obtained, for example, from the deceased's trade union or employer.

Conversely, there may be evidence of likely loss of earning capacity, for example because of redundancy.

(b)   *Services rendered by the deceased.* The deceased may have been contributing to the support of the family not only in terms of a percentage of his earnings but also by rendering services to the family free of charge. Examples of such services include:

(i)   do-it-yourself jobs (eg, painting the house annually);

(ii)   vegetable gardening (therefore saving on grocery bills);

(iii)   nursing services to a sick member of the family;

(iv) 'perks' of employment (eg, the deceased was provided with a company car which was also used by the family, saving the family the capital cost of the car and the expense of maintenance and insurance

On the deceased's death, such free services will be lost. The family will have to pay for the services (eg, by employing a decorator) and thus incur a loss. The value of these services can add considerably to the multiplicand. Evidence must be obtained, for example, by quotations from the appropriate source.

15.6.2.2 The multiplier – the period of loss

Having calculated the multiplicand, the other side of the equation is to calculate the number of years' loss of dependency.

Commencement of period of loss

The starting point for the number of years' loss is the date of death (not the date of trial: *Graham v Dodds* [1983] 2 All ER 953; *White v ESAB Group (UK) Ltd* [2002] All ER (D) 02 (Jan) and *ATM v MS* (2002) *The Times*, 3 July. However, see the fifth edition of the Ogden Tables (**Appendix 5**) for further commentary on this point.

End of the period of loss

In the case of a deceased wage earner, prima facie the number of years' loss will extend to the end of the deceased's working life (ie, usually up to what would have been the deceased's retiring age). Direct evidence should be called on this point. (It must be remembered that certain items of loss such as the claim for the cost of DIY may extend beyond retirement age as the deceased would not necessarily have stopped doing DIY when he retired from work.)

However, each case will turn upon its own facts and the period of dependency may end before or after what would have been the normal date of the deceased's retirement. For example, where the deceased was a professional person, he may have been expected to work and support his dependants beyond normal retirement age. Equally, if the deceased would have enjoyed a pension, it may be argued that he would have continued to provide for his dependants beyond normal retirement age (although evidence would be needed to substantiate this: *Auty v National Coal Board* [1985] 1 All ER 930; see **Chapter 13**).

Conversely, the period of dependency may stop before what would have been the normally expected retirement age of the deceased. For example, if the deceased was already in a poor state of health, he may not have been expected to work until normal retirement age, and the financial support for the dependants would therefore have ended earlier. Similarly, if the dependant himself is in a poor state of health and has a short life-expectancy, the period of dependency will be shorter.

Where there is a claim by a widow as dependant, the likelihood that the marriage would have ended in divorce may be taken into account in assessing the period of dependency. In *Owen v Martin* [1992] PIQR Q151, the judge adopted a multiplier of 15, but the Court of Appeal reduced this to 11 on the basis that the widow's attitude towards her marriage vows as shown by her personal history led the court to believe that the marriage may not have lasted the whole of the natural life of the deceased. The court should take this approach only provided there is some evidence of likelihood of divorce (*Wheatley v Cunningham* [1992] PIQR Q100). See also *D and D v Donald* [2001] PIQR Q44, concerning an extra-marital affair. In *O'Loughlin v Cape Distribution Ltd* [2001] EWCA Civ 178, (2001) JPIL, Issue 2/01,

191, the court confirmed that there is no prescribed method by which damages for loss of dependency had to be identified. The key factor was showing economic loss. However, the widow's prospects of remarriage or actual remarriage is to be ignored (FAA 1976, s 3(3)). Therefore, the period of the widow's dependency on her deceased husband is calculated without regard to the fact that she is or may be financially supported by a new husband.

15.6.2.3   Conversion of the period of loss to a multiplier

Once the number of years' loss of dependency has been ascertained, this is then converted to a multiplier.

15.6.2.4   The deceased non-wage earner

Where the deceased was a wage earner, the valuation of the multiplicand in the dependency claim is predominantly based on a proportion of the deceased's earnings (see above). This is so whether the deceased was male or female (eg, whether husband, father, wife or mother). It is not uncommon, however, that the deceased was not in paid employment. In this case, the value of the services rendered to the family becomes the vital issue. For example, if the deceased was the wife and mother of the family and was not a wage earner at the date of her death, the services rendered by her to the family might be quantified in the terms of employing a housekeeper to provide the same services. In *Regan v Williamson* [1976] 1 WLR 305, Watkins J said that in this context 'the word "services" [has] been too narrowly construed. It should at least include an acknowledgement that a wife and mother does not work to set hours, and, still less, to rule'. Accordingly, a value in excess of a housekeeper was awarded in that case. In *Mehmet v Perry* [1977] 2 All ER 529, the claimant widower, on the death of his wife, reasonably gave up his job in order to look after his young children. The starting point for the value of the services of the deceased wife was taken as the husband's loss of earnings.

15.6.2.5   Claims by parents, if children unmarried

A claim can be made by a parent (who is often unemployed or ill) who was dependent on the support from his unmarried child. When the court considers this type of case, it will have regard to the fact that the child may have married and the financial assistance provided by the child may have ceased.

15.6.2.6   Claims by child dependants

Where a claim is made by a surviving spouse and child, the court's approach is often to assess the claim for dependency of the widow alone, and then to apportion a small amount ('pocket money') to the child. This approach may be justified on the basis that:

(a)   the surviving spouse will be expected to provide for the child out of her damages;

(b)   compared to the surviving spouse, the period of dependency of the child will often be short (ending probably between the ages of 16 to 21 depending on whether the child is expected to go on to higher education); and

(c)   it avoids repeated applications to the court for the release of invested funds for the benefit of the child.

However, the court is keen to protect the child's interest, and this approach may not be followed in every case. For example, if the surviving spouse is a known spendthrift and cannot be trusted to provide for the child, the court may assess the claims of the surviving spouse and child separately (see *H and Another v S*

[2002] EWCA Civ 792, [2003] QB 965 concerning the protection of any damages for child dependants).

If the claim is brought by a child alone (eg, if the death of a parent has left a child orphaned), the court may assess the child's dependency by the use of the 'nanny formula', that is to quantify the loss in the terms of employing a professional (a nanny) to care for the child or to have regard to the cost of employing a housekeeper. (See also *R v Criminal Injuries Compensation Board, ex p K* [1998] 2 FLR 1071, which held that while the child had the benefit of new parental sources after the death of the mother, for example, by an aunt or uncle, it was not the case that the child had suffered 'no loss' for the purposes of the FAA 1976; see also *Stanley v Saddique* [1992] 1 QB 1 and *Laniyan v Barry May Haulage* (2001) LTL, 2 August.)

Where the claim involves a minor dependant, the court's approval of any settlement should be sought as it will be necessary to satisfy the court that the child's interests are protected (see *M v S* (2001) CLI, May, concerning the payment of the award of damages to the dependants and not to their carer).

15.6.2.7   The multiplication

Having established the appropriate multiplicand and the overall multiplier, one method of calculating the award for loss of dependency is as follows:

(a)   special damages: calculate the actual number of years' loss from the date of death until the trial;

(b)   deduct the number of pre-trial years from the overall multiplier;

(c)   apply the balance of the multiplier to the multiplicand (or multiplicands).

Example

Tom is killed in a road traffic accident. At the time of his death, Tom was 30 years' old. Tom has left a widow, Lucy, aged 29, and twin boys, Mark and James, both aged 9. Tom was a do-it-yourself enthusiast and performed many decorating and maintenance tasks in the family home. The value of the services to the family was £750 per year. Prior to the accident, Tom was in good health and was expected to work until he was 65. His net annual earnings at trial have been calculated as £10,000. At the age of 40, Tom would have been promoted and would have been earning £15,000 net per year. At the age of 50, Tom would have been further promoted and would have been earning £20,000 net per year until his retirement. Mark and James will become independent at the age of 18. The case comes to trial three years after the accident.

The significant factors in the calculation are as follows:

(a)   The length of dependency is likely to be based on Tom's age of 30 and his retirement age of 65, that is a period of 35 years. This is likely to produce an overall multiplier of, say, 21.

(b)   There will be three years' special damages (pre-trial). This will leave 18 as the balance of the overall multiplier for post-trial losses.

(c)   The multiplicand is likely to be based not only on the net annual earnings but also on the value of the services.

(d)   The calculation may be split into various sub-calculations to reflect, for example, that for the first nine years after the accident (but for his death) Tom would have been supporting a wife and children (therefore he might have been expected to spend one-quarter of his net earnings on his own maintenance), but for the remaining 26 years of his working life (after the children became independent) he would have been supporting only a wife (and therefore he might be expected to spend one-third of his net earnings on his own maintenance). Another reason for splitting the calculation may be to reflect his increased earnings because of promotion 10 years and 20 years after the accident.

The above example is given merely to illustrate the general principles of quantifying a claim. It will be appreciated that, in practice, it will be rare that a person's working and family life can be predicted with such certainty and other methods of calculating the loss of dependency (eg, nil discount tables issued by the Government's Actuary's Department) have been advocated.

It should also be remembered that different multipliers must be applied to items that would not have ceased at the age of 65. Detailed instructions need to be obtained from the client on this point. In practice, therefore, the facts of a particular case are usually such as to defy precise mathematical calculation. The assessment of dependency damages is a difficult matter and the court has to anticipate what would have occurred in the future. To assist the court, as much evidence as possible should be obtained.

Are bereavement damages awarded to the parents of unmarried children over 18? Normally not, however in an article in *The Lawyer*, 7 March 2005, there is a report of an out of court settlement by a NHS trust for a payment of £10,000 (an amount equivalent to bereavement damages) to a mother for the death of an unmarried child over 18, by using arguments under the Human Rights Act.

15.6.3 Assessing loss of dependency – the Ogden Tables

The above paragraphs set out the 'traditional method' of calculating the dependency figure in a FAA 1976 case. However, in the fifth edition of the Ogden Tables (see **Appendix 5**), an alternative method is adopted and recommended for the calculation of the dependency claim. The introduction to the Ogden Tables states that the cases prior to *Page v Sheerness Steel Co Ltd; Wells v Wells; Thomas v Brighton Health Authority* [1998] 3 WLR 329 (see **Chapter 13**) do not preclude the use of the new method suggested in the Ogden Tables.

It would appear that the above approach is, however, contrary to *Cookson v Knowles* [1979] AC 556, see also *White v ESAB Group* [2002] All ER (D) 02 (Jan) and *A and Others v MS* [2003] PIQR Q1 (see **15.6.2.1**). It would appear that, unless the matter is reconsidered by the House of Lords or Parliament, courts will continue to adopt the traditional method.

15.6.4 Bereavement

15.6.4.1 The claimants

The claim for bereavement is open only to a limited class (not just 'dependants' generally: see **15.6.1**). The possible claimants are:

(a)   the spouse of the deceased; or

(b)   the parents of a legitimate unmarried deceased minor;

(c)   the mother of an illegitimate unmarried deceased minor.

It should be noted therefore that, for example, a child is not entitled to the award of bereavement on the death of his parent, and in a case where both parents can claim, the damages are divided equally between them (FAA 1976, s 1A(4)). However, in *Navaei v Navaei* (1995) *Halsbury's Laws* June 1995/1784, the mother was negligent and this resulted in the death of her daughter. The father claimed all of the bereavement damages and stated that they should not be shared with the mother. He argued that if he were to be paid only half of the damages, the mother/tortfeasor would be benefiting contrary to public policy. The court held that in bringing a claim under the FAA 1976, a claimant is under a duty to act on behalf of all dependants and the father was allowed only half the damages.

In the case of *Griffiths and Others v British Coal Corporation* (QBD, 23 February 1998), it was held that the FAA 1976 did not require an apportionment of damages for bereavement where there were two causes of death (in this case, smoking and exposure to mine dust), and therefore the claimant recovered the full statutory sum.

The claim for the bereavement award by parents depends on the deceased being a minor at the date of death, not at the date of the accident (*Doleman v Deakin* (1990) *The Times,* 30 January).

15.6.4.2   The amount of the bereavement award

The award is a fixed amount of £10,000 in respect of causes of action arising on or after 1 April 2002. Many people have criticised the level of award. It should be noted that a cohabitee is excluded from the definition, despite the fact that a cohabitee can pursue a dependency claim as noted above. In certain cases, especially those with a media interest, defendants have offered a higher figure than the statutory minimum, so as to avoid allegations by the press that they have undervalued a life.

15.6.5   Funeral expenses (FAA 1976, s 3(5))

Funeral expenses can be claimed if reasonable and paid by a dependant. The question of reasonableness will be a decision on the facts of each case. Reference should be made to previous case law in circumstances where the client puts forward an unusual claim so as to determine whether the court will regard the claim as reasonable or otherwise.

If the funeral expenses are paid by the estate then they are claimed as part of a LR(MP)A 1934 claim (see **15.5.3**). Clearly, funeral expenses cannot be claimed under both the LR(MP)A 1934 and the FAA 1976.

15.6.6   Disregarding benefits

Section 4 of the FAA 1976 provides:

> In assessing damages in respect of a person's death in an action under this Act, benefits which have accrued or will or may accrue to any person from his estate or otherwise as a result of his death shall be disregarded.

For example, if a dependant receives insurance money as a result of the deceased's death, the dependant does not have to give credit for that money against the FAA 1976 damages. Similarly, if damages awarded to the estate under a LR(MP)A 1934 claim end up in the hands of a dependant by reason of the deceased's will or rules of intestacy, those damages do not necessarily reduce any FAA 1976 damages which may be awarded to that dependant.

See also *H and Another v S* [2002] EWCA Civ 792, [2003] QB 965 concerning support now being given by a surviving parent which was unlikely to have supported the children if the death had not occurred.

15.6.7   Recoupment and offsetting of benefits

Any payment made in consequence of a claim under the FAA 1976 is not subject to recoupment under the Social Security (Recovery of Benefits) Act 1997 (see **Chapter 12**).

15.7   Interest

Interest on the bereavement damages may be awarded at the full short-term investment rate (*Sharman v Sheppard* [1989] CLY 1190) from the date of death.

The pecuniary losses to the date of the trial are treated as special damages in a fatal injury claim and therefore are often awarded interest at half the short-term investment rate, although it is arguable that interest can be awarded at the full rate in certain circumstances. Future pecuniary loss attracts no interest.

15.8   Pension loss

Investigations should be made as to whether there will be a reduced pension fund available to the deceased's dependants due to the early death, and this should be included within the claim if appropriate (see also **13.3.6**).

15.9   Establishing the case

A fatal accident case will be dealt with in essentially the same way as any other personal injury or clinical negligence claim. Evidence is needed to establish liability and the highest level of damages. The claimant's solicitor must remember to obtain a signed proof of evidence or statement from a client as soon as possible in every case, as this will be of considerable assistance if the client dies either due to the injuries sustained in the accident or otherwise. If the solicitor has failed to take this precaution he will make proving the case more difficult. Under the Civil Evidence Act 1995, the client's statement or proof can now be put before the court and it should be regarded by the court as important evidence.

It should also be remembered that the inquest will be an important source of information (see **Chapter 14**), and as much information as possible should be obtained.

15.10   Conduct

To avoid conflicts of interest arising, it is good practice to ensure that none of the dependants who could be to blame in whole or part for the accident that resulted in the death are appointed as personal representatives.

The conduct of a fatal accident claim clearly requires sympathy and diplomacy on the part of the solicitor. There are frequently conflicts of personality between the dependants and personal representatives and this is compounded by the fact that only one claim can be brought in respect of the claim. If, after the fatal accident, it comes to light that the deceased had more than one dependent family, it can be anticipated that any interviews with the deceased's wife may be difficult!

15.11 Simplified example of a schedule of loss in a fatal accident case – traditional method (see 15.6.2)

COLLAWS SOLICITORS

SCHEDULE OF LOSS AS AT TRIAL IN THE CASE OF LUCY BROWN

Date of birth	1 January 1957
Date of accident/death	1 January 2004
Net pre-accident wage	£133.33 per week
Date of schedule/trial	1 January 2006

Reduction for deceased own needs: 25% so initial multiplicand = £100

Loss of earnings to date of schedule:

1 January 2004 to 4 April 2004	14 weeks × £100	£1,400.00
Thereafter annual payrise having the effect of a		
5% rise on net pay effective from 5 April each year		
5 April 2004 to 4 April 2005	52 weeks at £105	£5,460.00
5 April 2005 to 1 January 2006	38 weeks at £110.25	£4,189.50
TOTAL		£11,049.50
Other services to family per annum	2 × £800	£1,600.00
(eg, gardening, housework, DIY)		
TOTAL		£12,649.50
Bereavement	£10,000	
Funeral expenses	£1,390.50	

Loss of dependency

Earnings		
At a weekly rate of	£110.25	
Annual rate of		£5,733.00
Other services to the family		
Annual rate of		£800.00
TOTAL		£6,533.00

A multiplier of, say, 12 (in this simplistic example the multiplier of 12 is a hypothetical figure) from the date of death is used on the basis that the deceased would have worked until the age of 65. The multiplier from the date of trial two years post-accident is 10 (the original multiplier of 12 less the 2 years between the death and the trial).

Total future loss of dependency:	10 × £6,533 = £65,330

SUMMARY

Pre-trial loss	£12,649.50
Future loss	£65,330.00
Bereavement damages	£10,000.00
Funeral expenses	£1,390.50
TOTAL	£89,370.00

In addition, interest is claimed on the items of loss to the date of trial at half the short-term rate and on bereavement damages at the full short-term investment account rate.

15.12 Conclusion

It should be noted that the Law Commission has published proposals to extend the definition of 'dependants' and to increase the level of bereavement damages, but the proposals have not been taken further at this point.

Finally, acting on behalf of the relatives in a fatal accident claim requires the personal injury/clinical negligence solicitor to have tact, sympathy and a detailed understanding of the law involved. It should be appreciated that each case will be dealt with on its own facts, and only broad principles have been established by the case law in this area. In fatal accident cases the court is required to anticipate what would have occurred in the future, which will be different in every case.

15.13 Further reading

Kemp and Kemp, *The Quantum of Damages* (Sweet & Maxwell).

Chapter 16
Other Matters Relating to Personal Injury and Clinical Negligence Matters

16.1 Criminal Injuries Compensation Authority

Victims of crimes of violence who have suffered injuries can apply for compensation from the Criminal Injuries Compensation Authority (CICA). The Criminal Injuries Compensation Scheme (2001) (the scheme) was made pursuant to ss 1–6 and s 12 of the Criminal Injuries Compensation Act 1995 and deals with all claims received on or after 1 April 2001.

To be eligible to make an application under the scheme, an applicant must have sustained a criminal injury on or after 1 August 1964 (in the case of a victim and assailant living in the same household, the injury must have been sustained on or after 1 October 1979). The personal injury must be directly attributable to a crime of violence that occurred in Great Britain. The applicant must have an injury serious enough to qualify for at least the minimum award (see below) available under the scheme for the application to be considered.

The CICA also requires that, unless good reasons can be shown, the incident should have been reported to the police as soon as possible after it occurred and any application should be received within two years from the date of the incident. (The CICA has a discretion to waive this time limit, if appropriate.)

If an application is to be made, the appropriate form should be obtained from the CICA. The correct form must be used as different application forms are required for personal injury and fatal accident claims.

The procedure adopted by the CICA is that once the application has been received at its offices, it will acknowledge receipt of the application and send out routine enquiry forms to the police and medical authorities. The CICA retains the right to withhold or reduce an award if the applicant persistently fails to assist the CICA in its requests for information, fails to attend medical examinations or otherwise fails to give reasonable assistance. The CICA also has the power to withhold or reduce an award if the applicant has failed to take all reasonable steps to inform or co-operate with the police or, more significantly, if the conduct of the applicant makes it inappropriate for a full award to be made.

The CICA will have regard not only to the applicant's behaviour connected with the incident, but also the applicant's character as shown by his criminal convictions even if they are unrelated to the incident. In assessing an applicant's character, the CICA adopts a scheme of awarding 'penalty points' for any convictions of the applicant. Full details of the Criminal Injuries Compensation Scheme are set out in **Appendix 6**. However, it should be noted that there are new provisions in the Domestic Violence, Crime and Victims Act 2004 requiring offenders to repay CICA payments, and in the Law Society Gazette, 6 January 2005 it has been reported that, for the first time, the CICA has agreed to pay for a trust fund for a victim. Full details are beyond the scope of this text.

16.2 Claims on behalf of child claimants

16.2.1 Bringing the proceedings

In civil law, a child is a person who is not yet 18 years old. Under that age, a child is termed 'a person under a disability' (although this term is not used in the CPR 1998). While under a disability the limitation period does not run against the child (see **Chapter 6**), but during that time the child cannot normally bring proceedings in his own name. The solutions therefore are either:

(a)   to wait until the child reaches the age of 18; or

(b)   during his minority to bring proceedings through a 'litigation friend' (usually a parent).

It is important to ensure that there is no conflict of interest between the child and the person who is bringing the claim on the child's behalf. For example, if a child is injured in a road traffic accident while a passenger in a car being driven by his father, it would be sensible to appoint the child's mother as litigation friend (rather than the father) as the father may eventually be a defendant in the proceedings.

16.2.2 Court's approval of settlements

In all settlements involving a child (including the acceptance of money paid into court and a claim in a fatal accident case where there is a child dependant), the court's approval of the proposed settlement should be sought in order to validate the settlement, bind the claimant and give a discharge to the defendant.

16.2.3 Procedure for court settlement

If an agreement is made between the parties prior to proceedings being issued and the sole purpose of issuing proceedings is to obtain the court's approval, then the solicitor must follow the procedure set out in Part 8 of the CPR and a specific request must be included with the claim form for approval of the settlement. In addition, a draft consent order must be provided to the court using practice form N292. If the child reaches a settlement during the course of a claim, or the defendant makes a Part 36 payment which is accepted, then the claimant will require an order from the court seeking:

(a)   the court's approval of the settlement; and

(b)   directions for investment of the damages.

16.2.4 The approval hearing

The aim of the hearing is to ensure that the settlement agreed is a reasonable one, and is in the child's best interests. At the hearing, the court will wish to have made available a number of documents including the following:

(a)   the child's birth certificate (certainly details of the child's age);

(b)   the statements of case and other documents already on the court file;

(c)   evidence on liability (information as to whether liability is in dispute or the extent to which the defendant admits liability) and documents such as the police accident report, inquest report and details of any prosecutions brought;

(d)   up-to-date calculation of past and future losses (with supporting documentation);

(e)   up-to-date medical report or reports;

(f)   litigation friend's approval of the settlement;

(g)   interest calculation to date; and

(h)   a copy of an opinion on the merits of the agreed settlement given to counsel or a solicitor (while the case is a simple one).

Full details of the court's requirements are set out in Part 21 of the CPR and the accompanying Practice Direction.

16.2.5   Further requirements at the hearing

The litigation friend should also provide a Court Funds Office, CFO form 320 (request for investment) which the district judge will complete.

16.2.6   The order

If the proposed settlement is approved, the court will give directions as to the investment of the damages. In the case of *Beatham v Carlisle Hospitals NHS Trust* (1999) *The Times*, 20 May, it was held that the court's approval of a settlement on behalf of a child or indeed a patient should normally be given in public.

It should be noted that the court has an obligation to consider using a periodic payments order in certain circumstances (see **16.4**).

16.2.7   Investment of the damages

Money recovered on behalf of a child must be dealt with in accordance with directions of the court, which will be concerned that the damages are invested wisely for the child's benefit.

The court and the claimant's solicitor may need to know such things as whether:

(a)   regular income is required;

(b)   capital growth is required;

(c)   the child has other income;

(d)   the child is liable for tax;

(e)   there are any specific liabilities;

(f)   an address to which all future income is to be sent.

16.2.8   Possible orders with regard to investment

It is likely that the court will consider the following options when making an order for investment.

16.2.8.1   Payment out of part of or the whole sum immediately

In the case of small sums the court may consider that proper investment can be achieved by placing the sums in the hands of the litigation friend, for example, to invest in a National Savings Bank investment account or building society account. In the case of a larger sum of damages, the court may authorise the immediate payment out of part of those damages to meet expenses already incurred on behalf of the child (eg, the accrued cost of care) or expenses to be incurred in the immediate future.

16.2.8.2   Investment of the sum in court

The precise nature of the investment (eg, government or local government stock, unit trusts, special account) is likely to be decided by the investment managers of the Public Trust Office according to the policy of investment laid down by the court at the hearing, bearing in mind the requirements of the child (eg, a requirement as to capital growth rather than income).

16.2.9   Refusal of approval by the court

If there is no dispute on liability, the court's refusal to approve the settlement will normally lead to renegotiation of the settlement figure. If the court continues not to approve the settlement, the claimant must bring proceedings in the normal manner. If liability is in dispute, the defendant may wish to continue to defend the case.

16.3   Provisional damages

16.3.1   The problem which provisional damages are intended to solve

When the court makes a lump sum award of damages, it will be designed to cover both past and future pain and suffering (and other losses).

The problem lies in cases where the deterioration, although possible, is less than probable.

Example

Fred is injured. At the time of the trial he has no loss of sight, but there is a 10% possibility that in the future he will lose the sight in one eye. Bearing in mind that quantum for pain and suffering and loss of amenity for the loss of sight in one eye is, say, £20,000, how does the judge award damages to Fred?

If the judge awards £2,000 (10% of £20,000) and Fred does lose the sight in his eye in the future, Fred will be under-compensated by £18,000, but cannot return to court for more damages. If Fred does not lose the sight in his eye in the future, Fred is unjustly enriched by £2,000 and the defendant cannot recover the excess damages.

Provisional damages are aimed at solving the above problem by providing an exception to the basic rule (see also periodic payments at **16.4**) that, once a compensation payment has been made, it is in full and final settlement and further compensation cannot be claimed if the client's condition deteriorates unexpectedly. Therefore, in certain limited circumstances the claimant can be compensated for his injuries with the proviso that if a specific condition occurs in the future, he will be allowed to return to court so that further damages can be awarded.

16.3.2   The statutory provision

Section 32A of the Supreme Court Act 1981 provides:

> This section applies to an action for damages for personal injuries in which there is proved or admitted to be a chance that at some definite or indefinite time in the future the injured person will, as a result of the act or omission which gave rise to the cause of action, develop some serious disease or suffer some serious deterioration in his physical or mental condition.

A similar provision applies in the county court (County Courts Act 1984, s 51).

The CPR state that the court may make an order for provisional damages providing the claimant comes within the definitions set out in s 32A of the Supreme Court Act 1981 or s 51 of the County Courts Act 1984.

16.3.2.1 'Chance'

The expression 'chance' is not defined in the Supreme Court Act 1981. It clearly indicates something less than a probability. However, it must be measurable rather than merely fanciful (*Willson v Ministry of Defence* [1991] 1 All ER 638, in which it was held that the possibility that the claimant would incur further injury from a fall as a result of an ankle injury was held not to be within s 32A of the Supreme Court Act 1981. See also *Curi v Colina* [1998] EWCA Civ 1326).

While it is difficult to say with great certainty, where the likelihood can be expressed in the terms of single figure percentages, this is likely to be sufficient 'chance'. If there is doubt as to whether the case is appropriate for a provisional damages claim, then advice from an experienced solicitor or barrister should be sought.

16.3.2.2 'Serious deterioration'

'Serious deterioration' is not defined in the Supreme Court Act 1981. In *Willson* (above) it was held that 'serious deterioration' meant:

(a)   a clear and severable risk of deterioration (not merely the natural progression of the injury); and

(b)   something beyond ordinary deterioration.

(On the facts of *Willson,* the court held that the chance of arthritis was merely a natural progression of the injury and was not a suitable case for provisional damages.)

Clearly, the claimant will base his claim for provisional damages on medical evidence indicating that there is a 'chance' of a 'serious disease or deterioration' developing.

The most common examples of conditions in which provisional damages have been awarded in practice are where there is the chance of the claimant suffering from epilepsy or from a disease such as cancer or asbestosis as a result of exposure to a dangerous substance.

The mere fact that the claimant's medical prognosis will not be certain for a considerable time (eg, two or three years) does not justify a claim for provisional damages. In such circumstances, consideration should be given to an application for an interim payment (see *Adefunke Fashade v North Middlesex Hospital* (2001) PMILL, January as an example of a recent case where provisional damages had been refused). See also *Adan v Securicor Custodial Services* [2004] EWHC 394 (QB).

For a provisional damages award to be made, there must be sufficient certainty as to which circumstances must arise before the claimant is allowed to return to court. The court will wish to avoid a situation where there would be a dispute as to whether the proper circumstances had arisen.

16.3.3 The court's approach to provisional damages

If the court considers that there is a suitable case for provisional damages (see Part 41 and PD 41 to the CPR), it will:

(a)   assess damages on the assumption that the injured person will not develop the disease or suffer the deterioration in his condition;

(b)   identify the disease or deterioration that has been disregarded;

(c)   stipulate a period (which may be indefinite) during which the claimant may return to court for further damages if he develops the disease or suffers the deterioration;

(d)   make an order that relevant documents are to be kept by the court.

Even where the claimant's claim falls within the realm of provisional damages, the claimant may not want to pursue an open-ended claim, preferring, instead, that the claim is satisfied once and for all by the award of a lump sum. The claimant's solicitor must take careful instructions on this aspect. It must be explained to the client that he will be able to return to court only if the deterioration is the 'specified disease or deterioration', and not for any other reason.

16.3.4   The claim for provisional damages must be included within the court documents

The claim for provisional damages must be included in the particulars of claim, and, if the possibility of provisional damages emerges after these documents have been served, the documents must be amended. Part 16 of the CPR and the accompanying Practice Direction set out the necessary information which must be included.

16.3.5   Consequences of a provisional damages claim

If the claimant claims provisional damages, the client must be informed of the consequences of the court's order and any time limit imposed. Solicitors must also ensure that they preserve their own files for the appropriate length of time.

16.3.6   The court order

The only basis for an award of provisional damages is a court order. Any application by consent for an award of provisional damages should follow the procedure set out in Part 23 of the CPR.

16.3.7   Further award

If the specified disease or deterioration occurs within the specified period, the claimant must give at least 28 days' written notice to the defendant of his intention to apply for further damages.

It is possible to apply to extend the period of time for claiming further damages, and a medical report should be filed in support of such an application. Such an application must be made within the original time limit.

16.3.8   Provisional damages and the Fatal Accidents Act 1976

Section 3 of the Damages Act 1996 now allows an application to the court under the FAA 1976 where a person is awarded provisional damages and subsequently dies.

16.3.9   Provisional damages and Part 36 of the CPR

The Part 36 payment notice must specify whether or not the defendant is offering to agree to the making of a provisional damages award (see r 36.7).

16.4   Periodic payments

With effect from 1 April 2005 the court now has the power to award periodic payments under the Damages Act 1996. Full reference should be made to the statutory provisions, Part 41 of the CPR and the accompanying Practice Direction.

In essence, the court must consider, in every case involving a future pecuniary loss, whether periodical payments are appropriate and, if appropriate, make such an order.

The parties may identify to the court that they believe the matter is suitable for a periodic payments order by making a claim within their statement of case, or the court may indicate to the parties that it considers of its own motion that periodical payments or a lump sum are the more appropriate form of damages. With the parties' consent, the court can make a periodical payment order for pain and suffering and special damages.

The factors that the court will have to take into account in deciding whether to make a periodic payment order are contained within the Practice Direction that accompanies Part 41. The relevant factors include:

(a)   the scale of the annual payments, taking into account any deduction for contributory negligence;

(b)   the form of award preferred by the claimant including:

    (i)   the reasons for the claimant's preference; and

    (ii)   the nature of any financial advice received by the claimant; and

(c)   the form of award preferred by the defendant.

So as to ensure that the claimant continues to receive the payments (ie, that they are secure), the court must have specific regard to this point prior to making the order (see s 2(3) of the Damages Act 1996).

As a consequence of these new provisions an amendment has been made to Part 36 of the CPR: a new r 36.2A has been added, relating to all future pecuniary loss. Full reference must be made to Part 36, in particular r 36.2A(4) and r 36.2A(5). An amendment to the Practice Direction confirms that Part 36 offers must comply with the specific requirements.

These changes have been introduced only a short time prior to the writing of this text. It is therefore not possible to take a view on whether the new provisions will become popular with the court or practitioners. However, in an article in the Law Society Gazette of 12 May 2005, it is reported that the new regime has been used for a brain damaged woman who suffered from cerebral palsy. The periodic payments are reported to be worth £4.5 million. (See also *Walton v Calderdale Healthcare NHS Trust* [2005] EWHC 1053.)

16.5   Choice of jurisdiction

A personal injury solicitor may have a client who has been injured abroad or who wishes to bring a claim in a different jurisdiction, normally on the basis that a higher level of damages may be awarded. (For example, clients may have heard of the case against McDonalds where the claimant was awarded $2.9 million (this amount was reduced on appeal) following hot coffee being spilt.) In such circumstances, the solicitor can refer the client to a specialist or seek the assistance of a barrister who is experienced in the area. However, the solicitor should be familiar with a basic outline of the law and procedure, and further details are supplied in the Legal Practice Guide, *Civil Litigation*. It is important that the personal injury solicitor considers which is the most appropriate 'forum' for the litigation (see *Harding v Wealands* [2004] EWHC 1957 (QB) in relation to determining the appopriate law to decide the claimant's damages where an accident occurred outside the jurisdiction).

16.5.1 Claims within the European Union

If a claim is brought within another EU country then it must be remembered that there are many differences between the various legal systems of the Member States. For example, many European countries' judicial authorities have a far more inquisitorial role, with 'statutory settlement procedures' and obligations on the parties to participate in the judicial investigation if they wish to pursue a civil claim. The economics of pursuing the case also have to be considered. It also needs to be explained to the client that, in certain countries, costs are not recoverable from the defendant in addition to damages.

It must also be remembered that limitation periods differ between EU Member States, ranging from 1 to 30 years.

Consideration should be given as to which jurisdiction will give rise to the most satisfactory outcome for the client (often the highest level of damages is a significant factor). In *Edmunds v Simmonds* [2001] 1 WLR 1003, it was held that, despite the accident occurring in Spain, where both parties were English and the major heads of damages arose wholly in England, it was possible under s 12(1)(b) of the Private International Law (Miscellaneous Provisions) Act 1995, for English law to be the applicable law (see also *Hulse and Others v Chambers* [2002] 1 WLR 2386 relating to the quantification of damages being a matter of procedure and being governed by English law; *Henderson v Jaouen and Another* [2002] EWCA Civ 75, [2002] 2 All ER 705 and *Harding v Wealands* [2004] EWCA Civ 1735).

16.5.2 Claims outside the EU

The main non-European country where a personal injury solicitor may consider bringing proceedings is the USA. It is very likely that a US court will award a higher level of damages for a personal injury case than an English court, and this is the potential attraction of a US claim. As a consequence, any defendant is likely to object to the proceedings being taken in the USA and will seek to rely on the doctrine of *forum non conveniens* to show that an alternative forum is available and that private and public interests favour the case being dealt with outside the USA.

16.5.3 Package holidays

If an accident occurs while a client is on holiday, then consideration must be given to whether the holiday falls within any specific provisions, such as the Package Travel, Package Holidays and Package Tours Regulations 1992 (SI 1992/3288).

16.6 Conclusion

Some of the areas dealt with in this chapter arise infrequently in day-to-day practice, and reference must always be made to the appropriate Rules of Court and more specialist practitioner works. The aim of this chapter is simply to serve as an introduction to these topics and reference should be made to other sources.

16.7 Further reading

Kemp and Kemp, *The Quantum of Damages* (Sweet & Maxwell).

Powers and Harris, *Medical Negligence* (Butterworths).

16.8 Key points

Criminal Injuries Compensation Authority	(a) Matter should normally be reported to the police (b) Two-year time limit (c) CICA has power to withhold or revise an award in certain circumstances (d) Scheme does not provide compensation for lost earnings in first 28 weeks

Claims on behalf of children	(a) Need to appoint a 'litigation friend' (b) Court should approve settlement (c) See Part 21 and Part 8 of the CPR

Provisional damages	Damages assessed on the basis that a particular disease or deterioration will not occur but, if it does, the claimant can return to court for damages (within a specified period). See Part 23 of the CPR

Appendices

Appendix 1
The Law Society Conditional Fee Agreement

Conditional Fee Agreement

For use in personal injury and clinical negligence cases only.

This agreement is a binding legal contract between you and your solicitor/s. Before you sign, please read everything carefully. This agreement must be read in conjunction with the Law Society document 'What you need to know about a CFA'.

Agreement date [...]

I/We, the solicitor/s [..]

You, the client [...]

What is covered by this agreement

- Your claim against [....................................] for damages for personal injury suffered on [..........................]. *(if either the name of the opponent or the date of the incident are unclear then set out here in as much detail as possible to give sufficient information for the client and solicitor to understand the basis of the claim being pursued)*
- Any appeal by your opponent.
- Any appeal you make against an interim order.
- Any proceedings you take to enforce a judgment, order or agreement.
- Negotiations about and/or a court assessment of the costs of this claim.

What is not covered by this agreement

- Any counterclaim against you.
- Any appeal you make against the final judgment order.

Paying us

If you win your claim, you pay our basic charges, our disbursements and a success fee. You are entitled to seek recovery from your opponent of part or all of our basic charges, our disbursements, a success fee and insurance premium as set out in the document 'What you need to know about a CFA.'

It may be that your opponent makes a Part 36 offer or payment which you reject on our advice, and your claim for damages goes ahead to trial where you recover damages that are less than that offer or payment. If this happens, we will *[not add our success fee to the basic charges] [not claim any costs]* for the work done after we received notice of the offer or payment.

If you receive interim damages, we may require you to pay our disbursements at that point and a reasonable amount for our future disbursements.

If you receive provisional damages, we are entitled to payment of our basic charges our disbursements and success fee at that point.

If you lose you remain liable for the other sides costs.

The Success Fee

The success fee is set at [............]% of basic charges, where the claim concludes at trial; or [............] % where the claim concludes before a trial has commenced. In addition [............]% relates to the postponement of payment of our fees and expenses and cannot be recovered from your opponent. The success fee inclusive of any additional percentage relating to postponement cannot be more than 100% of the basic charges in total.

Other points

The parties acknowledge and agree that this agreement is not a Contentious Business Agreement within the terms of the Solicitors Act 1974.

Signatures

Signed by the solicitor(s): ....

Signed by the client: ....

Conditional Fee Agreements: what you need to know

Definitions of words used in this document and the accompanying CFA are explained at the end of this document.

What do I pay if I win?

If you win your claim, you pay our basic charges, our disbursements and a success fee. The amount of these is not based on or limited by the damages. You can claim from your opponent part or all of our basic charges, our disbursements, a success fee and insurance premium.

It may be that your opponent makes a Part 36 offer or payment which you reject on our advice, and your claim for damages goes ahead to trial where you recover damages that are less than that offer or payment. Refer to the 'Paying Us' section in the CFA document to establish costs we will be seeking for the work done after we received notice of the offer or payment.

If you receive interim damages, we may require you to pay our disbursements at that point as well as a reasonable amount for our future disbursements.

If you receive provisional damages, we are entitled to payment of our basic charges, our disbursements and success fee at that point.

If you win overall but on the way lose an interim hearing, you may be required to pay your opponent's charges of that hearing.

If on the way to winning or losing you are awarded any costs, by agreement or court order, then we are entitled to payment of those costs, together with a success fee on those charges if you win overall.

What do I pay if I lose?

If you lose, you pay your opponent's charges and disbursements. You may be able to take out an insurance policy against this risk. If you lose, you do not pay our charges but we may require you to pay our disbursements.

Ending this agreement

If you end this agreement before you win or lose, you pay our basic charges and disbursements. If you go on to win, you also pay a success fee.

We may end this agreement before you win or lose.

Basic charges

These are for work done from now until this agreement ends. These are subject to review.

How we calculate our basic charges

These are calculated for each hour engaged on your matter. Routine letters and telephone calls will be charged as units of one tenth of an hour. Other letters and telephone calls will be charged on a time basis. The hourly rates are:

Grade of Fee Earner	Hourly Rate
1 Solicitors with over 8 years experience after qualification	
2 Solicitors with over four years' experience after qualification	
3 Other solicitors and legal executives and other staff of equivalent experience	
4 Trainee solicitors and other staff of equivalent experience	

We review the hourly rate on [review date] and we will notify you of any change in the rate in writing.

Road Traffic Accidents

[If your claim is settled before proceedings are issued, for less than £10,000, our basic costs will be £800; plus 20% of the damages agreed up to £5,000; and 15% of the damages agreed between £5,000 and £10,000.] [If you live in London, these costs will be increased by 12.5%]. These costs are fixed by the Civil Procedure Rules.

Success fee

The success fee percentage set out in the agreement reflects the following:

(a)   the fact that if you lose, we will not earn anything;
(b)   our assessment of the risks of your case;
(c)   any other appropriate matters;
(d)   the fact that if you win we will not be paid our basic charges until the end of the claim;
(e)   our arrangements with you about paying disbursements.

Value added tax (VAT)

We add VAT, at the rate (now [.............]%) that applies when the work is done, to the total of the basic charges and success fee.

The Insurance Policy

In all the circumstances and on the information currently available to us, we believe that a contract of insurance with [.......................] is appropriate to cover your opponent's charges and disbursements in case you lose.

This is because

> *You do not have an existing or satisfactory insurance that would cover the costs of making this claim. The policy we recommend will pay:*
>
> (a)   *the costs of the other party in the event that the claim fails, to a maximum of £X;*
>
> (b)   *all your disbursements if your claim fails.*
>
> (c)   *[add other key features where necessary such as, our costs and the other side's costs (without deduction from your damages) if you fail to beat an (Part 36) Offer to Settle your claim, which you rejected following our advice].*
>
> or:
>
> [We cannot identify a policy which meets your needs but our recommended policy is the closest that we can discover within the products that we have searched. It does not meet your needs in the following respects:
>
> (a)   *it has an excess of £Z*
>
> (b)   *the maximum cover is £ZZ]*
>
> or:
>
> *[We cannot obtain an insurance policy at this stage but we shall continue to look for one and if we are successful in our search then we shall advise you at that stage of the benefits of the policy and purchasing it]*
>
> **[NB. The italicised reasons set out are examples only. Your solicitor must consider your individual circumstances and set out the reasons that apply].**

Law Society Conditions

The Law Society Conditions below are part of this agreement. Any amendments or additions to them will apply to you. You should read the conditions carefully and ask us about anything you find unclear.

Our responsibilities

We must:

- always act in your best interests, subject to our duty to the court;
- explain to you the risks and benefits of taking legal action;
- give you our best advice about whether to accept any offer of settlement;
- give you the best information possible about the likely costs of your claim for damages.

Your responsibilities

You must:

- give us instructions that allow us to do our work properly;
- not ask us to work in an improper or unreasonable way;

- not deliberately mislead us;
- co-operate with us;
- go to any medical or expert examination or court hearing.

Dealing with costs if you win

- You are liable to pay all our basic charges, our disbursements and success fee.
- Normally, you can claim part or all of our basic charges, our disbursements success fee and insurance premium from your opponent.
- If we and your opponent cannot agree the amount, the court will decide how much you can recover. If the amount agreed or allowed by the court does not cover all our basic charges and our disbursements, then you pay the difference.
- You will not be entitled to recover from your opponent the part of the success fee that relates to the cost to us of postponing receipt of our charges and our disbursements. This remains payable by you.
- You agree that after winning, the reasons for setting the success fee at the amount stated may be disclosed:
  (i)   to the court and any other person required by the court;
  (ii)   to your opponent in order to gain his or her agreement to pay the success fee.
- If the court carries out an assessment and reduces the success fee because the percentage agreed was unreasonable in view of what we knew or should have known when it was agreed, then the amount reduced ceases to be payable unless the court is satisfied that it should continue to be payable.
- If we agree with your opponent that the success fee is to be paid at a lower percentage than is set out in this agreement, then the success fee percentage will be reduced accordingly unless the court is satisfied that the full amount is payable.
- It may happen that your opponent makes an offer of one amount that includes payment of our basic charges and a success fee. If so, unless we consent, you agree not to tell us to accept the offer if it includes payment of the success fee at a lower rate than is set out in this agreement.
- If your opponent is receiving Community Legal Service funding, we are unlikely to get any money from him or her. So if this happens, you have to pay us our basic charges, disbursements and success fee.

As with the costs in general, you remain ultimately responsible for paying our success fee.

You agree to pay into a designated account any cheque received by you or by us from your opponent and made payable to you. Out of the money, you agree to let us take the balance of the basic charges; success fee; insurance premium; our remaining disbursements; and VAT.

You take the rest.

We are allowed to keep any interest your opponent pays on the charges.

If your opponent fails to pay

If your opponent does not pay any damages or charges owed to you, we have the right to take recovery action in your name to enforce a judgment, order or agreement. The charges of this action become part of the basic charges.

Payment for advocacy

The cost of advocacy and any other work by us, or by any solicitor agent on our behalf, forms part of our basic charges. We shall discuss with you the identity of any barrister instructed, and the arrangements made for payment.

Barristers who have a conditional fee agreement with us

If you win, you are normally entitled to recover their fee and success fee from your opponent. The barrister's success fee is shown in the separate conditional fee agreement we make with the barrister. We will discuss the barrister's success fee with you before we instruct him or her. If you lose, you pay the barrister nothing.

Barristers who do not have a conditional fee agreement with us

If you win, then you will normally be entitled to recover all or part of their fee from your opponent. If you lose, then you must pay their fee.

What happens when this agreement ends before your claim for damages ends?

(a) *Paying us if you end this agreement*

You can end the agreement at any time. We then have the right to decide whether you must:

- pay our basic charges and our disbursements including barristers' fees but not the success fee when we ask for them; or
- pay our basic charges, and our disbursements including barristers' fees and success fees if you go on to win your claim for damages.

(b) *Paying us if we end this agreement*

(i)   We can end this agreement if you do not keep to your responsibilities. We then have the right to decide whether you must:

- pay our basic charges and our disbursements including barristers' fees but not the success fee when we ask for them; or
- pay our basic charges and our disbursements including barristers' fees and success fees if you go on to win your claim for damages.

(ii) We can end this agreement if we believe you are unlikely to win. If this happens, you will only have to pay our disbursements. These will include barristers' fees if the barrister does not have a conditional fee agreement with us.

(iii) We can end this agreement if you reject our opinion about making a settlement with your opponent. You must then:

- pay the basic charges and our disbursements, including barristers' fees;
- pay the success fee if you go on to win your claim for damages.

If you ask us to get a second opinion from a specialist solicitor outside our firm, we will do so. You pay the cost of a second opinion.

(iv) We can end this agreement if you do not pay your insurance premium when asked to do so.

(c) *Death*

This agreement automatically ends if you die before your claim for damages is concluded. We will be entitled to recover our basic charges up to the date of your death from your estate.

If your personal representatives wish to continue your claim for damages, we may offer them a new conditional fee agreement, as long as they agree to pay the success fee on our basic charges from the beginning of the agreement with you.

What happens after this agreement ends

After this agreement ends, we may apply to have our name removed from the record of any court proceedings in which we are acting unless you have another form of funding and ask us to work for you.

We have the right to preserve our lien unless another solicitor working for you undertakes to pay us what we are owed including a success fee if you win.

Explanation of words used

(a) *Advocacy*

Appearing for you at court hearings.

(b) *Basic charges*

Our charges for the legal work we do on your claim for damages.

(c) *Claim*

Your demand for damages for personal injury whether or not court proceedings are issued.

(d) *Counterclaim*

A claim that your opponent makes against you in response to your claim.

(e) *Damages*

Money that you win whether by a court decision or settlement.

(f) *Our disbursements*

Payment we make on your behalf such as:

- court fees;
- experts' fees;
- accident report fees;
- travelling expenses.

(g) *Interim damages*

Money that a court says your opponent must pay or your opponent agrees to pay while waiting for a settlement or the court's final decision.

(h) *Interim hearing*

A court hearing that is not final.

(i) *Lien*

Our right to keep all papers, documents, money or other property held on your behalf until all money due to us is paid. A lien may be applied after this agreement ends.

(j) *Lose*

The court has dismissed your claim or you have stopped it on our advice.

(k) *Part 36 offers or payments*

An offer to settle your claim made in accordance with Part 36 of the Civil Procedure Rules.

(l) *Provisional damages*

Money that a court says your opponent must pay or your opponent agrees to pay, on the basis that you will be able to go back to court at a future date for further damages if:

- you develop a serious disease; or
- your condition deteriorates;

in a way that has been proved or admitted to be linked to your personal injury claim.

(m) *Success fee*

The percentage of basic charges that we add to your bill if you win your claim for damages and that we will seek to recover from your opponent.

(n) *Trial*

The final contested hearing or the contested hearing of any issue to be tried separately and a reference to a claim concluding at trial includes a claim settled after the trial has commenced or a judgment.

(o) *Win*

Your claim for damages is finally decided in your favour, whether by a court decision or an agreement to pay you damages or in any way that you derive benefit from pursuing the claim.

'Finally' means that your opponent:

- is not allowed to appeal against the court decision; or
- has not appealed in time; or
- has lost any appeal.

Appendix 2
Medical Information

Common abbreviations used in medical records

AAL	Anterior axillary line
ACTH	Adrenocorticotrophic hormone
ADH	Antidiuretic hormone
AE	Air entry
AF	Atrial fibrillation
AFB	Acid fast bacillus (TB)
AFP	Alpha-fetoprotein
AJ	Ankle jerk (reflex)
Alk	Alkaline (phos = phosphatase)
An	Anaemia
ANF	Antinuclear factor
Anti-D	This gamma globulin must be given by injection to Rhesus negative mother who delivers/aborts Rhesus positive child/foetus to prevent mother developing antibodies which could damage a subsequent Rhesus positive baby
Apgar	Apgar score: means of recording baby's condition at and shortly after birth by observing and 'scoring' (0, 1 or 2) 5 parameters
AP	Anteroposterior
APH	Antepartum haemorrhage
ARM	Artificial rupture of membranes (labour)
ASO	Antistreptolysin O
ATN	Acute tubular necrosis
A/V	(a) Anteverted
	(b) Arterio venous
AXR	Abdominal x-ray (plain)
Ba	Barium
BD	To be given/taken twice a day
BJ	Biceps jerk (reflex, see AJ)
BMJ	British Medical Journal
BMR	Basal metabolic rate
BO	Bowels open
BP	British Pharmacopoeia
BP	Blood pressure
BS	(a) Breath sounds
	(b) Bowel sounds
	(c) Blood sugar
C_2H_5OH	Alcohol
ca	Carcinoma/cancer
Ca	Calcium

Caps	Capsules
CAT scan	Computed axial tomograph scan
CBD	Common bile duct
cc	(a) Carcinoma (cancer)
	(b) Cubic centimetre
CCF	Congestive cardiac failure
Ch VS	Chorionic villus sampling
CI	Contraindications
Cl	Clubbing (of finger or toe nails)
CLL	Chronic lymphocytic leukaemia
CML	Chronic myeloid leukaemia
CMV	Cytomegalovirus
CN I-XII	Cranial nerves 1 – 12
CNS	Central nervous system
C/O	Complaining of
CO$_2$	Carbon dioxide
COETT	Cuffed oral endotracheal tube
COT	Cuffed oral tube (an endotracheal tube used for ventilating a patient who cannot breathe unaided)
CPD	Cephalo-pelvic disproportion (baby too large to fit through pelvis)
CSF	Cerebro-spinal fluid
CT	Computerised tomography
CTG	Cardiotocograph (trace during labour of baby's heart and mother's contractions)
CVA	Cardiovascular accident (stroke)
CVP	Central venous pressure
CVS	Cardiovascular system
Cx	Cervix
CXR	Chest x-ray
Cy	Cyanosis
DB	Decibel
D&C	Dilation (cervical) and curettage
DM	Diabetes mellitus
DNA	Deoxyribonucleic acid (also 'did not attend')
DOA	Dead on arrival
D&V	Diarrhoea and vomiting
DVT	Deep venous thrombosis
D/W	Discussed with
Dx	Diagnosis
ECG	Electrocardiography
ECT	Electroconvulsive therapy
EDC	Expected date of confinement
EDD	Expected date of delivery
EEG	Electroencephalogram/graph (brain scan)
ENT	Ear, nose and throat
ERCP	Endoscopic retrograde choledochopancreatico/graphy/scope
ERPC	Evacuation of retained products of conception

ESR	Erythrocyte sedimentation rate (blood)
ETR	Examined through clothes
EtoH	Alcohol
ET(T)	Endotracheal (tube)
EUA	Examined under anaesthesia
FB	(a) Finger's breadth
	(b) Foreign body
FBC	Full blood count
FBS	Foetal blood sampling (a procedure which is carried out during labour to check on the baby's condition)
FH	Family history
FHH	Foetal heart heard
FHHR	Foetal heart heard regular
FHR	Foetal heart rate
FMF	Foetal movements felt
FSE	Foetal scalp electrode
FSH	Follicle-stimulating hormone
G	gram
GA	General anaesthesia
GB	Gall bladder
GFR	Glomerular filtration rate
GI	Gastro-intestinal
GIT	Gastro-intestinal tract
G6PD	Glucose 6 phosphate dehydrogenase
GP	General practitioner
GTT	Glucose tolerance test (for diabetes)
GU	Genito-urinary
GUT	Genito-urinary tract
h	Hour
Hb	Haemoglobin
Hct	Haemocrit
HOCM	Hypertrophic obstructive cardiomyopathy
HPC	History of presenting complaint
HRT	Hormone replacement therapy
HS	Heart sounds
HVS	High vaginal swab
Hx	History
ICP	Intracranial pressure
ICS	Intercostal space
IDA	Iron deficiency anaemia
IDDM	Insulin dependent diabetes mellitus
Ig	Immunoglobulin
IJ	Internal jugular vein
IM	Intramuscular
ISQ	In status quo
IT	Intrathecal
ITP	Idiopathic thrombocytopenic purpura

ITU	Intensive therapy unit
iu	International unit
IUCD	Intrauterine contraceptive device
IV	Intravenous
IVC	Inferior vena cava
IVI	Intravenous infusion (drip)
IVU	Intravenous urography
Ix	Investigations
J	Jaundice
°JACCO	No jaundice, anaemia, cyanosis, clubbing or oedema
JVP	Jugular venous pressure
K$^+$	Potassium
kg	Kilogram
KJ	Knee jerk (reflex, see AJ)
kPa	Kilopascal, approximately 7.5 mmHg
L	(a) Litre
	(b) Left
LA	Local anaesthesia
LBBB	Left bundle branch block
LFTs	Liver function tests
LH	Luteinising hormone
LIF	Left iliac fossa
LIH	Left inguinal hernia
LMN	Lower motor neurone
LMP	First day of the last menstrual period
LN	Lymph node
LOA	Left occiput anterior (position of baby's head at delivery, see also LOP, ROA, ROP, LOL, ROL, OA, OP)
LOC	Loss of consciousness
LOL	Left occipitolateral (see LOA)
LOP	Left occiput posterior (see LOA above)
LP	Lumbar puncture
LS	Letter sent
LSCS	Lower segment caesarean section (the 'normal' type of caesarean section)
LSKK	Liver, spleen and kidneys
LUQ	Left upper quadrant
LVF	Left ventricular failure
LVH	Left ventricular hypertrophy
mane	In the morning
mcg	Microgram
MCL	Mid clavicular line
MCV	Mean cell volume
µg	Microgram
mg	Milligram
mist	mixture
mitte 1/12	Supply/give/send/provide

ml	Millilitres
mmHg	Millimetres of mercury (pressure)
mMol	Millimol
MRI	Magnetic resonance imaging (=NMRI)
MS	Multiple sclerosis
MSU	Mid stream urine
N&V	Nausea and vomiting
Na	Sodium
NaHCO$_3$	Sodium bicarbonate
NAD	Nothing abnormal diagnosed/detected
NBM	Nil by mouth
ND	Notifiable disease
ng	Nanogram
NG	(a) Naso-gastric
	(b) Carcinoma/cancer (neoplastic growth)
NMCS	No malignant cells seen
NMR	Nuclear magnetic resonance (scan)
noct/nocte	At night
NOF	Neck of femur
N/S	Normal size
NSAID	Non-steroidal anti-inflammatory drugs
O$_2$	Oxygen
OA	(a) Occipito-anterior (see LOA)
	(b) Osteoarthritis
OCP	Oral contraceptive pill
OE	On examination
OP	Occipito-posterior (see LOA)
Orthop.	Orthopnoea (breathlessness on lying flat)
P	Pulse
P or π	Period
PA	Posteroanterior
PAN	Polyarteritis nodosa
PC	Post cibum (after food)
pCO$_2$	Partial pressure of carbon dioxide (normally in blood)
PCV	Packed cell volume
PERLA	Pupils are equal and react to light and accommodation
PE	(a) Pulmonary embolism
	(b) Pre eclampsia
PEFR	Peak expiratory flow rate
PET	Pre-eclamptic toxaemia
pg	Picogram
pH	Acidity and alkalinity scale. Low is acidic. High is alkaline. pH7 is about neutral
PH	Past/previous history
PID	(a) Pelvic inflammatory disease
	(b) Prolapsed intervertebral disc
PIP	Proximal interphalangeal

PL	Prolactin
PMH	Past/previous medical history
PND	Paroxysmal nocturnal dyspnoea
PN (R)	Percussion note (resonant)
po	Per os (by mouth)
pO$_2$	Partial pressure of oxygen (normally in blood)
POH	Past/previous obstetric history
POP	Plaster of Paris
PoP	Progesterone only pill
PPH	Post-partum haemorrhage
pr	Per rectum (by the rectum)
prn	As required – of eg, pain killers
PRV	Polycythaemia rubra vera
PTH	Parathyroid hormone
PTT	Prothrombin time
PU	Peptic ulcer
PV	Per vaginam (by the vagina)
QDS	To be given/taken 4 times a day
R	Right *or* respiration
RA	Rheumatoid arthritis
RBBB	Right bundle branch block
RBC	Red blood cell (erythrocyte)
RE	Rectal examination
Rh	Rhesus factor
RIC	Raised intracranial pressure
RIF	Right iliac fossa
RIH	Right inguinal hernia
ROA	Right occiput anterior (see LOA)
ROL	Right occipito-lateral (see LOA)
ROM	Range of movement
ROP	Right occiput posterior (see LOA)
RS	Respiratory system
RT	Radiotherapy
RTA	Road traffic accident
RTI	Respiratory tract infection
RUQ	Right upper quadrant
SB	Serum bilirubin
S/B	Seen by
SBE	Subacute bacterial endocarditis
SC	Subcutaneous
S/D	Systolic/diastolic (heart and circulation)
SE	Side effects
SH	Social history
SJ	Supinator jerk (reflex: see AJ)
SL	Sub linguinal (under the tongue)
SLE	Systemic lupus erythematosus
SOA	Swelling of ankles

SOB (OE)	Shortness of breath
SOS	(a) if necessary
	(b) see other sheet
SROM	Spontaneous rupture of membranes
stat	Immediately
Supp	Suppositories
SVC	Superior vena cava
SVD	Spontaneous vaginal delivery
SVT	Supraventricular tachycardia
SXR	Skull x-ray
Ts and As	Tonsils and Adenoids
TCI 2/52	To come in (to be admitted to hospital), in 2 weeks' time
tds	To be given/taken 3 times a day
TGH	To go home
THR	Total hip replacement
TIA	Transient ischaemic attack
TJ	Triceps jerk (reflex: see AJ)
TPR	Temperature, pulse and respiration
TSH	Thyroid stimulating hormone
TTA	To take away
TVF	Tactile vocal fremitus
TX	Transfusion
UC	Ulcerative colitis
U&E	Urea and electrolytes (biochemical tests)
UG	Urogenital
UMN	Upper motor neurone
URTI	Upper respiratory tract infection
USS	Ultra sound scan
UTI	Urinary tract infection
VA	Visual acuity
VE	Vaginal examination
VF	Ventricular fibrillation
VT	Ventricular tachycardia
V/V	Vulva and vagina
VVs	Varicose veins
WBC	White blood corpuscle/white blood cell count
WCC	White blood cell count
WR	Wasserman reaction
wt	Weight
XR	X-ray

Appendix 3

Pre-action Protocols

Pre-action protocol for the resolution of clinical disputes

Contents

Executive Summary

1   The Clinical Disputes Forum is a multi-disciplinary body which was formed in 1997, as a result of Lord Woolf's 'Access to Justice' inquiry. One of the aims of the Forum is to find less adversarial and more cost effective ways of resolving disputes about healthcare and medical treatment. The names and addresses of the Chairman and Secretary of the Forum can be found at Annex E.

2   This protocol is the Forum's first major initiative. It has been drawn up carefully, including extensive consultations with most of the key stakeholders in the medico-legal system.

3   The protocol—

   •   encourages a climate of openness when something has 'gone wrong' with a patient's treatment or the patient is dissatisfied with that treatment and/or the outcome. This reflects the new and developing requirements for clinical governance within healthcare;

   •   provides **general guidance** on how this more open culture might be achieved when disputes arise;

   •   recommends **a timed sequence** of steps for patients and healthcare providers, and their advisers, to follow when a dispute arises. This should facilitate and speed up exchanging relevant information and increase the prospects that disputes can be resolved without resort to legal action.

4   This protocol has been prepared by a working party of the Clinical Disputes Forum. It has the support of the Lord Chancellor's Department, the Department of Health and NHS Executive, the Law Society, the Legal Aid Board and many other key organisations.

1 Why this Protocol?

Mistrust in healthcare disputes

1.1   The number of complaints and claims against hospitals, GPs, dentists and private healthcare providers is growing as patients become more prepared to question the treatment they are given, to seek explanations of what happened, and to seek appropriate redress. Patients may require further treatment, an apology, assurances about future action, or compensation. These trends are unlikely to change. The Patients' Charter encourages patients to have high expectations, and a revised NHS Complaints Procedure was implemented in 1996. The civil justice reforms and new Rules of Court should make litigation quicker, more user friendly and less expensive.

1.2   It is clearly in the interests of patients, healthcare professionals and providers that patients' concerns, complaints and claims arising from their treatment are resolved as quickly, efficiently and professionally as possible. A climate of mistrust and lack of openness can seriously damage the patient/clinician relationship, unnecessarily prolong disputes (especially litigation), and reduce the resources available for treating patients. It may also cause additional work for, and lower the morale of, healthcare professionals.

1.3   At present there is often mistrust by both sides. This can mean that patients fail to raise their concerns with the healthcare provider as early as possible. Sometimes patients may pursue a complaint or claim which has little merit, due to a lack of sufficient information and understanding. It can also mean that patients become reluctant, once advice has been taken on a potential claim, to disclose sufficient information to enable the provider to investigate that claim efficiently and, where appropriate, resolve it.

1.4   On the side of the healthcare provider this mistrust can be shown in a reluctance to be honest with patients, a failure to provide prompt clear explanations, especially of adverse outcomes (whether or not there may have been negligence) and a tendency to 'close ranks' once a claim is made.

What needs to change

1.5   If that mistrust is to be removed, and a more co-operative culture is to develop—

• healthcare professionals and providers need to adopt a constructive approach to complaints and claims. They should accept that concerned patients are entitled to an explanation and an apology, if warranted, and to appropriate redress in the event of negligence. An overly defensive approach is not in the long-term interest of their main goal: patient care;

• patients should recognise that unintended and/or unfortunate consequences of medical treatment can only be rectified if they are brought to the attention of the healthcare provider as soon as possible.

1.6   A protocol which sets out 'ground rules' for the handling of disputes at their early stages should, if it is to be subscribed to, and followed—

• encourage greater openness between the parties;

• encourage parties to find the most appropriate way of resolving the particular dispute;

• reduce delay and costs;

• reduce the need for litigation.

Why this protocol now?

1.7   Lord Woolf in his Access to Justice Report in July 1996, concluded that major causes of costs and delay in medical negligence litigation occur at the pre-action stage. He recommended that patients and their advisers, and healthcare providers, should work more closely together to try to resolve disputes co-operatively, rather than proceed to litigation. He specifically recommended a pre-action protocol for medical negligence cases.

1.8   A fuller summary of Lord Woolf's recommendations is at Annex D.

Where the protocol fits in

1.9   Protocols serve the needs of litigation and pre-litigation practice, especially—

- predictability in the time needed for steps pre-proceedings;
- standardisation of relevant information, including records and documents to be disclosed.

1.10   Building upon Lord Woolf's recommendations, the Lord Chancellor's Department is now promoting the adoption of protocols in specific areas, including medical negligence.

1.11   It is recognised that contexts differ significantly. For example, patients tend to have an ongoing relationship with a GP, more so than with a hospital; clinical staff in the National Health Service are often employees, while those in the private sector may be contractors; providing records quickly may be relatively easy for GPs and dentists, but can be a complicated procedure in a large multi-department hospital. The protocol which follows is intended to be sufficiently broadly based, and flexible, to apply to all aspects of the health service: primary and secondary; public and private sectors.

Enforcement of the protocol and sanctions

1.12   The civil justice reforms will be implemented in April 1999. One new set of Court Rules and procedures is replacing the existing rules for both the High Court and county courts. This and the personal injury protocol are being published with the Rules, Practice Directions and key court forms. The courts will be able to treat the standards set in protocols as the normal reasonable approach to pre-action conduct.

1.13   If proceedings are issued it will be for the court to decide whether non-compliance with a protocol should merit sanctions. Guidance on the court's likely approach will be given from time to time in practice directions.

1.14   If the court has to consider the question of compliance after proceedings have begun it will not be concerned with minor infringements, eg, failure by a short period to provide relevant information. One minor breach will not entitle the 'innocent' party to abandon following the protocol. The court will look at the effect of non-compliance on the other party when deciding whether to impose sanctions.

2 The aims of the Protocol

2.1   The **general** aims of the protocol are—

- to maintain/restore the patient/healthcare provider relationship;
- to resolve as many disputes as possible without litigation.

2.2   The **specific** objectives are—

Openness

- to encourage early communication of the perceived problem between patients and healthcare providers;
- to encourage patients to voice any concerns or dissatisfaction with their treatment as soon as practicable;
- to encourage healthcare providers to develop systems of early reporting and investigation for serious adverse treatment outcomes and to provide full and prompt explanations to dissatisfied patients;
- to ensure that sufficient information is disclosed by both parties to enable each to understand the other's perspective and case, and to encourage early resolution.

Timeliness

- to provide an early opportunity for healthcare providers to identify cases where an investigation is required and to carry out that investigation promptly;
- to encourage primary and private healthcare providers to involve their defence organisations or insurers at an early stage;
- to ensure that all relevant medical records are provided to patients or their appointed representatives on request, to a realistic timetable by any healthcare provider;
- to ensure that relevant records which are not in healthcare providers' possession are made available to them by patients and their advisers at an appropriate stage;
- where a resolution is not achievable to lay the ground to enable litigation to proceed on a reasonable timetable, at a reasonable and proportionate cost and to limit the matters in contention;
- to discourage the prolonged pursuit of unmeritorious claims and the prolonged defence of meritorious claims.

Awareness of options

- to ensure that patients and healthcare providers are made aware of the available options to pursue and resolve disputes and what each might involve.

2.3   This protocol does not attempt to be prescriptive about a number of related clinical governance issues which will have a bearing on healthcare providers' ability to meet the standards within the protocol. Good clinical governance requires the following to be considered—

    (a)   **Clinical risk management:** the protocol does not provide any detailed guidance to healthcare providers on clinical risk management or the adoption of risk management systems and procedures. This must be a matter for the NHS Executive, the National Health Service Litigation Authority, individual trusts and providers, including GPs, dentists and the private sector. However, effective co-ordinated, focused clinical risk management strategies and procedures can help in managing risk and in the early identification and investigation of adverse outcomes.

    (b)   **Adverse outcome reporting:** the protocol does not provide any detailed guidance on which adverse outcomes should trigger an investigation. However, healthcare providers should have in place procedures for such investigations, including recording of statements of key witnesses. These procedures should also cover when and how to inform patients that an adverse outcome has occurred.

(c)   **The professional's duty to report:** the protocol does not recommend changes to the codes of conduct of professionals in healthcare, or attempt to impose a specific duty on those professionals to report known adverse outcomes or untoward incidents. Lord Woolf in his final report suggested that the professional bodies might consider this. The General Medical Council is preparing guidance to doctors about their duty to report adverse incidents and to co-operate with inquiries.

3 The Protocol

3.1   This protocol is not a comprehensive code governing all the steps in clinical disputes. Rather it attempts to set out **a code of good practice** which parties should follow when litigation might be a possibility.

3.2   The **commitments** section of the protocol summarises the guiding principles which healthcare providers and patients and their advisers are invited to endorse when dealing with patient dissatisfaction with treatment and its outcome, and with potential complaints and claims.

3.3   The **steps** section sets out in a more prescriptive form, a recommended sequence of actions to be followed if litigation is a prospect.

Good practice commitments

3.4   **Healthcare providers** should—

(i)   ensure that **key staff**, including claims and litigation managers, are appropriately trained and have some knowledge of healthcare law, and of complaints procedures and civil litigation practice and procedure;

(ii)   develop an approach to **clinical governance** that ensures that clinical practice is delivered to commonly accepted standards and that this is routinely monitored through a system of clinical audit and clinical risk management (particularly adverse outcome investigation);

(iii) set up **adverse outcome reporting systems** in all specialties to record and investigate unexpected serious adverse outcomes as soon as possible. Such systems can enable evidence to be gathered quickly, which makes it easier to provide an accurate explanation of what happened and to defend or settle any subsequent claims;

(iv)   use the results of **adverse incidents and complaints positively** as a guide to how to improve services to patients in the future;

(v)   ensure **that patients receive clear and comprehensible information** in an accessible form about how to raise their concerns or complaints;

(vi)   establish **efficient and effective systems of recording and storing patient records,** notes, diagnostic reports and x-rays, and to retain these in accordance with Department of Health guidance (currently for a minimum of eight years in the case of adults, and all obstetric and paediatric notes for children until they reach the age of 25);

(vii) **advise patients** of a serious adverse outcome and provide on request to the patient or the patient's representative an oral or written explanation of what happened, information on further steps open to the patient, including where appropriate an offer of future treatment to rectify the problem, an apology, changes in procedure which will benefit patients and/or compensation.

3.5   **Patients and their advisers** should—

(i)   **report any concerns and dissatisfaction** to the healthcare provider as soon as is reasonable to enable that provider to offer clinical advice where possible, to advise the patient if anything has gone wrong and take appropriate action;

(ii)   consider the **full range of options** available following an adverse outcome with which a patient is dissatisfied, including a request for an explanation, a meeting, a complaint, and other appropriate dispute resolution methods (including mediation) and negotiation, not only litigation;

(iii) **inform the healthcare provider when the patient is satisfied** that the matter has been concluded: legal advisers should notify the provider when they are no longer acting for the patient, particularly if proceedings have not started.

Protocol steps

3.6   The steps of this protocol which follow have been kept deliberately simple. An illustration of the likely sequence of events in a number of healthcare situations is at Annex A.

Obtaining the health records

3.7   Any request for records by the **patient** or their adviser should—

- **provide sufficient information** to alert the healthcare provider where an adverse outcome has been serious or had serious consequences;

- be as **specific as possible** about the records which are required.

3.8   Requests for copies of the patient's clinical records should be made using the Law Society and Department of Health approved **standard forms** (enclosed at Annex B), adapted as necessary.

3.9   The copy records should be provided **within 40 days** of the request and for a cost not exceeding the charges permissible under the Access to Health Records Act 1990 (currently a maximum of £10 plus photocopying and postage).[1]

3.10 In the rare circumstances that the healthcare provider is in difficulty in complying with the request within 40 days, the **problem should be explained** quickly and details given of what is being done to resolve it.

3.11 It will not be practicable for healthcare providers to investigate in detail each case when records are requested. But healthcare providers should **adopt a policy on which cases will be investigated** (see paragraph 3.5 on clinical governance and adverse outcome reporting).

3.12 If the healthcare provider fails to provide the health records within 40 days, the patient or their adviser can then apply to the court for an **order for pre-action disclosure.** The new Civil Procedure Rules should make pre-action applications to the court easier. The court will also have the power to impose costs sanctions for unreasonable delay in providing records.

3.13 If either the patient or the healthcare provider considers **additional health records are required from a third party**, in the first instance these should be requested by or through the patient. Third party healthcare providers are expected to co-operate. The Civil Procedure Rules will enable patients and healthcare providers to apply to the court for pre-action disclosure by third parties.

---

1 Note that the relevant legislation is now the Data Protection Act 1998, and the relevant fee is £50 plus copying charges and postage.

Letter of claim

3.14 Annex C1 to this protocol provides **a template for the recommended contents of a letter of claim:** the level of detail will need to be varied to suit the particular circumstances.

3.15 If, following the receipt and analysis of the records, and the receipt of any further advice (including from experts if necessary – see Section 4), the patient/adviser decides that there are grounds for a claim, they should then send, as soon as practicable, to the healthcare provider/potential defendant, a **letter of claim.**

3.16 This letter should contain a **clear summary of the facts** on which the claim is based, including the alleged adverse outcome, and the **main allegations of negligence.** It should also describe the **patient's injuries,** and present condition and prognosis. The **financial loss** incurred by the plaintiff should be outlined with an indication of the heads of damage to be claimed and the scale of the loss, unless this is impracticable.

3.17 In more complex cases a **chronology** of the relevant events should be provided, particularly if the patient has been treated by a number of different healthcare providers.

3.18 The letter of claim **should refer to any relevant documents,** including health records, and if possible enclose copies of any of those which will not already be in the potential defendant's possession, eg any relevant general practitioner records if the plaintiff's claim is against a hospital.

3.19 **Sufficient information** must be given to enable the healthcare provider defendant to **commence investigations** and to put an initial valuation on the claim.

3.20 Letters of claim are **not** intended to have the same formal status as a pleading, nor should any sanctions necessarily apply if the letter of claim and any subsequent statement of claim in the proceedings differ.

3.21 **Proceedings should not be issued until after three months from the letter of claim,** unless there is a limitation problem and/or the patient's position needs to be protected by early issue.

3.22 The patient or their adviser may want to make an **offer to settle** the claim at this early stage by putting forward an amount of compensation which would be satisfactory (possibly including any costs incurred to date). If an offer to settle is made, generally this should be supported by a medical report which deals with the injuries, condition and prognosis, and by a schedule of loss and supporting documentation. The level of detail necessary will depend on the value of the claim. Medical reports may not be necessary where there is no significant continuing injury, and a detailed schedule may not be necessary in a low value case. The Civil Procedure Rules are expected to set out the legal and procedural requirements for making offers to settle.

The response

3.23 Attached at Annex C2 is a template for the suggested contents of the **letter of response.**

3.24 The healthcare provider should **acknowledge** the letter of claim **within 14 days of receipt** and should identify who will be dealing with the matter.

3.25 The healthcare provider should, **within three months** of the letter of claim, provide a **reasoned answer—**

- if the **claim is admitted** the healthcare provider should say so in clear terms;

- if only **part of the claim is admitted** the healthcare provider should make clear which issues of breach of duty and/or causation are admitted and which are denied and why;

- if it is intended that any **admissions will be binding;**

- if the claim is denied, this should include specific comments on the allegations of negligence, and if a synopsis or chronology of relevant events has been provided and is disputed, the healthcare provider's version of those events;

- where additional documents are relied upon, eg an internal protocol, copies should be provided.

3.26 If the patient has made an offer to settle, the healthcare provider should **respond to that offer** in the response letter, preferably with reasons. The provider may make its own offer to settle at this stage, either as a counter-offer to the patient's, or of its own accord, but should accompany any offer by any supporting medical evidence, and/or by any other evidence in relation to the value of the claim which is in the healthcare provider's possession.

3.27 If the parties reach agreement on liability, but time is needed to resolve the value of the claim, they should aim to agree a reasonable period.

4 Experts

4.1 In clinical negligence disputes expert opinions may be needed—

- on breach of duty and causation;

- on the patient's condition and prognosis;

- to assist in valuing aspects of the claim.

4.2 The civil justice reforms and the new Civil Procedure Rules will encourage economy in the use of experts and a less adversarial expert culture. It is recognised that in clinical negligence disputes, the parties and their advisers will require flexibility in their approach to expert evidence. Decisions on whether experts might be instructed jointly, and on whether reports might be disclosed sequentially or by exchange, should rest with the parties and their advisers. Sharing expert evidence may be appropriate on issues relating to the value of the claim. However, this protocol does not attempt to be prescriptive on issues in relation to expert evidence.

4.3 Obtaining expert evidence will often be an expensive step and may take time, especially in specialised areas of medicine where there are limited numbers of suitable experts. Patients and healthcare providers, and their advisers, will therefore need to consider carefully how best to obtain any necessary expert help quickly and cost-effectively. Assistance with locating a suitable expert is available from a number of sources.

5 Alternative Approaches to Settling Disputes

5.1 It would not be practicable for this protocol to address in any detail how a patient or their adviser, or healthcare provider, might decide which method to adopt to resolve the particular problem. But, the courts increasingly expect parties to try to settle their differences by agreement before issuing proceedings.

5.2 Most disputes are resolved by **discussion and negotiation.** Parties should bear in mind that carefully planned face-to-face meetings may be particularly helpful in exploring further treatment for the patient, in reaching understandings about what happened, and on both parties' positions, in narrowing the issues in dispute and, if the timing is right, in helping to settle the whole matter.

5.3   Summarised below are some other alternatives for resolving disputes—

- The revised NHS Complaints Procedure, which was implemented in April 1996, is designed to provide patients with an explanation of what happened and an apology if appropriate. It is not designed to provide compensation for cases of negligence. However, patients might choose to use the procedure if their only, or main, goal is to obtain an explanation, or to obtain more information to help them decide what other action might be appropriate.

- Mediation may be appropriate in some cases: this is a form of facilitated negotiation assisted by an independent neutral party. It is expected that the new Civil Procedure Rules will give the court the power to stay proceedings for one month for settlement discussions or mediation.

- Other methods of resolving disputes include arbitration, determination by an expert, and early neutral evaluation by a medical or legal expert. The Legal Services Commission has published a booklet on '**Alternatives to Court**', LSC August 2001, CLS information leaflet number 23, which lists a number of organisations that provide alternative dispute resolution services.

ANNEX A

Illustrative Flowchart

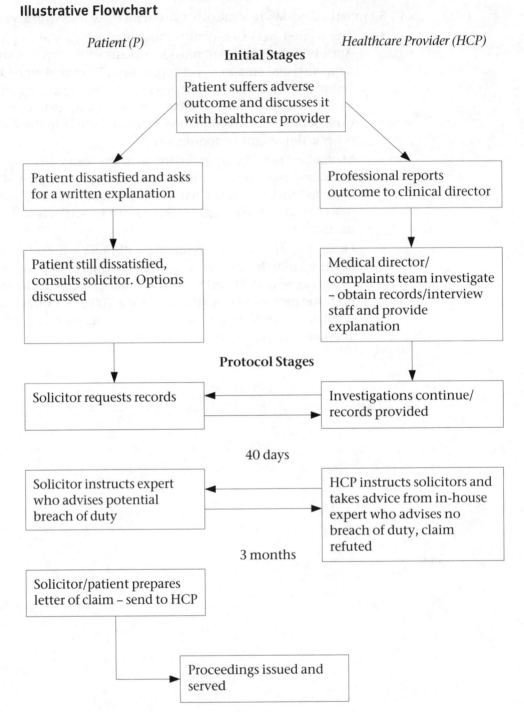

ANNEX B

Medical Negligence and Personal Injury Claims

Protocol for Obtaining Hospital Medical Records

(Revised Edition (June 1998); Civil Litigation Committee, The Law Society)

Application on Behalf of a Patient for Hospital Medical Records for Use When Court Proceedings are Contemplated

Purpose of the forms

This application form and response forms have been prepared by a working party of the Law Society's Civil Litigation Committee and approved by the Department of Health for use in NHS and Trust hospitals.

The purpose of the forms is to standardise and streamline the disclosure of medical records to a patient's solicitors, who are investigating pursuing a personal injury claim against a third party, or a medical negligence claim against the hospital to which the application is addressed and/or other hospitals or general practitioners.

Use of the forms

Use of the forms is entirely voluntary and does not prejudice any party's right under the Access to Health Records Act 1990, the Data Protection Act 1984, or ss 33 and 34 of the Supreme Court Act 1981. However, it is the Department of Health policy that patients be permitted to see what has been written about them, and that healthcare providers should make arrangements to allow patients to see all their records, not only those covered by the Access to Health Records Act 1990. The aim of the forms is to save time and costs for all concerned for the benefit of the patient and the hospital and in the interests of justice. Use of the forms should make it unnecessary in most cases for there to be exchanges of letters or other enquiries. If there is any unusual matter not covered by the form, the patient's solicitor may write a separate letter at the outset.

Charges for records

The Access to Health Records Act 1990 prescribes a maximum fee of £10. Photocopying and postage costs can be charged in addition. No other charges may be made.

The NHS Executive guidance makes it clear to healthcare providers that 'it is a perfectly proper use' of the 1990 Act to request records in that framework for the purpose of potential or actual litigation, whether against a third party or against the hospital or trust.

The 1990 Act does not permit differential rates of charges to be levied if the application is made by the patient, or by a solicitor on his or her behalf, or whether the response to the application is made by the healthcare provider directly (the medical records manager or a claims manager) or by a solicitor.

The NHS Executive guidance recommends that the same practice should be followed with regard to charges when the records are provided under a voluntary agreement as under the 1990 Act, except that in those circumstances the £10 access fee will not be appropriate.

The NHS Executive also advises—

- that the cost of photocopying may include 'the cost of staff time in making copies' and the costs of running the copier (but not costs of locating and sifting records);
- that the common practice of setting a standard rate for an application or charging an administration fee is not acceptable because there will be cases when this fails to comply with the 1990 Act.

Records: what might be included

X-rays and test results form part of the patient's records. Additional charges for copying x-rays are permissible. If there are large numbers of x-rays, the records officer should check with the patient/solicitor before arranging copying.

Reports on an 'adverse incident' and reports on the patient made for risk management and audit purposes may form part of the records and be disclosable: the exception will be any specific record or report made solely or mainly in connection with an actual or potential claim.

Records: quality standards

When copying records healthcare providers should ensure—

1   All documents are legible, and complete, if necessary by photocopying at less than 100% size.
2   Documents larger than A4 in the original, eg ITU charts, should be reproduced in A3, or reduced to A4 where this retains readability.
3   Documents are only copied on one side of paper, unless the original is two sided.
4   Documents should not be unnecessarily shuffled or bound and holes should not be made in the copied papers.

Enquiries/further information

Any enquiries about the forms should be made initially to the solicitors making the request. Comments on the use and content of the forms should be made to the Secretary, Civil Litigation Committee, The Law Society, 113 Chancery Lane, London WC2A 1PL, telephone (020) 7320 5739, or to the NHS Management Executive, Quarry House, Quarry Hill, Leeds LS2 7UE.

The Law Society

May 1998

Application on Behalf of a Patient for Hospital Medical Records for Use when Court Proceedings are Contemplated

This should be completed as fully as possible

Insert Hospital Name and Address

TO: Medical Records Officer   Hospital

1		
(a)	Full name of patient (including previous surnames)	
(b)	Address now	
(c)	Address at start of treatment	
(d)	Date of birth (and death, if applicable)	
(e)	Hospital ref no if available	
(f)	N.I. number, if available	
2	This application is made because the patient is considering	
(a)	a claim against your hospital as detailed in para 7 overleaf	YES/NO
(b)	pursuing an action against someone else	YES/NO
3	Department(s) where treatment was received	
4	Name(s) of consultant(s) at your hospital in charge of the treatment	
5	Whether treatment at your hospital was private or NHS, wholly or in part	
6	A description of the treatment received, with approximate dates	
7	If the answer to Q2(a) is 'Yes' details of	
	(a) the likely nature of the claim	
	(b) grounds for the claim	
	(c) approximate dates of the events involved	
8	If the answer to Q2(b) is 'Yes' insert	
	(a) the names of the proposed defendants	
	(b) whether legal proceedings yet begun	YES/NO
	(c) if appropriate, details of the claim and action number	
9	We confirm we will pay reasonable copying charges	
10	We request prior details of	
	(a) photocopying and administration charges for medical records	YES/NO
	(b) number of and cost of copying x-ray and scan films	YES/NO

11	Any other relevant information, particular requirements, or any particular documents *not* required (eg copies of computerised records)	
	Signature of Solicitor	
	Name	
	Address	
	Ref	
	Telephone number	
	Fax number	
	Please print name beneath each signature. *Signature by child over 12 but under* *18 years also requires signature by parent*	

Signature of patient

Signature of parent or next friend if appropriate

Signature of personal representative where patient has died

First Response to Application for Hospital Records

	NAME OF PATIENT Our ref Your ref	
1	Date of receipt of patient's application	
2	We intend that copy medical records will be dispatched within 6 weeks of that date	YES/NO
3	We require pre-payment of photocopying charges	YES/NO
4	If estimate of photocopying charges requested or pre-payment required the amount will be	£ /notified to you
5	The cost of x-ray and scan films will be	£ /notified to you
6	If there is any problem, we shall write to you within those 6 weeks	YES/NO
7	Any other information	
	Please address further correspondence to	
	Signed	
	Direct telephone number	
	Direct fax number	
	Dated	

Second Response Enclosing Patient's Hospital Medical Records

Address   Our Ref
                                                                       Your Ref

1	NAME OF PATIENT: We confirm that the enclosed copy medical records are all those within the control of the hospital, relevant to the application which you have made to the best of our knowledge and belief, subject to paras 2–5 below	YES/NO
2	Details of any other documents which have not yet been located	
3	Date by when it is expected that these will be supplied	
4	Details of any records which we are not producing	
5	The reasons for not doing so	
6	An invoice for copying and administration charges is attached	YES/NO
	Signed	
	Date	

ANNEX C

Templates for Letters of Claim and Response

C1 Letter of claim

Essential Contents

1   **Client's name, address, date of birth, etc**
2   **Dates of allegedly negligent treatment**
3   **Events giving rise to the claim:**
  - an outline of what happened, including details of other relevant treatments to the client by other healthcare providers.
4   **Allegation of negligence and causal link with injuries:**
  - an outline of the allegations or a more detailed list in a complex case;
  - an outline of the causal link between allegations and the injuries complained of.
5   **The client's injuries, condition and future prognosis**
6   **Request for clinical records (if not previously provided)**
  - use the Law Society form if appropriate or adapt;
  - specify the records required;
  - if other records are held by other providers, and may be relevant, say so;
  - state what investigations have been carried out to date, eg information from client and witnesses, any complaint and the outcome, if any clinical records have been seen or expert's advice obtained.

7   **The likely value of the claim**
- an outline of the main heads of damage, or, in straightforward cases, the details of loss.

Optional information

What investigations have been carried out

An offer to settle without supporting evidence

Suggestions for obtaining expert evidence

Suggestions for meetings, negotiations, discussion or mediation

Possible enclosures

Chronology

Clinical records request form and client's authorisation

Expert report(s)

Schedules of loss and supporting evidence

C2 Letter of response

Essential Contents

1   Provide **requested records** and invoice for copying:
- explain if records are incomplete or extensive records are held and ask for further instructions;
- request additional records from third parties.

2   **Comments on events and/or chronology:**
- if events are disputed or the healthcare provider has further information or documents on which they wish to rely, these should be provided, eg internal protocol;
- details of any further information needed from the patient or a third party should be provided.

3   **If breach of duty and causation are accepted:**
- suggestions might be made for resolving the claim and/or requests for further information;
- a response should be made to any offer to settle.

4   **If breach of duty and/or causation are denied:**
- a bare denial will not be sufficient. If the healthcare provider has other explanations for what happened, these should be given at least in outline;
- suggestions might be made for the next steps, eg further investigations, obtaining expert evidence, meetings/negotiations or mediation, or an invitation to issue proceedings.

Optional Matters

An offer to settle if the patient has not made one, or a counter offer to the patient's with supporting evidence

Possible Enclosures

Clinical records

Annotated chronology

Expert reports

ANNEX D

Lord Woolf's Recommendations

1   Lord Woolf in his Access to Justice Report in July 1996, following a detailed review of the problems of medical negligence claims, identified that one of the major sources of **costs and delay** is **at the pre-litigation stage** because—

   (a)   Inadequate incident reporting and record keeping in hospitals, and mobility of staff, make it difficult to establish facts, often several years after the event.

   (b)   Claimants must incur the cost of an expert in order to establish whether they have a viable claim.

   (c)   There is often a long delay before a claim is made.

   (d)   Defendants do not have sufficient resources to carry out a full investigation of every incident, and do not consider it worthwhile to start an investigation as soon as they receive a request for records, because many cases do not proceed beyond that stage.

   (e)   Patients often give the defendant little or no notice of a firm intention to pursue a claim. Consequently, many incidents are not investigated by the defendants until after proceedings have started.

   (f)   Doctors and other clinical staff are traditionally reluctant to admit negligence or apologise to, or negotiate with, claimants for fear of damage to their professional reputations or career prospects.

2   Lord Woolf acknowledged that under the present arrangements **healthcare providers,** faced with possible medical negligence claims, have a number of **practical problems** to contend with—

   (a)   Difficulties of finding patients' records and tracing former staff, which can be exacerbated by late notification and by the health-care provider's own failure to identify adverse incidents.

   (b)   The healthcare provider may have only treated the patient for a limited time or for a specific complaint: the patient's previous history may be relevant but the records may be in the possession of one of several other healthcare providers.

   (c)   The large number of potential claims do not proceed beyond the stage of a request for medical records, or an explanation; and that it is difficult for healthcare providers to investigate fully every case whenever a patient asks to see the records.

ANNEX E

How to Contact the Forum

The Clinical Disputes Forum

Chairman

Dr Alastair Scotland
Medical Director and Chief Officer
National Clinical Assessment Authority
9th Floor, Market Towers
London
SW8 5NQ
Telephone: (020) 7273 0850

Secretary

Sarah Leigh
c/o Margaret Dangoor
3 Clydesdale Gardens
Richmond
Surrey TW10 5EG
Telephone: (020) 8408 1012

Pre-action protocol for personal injury claims

Contents

1 Introduction

1.1   Lord Woolf in his final Access to Justice Report of July 1996 recommended the development of pre-action protocols:

> To build on and increase the benefits of early but well informed settlement which genuinely satisfy both parties to dispute.

1.2   The aims of pre-action protocols are:

- more pre-action contact between the parties
- better and earlier exchange of information
- better pre-action investigation by both sides
- to put the parties in a position where they may be able to settle cases fairly and early without litigation
- to enable proceedings to run to the court's timetable and efficiently, if litigation does become necessary
- to promote the provision of medical or rehabilitation treatment (not just in high value cases) to address the needs of the claimant

1.3   The concept of protocols is relevant to a range of initiatives for good litigation and pre-litigation practice, especially:

- predictability in the time needed for steps pre-proceedings
- standardisation of relevant information, including documents to be disclosed.

1.4   The Courts will be able to treat the standards set in protocols as the normal reasonable approach to pre-action conduct. If proceedings are issued, it will be for the court to decide whether non-compliance with a protocol should merit adverse consequences. Guidance on the court's likely approach will be given from time to time in practice directions.

1.5   If the court has to consider the question of compliance after proceedings have begun, it will not be concerned with minor infringements, e.g. failure by a short period to provide relevant information. One minor breach will not exempt the 'innocent' party from following the protocol. The court will look at the effect of non-compliance on the other party when deciding whether to impose sanctions.

2 Notes of Guidance

2.1   The protocol has been kept deliberately simple to promote ease of use and general acceptability. The notes of guidance which follows relate particularly to issues which arose during the piloting of the protocol.

Scope of the protocol

2.2   This protocol is intended to apply to all claims which include a claim for personal injury (except those claims covered by the Clinical Disputes and Disease and Illness Protocols) and to the entirety of those claims: not only to the personal injury element of a claim which also includes, for instance, property damage.

2.3   This protocol is primarily designed for those road traffic, tripping and slipping and accident at work cases which include an element of personal injury with a value of less than £15,000 which are likely to be allocated to the fast track. This is because time will be of the essence, after proceedings are issued, especially for the defendant, if a case is to be ready for trial within 30 weeks of allocation. Also, proportionality of work and costs to the value of what is in dispute is particularly important in lower value claims. For some claims within the value 'scope' of the fast track some flexibility in the timescale of the protocol may be necessary, see also paragraph 3.8.

2.4   However, the 'cards on the table' approach advocated by the protocol is equally appropriate to higher value claims. The spirit, if not the letter of the protocol, should still be followed for multi-track type claims. In accordance with the sense of the civil justice reforms, the court will expect to see the spirit of reasonable pre-action behaviour applied in all cases, regardless of the existence of a specific protocol. In particular with regard to personal injury cases worth more than £15,000, with a view to avoiding the necessity of proceedings parties are expected to comply with the protocol as far as possible e.g. in respect of letters before action, exchanging information and documents and agreeing experts.

2.5   The timetable and the arrangements for disclosing documents and obtaining expert evidence may need to be varied to suit the circumstances of the case. Where one or both parties consider the detail of the protocol is not appropriate to the case, and proceedings are subsequently issued, the court will expect an explanation as to why the protocol has not been followed, or has been varied.

Early notification

2.6   The claimant's legal representative may wish to notify the defendant and/or his insurer as soon as they know a claim is likely to be made, but before they are able to send a detailed letter of claim, particularly for instance, when the defendant has no or limited knowledge of the incident giving rise to the claim or where the claimant is incurring significant expenditure as a result of the accident which he hopes the defendant might pay for, in whole or in part. If the claimant's representative chooses to do this, it will not start the timetable for responding.

The letter of claim

2.7   The specimen letter of claim at Annex A will usually be sent to the individual defendant. In practice, he/she may have no personal financial interest in the financial outcome of the claim/dispute because he/she is insured. Court imposed sanctions for non-compliance with the protocol may be ineffective against an insured. This is why the protocol emphasises the importance of passing the letter of claim to the insurer and the possibility that the insurance cover might be affected. If an insurer receives the letter of claim only after some delay by the insured, it would not be unreasonable for the insurer to ask the claimant for additional time to respond.

2.8   In road traffic cases, the letter of claim should always contain the name and address of the hospital where the claimant was treated and, where available, the claimant's hospital reference number.

2.9   The priority at letter of claim stage is for the claimant to provide sufficient information for the defendant to assess liability. Sufficient information should also be provided to enable the defendant to estimate the likely size of the claim.

2.10   Once the claimant has sent the letter of claim no further investigation on liability should normally be carried out until a response is received from the defendant indicating whether liability is disputed.

Reasons for early issue

2.11   The protocol recommends that a defendant be given three months to investigate and respond to a claim before proceedings are issued. This may not always be possible, particularly where a claimant only consults a solicitor close to the end of any relevant limitation period. In these circumstances, the claimant's solicitor should give as much notice of the intention to issue proceedings as is practicable and the parties should consider whether the court might be invited to extend time for service of the claimant's supporting documents and for service of any defence, or alternatively, to stay the proceedings while the recommended steps in the protocol are followed.

Status of letters of claim and response

2.12   Letters of claim and response are not intended to have the same status as a statement of case in proceedings. Matters may come to light as a result of investigation after the letter of claim has been sent, or after the defendant has responded, particularly if disclosure of documents takes place outside the recommended three-month period. These circumstances could mean that the 'pleaded' case of one or both parties is presented slightly differently than in the letter of claim and response. It would not be consistent with the spirit of the protocol for a party to 'take a point' on this in the proceedings, provided that there was no obvious intention by the party who changed their position to mislead the other party.

Disclosure of documents

2.13   The aim of the early disclosure of documents by the defendant is not to encourage 'fishing expeditions' by the claimant, but to promote an early exchange of relevant information to help in clarifying or resolving issues in dispute. The claimant's solicitor can assist by identifying in the letter of claim or in a subsequent letter the particular categories of documents which they consider are relevant.

Experts

2.14   The protocol encourages joint selection of, and access to, experts. The report produced is not a joint report for the purposes of CPR Part 35. Most frequently this will apply to the medical expert, but on occasions also to liability experts, e.g. engineers. The protocol promotes the practice of the claimant obtaining a medical report, disclosing it to the defendant who then asks questions and/or agrees it and does not obtain his own report. The Protocol provides for nomination of the expert by the claimant in personal injury claims because of the early stage of the proceedings and the particular nature of such claims. If proceedings have to be issued, a medical report must be attached to these proceedings. However, if necessary after proceedings have commenced and with the permission of the court, the parties may obtain further expert reports. It would be for the court to decide whether the costs of more than one expert's report should be recoverable.

2.15 Some solicitors choose to obtain medical reports through medical agencies, rather than directly from a specific doctor or hospital. The defendant's prior consent to the action should be sought and, if the defendant so requests, the agency should be asked to provide in advance the names of the doctor(s) whom they are considering instructing.

Negotiations/settlement

2.16 Parties and their legal representatives are encouraged to enter into discussions and/or negotiations prior to starting proceedings. The protocol does not specify when or how this might be done but parties should bear in mind that the courts increasingly take the view that litigation should be a last resort, and that claims should not be issued prematurely when a settlement is in reasonable prospect.

Stocktake

2.17 Where a claim is not resolved when the protocol has been followed, the parties might wish to carry out a 'stocktake' of the issues in dispute, and the evidence that the court is likely to need to decide those issues, before proceedings are started. Where the defendant is insured and the pre-action steps have been conducted by the insurer, the insurer would normally be expected to nominate solicitors to act in the proceedings and the claimant's solicitor is recommended to invite the insurer to nominate solicitors to act in the proceedings and do so 7–14 days before the intended issue date.

3 The protocol

Letter of claim

3.1 The claimant shall send to the proposed defendant two copies of a letter of claim, immediately sufficient information is available to substantiate a realistic claim and before issues of quantum are addressed in detail. One copy of the letter is for the defendant, the second for passing on to his insurers.

3.2 The letter shall contain **a clear summary of the facts** on which the claim is based together with an indication of the **nature of any injuries** suffered and of **any financial loss incurred**. In cases of road traffic accidents, the letter should provide the name and address of the hospital where treatment has been obtained and the claimant's hospital reference number. Where the case is funded by a conditional fee agreement (or collective conditional fee agreement), notification should be given of the existence of the agreement and where appropriate, that there is a success fee and/or insurance premium, although not the level of the success fee or premium.

3.3 Solicitors are recommended to use a **standard format** for such a letter – an example is at Annex A: this can be amended to suit the particular case.

3.4 The letter should ask for **details of the insurer** and that a copy should be sent by the proposed defendant to the insurer where appropriate. If the insurer is known, a copy shall be sent directly to the insurer. Details of the claimant's National Insurance number and date of birth should be supplied to the defendant's insurer once the defendant has responded to the letter of claim and confirmed the identity of the insurer. This information should not be supplied in the letter of claim.

3.5 **Sufficient information** should be given in order to enable the defendant's insurer/solicitor to commence investigations and at least put a broad valuation on the 'risk'.

3.6 The **defendant should reply within 21 calendar days** of the date of posting of the letter identifying the insurer (if any) and, if necessary, identifying specifically any significant omissions from the letter of claim. If there has been no reply by the defendant or insurer within 21 days, the claimant will be entitled to issue proceedings.

3.7 The **defendant**('s insurers) will have a **maximum of three months** from the date of acknowledgment of the claim **to investigate**. No later than the end of that period the defendant (insurer) shall reply, stating whether liability is denied and, if so, giving reasons for their denial of liability including any alternative version of events relied upon.

3.8 Where the accident occurred outside England and Wales and/or where the defendant is outside the jurisdiction, the time periods of 21 days and three months should normally be extended up to 42 days and six months.

3.9 Where **liability is admitted**, the presumption is that the defendant will be bound by this admission for all claims with a total value of up to £15,000. Where the claimant's investigation indicates that the value of the claim has increased to more than £15,000 since the letter of claim, the claimant should notify the defendant as soon as possible.

Documents

3.10 If the **defendant denies liability**, he should enclose with the letter of reply, **documents** in his possession which are **material to the issues** between the parties, and which would be likely to be ordered to be disclosed by the court, either on an application for pre-action disclosure, or on disclosure during proceedings.

3.11 Attached at Annex B are **specimen**, but non-exhaustive, **lists** of documents likely to be material in different types of claim. Where the claimant's investigation of the case is well advanced, the letter of claim could indicate which classes of documents are considered relevant for early disclosure. Alternatively these could be identified at a later stage.

3.12 Where the defendant admits primary liability, but alleges contributory negligence by the claimant, the defendant should give reasons supporting those allegations and disclose those documents from Annex B which are relevant to the issues in dispute. The claimant should respond to the allegations of contributory negligence before proceedings are issued.

3.13 No charge will be made for providing copy documents under the Protocol.

Special damages

3.14 The claimant will send to the defendant as soon as practicable a Schedule of Special Damages with supporting documents, particularly where the defendant has admitted liability.

Experts

3.15 Before any party instructs an expert he should give the other party a list of the **name**(s) of **one or more experts** in the relevant speciality whom he considers are suitable to instruct.

3.16 Where a medical expert is to be instructed the claimant's solicitor will organise access to relevant medical records – see specimen letter of instruction at Annex C.

3.17 **Within 14 days** the other party may indicate **an objection** to one or more of the named experts. The first party should then instruct a mutually acceptable expert (which is not the same as a joint expert). It must be emphasised that if the Claimant nominates an expert in the original letter of claim, the defendant has 14 days to object to one or more of the named experts after expiration of the period of 21 days within which he has to reply to the letter of claim, as set out in paragraph 3.6.

3.18 If the second party objects to all the listed experts, the parties may then instruct **experts of their own choice**. It would be for the court to decide subsequently, if proceedings are issued, whether either party had acted unreasonably.

3.19 If the **second party does not object to an expert nominated**, he shall not be entitled to rely on his own expert evidence within that particular speciality unless:

(a) the first party agrees,

(b) the court so directs, or

(c) the first party's expert report has been amended and the first party is not prepared to disclose the original report.

3.20 **Either party may send to an agreed expert written questions** on the report, relevant to the issues, via the first party's solicitors. The expert should send answers to the questions separately and directly to each party.

3.21 The cost of a report from an agreed expert will usually be paid by the instructing first party: the costs of the expert replying to questions will usually be borne by the party which asks the questions.

4 Rehabilitation

4.1 The claimant or the defendant or both shall consider as early as possible whether the claimant has reasonable needs that could be met by rehabilitation treatment or other measures.

4.2 The parties shall consider, in such cases, how those needs might be addressed. The Rehabilitation Code (which is attached at Annex D) may be helpful in considering how to identify the claimant's needs and how to address the cost of providing for those needs.

4.3 The time limit set out in paragraph 3.7 of this Protocol shall not be shortened, except by consent to allow these issues to be addressed.

4.4 The provision of any report obtained for the purposes of assessment of provision of a party's rehabilitation needs shall not be used in any litigation arising out of the accident, the subject of the claim, save by consent and shall in any event be exempt from the provisions of paragraphs 3.15 to 3.21 inclusive of this protocol.

5 Resolution of issues

5.1 Where the defendant admits liability in whole or in part, before proceedings are issued, any medical reports obtained under this protocol on which a party relies should be disclosed to the other party. The claimant should delay issuing proceedings for 21 days from disclosure of the report (unless such delay would cause his claim to become time-barred), to enable the parties to consider whether the claim is capable of settlement.

5.2   The Civil Procedure Rules Part 36 permit claimants and defendants to make offers to settle pre-proceedings. Parties should always consider before issuing if it is appropriate to make Part 36 Offer. If such an offer is made, the party making the offer must always supply sufficient evidence and/or information to enable the offer to be properly considered.

5.3   Where the defendant has admitted liability, the claimant should send to the defendant schedules of special damages and loss at least 21 days before proceedings are issued (unless that would cause the claimant's claim to become time-barred).

ANNEX A

Letter of claim

To

Defendant

Dear Sirs

Re: **Claimant's full name**
     Claimant's full address
     Claimant's Clock or Works Number
     Claimant's Employer (name and address)

We are instructed by the above named to claim damages in connection with an *accident at work/road traffic accident/tripping accident* on   day of   *(year)* at *(place of accident which must be sufficiently detailed to establish location)*

Please confirm the identity of your insurers. Please note that the insurers will need to see this letter as soon as possible and it may affect your insurance cover and/or the conduct of any subsequent legal proceedings if you do not send this letter to them.

The circumstances of the accident are:
(brief outline)

The reason why we are alleging fault is:
(simple explanation e.g. defective machine, broken ground)

A description of our clients' injuries is as follows:
(brief outline)

(In cases of road traffic accidents)

Our client (state hospital reference number) received treatment for the injuries at name and address of hospital).

Our client is still suffering from the effects of his/her injury. We invite you to participate with us in addressing his/her immediate needs by use of rehabilitation.

He is employed as *(occupation)* and has had the following time off work *(dates of absence)*. His approximate weekly income is (insert if known).

If you are our client's employers, please provide us with the usual earnings details which will enable us to calculate his financial loss.

We are obtaining a police report and will let you have a copy of the same upon your undertaking to meet half the fee.

We have also sent a letter of claim to *(name and address)* and a copy of that letter is attached. We understand their insurers are *(name, address and claims number if known)*.

At this stage of our enquiries we would expect the documents contained in parts *(insert appropriate parts of standard disclosure list)* to be relevant to this action.

Please note that we have entered into a conditional fee agreement with our client dated   in relation to this claim which provides for a success fee within the meaning of section 58(2) of the Courts and Legal Services Act 1990. Our client has taken out an insurance policy with [name of insurance company] of [address of insurance company] to which section 29 of the Access Justice Act 1999 applies. The policy number is   and the policy is dated   . Where the funding arrangement is an insurance policy, the party must state the name and address of the insurer, the policy number and the date of the policy, and must identify the claim or claims to which it relates (including Part 20 claims if any).

A copy of this letter is attached for you to send to your insurers. Finally we expect an acknowledgment of this letter within 21 days by yourselves or your insurers.

Yours faithfully

ANNEX B

Pre-action personal injury protocol standard disclosure lists

Fast track disclosure

RTA Cases

Section A

In all cases where liability is at issue—

(i)   Documents identifying nature, extent and location of damage to defendant's vehicle where there is any dispute about point of impact.

(ii)   MOT certificate where relevant.

(iii)   Maintenance records where vehicle defect is alleged or it is alleged by defendant that there was an unforeseen defect which caused or contributed to the accident.

Section B

Accident involving commercial vehicle as defendant—

(i)   Tachograph charts or entry from individual control book.

(ii)   Maintenance and repair records required for operators' licence where vehicle defect is alleged or it is alleged by defendant that there was an unforeseen defect which caused or contributed to the accident.

Section C

Cases against local authorities where highway design defect is alleged.

(i)   Documents produced to comply with Section 39 of the Road Traffic Act 1988 in respect of the duty designed to promote road safety to include studies into road accidents in the relevant area and documents relating to measures recommended to prevent accidents in the relevant area.

Highway tripping claims

Documents from Highway Authority for a period of 12 months prior to the accident—

(i)   Records of inspection for the relevant stretch of highway.

(ii)   Maintenance records including records of independent contractors working in relevant area.

(iii)   Records of the minutes of Highway Authority meetings where maintenance or repair policy has been discussed or decided.

(iv)   Records of complaints about the state of highways.

(v)   Records of other accidents which have occurred on the relevant stretch of highway.

Workplace claims

(i)   Accident book entry.

(ii)   First aider report.

(iii)   Surgery record.

(iv)   Foreman/supervisor accident report.

(v)   Safety representatives accident report.

(vi)   RIDDOR (Reporting of Injuries, Diseases and Dangerous Occurrences Regulations) report to HSE.

(vii) Other communications between defendants and HSE.

(viii) Minutes of Health and Safety Committee meeting(s) where accident/matter considered.

(ix)   Report to DSS.

(x)   Documents listed above relative to any previous accident/matter identified by the claimant and relied upon as proof of negligence.

(xi)   Earnings information where defendant is employer.

Documents produced to comply with requirements of the Management of Health and Safety at Work Regulations 1992—

(i)   Pre-accident Risk Assessment required by Regulation 3.

(ii)   Post-accident Re-Assessment required by Regulation 3.

(iii)   Accident Investigation Report prepared in implementing the requirements of Regulations 4, 6 and 9.

(iv)   Health Surveillance Records in appropriate cases required by Regulation 5.

(v)   Information provided to employees under Regulation 8.

(vi)   Documents relating to the employees health and safety training required by Regulation 11.

Workplace claims – disclosure where specific regulations apply

Section A – Workplace (Health Safety and Welfare) Regulations 1992

(i)   Repair and maintenance records required by Regulation 5.

(ii)   Housekeeping records to comply with the requirements of Regulation 9.

(iii)   Hazard warning signs or notices to comply with Regulation 17 (Traffic Routes).

Section B – Provision and Use of Work Equipment Regulations 1998

(i)   Manufacturers' specifications and instructions in respect of relevant work equipment establishing its suitability to comply with Regulation 5.

(ii)   Maintenance log/maintenance records required to comply with Regulation 6.

(iii) Documents providing information and instructions to employees to comply with Regulation 8.

(iv)   Documents provided to the employee in respect of training for use to comply with Regulation 9.

(v)   Any notice, sign or document relied upon as a defence to alleged breaches of Regulations 14 to 18 dealing with controls and control systems.

(vi)   Instruction/training documents issued to comply with the requirements of regulation 22 insofar as it deals with maintenance operations where the machinery is not shut down.

(vii) Copies of markings required to comply with Regulation 23.

(viii) Copies of warnings required to comply with Regulation 24.

Section C – Personal Protective Equipment at Work Regulations 1992

(i)   Documents relating to the assessment of the Personal Protective Equipment to comply with Regulation 6.

(ii)   Documents relating to the maintenance and replacement of Personal Protective Equipment to comply with Regulation 7.

(iii) Record of maintenance procedures for Personal Protective Equipment to comply with Regulation 7.

(iv)   Records of tests and examinations of Personal Protective Equipment to comply with Regulation 7.

(v)   Documents providing information, instruction and training in relation to the Personal Protective Equipment to comply with Regulation 9.

(vi)   Instructions for use of Personal Protective Equipment to include the manufacturers' instructions to comply with Regulation 10.

Section D – Manual Handling Operations Regulations 1992

(i)   Manual Handling Risk Assessment carried out to comply with the requirements of Regulation 4(1)(b)(i).

(ii)   Re-assessment carried out post-accident to comply with requirements of Regulation 4(1)(b)(i).

(iii) Documents showing the information provided to the employee to give general indications related to the load and precise indications on the weight of the load and the heaviest side of the load if the centre of gravity was not positioned centrally to comply with Regulation 4(1)(b)(iii).

(iv)   Documents relating to training in respect of manual handling operations and training records.

Section E – Health and Safety (Display Screen Equipment) Regulations 1992

(i)   Analysis of work stations to assess and reduce risks carried out to comply with the requirements of Regulation 2.

(ii)   Re-assessment of analysis of work stations to assess and reduce risks following development of symptoms by the claimant.

(iii) Documents detailing the provision of training including training records to comply with the requirements of Regulation 6.

(iv)   Documents providing information to employees to comply with the requirements of Regulation 7.

Section F – Control of Substances Hazardous to Health Regulations 1999

(i)   Risk assessment carried out to comply with the requirements of Regulation 6.

(ii)   Reviewed risk assessment carried out to comply with the requirements of Regulation 6.

(iii)   Copy labels from containers used for storage handling and disposal of carcinogenics to comply with the requirements of Regulation 7(2A)(h).

(iv)   Warning signs identifying designation of areas and installations which may be contaminated by carcinogenics to comply with the requirements of Regulation 7(2A)(h).

(v)   Documents relating to the assessment of the Personal Protective Equipment to comply with Regulation 7(3A).

(vi)   Documents relating to the maintenance and replacement of Personal Protective Equipment to comply with Regulation 7(3A).

(vii) Record of maintenance procedures for Personal Protective Equipment to comply with Regulation 7(3A).

(viii) Records of tests and examinations of Personal Protective Equipment to comply with Regulation 7(3A).

(ix)   Documents providing information, instruction and training in relation to the Personal Protective Equipment to comply with Regulation 7(3A).

(x)   Instructions for use of Personal Protective Equipment to include the manufacturers' instructions to comply with Regulation 7(3A).

(xi)   Air monitoring records for substances assigned a maximum exposure limit or occupational exposure standard to comply with the requirements of Regulation 7.

(xii) Maintenance examination and test of control measures records to comply with Regulation 9.

(xiii) Monitoring records to comply with the requirements of Regulation 10.

(xiv) Health surveillance records to comply with the requirements of Regulation 11.

(xv)   Documents detailing information, instruction and training including training records for employees to comply with the requirements of Regulation 12.

(xvi) Labels and Health and Safety data sheets supplied to the employers to comply with the CHIP Regulations.

Section G – Construction (Design and Management) (Amendment) Regulations 2000

(i)   Notification of a project form (HSE F10) to comply with the requirements of Regulation 7.

(ii)   Health and Safety Plan to comply with requirements of Regulation 15.

(iii) Health and Safety file to comply with the requirements of Regulations 12 and 14.

(iv)   Information and training records provided to comply with the requirements of Regulation 17.

(v)   Records of advice from and views of persons at work to comply with the requirements of Regulation 18.

Section H – Pressure Systems and Transportable Gas Containers Regulations 1989

(i)   Information and specimen markings provided to comply with the requirements of Regulation 5.

(ii)   Written statements specifying the safe operating limits of a system to comply with the requirements of Regulation 7.

(iii)   Copy of the written scheme of examination required to comply with the requirements of Regulation 8.

(iv)   Examination records required to comply with the requirements of Regulation 9.

(v)   Instructions provided for the use of operator to comply with Regulation 11.

(vi)   Records kept to comply with the requirements of Regulation 13.

(vii)   Records kept to comply with the requirements of Regulation 22.

Section I – Lifting Operations and Lifting Equipment Regulations 1998

(i)   Record kept to comply with the requirements of Regulation 6.

Section J – The Noise at Work Regulations 1989

(i)   Any risk assessment records required to comply with the requirements of Regulations 4 and 5.

(ii)   Manufacturers' literature in respect of all ear protection made available to claimant to comply with the requirements of Regulation 8.

(iii)   All documents provided to the employee for the provision of information to comply with Regulation 11.

Section K – Construction (Head Protection) Regulations 1989

(i)   Pre-accident assessment of head protection required to comply with Regulation 3(4).

(ii)   Post-accident re-assessment required to comply with Regulation 3(5).

Section L – The Construction (General Provisions) Regulations 1961

(i)   Report prepared following inspections and examinations of excavations etc. to comply with the requirements of Regulation 9.

Section M – Gas Containers Regulations 1989

(i)   Information and specimen markings provided to comply with the requirements of Regulation 5.

(ii)   Written statements specifying the safe operating limits of a system to comply with the requirements of Regulation 7.

(iii)   Copy of the written scheme of examination required to comply with the requirements of Regulation 8.

(iv)   Examination records required to comply with the requirements of Regulation 9.

(v)   Instructions provided for the use of operator to comply with Regulation 11.

Annex C

Letter of Instruction to Medical Expert

Dear Sir,

Re: *(Name and Address)*

D.O.B. –

Telephone No. –

Date of Accident –

We are acting for the above named in connection with injuries received in an accident which occurred on the above date. The main injuries appear to have been *(main injuries)*.

We should be obliged if you would examine our Client and let us have a full and detailed report dealing with any relevant pre-accident medical history, the injuries sustained, treatment received and present condition, dealing in particular with the capacity for work and giving a prognosis.

It is central to our assessment of the extent of our Client's injuries to establish the extent and duration of any continuing disability. Accordingly, in the prognosis section we would ask you to specifically comment on any areas of continuing complaint or disability or impact on daily living. If there is such continuing disability you should comment upon the level of suffering or inconvenience caused and, if you are able, give your view as to when or if the complaint or disability is likely to resolve.

Please send our Client an appointment direct for this purpose. Should you be able to offer a cancellation appointment please contact our Client direct. We confirm we will be responsible for your reasonable fees.

We are obtaining the notes and records from our Client's GP and Hospitals attended and will forward them to you when they are to hand/or please request the GP and Hospital records direct and advise that any invoice for the provision of these records should be forwarded to us.

In order to comply with Court Rules we would be grateful if you would insert above your signature a statement that the contents are true to the best of your knowledge and belief.

In order to avoid further correspondence we can confirm that on the evidence we have there is no reason to suspect we may be pursuing a claim against the hospital or its staff.

We look forward to receiving your report within _____ weeks. If you will not be able to prepare your report within this period please telephone us upon receipt of these instructions.

When acknowledging these instructions it would assist if you could give an estimate as to the likely time scale for the provision of your report and also an indication as to your fee.

Yours faithfully

Annex D

The Rehabilitation Code

(Code of Best Practice on Rehabilitation, Early Intervention and Medical Treatment in Personal Injury Claims)

The main aim of this Code, first introduced in 1999, is to promote the use of rehabilitation and early intervention in the claims process so that the injured person makes the best and quickest possible medical, social and psychological recovery. This objective applies whatever the severity of the injury sustained by the claimant. The Code provides a framework supported by all the main associations for insurers and personal injury lawyers in the UK, but is neither compulsory nor the only way to approach rehabilitation. The objectives of the Rehabilitation Code will be met whenever the parties co-operate to assess and then provide for the claimant's rehabilitation needs.

1. Introduction

1.1   It is recognised that, in many claims for damages for personal injuries, the claimant's current medical situation, and/or the long-term prognosis, may be improved by appropriate medical treatment, including surgery, being given at the earliest practicable opportunity, rather than waiting until the claim has been settled. Similarly, claims may involve a need for non-medical treatment, such as physiotherapy, counselling, occupational therapy, speech therapy and so forth ('rehabilitation'): again, there is a benefit in these services being provided as early as practicable.

1.2   It is also recognised that (predominantly in cases of serious injury) the claimant's quality of life can be immediately improved by undertaking some basic home adaptations and/or by the provision of aids and equipment and/ or appropriate medical treatment as soon as these are needed ('early intervention'), rather than when the claim is finally settled.

1.3   It is further recognised that, where these medical or other issues have been dealt with, there may be employment issues that can be addressed for the benefit of the claimant, to enable the claimant to keep his/her existing job, to obtain alternative suitable employment with the same employer or to retrain for new employment. Again, if these needs are addressed at the proper time, the claimant's quality of life and long-term prospects may be greatly improved.

1.4   Solicitors acting for claimants understand that, taking all these matters into account, they can achieve more for the claimant – by making rehabilitation available – than just the payment of compensation. The insurance industry realises that great benefit may be had in considering making funds available for these purposes.

1.5   The aim of this Rehabilitation Code is therefore to ensure that the claimant's solicitor and the insurer (and the insurer's solicitor or handling agent) both actively consider the use of rehabilitation services and the benefits of an early assessment of the claimant's needs. The further aim is that both should treat the possibility of improving the claimant's quality of life and their present and long-term physical and mental well-being as issues equally as important as the payment of just, full and proper compensation.

1.6   The report mentioned in section 6 of the Code focuses on the early assessment of the claimant's needs in terms of treatment and/or rehabilitation. The assessment report is not intended to determine the claimant's long-term needs for care or medical treatment, other than by way of general indication and comment.

2. The Claimant's Solicitor's Duty

2.1   It shall be the duty of every claimant's solicitor to consider, from the earliest practicable stage, and in consultation with the claimant and/or the claimant's family, whether it is likely or possible that early intervention, rehabilitation or medical treatment would improve their present and/or long-term physical or mental well-being. This duty is ongoing throughout the life of the case but is of most importance in the early stages.

2.2   It shall be the duty of a claimant's solicitor to consider, with the claimant and/or the claimant's family, whether there is an immediate need for aids, adaptations or other matters that would seek to alleviate problems caused by disability, and then to communicate with the insurer as soon as practicable about any rehabilitation needs, with a view to putting this Code into effect.

2.3   It shall not be the responsibility of the solicitor to decide on the need for treatment or rehabilitation or to arrange such matters without appropriate medical consultation. Such medical consultation should involve the claimant and/or the claimant's family, the claimant's primary care physician and, where appropriate, any other medical practitioner currently treating the claimant.

2.4   Nothing in this Code shall in any way affect the obligations placed on a claimant's solicitor by the Pre-Action Protocol for Personal Injury Claims ('the Protocol'). However, it must be appreciated that very early communication with the insurer will enable the matters dealt with here to be addressed more effectively.

2.5   It must be recognised that the insurer will need to receive from the claimant's solicitor sufficient information for the insurer to make a proper decision about the need for intervention, rehabilitation or treatment. To this extent, the claimant's solicitor must comply with the requirements of the Protocol to provide the insurer with full and adequate details of the injuries sustained by the claimant, the nature and extent of any, or any likely, continuing disability and any suggestions that may already have been made concerning rehabilitation and/or early intervention. There is no requirement under the Protocol, or this Code, for the claimant's solicitor to have obtained a full medical report. It is recognised that many cases will be identified for consideration under this Code before medical evidence has actually been commissioned.

The Insurer

3.1   It shall be the duty of the insurer to consider, from the earliest practicable stage in any appropriate case, whether it is likely that the claimant will benefit in the immediate, medium or longer term from further medical treatment, rehabilitation or early intervention. This duty is ongoing throughout the life of the case but is of most importance in the early stages.

3.2   If the insurer considers that a particular claim might be suitable for intervention, rehabilitation or treatment, the insurer will communicate this to the claimant's solicitor as soon as practicable.

3.3   On receipt of such communication, the claimant's solicitor will immediately discuss these issues with the claimant and/or the claimant's family pursuant to his duty as set out above and, where appropriate, will seek advice from the claimant's treating physicians/surgeons.

3.4   Nothing in this or any other Code of Practice shall in any way modify the obligations of the insurer under the Protocol to investigate claims rapidly and in any event within three months (except where time is extended by the claimant's solicitor) from the date of the formal claim letter. It is recognised that, although the rehabilitation assessment can be done even where liability investigations are outstanding, it is essential that such investigations proceed with the appropriate speed.

4. Assessment

4.1   Unless the need for intervention, rehabilitation or treatment has already been identified by medical reports obtained and disclosed by either side, the need for and extent of such intervention, rehabilitation or treatment will be considered by means of an independent assessment.

4.2   'Independent assessment' in this context means that the assessment will be carried out by either:

a.   One or more of the treating physicians/surgeons, or

b.   By an agency suitably qualified and/or experienced in such matters, which is financially and managerially independent of the claimant's solicitor's firm and the insurers dealing with the claim.

4.3   It is essential that the process of assessment and recommendation be carried out by those who have an appropriate qualification (to include physiotherapists, occupational therapists, psychologists, psychotherapists and so forth). It would be inappropriate for assessments to be done by someone who does not have a medical or other appropriate qualification. Those doing the assessments should not only have an appropriate qualification but should have experience in treating the type of disability from which the individual claimant suffers.

5. The Assessment Process

5.1   Where possible, the agency to be instructed to provide the assessment should be agreed between the claimant's solicitor and the insurer. The instruction letter will be sent by the claimant's solicitor to the medical agency and a copy of the instruction letter will be sent to the insurer.

5.2   The medical agency will be asked to interview the claimant at home (or in hospital, if the claimant is still in hospital, with a subsequent visit to the claimant's home) and will be asked to produce a report, which covers the following headings:

1.   The injuries sustained by the claimant

2.   The claimant's present medical condition (medical conditions that do not arise from the accident should also be noted where relevant to the overall picture of the claimant's needs)

3.   The claimant's domestic circumstances (including mobility, accommodation and employment), where relevant

4.   The injuries/disability in respect of which early intervention or early rehabilitation is suggested

5.   The type of intervention or treatment envisaged

6.   The likely cost

7.   The likely short/medium-term benefit to the claimant

5.3   The report will not deal with diagnostic criteria, causation issues or long-term care requirements.

6. The Assessment Report

6.1 The reporting agency will, on completion of the report, send copies to both the instructing solicitor and the insurer simultaneously. Both parties will have the right to raise queries on the report, disclosing such correspondence to the other party.

6.2 It is recognised that for this independent assessment report to be of benefit to the parties, it should be prepared and used wholly outside the litigation process. Neither side can therefore rely on its contents in any subsequent litigation. With that strict proviso, to be confirmed in writing by the individual solicitor and insurer if required, the report shall be disclosed to both parties.

6.3 The report, any correspondence relating to it and any notes created by the assessing agency will be covered by legal privilege and will not under any circumstances be disclosed in any legal proceedings. Any notes or documents created in connection with the assessment process will not be disclosed in any litigation, and any person involved in the preparation of the report or involved in the assessment process shall not be a compellable witness at court.

6.4 The provision in paragraph 6.3 above as to treating the report, etc. as outside the litigation process is limited to the assessment report and any notes relating to it. Once the parties have agreed, following an assessment report, that a particular regime of rehabilitation or treatment should be put in place, the case management of that regime falls outside this Code and paragraph 6.3 does not therefore apply. Any notes and reports created during the subsequent case management will be governed by the usual principles relating to disclosure of documents and medical records relating to the claimant.

6.5 The insurer will pay for the report within 28 days of receipt.

6.6 The need for any further or subsequent assessment shall be agreed between the claimant's solicitor and the insurer. The provisions of this Code shall apply to such assessments.

7. Recommendations

7.1 When the assessment report is disclosed to the insurer, the insurer will be under a duty to consider the recommendations made and the extent to which funds will be made available to implement all or some of the recommendations. The insurer will not be required to pay for intervention or treatment that is unreasonable in nature, content or cost. The claimant will be under no obligation to undergo intervention, medical investigation or treatment that is unreasonable in all the circumstances of the case.

7.2 Any funds made available shall be treated as an interim payment on account of damages. However, if the funds are provided to enable specific intervention, rehabilitation or treatment to occur, the insurers warrant that they will not, in any legal proceedings connected with the claim, dispute the reasonableness of that treatment nor the agreed cost, provided of course that the claimant has had the recommended treatment.

Pre-action protocol for disease and illness claims

Contents

Annexes

1   Introduction

1.1   Lord Woolf in his final Access to Justice Report of July 1996 recommended the development of protocols: 'To build on and increase the benefits of early but well informed settlement which genuinely satisfy both parties to dispute.'

1.2   The aims of these protocols are:
- more contact between the parties
- better and earlier exchange of information
- better investigation by both sides
- to put the parties in a position where they may be able to settle cases fairly and early without litigation
- to enable proceedings to run to the court's timetable and efficiently, if litigation does become necessary.

1.3   The concept of protocols is relevant to a range of initiatives for good claims practice, especially:
- predictability in the time needed for steps to be taken
- standardisation of relevant information, including documents to be disclosed.

1.4   The Courts will be able to treat the standards set in protocols as the normal reasonable approach. If proceedings are issued, it will be for the court to decide whether non-compliance with a protocol should merit adverse consequences. Guidance on the court's likely approach will be given from time to time in practice directions.

1.5   If the court has to consider the question of compliance after proceedings have begun, it will not be concerned with minor infringements, eg, failure by a short period to provide relevant information. One minor breach will not exempt the 'innocent' party from following the protocol.

The court will look at the effect of non-compliance on the other party when deciding whether to impose sanctions.

2   NOTES OF GUIDANCE

Scope of the protocol

2.1   This protocol is intended to apply to all personal injury claims where the injury is not as the result of an accident but takes the form of an illness or disease.

2.2   This protocol covers disease claims which are likely to be complex and frequently not suitable for fast-track procedures even though they may fall within fast track limits. Disease for the purpose of this protocol primarily covers any illness physical or psychological, any disorder, ailment, affliction, complaint, malady, or derangement other than a physical or psychological injury solely caused by an accident or other similar single event.

2.3   This protocol is not limited to diseases occurring in the workplace but will embrace diseases occurring in other situations for example through occupation of premises or the use of products. It is not intended to cover those cases, which are dealt with as a 'group' or 'class' action.

2.4   The 'cards on the table' approach advocated by the personal injury protocol is equally appropriate to disease claims. The spirit of that protocol, and of the clinical negligence protocol is followed here, in accordance with the sense of the civil justice reforms.

2.5   The timetable and the arrangements for disclosing documents and obtaining expert evidence may need to be varied to suit the circumstances of the case. If a party considers the detail of the protocol to be inappropriate they should communicate their reasons to all of the parties at that stage. If proceedings are subsequently issued, the court will expect an explanation as to why the protocol has not been followed, or has been varied. In a terminal disease claim with short life expectancy, for instance for a claimant who has a disease such as mesothelioma, the time scale of the protocol is likely to be too long. In such a claim, the claimant may not be able to follow the protocol and the defendant would be expected to treat the claim with urgency.

3 THE AIMS OF THE PROTOCOL

3.1   The *general* aims of the protocol are –

- to resolve as many disputes as possible without litigation;
- where a claim cannot be resolved to identify the relevant issues which remain in dispute.

3.2   The specific objectives are –

Openness

- to encourage early communication of the perceived problem between the parties or their insurers;
- to encourage employees to voice any concerns or worries about possible work related illness as soon as practicable;
- to encourage employers to develop systems of early reporting and investigation of suspected occupational health problems and to provide full and prompt explanations to concerned employees or former employees;

- to apply such principles to perceived problems outside the employer/ employee relationship, for example occupiers of premises or land and producers of products;
- to ensure that sufficient information is disclosed by both parties to enable each to understand the other's perspective and case, and to encourage early resolution;

Timeliness

- to provide an early opportunity for employers (past or present) or their insurers to identify cases where an investigation is required and to carry out that investigation promptly;
- to encourage employers (past or present) or other defendants to involve and identify their insurers at an early stage;
- to ensure that all relevant records including health and personnel records are provided to employees (past or present) or their appointed representatives promptly on request, by any employer (past or present) or their insurers. This should be complied with to a realistic timetable;
- to ensure that relevant records which are in the claimant's possession are made available to the employers or their insurers by claimants or their advisers at an appropriate stage;
- to proceed on a reasonable timetable where a resolution is not achievable to lay the ground to enable litigation to proceed at a reasonable and proportionate cost, and to limit the matters in contention;
- to communicate promptly where any of the requested information is not available or does not exist;
- to discourage the prolonged pursuit of unmeritorious claims and the prolonged defence of meritorious claims.
- To encourage all parties, at the earliest possible stage, to disclose voluntarily any additional documents which will assist in resolving any issue.

4 THE PROTOCOL

This protocol is not a comprehensive code governing all the steps in disease claims. Rather it attempts to set out **a code of good practice** which parties should follow.

Obtaining occupational records including health records

4.1 In appropriate cases, a **potential claimant** may request Occupational Records including Health Records and Personnel Records before sending a Letter of Claim.

4.2 Any request for records by the **potential claimant** or his adviser should **provide sufficient information** to alert the **potential defendant** or his insurer where a possible disease claim is being investigated; Annex A1 provides a suggested form for this purpose for use in cases arising from employment. Similar forms can be prepared and used in other situations.

4.3 The copy records should be provided **within a maximum of 40 days** of the request at no cost. Although these will primarily be occupational records, it will be good practice for a **potential defendant** to disclose product data documents identified by a **potential claimant** at this stage which may resolve a causation issue.

4.4 In the rare circumstances that the **potential defendant** or his insurer is in difficulty in providing information quickly details should be given of what is being done to resolve it with a reasonable time estimate for doing so.

4.5 If the **potential defendant** or his insurer fails to provide the records including health records within 40 days and fails to comply with paragraph 4.4 above, the **potential claimant** or his adviser may then apply to the court for an **order for pre-action disclosure**. The Civil Procedure Rules make pre-action applications to the court easier. The court also has the power to impose costs sanctions for unreasonable delay in providing records.

5 COMMUNICATION

5.1 If either the **potential claimant** or his adviser considers **additional records are required from a third party**, such as records from previous employers or general practitioner records, in the first instance these should be requested by the **potential claimant** or their advisers. Third party record holders would be expected to co-operate. The Civil Procedure Rules enable parties to apply to the court for pre-action disclosure by third parties.

5.2 As soon as the records have been received and analysed, the **potential claimant** or his adviser should consider whether a claim should be made. General practitioner records will normally be obtained before a decision is reached.

5.3 If a decision is made not to proceed further at this stage against a party identified as a **potential defendant**, the **potential claimant** or his adviser should notify that **potential defendant** as soon as practicable.

6 LETTER OF CLAIM

6.1 Where a decision is made to make a claim, the claimant shall send to the proposed defendant two copies of a letter of claim, as soon as sufficient information is available to substantiate a realistic claim and before issues of quantum are addressed in detail. One copy is for the defendants, the second for passing on to his insurers.

6.2 This letter shall contain a **clear summary of the facts** on which the claim is based, including details of the illness alleged, and the **main allegations of fault**. It shall also give details of present condition and prognosis. The **financial loss** incurred by the claimant should be outlined. Where the case is funded by a conditional fee agreement, notification should be given of the existence of the agreement and where appropriate, that there is a success fee and insurance premium, although not the level of the success fee or premium.

6.3 Solicitors are recommended to use a **standard format** for such a letter – an example is at Annex B: this can be amended to suit the particular case, for example, if the client has rehabilitation needs these can also be detailed in the letter.

6.4 A **chronology** of the relevant events (e.g. dates or periods of exposure) should be provided. In the case of alleged occupational disease an appropriate employment history should also be provided, particularly if the claimant has been employed by a number of different employers and the illness in question has a long latency period.

6.5 The letter of claim should identify any **relevant documents**, including health records not already in the defendant's possession e.g. any relevant general practitioner records. These will need to be disclosed in confidence to the nominated insurance manager or solicitor representing the defendant following receipt of their letter of acknowledgement. Where the action is brought under the Law Reform Act 1934 or the Fatal Accidents Act 1976 then **relevant documents** will normally include copies of the death certificate, the post mortem report, the inquest depositions and if obtained by that date the grant of probate or letters of administration.

6.6   The letter of claim should indicate whether a claim is also being made against any **other potential defendant** and identify any known insurer involved.

6.7   Sufficient information should be given to enable the defendant's insurer/ solicitor to commence **investigations** and at least to put a broad valuation on the 'risk'.

6.8   It is not a requirement for the claimant to provide **medical evidence** with the letter of claim, but the claimant may choose to do so in very many cases.

6.9   **Letters of claim and response** are not intended to have the same **status** as a statement of case in proceedings. Matters may come to light as a result of investigation after the letter of claim has been sent, or after the defendant has responded, particularly if disclosure of documents takes place outside the recommended three-month period. These circumstances could mean that the 'pleaded' case of one or both parties is presented slightly differently than in the letter of claim or response. It would not be consistent with the spirit of the protocol for a party to 'take a point' on this in the proceedings, provided that there was no obvious intention by the party who changed their position to mislead the other party.

6.10   **Proceedings should not be issued until after three months from the date of acknowledgement** (see paragraph 7), unless there is a limitation problem and/or the claimant's position needs to be protected by early issue. (See paragraph 2.5)

7 THE RESPONSE

7.1   The defendant should **send an acknowledgement within 21 calendar days** of the date of posting of the letter of claim, identifying the liability insurer (if any) who will be dealing with the matter and, if necessary, identifying specifically any significant omissions from the Letter of Claim. If there has been no acknowledgement by the defendant or insurer within 21 days, the claimant will be entitled to issue proceedings.

7.2   The identity of all relevant insurers, if more than one, should be notified to the claimant by the insurer identified in the acknowledgement letter, within one calendar month of the date of that acknowledgement.

7.3   The defendant or his representative should, **within three months of the date of the acknowledgement letter**, provide a **reasoned answer**: –

- if the **claim is admitted**, they should say so in clear terms;
- if only **part of the claim is admitted** they should make clear which issues of fault and/or causation and/or limitation are admitted and which remain in issue and why;
- if the **claim is not admitted in full**, they should explain why and should, **for example**, include comments on the employment status of the claimant, (including job description(s) and details of the department(s) where the claimant worked), the allegations of fault, causation and of limitation, and if a synopsis or chronology of relevant events has been provided and is disputed, their version of those events;
- if the **claim is not admitted in full**, the defendant should enclose with his letter of reply **documents** in his possession which are **material to**

the issues between the parties and which would be likely to be ordered to be disclosed by the court, either on an application for pre-action disclosure, or on disclosure during proceedings. Reference can be made to the documents annexed to the personal injury protocol.

- where more than one defendant receives a letter of claim, the timetable will be activated for each defendant by the date on the letter of claim addressed to them. If any defendant wishes to extend the timetable because the number of defendants will cause complications, they should seek agreement to a different timetable as soon as possible.

7.4 If the parties reach agreement on liability and/or causation, but time is needed to resolve other issues including the value of the claim, they should aim to agree a reasonable period.

7.5 Where it is not practicable for the defendant to complete his investigations within 3 months, the defendant should indicate the difficulties and outline the further time needed. Any request for an extension of time should be made, with reasons, as soon as the defendant becomes aware that an extension is needed and normally before the 3 month period has expired. Such an extension of time should be agreed in circumstances where reasonable justification has been shown. Lapse of many years since the circumstances giving rise to the claim does not, by itself, constitute reasonable justification for further time.

7.6 Where the relevant negligence occurred outside England and Wales and/or where the defendant is outside the jurisdiction, the time periods of 21 days and three months should normally be extended up to 42 days and six months.

8 SPECIAL DAMAGES

8.1 The claimant will send to the defendant as soon as practicable a Schedule of Special Damages with supporting documents, particularly where the defendant has admitted liability.

9 EXPERTS

9.1 In disease claims expert opinions will usually be needed:
- on knowledge, fault and causation;
- on condition and prognosis;
- to assist in valuing aspects of the claim.

9.2 The civil justice reforms and the Civil Procedure Rules encourage economy in the use of experts and a less adversarial expert culture. It is recognised that in disease claims, the parties and their advisers will require flexibility in their approach to expert evidence. Decisions on whether experts might be instructed jointly, and on whether reports might be disclosed sequentially or by exchange, should rest with the parties and their advisers. Sharing expert evidence may be appropriate on various issues including those relating to the value of the claim. However, this protocol does not attempt to be prescriptive on issues in relation to expert evidence.

9.3 Obtaining expert evidence will often be an expensive step and may take time, especially in specialised areas where there are limited numbers of suitable experts. Claimants, defendants and their advisers, will therefore need to consider carefully how best to obtain any necessary expert help quickly and cost-effectively.

9.4 The protocol recognises that a flexible approach must be adopted in the obtaining of medical reports in claims of this type. There will be very many occasions where the claimant will need to obtain a medical report before writing the letter of claim. In such cases the defendant will be entitled to obtain their own medical report. In some other instances it may be more appropriate to send the letter of claim before the medical report is obtained. Defendants will usually need to see a medical report before they can reach a view on causation.

9.5   Where the parties agree the nomination of a single expert is appropriate, before any party instructs an expert he should give the other party a list of the **name**(s) of **one or more experts** in the relevant speciality whom he considers are suitable to instruct. The parties are encouraged to agree the instruction of a single expert to deal with discrete areas such as cost of care.

9.6   **Within 14 days** the other party may indicate **an objection** to one or more of the named experts. The first party should then instruct a mutually acceptable expert. If the Claimant nominates an expert in the original letter of claim, the 14 days is in addition to the 21 days in paragraph 7.1.

9.7   If the second party objects to all the listed experts, the parties may then instruct **experts of their own choice**. It would be for the court to decide subsequently, if proceedings are issued, whether either party had acted unreasonably.

9.8   If the **second party does not object to an expert nominated**, he shall not be entitled to rely on his own expert evidence within that particular speciality unless:

(a)   the first party agrees,

(b)   the court so directs, or

(c)   the first party's expert report has been amended and the first party is not prepared to disclose the original report.

9.9   **Either party may send to an agreed expert written questions** on the report, relevant to the issues, via the first party's solicitors. The expert should send answers to the questions separately and directly to each party.

9.10   The cost of a report from an agreed expert will usually be paid by the instructing first party: the costs of the expert replying to questions will usually be borne by the party which asks the questions.

9.11   Where the defendant admits liability in whole or in part, before proceedings are issued, any medical report obtained under this protocol which **the claimant** relies upon, should be disclosed to the other party.

9.12   Where the defendant admits liability in whole or in part before proceedings are issued, any medical report obtained under this protocol which **the defendant** relies upon, should be disclosed to the claimant.

10 RESOLUTION OF ISSUES

10.1   The Civil Procedure Rules Part 36 enable claimants and defendants to make formal offers to settle before proceedings are started. Parties should consider making such an offer, since to do so often leads to settlement. If such an offer is made, the party making the offer must always supply sufficient evidence and/or information to enable the offer to be properly considered.

10.2   Where a claim is not resolved when the protocol has been followed, the parties might wish to carry out a 'stocktake' of the issues in dispute, and the evidence that the court is likely to need to decide those issues, before proceedings are started.

10.3 Prior to proceedings it will be usual for all parties to disclose those expert reports relating to liability and causation upon which they propose to rely.

10.4 The claimant should delay issuing proceedings for 21 days from disclosure of reports to enable the parties to consider whether the claim is capable of settlement.

10.5 Where the defendant is insured and the pre-action steps have been conducted by the insurer, the insurer would normally be expected to nominate solicitors to act in the proceedings and the claimant's solicitor is recommended to invite the insurer to nominate solicitors to act in the proceedings and to do so 7–14 days before the intended issue date.

11 LIMITATION

11.1 If by reason of complying with any part of this protocol a claimant's claim may be time-barred under any provision of the Limitation Act 1980, or any other legislation which imposes a time limit for bringing an action, the claimant may commence proceedings without complying with this protocol. In such circumstances, a claimant who commences proceedings without complying with all, or any part, of this protocol may apply to the court on notice for directions as to the timetable and form of procedure to be adopted, at the same time as he requests the court to issue proceedings. The court will consider whether to order a stay of the whole or part of the proceedings pending compliance with this protocol.

ANNEX A

Letter requesting occupational records including health records

Dear Sirs,

We are acting on behalf of the above-named who has developed the following *(insert disease)*. We are investigating whether this disease may have been caused: -

- *during the course of his employment with you / name of employer if different*
- *whilst at your premises at (address)*
- *as a result of your product (name)*

We are writing this in accordance with the Protocol for Disease and Illness Claims

We seek the following records:-

(Insert details eg, personnel / occupational health)

Please note your insurers may require you to advise them of this request.

We enclose a request form and expect to receive the records within 40 days.

If you are not able to comply with this request within this time, please advise us of the reason.

Yours faithfully

ANNEX A1

Application on behalf of a potential claimant for use where a disease claim is being investigated

This should be completed as fully as possible

Company
    Name
    And
    Address

1 a)	Full name of claimant (including previous surnames)	
b)	Address now	
c)	Address at date of termination of employment, if different	
d)	Date of birth (and death, if applicable)	
e)	National Insurance number, if available	
2	Department(s) where claimant worked	
3	This application is made because the claimant is considering	
a)	a claim against you as detailed in para 4	YES/NO
b)	Pursuing an action against someone else	YES/NO
4	If the answer to Q3(a) is 'Yes' details of	
	a) the likely nature of the claim, eg dermatitis	
	b) grounds for the claim, eg exposure to chemical	
	c) approximate dates of the events involved	
5	If the answer to Q3(b) is 'Yes' insert	
	a) the names of the proposed defendants	
	b) have legal proceedings been started?	YES/NO
	c) if appropriate, details of the claim and action number	
6	Any other relevant information or documents requested	
	Signature of Solicitor	
	Name	
	Address	
	Ref.	
	Telephone Number	
	Fax number	

I authorise you to disclose all of your records relating to me/the claimant to my solicitor and to your legal and insurance representatives.

Signature of Claimant

Signature of personal representative where claimant has died

ANNEX B

Template for letter of claim

To: Defendant

Dear Sirs

Re: **Claimant's full name**
     Claimant's full address
     Claimant's National Insurance Number
     Claimant's Date of Birth
     Claimant's Clock or Works Number
     Claimant's Employer *(name and address)*

We are instructed by the above named to claim damages in connection with a claim for: - *Specify occupational disease*

We are writing this letter in accordance with the pre-action protocol for disease and illness claims.

Please confirm the identity of your insurers. Please note that your insurers will need to see this letter as soon as possible and it may affect your insurance cover if you do not send this to them.

The Claimant was employed by you *(if the claim arises out of public or occupiers' liability give appropriate details)* as *job description* from *date* to *date.* During the relevant period of his employment he worked:
description of precisely where the Claimant worked and what he did to include a description of any machines used and details of any exposure to noise or substances

The circumstances leading to the development of this condition are as follows:
Give chronology of events

The reason why we are alleging fault is:
Details should be given of contemporary and comparable employees who have suffered from similar problems if known; any protective equipment provided; complaints; the supervisors concerned, if known.

Our client's employment history is attached.

We have also made a claim against:
Insert details

Their insurers' details are:
Insert if known

We have the following documents in support of our client's claim and will disclose these in confidence to your nominated insurance manager or solicitor when we receive their acknowledgement letter.
eg, Occupational health notes; GP notes

We have obtained a medical report from (name) and will disclose this when we receive your acknowledgement of this letter.
(This is optional at this stage)

From the information we presently have:

(i)   the Claimant first became aware of symptoms on *(insert approximate date)*

(ii)   the Claimant first received medical advice about those symptoms on *(insert date) (give details of advice given if appropriate)*

(iii) the Claimant first believed that those symptoms might be due to exposure leading to this claim on *(insert approximate date)*

A description of our client's condition is as follows:
This should be sufficiently detailed to allow the Defendant to put a broad value on the claim

He has the following time off work:
Insert dates

He is presently employed as a *job description* and his average net weekly income is £

If you are our client's employers, please provide us with the usual earnings details, which will enable us to calculate his financial loss.

Please note that we have entered into a conditional fee agreement with our client dated in relation to this claim which provides for a success fee within the meaning of section 58(2) of the Courts and Legal Services Act 1990. Our client has taken out an insurance policy dated with (name of insurance company) to which section 29 of the Access to Justice Act 1999 applies in respect of this claim.

A copy of this letter is attached for you to send to your insurers. Finally we expect an acknowledgement of this letter within 21 days by yourselves or your insurers.

Yours faithfully

Appendix 4

Questionnaire – Accident at Place of Work

Section A – Personal Details

Your name:

Your address:

Your telephone number   daytime:

                                    evening:

Your age:

Your date of birth:

If you are under 18, the full names and address of your parents:

Your marital status:

Your spouse's name:

Your spouse's age:

Your spouse's date of birth:

Do you have children? If so, please state their names and ages:

Your National Insurance number:

What do you earn net (take home pay) each week?
(please bring with you your wages slip for the last month)

What does your spouse earn net (take home pay each week)?

Are you a member of a trade union?

If so, which trade union?

Have you asked your trade union to help you make a claim regarding the accident?

If so, what was the result?

Are you covered by insurance for legal costs?

Section B – Details of your Present Employer

Your present employer's name:

Your present employer's address:

Your employee number:

What is your present job?

What is your job title?

What is your present employer's business?

How long have you worked for your present employer?

Section C – Details of your Employer at the Time of the Accident

Name and address of your employer at the time of your accident:

Your employee number at the time of the accident:

What was your job at the time of the accident?

What was your job title at the time of the accident?

How long had you worked for your employer at the time of the accident?

How many other employees did your employer have at the time of your accident?

Please give the details of your employer's insurers:

Section D – Details of the Accident

On what date did the accident occur?

At what time of day did the accident occur?

Did the accident occur in your normal working hours?

Were you doing your job when the accident occurred?

Where did the accident take place?

If the accident occurred in a building:

> what is the address of the building where the accident took place?
> who owns that building?
> what type of building is it?
> was this building your usual place of work at the time of the accident?
> if not, where was your usual place of work?

What were you doing at the time of the accident?

What caused the accident?

What equipment were you using at the time of the accident?

Who gave you this equipment?

Who do you think was to blame for the accident?

Why do you think that this person was to blame for the accident?

What job is this person employed to do?

What is this person's job title?

Has this person admitted he was to blame for the accident?

Do you think you were to blame for the accident?

Do you know if anyone has made a complaint about similar accidents?

Have you reported the accident to your employer?

To whom did you report it?

When did you report it?

Were details of the accident recorded in your employer's accident report book?

Did anyone else witness the accident?

If so, give the names and addresses of the witnesses.

Have you made a written statement about the accident to anyone?

Have you been asked to make a statement?

Have you made a claim for compensation against your employer or anyone else regarding the accident?

If so, to whom did you make your claim?

What was his response?

Do you know whether your employer was prosecuted as a result of your accident?

If so, what was the result?

Section E – Details of your Injuries and Medical Treatment

What injuries did you receive as a result of the accident?

Who is your doctor (general practitioner)?

What is his address?

What is your patient number?

Have you consulted him about your injuries?

When did you consult him?

Please bring with you to the interview your appointment card (if you have one).

Have you received hospital treatment for your injuries?

If so, what was the name and address of the hospital?

Name of the doctor who treated you:

Your hospital record number:

Please bring with you to the interview your appointment card (if you have one).

What was your state of health before the accident?

What has your state of health been since the accident?

Did you have time off work as result of the accident?

If so, how long?

How long did you spend in hospital?

Did you receive any money while you were off work?

If so, how much did you receive?

Who paid you the money?

Did anyone look after you after you left hospital?

    professional help, (eg district nurse):

    non-professional help (eg, your spouse, another relative, a friend):

How long did you receive this care?

What sort of care was it?

Did you have to pay for this care?

If so, how much?

Section F – Expenses you have Incurred as a Result of the Accident

What expenses have you incurred as a result of the accident?

Please make sure to keep a careful note of all expenses you incur from now on as a result of the accident (and, if possible, please obtain a receipt for these expenses).

Appendix 5
Actuarial Tables

With explanatory notes for use in Personal Injury and Fatal Accident Cases

Prepared by an Inter-disciplinary Working Party of Actuaries, Lawyers, Accountants and other interested parties (Fifth edition)

London: Her Majesty's Stationery Office

Contents

INTRODUCTION TO THE FIFTH EDITION

"When it comes to the explanatory notes we must make sure that they are readily comprehensible. We must assume the most stupid circuit judge in the country and before him are the two most stupid advocates. All three of them must be able to understand what we are saying".

Sir Michael Ogden QC,
on his explanatory notes to the
First Edition of the Ogden Tables.[1]

Vale

1. This is the first Edition to which neither Michael Ogden nor David Kemp has been a party.

2. Michael Ogden believed that the task of chairing his Working Party would be one which, when completed, would be put away and forgotten. He never foresaw that it would produce an industry, all of its own, and not end with the classic decision of *Wells v Wells* [1999] 1 AC 345. When he passed on the Chairmanship to me, I said, when accepting, that he had passed a 19-year sentence upon me, for that was the period of his rôle in the post of Chairman. He laughed. It is not to everyone to become eponymous with a set of Tables, but when he spoke to the parliamentary draftsman about his mention in the Civil Evidence Act 1995, he was told that it was simpler to refer to his name and the Tables rather than use the full title of the Working Party.

3. David Kemp started his work with his first wife, whom he commemorated by her photograph in Volume 1 of Kemp & Kemp, shortly after he came down from Cambridge. It was not his area of work as such, which was in the field of restrictive trade practice. He was due to go from Winchester College to Cambridge on a classics scholarship in 1939. World events intervened. When he did go to Corpus Christi, Cambridge, he elected to read law rather than classics, on the grounds that he had forgotten all his classics as a result of his war service. He obtained a 1st Class in Law. He regretted in retrospect, he said, not reading classics. He was skiing with his grandchildren in his 81st year.

4. Each of them, in his own way, reformed the law of damages, put it on a more professional footing, and persuaded the courts that personal injury compensation was not a subject to be treated by merely wetting one's finger and holding it in the air to discern the direction of the wind. It is right that both should be remembered for what they did for those who have been and will be injured.

The purpose of the Ogden Tables

5. The purpose of these Tables is to enable the simple calculation of full compensation for those victims who have suffered future loss as a result of wrongful injury. It is well established that such victims are entitled to full compensation.

6. This is in accordance with the law. The rule was first stated by Lord Blackburn in those famous words to be found in *Livingstone v Rawyards Coal Company* (1880) 5 App Cas 25 at 39.

---

[1] Memoirs of Sir Michael Ogden QC, 'Variety is the Spice of Legal Life', p.182; The Book Guild, 2002

7. Compensation should be both adequate and sufficient. The authority for that can be found in the speech of Lord Lloyd of Berwick in *Wells v Wells* [1999] 1 AC 345 at 362 and following.

8. The problem is to attain this worthy aim; whether it is currently attainable is debatable.

9. In order to achieve that aim it is necessary for both the courts and society to look into the future. This is a perilous task and requires uncommon abilities. One Victorian judge described the quality necessary as demanding both the agility of an acrobat and the foresight of an Hebrew prophet.

10. Money will always produce problems for the value today will not necessarily be the same in the future. Inflation is more likely to occur than deflation, but there have been periods in Britain, albeit usually short periods, where deflation has occurred.

11. Any calculation of a rate of inflation must relate to some 'basket' of goods and services, and perhaps also of assets, whose prices are to be measured. There need be no unique definition or measured rate of inflation: different measures serve different purposes. For example, the retail prices index (RPI) gives a measure of inflation based on the cost of living appropriate to the expenditure patterns of typical households; its historic forbear was the price of corn. The RPI is also the measure used to uprate interest and principal on index-linked gilts. The average earnings index gives a measure of wage inflation, which has typically exceeded RPI inflation, on account of economy-wide productivity growth.

12. The present value of future monetary amounts must also depend on real interest returns, as well as inflation, over the intervening period, and therefore calculated amounts of damages require assumptions to be made for such returns, including what, if any, investment risks for which they compensate. In fact, the precedent set by *Wells v Wells* [1999] 1 AC 345 was that the appropriate discount rate should be based on the 'risk free' rate.

13. The Ogden Tables were originally devised to enable future losses to be simply calculated through the application of a given discount rate defined in real terms, that is, after making allowance for the effects of future inflation. This was achieved by exploiting the properties of index-linked gilts to derive a market-related measure of prevailing real interest rates over an appropriate investment horizon. The use of index-linked gilts, being tradeable British Government securities, should, in general, be expected to yield discount rates close to risk-free returns.

14. The Ogden Tables also depend on the Expectation of Life figures, which are supplied by the Government Actuary. Those figures have been consistently rising as a result of better diet, care, housing and medical treatment. This means that the average length of life has risen dramatically. This is demonstrated by the figures issued by the Government Actuary on 18th December 2003, arising from the most recent census.

15. Apart from life expectancy the main factor in using the Ogden Tables is the appropriate choice of the discount rate, now fixed by the Lord Chancellor since 25th June 2001, and revisited on 27th July 2001, at 2½%. The right choice of discount rate is vital if the proper aim of full and adequate compensation is to be achieved. It has never, since the Lord Chancellor made his first announcement, been within ½% of the correct rate of return from Index Linked Gilts, after taking tax into account.

16. The Damages Act 1996 appreciated that the search for the most appropriate method would not necessarily be a single prescribed rate in all cases and at

all times. Section 1(2) of the Damages Act 1996 therefore made provision for the Court to make variations to the discount rate if any party to the proceedings shows that it is more appropriate in the case in question. Unfortunately, in two separate cases[1], the Court of Appeal has emasculated that provision in large and complex cases. It has ruled in each case that consistency and fairness and the use of the Lord Chancellor's chosen discount rate should be preferred. Neither decision is helpful in the desire to achieve full and proper compensation.

Other methods of calculating future pecuniary loss

17.   It needs to be emphasised that the Ogden Tables are not the only way, or even the best way, of calculating and estimating future losses.

18.   Actuaries, who are those chosen to value those most complex of entities, pension funds, calculate future claims and losses in a different and more subtle way than the methods used in the Ogden Tables. In the United States, professional economists are called to give evidence about future losses.

19.   For that reason, the Government Actuary has written an Appendix on this issue. He explains how actuaries do value future claims and losses.

20.   I believe that it is essential that everyone understands the limits of the Ogden Tables. A failure to understand those limits could lead to the Ogden Tables being devalued. As with justice, the Tables need to be both fair and seen to be fair, as well as properly applied.

Removal of the previous Tables 1 to 18

21.   This has been done as they relate to the past rather than the future. However, the fact that they are no longer published, saving valuable space, does not mean that in very particular circumstances, they may not be relevant to the calculations of damages.

Fatal Accident Act claims

22.   The courts do not, at present, appear inclined to accept the guidance which we offered in the 4th Edition of these Tables. The courts consider themselves bound by the speech of Lord Fraser in *Cookson v Knowles* [1979] AC 556 at 574. Nelson J. in *White v ESAB Group (UK) Limited* [2002] PIQR Q6 would have decided differently but for the words of Lord Fraser. In reality, in complex cases, the position is that financial experts often agree that the actual method we suggest is, in fact, the correct method.

23.   These tables are designed for losses that occur after the date of trial. In the Explanatory Notes it is made clear that the purpose of the Tables is for the assessment of future pecuniary loss. The Tables use discount rates which are applicable to future losses. This is because it is assumed that once the claimant has received compensation he will invest it to produce an income. It is therefore fundamental that the discounted columns in the Tables should only be used for losses that arise after the date of trial or assessment.

24.   If the guidance on multipliers in fatal accident cases given in section D of the Explanatory Notes is not followed, in order to select them from the date of death, it is essential that the 0% columns are used for the period prior to the trial (see paragraph 64).

---

[1] *Warriner v Warriner* [2002] 1 WLR 1703; *Cooke & Others v United Bristol Health Care & Others* [2004] 1 WLR 251.

Contingencies other than mortality

25.   Certain inaccuracies have been noted in the figures used in Tables A, B and C for contingencies other than mortality. These inaccuracies were first revealed in the paper by Professors Lewis and McNabb[1]. They have since been confirmed by and acknowledged by the authors of the original paper, Haberman & Bloomfield[2], as due to incomplete data. We have not been inclined to remove those Tables completely, for they do give an indication of the factors that should be considered. We are attempting to commission new work on this aspect for later editions of these Tables. Better figures may take some time to produce and a 'health warning' exists on those presently produced.

Final matters

26.   The core of the work which constitutes these Tables is produced by the Government Actuary and his team. The lawyers are merely an encumbrance, welcomed by him, so that the process can be refined and improved. He has to listen to arcane matters such as the 'lost years' argument and other delights from the lawyers, but the Tables are intended as a mathematical tool to be used in the most simple way so that future pecuniary losses can be calculated without great stress and in the most accurate way that is easily available.

31st July 2004   Robin de Wilde QC

EXPLANATORY NOTES

Section A: general

Purpose of tables

1.   The tables have been prepared by the Government Actuary's Department. They provide an aid for those assessing the lump sum appropriate as compensation for a continuing future pecuniary loss or consequential expense or cost of care in personal injury and fatal accident cases.

Application of tables

2.   The tables set out multipliers. These multipliers enable the user to assess the present capital value of future annual loss (net of tax) or annual expense calculated on the basis of various assumptions which are explained below. Accordingly, to find the present capital value of a given annual loss or expense, it is necessary to select the appropriate table, find the appropriate multiplier and then multiply the amount of the annual loss or expense by that figure.

3.   Tables 1 to 26 deal with annual loss or annual expense extending over three different periods of time. In each case there are separate tables for men and women.

•   In Tables 1 and 2 the loss or expense is assumed to begin immediately and to continue for the whole of the rest of the claimant's life, allowing for different potential lifespans, including the possibility of early death or prolonged life. The tables apply to both the deceased and the dependants' lives in fatal accident cases.

---

[1] Journal of Law and Society Vol 29, No 3, Sept 2002.
[2] Their paper is entitled: 'Work Time Lost to Sickness, Unemployment and Stoppages: Measurement and Application'; (1990) Journal of the Institute of Actuaries Volume 117, 533.

- In Tables 3 to 14 the loss or expense is assumed to begin immediately but to continue only until the claimant's retirement or earlier death. The age of retirement is assumed to be 50 in Tables 3 and 4, 55 in Tables 5 and 6, 60 in Tables 7 and 8, 65 in Tables 9 and 10, 70 in Tables 11 and 12, and 75 in Tables 13 and 14.

- In Tables 15 to 26 it is assumed that the annual loss or annual expense will not begin until the claimant reaches retirement but will then continue for the whole of the rest of his or her life.

4.   In Table 19 (males) and Table 20 (females) the age of retirement is assumed to be 60. In Table 21 (males) and Table 22 (females) the age of retirement is assumed to be 65 (and similarly for retirement ages 50, 55, 70 and 75). These tables all make due allowance for the chance that the claimant may not live to reach the age of retirement.

Mortality assumptions

5.   In previous editions of these tables, tables have been included based on the mortality rates experienced in England & Wales in a historical three-year period. Tables based on mortality experienced in the years 1990 to 1992, published by the Government Actuary's Department as English Life Table No. 15 (ELT15), were set out in the 4th Edition of the tables. The Working Party has decided that it is not necessary to publish these historic tables again in this edition and have correspondingly agreed that the tables to be published should be based on a reasonable estimate of the future mortality likely to be experienced by average members of the population alive today.

6.   On the basis of some reported cases, it appears that tables for pecuniary loss for life, e.g. cost of care, may have been misunderstood. The tables do not assume that the claimant dies after a period equating to the expectation of life, but take account of the possibilities that the claimant will live for different periods, e.g. die soon or live to be very old. The mortality assumptions relate to the general population of England & Wales. Unless there is clear evidence in an individual case to support the view that the individual is atypical and will enjoy longer or shorter expectation of life, no further increase or reduction is required for mortality alone.

7.   For the purposes of preparing the official national population projections, the Government Actuary makes an estimate of the extent of future improvements in mortality. Tables 1 to 26 in this edition show the multipliers which result from the application of these projected mortality rates (derived from the 2002-based population projections for England & Wales, which were published in December 2003 on the GAD website www.gad.gov.uk. Details can also be found in the publication *National Population Projections 2002-based. PP2 No.24* from the Office of National Statistics). The actuaries on the Working Party consider that these alternative tables provide a more appropriate estimate of the value of future income streams than tables based on historic mortality which, given the rate at which mortality experience has improved, and continues to improve, are likely to underestimate future longevity to a significant extent. The Working Party therefore recommends the Courts to use Tables 1 to 26 contained in this latest edition of the tables.

Use of tables

8.   To find the appropriate figure for the present value of a particular loss or expense, the user must first choose that table which relates to the period of

loss or expense for which the individual claimant is to be compensated and to the sex of the claimant, or, where appropriate, the claimant's dependants.

9.   If, for some reason, the facts in a particular case do not correspond with the assumptions on which one of the tables is based (e.g. it is known that the claimant will have a different retiring age from that assumed in the tables), then the tables can only be used if an appropriate allowance is made for this difference; for this purpose the assistance of an actuary should be sought, except for situations where specific guidance is given in these explanatory notes.

Rate of return

10.   The basis of the multipliers set out in the tables is that the lump sum will be invested and yield income (but that over the period in question the claimant will gradually reduce the capital sum, so that at the end of the period it is exhausted). Accordingly, an essential factor in arriving at the right figure is the choice of the appropriate rate of return.

11.   The annual rate of return currently to be applied is 2½% (net of tax), as fixed by the Lord Chancellor on 25 June 2001, and reassessed on 27 July 2001, under the provisions of the Damages Act 1996 Section 1. An annual rate of return of 2½% has also been set for Scotland by the Scottish Ministers on 8 February 2002. The Lord Chancellor may make a fresh determination of this rate, after receiving advice from the Government Actuary and the Treasury (and, in Scotland, by the Scottish Ministers after consultation with the Government Actuary). Tables are accordingly shown for a range of possible annual rates of return ranging from ½% to 5%, as in the previous edition. In addition, a 0% column has been included to show the multiplier without any discount for interest (i.e. expectations of life, or the equivalent for different periods). These are supplied to assist in the calculation of multipliers in Fatal Accident Act cases (see Section D).

12.   Section 1(2) of the Damages Act 1996 makes provision for the Courts to make variations to the discount rate if any party to the proceedings shows that it is more appropriate in the case in question. Variations to the discount rate under this provision have, however, been rejected by the Court of Appeal in the cases of *Warriner v Warriner* [2002] 1 WLR 1703 and *Cooke & Others v United Bristol Health Care & Others* [2004] 1 WLR 251. A note by the Government Actuary in Appendix A of this edition describes how appropriate account could be taken by the Courts of different inflationary conditions. Use of such sound actuarial methodology would require tables at rates of return other than the rate set by the Lord Chancellor and for this reason also it has been deemed appropriate to continue to show a range of rates of return.

13.   Previous editions of these tables explained how the current yields on index-linked government bonds could be used as an indicator of the appropriate real rate of return for valuing future income streams. Such considerations were endorsed by the House of Lords in *Wells v Wells* and the same argumentation was adopted by the Lord Chancellor when he set the rate on commencement of Section 1 of the Damages Act 1996. In cases outwith the scope of these tables, the advice of an actuary should be sought.

Different retirement ages

14.   In paragraph 9 above, reference was made to the problem that will arise when the claimant's retiring age is different from that assumed in the tables. Such a problem may arise in valuing a loss or expense beginning

immediately but ending at retirement; or in valuing a loss or expense which will not begin until the claimant reaches retirement but will then continue until death. Tables are provided for retirement ages of 50, 55, 60, 65, 70 and 75. Where the claimant's actual retiring age would have been between two of these retirement ages for which tables are provided, the correct multiplier can be obtained by consideration of the tables for retirement age immediately above and below the actual retirement age, keeping the period to retirement age the same. Thus a woman of 42 who would have retired at 58 can be considered as being in between the cases of a woman of 39 with a retirement age of 55 and a woman of 44 with a retirement age of 60. The steps to take are as follows:

(1) Determine between which retirement ages, for which tables are provided, the claimant's actual retirement age R lies. Let the lower of these ages be A and the higher be B.

(2) Determine how many years must be subtracted from the claimant's actual retirement age to get to A and subtract that period from the claimant's age. If the claimant's age is x, the result of this calculation is $(x+A-R)$.

(3) Look up this new reduced age in the Table corresponding to retirement age A at the appropriate rate of return. Let the resulting multiplier be M.

(4) Determine how many years must be added to the claimant's actual retirement age to get to B and add that period to the claimant's age. The result of this calculation is $(x+B-R)$.

(5) Look up this new increased age in the Table corresponding to retirement age B at the appropriate rate of return. Let the resulting multiplier be N.

(6) Interpolate between M and N. In other words, calculate:

$(B-R) \times M + (R-A) \times N$

and divide the result by 5.

15. In the example given in paragraph 14, the steps would be as follows:

(1) A is 55 and B is 60.

(2) Subtracting 3 years from the claimant's age gives 39.

(3) Looking up age 39 in Table 6 (for retirement age 55) gives 13.08 at a rate of return of 2½%.

(4) Adding 2 years to the claimant's age gives 44.

(5) Looking up age 44 in Table 8 (for retirement age 60) gives 13.01 at a rate of return of 2½%.

(6) Calculating 2 x 13.08 + 3 x 13.01 and dividing by 5 gives 13.04 as the multiplier.

16. When the loss or expense to be valued is that from the date of retirement to death, and the claimant's date of retirement differs from that assumed in the tables, a different approach is necessary, involving the following three steps.

(1) Assume that there is a present loss which will continue for the rest of the claimant's life and from Table 1 or 2 establish the value of that loss or expense over the whole period from the date of assessment until the claimant's death.

(2) Establish the value of such loss or expense over the period from the date of assessment until the claimant's expected date of retirement following the procedure explained in paragraphs 14 and 15 above.

(3)   Subtract the second figure from the first. The balance remaining represents the present value of the claimant's loss or expense between retirement and death.

17.   If the claimant's actual retiring age would have been earlier than 50, or later than 75, the advice of an actuary should be sought.

Younger ages

18.   Tables 1 and 2, which concern pecuniary loss for life, and Tables 15 to 26, which concern loss of pension from retirement age, have been extended down to age 0. In some circumstances the multiplier at age 0 is slightly lower than that at age 1; this arises because of the relatively high incidence of deaths immediately after birth.

19.   Tables for multipliers for loss of earnings (Tables 3 to 14) have not been extended below age 16. In order to determine the multiplier for loss of earnings for someone who has not yet started work, it is first necessary to determine an assumed age at which the claimant would have commenced work and to find the appropriate multiplier for that age from Tables 3 to 14, according to the assumed retirement age. This multiplier should then be multiplied by the deferment factor from Table 27 which corresponds to the appropriate rate of return and the period from the date of the trial to the date on which it is assumed that the claimant would have started work. A similar approach can be used for determining a multiplier for pecuniary loss for life where the loss is assumed to commence a fixed period of years from the date of the trial. For simplicity the factors in Table 27 relate purely to the impact of compound interest and ignore mortality. At ages below 30 this is a reasonable approximation but at higher ages it would normally be appropriate to allow explicitly for mortality and the advice of an actuary should be sought.

Contingencies

20.   Tables 1 to 26 make reasonable provision for the levels of mortality which members of the population of England & Wales alive today may expect to experience in future. The tables do not take account of the other risks and vicissitudes of life, such as the possibility that the claimant would for periods have ceased to earn due to ill-health or loss of employment. Nor do they take account of the fact that many people cease work for substantial periods to care for children or other dependants. Section B suggests ways in which allowance may be made to the multipliers for loss of earnings, to allow for certain risks other than mortality.

Impaired lives

21.   In some cases, medical evidence may be available which asserts that a claimant's health impairments are equivalent to adding a certain number of years to their current age, or to treating the individual as having a specific age different from their actual age. In such cases, Tables 1 and 2 can be used with respect to the deemed higher age. For the other tables the adjustment is not so straightforward, as adjusting the age will also affect the assumed retirement age, but the procedures described in paragraphs 14 to 16 may be followed, or the advice of an actuary should be sought.

Fixed periods

22.   In cases where pecuniary loss is to be valued for a fixed period, the multipliers in Table 28 may be used. These make no allowance for mortality or any other contingency but assume that regular frequent payments (e.g.

weekly or monthly) will continue throughout the period. These figures should in principle be adjusted if the periodicity of payment is less frequent, especially if the payments in question are annually in advance or in arrears.

Variable loss or expense

23. The tables do not provide an immediate answer when the annual loss or expense to be valued is not assumed to be stable; where, for instance, the claimant's lost earnings were on a sliding scale or promotion was likely to be achieved. It may be possible to use the tables to deal with such situations by increasing the basic figure of annual loss or expenses or it may be appropriate to split the overall multiplier into two or more parts and apply different multiplicands to each. In addition to contingent widows' pensions, cases such as *Singapore Bus v Lim Soon Yong* [1985] 1 WLR 1075 at 1079D – 1080A, *Taylor v O'Connor* [1971] AC 115 at 127, 130, *Davies and Others v Whiteways Cyder Co Ltd and Another* [1974] 3 All ER 168 etc may necessitate actuarial advice with regard to other losses.

Spouses' pension benefits

24. If doubt exists whether the tables are appropriate to a particular case which appears to present significant difficulties of substance, it would be prudent to take actuarial advice. This might be appropriate in relation to the level of spouses' benefits, if these are to be assessed, since these are not readily valued using Tables 1 to 26. As a rough rule of thumb, if spouse's benefits are to be included when valuing pension loss from normal pension age, the multipliers in tables 15 to 26 should be increased by 5% for a female claimant (i.e. benefits to the male spouse) and by 15% for a male claimant if the spouse's pension would be half of the pension that the member was receiving at death. If the spouse's pension would be payable at a rate of two-thirds the member's pension at death the multipliers should be increased by 7% for a female claimant and by 20% for a male claimant.

SECTION B: CONTINGENCIES OTHER THAN MORTALITY

25. As stated in paragraph 20, the tables for loss of earnings (Tables 3 to 14) take no account of risks other than mortality. This section shows how the multipliers in these tables may be reduced to take account of risks other than mortality. This is based on work commissioned by the Institute of Actuaries and carried out by Professor S Haberman and Mrs D S F Bloomfield *(Work time lost to sickness, unemployment and stoppages: measurement and application* (1990), Journal of the Institute of Actuaries 117, 533–595). Although there was some debate within the actuarial profession about the details of this work, and in particular about the scope for developing it further, the findings were broadly accepted and were adopted by the Government Actuary and the other actuaries who were members of the Working Party when the Second Edition of the Tables was published.

26. Since the risk of mortality (including the risks of dying early or living longer) has already been taken into account in the tables, the principal contingencies in respect of which a further reduction is to be made, particularly for earnings loss up to retirement age, are illness and unemployment. Even with the effective disappearance of the "job for life" there appears to be no scientific justification in the generality of cases for assuming significantly larger deductions than those given in this section. It should be noted that the authors of the 1990 paper (Professor Haberman and Mrs Bloomfield) wrote "All the results discussed in this paper should be

further qualified by the caveat that the underlying models ... assume that economic activity rates and labour force separation and accession rated do not vary in the future from the bases chosen. As mentioned already in the text, it is unlikely to be true that the future would be free from marked secular trends." The paper relied on Labour Force Surveys for 1973, 1977, 1981 and 1985 and English Life Tables No. 14 (1980–82). However, although it is now somewhat out of date, it is the best study presently available. Some related work has recently been published by Lewis, McNabb and Wass (*Methods of calculating damages for loss of future earnings,* Journal of Personal Injury Law, 2002 Number 2). It is hoped that further research into the impact of contingencies other than mortality will be carried out in due course and the Ogden Working Party is in discussion with potential researchers in the hope of carrying this forward.

27.   Specific factors in individual cases may necessitate larger reductions. By contrast, there will also be cases where the standard multipliers should be increased, to take into account positive factors of lifestyle, employment prospects and life expectancy.

28.   The extent to which the multiplier needs to be reduced will reflect individual circumstances such as occupation and geographical region. In the short term, levels of economic activity and unemployment, including time lost through industrial action, are relevant. Reductions may be expected to be smaller for clerical workers than for manual workers, for those living in the South rather than the North, and for those in 'secure' jobs and in occupations less affected by redundancy or industrial action.

29.   The factors described in subsequent paragraphs are for use in calculating loss of earnings up to retirement age. The research work did not investigate the impact of contingencies other than mortality on the value of future pension rights. Some reduction to the multiplier for loss of pension would often be appropriate when a reduction is being applied for loss of earnings. This may be less of a reduction than in the case of loss of earnings because of the ill-health contingency (as opposed to the unemployment contingency), particularly in cases where there are significant ill-health retirement pension rights. A bigger reduction may be necessary in cases where there is significant doubt whether pension rights would have continued to accrue (to the extent not already allowed for in the post-retirement multiplier) or in cases where there may be doubt over the ability of the pension fund to pay promised benefits. In the case of a defined contribution pension scheme, loss of pension rights may be able to be allowed for simply by increasing the future earnings loss (adjusted for contingencies other than mortality) by the percentage which the employer pays to the scheme in contributions.

30.   The suggestions which follow are intended only to provide a 'ready reckoner', as opposed to precise figures.

The basic deduction for contingencies other than mortality

31.   Subject to the adjustments which may be made as described below, the multiplier which has been selected from the tables, i.e. in respect of risks of mortality only, should be reduced by *multiplying* it by a figure selected from the table below, under the heading 'Medium'.

Levels of economic activity and employment

32.   The medium set of reductions is appropriate if it is anticipated that economic activity is likely to correspond to that in the 1970s and 1980s (ignoring periods of high and low unemployment). The high set is

appropriate if higher economic activity and lower unemployment rates are anticipated. The low set is appropriate if lower economic activity and higher unemployment rates are anticipated.

Table A
Loss of Earnings to Pension Age 65 (Males)

Age at date of trial	High	Medium	Low
20	0.99	0.98	0.97
25	0.99	0.98	0.96
30	0.99	0.97	0.95
35	0.98	0.96	0.93
40	0.98	0.96	0.92
45	0.97	0.95	0.90
50	0.96	0.93	0.87
55	0.95	0.90	0.82
60	0.95	0.90	0.81

Lower pension ages (Males)

33.   The figures will be higher for a lower pension age. For example, if pension age is 60, the figures should be as shown in Table B.

Table B
Loss of Earnings to Pension Age 60 (Males)

Age at date of trial	High	Medium	Low
20	0.99	0.99	0.98
25	0.99	0.99	0.97
30	0.99	0.98	0.97
35	0.99	0.98	0.96
40	0.98	0.97	0.94
45	0.98	0.96	0.93
50	0.97	0.94	0.92
55	0.96	0.93	0.88

Female lives

34.   As a rough guide, for female lives between ages 35 and 55 with a pension age of 60, the figures should be as shown in Table C. As for males, the factors will be lower if the pension age is higher (e.g. 65) and higher if the pension age is lower (e.g. 55).

Table C
Loss of Earnings to Pension Age 60 (Females)

Age at date of trial	High	Medium	Low
35	0.95	0.95	0.94
40	0.93	0.93	0.92
45	0.90	0.90	0.88
50	0.91	0.90	0.88
55	0.95	0.94	0.93

Variations by occupation

35.   The risks of illness, injury and disability are less for persons in clerical or similar jobs, e.g. civil servants, the professions and financial services industries, and greater for those in manual jobs, e.g. construction, mining, quarrying and ship-building. However, what matters is the precise nature of the work undertaken by the person in question, rather than the industry as

such; for example, a secretary in the headquarters office of a large construction company may be at no greater risk than a secretary in a solicitor's office.

36. In less risky occupations the figures in Tables A to C should be *increased* by a maximum of the order of 0.01 up to age 40, rising to 0.03 at age 55.

37. In more risky occupations the figures in Tables A to C should be *reduced* by a maximum of the order of 0.01 at age 25, 0.02 at age 40 and 0.05 at age 55.

Variations by geographical region

38. For persons resident in the South East, East Anglia, South West and East Midlands, the figures in Tables A to C should be *increased* by a maximum of the order of 0.01 up to age 40, rising to 0.03 at age 55.

39. For persons resident in the North, North West, Wales and Scotland, the figures in Tables A to C should be reduced by a maximum of the order of 0.01 at age 25, 0.02 at age 40 and 0.05 at age 55.

SECTION C: SUMMARY OF PERSONAL INJURY APPLICATIONS

40. To use the tables take the following steps:

    (1) Choose the tables relating to the appropriate period of loss or expense.

    (2) Choose the table, relating to that period, appropriate to the sex of the claimant (Tables 1 to 26).

    (3) Choose the appropriate rate of return, as determined under Section 1 of the Damages Act 1996.

    (4) Find the figure under the column in the table chosen given against the age at trial of the claimant.

    (5) Adjust the figure to take account of contingencies other than mortality, as specified in Section B above.

    (6) Multiply the annual loss (net of tax) or expense by that figure.

41. In cases where the claimant's expected age of retirement differs from that assumed in the tables, the more complicated procedure explained in paragraphs 14 to 17 should be followed.

Example 1

42. The following is an example of the use of the tables in a personal injury case:

    The claimant is female, aged 35 at the date of the trial. She lives in London and is an established civil servant who was working in an office at a salary of £25,000 net of tax. As a result of her injuries, she has lost her job. Her loss of earnings to retirement age of 60 is assessed as follows:

    (1) Look up Table 8 for loss of earnings to pension age 60 for females.

    (2) The appropriate rate of return is determined to be 2½% (the rate set under Section 1 of the Damages Act 1996).

    (3) Table 8 shows that, on the basis of a 2½% rate of return, the multiplier for a female aged 35 is 18.39.

    (4) Now take account of risks other than mortality. On the assumption of high economic activity for the next few years, Table C would require 18.39 to be multiplied by 0.95.

    (5) Based on Section B, further adjustment is necessary because the claimant (a) is in a secure non-manual job, and (b) lives in the South East.

(6)   The adjustments should be made as follows:

Basic adjustment to allow for short-term high economic activity (Table C)	0.95
Adjustment to allow for occupation, say	+0.01
	0.96
Adjustment for geographical region, say	+ 0.01
	0.97

(7)   The original multiplier taken from Table 8, namely 18.39, must therefore be multiplied by 0.97, resulting in a revised multiplier of 17.84.

(8)   The damages for loss of earnings are assessed as £446,000 (17.84 x 25,000).

Example 2

43.   The following is a second example of the use of the tables in a personal injury case:

The claimant is male, aged 48 at the date of the trial. He lives in Manchester and was working in a factory. His retirement age was 65 and his pre-retirement multiplicand has been determined as £20,000 a year net of tax. The multiplicand for costs of care is deemed to be £50,000 a year. As a result of his injuries, he has lost his job. His loss of earnings to retirement age of 65 is assessed as follows:

(1)   Look up Table 9 for loss of earnings to pension age 65 for males.

(2)   The appropriate rate of return is determined to be 2½% (the rate set under Section 1 of the Damages Act 1996).

(3)   Table 9 shows that, on the basis of a 2½% rate of return, the multiplier for a male aged 48 is 13.38.

(4)   Now take account of risks other than mortality. On the assumption of medium economic activity for the next few years, Table A would require 13.38 to be multiplied by 0.93.

(5)   Based on Section B, further adjustment is necessary because the Plaintiff (a) is in a risky manual job, and (b) lives in the North West.

(6)   The adjustments should be made as follows:

Basic adjustment to allow for short-term medium economic activity (Table A)	0.93
Adjustment to allow for occupation, say	- 0.02
	0.91
Adjustment for geographical region, say	- 0.03
	0.88

(7)   The original multiplier taken from Table 9, namely 13.38, must therefore be multiplied by 0.88, resulting in a revised multiplier of 11.77.

(8)   The damages for loss of earnings are assessed as £235,400 (11.77 x 20,000).

44.   The damages for cost of care are assessed as follows:

(1)   Look up Table 1 for the multiplier at age 48.

(2)   The appropriate rate of return is 2½%.

(3)   Table 1 shows that, on the basis of a 2½% rate of return, the multiplier at age 48 is 22.51.

(4)   No further adjustment is made for risks other than mortality.

(5)   The damages for cost of care are assessed at £1,125,500 (22.51 x 50,000).

SECTION D: APPLICATION OF TABLES TO FATAL ACCIDENT CASES

45.   Whereas in personal injury cases the problem to be solved is that of setting a value on an income stream during the potential life of one person (the claimant), the situation is generally more complicated in fatal accident cases. Here the compensation is intended to reflect the value of an income stream during the lifetime of one or more dependants of the deceased (or the expected period for which the dependants would have expected to receive the dependency, if shorter) but limited according to the expectation of how long the deceased would have been able to provide the financial support, had he or she not been involved in the fatal accident.

46.   In principle, therefore, the compensation for post-trial dependency should be based on the present value at the date of the trial of the dependency during the expected future joint lifetime of the deceased and the dependant or claimant (had the deceased survived naturally to the date of the trial), subject to any limitations on the period of dependency and any expected future changes in the level of dependency, for example, on attaining retirement age. In addition there should be compensation for the period between the date of accident and the date of trial.

47.   A set of actuarial tables to make such calculations accurately would require tables similar to Tables 1 to 26 but for each combination of ages as at the date of the trial of the deceased and the dependant to whom compensation is to be paid. The Working Party concluded that this would not meet the criterion of simplicity of application which was a central objective of these tables and recommends that, in complex cases, or cases where the accuracy of the multiplier is thought by the parties to be of critical importance and material to the resulting amount of compensation (for example in cases potentially involving very large claims where the level of the multiplicand is unambiguously established), the advice of a professionally qualified actuary should be sought. However, for the majority of cases, a certain amount of approximation will be appropriate, bearing in mind the need for a simple and streamlined process, and taking into consideration the other uncertainties in the determination of an appropriate level of compensation. The following paragraphs describe a methodology using Tables 1 to 26 which can be expected to yield satisfactory answers.

Damages for the period from the fatal accident to the date of trial

48.   The period of pre-trial dependency will normally be equal to the period between the date of the fatal accident and the date of the trial, substituting where appropriate the lower figure of the expected period for which the deceased would have provided the dependency, had he or she not been killed in the accident, or if the period of dependency would have been limited in some way, for example if the dependant is a child.

49.   A deduction may be made for the risk that the deceased might have died anyway, in the period between the date of the fatal accident and the date at which the trial takes place. In many cases this deduction will be small and could usually be regarded as *de minimis*. The need for a deduction becomes more necessary the longer the period from the date of accident to the date of trial and the older the deceased at the date of death. As an illustration of the order of magnitude of the deduction, Table D shows some examples of factors by which the multiplier should be multiplied for different ages of the

deceased and for different periods from the date of accident to the date of the trial.

TABLE D

Factor by which pre-trial damages should be multiplied to allow for the likelihood that the deceased would not in any case have survived to provide the dependency for the full period to the date of trial.

Age of deceased at date of accident	Period from date of accident to date of trial or date of cessation of dependency, if earlier (years)					
	Male deceased			Female deceased		
	3	6	9	3	6	9
10	1.00	1.00	1.00	1.00	1.00	1.00
20	1.00	1.00	1.00	1.00	1.00	1.00
30	1.00	1.00	1.00	1.00	1.00	1.00
40	1.00	0.99	0.99	1.00	1.00	0.99
50	0.99	0.99	0.98	1.00	0.99	0.99
60	0.98	0.97	0.95	0.99	0.98	0.97
65	0.98	0.95	0.92	0.99	0.97	0.95
70	0.96	0.92	0.87	0.98	0.95	0.92
75	0.93	0.86	0.79	0.96	0.91	0.85
80	0.89	0.79	0.69	0.93	0.84	0.76

Note: The factor for a period of zero years is clearly 1.00. Factors for other ages and periods not shown in the table may be obtained approximately by interpolation.

50.   The resultant multiplier, after application of any discount for the possibility of early death of the deceased before the date of trial, even had the accident not taken place, is to be applied to the multiplicand, which is determined in the usual way. Interest will then be added up to the date of trial on the basis of special damages.

Damages from the date of trial to retirement age

51.   The assessment of the multiplier involves the following steps:

(1)   Determine the expected period for which the deceased would have been able to provide the dependency (see paragraph 52).

(2)   Determine the expected period for which the dependant would have been able to receive the dependency (see paragraph 52).

(3)   Take the lesser of the two periods.

(4)   Treat the resulting period as a term certain for which the multiplier is to be determined and look up the figure in Table 28 for this period at the appropriate rate of interest.

(5)   Apply any adjustment for contingencies other than mortality in accordance with Section B.

(6)   If necessary, make an allowance for the risk that the deceased might have died anyway before the date of the trial (see paragraph 54).

52.   The expected periods at (1) and (2) of paragraph 51 may be obtained from the 0% column of the appropriate table at the back of this booklet. For (1), Tables 3 to 14 will be relevant, according to the sex of the deceased and the expected age of retirement. The age at which the table should be entered is

the age which the deceased would have been at the date of the trial. For (2) Tables 1 and 2 can be used, according to the sex of the dependant and looking up the table at the age of the dependant at the date of the trial.

53. If the period for which the dependency would have continued is a short fixed period, as in the case of a child, the figure at (2) would be the outstanding period at the date of the trial.

54. A deduction may be made for the risk that the deceased might have died anyway before the date of trial. The need for such a deduction becomes more necessary the longer the period from the date of accident to the date of trial and the older the deceased at the date of death. As an illustration of the order of magnitude of the deduction, Table E shows some examples of the factor by which the multiplier, determined as above, should be multiplied for different ages of the deceased and for different periods from the date of accident to the date of the trial.

TABLE E

Factor by which post-trial damages should be multiplied to allow for the likelihood that the deceased would not in any case have survived to the date of trial in order to provide any post-trial dependency.

Age of deceased at date of accident	Period from date of accident to date of trial (years)					
	Male deceased			Female deceased		
	3	6	9	3	6	9
10	1.00	1.00	1.00	1.00	1.00	1.00
20	1.00	1.00	0.99	1.00	1.00	1.00
30	1.00	0.99	0.99	1.00	1.00	1.00
40	1.00	0.99	0.98	1.00	0.99	0.99
50	0.99	0.97	0.96	0.99	0.98	0.97
60	0.97	0.93	0.89	0.98	0.96	0.93
65	0.95	0.90	0.83	0.97	0.94	0,89
70	0.92	0.83	0.73	0.95	0.89	0.82
75	0.87	0.72	0.58	0.91	0.81	0.68
80	0.79	0.58	0.39	0.85	0.68	0.50

Note: The factor for a period of zero years is clearly 1.00. Factors for other ages and periods not shown in the table may be obtained approximately by interpolation.

55. The resulting multiplier, after application of any discount for the possibility of early death of the deceased before the date of trial, even had the accident not taken place, is to be applied to the appropriate multiplicand, determined in relation to dependency as assessed for the period up to retirement age.

56. If there are several dependants, to whom damages are to be paid in respect of their own particular lifetime (or for a fixed period of dependency), separate multipliers should be determined for each and multiplied by the appropriate multiplicand using the procedure in paragraphs 51 to 55. The total amount of damages is then obtained by adding the separate components. If a single multiplicand is determined, but the damages are to be shared among two or more dependants so long as they are each alive, or during a period of common dependency, then the multiplier will be calculated using the procedure in paragraphs 51 to 55. However, at step (2) of paragraph 51 the

expected period will be the longest of the expected periods for which the dependency might last.

Damages for the period of dependency after retirement age

57.   The method described in paragraphs 51 to 56 for pre-retirement age dependency cannot satisfactorily be applied directly to post-retirement age dependency with a sufficient degree of accuracy. We therefore propose a method which involves determining the multiplier by looking at dependency for the rest of life from the date of trial and then subtracting the multiplier for dependency up to retirement age.

58.   The assessment of the multiplier for whole of life dependency involves the following steps:

   (1)   Determine the expectation of life which the deceased would have had as at the date of trial, or such lesser period for which the deceased would have been able to provide the dependency (see paragraph 59).

   (2)   Determine the expected period for which the dependant would have been able to receive the dependency (see paragraph 59).

   (3)   Take the lesser of the two periods.

   (4)   Treat the resulting period as a term certain for which the multiplier is to be determined and look up the figure in Table 28 for this period at the appropriate rate of interest.

59.   The expected periods at (1) and (2) of paragraph 58 may be obtained from the 0% column of the appropriate table at the back of this booklet. For (1) Tables 1 or 2 will be relevant, according to the sex of the deceased. The age at which the table should be entered is the age which the deceased would have attained at the date of the trial. For (2) Tables 1 and 2 can be used, according to the sex of the dependant and looking up the table at the age of the dependant at the date of the trial.

60.   Deduct the corresponding multiplier for post-trial pre-retirement dependency, as determined in paragraphs 51 to 56, but without any adjustment for contingencies other than mortality, or that the deceased may have died anyway before the date of trial. The result is the multiplier for post-retirement dependency, which must then be applied to the appropriate multiplicand, assessed in relation to dependency after retirement age. The adjustment for contingencies other than mortality in respect of the damages for the period of dependency after retirement age will often be less than that required for pre-retirement age damages (see paragraph 29).

61.   A deduction may finally be made for the risk that the deceased might have died anyway before the date of trial. The need for such a deduction becomes more necessary the longer the period from the date of accident to the date of trial and the older the deceased at the date of death. As an illustration of the order of magnitude of the deduction, Table E shows some examples of the factor by which the multiplier, determined as above, should be multiplied for different ages of the deceased and for different periods from the date of accident to the date of the trial. The factors for this purpose are exactly the same deductions as used in the calculation at paragraphs 51 to 56.

Cases where dependency is not related to employment

62.   The layout of paragraphs 51 to 61 is based on the assumption that the dependency provided by the deceased would have changed at retirement age. This may not be appropriate in some cases, particularly in the important case of the deceased wife and mother whose contribution has been solely in

the home or in the case of an adult child caring for an elderly parent or parents. In cases like this, where the deceased might have provided the dependency throughout their lifetime, paragraphs 57 to 61 should be ignored and paragraphs 51 to 56 used, with the difference that the expected period required at step (1) of paragraph 51 should be a whole of life expectancy, taken from Tables 1 and 2. This is also the approach to use when the deceased was already a pensioner.

Example 3

63. The dependant is female, aged 38 at the date of the trial, which is taking place 6 years after the date of the fatal accident which killed the male deceased, at that time aged 37, on whom the dependant was financially dependent. The Court has determined a multiplicand, up to the deceased's normal retirement age of 65, of £30,000 and has decided that no post-retirement damages are payable. The damages are to be calculated as follows:

Pre-trial damages:

(1) Period between fatal accident and trial: 6 years

(2) Factor for possible early death (Table D for male aged 37 and 6 years): 0.99

(3) Pre-trial damages = 6 x 0.99 x £30,000

= £178,200 (plus interest as special damages)

Post-trial damages:

(1) Expected period for which the deceased would have provided the dependency (Table 9 at 0% for male aged 43, the age as at the date of trial): 21.15

(2) Expected period for which the dependant would have been able to receive the dependency (Table 2 at 0% for female aged 38): 48.44

(3) Lesser of two periods at (1) and (2) = 21.15

(4) Multiplier for term certain of 21.15 years at 2½% rate of return (interpolating between the values for 21 and 22 years in Table 28)

= (22 – 21.15) x 16.39 + (21.15 – 21) x 16.97

= 16.48

(5) Adjustment factor for contingencies other than mortality (in accordance with Section B). Assume medium economic activity. Factor from Table A: 0.96

(6) Adjustment factor for the risk that the deceased might have died anyway before the date of trial (Table E for male aged 37 and 6 years): 0.99

(7) Post-trial damages = 16.48 x 0.96 x 0.99 x £30,000

= £469,878

64. If the court wishes to select multipliers from the date of death instead of following the guidance given above, it is essential to ensure that the period before the trial does not include a discount for early receipt. This could be achieved by selecting multipliers from the 0% columns of the appropriate tables and then applying the discount for early receipt to the period after the trial (using the discount rate set under Section 1 of the Damages Act 1996). Thus, the calculations for example 3 above would then be:

(1) Expected period for which the deceased would have provided the dependency (Table 9 at 0% for male aged 37, the age as at the date of trial): 26.99

(2)   Deduct period between accidental death and date of trial of 6 years to give post-trial period: 20.99

(3)   Expected post-trial period for which the dependant would have been able to receive the dependency (Table 2 at 0% for female aged 38): 48.44

(4)   Lesser of two periods at (2) and (3) = 20.99

(5)   Multiplier for term certain of 20.99 years at 2.5% rate of return (Table 28) = 16.38

(6)   Adjustment factor for contingencies other than mortality (in accordance with Section B). Assume medium economic activity. Factor from Table A: 0.96

(7)   Pre-trial damages = 6 x £30,000

$$= £180,000 \text{ (plus interest as special damages)}$$

(8)   Post-trial damages = 16.38 x 0.96 x £30,000

$$= £471,744$$

This method can be extended to the following examples.

Example 4

65.   The dependant is female, aged 50 at the date of the trial, which is taking place 4 years after the date of the fatal accident which killed the man, at that time aged 47, on whom she was financially dependent. The Court has determined a multiplicand, up to the deceased's normal retirement age of 60, of £50,000 and has decided that post-retirement damages should be payable based on a multiplicand of £30,000. The damages are to be calculated as follows:

Pre-trial damages:

(1)   Period between fatal accident and trial: 4 years

(2)   Factor for possible early death (Table D for male aged 47 and 4 years): 0.99

(3)   Pre-trial damages = 4 x 0.99 x £50,000

$$= £198,000 \text{ (plus interest as special damages)}$$

Post-trial pre-retirement damages:

(1)   Expected period for which the deceased would have provided the dependency (Table 7 at 0% for male aged 51, the age as at the date of trial): 8.81

(2)   Expected period for which the dependant would have been able to receive the dependency (Table 2 at 0% for female aged 50): 36.29

(3)   Lesser of two periods at (1) and (2) = 8.81

(4)   Multiplier for term certain of 8.81 years at 2½% rate of return (interpolating between the values for 8 and 9 in Table 28)

$$= (9 - 8.81) \times 7.26 + (8.81 - 8) \times 8.07$$

$$= 7.92$$

(5)   Adjustment factor for contingencies other than mortality (in accordance with Section B). Assume medium economic activity. Factor from Table B: 0.94

(6)   Adjustment factor for the risk that the deceased might have died anyway before the date of trial (Table E for male aged 47 and 4 years): 0.99

(7)   Post-trial pre-retirement damages = 7.92 x 0.94 x 0.99 x £50,000

$$= £368,518$$

Post-retirement damages:

(1)   Expectation of life of deceased at date of trial (Table 1 at 0% for male aged 51): 31.85

(2)   Expected period for which the dependant would have been able to receive the dependency (Table 2 at 0% for female aged 50): 36.29

(3)   Lesser of two periods at (1) and (2) = 31.85

(4)   Multiplier for time certain of 31.85 years at 2½% rate of return (interpolating between the values for 31 and 32 in Table 28)

= (32 – 31.85) x 21.66 + (31.85 – 31) x 22.12 = 22.05

(5)   Deduct multiplier for post-trial pre-retirement damages before application of adjustment factors for contingencies other than mortality and for the risk that the deceased might have died anyway before the date of trial: 22.05 – 7.92 = 14.13

(6)   Adjustment factor for the risk that the deceased might have died anyway before the date of trial (Table E for male aged 47 and 4 years): 0.99

(7)   Post-trial pre-retirement damages = 14.13 x 0.99 x £30,000

= £419,661

Example 5

66.   There are two dependants, respectively a child aged 10 and a male aged 41 at the date of the trial, which is taking place 3 years after the date of the fatal accident which killed the woman, at that time aged 35, on whom both were financially dependent. She worked in London for a computer company and future economic activity is deemed by the Court to be high. The Court has determined a multiplicand, up to the deceased's normal retirement age of 62, of £50,000 for the male dependant and £10,000 for the child, up to the age of 21, and has decided that post-retirement damages should be payable based on a multiplicand of £20,000. The damages are to be calculated as follows:

Pre-trial damages:

(1)   Period between fatal accident and trial: 3 years

(2)   Factor for possible early death (Table D for female aged 35 and 3 years): 1.00

(3)   Pre-trial damages = 3 x 1.00 x (£50,000 + £10,000)

= £180,000 (plus interest as special damages)

Post-trial pre-retirement damages:

(1)   Expected period for which the deceased would have provided the dependency should be based on female aged 38 at the date of trial with retirement age of 62. First calculate as though deceased were aged 36 and had retirement age of 60 (Table 8 at 0% for female aged 36): 23.61

Then calculate as though deceased were aged 41 and had retirement age of 65 (Table 10 at 0% for female aged 41): 23.38

Interpolate for age 38 with retirement age of 62

= (3 x 23.61 + 2 x 23.38)/5 = 23.52

(2)   Expected period for which the male dependant would have been able to receive the dependency (Table 1 at 0% for male aged 41): 41.80

Expected period for which child would have been able to receive the dependency = 11.00

(3)   Lesser of two periods at (1) and (2) = 11.00 (in case of child)

= 23.52 (in case of man)

(4)   Multiplier for term certain of 11 years at 2½% (Table 28): 9.63

Multiplier for term certain of 23.52 years at 2½% rate of return (interpolating between the values for 23 and 24 in Table 28)

$$= (24 - 23.52) \times 17.55 + (23.52 - 23) \times 18.11$$

$$= 17.84$$

(5)   Adjustment factor for contingencies other than mortality (in accordance with Section B). Factor from Table C, allowing for occupation and geographical area: 0.96 (does not apply to child)

(6)   Adjustment factor for the risk that the deceased might have died anyway before the date of trial (Table E for female aged 35 and 3 years): 1.00

(7)   Pre-retirement damages = 9.63 x 1.00 x £10,000 + 17.84 x 0.96 x 1.00 x £50,000

$$= 96,300 + £856,320$$

$$= 952,620$$

Post-retirement damages:

(1)   Expectation of life of deceased at date of trial (Table 2 at 0% for female aged 38): 48.44

(2)   Expected period for which the dependant would have been able to receive the dependency (Table 1 at 0% for male aged 41): 41.80 (no post retirement dependency for child)

(3)   Lesser of two periods at (1) and (2) = 41.80

(4)   Multiplier for time certain of 41.80 years at 2½% rate of return (interpolating between the values for 41 and 42 in Table 28)

$$= (42 - 41.80) \times 25.78 + (41.80 - 41) \times 26.14 = 26.07$$

(5)   Deduct multiplier for post-trial pre-retirement damages before application of adjustment factors for contingencies other than mortality and for the risk that the deceased might have died anyway before the date of trial: 26.07 – 17.84 = 8.23

(6)   Adjustment factor for the risk that the deceased might have died anyway before the date of trial (Table E for female aged 35 and 3 years) = 1.00

(7)   Post-retirement damages = 8.23 x 1.00 x £20,000

$$= £164,600$$

SECTION E: CONCLUDING REMARKS

67.   These tables are designed to assist the courts to arrive at suitable multipliers in a range of possible situations. However, they do not cover all possibilities and in more complex situations advice should be sought from a Fellow of the Institute of Actuaries or a Fellow of the Faculty of Actuaries.

68.   In cases in which the award will be large, say, about £2 million or more at current prices, or where there are significant pension rights to be taken into consideration, more accurate calculations may be necessary. In such cases advice from an actuary will be desirable.

CHRISTOPHER DAYKIN CB, MA, FIA   London

Government Actuary   September 2004

Table 1   Multipliers for pecuniary loss for life (males)

Age at date of trial	Multiplier calculated with allowance for projected mortality from the 2002-based population projections and rate of return of											Age at date of trial
	0.0%	0.5%	1.0%	1.5%	2.0%	2.5%	3.0%	3.5%	4.0%	4.5%	5.0%	
0	83.24	67.69	56.00	47.08	40.18	34.76	30.46	27.00	24.17	21.83	19.88	0
1	82.62	67.34	55.82	47.00	40.16	34.79	30.51	27.06	24.23	21.90	19.95	1
2	81.62	66.68	55.37	46.70	39.96	34.65	30.42	26.99	24.19	21.87	19.93	2
3	80.60	66.00	54.92	46.39	39.75	34.51	30.32	26.92	24.14	21.84	19.91	3
4	79.58	65.31	54.45	46.08	39.53	34.36	30.21	26.85	24.09	21.80	19.88	4
5	78.55	64.62	53.98	45.75	39.31	34.20	30.10	26.77	24.03	21.76	19.85	5
6	77.52	63.92	53.50	45.42	39.08	34.04	29.98	26.69	23.97	21.71	19.82	6
7	76.48	63.21	53.01	45.08	38.84	33.87	29.87	26.60	23.91	21.67	19.78	7
8	75.45	62.50	52.52	44.74	38.60	33.70	29.74	26.51	23.84	21.62	19.74	8
9	74.41	61.78	52.02	44.39	38.35	33.52	29.61	26.42	23.77	21.57	19.71	9
10	73.38	61.06	51.52	44.03	38.10	33.34	29.48	26.32	23.70	21.51	19.67	10
11	72.34	60.34	51.01	43.67	37.84	33.16	29.35	26.22	23.63	21.46	19.62	11
12	71.30	59.61	50.49	43.31	37.58	32.96	29.21	26.12	23.55	21.40	19.58	12
13	70.26	58.88	49.97	42.93	37.31	32.77	29.06	26.01	23.47	21.34	19.53	13
14	69.22	58.14	49.45	42.56	37.04	32.57	28.92	25.90	23.39	21.27	19.48	14
15	68.18	57.40	48.92	42.17	36.76	32.36	28.76	25.79	23.30	21.21	19.43	15
16	67.15	56.66	48.38	41.79	36.47	32.15	28.61	25.67	23.21	21.14	19.38	16
17	66.11	55.92	47.85	41.40	36.19	31.94	28.45	25.55	23.12	21.07	19.32	17
18	65.09	55.19	47.32	41.01	35.90	31.73	28.29	25.43	23.03	21.00	19.27	18
19	64.08	54.46	46.79	40.62	35.61	31.52	28.13	25.31	22.94	20.93	19.22	19
20	63.08	53.73	46.25	40.23	35.32	31.30	27.97	25.19	22.85	20.86	19.16	20
21	62.07	52.99	45.71	39.83	35.03	31.08	27.80	25.06	22.75	20.79	19.10	21
22	61.06	52.25	45.16	39.42	34.72	30.85	27.63	24.93	22.65	20.71	19.04	22
23	60.05	51.50	44.61	39.01	34.41	30.62	27.45	24.79	22.54	20.63	18.98	23
24	59.03	50.75	44.05	38.59	34.10	30.38	27.27	24.65	22.43	20.54	18.91	24
25	58.02	50.00	43.49	38.16	33.78	30.13	27.08	24.51	22.32	20.45	18.84	25
26	57.01	49.24	42.92	37.73	33.45	29.88	26.89	24.36	22.20	20.36	18.77	26
27	56.00	48.48	42.34	37.30	33.11	29.62	26.69	24.20	22.08	20.26	18.69	27
28	54.99	47.72	41.76	36.85	32.77	29.36	26.48	24.04	21.96	20.16	18.61	28
29	53.98	46.95	41.18	36.40	32.42	29.09	26.27	23.88	21.83	20.06	18.53	29
30	52.97	46.18	40.58	35.94	32.07	28.81	26.05	23.70	21.69	19.95	18.44	30
31	51.96	45.40	39.98	35.48	31.71	28.53	25.83	23.53	21.55	19.84	18.35	31
32	50.94	44.62	39.38	35.01	31.34	28.24	25.60	23.34	21.40	19.72	18.25	32
33	49.93	43.83	38.76	34.53	30.96	27.94	25.36	23.15	21.24	19.59	18.15	33
34	48.91	43.04	38.15	34.04	30.57	27.63	25.11	22.95	21.09	19.46	18.04	34
35	47.90	42.25	37.52	33.54	30.18	27.31	24.86	22.75	20.92	19.33	17.93	35
36	46.88	41.45	36.89	33.04	29.78	26.99	24.60	22.54	20.75	19.18	17.81	36
37	45.86	40.64	36.25	32.53	29.37	26.66	24.33	22.32	20.57	19.03	17.69	37
38	44.85	39.83	35.60	32.01	28.95	26.32	24.05	22.09	20.38	18.88	17.56	38
39	43.83	39.02	34.95	31.48	28.52	25.97	23.77	21.85	20.18	18.72	17.42	39
40	42.81	38.20	34.29	30.95	28.08	25.61	23.47	21.61	19.98	18.55	17.28	40
41	41.80	37.38	33.62	30.41	27.64	25.25	23.17	21.36	19.77	18.37	17.13	41
42	40.78	36.56	32.96	29.86	27.19	24.88	22.86	21.10	19.56	18.19	16.98	42
43	39.78	35.74	32.28	29.31	26.73	24.50	22.55	20.84	19.33	18.00	16.82	43
44	38.77	34.92	31.61	28.75	26.27	24.11	22.23	20.57	19.10	17.81	16.66	44
45	37.77	34.09	30.93	28.19	25.80	23.72	21.90	20.29	18.87	17.61	16.48	45
46	36.78	33.27	30.25	27.62	25.33	23.32	21.56	20.00	18.63	17.40	16.31	46
47	35.79	32.45	29.56	27.05	24.85	22.92	21.22	19.71	18.38	17.19	16.12	47
48	34.80	31.63	28.88	26.47	24.36	22.51	20.87	19.41	18.12	16.97	15.93	48
49	33.82	30.81	28.18	25.89	23.87	22.08	20.51	19.11	17.86	16.74	15.73	49
50	32.84	29.98	27.48	25.29	23.36	21.65	20.14	18.79	17.58	16.50	15.53	50
51	31.85	29.15	26.78	24.69	22.85	21.21	19.76	18.46	17.30	16.25	15.31	51
52	30.87	28.32	26.07	24.08	22.32	20.76	19.37	18.12	17.00	15.99	15.08	52
53	29.90	27.48	25.35	23.47	21.79	20.30	18.97	17.77	16.69	15.72	14.85	53
54	28.93	26.65	24.64	22.85	21.26	19.84	18.56	17.41	16.38	15.45	14.60	54
55	27.97	25.82	23.92	22.23	20.72	19.37	18.15	17.05	16.06	15.17	14.35	55
56	27.02	25.01	23.21	21.61	20.18	18.89	17.73	16.69	15.74	14.88	14.10	56
57	26.09	24.20	22.51	21.00	19.64	18.42	17.32	16.32	15.41	14.59	13.84	57
58	25.17	23.40	21.81	20.38	19.10	17.94	16.89	15.94	15.08	14.29	13.57	58
59	24.27	22.61	21.11	19.77	18.56	17.46	16.47	15.57	14.74	13.99	13.30	59
60	23.37	21.82	20.42	19.16	18.02	16.98	16.04	15.18	14.40	13.68	13.02	60
61	22.50	21.05	19.74	18.56	17.48	16.50	15.61	14.80	14.05	13.37	12.74	61
62	21.64	20.29	19.06	17.95	16.94	16.02	15.18	14.41	13.71	13.06	12.46	62
63	20.79	19.53	18.39	17.35	16.40	15.54	14.75	14.02	13.35	12.73	12.17	63
64	19.94	18.78	17.71	16.75	15.86	15.05	14.30	13.62	12.99	12.40	11.86	64
65	19.10	18.02	17.03	16.13	15.31	14.55	13.85	13.21	12.61	12.06	11.55	65
66	18.25	17.26	16.35	15.51	14.74	14.03	13.38	12.78	12.22	11.70	11.22	66
67	17.41	16.49	15.65	14.88	14.17	13.51	12.90	12.34	11.82	11.33	10.88	67
68	16.56	15.72	14.95	14.24	13.58	12.97	12.41	11.89	11.40	10.95	10.53	68
69	15.72	14.95	14.25	13.60	12.99	12.43	11.91	11.43	10.97	10.55	10.16	69
70	14.89	14.19	13.55	12.95	12.40	11.88	11.41	10.96	10.54	10.15	9.78	70

continued

Table 1   Multipliers for pecuniary loss for life (males) *continued*

Age at date of trial	Multiplier calculated with allowance for projected mortality from the 2002-based population projections and rate of return of											Age at date of trial
	0.0%	0.5%	1.0%	1.5%	2.0%	2.5%	3.0%	3.5%	4.0%	4.5%	5.0%	
71	14.08	13.45	12.86	12.32	11.81	11.34	10.90	10.49	10.10	9.74	9.41	71
72	13.29	12.72	12.19	11.69	11.23	10.80	10.40	10.02	9.67	9.34	9.03	72
73	12.53	12.01	11.54	11.09	10.67	10.28	9.91	9.56	9.24	8.94	8.65	73
74	11.80	11.34	10.91	10.50	10.12	9.77	9.43	9.12	8.82	8.54	8.27	74
75	11.10	10.69	10.30	9.94	9.59	9.27	8.96	8.68	8.41	8.15	7.91	75
76	10.44	10.07	9.72	9.39	9.08	8.79	8.51	8.25	8.01	7.77	7.55	76
77	9.81	9.48	9.16	8.87	8.59	8.33	8.08	7.84	7.62	7.40	7.20	77
78	9.21	8.91	8.63	8.37	8.12	7.88	7.65	7.44	7.24	7.04	6.86	78
79	8.64	8.38	8.12	7.89	7.66	7.45	7.24	7.05	6.87	6.69	6.52	79
80	8.09	7.86	7.63	7.42	7.22	7.03	6.84	6.67	6.50	6.34	6.19	80
81	7.56	7.35	7.15	6.96	6.78	6.61	6.45	6.29	6.14	6.00	5.86	81
82	7.04	6.86	6.68	6.52	6.36	6.20	6.06	5.92	5.78	5.66	5.53	82
83	6.55	6.39	6.24	6.09	5.95	5.81	5.68	5.56	5.44	5.32	5.22	83
84	6.10	5.95	5.82	5.69	5.56	5.44	5.33	5.22	5.11	5.01	4.91	84
85	5.67	5.55	5.43	5.31	5.20	5.09	4.99	4.89	4.80	4.71	4.62	85
86	5.28	5.17	5.06	4.96	4.86	4.77	4.68	4.59	4.51	4.43	4.35	86
87	4.92	4.82	4.73	4.64	4.55	4.47	4.39	4.31	4.23	4.16	4.09	87
88	4.59	4.50	4.42	4.34	4.26	4.19	4.12	4.05	3.98	3.92	3.86	88
89	4.29	4.21	4.14	4.07	4.00	3.94	3.87	3.81	3.75	3.69	3.64	89
90	4.01	3.95	3.88	3.82	3.76	3.70	3.64	3.59	3.54	3.48	3.43	90
91	3.75	3.69	3.63	3.58	3.52	3.47	3.42	3.37	3.32	3.28	3.23	91
92	3.50	3.45	3.40	3.35	3.30	3.25	3.21	3.16	3.12	3.08	3.04	92
93	3.29	3.24	3.19	3.15	3.11	3.07	3.03	2.99	2.95	2.91	2.88	93
94	3.11	3.06	3.02	2.99	2.95	2.91	2.87	2.84	2.80	2.77	2.74	94
95	2.93	2.90	2.86	2.83	2.79	2.76	2.73	2.69	2.66	2.63	2.60	95
96	2.76	2.73	2.69	2.66	2.63	2.60	2.57	2.55	2.52	2.49	2.47	96
97	2.59	2.56	2.53	2.50	2.47	2.45	2.42	2.40	2.37	2.35	2.33	97
98	2.42	2.39	2.36	2.34	2.32	2.29	2.27	2.25	2.23	2.20	2.18	98
99	2.25	2.23	2.21	2.18	2.16	2.14	2.12	2.10	2.08	2.06	2.05	99
100	2.10	2.08	2.06	2.04	2.02	2.00	1.98	1.97	1.95	1.93	1.92	100

Table 2   Multipliers for pecuniary loss for life (females)

Age at date of trial	Multiplier calculated with allowance for projected mortality from the 2002-based population projections and rate of return of											Age at date of trial
	0.0%	0.5%	1.0%	1.5%	2.0%	2.5%	3.0%	3.5%	4.0%	4.5%	5.0%	
0	87.08	70.28	57.76	48.29	41.02	35.35	30.88	27.30	24.39	22.00	20.01	0
1	86.43	69.92	57.57	48.21	41.00	35.38	30.93	27.36	24.45	22.06	20.07	1
2	85.43	69.27	57.15	47.93	40.82	35.26	30.85	27.30	24.42	22.04	20.06	2
3	84.42	68.61	56.71	47.64	40.63	35.13	30.76	27.24	24.38	22.01	20.04	3
4	83.40	67.94	56.27	47.35	40.43	34.99	30.67	27.18	24.33	21.98	20.02	4
5	82.38	67.26	55.82	47.04	40.22	34.86	30.57	27.11	24.29	21.95	19.99	5
6	81.36	66.58	55.36	46.73	40.01	34.71	30.47	27.05	24.24	21.91	19.97	6
7	80.34	65.89	54.90	46.42	39.80	34.56	30.37	26.97	24.19	21.88	19.94	7
8	79.31	65.20	54.43	46.10	39.58	34.41	30.26	26.90	24.13	21.84	19.91	8
9	78.28	64.51	53.96	45.78	39.36	34.26	30.16	26.82	24.08	21.80	19.89	9
10	77.25	63.81	53.48	45.45	39.13	34.09	30.04	26.74	24.02	21.76	19.85	10
11	76.23	63.11	52.99	45.11	38.89	33.93	29.93	26.66	23.96	21.71	19.82	11
12	75.20	62.40	52.51	44.77	38.65	33.76	29.81	26.57	23.90	21.67	19.79	12
13	74.17	61.69	52.01	44.42	38.41	33.59	29.68	26.48	23.83	21.62	19.75	13
14	73.14	60.97	51.51	44.07	38.16	33.41	29.55	26.39	23.77	21.57	19.72	14
15	72.11	60.26	51.01	43.72	37.91	33.23	29.42	26.29	23.70	21.52	19.68	15
16	71.09	59.54	50.50	43.36	37.65	33.05	29.29	26.20	23.62	21.47	19.64	16
17	70.06	58.82	49.99	43.00	37.39	32.86	29.15	26.10	23.55	21.41	19.60	17
18	69.04	58.09	49.48	42.63	37.13	32.67	29.01	25.99	23.47	21.35	19.55	18
19	68.02	57.37	48.96	42.25	36.86	32.47	28.87	25.89	23.40	21.29	19.51	19
20	66.99	56.63	48.43	41.87	36.58	32.27	28.72	25.78	23.31	21.23	19.46	20
21	65.96	55.90	47.90	41.49	36.30	32.06	28.57	25.66	23.23	21.17	19.41	21
22	64.94	55.16	47.36	41.09	36.01	31.84	28.41	25.54	23.14	21.10	19.36	22
23	63.91	54.41	46.82	40.69	35.71	31.63	28.24	25.42	23.04	21.03	19.30	23
24	62.88	53.66	46.27	40.29	35.41	31.40	28.07	25.29	22.94	20.95	19.25	24
25	61.85	52.90	45.71	39.88	35.10	31.17	27.90	25.16	22.84	20.87	19.18	25
26	60.82	52.14	45.15	39.46	34.79	30.93	27.72	25.02	22.74	20.79	19.12	26
27	59.79	51.38	44.58	39.03	34.47	30.69	27.53	24.88	22.63	20.70	19.05	27
28	58.76	50.61	44.00	38.60	34.14	30.44	27.34	24.73	22.51	20.61	18.98	28
29	57.72	49.84	43.42	38.16	33.81	30.18	27.14	24.58	22.39	20.52	18.91	29
30	56.69	49.06	42.83	37.71	33.46	29.92	26.94	24.42	22.27	20.42	18.83	30
31	55.66	48.28	42.24	37.26	33.12	29.65	26.73	24.25	22.14	20.32'	18.75	31
32	54.63	47.50	41.64	36.80	32.76	29.37	26.52	24.08	22.00	20.21	18.66	32
33	53.59	46.71	41.04	36.33	32.40	29.09	26.29	23.91	21.86	20.10	18.57	33
34	52.56	45.92	40.43	35.86	32.03	28.80	26.07	23.73	21.72	19.99	18.48	34
35	51.53	45.12	39.81	35.38	31.65	28.51	25.83	23.54	21.57	19.86	18.38	35
36	50.50	44.32	39.19	34.89	31.27	28.20	25.59	23.35	21.41	19.74	18.28	36
37	49.47	43.52	38.56	34.40	30.88	27.89	25.34	23.15	21.25	19.61	18.17	37
38	48.44	42.72	37.93	33.89	30.48	27.57	25.09	22.94	21.09	19.47	18.06	38
39	47.41	41.91	37.29	33.39	30.08	27.25	24.82	22.73	20.91	19.33	17.94	39
40	46.39	41.10	36.64	32.87	29.66	26.92	24.55	22.51	20.73	19.18	17.82	40
41	45.36	40.28	35.99	32.35	29.24	26.58	24.28	22.28	20.55	19.03	17.69	41
42	44.34	39.47	35.34	31.83	28.82	26.23	24.00	22.05	20.36	18.87	17.56	42
43	43.32	38.65	34.69	31.30	28.39	25.88	23.71	21.81	20.16	18.70	17.42	43
44	42.31	37.84	34.02	30.76	27.95	25.52	23.41	21.57	19.96	18.53	17.28	44
45	41.30	37.02	33.36	30.22	27.51	25.16	23.11	21.32	19.75	18.36	17.13	45
46	40.29	36.20	32.69	29.67	27.06	24.78	22.80	21.06	19.53	18.18	16.98	46
47	39.29	35.38	32.02	29.12	26.60	24.40	22.48	20.79	19.31	17.99	16.82	47
48	38.28	34.56	31.34	28.56	26.13	24.01	22.16	20.52	19.08	17.79	16.65	48
49	37.29	33.73	30.66	27.99	25.66	23.62	21.82	20.24	18.84	17.59	16.48	49
50	36.29	32.91	29.98	27.42	25.18	23.22	21.48	19.95	18.59	17.38	16.30	50
51	35.30	32.09	29.29	26.84	24.70	22.81	21.14	19.66	18.34	17.16	16.11	51
52	34.32	31.26	28.60	26.26	24.20	22.39	20.78	19.35	18.08	16.94	15.91	52
53	33.34	30.44	27.90	25.67	23.70	21.96	20.42	19.04	17.81	16.71	15.71	53
54	32.36	29.62	27.20	25.08	23.20	21.53	20.05	18.72	17.54	16.47	15.51	54
55	31.39	28.80	26.51	24.49	22.69	21.10	19.67	18.40	17.25	16.22	15.29	55
56	30.44	27.98	25.81	23.89	22.18	20.66	19.29	18.07	16.97	15.97	15.07	56
57	29.49	27.17	25.12	23.29	21.66	20.21	18.90	17.73	16.67	15.71	14.85	57
58	28.54	26.36	24.42	22.69	21.14	19.76	18.51	17.39	16.37	15.45	14.61	58
59	27.61	25.56	23.72	22.09	20.62	19.30	18.11	17.04	16.06	15.18	14.37	59
60	26.69	24.75	23.03	21.48	20.09	18.84	17.70	16.68	15.75	14.90	14.12	60
61	25.77	23.96	22.33	20.87	19.56	18.37	17.29	16.31	15.42	14.61	13.87	61
62	24.86	23.16	21.64	20.26	19.02	17.89	16.87	15.94	15.09	14.32	13.61	62
63	23.95	22.36	20.94	19.64	18.47	17.41	16.44	15.56	14.75	14.01	13.33	63
64	23.04	21.56	20.23	19.02	17.92	16.91	16.00	15.16	14.40	13.69	13.05	64
65	22.12	20.75	19.51	18.38	17.34	16.40	15.54	14.75	14.03	13.36	12.75	65
66	21.20	19.93	18.77	17.72	16.76	15.88	15.07	14.33	13.64	13.01	12.43	66
67	20.27	19.10	18.03	17.05	16.16	15.33	14.58	13.88	13.24	12.64	12.09	67
68	19.33	18.25	17.27	16.37	15.54	14.77	14.07	13.42	12.82	12.26	11.74	68
69	18.39	17.40	16.50	15.67	14.90	14.20	13.54	12.94	12.38	11.86	11.37	69
70	17.45	16.55	15.73	14.96	14.26	13.61	13.01	12.45	11.92	11.44	10.99	70

continued

Table 2   Multipliers for pecuniary loss for life (females) *Continued*

Age at date of trial	Multiplier calculated with allowance for projected mortality from the 2002-based population projections and rate of return of											Age at date of trial
	0.0%	0.5%	1.0%	1.5%	2.0%	2.5%	3.0%	3.5%	4.0%	4.5%	5.0%	
71	16.52	15.71	14.96	14.26	13.62	13.02	12.46	11.95	11.46	11.02	10.60	71
72	15.62	14.88	14.20	13.56	12.98	12.43	11.92	11.44	11.00	10.59	10.20	72
73	14.74	14.07	13.45	12.88	12.34	11.84	11.38	10.94	10.54	10.15	9.79	73
74	13.88	13.29	12.73	12.21	11.72	11.27	10.85	10.45	10.07	9.72	9.39	74
75	13.07	12.53	12.03	11.56	11.12	10.71	10.32	9.96	9.62	9.30	9.00	75
76	12.29	11.81	11.36	10.93	10.54	10.17	9.81	9.49	9.17	8.88	8.60	76
77	11.55	11.12	10.71	10.33	9.97	9.64	9.32	9.02	8.74	8.47	8.22	77
78	10.83	10.45	10.09	9.75	9.43	9.12	8.84	8.57	8.31	8.07	7.84	78
79	10.15	9.81	9.48	9.18	8.89	8.62	8.36	8.12	7.89	7.67	7.46	79
80	9.49	9.18	8.90	8.63	8.37	8.13	7.89	7.68	7.47	7.27	7.08	80
81	8.85	8.58	8.33	8.09	7.86	7.64	7.43	7.24	7.05	6.87	6.70	81
82	8.23	8.00	7.77	7.56	7.36	7.17	6.98	6.81	6.64	6.48	6.33	82
83	7.64	7.44	7.24	7.05	6.88	6.71	6.54	6.39	6.24	6.10	5.96	83
84	7.09	6.91	6.73	6.57	6.41	6.26	6.12	5.98	5.85	5.72	5.60	84
85	6.56	6.40	6.25	6.11	5.97	5.84	5.71	5.59	5.48	5.36	5.26	85
86	6.07	5.93	5.80	5.68	5.56	5.44	5.33	5.22	5.12	5.02	4.93	86
87	5.61	5.49	5.38	5.27	5.16	5.06	4.96	4.87	4.78	4.69	4.61	87
88	5.18	5.08	4.98	4.89	4.79	4.71	4.62	4.54	4.46	4.38	4.31	88
89	4.79	4.70	4.62	4.54	4.45	4.38	4.30	4.23	4.16	4.09	4.03	89
90	4.44	4.36	4.28	4.21	4.14	4.07	4.01	3.94	3.88	3.82	3.77	90
91	4.11	4.04	3.97	3.91	3.85	3.79	3.73	3.68	3.62	3.57	3.52	91
92	3.81	3.75	3.70	3.64	3.59	3.53	3.48	3.43	3.39	3.34	3.30	92
93	3.55	3.50	3.45	3.40	3.35	3.31	3.26	3.22	3.18	3.14	3.10	93
94	3.32	3.27	3.23	3.18	3.14	3.10	3.06	3.02	2.98	2.95	2.91	94
95	3.09	3.05	3.01	2.98	2.94	2.90	2.87	2.83	2.80	2.77	2.74	95
96	2.88	2.85	2.82	2.78	2.75	2.72	2.69	2.66	2.63	2.60	2.57	96
97	2.69	2.66	2.63	2.60	2.57	2.55	2.52	2.49	2.47	2.44	2.42	97
98	2.51	2.49	2.46	2.43	2.41	2.38	2.36	2.34	2.31	2.29	2.27	98
99	2.34	2.31	2.29	2.27	2.25	2.22	2.20	2.18	2.16	2.14	2.12	99
100	2.16	2.14	2.12	2.10	2.08	2.06	2.05	2.03	2.01	1.99	1.98	100

Table 3   Multipliers for loss of earnings to pension age 50 (males)

Age at date of trial	Multiplier calculated with allowance for projected mortality from the 2002-based population projections and rate of return of											Age at date of trial
	0.0%	0.5%	1.0%	1.5%	2.0%	2.5%	3.0%	3.5%	4.0%	4.5%	5.0%	
16	33.53	30.86	28.48	26.35	24.45	22.74	21.21	19.83	18.59	17.46	16.44	16
17	32.54	30.02	27.76	25.74	23.93	22.30	20.84	19.51	18.31	17.23	16.24	17
18	31.55	29.17	27.04	25.13	23.41	21.86	20.45	19.18	18.03	16.99	16.03	18
19	30.57	28.33	26.32	24.51	22.88	21.40	20.06	18.85	17.74	16.74	15.82	19
20	29.58	27.49	25.60	23.89	22.34	20.94	19.66	18.50	17.45	16.48	15.59	20
21	28.60	26.64	24.86	23.25	21.79	20.46	19.25	18.15	17.13	16.21	15.36	21
22	27.62	25.79	24.12	22.61	21.23	19.97	18.83	17.77	16.81	15.93	15.11	22
23	26.63	24.93	23.37	21.95	20.66	19.47	18.39	17.39	16.47	15.63	14.85	23
24	25.65	24.06	22.62	21.29	20.07	18.96	17.94	16.99	16.12	15.32	14.58	24
25	24.67	23.20	21.85	20.62	19.48	18.43	17.47	16.58	15.76	15.00	14.29	25
26	23.68	22.33	21.08	19.93	18.87	17.90	16.99	16.16	15.38	14.66	14.00	26
27	22.70	21.45	20.30	19.24	18.26	17.34	16.50	15.72	14.99	14.31	13.68	27
28	21.72	20.57	19.52	18.53	17.62	16.78	15.99	15.26	14.58	13.94	13.35	28
29	20.73	19.69	18.72	17.82	16.98	16.20	15.47	14.79	14.16	13.56	13.01	29
30	19.75	18.80	17.92	17.10	16.33	15.61	14.93	14.30	13.71	13.16	12.64	30
31	18.77	17.91	17.11	16.36	15.66	15.00	14.38	13.80	13.26	12.74	12.26	31
32	17.78	17.01	16.29	15.61	14.97	14.37	13.81	13.28	12.78	12.31	11.86	32
33	16.80	16.11	15.46	14.85	14.28	13.73	13.22	12.74	12.28	11.85	11.44	33
34	15.82	15.21	14.63	14.08	13.57	13.08	12.62	12.18	11.76	11.37	11.00	34
35	14.83	14.29	13.78	13.30	12.84	12.41	11.99	11.60	11.23	10.87	10.54	35
36	13.85	13.38	12.93	12.51	12.10	11.72	11.35	11.00	10.67	10.35	10.05	36
37	12.86	12.46	12.07	11.70	11.35	11.01	10.69	10.38	10.09	9.81	9.54	37
38	11.88	11.53	11.20	10.88	10.58	10.28	10.01	9.74	9.48	9.24	9.00	38
39	10.89	10.60	10.32	10.05	9.79	9.54	9.30	9.07	8.85	8.64	8.44	39
40	9.90	9.66	9.43	9.20	8.99	8.78	8.58	8.38	8.20	8.02	7.84	40
41	8.92	8.72	8.53	8.35	8.17	8.00	7.83	7.67	7.52	7.37	7.22	41
42	7.93	7.77	7.62	7.48	7.33	7.20	7.06	6.93	6.81	6.69	6.57	42
43	6.94	6.82	6.71	6.59	6.48	6.38	6.27	6.17	6.07	5.98	5.88	43
44	5.95	5.87	5.78	5.70	5.61	5.54	5.46	5.38	5.31	5.23	5.16	44
45	4.97	4.90	4.84	4.79	4.73	4.67	4.62	4.56	4.51	4.46	4.41	45
46	3.98	3.94	3.90	3.86	3.82	3.79	3.75	3.72	3.68	3.65	3.61	46
47	2.99	2.96	2.94	2.92	2.90	2.88	2.86	2.84	2.82	2.80	2.78	47
48	1.99	1.98	1.97	1.96	1.95	1.95	1.94	1.93	1.92	1.91	1.90	48
49	1.00	1.00	0.99	0.99	0.99	0.99	0.98	0.98	0.98	0.98	0.97	49

Table 4   Multipliers for loss of earnings to pension age 50 (females)

Age at date of trial	Multiplier calculated with allowance for projected mortality from the 2002-based population projections and rate of return of											Age at date of trial
	0.0%	0.5%	1.0%	1.5%	2.0%	2.5%	3.0%	3.5%	4.0%	4.5%	5.0%	
16	33.79	31.08	28.68	26.53	24.61	22.89	21.34	19.95	18.69	17.55	16.52	16
17	32.79	30.24	27.96	25.93	24.10	22.45	20.97	19.63	18.42	17.33	16.33	17
18	31.80	29.40	27.24	25.31	23.57	22.00	20.59	19.31	18.14	17.09	16.12	18
19	30.80	28.55	26.52	24.69	23.04	21.55	20.20	18.97	17.85	16.84	15.91	19
20	29.81	27.69	25.78	24.06	22.49	21.08	19.79	18.62	17.55	16.58	15.68	20
21	28.81	26.83	25.04	23.41	21.94	20.60	19.37	18.26	17.24	16.30	15.45	21
22	27.82	25.97	24.29	22.76	21.37	20.10	18.94	17.88	16.91	16.02	15.20	22
23	26.83	25.10	23.53	22.10	20.79	19.60	18.50	17.50	16.57	15.72	14.94	23
24	25.83	24.23	22.77	21.43	20.20	19.08	18.05	17.09	16.22	15.41	14.66	24
25	24.84	23.35	22.00	20.75	19.60	18.55	17.58	16.68	15.85	15.08	14.37	25
26	23.84	22.47	21.22	20.06	18.99	18.00	17.09	16.25	15.47	14.74	14.07	26
27	22.85	21.59	20.43	19.36	18.36	17.45	16.59	15.80	15.07	14.39	13.75	27
28	21.85	20.70	19.63	18.64	17.73	16.87	16.08	15.34	14.66	14.02	13.42	28
29	20.86	19.81	18.83	17.92	17.08	16.29	15.55	14.87	14.23	13.63	13.07	29
30	19.86	18.91	18.02	17.19	16.41	15.69	15.01	14.38	13.78	13.22	12.70	30
31	18.87	18.01	17.20	16.44	15.74	15.07	14.45	13.87	13.32	12.80	12.32	31
32	17.88	17.10	16.37	15.69	15.05	14.44	13.87	13.34	12.84	12.36	11.91	32
33	16.88	16.19	15.54	14.92	14.34	13.80	13.28	12.79	12.33	11.90	11.49	33
34	15.89	15.27	14.69	14.14	13.63	13.13	12.67	12.23	11.81	11.42	11.04	34
35	14.90	14.36	13.84	13.36	12.89	12.46	12.04	11.65	11.27	10.91	10.58	35
36	13.91	13.43	12.98	12.56	12.15	11.76	11.39	11.04	10.71	10.39	10.08	36
37	12.91	12.50	12.11	11.74	11.39	11.05	10.73	10.42	10.12	9.84	9.57	37
38	11.92	11.57	11.24	10.92	10.61	10.32	10.04	9.77	9.51	9.27	9.03	38
39	10.93	10.63	10.35	10.08	9.82	9.57	9.33	9.10	8.88	8.67	8.46	39
40	9.94	9.69	9.46	9.23	9.02	8.81	8.61	8.41	8.22	8.04	7.87	40
41	8.94	8.75	8.56	8.37	8.19	8.02	7.86	7.70	7.54	7.39	7.24	41
42	7.95	7.80	7.65	7.50	7.36	7.22	7.08	6.95	6.83	6.71	6.59	42
43	6.96	6.84	6.73	6.61	6.50	6.39	6.29	6.19	6.09	5.99	5.90	43
44	5.97	5.88	5.80	5.71	5.63	5.55	5.47	5.40	5.32	5.25	5.18	44
45	4.98	4.92	4.86	4.80	4.74	4.68	4.63	4.57	4.52	4.47	4.42	45
46	3.99	3.95	3.91	3.87	3.83	3.79	3.76	3.72	3.69	3.65	3.62	46
47	2.99	2.97	2.95	2.93	2.90	2.88	2.86	2.84	2.82	2.80	2.78	47
48	2.00	1.99	1.98	1.97	1.96	1.95	1.94	1.93	1.92	1.91	1.90	48
49	1.00	1.00	0.99	0.99	0.99	0.99	0.98	0.98	0.98	0.98	0.97	49

Table 5   Multipliers for loss of earnings to pension age 55 (males)

Age at date of trial	Multiplier calculated with allowance for projected mortality from the 2002-based population projections and rate of return of											Age at date of trial
	0.0%	0.5%	1.0%	1.5%	2.0%	2.5%	3.0%	3.5%	4.0%	4.5%	5.0%	
16	38.32	34.85	31.80	29.13	26.77	24.69	22.84	21.20	19.73	18.42	17.25	16
17	37.32	34.02	31.12	28.56	26.30	24.30	22.51	20.92	19.50	18.23	17.09	17
18	36.33	33.20	30.44	27.99	25.83	23.90	22.18	20.65	19.27	18.04	16.92	18
19	35.35	32.38	29.75	27.42	25.35	23.50	21.84	20.36	19.03	17.83	16.75	19
20	34.37	31.56	29.06	26.84	24.86	23.09	21.50	20.07	18.79	17.63	16.58	20
21	33.39	30.73	28.36	26.25	24.36	22.66	21.14	19.77	18.53	17.41	16.39	21
22	32.41	29.90	27.66	25.65	23.85	22.23	20.77	19.45	18.26	17.18	16.20	22
23	31.42	29.06	26.95	25.04	23.33	21.79	20.39	19.13	17.98	16.94	15.99	23
24	30.44	28.22	26.23	24.43	22.80	21.33	20.00	18.79	17.69	16.69	15.78	24
25	29.46	27.38	25.50	23.80	22.26	20.87	19.60	18.45	17.39	16.43	15.55	25
26	28.48	26.53	24.77	23.17	21.71	20.39	19.19	18.09	17.08	16.16	15.32	26
27	27.50	25.68	24.03	22.52	21.15	19.90	18.76	17.72	16.76	15.88	15.07	27
28	26.52	24.82	23.28	21.87	20.58	19.40	18.32	17.33	16.42	15.58	14.81	28
29	25.54	23.96	22.52	21.21	20.00	18.89	17.87	16.93	16.07	15.27	14.54	29
30	24.56	23.10	21.76	20.53	19.41	18.37	17.41	16.52	15.71	14.95	14.25	30
31	23.58	22.23	20.99	19.85	18.80	17.83	16.93	16.10	15.33	14.61	13.95	31
32	22.60	21.36	20.22	19.16	18.18	17.28	16.44	15.66	14.94	14.26	13.64	32
33	21.62	20.48	19.43	18.46	17.55	16.71	15.93	15.20	14.53	13.89	13.31	33
34	20.64	19.60	18.64	17.74	16.91	16.13	15.41	14.73	14.10	13.51	12.96	34
35	19.66	18.71	17.84	17.02	16.25	15.54	14.87	14.25	13.66	13.11	12.59	35
36	18.67	17.82	17.03	16.28	15.58	14.93	14.32	13.74	13.20	12.69	12.21	36
37	17.69	16.93	16.21	15.54	14.90	14.31	13.75	13.22	12.72	12.25	11.81	37
38	16.71	16.03	15.38	14.78	14.21	13.67	13.16	12.68	12.22	11.80	11.39	38
39	15.73	15.12	14.55	14.01	13.50	13.01	12.55	12.12	11.71	11.32	10.95	39
40	14.75	14.21	13.71	13.23	12.77	12.34	11.93	11.54	11.17	10.82	10.48	40
41	13.77	13.30	12.86	12.44	12.03	11.65	11.29	10.94	10.61	10.30	10.00	41
42	12.79	12.38	12.00	11.63	11.28	10.95	10.63	10.32	10.03	9.75	9.49	42
43	11.81	11.46	11.13	10.82	10.52	10.23	9.95	9.69	9.43	9.19	8.95	43
44	10.83	10.54	10.26	9.99	9.74	9.49	9.25	9.02	8.81	8.59	8.39	44
45	9.85	9.61	9.38	9.15	8.94	8.73	8.53	8.34	8.16	7.98	7.80	45
46	8.87	8.68	8.49	8.30	8.13	7.96	7.79	7.64	7.48	7.33	7.19	46
47	7.89	7.74	7.59	7.44	7.30	7.17	7.03	6.90	6.78	6.66	6.54	47
48	6.91	6.80	6.68	6.57	6.46	6.35	6.25	6.15	6.05	5.95	5.86	48
49	5.93	5.85	5.76	5.68	5.60	5.52	5.44	5.36	5.29	5.22	5.15	49
50	4.95	4.89	4.83	4.77	4.72	4.66	4.60	4.55	4.50	4.45	4.40	50
51	3.97	3.93	3.89	3.85	3.81	3.78	3.74	3.71	3.67	3.64	3.61	51
52	2.98	2.96	2.94	2.92	2.89	2.87	2.85	2.83	2.81	2.79	2.77	52
53	1.99	1.98	1.97	1.96	1.95	1.94	1.93	1.92	1.91	1.91	1.90	53
54	1.00	0.99	0.99	0.99	0.99	0.99	0.98	0.98	0.98	0.98	0.97	54

Table 6   Multipliers for loss of earnings to pension age 55 (females)

Age at date of trial	Multiplier calculated with allowance for projected mortality from the 2002-based population projections and rate of return of											Age at date of trial
	0.0%	0.5%	1.0%	1.5%	2.0%	2.5%	3.0%	3.5%	4.0%	4.5%	5.0%	
16	38.66	35.15	32.07	29.36	26.98	24.87	23.00	21.34	19.86	18.54	17.35	16
17	37.67	34.33	31.39	28.80	26.51	24.48	22.68	21.07	19.64	18.35	17.19	17
18	36.68	33.50	30.71	28.23	26.04	24.09	22.35	20.80	19.41	18.16	17.03	18
19	35.68	32.67	30.01	27.65	25.55	23.68	22.01	20.51	19.17	17.96	16.86	19
20	34.69	31.84	29.31	27.06	25.06	23.27	21.66	20.22	18.92	17.75	16.69	20
21	33.69	31.00	28.61	26.47	24.55	22.84	21.30	19.91	18.66	17.52	16.50	21
22	32.70	30.16	27.89	25.86	24.04	22.40	20.93	19.59	18.39	17.29	16.30	22
23	31.70	29.31	27.17	25.25	23.52	21.95	20.54	19.27	18.11	17.05	16.10	23
24	30.71	28.46	26.44	24.62	22.98	21.49	20.15	18.93	17.82	16.80	15.88	24
25	29.71	27.61	25.71	23.99	22.43	21.02	19.74	18.58	17.51	16.54	15.65	25
26	28.72	26.75	24.96	23.35	21.88	20.54	19.32	18.21	17.20	16.27	15.41	26
27	27.73	25.89	24.21	22.69	21.31	20.05	18.89	17.84	16.87	15.98	15.16	27
28	26.73	25.02	23.46	22.03	20.73	19.54	18.45	17.45	16.53	15.68	14.90	28
29	25.74	24.15	22.69	21.36	20.14	19.02	17.99	17.05	16.17	15.37	14.62	29
30	24.74	23.27	21.92	20.68	19.54	18.49	17.52	16.63	15.80	15.04	14.33	30
31	23.75	22.39	21.14	19.99	18.93	17.94	17.04	16.20	15.42	14.70	14.03	31
32	22.76	21.51	20.35	19.29	18.30	17.39	16.54	15.75	15.02	14.35	13.71	32
33	21.77	20.62	19.56	18.58	17.66	16.82	16.03	15.29	14.61	13.97	13.38	33
34	20.77	19.73	18.76	17.85	17.01	16.23	15.50	14.82	14.18	13.59	13.03	34
35	19.78	18.83	17.95	17.12	16.35	15.63	14.96	14.33	13.74	13.18	12.66	35
36	18.79	17.93	17.13	16.38	15.68	15.02	14.40	13.82	13.27	12.76	12.28	36
37	17.80	17.03	16.31	15.63	14.99	14.39	13.82	13.29	12.79	12.32	11.87	37
38	16.81	16.12	15.47	14.86	14.29	13.74	13.23	12.75	12.29	11.86	11.45	38
39	15.82	15.21	14.63	14.09	13.57	13.08	12.62	12.18	11.77	11.38	11.00	39
40	14.83	14.30	13.78	13.30	12.84	12.41	11.99	11.60	11.23	10.87	10.54	40
41	13.85	13.38	12.93	12.50	12.10	11.72	11.35	11.00	10.67	10.35	10.05	41
42	12.86	12.45	12.07	11.70	11.34	11.01	10.69	10.38	10.08	9.80	9.53	42
43	11.87	11.53	11.19	10.88	10.57	10.28	10.00	9.73	9.48	9.23	9.00	43
44	10.89	10.59	10.31	10.04	9.79	9.54	9.30	9.07	8.85	8.64	8.43	44
45	9.90	9.66	9.43	9.20	8.99	8.78	8.58	8.38	8.20	8.02	7.84	45
46	8.91	8.72	8.53	8.34	8.17	8.00	7.83	7.67	7.52	7.37	7.22	46
47	7.93	7.77	7.62	7.48	7.33	7.20	7.06	6.93	6.81	6.69	6.57	47
48	6.94	6.82	6.71	6.59	6.48	6.38	6.27	6.17	6.07	5.98	5.88	48
49	5.95	5.87	5.78	5.70	5.62	5.54	5.46	5.38	5.31	5.24	5.16	49
50	4.97	4.91	4.85	4.79	4.73	4.67	4.62	4.56	4.51	4.46	4.41	50
51	3.98	3.94	3.90	3.86	3.82	3.79	3.75	3.72	3.68	3.65	3.61	51
52	2.99	2.96	2.94	2.92	2.90	2.88	2.86	2.84	2.82	2.80	2.78	52
53	1.99	1.98	1.97	1.96	1.95	1.95	1.94	1.93	1.92	1.91	1.90	53
54	1.00	1.00	0.99	0.99	0.99	0.99	0.98	0.98	0.98	0.98	0.97	54

Table 7   Multipliers for loss of earnings to pension age 60 (males)

Age at date of trial	Multiplier calculated with allowance for projected mortality from the 2002-based population projections and rate of return of											Age at date of trial
	0.0%	0.5%	1.0%	1.5%	2.0%	2.5%	3.0%	3.5%	4.0%	4.5%	5.0%	
16	43.02	38.67	34.92	31.66	28.84	26.38	24.22	22.33	20.66	19.18	17.87	16
17	42.02	37.86	34.26	31.14	28.41	26.03	23.93	22.09	20.47	19.02	17.74	17
18	41.03	37.06	33.61	30.60	27.98	25.67	23.65	21.86	20.27	18.86	17.61	18
19	40.05	36.26	32.96	30.07	27.54	25.31	23.35	21.61	20.07	18.70	17.47	19
20	39.07	35.46	32.30	29.53	27.10	24.95	23.05	21.37	19.87	18.53	17.33	20
21	38.09	34.65	31.63	28.98	26.64	24.57	22.74	21.11	19.65	18.35	17.19	21
22	37.11	33.84	30.96	28.42	26.18	24.19	22.42	20.84	19.43	18.17	17.03	22
23	36.13	33.02	30.28	27.86	25.71	23.79	22.09	20.57	19.20	17.97	16.87	23
24	35.15	32.20	29.60	27.28	25.23	23.39	21.75	20.28	18.96	17.77	16.70	24
25	34.17	31.38	28.90	26.70	24.74	22.98	21.40	19.99	18.71	17.56	16.52	25
26	33.19	30.55	28.21	26.11	24.24	22.55	21.04	19.68	18.45	17.34	16.33	26
27	32.21	29.72	27.50	25.51	23.73	22.12	20.67	19.37	18.18	17.11	16.13	27
28	31.23	28.89	26.79	24.91	23.21	21.68	20.29	19.04	17.90	16.87	15.93	28
29	30.25	28.05	26.07	24.29	22.68	21.22	19.90	18.70	17.61	16.62	15.71	29
30	29.27	27.21	25.35	23.67	22.14	20.76	19.50	18.36	17.31	16.36	15.49	30
31	28.29	26.36	24.62	23.03	21.59	20.28	19.09	18.00	17.00	16.09	15.25	31
32	27.31	25.51	23.88	22.39	21.03	19.79	18.66	17.62	16.67	15.80	15.00	32
33	26.34	24.66	23.13	21.73	20.46	19.29	18.22	17.24	16.34	15.50	14.74	33
34	25.36	23.80	22.37	21.07	19.88	18.78	17.77	16.84	15.98	15.19	14.46	34
35	24.38	22.94	21.61	20.40	19.28	18.25	17.30	16.43	15.62	14.87	14.18	35
36	23.40	22.07	20.84	19.72	18.67	17.71	16.82	16.00	15.24	14.53	13.87	36
37	22.42	21.20	20.07	19.02	18.06	17.16	16.33	15.56	14.84	14.18	13.56	37
38	21.44	20.32	19.28	18.32	17.42	16.59	15.82	15.10	14.43	13.81	13.22	38
39	20.46	19.44	18.49	17.60	16.78	16.01	15.30	14.63	14.00	13.42	12.87	39
40	19.49	18.56	17.69	16.88	16.13	15.42	14.76	14.14	13.56	13.02	12.51	40
41	18.51	17.67	16.88	16.15	15.46	14.81	14.21	13.64	13.10	12.60	12.12	41
42	17.54	16.78	16.07	15.40	14.78	14.19	13.64	13.12	12.62	12.16	11.72	42
43	16.56	15.89	15.25	14.65	14.09	13.55	13.05	12.58	12.13	11.70	11.30	43
44	15.59	14.99	14.42	13.89	13.38	12.90	12.45	12.02	11.62	11.23	10.86	44
45	14.62	14.09	13.59	13.12	12.67	12.24	11.83	11.45	11.08	10.74	10.40	45
46	13.65	13.19	12.75	12.33	11.94	11.56	11.20	10.86	10.53	10.22	9.92	46
47	12.68	12.28	11.90	11.54	11.19	10.86	10.55	10.25	9.96	9.68	9.42	47
48	11.71	11.37	11.05	10.74	10.44	10.15	9.88	9.62	9.36	9.12	8.89	48
49	10.75	10.46	10.19	9.92	9.67	9.42	9.19	8.96	8.75	8.54	8.34	49
50	9.78	9.54	9.31	9.09	8.88	8.67	8.48	8.29	8.10	7.93	7.75	50
51	8.81	8.62	8.43	8.25	8.07	7.91	7.74	7.59	7.43	7.29	7.14	51
52	7.84	7.69	7.54	7.39	7.25	7.12	6.99	6.86	6.74	6.62	6.50	52
53	6.87	6.75	6.63	6.52	6.41	6.31	6.21	6.11	6.01	5.92	5.82	53
54	5.89	5.81	5.72	5.64	5.56	5.48	5.40	5.33	5.26	5.18	5.11	54
55	4.92	4.86	4.80	4.74	4.68	4.63	4.57	4.52	4.47	4.42	4.37	55
56	3.94	3.91	3.87	3.83	3.79	3.76	3.72	3.69	3.65	3.62	3.58	56
57	2.97	2.94	2.92	2.90	2.88	2.86	2.84	2.82	2.80	2.78	2.76	57
58	1.98	1.97	1.96	1.95	1.94	1.94	1.93	1.92	1.91	1.90	1.89	58
59	1.00	0.99	0.99	0.99	0.99	0.98	0.98	0.98	0.98	0.97	0.97	59

Table 8   **Multipliers for loss of earnings to pension age 60 (females)**

Age at date of trial	Multiplier calculated with allowance for projected mortality from the 2002-based population projections and rate of return of											Age at date of trial
	0.0%	0.5%	1.0%	1.5%	2.0%	2.5%	3.0%	3.5%	4.0%	4.5%	5.0%	
16	43.48	39.07	35.26	31.96	29.10	26.60	24.42	22.50	20.81	19.31	17.99	16
17	42.48	38.26	34.61	31.44	28.67	26.26	24.14	22.27	20.62	19.16	17.86	17
18	41.49	37.46	33.96	30.91	28.24	25.90	23.85	22.04	20.43	19.01	17.74	18
19	40.50	36.65	33.30	30.37	27.80	25.54	23.55	21.79	20.23	18.84	17.60	19
20	39.50	35.83	32.63	29.82	27.35	25.17	23.25	21.54	20.03	18.67	17.46	20
21	38.51	35.02	31.95	29.26	26.89	24.80	22.94	21.28	19.81	18.49	17.31	21
22	37.51	34.19	31.27	28.70	26.42	24.41	22.61	21.02	19.59	18.31	17.16	22
23	36.52	33.37	30.59	28.13	25.95	24.01	22.28	20.74	19.35	18.11	16.99	23
24	35.52	32.54	29.89	27.55	25.46	23.60	21.94	20.45	19.11	17.91	16.82	24
25	34.53	31.70	29.19	26.96	24.96	23.18	21.59	20.15	18.86	17.69	16.64	25
26	33.53	30.86	28.48	26.36	24.46	22.75	21.22	19.84	18.60	17.47	16.45	26
27	32.54	30.02	27.77	25.75	23.94	22.32	20.85	19.52	18.33	17.24	16.25	27
28	31.54	29.17	27.05	25.14	23.42	21.87	20.46	19.19	18.04	17.00	16.04	28
29	30.55	28.32	26.32	24.51	22.88	21.40	20.07	18.85	17.75	16.74	15.83	29
30	29.56	27.47	25.58	23.88	22.33	20.93	19.66	18.50	17.44	16.48	15.60	30
31	28.56	26.61	24.84	23.23	21.77	20.45	19.24	18.14	17.13	16.20	15.36	31
32	27.57	25.75	24.09	22.58	21.21	19.95	18.81	17.76	16.80	15.92	15.10	32
33	26.58	24.88	23.33	21.92	20.63	19.45	18.36	17.37	16.46	15.61	14.84	33
34	25.59	24.01	22.57	21.25	20.04	18.93	17.91	16.97	16.10	15.30	14.56	34
35	24.60	23.14	21.80	20.57	19.44	18.39	17.43	16.55	15.73	14.97	14.27	35
36	23.61	22.26	21.02	19.88	18.82	17.85	16.95	16.12	15.35	14.63	13.97	36
37	22.62	21.38	20.23	19.18	18.20	17.29	16.45	15.67	14.95	14.28	13.65	37
38	21.63	20.49	19.44	18.47	17.56	16.72	15.94	15.21	14.54	13.90	13.31	38
39	20.64	19.61	18.64	17.75	16.91	16.14	15.41	14.74	14.11	13.52	12.96	39
40	19.65	18.71	17.84	17.02	16.25	15.54	14.87	14.25	13.66	13.11	12.59	40
41	18.67	17.82	17.02	16.28	15.58	14.93	14.31	13.74	13.20	12.69	12.21	41
42	17.69	16.92	16.20	15.53	14.90	14.30	13.74	13.21	12.72	12.25	11.81	42
43	16.70	16.02	15.38	14.77	14.20	13.66	13.15	12.67	12.22	11.79	11.38	43
44	15.72	15.11	14.54	14.00	13.49	13.01	12.55	12.11	11.70	11.31	10.94	44
45	14.74	14.21	13.70	13.22	12.77	12.33	11.93	11.54	11.17	10.81	10.48	45
46	13.76	13.29	12.85	12.43	12.03	11.65	11.28	10.94	10.61	10.29	9.99	46
47	12.78	12.38	11.99	11.63	11.28	10.94	10.63	10.32	10.03	9.75	9.48	47
48	11.80	11.46	11.13	10.81	10.51	10.22	9.95	9.68	9.43	9.18	8.95	48
49	10.82	10.53	10.26	9.99	9.73	9.49	9.25	9.02	8.80	8.59	8.39	49
50	9.85	9.61	9.37	9.15	8.94	8.73	8.53	8.34	8.15	7.97	7.80	50
51	8.87	8.67	8.48	8.30	8.13	7.96	7.79	7.63	7.48	7.33	7.19	51
52	7.89	7.73	7.58	7.44	7.30	7.16	7.03	6.90	6.78	6.65	6.54	52
53	6.91	6.79	6.67	6.56	6.45	6.35	6.24	6.14	6.04	5.95	5.86	53
54	5.93	5.84	5.75	5.67	5.59	5.51	5.43	5.36	5.28	5.21	5.14	54
55	4.95	4.89	4.83	4.77	4.71	4.65	4.60	4.55	4.49	4.44	4.39	55
56	3.96	3.92	3.89	3.85	3.81	3.77	3.74	3.70	3.67	3.64	3.60	56
57	2.98	2.96	2.93	2.91	2.89	2.87	2.85	2.83	2.81	2.79	2.77	57
58	1.99	1.98	1.97	1.96	1.95	1.94	1.93	1.92	1.91	1.90	1.90	58
59	1.00	0.99	0.99	0.99	0.99	0.99	0.98	0.98	0.98	0.98	0.97	59

Table 9   Multipliers for loss of earnings to pension age 65 (males)

Age at date of trial	Multiplier calculated with allowance for projected mortality from the 2002-based population projections and rate of return of											Age at date of trial
	0.0%	0.5%	1.0%	1.5%	2.0%	2.5%	3.0%	3.5%	4.0%	4.5%	5.0%	
16	47.58	42.29	37.79	33.95	30.66	27.82	25.37	23.25	21.39	19.77	18.34	16
17	46.58	41.50	37.16	33.45	30.26	27.51	25.12	23.05	21.23	19.64	18.24	17
18	45.59	40.71	36.54	32.96	29.87	27.19	24.87	22.84	21.07	19.51	18.13	18
19	44.61	39.93	35.92	32.46	29.47	26.87	24.61	22.64	20.90	19.37	18.02	19
20	43.63	39.15	35.29	31.95	29.06	26.55	24.35	22.42	20.73	19.23	17.91	20
21	42.65	38.36	34.65	31.44	28.65	26.21	24.08	22.20	20.55	19.09	17.79	21
22	41.67	37.56	34.01	30.92	28.23	25.87	23.80	21.98	20.36	18.94	17.66	22
23	40.69	36.77	33.36	30.39	27.79	25.52	23.51	21.74	20.17	18.78	17.53	23
24	39.71	35.97	32.71	29.86	27.35	25.16	23.21	21.50	19.97	18.61	17.40	24
25	38.73	35.16	32.05	29.31	26.91	24.79	22.91	21.24	19.76	18.44	17.25	25
26	37.75	34.35	31.38	28.76	26.45	24.41	22.60	20.98	19.54	18.26	17.10	26
27	36.77	33.54	30.71	28.20	25.99	24.02	22.27	20.71	19.32	18.07	16.94	27
28	35.79	32.73	30.03	27.64	25.51	23.63	21.94	20.44	19.09	17.87	16.78	28
29	34.81	31.91	29.34	27.06	25.03	23.22	21.60	20.15	18.84	17.67	16.60	29
30	33.83	31.09	28.65	26.48	24.54	22.81	21.25	19.85	18.59	17.45	16.42	30
31	32.86	30.26	27.95	25.89	24.04	22.38	20.89	19.54	18.33	17.23	16.23	31
32	31.88	29.43	27.25	25.29	23.53	21.94	20.52	19.22	18.06	17.00	16.03	32
33	30.90	28.60	26.53	24.68	23.01	21.50	20.13	18.90	17.77	16.75	15.82	33
34	29.92	27.76	25.81	24.06	22.47	21.04	19.74	18.56	17.48	16.50	15.60	34
35	28.95	26.92	25.09	23.43	21.93	20.57	19.33	18.20	17.18	16.23	15.37	35
36	27.97	26.07	24.35	22.80	21.38	20.09	18.91	17.84	16.86	15.96	15.13	36
37	26.99	25.22	23.61	22.15	20.82	19.60	18.48	17.46	16.53	15.67	14.88	37
38	26.01	24.37	22.86	21.49	20.24	19.09	18.04	17.07	16.18	15.37	14.61	38
39	25.04	23.51	22.11	20.83	19.65	18.58	17.58	16.67	15.83	15.05	14.33	39
40	24.06	22.65	21.35	20.15	19.06	18.05	17.11	16.25	15.46	14.72	14.04	40
41	23.09	21.78	20.58	19.47	18.45	17.51	16.63	15.83	15.08	14.38	13.73	41
42	22.12	20.92	19.81	18.78	17.83	16.95	16.14	15.38	14.68	14.02	13.41	42
43	21.15	20.05	19.03	18.08	17.20	16.39	15.63	14.93	14.27	13.65	13.08	43
44	20.18	19.17	18.24	17.37	16.57	15.81	15.11	14.45	13.84	13.27	12.73	44
45	19.21	18.30	17.45	16.66	15.92	15.22	14.58	13.97	13.40	12.87	12.37	45
46	18.25	17.43	16.66	15.93	15.26	14.62	14.03	13.47	12.95	12.45	11.99	46
47	17.29	16.55	15.85	15.20	14.59	14.01	13.47	12.96	12.47	12.02	11.59	47
48	16.33	15.67	15.05	14.46	13.91	13.38	12.89	12.43	11.98	11.57	11.17	48
49	15.37	14.79	14.23	13.71	13.21	12.74	12.30	11.88	11.48	11.10	10.74	49
50	14.42	13.90	13.41	12.94	12.50	12.08	11.69	11.31	10.95	10.61	10.28	50
51	13.46	13.01	12.58	12.17	11.78	11.41	11.06	10.72	10.40	10.10	9.80	51
52	12.50	12.11	11.74	11.38	11.04	10.72	10.41	10.11	9.83	9.56	9.30	52
53	11.54	11.21	10.89	10.58	10.29	10.01	9.74	9.49	9.24	9.00	8.78	53
54	10.58	10.30	10.03	9.78	9.53	9.29	9.06	8.84	8.62	8.42	8.22	54
55	9.63	9.40	9.17	8.96	8.75	8.55	8.35	8.17	7.99	7.81	7.65	55
56	8.68	8.49	8.31	8.13	7.96	7.79	7.63	7.48	7.33	7.18	7.04	56
57	7.73	7.58	7.43	7.29	7.15	7.02	6.89	6.77	6.65	6.53	6.41	57
58	6.78	6.66	6.55	6.44	6.33	6.23	6.13	6.03	5.93	5.84	5.75	58
59	5.82	5.74	5.65	5.57	5.49	5.42	5.34	5.27	5.20	5.13	5.06	59
60	4.87	4.81	4.75	4.69	4.64	4.58	4.53	4.48	4.43	4.37	4.33	60
61	3.91	3.87	3.83	3.80	3.76	3.73	3.69	3.66	3.62	3.59	3.56	61
62	2.95	2.92	2.90	2.88	2.86	2.84	2.82	2.80	2.78	2.76	2.74	62
63	1.97	1.97	1.96	1.95	1.94	1.93	1.92	1.91	1.90	1.89	1.88	63
64	0.99	0.99	0.99	0.99	0.98	0.98	0.98	0.98	0.97	0.97	0.97	64

Table 10   Multipliers for loss of earnings to pension age 65 (females)

Age at date of trial	Multiplier calculated with allowance for projected mortality from the 2002-based population projections and rate of return of											Age at date of trial
	0.0%	0.5%	1.0%	1.5%	2.0%	2.5%	3.0%	3.5%	4.0%	4.5%	5.0%	
16	48.20	42.81	38.23	34.32	30.98	28.10	25.61	23.45	21.57	19.92	18.48	16
17	47.20	42.03	37.61	33.84	30.59	27.79	25.37	23.26	21.42	19.80	18.38	17
18	46.21	41.24	36.99	33.34	30.20	27.48	25.12	23.06	21.26	19.67	18.28	18
19	45.22	40.45	36.36	32.84	29.80	27.16	24.86	22.85	21.09	19.54	18.17	19
20	44.22	39.65	35.72	32.33	29.39	26.83	24.59	22.64	20.92	19.40	18.06	20
21	43.22	38.85	35.08	31.81	28.97	26.49	24.32	22.42	20.74	19.25	17.94	21
22	42.23	38.05	34.43	31.28	28.54	26.14	24.04	22.19	20.55	19.10	17.81	22
23	41.23	37.24	33.77	30.75	28.11	25.79	23.75	21.95	20.36	18.94	17.68	23
24	40.24	36.43	33.11	30.21	27.66	25.42	23.45	21.70	20.16	18.78	17.54	24
25	39.24	35.61	32.44	29.65	27.21	25.05	23.14	21.45	19.94	18.60	17.40	25
26	38.25	34.79	31.76	29.10	26.75	24.67	22.83	21.19	19.73	18.42	17.25	26
27	37.25	33.97	31.08	28.53	26.28	24.28	22.50	20.92	19.50	18.23	17.09	27
28	36.25	33.14	30.39	27.95	25.80	23.88	22.16	20.63	19.26	18.03	16.92	28
29	35.26	32.31	29.69	27.37	25.31	23.46	21.82	20.34	19.02	17.82	16.75	29
30	34.26	31.47	28.99	26.78	24.81	23.04	21.46	20.04	18.76	17.61	16.56	30
31	33.27	30.63	28.28	26.18	24.30	22.61	21.10	19.73	18.50	17.38	16.37	31
32	32.28	29.79	27.56	25.57	23.78	22.17	20.72	19.41	18.22	17.15	16.17	32
33	31.28	28.94	26.84	24.95	23.25	21.72	20.33	19.08	17.94	16.90	15.96	33
34	30.29	28.09	26.11	24.33	22.71	21.26	19.93	18.73	17.64	16.65	15.74	34
35	29.30	27.24	25.38	23.69	22.17	20.78	19.52	18.38	17.33	16.38	15.51	35
36	28.31	26.38	24.63	23.05	21.61	20.30	19.10	18.01	17.01	16.10	15.26	36
37	27.32	25.52	23.89	22.40	21.04	19.80	18.67	17.63	16.68	15.81	15.01	37
38	26.33	24.66	23.13	21.74	20.46	19.29	18.22	17.24	16.34	15.51	14.74	38
39	25.35	23.79	22.37	21.06	19.87	18.77	17.77	16.84	15.98	15.19	14.46	39
40	24.36	22.92	21.60	20.39	19.27	18.24	17.29	16.42	15.61	14.86	14.17	40
41	23.38	22.05	20.83	19.70	18.66	17.70	16.81	15.99	15.23	14.52	13.86	41
42	22.40	21.17	20.04	19.00	18.04	17.14	16.31	15.54	14.83	14.16	13.54	42
43	21.42	20.30	19.26	18.30	17.40	16.58	15.80	15.09	14.42	13.79	13.21	43
44	20.44	19.42	18.47	17.58	16.76	16.00	15.28	14.61	13.99	13.41	12.86	44
45	19.46	18.53	17.67	16.86	16.11	15.40	14.74	14.13	13.55	13.00	12.50	45
46	18.49	17.65	16.86	16.13	15.44	14.79	14.19	13.62	13.09	12.59	12.11	46
47	17.51	16.76	16.05	15.39	14.76	14.17	13.62	13.10	12.61	12.15	11.71	47
48	16.54	15.86	15.23	14.63	14.07	13.54	13.04	12.56	12.12	11.69	11.29	48
49	15.57	14.97	14.40	13.87	13.37	12.89	12.44	12.01	11.60	11.22	10.85	49
50	14.60	14.07	13.57	13.10	12.65	12.22	11.82	11.43	11.07	10.72	10.39	50
51	13.63	13.17	12.73	12.31	11.92	11.54	11.18	10.84	10.52	10.21	9.91	51
52	12.66	12.26	11.88	11.52	11.17	10.85	10.53	10.23	9.94	9.67	9.40	52
53	11.69	11.35	11.03	10.71	10.42	10.13	9.86	9.60	9.35	9.11	8.87	53
54	10.72	10.44	10.16	9.90	9.65	9.40	9.17	8.94	8.73	8.52	8.32	54
55	9.76	9.52	9.29	9.07	8.86	8.65	8.46	8.27	8.08	7.91	7.74	55
56	8.79	8.60	8.41	8.23	8.06	7.89	7.73	7.57	7.42	7.27	7.13	56
57	7.82	7.67	7.52	7.38	7.24	7.11	6.97	6.85	6.72	6.60	6.49	57
58	6.86	6.74	6.63	6.51	6.41	6.30	6.20	6.10	6.00	5.91	5.82	58
59	5.89	5.80	5.72	5.63	5.55	5.48	5.40	5.32	5.25	5.18	5.11	59
60	4.92	4.86	4.80	4.74	4.68	4.63	4.57	4.52	4.47	4.42	4.37	60
61	3.94	3.91	3.87	3.83	3.79	3.76	3.72	3.69	3.65	3.62	3.59	61
62	2.97	2.95	2.92	2.90	2.88	2.86	2.84	2.82	2.80	2.78	2.76	62
63	1.98	1.97	1.97	1.96	1.95	1.94	1.93	1.92	1.91	1.90	1.89	63
64	1.00	0.99	0.99	0.99	0.99	0.98	0.98	0.98	0.98	0.97	0.97	64

Table 11   Multipliers for loss of earnings to pension age 70 (males)

Age at date of trial	Multiplier calculated with allowance for projected mortality from the 2002-based population projections and rate of return of											Age at date of trial
	0.0%	0.5%	1.0%	1.5%	2.0%	2.5%	3.0%	3.5%	4.0%	4.5%	5.0%	
16	51.94	45.66	40.40	35.98	32.23	29.05	26.33	23.99	21.97	20.22	18.70	16
17	50.94	44.89	39.80	35.51	31.87	28.77	26.11	23.82	21.84	20.11	18.61	17
18	49.95	44.12	39.21	35.04	31.51	28.48	25.88	23.64	21.70	20.00	18.52	18
19	48.97	43.35	38.61	34.58	31.14	28.19	25.65	23.46	21.55	19.89	18.43	19
20	47.99	42.59	38.01	34.10	30.77	27.90	25.42	23.28	21.41	19.78	18.34	20
21	47.01	41.81	37.40	33.62	30.39	27.60	25.18	23.09	21.26	19.65	18.24	21
22	46.02	41.04	36.78	33.13	30.00	27.29	24.94	22.89	21.10	19.53	18.14	22
23	45.04	40.26	36.16	32.64	29.60	26.97	24.68	22.68	20.93	19.39	18.03	23
24	44.06	39.47	35.53	32.14	29.20	26.64	24.42	22.47	20.76	19.25	17.92	24
25	43.08	38.68	34.90	31.63	28.79	26.31	24.15	22.25	20.58	19.11	17.80	25
26	42.10	37.89	34.26	31.11	28.37	25.97	23.87	22.03	20.40	18.96	17.68	26
27	41.12	37.10	33.62	30.59	27.94	25.62	23.59	21.80	20.21	18.80	17.55	27
28	40.14	36.30	32.97	30.05	27.51	25.27	23.30	21.56	20.01	18.64	17.41	28
29	39.16	35.50	32.31	29.52	27.06	24.90	23.00	21.31	19.81	18.47	17.27	29
30	38.18	34.70	31.65	28.97	26.61	24.53	22.69	21.05	19.59	18.29	17.12	30
31	37.20	33.89	30.98	28.41	26.15	24.15	22.37	20.78	19.37	18.10	16.97	31
32	36.23	33.08	30.30	27.85	25.68	23.75	22.04	20.51	19.14	17.91	16.80	32
33	35.25	32.26	29.62	27.28	25.20	23.35	21.70	20.23	18.90	17.71	16.63	33
34	34.27	31.44	28.93	26.70	24.71	22.94	21.36	19.93	18.65	17.50	16.45	34
35	33.29	30.61	28.23	26.11	24.22	22.52	21.00	19.63	18.39	17.28	16.27	35
36	32.31	29.79	27.53	25.52	23.71	22.09	20.63	19.31	18.12	17.05	16.07	36
37	31.34	28.95	26.82	24.91	23.19	21.65	20.25	18.99	17.84	16.81	15.86	37
38	30.36	28.12	26.10	24.30	22.66	21.19	19.86	18.65	17.55	16.55	15.64	38
39	29.38	27.28	25.38	23.67	22.13	20.73	19.46	18.30	17.25	16.29	15.42	39
40	28.41	26.43	24.65	23.04	21.58	20.25	19.04	17.94	16.94	16.02	15.18	40
41	27.43	25.59	23.92	22.40	21.02	19.77	18.62	17.57	16.62	15.74	14.93	41
42	26.46	24.74	23.18	21.76	20.46	19.27	18.19	17.19	16.28	15.44	14.67	42
43	25.49	23.89	22.43	21.10	19.88	18.77	17.74	16.80	15.93	15.14	14.40	43
44	24.53	23.04	21.68	20.44	19.30	18.25	17.29	16.40	15.58	14.82	14.12	44
45	23.56	22.19	20.93	19.77	18.71	17.72	16.82	15.98	15.21	14.49	13.82	45
46	22.60	21.34	20.17	19.10	18.11	17.19	16.34	15.55	14.82	14.15	13.52	46
47	21.65	20.49	19.41	18.42	17.50	16.64	15.85	15.11	14.43	13.79	13.20	47
48	20.70	19.63	18.64	17.73	16.88	16.08	15.35	14.66	14.02	13.42	12.87	48
49	19.75	18.77	17.87	17.03	16.24	15.51	14.83	14.19	13.60	13.04	12.52	49
50	18.79	17.91	17.09	16.32	15.60	14.93	14.30	13.71	13.16	12.64	12.15	50
51	17.84	17.05	16.30	15.60	14.95	14.33	13.76	13.21	12.70	12.22	11.77	51
52	16.89	16.18	15.50	14.87	14.28	13.72	13.19	12.70	12.23	11.79	11.37	52
53	15.95	15.31	14.70	14.14	13.60	13.09	12.62	12.17	11.74	11.34	10.95	53
54	15.00	14.43	13.90	13.39	12.91	12.46	12.03	11.62	11.23	10.87	10.52	54
55	14.06	13.56	13.09	12.64	12.21	11.81	11.42	11.06	10.71	10.38	10.06	55
56	13.12	12.69	12.27	11.88	11.50	11.15	10.80	10.48	10.17	9.87	9.59	56
57	12.19	11.82	11.46	11.11	10.79	10.47	10.17	9.89	9.61	9.35	9.10	57
58	11.27	10.95	10.64	10.34	10.06	9.79	9.53	9.28	9.04	8.81	8.59	58
59	10.35	10.07	9.81	9.56	9.32	9.09	8.87	8.65	8.44	8.25	8.06	59
60	9.42	9.20	8.98	8.77	8.57	8.37	8.19	8.00	7.83	7.66	7.50	60
61	8.50	8.32	8.14	7.97	7.80	7.64	7.49	7.34	7.19	7.05	6.91	61
62	7.59	7.44	7.30	7.16	7.03	6.90	6.77	6.65	6.53	6.42	6.30	62
63	6.66	6.55	6.44	6.33	6.23	6.13	6.03	5.93	5.84	5.75	5.66	63
64	5.74	5.65	5.57	5.49	5.41	5.34	5.26	5.19	5.12	5.05	4.99	64
65	4.81	4.75	4.69	4.63	4.58	4.52	4.47	4.42	4.37	4.32	4.27	65
66	3.87	3.83	3.79	3.75	3.72	3.68	3.65	3.61	3.58	3.55	3.52	66
67	2.92	2.90	2.88	2.85	2.83	2.81	2.79	2.77	2.75	2.74	2.72	67
68	1.96	1.95	1.94	1.93	1.92	1.91	1.90	1.89	1.89	1.88	1.87	68
69	0.99	0.99	0.98	0.98	0.98	0.98	0.97	0.97	0.97	0.97	0.97	69

Table 12   **Multipliers for loss of earnings to pension age 70 (females)**

Age at date of trial	Multiplier calculated with allowance for projected mortality from the 2002-based population projections and rate of return of											Age at date of trial
	0.0%	0.5%	1.0%	1.5%	2.0%	2.5%	3.0%	3.5%	4.0%	4.5%	5.0%	
16	52.79	46.36	40.98	36.46	32.63	29.39	26.61	24.23	22.18	20.40	18.85	16
17	51.79	45.59	40.39	36.00	32.28	29.11	26.40	24.07	22.05	20.30	18.77	17
18	50.79	44.82	39.79	35.54	31.92	28.83	26.18	23.90	21.92	20.19	18.69	18
19	49.80	44.05	39.19	35.06	31.55	28.54	25.95	23.72	21.78	20.08	18.60	19
20	48.80	43.27	38.58	34.59	31.18	28.25	25.72	23.53	21.63	19.97	18.51	20
21	47.80	42.48	37.96	34.10	30.79	27.94	25.48	23.34	21.48	19.85	18.41	21
22	46.81	41.70	37.34	33.61	30.40	27.63	25.23	23.15	21.32	19.72	18.31	22
23	45.81	40.90	36.71	33.11	30.00	27.32	24.98	22.94	21.16	19.59	18.20	23
24	44.81	40.11	36.08	32.60	29.60	26.99	24.72	22.73	20.99	19.45	18.09	24
25	43.81	39.31	35.43	32.08	29.18	26.65	24.45	22.51	20.81	19.31	17.98	25
26	42.82	38.51	34.79	31.56	28.76	26.31	24.17	22.29	20.63	19.16	17.85	26
27	41.82	37.70	34.13	31.03	28.33	25.96	23.88	22.05	20.43	19.00	17.72	27
28	40.82	36.89	33.47	30.49	27.89	25.60	23.59	21.81	20.24	18.84	17.59	28
29	39.82	36.07	32.80	29.95	27.44	25.23	23.28	21.56	20.03	18.67	17.45	29
30	38.83	35.26	32.13	29.39	26.98	24.85	22.97	21.30	19.81	18.49	17.30	30
31	37.83	34.43	31.45	28.83	26.51	24.47	22.65	21.03	19.59	18.30	17.14	31
32	36.84	33.61	30.77	28.26	26.04	24.07	22.32	20.76	19.36	18.11	16.98	32
33	35.84	32.78	30.08	27.68	25.56	23.67	21.98	20.47	19.12	17.90	16.81	33
34	34.85	31.95	29.38	27.10	25.06	23.25	21.63	20.18	18.87	17.69	16.63	34
35	33.86	31.11	28.67	26.50	24.56	22.83	21.27	19.87	18.61	17.47	16.44	35
36	32.87	30.27	27.96	25.90	24.05	22.39	20.90	19.56	18.34	17.24	16.25	36
37	31.88	29.43	27.25	25.29	23.53	21.95	20.52	19.23	18.06	17.00	16.04	37
38	30.89	28.59	26.52	24.67	23.00	21.49	20.13	18.89	17.77	16.75	15.82	38
39	29.90	27.74	25.80	24.04	22.46	21.03	19.73	18.55	17.47	16.49	15.60	39
40	28.91	26.89	25.06	23.41	21.91	20.55	19.32	18.19	17.16	16.22	15.36	40
41	27.93	26.04	24.32	22.77	21.35	20.07	18.89	17.82	16.84	15.94	15.12	41
42	26.95	25.18	23.58	22.12	20.79	19.57	18.46	17.44	16.51	15.65	14.86	42
43	25.97	24.33	22.83	21.46	20.21	19.06	18.01	17.05	16.16	15.35	14.59	43
44	24.99	23.47	22.07	20.79	19.62	18.55	17.56	16.65	15.81	15.03	14.31	44
45	24.02	22.61	21.31	20.12	19.03	18.02	17.09	16.23	15.44	14.70	14.02	45
46	23.04	21.74	20.54	19.44	18.42	17.48	16.61	15.80	15.05	14.36	13.71	46
47	22.07	20.88	19.77	18.75	17.80	16.93	16.11	15.36	14.66	14.00	13.40	47
48	21.11	20.01	18.99	18.05	17.18	16.36	15.61	14.90	14.25	13.63	13.06	48
49	20.14	19.14	18.21	17.34	16.54	15.79	15.09	14.43	13.82	13.25	12.71	49
50	19.17	18.27	17.42	16.63	15.89	15.20	14.55	13.95	13.38	12.85	12.35	50
51	18.21	17.39	16.62	15.90	15.23	14.60	14.00	13.45	12.92	12.43	11.97	51
52	17.25	16.51	15.82	15.17	14.56	13.98	13.44	12.93	12.45	12.00	11.57	52
53	16.29	15.63	15.01	14.42	13.87	13.35	12.86	12.40	11.96	11.54	11.15	53
54	15.33	14.75	14.20	13.67	13.18	12.71	12.27	11.85	11.45	11.07	10.71	54
55	14.38	13.86	13.38	12.91	12.47	12.05	11.66	11.28	10.92	10.58	10.26	55
56	13.43	12.98	12.55	12.14	11.75	11.39	11.03	10.70	10.38	10.07	9.78	56
57	12.48	12.09	11.72	11.36	11.02	10.70	10.39	10.10	9.82	9.55	9.29	57
58	11.53	11.20	10.88	10.57	10.28	10.00	9.73	9.48	9.23	8.99	8.77	58
59	10.58	10.30	10.03	9.77	9.53	9.29	9.06	8.84	8.62	8.42	8.22	59
60	9.64	9.40	9.18	8.96	8.76	8.55	8.36	8.17	7.99	7.82	7.65	60
61	8.69	8.50	8.32	8.14	7.97	7.80	7.64	7.49	7.34	7.19	7.05	61
62	7.74	7.59	7.45	7.30	7.17	7.03	6.90	6.78	6.66	6.54	6.43	62
63	6.79	6.68	6.56	6.45	6.35	6.24	6.14	6.04	5.95	5.85	5.76	63
64	5.84	5.75	5.67	5.59	5.51	5.43	5.35	5.28	5.21	5.14	5.07	64
65	4.88	4.82	4.76	4.70	4.65	4.59	4.54	4.49	4.43	4.38	4.33	65
66	3.92	3.88	3.84	3.80	3.77	3.73	3.70	3.66	3.63	3.59	3.56	66
67	2.95	2.93	2.91	2.89	2.86	2.84	2.82	2.80	2.78	2.76	2.75	67
68	1.98	1.97	1.96	1.95	1.94	1.93	1.92	1.91	1.90	1.89	1.88	68
69	0.99	0.99	0.99	0.99	0.98	0.98	0.98	0.98	0.97	0.97	0.97	69

Table 13   Multipliers for loss of earnings to pension age 75 (males)

Age at date of trial	Multiplier calculated with allowance for projected mortality from the 2002-based population projections and rate of return of											Age at date of trial
	0.0%	0.5%	1.0%	1.5%	2.0%	2.5%	3.0%	3.5%	4.0%	4.5%	5.0%	
16	56.02	48.74	42.73	37.74	33.57	30.06	27.10	24.58	22.42	20.56	18.96	16
17	55.02	47.98	42.15	37.30	33.23	29.80	26.90	24.42	22.30	20.47	18.88	17
18	54.02	47.22	41.57	36.85	32.89	29.54	26.70	24.27	22.18	20.37	18.81	18
19	53.04	46.47	41.00	36.41	32.55	29.28	26.49	24.11	22.06	20.28	18.73	19
20	52.06	45.72	40.42	35.97	32.21	29.01	26.29	23.95	21.93	20.18	18.66	20
21	51.07	44.96	39.83	35.51	31.85	28.74	26.07	23.78	21.80	20.08	18.57	21
22	50.09	44.20	39.24	35.05	31.49	28.46	25.85	23.61	21.66	19.97	18.49	22
23	49.10	43.43	38.64	34.58	31.13	28.17	25.62	23.43	21.52	19.85	18.40	23
24	48.12	42.66	38.04	34.11	30.75	27.87	25.39	23.24	21.37	19.74	18.30	24
25	47.13	41.88	37.43	33.63	30.37	27.57	25.15	23.05	21.22	19.61	18.20	25
26	46.15	41.11	36.81	33.14	29.98	27.26	24.90	22.85	21.06	19.48	18.10	26
27	45.17	40.33	36.19	32.64	29.59	26.94	24.65	22.65	20.89	19.35	17.99	27
28	44.19	39.55	35.57	32.14	29.18	26.62	24.39	22.43	20.72	19.21	17.88	28
29	43.21	38.76	34.93	31.63	28.77	26.29	24.12	22.22	20.54	19.07	17.76	29
30	42.23	37.97	34.30	31.12	28.36	25.95	23.84	21.99	20.36	18.92	17.63	30
31	41.24	37.17	33.65	30.59	27.93	25.60	23.56	21.76	20.17	18.76	17.50	31
32	40.26	36.37	33.00	30.06	27.49	25.24	23.26	21.51	19.97	18.59	17.37	32
33	39.28	35.57	32.34	29.52	27.05	24.88	22.96	21.26	19.76	18.42	17.22	33
34	38.30	34.77	31.68	28.98	26.60	24.50	22.65	21.01	19.55	18.24	17.07	34
35	37.32	33.96	31.01	28.42	26.14	24.12	22.33	20.74	19.32	18.05	16.92	35
36	36.34	33.14	30.33	27.86	25.67	23.73	22.00	20.46	19.09	17.86	16.75	36
37	35.36	32.33	29.65	27.28	25.19	23.32	21.66	20.18	18.85	17.65	16.58	37
38	34.38	31.50	28.96	26.70	24.70	22.91	21.31	19.88	18.60	17.44	16.39	38
39	33.40	30.68	28.26	26.11	24.20	22.49	20.95	19.58	18.34	17.22	16.20	39
40	32.42	29.85	27.56	25.52	23.69	22.06	20.58	19.26	18.07	16.98	16.00	40
41	31.44	29.02	26.85	24.91	23.18	21.61	20.21	18.94	17.79	16.74	15.80	41
42	30.47	28.19	26.14	24.30	22.65	21.16	19.82	18.60	17.50	16.49	15.58	42
43	29.50	27.35	25.43	23.69	22.12	20.70	19.42	18.26	17.20	16.24	15.35	43
44	28.53	26.52	24.70	23.07	21.58	20.24	19.02	17.90	16.89	15.97	15.12	44
45	27.57	25.69	23.98	22.44	21.03	19.76	18.60	17.54	16.57	15.69	14.88	45
46	26.61	24.85	23.25	21.80	20.48	19.28	18.18	17.17	16.25	15.40	14.62	46
47	25.66	24.02	22.52	21.16	19.92	18.78	17.74	16.79	15.91	15.10	14.36	47
48	24.71	23.18	21.79	20.51	19.35	18.28	17.30	16.39	15.56	14.79	14.09	48
49	23.76	22.34	21.05	19.86	18.77	17.76	16.84	15.99	15.20	14.47	13.80	49
50	22.81	21.50	20.30	19.20	18.18	17.24	16.37	15.57	14.83	14.14	13.50	50
51	21.87	20.66	19.55	18.52	17.58	16.70	15.89	15.14	14.44	13.79	13.19	51
52	20.92	19.81	18.79	17.84	16.96	16.15	15.39	14.69	14.04	13.43	12.86	52
53	19.98	18.96	18.02	17.15	16.34	15.59	14.89	14.23	13.62	13.05	12.52	53
54	19.04	18.11	17.26	16.46	15.71	15.02	14.37	13.76	13.19	12.66	12.16	54
55	18.11	17.27	16.49	15.76	15.08	14.44	13.84	13.28	12.75	12.26	11.79	55
56	17.18	16.43	15.72	15.05	14.43	13.85	13.30	12.79	12.30	11.84	11.41	56
57	16.27	15.59	14.95	14.35	13.79	13.25	12.75	12.28	11.84	11.42	11.02	57
58	15.36	14.75	14.18	13.64	13.13	12.65	12.20	11.77	11.36	10.98	10.61	58
59	14.46	13.92	13.41	12.93	12.47	12.04	11.63	11.24	10.87	10.52	10.19	59
60	13.56	13.08	12.63	12.21	11.80	11.42	11.05	10.70	10.37	10.06	9.76	60
61	12.67	12.25	11.86	11.48	11.13	10.79	10.46	10.15	9.85	9.57	9.30	61
62	11.79	11.43	11.08	10.75	10.44	10.14	9.86	9.58	9.32	9.07	8.83	62
63	10.90	10.59	10.30	10.02	9.75	9.49	9.24	9.00	8.77	8.55	8.34	63
64	10.02	9.76	9.51	9.27	9.04	8.82	8.60	8.40	8.20	8.01	7.83	64
65	9.14	8.92	8.71	8.51	8.32	8.13	7.95	7.78	7.61	7.45	7.29	65
66	8.25	8.07	7.90	7.74	7.58	7.42	7.27	7.13	6.99	6.85	6.72	66
67	7.36	7.22	7.08	6.95	6.82	6.70	6.58	6.46	6.35	6.24	6.13	67
68	6.47	6.36	6.25	6.15	6.05	5.95	5.86	5.77	5.68	5.59	5.50	68
69	5.57	5.49	5.41	5.34	5.26	5.19	5.12	5.05	4.98	4.91	4.85	69
70	4.67	4.62	4.56	4.51	4.45	4.40	4.35	4.30	4.25	4.20	4.16	70
71	3.77	3.73	3.70	3.66	3.63	3.59	3.56	3.53	3.49	3.46	3.43	71
72	2.86	2.84	2.81	2.79	2.77	2.75	2.74	2.72	2.70	2.68	2.66	72
73	1.93	1.92	1.91	1.90	1.89	1.88	1.87	1.87	1.86	1.85	1.84	73
74	0.98	0.98	0.98	0.97	0.97	0.97	0.97	0.96	0.96	0.96	0.96	74

Table 14   Multipliers for loss of earnings to pension age 75 (females)

Age at date of trial	Multiplier calculated with allowance for projected mortality from the 2002-based population projections and rate of return of											Age at date of trial
	0.0%	0.5%	1.0%	1.5%	2.0%	2.5%	3.0%	3.5%	4.0%	4.5%	5.0%	
16	57.18	49.67	43.48	38.35	34.07	30.48	27.44	24.86	22.66	20.77	19.13	16
17	56.18	48.92	42.92	37.92	33.74	30.23	27.25	24.72	22.55	20.68	19.06	17
18	55.18	48.16	42.34	37.49	33.41	29.97	27.06	24.57	22.43	20.59	19.00	18
19	54.18	47.40	41.76	37.04	33.07	29.71	26.86	24.42	22.32	20.50	18.92	19
20	53.18	46.64	41.18	36.59	32.73	29.45	26.65	24.26	22.19	20.40	18.85	20
21	52.18	45.87	40.59	36.14	32.37	29.17	26.44	24.09	22.06	20.30	18.77	21
22	51.18	45.10	39.99	35.67	32.01	28.89	26.22	23.92	21.93	20.20	18.68	22
23	50.18	44.32	39.38	35.20	31.65	28.61	25.99	23.74	21.79	20.09	18.60	23
24	49.18	43.54	38.77	34.73	31.27	28.31	25.76	23.56	21.64	19.97	18.50	24
25	48.18	42.76	38.16	34.24	30.89	28.01	25.52	23.37	21.49	19.85	18.41	25
26	47.18	41.97	37.54	33.75	30.50	27.70	25.28	23.17	21.33	19.72	18.31	26
27	46.18	41.18	36.91	33.25	30.10	27.38	25.02	22.97	21.17	19.59	18.20	27
28	45.18	40.38	36.27	32.74	29.69	27.06	24.76	22.76	21.00	19.45	18.09	28
29	44.18	39.58	35.63	32.23	29.28	26.72	24.49	22.54	20.82	19.31	17.97	29
30	43.18	38.78	34.99	31.71	28.86	26.38	24.21	22.31	20.64	19.16	17.85	30
31	42.18	37.97	34.33	31.18	28.43	26.03	23.93	22.08	20.45	19.00	17.72	31
32	41.19	37.16	33.67	30.64	27.99	25.67	23.64	21.84	20.25	18.84	17.58	32
33	40.19	36.35	33.01	30.10	27.55	25.31	23.33	21.59	20.04	18.67	17.44	33
34	39.19	35.53	32.34	29.55	27.09	24.93	23.02	21.33	19.83	18.49	17.30	34
35	38.20	34.71	31.66	28.99	26.63	24.55	22.71	21.07	19.61	18.31	17.14	35
36	37.20	33.89	30.98	28.42	26.16	24.16	22.38	20.79	19.38	18.12	16.98	36
37	36.21	33.06	30.29	27.85	25.68	23.75	22.04	20.51	19.14	17.91	16.81	37
38	35.22	32.24	29.60	27.26	25.19	23.34	21.70	20.22	18.90	17.71	16.63	38
39	34.23	31.40	28.90	26.68	24.69	22.92	21.34	19.92	18.64	17.49	16.45	39
40	33.24	30.57	28.20	26.08	24.19	22.49	20.98	19.61	18.38	17.26	16.25	40
41	32.25	29.73	27.49	25.48	23.67	22.06	20.60	19.29	18.10	17.03	16.05	41
42	31.27	28.90	26.77	24.86	23.15	21.61	20.22	18.96	17.82	16.78	15.84	42
43	30.29	28.06	26.05	24.25	22.62	21.15	19.83	18.62	17.53	16.53	15.62	43
44	29.32	27.22	25.33	23.62	22.08	20.69	19.42	18.27	17.22	16.27	15.39	44
45	28.34	26.38	24.60	22.99	21.54	20.21	19.01	17.91	16.91	15.99	15.16	45
46	27.37	25.53	23.87	22.36	20.98	19.73	18.59	17.54	16.59	15.71	14.91	46
47	26.40	24.69	23.13	21.71	20.42	19.23	18.15	17.16	16.25	15.42	14.65	47
48	25.43	23.84	22.38	21.06	19.84	18.73	17.71	16.77	15.91	15.11	14.38	48
49	24.47	22.99	21.64	20.40	19.26	18.21	17.25	16.37	15.55	14.79	14.09	49
50	23.51	22.14	20.88	19.73	18.67	17.69	16.78	15.95	15.18	14.46	13.80	50
51	22.55	21.29	20.12	19.05	18.06	17.15	16.30	15.52	14.79	14.12	13.49	51
52	21.59	20.43	19.36	18.37	17.45	16.60	15.81	15.08	14.40	13.76	13.17	52
53	20.64	19.58	18.59	17.68	16.83	16.04	15.31	14.62	13.99	13.39	12.84	53
54	19.69	18.72	17.82	16.98	16.20	15.47	14.79	14.16	13.56	13.01	12.49	54
55	18.74	17.86	17.04	16.28	15.56	14.89	14.26	13.68	13.13	12.61	12.12	55
56	17.80	17.01	16.26	15.57	14.91	14.30	13.73	13.18	12.68	12.20	11.75	56
57	16.87	16.15	15.48	14.85	14.26	13.70	13.17	12.68	12.21	11.77	11.35	57
58	15.93	15.29	14.69	14.12	13.59	13.08	12.61	12.16	11.73	11.33	10.95	58
59	15.00	14.44	13.90	13.39	12.91	12.46	12.03	11.62	11.23	10.87	10.52	59
60	14.08	13.58	13.10	12.65	12.23	11.82	11.43	11.07	10.72	10.39	10.07	60
61	13.15	12.72	12.30	11.90	11.53	11.17	10.83	10.50	10.19	9.89	9.61	61
62	12.23	11.85	11.49	11.14	10.82	10.50	10.20	9.91	9.64	9.38	9.12	62
63	11.31	10.98	10.67	10.37	10.09	9.82	9.56	9.31	9.07	8.84	8.61	63
64	10.38	10.11	9.84	9.59	9.35	9.12	8.89	8.68	8.47	8.27	8.08	64
65	9.45	9.23	9.01	8.80	8.59	8.40	8.21	8.03	7.85	7.68	7.52	65
66	8.52	8.34	8.16	7.99	7.82	7.66	7.50	7.35	7.21	7.07	6.93	66
67	7.59	7.45	7.30	7.17	7.03	6.90	6.78	6.66	6.54	6.42	6.31	67
68	6.66	6.55	6.44	6.33	6.23	6.13	6.03	5.93	5.84	5.75	5.66	68
69	5.73	5.64	5.56	5.48	5.40	5.33	5.25	5.18	5.11	5.04	4.98	69
70	4.79	4.73	4.67	4.62	4.56	4.51	4.46	4.41	4.36	4.31	4.26	70
71	3.85	3.81	3.78	3.74	3.70	3.67	3.64	3.60	3.57	3.54	3.50	71
72	2.91	2.89	2.87	2.84	2.82	2.80	2.78	2.76	2.74	2.73	2.71	72
73	1.95	1.94	1.94	1.93	1.92	1.91	1.90	1.89	1.88	1.87	1.86	73
74	0.99	0.98	0.98	0.98	0.98	0.98	0.97	0.97	0.97	0.97	0.96	74

Appendix 6

The Criminal Injuries Compensation Scheme 2001

Table of contents

Tariff of injuries and standard amounts of compensation

Levels of compensation.
Descriptions of injury.
Notes to the Tariff.

The Criminal Injuries Compensation Scheme (2001)

1. This Scheme is made by the Secretary of State under the Criminal Injuries Compensation Act 1995. Applications received on or after 1 April 2001 for the payment of compensation to, or in respect of, persons who have sustained criminal injury will be considered under this Scheme (subject to paragraphs 83–86 below).

Administration of the Scheme

2. Claims officers in the Criminal Injuries Compensation Authority ('the Authority') will determine claims for compensation in accordance with this Scheme. Appeals against decisions taken on reviews under this Scheme will be determined by adjudicators. Persons appointed as adjudicators are appointed as members of the Criminal Injuries Compensation Appeals Panel ('the Panel'). The Secretary of State will appoint one of the adjudicators as Chairman of the Panel. The Secretary of State will also appoint persons as staff of the Panel to administer the provisions of this Scheme relating to the appeal system.

3. Claims officers will be responsible for deciding, in accordance with this Scheme, what awards (if any) should be made in individual cases, and how they should be paid. Their decisions will be open to review and thereafter to appeal to the Panel, in accordance with this Scheme. No decision, whether by a claims officer or the Panel, will be open to appeal to the Secretary of State.

4. The general working of this Scheme will be kept under review by the Secretary of State. The Accounting Officers for the Authority and the Panel must each submit reports to the Secretary of State and the Scottish Ministers

as soon as possible after the end of each financial year, dealing with the operation of this Scheme and the discharge of functions under it. The Accounting Officers must each keep proper accounts and proper records in relation to those accounts, and must each prepare a statement of accounts in each financial year in a form directed by the Secretary of State. These statements of accounts must be submitted to the Secretary of State and the Scottish Ministers as soon as possible after the end of each financial year.

5.   The Panel will advise the Secretary of State on matters on which he seeks its advice, as well as on such other matters and at such times as it considers appropriate. Any advice given by the Panel will be referred to by the Accounting Officer for the Panel in his annual report made under the preceding paragraph.

Eligibility to apply for compensation

6.   Compensation may be paid in accordance with this Scheme:

   (a)   to an applicant who has sustained a criminal injury on or after 1 August 1964;

   (b)   where the victim of a criminal injury sustained on or after 1 August 1964 has since died, to an applicant who is a qualifying claimant for the purposes of paragraph 38 (compensation in fatal cases).

   For the purposes of this Scheme, 'applicant' means any person for whose benefit an application for compensation is made, even where it is made on his behalf by another person.

7.   No compensation will be paid under this Scheme in the following circumstances:

   (a)   where the applicant has previously lodged any claim for compensation in respect of the same criminal injury under this or any other scheme for the compensation of the victims of violent crime in operation in Great Britain; or

   (b)   where the criminal injury was sustained before 1 October 1979 and the victim and the assailant were living together at the time as members of the same family.

8.   For the purposes of this Scheme, 'criminal injury' means one or more personal injuries as described in the following paragraph, being an injury sustained in Great Britain (see *Note 1)* and directly attributable to:

   (a)   a crime of violence (including arson, fire-raising or an act of poisoning); or

   (b)   an offence of trespass on a railway;or

   (c)   the apprehension or attempted apprehension of an offender or a suspected offender, the prevention or attempted prevention of an offence, or the giving of help to any constable who is engaged in any such activity.

9.   For the purposes of this Scheme, personal injury includes physical injury (including fatal injury), mental injury (that is temporary mental anxiety, medically verified, or a disabling mental illness confirmed by psychiatric diagnosis) and disease (that is a medically recognised illness or condition). Mental injury or disease may either result directly from the physical injury or from a sexual offence or may occur without any physical injury. Compensation will not be payable for mental injury or disease without physical injury, or in respect of a sexual offence, unless the applicant:

(a)   was put in reasonable fear of immediate physical harm to his own person; or

(b)   had a close relationship of love and affection with another person at the time when that person sustained physical and/or mental injury (including fatal injury) directly attributable to conduct within paragraph 8(a), (b) or (c), and

   (i)   that relationship still subsists (unless the victim has since died), and

   (ii) the applicant either witnessed and was present on the occasion when the other person sustained the injury, or was closely involved in its immediate aftermath; or

(c)   in a claim arising out of a sexual offence, was the non-consenting victim of that offence (which does not include a victim who consented in fact but was deemed in law not to have consented); or

(d)   being a person employed in the business of a railway, either witnessed and was present on the occasion when another person sustained physical (including fatal) injury directly attributable to an offence of trespass on a railway, or was closely involved in its immediate aftermath. Paragraph 12 below does not apply where mental anxiety or mental illness is sustained as described in this sub-paragraph.

10.   It is not necessary for the assailant to have been convicted of a criminal offence in connection with the injury. Moreover, even where the injury is attributable to conduct within paragraph 8 in respect of which the assailant cannot be convicted of an offence by reason of age, insanity or diplomatic immunity, the conduct may nevertheless be treated as constituting a criminal act.

11.   A personal injury is not a criminal injury for the purposes of this Scheme where the injury is attributable to the use of a vehicle, except where the vehicle was used so as deliberately to inflict, or attempt to inflict, injury on any person.

12.   Where an injury is sustained accidentally by a person who is engaged in:

(a)   any of the law-enforcement activities described in paragraph 8(c), or

(b)   any other activity directed to containing, limiting or remedying the consequences of a crime,

compensation will not be payable unless the person injured was, at the time he sustained the injury, taking an exceptional risk which was justified in all the circumstances.

Eligibility to receive compensation

13.   A claims officer may withhold or reduce an award where he considers that:

(a)   the applicant failed to take, without delay, all reasonable steps to inform the police, or other body or person considered by the Authority to be appropriate for the purpose, of the circumstances giving rise to the injury;or

(b)   the applicant failed to co-operate with the police or other authority in attempting to bring the assailant to justice; or

(c)   the applicant has failed to give all reasonable assistance to the Authority or other body or person in connection with the application; or

(d)   the conduct of the applicant before, during or after the incident giving rise to the application makes it inappropriate that a full award or any award at all be made; or

(e)   the applicant's character as shown by his criminal convictions (excluding convictions spent under the Rehabilitation of Offenders Act 1974 at the date of application or death) or by evidence available to the claims officer makes it inappropriate that a full award or any award at all be made.

14.   In considering the issue of conduct under paragraph 13(d) above, a claims officer may withhold or reduce an award where he considers that excessive consumption of alcohol or use of illicit drugs by the applicant contributed to the circumstances which gave rise to the injury in such a way as to make it inappropriate that a full award, or any award at all, be made.

15.   Where the victim has died since sustaining the injury (whether or not in consequence of it), paragraphs 13 and 14 will apply in relation both to the deceased and to any applicant for compensation under paragraphs 37–44 (fatal awards).

16.   A claims officer will make an award only where he is satisfied:

(a)   that there is no likelihood that an assailant would benefit if an award were made; or

(b)   where the applicant is under 18 years of age when the application is determined, that it would not be against his interest for an award to be made.

17.   Where a case is not ruled out under paragraph 7(b) (injury sustained before 1 October 1979) but at the time when the injury was sustained, the victim and any assailant (whether or not that assailant actually inflicted the injury) were living in the same household as members of the same family, an award will be withheld unless:

(a)   the assailant has been prosecuted in connection with the offence, except where a claims officer considers that there are practical, technical or other good reasons why a prosecution has not been brought; and

(b)   in the case of violence between adults in the family, a claims officer is satisfied that the applicant and the assailant stopped living in the same household before the application was made and are unlikely to share the same household again.

For the purposes of this paragraph, a man and woman living together as husband and wife will be treated as members of the same family.

Consideration of applications

18.   An application for compensation under this Scheme in respect of a criminal injury ('injury' hereafter in this Scheme) must be made in writing on a form obtainable from the Authority. It should be made as soon as possible after the incident giving rise to the injury and must be received by the Authority within two years of the date of the incident. A claims officer may waive this time limit where he considers that, by reason of the particular circumstances of the case, it is reasonable and in the interests of justice to do so.

19.   It will be for the applicant to make out his case including, where appropriate:

(a)   making out his case for a waiver of the time limit in the preceding paragraph; and

(b)   satisfying the claims officer dealing with his application (including an officer reviewing a decision under paragraph 60) that an award should not be reconsidered, withheld or reduced under any provision of this Scheme.

Where an applicant is represented, the costs of representation will not be met by the Authority.

20.   A claims officer may make such directions and arrangements for the conduct of an application, including the imposition of conditions, as he considers appropriate in all the circumstances. The standard of proof to be applied by a claims officer in all matters before him will be the balance of probabilities.

21.   Where a claims officer considers that an examination of the injury is required before a decision can be reached, the Authority will make arrangements for such an examination by a duly qualified medical practitioner. Reasonable expenses incurred by the applicant in that connection will be met by the Authority.

22.   A Guide to the operation of this Scheme will be published by the Authority. In addition to explaining the procedures for dealing with applications, the Guide will set out, where appropriate, the criteria by which decisions will normally be reached.

Types and limits of compensation

23.   Subject to the other provisions of this Scheme, the compensation payable under an award will be:

(a)   a standard amount of compensation determined by reference to the nature of the injury in accordance with paragraphs 26–29;

(b)   where the applicant has lost earnings or earning capacity for longer than 28 weeks as a direct consequence of the injury (other than injury leading to his death), an additional amount in respect of such loss of earnings, calculated in accordance with paragraphs 30–34;

(c)   where the applicant has lost earnings or earning capacity for longer than 28 weeks as a direct consequence of the injury (other than injury leading to his death) or, if not normally employed, is incapacitated to a similar extent, an additional amount in respect of any special expenses, calculated in accordance with paragraphs 35–36;

(d)   where the victim has died in consequence of the injury, the amount or amounts calculated in accordance with paragraphs 37–43;

(e)   where the victim has died otherwise than in consequence of the injury, a supplementary amount calculated in accordance with paragraph 44.

24.   The maximum award that may be made (before any reduction under paragraphs 13–15 above) in respect of the same injury will not exceed £500,000. For these purposes, where the victim has died in consequence of the injury, any application made by the victim before his death and any application made by any qualifying claimant or claimants after his death will be regarded as being in respect of the same injury.

25.   The injury, or any exacerbation of a pre-existing condition, must be sufficiently serious to qualify for compensation equal at least to the minimum award under this Scheme in accordance with paragraph 26, but lesser compensation may be paid if an award is reduced under paragraphs 13, 14, or 15 of the Scheme.

Standard amount of compensation

26.   The standard amount of compensation will be the amount shown in respect of the relevant description of injury in the Tariff, which sets out:

(a)   a scale of fixed levels of compensation;

(b)   the level and corresponding amount of compensation for each description of injury; and

(c)   qualifying notes.

Level 1 represents the minimum award under this Scheme, and Level 25 represents the maximum award for any single description of injury. Where the injury has the effect of accelerating or exacerbating a pre-existing condition, the compensation awarded will reflect only the degree of acceleration or exacerbation.

27.   Minor multiple injuries will be compensated in accordance with *Note 12* to the Tariff. The standard amount of compensation for more serious but separate multiple injuries will, unless expressly provided for otherwise in the Tariff, be calculated as:

(a)   the Tariff amount for the highest-rated description of injury; plus

(b)   30 per cent of the Tariff amount for the second highest-rated description of injury; plus, where there are three or more injuries,

(c)   15 per cent of the Tariff amount for the third highest-rated description of injury.

28.   Where the Authority considers that any description of injury for which no provision is made in the Tariff is sufficiently serious to qualify for at least the minimum award under this Scheme, it will, following consultation with the Panel, refer the injury to the Secretary of State. In doing so the Authority will recommend to the Secretary of State both the inclusion of that description of injury in the Tariff and also the amount of compensation for which it should qualify. Any such consultation with the Panel or reference to the Secretary of State must not refer to the circumstances of any individual application for compensation under this Scheme other than the relevant medical reports.

29.   Where an application for compensation is made in respect of an injury for which no provision is made in the Tariff and the Authority decides to refer the injury to the Secretary of State under the preceding paragraph, an interim award may be made of up to half the amount of compensation for which it is recommended that such description of injury should qualify if subsequently included in the Tariff. No part of such an interim award will be recoverable if the injury is not subsequently included in the Tariff or, if included, qualifies for less compensation than the interim award paid.

Compensation for loss of earnings

30.   Where the applicant has lost earnings or earning capacity for longer than 28 weeks as a direct consequence of the injury (other than injury leading to his death), no compensation in respect of loss of earnings or earning capacity will be payable for the first 28 weeks of loss. The period of loss for which compensation may be payable will begin after 28 weeks incapacity for work and continue for such period as a claims officer may determine.

31.   For a period of loss ending before or continuing to the time the claim is assessed, the net loss of earnings or earning capacity will be calculated on the basis of:

(a)   the applicant's emoluments (being any profit or gain accruing from an office or employment) at the time of the injury and what those emoluments would have been during the period of loss; and

(b)   any emoluments which have become payable to the applicant in respect of the whole or part of the period of loss, whether or not as a result of the injury; and

(c)   any changes in the applicant's pension rights; and

(d)   in accordance with paragraphs 45–47 (reductions to take account of other payments), any social security benefits, insurance payments and pension which have become payable to the applicant during the period of loss; and

(e)   any other pension which has become payable to the applicant during the period of loss, whether or not as a result of the injury.

32.   Where, at the time the claim is assessed, a claims officer considers that the applicant is likely to suffer continuing loss of earnings and/or earning capacity, an annual rate of net loss (the multiplicand) or, where appropriate, more than one such rate will be calculated on the basis of:

(a)   the current rate of net loss calculated in accordance with the preceding paragraph; and

(b)   such future rate or rates of net loss (including changes in the applicant's pension rights) as the claims officer may determine; and

(c)   the claims officer's assessment of the applicant's future earning capacity; and

(d)   in accordance with paragraphs 45–47 (reductions to take account of other payments), any social security benefits, insurance payments and pension which will become payable to the applicant in future; and

(e)   any other pension which will become payable to the applicant in future, whether or not as a result of the injury.

The compensation payable in respect of each period of continuing loss will be a lump sum, which is the product of that multiplicand and an appropriate multiplier. When the loss does not start until a future date, the lump sum will be discounted to provide for the present value of the money. The claims officer will assess an appropriate multiplier, discount factor, or life expectancy by reference to the tables in *Note 3*, and may make such adjustments as he considers appropriate to take account of any factors and contingencies which appear to him to be relevant. The tables in *Note 3* set out the multipliers and (where applicable) discounts and life expectancies to be applied.

(a)   Table A is to be applied to various periods of future loss to allow for the accelerated receipt of compensation;

(b)   Table B sets out the discount factor, by which the lump sum is to be multiplied, when the loss does not start until various periods in the future;

(c)   Table C is a life expectancy table, and in the absence of other factors affecting life expectancy, the table sets out the age to be applied when assessing a multiplier based on pecuniary loss for life.

33.   Where a claims officer considers that the approach in the preceding paragraph is impracticable, the compensation payable in respect of continuing loss of earnings and/or earning capacity will be such other lump sum as he may determine.

34.   Any rate of net loss of earnings or earning capacity (before any reduction in accordance with this Scheme) which is to be taken into account in calculating any compensation payable under paragraphs 30–33 must not exceed one and a half times the gross average industrial earnings at the time of assessment according to the latest figures published by the Office for National Statistics.

Compensation for special expenses

35. Where the applicant has lost earnings or earning capacity for longer than 28 weeks as a direct consequence of the injury (other than injury leading to his death), or, if not normally employed, is incapacitated to a similar extent, additional compensation may be payable in respect of any special expenses incurred by the applicant from the date of the injury for:

(a) loss of or damage to property or equipment belonging to the applicant on which he relied as a physical aid, where the loss or damage was a direct consequence of the injury;

(b) costs (other than by way of loss of earnings or earning capacity) associated with National Health Service treatment for the injury;

(c) the cost of private health treatment for the injury, but only where a claims officer considers that, in all the circumstances, both the private treatment and its cost are reasonable;

(d) the reasonable cost, to the extent that it falls to the applicant, of

(i) special equipment, and/or

(ii) adaptations to the applicant's accommodation, and/or

(iii) care, whether in a residential establishment or at home, which are not provided or available free of charge from the National Health Service, local authorities or any other agency, provided that a claims officer considers such expense to be necessary as a direct consequence of the injury; and

(iv) the cost of the Court of Protection or of the curator bonis.

In the case of (d)(iii), the expense of unpaid care provided at home by a relative or friend of the victim will be compensated by having regard to the level of care required, the cost of a carer, assessing the carer's loss of earnings or earning capacity and/or additional personal and living expenses, as calculated on such basis as a claims officer considers appropriate in all the circumstances. Where the foregoing method of assessment is considered by the claims officer not to be relevant in all the circumstances, the compensation payable will be such sum as he may determine having regard to the level of care provided.

36. Where, at the time the claim is assessed, a claims officer is satisfied that the need for any of the special expenses mentioned in the preceding paragraph is likely to continue, he will determine the annual cost and select an appropriate multiplier in accordance with paragraph 32 (future loss of earnings), taking account of any other factors and contingencies which appear to him to be relevant.

Compensation in fatal cases

37. Where the victim has died in consequence of the injury, no compensation other than funeral expenses will be payable for the benefit of his estate. Such expenses will, subject to the application of paragraphs 13 and 14 in relation to the actions, conduct and character of the deceased, be payable up to an amount considered reasonable by a claims officer, even where the person bearing the cost of the funeral is otherwise ineligible to claim under this Scheme.

38. Where the victim has died since sustaining the injury, compensation may be payable, subject to paragraphs 13–15 (actions, conduct and character), to any claimant (a 'qualifying claimant') who at the time of the deceased's death was:

(a) the partner of the deceased, being only, for these purposes:

(i) a person who was living together with the deceased as husband and wife or as a same sex partner in the same household immediately before the date of death and who, unless formally married to him, had been so living throughout the two years before that date, or

(ii) a spouse or former spouse of the deceased who was financially supported by him immediately before the date of death; or

(b) a natural parent of the deceased, or a person who was not the natural parent, provided that he was accepted by the deceased as a parent of his family; or

(c) a natural child of the deceased, or a person who was not the natural child, provided that he was accepted by the deceased as a child of his family or was dependent on him.

Where the victim has died in consequence of the injury, compensation may be payable to a qualifying claimant under paragraphs 39–42 (standard amount of compensation, dependency, and loss of parent). Where the victim has died otherwise than in consequence of the injury, and before title to the award has been vested in the victim (see paragraph 50), no standard amount or other compensation will be payable to the estate or to a qualifying claimant other than under paragraph 44 (supplementary compensation).

39. A person who was criminally responsible for the death of a victim may not be a qualifying claimant. In cases where there is only one qualifying claimant, the standard amount of compensation will be Level 13 of the Tariff, save that where a claims officer is aware of the existence of one or more other persons who would in the event of their making a claim become a qualifying claimant, the standard amount of compensation will be level 10 of the tariff. Where there is more than one qualifying claimant, the standard amount of compensation for each claimant will be Level 10 of the Tariff. A former spouse of the deceased is not a qualifying claimant for the purposes of this paragraph.

40. Additional compensation calculated in accordance with the following paragraph may be payable to a qualifying claimant where a claims officer is satisfied that the claimant was financially or physically dependent on the deceased. A financial dependency will not be established where the deceased's only normal income was from:

(a) United Kingdom social security benefits; or

(b) social security benefits or similar payments from the funds of other countries.

41. The amount of compensation payable in respect of dependency will be calculated on a basis similar to paragraphs 31–34 (loss of earnings) and paragraph 35 (d) (iii) (cost of care). The period of loss will begin from the date of the deceased's death and continue for such period as a claims officer may determine, with no account being taken, where the qualifying claimant was formally married to the deceased, of remarriage or prospects of remarriage. In assessing the dependency, the claims officer will take account of the qualifying claimant's income and emoluments (being any profit or gain accruing from an office or employment), if any. Where the deceased had been living in the same household as the qualifying claimant before his death, the claims officer will, in calculating the multiplicand, make such proportional reduction as he considers appropriate to take account of the deceased's own personal and living expenses.

42. Where a qualifying claimant was under 18 years of age at the time of the deceased's death and was dependent on him for parental services, the following additional compensation may also be payable:

    (a) a payment for loss of that parent's services at an annual rate of Level 5 of the Tariff; and

    (b) such other payments as a claims officer considers reasonable to meet other resultant losses.

    Each of these payments will be multiplied by an appropriate multiplier selected by a claims officer in accordance with paragraph 32 (future loss of earnings), taking account of the period remaining before the qualifying claimant reaches age 18 and of any other factors and contingencies which appear to the claims officer to be relevant.

43. Application may be made under paragraphs 37–42 (compensation in fatal cases) even where an award had been made to the victim in respect of the same injury before his death. Any such application will be subject to the conditions set out in paragraphs 56–57 for the re-opening of cases, and any compensation payable to the qualifying claimant or claimants, except payments made under paragraphs 37 and 39 (funeral expenses and standard amount of compensation), will be reduced by the amount paid to the victim. The amounts payable to the victim and the qualifying claimant or claimants will not in total exceed £500,000.

44. Where a victim who would have qualified for additional compensation under paragraph 23(b) (loss of earnings) and/or paragraph 23(c) (special expenses) has died, otherwise than in consequence of the injury, before such compensation was awarded, supplementary compensation under this paragraph may be payable to a qualifying claimant who was financially dependent on the deceased within the terms of paragraph 40 (dependency), whether or not a relevant application was made by the victim before his death. Payment may be made in accordance with paragraph 31 in respect of the victim's loss of earnings (except for the first 28 weeks of the victim's loss of earnings and/or earning capacity) and in accordance with paragraph 35 in respect of any special expenses incurred by the victim before his death. The amounts payable to the victim and the qualifying claimant or claimants will not in total exceed £500,000.

Effect on awards of other payments

45. All awards payable under this Scheme, except those payable under paragraphs 26, 27, 39 and 42(a) (Tariff-based amounts of compensation), will be subject to a reduction to take account of social security benefits (or other state benefits) or insurance payments made by way of compensation for the same contingency. The reduction will be applied to those categories or periods of loss or need for which additional or supplementary compensation is payable, including compensation calculated on the basis of a multiplicand or annual cost. The amount of the reduction will be the full value of any relevant payment which the applicant has received, or to which he has or may have any present or future entitlement, by way of:

    (a) United Kingdom social security benefits (or other state benefits);

    (b) social security benefits or similar payments from the funds of other countries;

    (c) payments under insurance arrangements, including, where a claim is made under paragraphs 35(c) and (d) and 36 (special expenses), insurance personally effected, paid for and maintained by the personal income of the victim or, in the case of a person under 18 years of age, by his parent. Insurance so personally effected will otherwise be disregarded.

In assessing the value of any such benefits and payments, account may be taken of any income tax liability likely to reduce their value.

46. Where, in the opinion of a claims officer, an applicant may be or may become eligible for any of the benefits and payments mentioned in the preceding paragraph, an award may be withheld until the applicant has taken such steps as the claims officer considers reasonable to claim them.

47. Where the victim is alive, any compensation payable under paragraphs 30–34 (loss of earnings) will be reduced to take account of any pension accruing as a result of the injury. Where the victim has died in consequence of the injury, any compensation payable under paragraphs 40–41 (dependency) will similarly be reduced to take account of any pension payable, as a result of the victim's death, for the benefit of the applicant. Where such pensions are taxable, one half of their value will be deducted, but they will otherwise be deducted in full (where, for example, a lump sum payment not subject to income tax is made). For the purposes of this paragraph, 'pension' means any payment payable as a result of the injury or death in pursuance of pension or any other rights connected with the victim's employment, and includes any gratuity of that kind and similar benefits payable under insurance policies paid for by the victim's employers. Pension rights accruing solely as a result of payments by the victim or a dependant will be disregarded.

48. An award payable under this Scheme will be reduced by the full value of any payment in respect of the same injury which the applicant has received by way of:
   (a) any criminal injury compensation award made under or pursuant to arrangements in force at the relevant time in Northern Ireland;
   (b) any compensation award or similar payment from the funds of other countries;
   (c) any award where:
      (i) a civil court has made an order for the payment of damages;
      (ii) a claim for damages and/or compensation has been settled on terms providing for the payment of money;
      (iii) payment of compensation has been ordered by a criminal court in respect of personal injuries.

In the case of (a) or (b), the reduction will also include the full value of any payment to which the applicant has any present or future entitlement.

49. Where a person in whose favour an award under this Scheme is made subsequently receives any other payment in respect of the same injury in any of the circumstances mentioned in the preceding paragraph, but the award made under this Scheme was not reduced accordingly, he will be required to repay the Authority in full up to the amount of the other payment.

Determination of applications and payment of awards

50. An application for compensation under this Scheme will be determined by a claims officer, and written notification of the decision will be sent to the applicant or his representative. The claims officer may make such directions and arrangements, including the imposition of conditions, in connection with the acceptance, settlement or trust, payment, repayment and/or administration of an award as he considers appropriate in all the

circumstances. Any such directions and arrangements, including any settlement or trust may be made having regard to the interests of the applicant (whether or not a minor or a person under an incapacity) as well as to considerations of public policy (including the desirability of providing for the return of any parts of an award which may prove to be surplus to the purposes for which they were awarded) on terms which do not exhaust the beneficial interest in the award and which provide, either expressly or by operation of law, for the balance of any trust fund to revert to the Authority. Subject to any such arrangements, including the special procedures in paragraph 52 (purchase of annuities), and to paragraphs 53–55 (reconsideration of decisions), title to an award offered will be vested in the applicant when the Authority has received notification in writing that he accepts the award.

51.   Compensation will normally be paid as a single lump sum, but one or more interim payments may be made where a claims officer considers this appropriate. Once an award has been paid to an applicant or his representative, the following paragraph does not apply.

52.   Where prior agreement is reached between the Authority and the applicant or his representative, an award may consist in whole or in part of an annuity or annuities, purchased for the benefit of the applicant or to be held on trust for his benefit. Once that agreement is reached, the Authority will take the instructions of the applicant or his representative as to which annuity or annuities should be purchased. Any expenses incurred will be met from the award.

Reconsideration of decisions

53.   A decision made by a claims officer (other than a decision made in accordance with a direction by adjudicators on determining an appeal under paragraph 77) may be reconsidered at any time before actual payment of a final award where there is new evidence or a change in circumstances. In particular, the fact that an interim payment has been made does not preclude a claims officer from reconsidering issues of eligibility for an award.

54.   Where an applicant has already been sent written notification of the decision on his application, he will be sent written notice that the decision is to be reconsidered, and any representations which he sends to the Authority within 30 days of the date of such notice will be taken into account in reconsidering the decision. Whether or not any such representations are made, the applicant will be sent written notification of the outcome of the reconsideration, and where the original decision is not confirmed, such notification will include the revised decision.

55.   Where a decision to make an award has been made by a claims officer in accordance with a direction by adjudicators on determining an appeal under paragraph 77, but before the award has been paid the claims officer considers that there is new evidence or a change in circumstances which justifies reconsidering whether the award should be withheld or the amount of compensation reduced, the Authority will refer the case to the Panel for rehearing under paragraph 82.

Re-opening of cases

56.   A decision made by a claims officer and accepted by the applicant, or a direction by adjudicators, will normally be regarded as final, except where an appeal is reheard under paragraphs 79–82. A claims officer may, however, subsequently re-open a case where there has been such a material change in

the victim's medical condition that injustice would occur if the original assessment of compensation were allowed to stand, or where he has since died in consequence of the injury.

57.   A case will not be re-opened more than two years after the date of the final decision unless the claims officer is satisfied, on the basis of evidence presented in support of the application to re-open the case, that the renewed application can be considered without a need for further extensive enquiries.

Review of decisions

58.   An applicant may seek a review of any decision under this Scheme by a claims officer:

   (a)   not to waive the time limit in paragraph 18 (application for compensation) or paragraph 59 (application for review); or

   (b)   not to re-open a case under paragraphs 56–57; or

   (c)   to withhold an award, including such decision made on reconsideration of an award under paragraphs 53–54; or

   (d)   to make an award, including a decision to make a reduced award whether or not on reconsideration of an award under paragraphs 53–54; or

   (e)   to seek repayment of an award under paragraph 49.

An applicant may not, however, seek the review of any such decision where the decision was itself made on a review under paragraph 60 and either the applicant did not appeal against it or the appeal was not referred for determination on an oral hearing, or where the decision was made in accordance with a direction by adjudicators on determining an appeal under paragraph 77.

59.   An application for the review of a decision by a claims officer must be made in writing to the Authority and must be supported by reasons together with any relevant additional information. It must be received by the Authority within 90 days of the date of the decision to be reviewed, but this time limit may, in exceptional circumstances, be waived where a claims officer more senior than the one who made the original decision considers that:

   (a)   any extension requested by the applicant and received within the 90 days is based on good reasons; and

   (b)   it would be in the interests of justice to do so.

60.   All applications for review will be considered by a claims officer more senior than any claims officer who has previously dealt with the case. The officer conducting the review will reach his decision in accordance with the provisions of this Scheme applying to the original application, and he will not be bound by any earlier decision either as to the eligibility of the applicant for an award or as to the amount of an award. The applicant will be sent written notification of the outcome of the review, giving reasons for the review decision, and the Authority will, unless it receives notice of an appeal, ensure that a determination of the original application is made in accordance with the review decision.

Appeals against review decisions

61.   An applicant who is dissatisfied with a decision taken on a review under paragraph 60 may appeal against the decision by giving written notice of appeal to the Panel on a form obtainable from the Authority. Such notice of appeal must be supported by reasons for the appeal together with any

relevant additional material which the appellant wishes to submit, and must be received by the Panel within 90 days of the date of the review decision. The Panel will send to the Authority a copy of the notice of appeal and supporting reasons which it receives and of any other material submitted by the appellant. Where the applicant is represented for the purposes of the appeal, the costs of representation will not be met by the Authority or the Panel.

62.   A member of the staff of the Panel may, in exceptional circumstances, waive the time limit in the preceding paragraph where he considers that:

   (a)   any extension requested by the appellant and received within the 90 days is based on good reasons; and

   (b)   it would be in the interests of justice to do so.

   Where, on considering a request to waive the time limit, a member of the staff of the Panel does not waive it, he will refer the request to the Chairman of the Panel or to another adjudicator nominated by the Chairman to decide requests for waiver, and a decision by the adjudicator concerned not to waive the time limit will be final. Written notification of the outcome of the waiver request will be sent to the appellant and to the Authority, giving reasons for the decision where the time limit is not waived.

63.   Where the Panel receives notice of an appeal against a review decision relating to a decision mentioned in paragraph 58 (a) or (b), the appeal will be dealt with in accordance with paragraphs 66–68 (appeals concerning time limits and re-opening of cases). Where the Panel receives notice of an appeal against a review decision relating to a decision mentioned in paragraph 58(c), (d) or (e), the appeal will be dealt with in accordance with paragraphs 69–71 (appeals concerning awards) and may under those provisions be referred for an oral hearing in accordance with paragraphs 72–78. The Panel may publish information in connection with individual appeals, but such information must not identify any appellant or other person appearing at an oral hearing or referred to during an appeal, or enable identification to be made of any such person without that person's consent.

64.   The standard of proof to be applied by the Panel in all matters before it will be the balance of probabilities. It will be for the appellant to make out his case including, where appropriate:

   (a)   making out his case for a waiver of the time limit in paragraph 61 (time limit for appeals); and

   (b)   satisfying the adjudicator or adjudicators responsible for determining his appeal that an award should not be reconsidered, withheld or reduced under any provision of this Scheme. Subject to paragraph 78 (determination of appeal in appellant's absence), the adjudicator or adjudicators concerned must ensure, before determining an appeal, that the appellant has had an opportunity to submit representations on any evidence or other material submitted by or on behalf of the Authority.

65.   The Panel may make such arrangements for the inspection of the injury as it considers appropriate. Reasonable expenses incurred by the appellant in that connection will be met by the Panel.

Appeals concerning time limits and re-opening of cases

66.   The Chairman of the Panel or another adjudicator nominated by him will determine any appeal against a decision taken on a review:

(a)   not to waive the time limit in paragraph 18 (application for compensation) or paragraph 59 (application for review); or

(b)   not to re-open a case under paragraphs 56–57.

Where the appeal concerns a decision not to re-open a case and the application for re-opening was made more than two years after the date of the final decision, the adjudicator must be satisfied that the renewed application can be considered without a need for further extensive enquiries by the Authority.

67.   In determining an appeal under the preceding paragraph, the adjudicator will allow the appeal where he considers it appropriate to do so. Where he dismisses the appeal, his decision will be final. Written notification of the outcome of the appeal, giving reasons for the decision, will be sent to the appellant and to the Authority.

68.   Where the adjudicator allows an appeal in accordance with the preceding paragraph, he will direct the Authority:

(a)   in a case where the appeal was against a decision not to waive the time limit in paragraph 18, to arrange for the application for compensation to be dealt with under this Scheme as if the time limit had been waived by a claims officer;

(b)   in a case where the appeal was against a decision not to waive the time limit in paragraph 59, to conduct a review under paragraph 60;

(c)   in a case where the appeal was against a decision not to re-open a case, to re-open the case under paragraphs 56–57.

Appeals concerning awards

69.   A member of the staff of the Panel may refer for an oral hearing in accordance with paragraphs 72–78 any appeal against a decision taken on a review:

(a)   to withhold an award, including such decision made on reconsideration of an award under paragraphs 53–54; or

(b)   to make an award, including a decision to make a reduced award whether or not on reconsideration of an award under paragraphs 53–54; or

(c)   to seek repayment of an award under paragraph 49.

A request for an oral hearing in such cases may also be made by the Authority.

70.   Where a member of the staff of the Panel does not refer an appeal for an oral hearing under the preceding paragraph, he will refer it to an adjudicator. The adjudicator will refer the appeal for determination on an oral hearing in accordance with paragraphs 72–78 where, on the evidence available to him, he considers:

(a)   in a case where the review decision was to withhold an award on the ground that the injury was not sufficiently serious to qualify for an award equal to at least the minimum award payable under this Scheme, that an award in accordance with this Scheme could have been made; or

(b)   in any other case, that there is a dispute as to the material facts or conclusions upon which the review
decision was based and that a different decision in accordance with this Scheme could have been made.

He may also refer the appeal for determination on an oral hearing in accordance with paragraphs 72–78 where he considers that the appeal cannot be determined on the basis of the material before him or that for any other reason an oral hearing would be desirable.

71.   Where an appeal is not referred under paragraphs 69 or 70 for an oral hearing, the adjudicator's dismissal of the appeal will be final and the decision taken on the review will stand. Written notification of the dismissal of the appeal, giving reasons for the decision, will be sent to the appellant and to the Authority.

Oral hearing of appeals

72.   Where an appeal is referred for determination on an oral hearing, the hearing will take place before at least two adjudicators. Where the referral was made by an adjudicator under paragraph 70, that adjudicator will not take part in the hearing. On application by the appellant, pending determination, the Chairman or an adjudicator nominated by him may direct that an interim payment be made. Subject to the provisions of this Scheme, the procedure to be followed for any particular appeal will be a matter for the adjudicators hearing the appeal.

73.   Written notice of the date proposed for the oral hearing will normally be sent to the appellant and the Authority at least 21 days beforehand. Any documents to be submitted to the adjudicators for the purposes of the hearing by the appellant, or by or on behalf of the Authority, will be made available at the hearing, if not before, to the Authority or the appellant respectively.

74.   It will be open to the appellant to bring a friend or legal adviser to assist in presenting his case at the hearing, but the costs of representation will not be met by the Authority or the Panel. The adjudicators may, however, direct the Panel to meet reasonable expenses incurred by the appellant and any person who attends to give evidence at the hearing.

75.   The procedure at hearings will be as informal as is consistent with the proper determination of appeals. The adjudicators will not be bound by any rules of evidence which may prevent a court from admitting any document or other matter or statement in evidence. The appellant, the claims officer presenting the appeal and the adjudicators may call witnesses to give evidence and may cross-examine them.

76.   Hearings will take place in private. The Panel may, however, subject to the consent of the appellant, give permission for the hearing to be attended by observers such as representatives of the press, radio and television. Any such permission will be subject to written undertakings being given:

   (a)   that the identity of the appellant and of any other persons appearing at the hearing or referred to during the appeal will be kept confidential and will not be disclosed in any account of the proceedings which is broadcast or in any way published without that person's consent; and

   (b)   that no material will be disclosed or in any other way published from which those identities could be discovered without the consent of the subject.

77.   Where the adjudicators adjourn the hearing, they may direct that an interim payment be made. Where the only issue remaining is the determination of the amount of compensation, the adjudicators may remit the application for final determination by one of themselves in the absence of the appellant, but subject to the right of the appellant to have a further oral hearing if not satisfied with that determination, in which the adjudicator who made that determination will not take part. On determining the appeal, the

adjudicators will, where necessary, make such direction as they think fit as to the decision to be made by a claims officer on the application for compensation, but any such direction must be in accordance with the relevant provisions of this Scheme. Where they are of the opinion that the appeal was frivolous or vexatious, the adjudicators may reduce the amount of compensation to be awarded by such amount as they consider appropriate. The appellant and the Authority will be informed of the adjudicators' determination of the appeal and the reasons for it, normally at the end of the hearing, but otherwise by written notification as soon as is practicable thereafter.

78.   Adjudicators may determine an appeal on the available evidence in the absence of an appellant when they are satisfied that

(a)   he has so requested, or agreed; or

(b)   he has failed to attend a hearing and has given no reasonable excuse for his non-attendance; or

(c)   he is at the time of the hearing detained in custody or in hospital and is likely to remain so for a period of at least 6 months; or

(d)   he is not living in Great Britain

and it would not be against the interests of justice to do so.

Rehearing of appeals

79.   Where an appeal is determined in the appellant's absence, he may apply to the Panel in writing for his appeal to be reheard, giving the reasons for his non-attendance or otherwise why it should be reheard. Any such application must be received by the Panel within 30 days of the date of notification to the appellant of the outcome of the hearing which he did not attend. The Panel will send a copy of the application to the Authority.

80.   A member of the staff of the Panel may waive the time limit in the preceding paragraph where he considers that it would be in the interests of justice to do so. Where he does not waive the time limit, he will refer the application to the Chairman of the Panel or to another adjudicator nominated by the Chairman to decide such applications, and a decision by the adjudicator concerned not to waive the time limit will be final. Written notification of the waiver decision will be sent to the appellant and to the Authority, giving reasons for the decision where the time limit is not waived.

81.   Where a member of the staff of the Panel considers that there are good reasons for an appeal determined in the appellant's absence to be reheard, he will refer it for a rehearing. Where he does not refer it for a rehearing, he will refer the application to the Chairman of the Panel or to another adjudicator nominated by the Chairman to decide such applications, and a decision by the adjudicator concerned not to rehear the appeal will be final. Written notification of the decision on the application for a rehearing will be sent to the appellant and to the Authority, giving reasons for the decision where the application is refused.

82.   Where an appeal is to be reheard, any adjudicator or adjudicators who determined the appeal originally will not take part in the rehearing, and paragraphs 64 (onus on appellant), 65 (inspection of injury), and 72–78 (oral hearings) will apply.

Implementation and transitional provisions

83.   The provisions of this Scheme come into force on 1 April 2001. All applications for compensation received by the Authority on or after 1 April 2001 will be dealt

with under the terms of this Scheme, except that in relation to applications in respect of injuries incurred before that date paragraph 38 of this Scheme shall not apply, but only insofar as it applies to a same sex partner.

84. Applications for compensation received by the Authority or by the Criminal Injuries Compensation Board ('the Board') before 1 April 2001 will continue to be dealt with according to:

(a) the provisions of the Scheme which came into operation on 1 April 1996 ('the 1996 Scheme'); or

(b) the provisions of the non-statutory Scheme which came into operation on 1 February 1990 ('the old Scheme'). This includes provisions of the earlier non-statutory schemes referred to therein, insofar as they continue to have effect immediately before 1 April 2001 by virtue of the 1996 Scheme or the provisions of any non-statutory Scheme.

The following paragraphs of this Scheme will apply in addition to or in substitution for provisions of the 1996 Scheme as specified below –

(c) Paragraph 35 (d) (iv) will apply additionally to applications otherwise falling to be considered under the 1996 Scheme.

(d) Paragraphs 50, 61–62, 72, 77, and 78–82 of this Scheme will each apply in substitution for the same numbered paragraph of the 1996 Scheme.

85. From 1 April 2001 applications required by paragraph 84 to be dealt with according to the provisions of the old Scheme will continue to be so dealt with by the Authority, and :

(a) any decision authorised under the old Scheme to be made by a single member of the Board may be made by a single legally qualified member of the Panel appointed for the purposes of this Scheme;

(b) any decision authorised under the old Scheme to be made by at least two members of the Board may be made by at least two legally qualified members of the Panel; and

(c) any decision authorised under the old Scheme to be made by the Chairman of the Board may be made by the Chairman of the Panel or by another legally qualified adjudicator nominated by the Chairman to make such decisions.

In this paragraph legally qualified member means a member who is, or has been, qualified to practise as a solicitor, or as a barrister in England and Wales, or as an advocate in Scotland.

86. Cases which are reopened under paragraph 56 of this Scheme or any corresponding provision of any earlier scheme will be dealt with according to the terms of the scheme under which the initial application was decided.

Notes to the Scheme

(see paragraph 8)

Note 1   Definition of Great Britain

(a)   For the purposes of paragraph 8 of this Scheme, an injury is sustained in Great Britain where it is sustained:

(i)   on a British aircraft, hovercraft or ship (see Note 2); or

(ii)   on, under or above an installation in a designated area within the meaning of section 1(7) of the Continental Shelf Act 1964 or any waters within 500 metres of such an installation; or

(iii)   in a lighthouse off the coast of Great Britain.

(b)   For the purposes of paragraph 8 of this Scheme–

(i)   an injury is sustained in Great Britain where it is sustained in that part of the Channel Tunnel system incorporated into England under section 10 of the Channel Tunnel Act 1987. However, if such an injury is sustained or caused by a non-UK officer acting in the exercise of his functions under the 1993 and 1994 Orders no compensation shall be payable under this Scheme; and

(ii)   any injury caused in the following circumstances shall be treated for the purposes of any application for compensation under this Scheme as if the circumstances giving rise to the claim had occurred in Great Britain–

(a)   an injury sustained by a UK officer acting in the exercise of his functions within French or Belgian territory under the provisions of the 1993 and 1994 Orders; or

(b) an injury caused by a UK officer acting in the exercise of those functions within French or Belgian territory, other than an injury to any non-UK officer acting in the exercise of his functions.

In this Note 'the 1993 and 1994 Orders' mean the Channel Tunnel (International Arrangements) Order 1993 (SI 1993/1813) and the Channel Tunnel (Miscellaneous Provisions) Order 1994 (SI 1994/1405) and 'officer' has the same meaning as in those Orders.

Note 2   Definition of British craft In Note 1 above:

(a)   'British aircraft' means a British controlled aircraft within the meaning of section 92 of the Civil Aviation Act 1982 (application of criminal law to aircraft), or one of Her Majesty's aircraft;

(b)   'British hovercraft' means a British controlled hovercraft within the meaning of that section (as applied in relation to hovercraft by virtue of provision made under the Hovercraft Act 1968), or one of Her Majesty's hovercraft; and

(c)   'British ship' means one of Her Majesty's Ships or any vessel used in navigation which is owned wholly by persons of the following descriptions, namely:

   (i)   British citizens, or

   (ii)   bodies corporate incorporated under the law of some part of, and having their principal place of business in, the United Kingdom, or

   (iii) Scottish partnerships.

The references in this Note to Her Majesty's aircraft, hovercraft or ships are references to aircraft, hovercraft or ships which belong to, or are exclusively used in the service of, Her Majesty in right of the government of the United Kingdom.

Note 3   Multipliers and Discount Factors for assessing accelerated receipt of compensation, and life expectancy table. (See paragraph 32)

Table A

(This converts an annual loss over a period of years into a lump sum payable at the beginning of that period)

Years of loss	Multiplier	Years of loss	Multiplier
5	5	17	11.5
6	5.5	18	12
7	6	19	12.5
8	7	20	13
9	7.5	25	15
10	8	30	16
11	8.5	35	17
12	9	40	18
13	9.5	50	20

Years of loss	Multiplier	Years of loss	Multiplier
14	10		
15	10.5		
16	11		

Table B   Discount Factors

Period of Years	Discount in Future	Period of years in Future	Discount
5	.80	17	.48
6	.77	18	.46
7	.74	19	.44
8	.71	20	.42
9	.68	25	.34
10	.65	30	.27
11	.62	35	.22
12	.59	40	.18
13	.57	50	.12
14	.54		
15	.52		
16	.50		

Table C   Life expectancy table

Age at date of Assessment	Age to which expected to live for purposes of calculation	
	Males	Females
0–25	80 years of age	84 years of age
26–50	81	84
51–60	81	85
61–65	82	85
66–70	83	86
71–73	84	87
74–76	85	87
77–78	86	88
79–80	87	89
81	88	89
82	88	90
83	89	90
84–85	90	91
86	91	92
87–88	92	93
89	93	94
90	94	95

Criminal Injuries Compensation Scheme

Levels of compensation

Level 1	£1,000	Level 2	£1,250
Level 3	£1,500	Level 4	£1,750
Level 5	£2,000	Level 6	£2,500

Level 7	£3,300	Level 8	£3,800
Level 9	£4,400	Level 10	£5,500
Level 11	£6,600	Level 12	£8,200
Level 13	£11,000	Level 14	£13,500
Level 15	£16,500	Level 16	£19,000
Level 17	£22,000	Level 18	£27,000
Level 19	£33,000	Level 20	£44,000
Level 21	£55,000	Level 22	£82,000
Level 23	£110,000	Level 24	£175,000
Level 25	£250,000		

General Notes to Tariff of Injuries

(Notes 1–3 follow paragraph 86 of the Scheme)

4. *Where the tariff compensates for an operation the award includes provision for the normal operation scarring.*

5. *When compensation is paid for physical injury or for any sexual offence described in the tariff, a separate award for mental injury will not be made (as the tariff award includes an element of compensation for this); save that in the case of an award for physical injury, if the compensation for mental injury is the same as, or higher than, the level of compensation for the physical injury, the applicant will be entitled to awards for the separate injuries calculated in accordance with paragraph 27 of the Scheme (the serious multiple injury formula). When compensation is paid for any sexual offence, a separate award for mental injury will not be made.*

Tariff of injuries

General	401
Head and neck	405
Upper limbs	410
Torso	414

Lower limbs416 *(g)loss of fingernail*

Description of Injury	Level	Standard Amount £
GENERAL		
Fatal injury		
One qualifying claimant	13	11,000
Each qualifying claimant if more than one	10	5,500
Burns		
Note 6. For other burn injuries see under individual parts of the body		
Affecting multiple areas of body covering over 25% of skin area, with significant scarring	19	33,000
Infection with HIV/AIDS		
Note 7. Not subject to the multiple injuries formula and may be paid in addition to other awards		

Description of Injury	Level	Standard Amount £
Infection with HIV/AIDS	17	22,000
Loss of foetus	10	5,500
Major paralysis		
Hemiplegia (paralysis of one side of the body)	21	55,000
Paraplegia (paralysis of the lower limbs)	24	175,000
Quadriplegia/tetraplegia (paralysis of all four limbs)	25	250,000
Medically recognised illness/condition – not mental illness		
Moderately disabling disorder where the symptoms and disability persist for more than 6 weeks from the incident/ date of onset		
– lasting 6 to 13 weeks	1	1,000
– lasting up to 28 weeks	5	2,000
– lasting over 28 weeks		
– not permanent	7	3,300
– permanent	12	8,200
Seriously disabling disorder where the symptoms and disability persist for more than 6 weeks from the incident/ date of onset		
– lasting 6 to 13 weeks	5	2,000
– lasting up to 28 weeks	9	4,400
– lasting over 28 weeks		
– not permanent	12	8,200
– permanent	17	22,000

Mental illness and temporary mental anxiety

Notes:

8. *Mental illness includes conditions attributed to post-traumatic stress disorder, depression and similar generic terms within which there may be:*
   (a) such psychological symptoms as anxiety, tension, insomnia, irritability, loss of confidence, agoraphobia and preoccupation with thoughts of guilt or self-harm; and
   (b) related physical symptoms such as alopecia, asthma, eczema, enuresis and psoriasis.
9. *'Medically verified' means that the mental anxiety has been diagnosed by a registered medical practitioner.*
10. *'Psychiatric diagnosis/prognosis' means that the disabling mental illness has been diagnosed or the prognosis made by a psychiatrist or clinical psychologist.*
11. *A mental illness is disabling if it significantly impairs a person's functioning in some important aspect of her/his life e.g. impaired work or school performance or significant adverse effects on social relationships or sexual dysfunction.*

Disabling but temporary mental anxiety lasting more than 6 weeks, medically verified	1	1,000
Disabling mental illness, confirmed by psychiatric diagnosis:		

Description of Injury	Level	Standard Amount £
– lasting up to 28 weeks	6	2,500
– lasting over 28 weeks to 2 years	9	4,400
– lasting 2 years to 5 years	12	8,200
– lasting over 5 years but not permanent	14	13,500
Permanent mental illness, confirmed by psychiatric prognosis:		
– moderately disabling	16	19,000
– seriously disabling	18	27,000

Minor injuries: multiple

Note 12: Minor multiple physical injuries will qualify for compensation only where the applicant has sustained at least 3 separate physical injuries of the type illustrated below, at least one of which must still have had significant residual effects 6 weeks after the incident. The injuries must also have necessitated at least 2 visits to or by a medical practitioner within that 6-week period. Examples of qualifying injuries are:
(a) grazing, cuts, lacerations (no permanent scarring)
(b) severe and widespread bruising
(c) severe soft tissue injury (no permanent disability)
(d) black eye(s)
(e) bloody nose
(f) hair pulled from scalp
(g) loss of fingernail

Minor injuries: multiple	1	1,000

Peripheral sensory nerve damage

– lasting more than 13 weeks		
– substantial recovery expected	3	1,500
– permanent disability		
– minor loss	3	1,500
– significant loss (eg loss of sensation in large area of leg)	7	3,300
– serious loss (eg loss of sensation of hand)	12	8,200

Physical abuse of adults

Note 13: In the case of adult applicants where there has been a series of assaults (sexual and/or physical) over a period of time, it may be that an applicant will qualify for compensation only for the single most recent incident, if in relation to the earlier incidents she/he failed to report them to the police without delay and/or failed to co-operate with the police in bringing the assailant to justice. Where the applicant is entitled to compensation for the series of assaults, she/he will qualify for an award as the victim of a pattern of abuse, rather than for a separate award for each incident.

Serious abuse		
– intermittent physical assaults resulting in an accumulation of healed wounds, burns or scalds, but with no appreciable disfigurement	5	2,000
Severe abuse		

Description of Injury	Level	Standard Amount £
– pattern of repetitive violence resulting in minor disfigurement	10	5,500
Persistent pattern of severe abuse over a period exceeding 3 years	12	8,200

Physical abuse of children

Minor abuse
| – isolated or intermittent assault(s) resulting in weals, hair pulled from scalp etc. | 1 | 1,000 |

Serious abuse
| – intermittent physical assaults resulting in an accumulation of healed wounds, burns or scalds, but with no appreciable disfigurement | 5 | 2,000 |

Severe abuse
– persistent pattern of repetitive violence resulting in:
– moderate multiple injuries (eg bruising and minor fractures) and/or minor disfigurement	10	5,500
– significant multiple injuries	12	8,200
– severe multiple injuries	14	13,500

Sexual assault/abuse of victims any age (if not already compensated as a child)

Note 14: Note 13 (under Physical Abuse of Adults) applies here too.

Indecent assault
– minor – non-penetrative indecent physical act/or acts over clothing	1	1,000
– serious – non-penetrative indecent act/or acts under clothing	5	2,000
– severe – non-penile penetrative and/or oral-genital act or acts	7	3,300
– pattern of repetitive frequent severe abuse over a period		
– up to 3 years	11	6,600
– exceeding 3 years	12	8,200
– resulting in serious internal bodily injuries	17	22,000

Non-consensual vaginal and/or anal intercourse
– by one attacker	13	11,000
– by two or more attackers	14	13,500
– resulting in serious internal bodily injuries	17	22,000
– resulting in permanently disabling mental illness confirmed by psychiatric prognosis	18	27,000
– resulting in serious internal bodily injury with permanent disabling mental illness confirmed by psychiatric prognosis	19	33,000
– pattern of repeated incidents over a period		
– up to 3 years	15	16,500
– exceeding 3 years	17	22,000

Description of Injury	Level	Standard Amount £
Sexual assault/abuse of children (under age of 18 at time or commencement of abuse) and of adults who by reason of mental incapacity are incapable of giving consent		
Indecent assault		
– minor - non penetrative indecent physical act/or acts over clothing	1	1,000
– minor – non penetrative frequent assaults over clothing	3	1,500
– serious – non penetrative indecent act under clothing	5	2,000
– serious – pattern of repetitive indecent acts under clothing	7	3,300
Indecent assault		
– non-penile penetrative and/or oral genital acts		
– one incident	7	3,300
– two or more isolated incidents	9	4,400
– pattern of repetitive, frequent incidents		
– over a period up to 3 years	11	6,600
– over a period exceeding 3 years	12	8,200
– resulting in serious internal bodily injuries	17	22,000
Non-consensual vaginal and/or anal intercourse		
– one incident	13	11,000
– one incident involving two or more attackers	14	13,500
– repeated incidents over a period		
– up to 3 years	15	16,500
– exceeding 3 years	17	22,000
– resulting in serious internal bodily injuries	17	22,000
– resulting in permanently disabling mental illness confirmed by psychiatric prognosis	18	27,000
– resulting in serious internal bodily injury with permanent disabling mental illness confirmed by psychiatric prognosis	19	33,000
Sexual assault/abuse – additional awards where the following are directly attributable to sexual assault (whether of an adult or a child) – not subject to the multiple injuries formula & may be paid in addition to other awards		
Pregnancy	10	5,500
Sexually transmitted disease other than HIV/AIDS		
– substantial recovery	10	5,500
– permanent disability	13	11,000
Infection with HIV/AIDS	17	22,000

HEAD & NECK

	Level	Standard Amount £
Burns		
Head		
– minor visible disfigurement	5	2,000
– moderate	9	4,400
– severe	15	16,500
Face		
– minor disfigurement	5	2,000
– moderate	10	5,500

Description of Injury	Level	Standard Amount £
– severe	18	27,000
Neck		
– minor disfigurement	3	1,500
– moderate	9	4,400
– severe	15	16,500
Scarring		
Head		
– minor visible disfigurement	3	1,500
– significant disfigurement	7	3,300
– serious disfigurement	10	5,500
Face		
– minor disfigurement	3	1,500
– significant disfigurement	9	4,400
– serious disfigurement	13	11,000
Neck		
– minor disfigurement	3	1,500
– significant disfigurement	7	3,300
– serious disfigurement	11	6,600
Brain		
Balance impaired		
– lasting 6 to 28 weeks	3	1,500
– lasting over 28 weeks recovery expected	7	3,300
– permanent	12	8,200
Brain haemorrhage/stroke		
– substantial recovery	9	4,400
Brain damage – impairment of social/ intellectual functions		
– minor	12	8,200
– moderate	15	16,500
– serious	20	44,000
– very serious	23	110,000
– extremely serious (no effective control of functions)	25	250,000
Concussion		
– lasting at least one week	3	1,500
Epilepsy		
– post-traumatic epileptic fits – substantial recovery	5	2,000
– fully controlled	12	8,200
– partially controlled	14	13,500
– uncontrolled	20	44,000
Subdural or extradural haematoma		
– treated conservatively	9	4,400
– requiring evacuation	12	8,200
Ear		
Fractured mastoid	1	1,000
Deafness		
– temporary partial deafness		
– lasting 6 to 13 weeks	1	1,000
– lasting more than 13 weeks	3	1,500
– partial deafness (remaining hearing socially useful, with hearing aid if necessary)		

Description of Injury	Level	Standard Amount £
– one ear	8	3,800
– both ears	12	8,200
– total deafness		
– one ear	15	16,500
– both ears	20	44,000
Loss of ear		
– partial loss of ear(s)	9	4,400
– loss of ear	13	11,000
– loss of both ears	16	19,000
Perforated ear drum		
– one ear	4	1,750
– both ears	6	2,500
Tinnitus (ringing noise in ear(s))		
– lasting 6 to 13 weeks	1	1,000
– lasting more than 13 weeks	7	3,300
– permanent		
– other than very severe	12	8,200
– very severe	15	16,500
Vestibular damage (causing giddiness)		
– lasting 6 to 28 weeks	3	1,500
– lasting over 28 weeks – recovery expected	7	3,300
– permanent	12	8,200

Eye

Description of Injury	Level	Standard Amount £
Blow out or other fracture of orbital bone cavity containing eyeball		
– no operation	7	3,300
– requiring operation	9	4,400
Blurred or double vision		
– temporary		
– lasting 6 to 13 weeks	1	1,000
– lasting more than 13 weeks – recovery expected	4	1,750
– permanent		
– slight	9	4,400
– moderate	12	8,200
– serious	14	13,500
Cataracts		
– one eye		
– requiring operation	7	3,300
– permanent/inoperable	12	8,200
– both eyes		
– requiring operation	12	8,200
– permanent/inoperable	16	19,000
Corneal abrasions	5	2,000
Degeneration of optic nerve		
– one eye	5	2,000
– both eyes	10	5,500
Dislocation of lens		
– one eye	10	5,500
– both eyes	14	13,500

Description of Injury	Level	Standard Amount £
Glaucoma	6	2,500
Hyphaema requiring operation		
– one eye	3	1,500
– both eyes	6	2,500
Loss of eye		
– one eye	18	27,000
– both eyes	23	110,000
Loss of sight		
– one eye	17	22,000
– both eyes	23	110,000
Partial loss of vision		
– 6/12	11	6,600
– 6/18	12	8,200
– 6/24	14	13,500
– 6/36	15	16,500
– 6/60	16	19,000
substantial loss of vision (both eyes) at least 6/36 in each eye or worse	21	55,000
Residual central floater(s) affecting vision	7	3,300
Retina		
– damage not involving detachment		
– one eye	6	2,500
– both eyes	10	5,500
– detached		
– one eye	10	5,500
– both eyes	14	13,500
Significant penetrating injury		
– one eye	6	2,500
– both eyes	11	6,600
Traumatic angle recession	6	2,500
Face		
Clicking jaw		
– temporary		
– lasting 6 to 13 weeks	1	1,000
– lasting more than 13 weeks	3	1,500
– permanent	10	5,500
Dislocated jaw		
– substantial recovery	5	2,000
– continuing significant disability	10	5,500
Fractured ethmoid		
– no operation	5	2,000
– operation required	9	4,400
Fractured zygoma (malar/cheek bone)		
– no operation		
– substantial recovery	5	2,000
– continuing significant disability	9	4,400
– operation required		

Description of Injury	Level	Standard Amount £
– substantial recovery	6	2,500
– continuing significant disability	10	5,500
Fractured mandible and/or maxilla (jaw bones)		
– no operation		
– substantial recovery	7	3,300
– continuing significant disability	10	5,500
– operation required		
– substantial recovery	8	3,800
– continuing significant disability	12	8,200
Multiple fractures to face (eg, Le Fort fractures types 2 & 3)	13	11,000
Numbness/loss of feeling		
– temporary lasting more than 13 weeks – recovery expected	3	1,500
– permanent		
– moderate eg cheek, forehead	7	3,300
– severe eg lip interfering with function	9	4,400

Neck

Fractured hyoid (bone in windpipe)	1	1,000
Strained neck or whiplash injury		
– disabling		
– for 6 to 13 weeks	1	1,000
– for more than 13 weeks	6	2,500
– seriously disabling		
– not permanent	10	5,500
– permanent	13	11,000

Nose

Deviated nasal septum		
– no operation	1	1,000
– requiring septoplasty	5	2,000
Fracture of nasal bones		
– undisplaced	1	1,000
– displaced	3	1,500
– requiring manipulation	5	2,000
– requiring rhinoplasty	5	2,000
– requiring turbinectomy	5	2,000
Loss of smell/taste		
– partial loss of smell and/or taste	10	5,500
– total		
– loss of smell or taste	13	11,000
– loss of smell and taste	15	16,500
Partial loss of nose (at least 10%)	9	4,400

Skull

Fracture		
– simple		
– no operation	6	2,500
– depressed		
– no operation	9	4,400
– requiring operation	11	6,600

Description of Injury	Level	Standard Amount £
Teeth		
Damage to:		
– tooth/teeth requiring root-canal treatment	2	1,250
– front tooth/teeth requiring crown(s)	3	1,500
Fractured/chipped tooth/teeth requiring treatment	2	1,250
Fractured tooth/teeth requiring apicectomy (surgery to gum to reach root – root resection)	6	2,500
Loss of:		
– crowns	3	1,500
– front tooth/teeth (incisor or canine)		
– one front tooth	4	1,750
– two or three front teeth	6	2,500
– four or more front teeth	8	3,800
– tooth/teeth other than front		
– one tooth	2	1,250
– two or more teeth	4	1,750
Slackening of teeth requiring dental treatment	2	1,250
Tongue		
Impaired speech		
– slight	5	2,000
– moderate	10	5,500
– serious	13	11,000
– severe	16	19,000
Loss of speech – permanent	19	33,000
Loss of tongue	20	44,000

UPPER LIMBS

Description of Injury	Level	Standard Amount £
Burns		
Minor	3	1,500
Moderate	9	4,400
Severe	13	11,000
Scarring		
Minor disfigurement	2	1,250
Significant disfigurement	6	2,500
Serious disfigurement	10	5,500
Arm		
Loss of:		
– one arm	20	44,000
– both arms	23	110,000
Paralysis of or equivalent loss of function of:		
– one arm	19	33,000
– both arms	22	82,000
Elbow		
Dislocated/fractured		
– one elbow		
– substantial recovery	7	3,300
– continuing significant disability	12	8,200
– both elbows		

Description of Injury	Level	Standard Amount £
– substantial recovery	12	8,200
– continuing significant disability	13	11,000

Finger and Thumb
Fracture/dislocation of:
– thumb
  – one hand

	Level	Standard Amount £
– substantial recovery	5	2,000
– continuing significant disability	9	4,400

  – both hands

– substantial recovery	10	5,500
– continuing significant disability	12	8,200

– index finger
  – one hand

– substantial recovery	4	1,750
– continuing significant disability	8	3,800

  – both hands

– substantial recovery	9	4,400
– continuing significant disability	11	6,600

– one finger other than index finger
  – one hand

– substantial recovery	1	1,000
– continuing significant disability	5	2,000

  – both hands

– substantial recovery	4	1,750
– continuing significant disability	9	4,400

– two or more fingers other than index finger
  – one hand

– substantial recovery	2	1,250
– continuing significant disability	6	2,500

  – both hands

– substantial recovery	7	3,300
– continuing significant disability	11	6,600

Loss of:

– finger other than index finger	10	5,500
– two or more fingers	13	11,000
– index finger	12	8,200
– both index fingers	15	16,500
– thumb	15	16,500
– both thumbs	19	33,000

Partial loss of:

– finger other than thumb or index finger	6	2,500
– two or more fingers other than index finger or thumb	10	5,500
– thumb or index finger	9	4,400
– thumb or index finger – both hands	12	8,200
– thumb and index finger – one hand	12	8,200
– thumb and index finger – both hands	15	16,500

Hand
Fractured hand
– one hand

Description of Injury	Level	Standard Amount £
– substantial recovery	5	2,000
– continuing significant disability	10	5,500
– both hands		
– substantial recovery	8	3,800
– continuing significant disability	12	8,200
Loss of, or equivalent loss of function of:		
– one hand	20	44,000
– both hands	23	110,000
Permanently & seriously impaired grip		
– one hand	12	8,200
– both hands	15	16,500
Humerus (upper arm bone)		
Fractured		
– one arm		
– substantial recovery	7	3,300
– continuing significant disability	10	5,500
– both arms		
– substantial recovery	12	8,200
– continuing significant disability	13	11,000
Radius (a forearm bone)		
Fractured		
– one arm		
– substantial recovery	7	3,300
– continuing significant disability	10	5,500
– both arms		
– substantial recovery	12	8,200
– continuing significant disability	13	11,000
Shoulder		
Dislocated		
– one shoulder		
– substantial recovery	4	1,750
– continuing significant disability	10	5,500
– both shoulders		
– substantial recovery	8	3,800
– continuing significant disability	12	8,200
Frozen		
– one shoulder		
– substantial recovery	5	2,000
– continuing significant disability	10	5,500
– both shoulders		
– substantial recovery	7	3,300
– continuing significant disability	12	8,200
Tendon & Ligament		
Minor damage		
– one arm		
– substantial recovery	1	1,000
– continuing significant disability	6	2,500
– both arms		

Description of Injury	Level	Standard Amount £
– substantial recovery	5	2,000
– continuing significant disability	9	4,400
Moderate damage		
– one arm		
– substantial recovery	5	2,000
– continuing significant disability	9	4,400
– both arms		
– substantial recovery	9	4,400
– continuing significant disability	12	8,200
Severely damaged		
– one arm		
– substantial recovery	7	3,300
– continuing significant disability	10	5,500
– both arms		
– substantial recovery	11	6,600
– continuing significant disability	13	11,000
Ulna (a forearm bone)		
Fractured		
– one arm		
– substantial recovery	7	3,300
– continuing significant disability	10	5,500
– both arms		
– substantial recovery	12	8,200
– continuing significant disability	13	11,000
Wrist		
Fractured – colles type		
– one wrist		
– substantial recovery	9	4,400
– continuing significant disability	12	8,200
– both wrists		
– substantial recovery	12	8,200
– continuing significant disability	13	11,000
Fractured/dislocated – including scaphoid fracture		
– one wrist		
– substantial recovery	7	3,300
– continuing significant disability	11	6,600
– both wrists		
– substantial recovery	11	6,600
– continuing significant disability	13	11,000
Sprained		
– one wrist		
– disabling for 6 to 13 weeks	1	1,000
– disabling for more than 13 weeks	6	2,500
– both wrists		
– disabling for 6 to 13 weeks	5	2,000
– disabling for more than 13 weeks	8	3,800

Description of Injury	Level	Standard Amount £
TORSO		
Burns		
Minor	3	1,500
Moderate	9	4,400
Severe	13	11,000
Scarring		
Minor disfigurement	2	1,250
Significant disfigurement	6	2,500
Serious disfigurement	10	5,500
Abdomen		
Injury requiring laparotomy	8	3,800
– including removal or repair of multiple organs	17	22,000
Back		
Fracture of vertebra		
– one vertebra		
– substantial recovery	6	2,500
– continuing significant disability	10	5,500
– more than one vertebra		
– substantial recovery	9	4,400
– continuing significant disability	12	8,200
Prolapsed invertebral disc(s)		
– seriously disabling		
– not permanent	10	5,500
– permanent	12	8,200
Ruptured invertebral disc(s) – requiring surgical removal	13	11,000
Strained		
– disabling		
– for 6 to 13 weeks	1	1,000
– for more than 13 weeks	6	2,500
– seriously disabling		
– not permanent	10	5,500
– permanent	13	11,000
Chest		
Injury requiring thoracotomy	12	8,200
Clavicle (collar bone)		
Dislocated acromioclavicular joint	5	2,000
Fractured		
– one clavicle		
– substantial recovery	5	2,000
– continuing significant disability	9	4,400
– two clavicles		
– substantial recovery	9	4,400
– continuing significant disability	11	6,600
Coccyx (tail bone)		
Fractured	6	2,500

Description of Injury	Level	Standard Amount £
Genitalia		
Injury requiring medical treatment		
– no significant permanent damage	4	1,750
– permanent damage		
– moderate	10	5,500
– severe	13	11,000
Loss of fertility	21	55,000
Hernia		
– hernia	8	3,800
– hernias	10	5,500
Kidney		
Loss of kidney	17	22,000
Serious and permanent damage to or loss of both kidneys	21	55,000
Lung		
Punctured		
– one lung	7	3,300
– two lungs	11	6,600
Collapsed		
– one lung	8	3,800
– two lungs	12	8,200
Permanent and disabling damage to lungs from smoke or chemical inhalation	10	5,500
Pelvis		
Fractured		
– substantial recovery	9	4,400
– continuing significant disability	13	11,000
Rib		
Fractured (or bruised where significant pain lasts more than 6 weeks)		
– one rib	1	1,000
– two or more	3	1,500
Scapula (shoulder blade)		
Fractured		
– one scapula		
– substantial recovery	6	2,500
– continuing significant disability	9	4,400
– two scapulas		
– substantial recovery	9	4,400
– continuing significant disability	11	6,600
Spleen		
Loss of spleen	9	4,400
Sternum (breast bone)		
Fractured		
– substantial recovery	6	2,500

Description of Injury	Level	Standard Amount £
– continuing significant disability	10	5,500

LOWER LIMBS

Burns
Minor	3	1,500
Moderate	9	4,400
Severe	13	11,000

Scarring
Minor disfigurement	2	1,250
Significant disfigurement	6	2,500
Serious disfigurement	10	5,500

Ankle
Fractured or Dislocated
– one ankle
– substantial recovery	9	4,400
– continuing significant disability	13	11,000

– both ankles
– substantial recovery	12	8,200
– continuing significant disability	15	16,500

Sprained
– one ankle
– disabling for at least 6 to 13 weeks	1	1,000
– disabling for more than 13 weeks	6	2,500

– both ankles
– disabling for at least 6 to 13 weeks	5	2,000
– disabling for more than 13 weeks	8	3,800

Femur (thigh bone)
Fractured
– one leg
– substantial recovery	8	3,800
– continuing significant disability	11	6,600

– both legs
– substantial recovery	10	5,500
– continuing significant disability	13	11,000

Fibula (slender bone from knee to ankle)
Fractured
– one leg
– substantial recovery	6	2,500
– continuing significant disability	8	3,800

– both legs
– substantial recovery	7	3,300
– continuing significant disability	10	5,500

Foot
Fractured metatarsal bones
– one foot
– substantial recovery	6	2,500

Description of Injury	Level	Standard Amount £
– continuing significant disability	8	3,800
– both feet		
– substantial recovery	7	3,300
– continuing significant disability	10	5,500
Fractured tarsal bones		
– one foot		
– substantial recovery	7	3,300
– continuing significant disability	12	8,200
– both feet		
– substantial recovery	10	5,500
– continuing significant disability	14	13,500
Heel		
Fractured heel bone		
– one foot		
– substantial recovery	7	3,300
– continuing significant disability	12	8,200
– both feet		
– substantial recovery	10	5,500
– continuing significant disability	14	13,500
Hip		
Fractured/Dislocated		
– one hip		
– substantial recovery	9	4,400
– continuing significant disability	13	11,000
– both hips		
– substantial recovery	12	8,200
– continuing significant disability	15	16,500
Knee		
Arthroscopy (investigative surgery / repair to knee) – no fracture	5	2,000
Patella (knee cap)		
– dislocated		
– one knee		
– substantial recovery	1	1,000
– continuing significant disability	10	5,500
– both knees		
– substantial recovery	6	2,500
– continuing significant disability	12	8,200
– fractured		
– one knee		
– substantial recovery	6	2,500
– continuing significant disability	10	5,500
– both knees		
– substantial recovery	9	4,400
– continuing significant disability	12	8,200
– removal of:		
– one knee	8	3,800
– both knees	10	5,500

Description of Injury	Level	Standard Amount £
Leg		
Loss of:		
– one leg		
– below knee	19	33,000
– above knee	20	44,000
– both legs	23	110,000
Paralysis of leg	18	27,000
(see also major paralysis (paraplegia))		
Tendon & Ligament		
Minor damage		
– one leg		
– substantial recovery	1	1,000
– continuing significant disability	7	3,300
– both legs		
– substantial recovery	5	2,000
– continuing significant disability	10	5,500
Moderate damage		
– one leg		
– substantial recovery	5	2,000
– continuing significant disability	10	5,500
– both legs		
– substantial recovery	9	4,400
– continuing significant disability	13	11,000
Severe damage		
– one leg		
– substantial recovery	7	3,300
– continuing significant disability	12	8,200
– both legs		
– substantial recovery	11	6,600
– continuing significant disability	15	16,500
Tibia (shin bone)		
Fractured		
– one leg		
– substantial recovery	8	3,800
– continuing significant disability	11	6,600
– both legs		
– substantial recovery	10	5,500
– continuing significant disability	13	11,000
Toe		
Fractured		
– great toe		
– one foot		
– substantial recovery	6	2,500
– continuing significant disability	12	8,200
– both feet		
– substantial recovery	8	3,800
– continuing significant disability	14	13,500
– two or more toes		

Description of Injury	Level	Standard Amount £
– one foot		
– substantial recovery	1	1,000
– continuing significant disability	6	2,500
– both feet		
– substantial recovery	3	1,500
– continuing significant disability	9	4,400
Loss of:		
– great toe	12	8,200
– both great toes	14	13,500
– one toe (other than great toe)	1	1,000
– two or more toes	9	4,400
Partial loss of:		
– great toe	6	2,500
– both great toes	10	5,500

Appendix 7

Consent Form – Releasing Health Records Under the Data Protection Act 1998

About this form

In order to proceed with your claim, your solicitor may need to see your health records. Solicitors usually need to see all your records as they need to assess which parts are relevant to your case. (Past medical history is often relevant to a claim for compensation.) Also, if your claim goes ahead, the person you are making the claim against will ask for copies of important documents. Under court rules, they may see all your health records. So your solicitor needs to be familiar with all your records.

Part a – your, your solicitor's and the appropriate health professional's details

Your name:	
Your address:	
Solicitor's name:	
Solicitor's address:	
Health professional's name:	
Health professional's address:	

Part b – your declaration and signature

Please see the 'Notes for the client' over the page before you sign this form.

To the health professional

I understand that filling in and signing this form gives you permission to give all my health records to my solicitor whose details are given above.

Please give my solicitor copies of my health records, in line with the Data Protection Act 1998, within 40 days.

Your signature:		Date:	/ /

Part c – your solicitor's declaration and signature

Please see the 'Notes for the solicitor' over the page before you sign this form.

To the health professional

I have told my client the implications of giving me access to his or her health records. I confirm that I need the full records in this case.

Solicitor's signature:		Date:	/ /

- why you saw a health professional;
- details of clinical findings and diagnoses;
- any options for care and treatment the health professional discussed with you;
- the decisions made about your care and treatment, including evidence that you agreed; and
- details of action health professionals have taken and the outcomes.

By signing this form, you are agreeing to your solicitor receiving copies of your health records held by the health professional named on this form.

If you are making, or considering making, a legal claim against someone, your solicitor will need to see copies of all your health records so he or she can see if there is anything in your records that may affect your claim. Once you start your claim, the court can order you to give copies of your health records to the solicitor of the person you are making a claim against so he or she can see if any of the information in your records can be used to defend his or her client.

You do not have to give permission for your health records to be released but if you don't, the court may not let you go ahead with your claim and, in some circumstances, your solicitor may refuse to represent you.

Notes for the solicitor

Before you ask your client to fill in and sign this form you should explain that this will involve his or her full health records being released and how the information in them may be used. You should also tell your client to read the notes above.

If your client is not capable of giving his or her permission in this form, this form should be signed by:

- your client's litigation friend;
- someone who has enduring power of attorney to act for your client; or
- your client's receiver appointed by the Court of Protection.

When you send this form to the appropriate health professional, please also send a covering letter to confirm the authorised fees for getting access to records, and that you will pay those fees.

Unless your client agrees otherwise, you must use his or her health records only for the purpose for which the client signed this form (that is, making his or her claim). You should not keep health records for any longer than you need them. You should return them to the client at the end of the claim.

Notes for the health professional

This form shows your patient's permission for you to give copies of his or her full health records to his or her solicitor, in line with the Data Protection Act 1998.

© The Law Society and British Medical Association 2003

- is likely to cause serious physical or mental harm to the patient or another person; or
- relates to someone who would normally need to give their permission (where that person is not a health professional who has cared for the patient).

Your patient's permission for you to release information is valid only if that patient understands the consequences of his or her records being released, and how the information will be used. The solicitor named on this form must explain these issues to the patient. If you have any doubt about whether this has happened, contact the solicitor or your patient.

If your patient is not capable of giving his or her permission, this form should be signed by:

- a 'litigation friend' acting for your patient;
- someone with 'enduring power of attorney' to act for your patient; or
- a receiver appointed by the Court of Protection.

You may charge the usual fees authorised under the Data Protection Act for providing the records.

The BMA publishes detailed advice for doctors on giving access to health records, including the fees that you may charge. You can view that advice by visiting www.bma.org.uk/ap.nsf/Content/accesshealthrecords.

This form is published by the Law Society and British Medical Association.

Index

health and safety at work – *continued*
safe system of working 23-4
safety audit 32
seriousness factors 46-7
substances hazardous to health 40
training 33
work equipment, provision and use
34-6
workplace 38-9
young workers 31, 33
see also **work-based claims**
Health and Safety Executive
health and safety report 114
**Health Service Commissioner
(Ombudsman) 137**
Healthcare Commission 134
hemiplegia 11
highway authorities
breach of duty
to motorists 20
to pedestrians 20-1
duties 19-20
flooding 22
gritting the highway 22
maintenance of highway
duty 20
failure to maintain 21
state of highway 21
tripping/slipping claims 19, 20-1
human rights
access to medical records 117
coroner's courts 243-4
humerus 10
hydrocephalus 11
hypertrophic 11

incapacity benefit 97
indemnity principle
conditional fee agreements 72-3, 78
independent contractors
occupier's liability 43
industrial deafness 12
initial interview *see* **first interview**
inquests
apportionment of blame 238-9
criteria for 234
evidence at 236
evidence from 115
expert advice 236
funding representation 234-5
human rights and 243-4
preparation for hearing 235-6
publicity 242-3
refusal of 234
report 137
summation by coroner 239
transcripts 241
unnatural death 234
violent death 234
see also **coroner's court**
inquisition 239-40
inspection of documents 178-9
inspection of property 115, 168

insurance
after the event insurance (ATE) 72, 78-9
before the event 84-7
legal expenses insurance 84-7
choice of solicitor 85-7
level of success fee 79-80
recovery of cost 79
time for taking out 79
insurance moneys 213-14
interest
calculation 229
delay 229
fatal accident damages 260
general damages 228-9
included in settlements 229
pain and suffering 228
special damages 228, 229
interim payment
personal injury cases 178
recoupment of benefits 205
timing of application 177-8
**International Classification of Mental
and Behavioural Disorders (World
Health Organisation) 47**
intoxication 28
intracerebral 12
Investigative Help 70
issue of proceedings
acknowledgment of service 170
counterclaim 171
defence
contents 170-1
extension of time 170
filing 170
particulars of claim 169-70
reply to defence 171-2
contents 172
service of proceedings 170
statement of value 168-9

jargon *see* **medical terminology**
judgment 198
judicial review
refusal of inquest 234
juries
coroner's court 237
jurisdiction
choice of 269-70
claims in EU 270
claims outside EU 270
limitation periods 270
package holidays 270

laceration 11
legal expenses insurance 84-7
choice of solicitor 85-7
Legal Help 68
Legal Services Commission 68-7
letter of claim
clinical disputes 165-6
clinical negligence claims 106
personal injury claims 105-6, 161-2
response 162